THE GREEN GUIDE

S. Sauvignier/MICHELIN

Atlantic Coast
Poitou
Aquitaine
Basque Country

D0293650

Travel Publications

Hannay House, 39 Clarendon Road
Watford, Herts WD17 1JA, UK
☎ 01923 205 240 - Fax 01923 205 241
www.ViaMichelin.com
TheGreenGuide-uk@uk.michelin.com

Manufacture française des pneumatiques Michelin
Société en commandite par actions au capital de 304 000 000 EUR
Place des Carmes-Déchaux – 63 Clermont-Ferrand (France)
R.C.S. Clermont-Fd B 855 200 507

© Michelin et Cie, Propriétaires-éditeurs, 2001
Dépôt légal janvier 2001 – ISBN 2-06-000090-4 – ISSN 0763-1383
Printed in France 06-02/3.3

Typesetting, printing and binding: I.M.E. – Baume-les-Dames

Cover design: Carré Noir, Paris 17ᵉ arr.

THE GREEN GUIDE:
Spirit of Discovery

Leisure time spent with The Green Guide is also a time for refreshing your spirit, enjoying yourself, and taking advantage of our selection of fine restaurants, hotels and other places for relaxing: immerse yourself in the local culture, discover new horizons, experience the local lifestyle. The Green Guide opens the door for you.

Each year our writers go touring: visiting the sights, devising the driving tours, identifying the highlights, selecting the most attractive hotels and restaurants, checking the routes for the maps and plans.

Each title is compiled with great care, giving you the benefit of regular revisions and Michelin's first-hand knowledge. The Green Guide responds to changing circumstances and takes account of its readers' suggestions; all comments are welcome.

Share with us our enthusiasm for travel, which has led us to discover over 60 destinations in France and other countries. Like us, let yourself be guided by the desire to explore, which is the best motive for travel: the spirit of discovery.

Contents

Practical information   16

Introduction   50

Sights   94

In alphabetical order

Admission times and charges   396

Index   419

Vénus de Brassempouy

Photo JOSSE

Prow of a trawler

S. Sauvignier/MICHELIN

Maps
and Plans

Thematic maps

Monuments, sites and museums

Local maps for touring

Town plans

Monflanquin, a bastide town

"Green Venice" – the Marais Poitevin

Michelin maps

Michelin products are complementary: for each of the sites listed in The Green Guide, map references are indicated which help you find your location on our range of maps. The image below shows the maps to use for each geographic area covered in this guide. To travel the roads in this region, you may use any of the following:

● the **regional maps** at a scale of 1:200 000 nᵒˢ 232, 233, 234, 235 and 238, which cover the main roads and secondary roads, and include useful indications for finding tourist attractions. These are good maps to choose for travelling in a wide area. In a quick glance, you can locate and identify the main sights to see. In addition to identifying the nature of the road ways, the maps show castles, churches and other religious edifices, scenic view points, megalithic monuments, swimming beaches on lakes and rivers, swimming pools, golf courses, race tracks, air fields, and more.

● the **local maps** that cover all of France are illustrated on the map below.
And remember to travel with the latest edition of the map of France no 989, which gives an overall view of the region and the main access roads which connect it to the rest of France. The entire country is mapped at a 1:1 000 000 scale and clearly shows the main road network. Convenient Atlas formats (spiral, hard cover and "mini") are also available.

Michelin is pleased to offer a route-planning service on the Internet: **www.ViaMichelin.com**. Choose the shortest route, a route without tolls, or the Michelin recommended route to your destination; you can also access information about hotels and restaurants from The Red Guide, and tourists sites from The Green Guide.

Bon voyage!

Using this guide

● The summary maps on the following pages are designed to assist you in planning your trip: the **Map of principal sights** identifies major sights and attractions and the **Map of driving tours** proposes regional itineraries.

● The **Practical information** section offers useful information for planning your trip and seeking accommodation with the help of the **Map of places to stay**. Use it to find out more about recreation, festival and carnival dates; suggestions for thematic tours on scenic railways and through nature reserves, and more.

● We recommend that you read the **Introduction** before setting out on your trip. The background information it contains on history, the arts and traditional culture will prove most instructive and make your visit more meaningful.

● The main towns and attractions are presented in alphabetical order in the **Sights** section. In order to ensure quick, easy identification, original place names have been used throughout the guide. The clock symbol ☉, placed after monuments or other sights, refers to the **Admission times and charges** section at the end of the guide, in which the names appear in the same order as in the Sights section.

● The Green Guide also has suggestions for **places to stay, to dine and to enjoy entertainment** – addresses that we have selected for special local feeling and friendly atmosphere. Turn to the sections bordered in blue.

● The Index lists attractions, famous people and events, and other subjects covered in the guide.

Let us hear from you. We are interested in your reaction to our guide, in any ideas you have to offer or good addresses you would like to share. Send your comments to Michelin Travel Publications, Hannay House, 39 Clarendon Road, Watford, Herts WD17 1JA, U.K. or by e-mail to TheGreenGuide-uk@uk.michelin.com.

A. Thuillier/MICHELIN

Key

Selected monuments and sights

🎯 Tour - Departure point

🏛 ✝ Catholic church

🏛 ✝ Protestant church, other temple

✡ ◻ Synagogue - Mosque

🏛 Building

■ Statue, small building

✝ Calvary, wayside cross

◎ Fountain

●—■- Rampart - Tower - Gate

⤬ Château, castle, historic house

∴ Ruins

⌣ Dam

✿ Factory, power plant

☆ Fort

⌒ Cave

🕴 Prehistoric site

▼ Viewing table

Ⅶ Viewpoint

▲ Other place of interest

Special symbols

◈ Water park

🏖 Beach

🚣 Boat trips departure

⦂⦂⦂ Fortified town (bastide): in southwest France, a new town built in the 13-14C and typified by a geometrical layout.

Sports and recreation

🏇 Racecourse

⛸ Skating rink

🏊 🏊 Outdoor, indoor swimming pool

🎥 Multiplex Cinema

⛵ Marina, sailing centre

⛺ Trail refuge hut

◻-■-■-◻ Cable cars, gondolas

◻-+++-◻ Funicular, rack railway

🚂 Tourist train

◇ Recreation area, park

🎭 Theme, amusement park

🦌 Wildlife park, zoo

✿ Gardens, park, arboretum

🕊 Bird sanctuary, aviary

🚶 Walking tour, footpath

👶 Of special interest to children

Abbreviations

A Agricultural office (Chambre d'agriculture)

C Chamber of Commerce (Chambre de commerce)

H Town hall (Hôtel de ville)

J Law courts (Palais de justice)

M Museum (Musée)

P Local authority offices (Préfecture, sous-préfecture)

POL. Police station (Police)

🛡 Police station (Gendarmerie)

T Theatre (Théâtre)

U University (Université)

8

	Sight	Seaside resort	Winter sports resort	Spa
Highly recommended	★★★	⚱⚱⚱	❄❄❄	⚕⚕⚕
Recommended	★★	⚱⚱	❄❄	⚕⚕
Interesting	★	⚱	❄	⚕

Additional symbols

🛈		Tourist information
═══	═══	Motorway or other primary route
❶	❶	Junction: complete, limited
⊨═⊨	═══	Pedestrian street
⊥ ═ ═ ═ ⊥		Unsuitable for traffic, street subject to restrictions
⊥⊥⊥⊥	- - - -	Steps - Footpath
🚆	🚉	Train station - Auto-train station
🚐	S.N.C.F.	Coach (bus) station
──┼──		Tram
⌒		Metro, underground
P⊦R		Park-and-Ride
♿		Access for the disabled
✉		Post office
☎		Telephone
✉		Covered market
⋅×⋅		Barracks
△		Drawbridge
∪		Quarry
⚒		Mine
B	F	Car ferry (river or lake)
⛴		Ferry service: cars and passengers
⛵		Foot passengers only
③		Access route number common to Michelin maps and town plans
Bert (R.)...		Main shopping street
AZ B		Map co-ordinates
►►		Visit if time permits

Hotels and restaurants

20 rooms: *38.57/57.17€*	Number of rooms: price for one person/ double room
half-board or full board: *42.62€*	Price per person, based on double occupancy
⇌ *6.85€*	Price of breakfast; when not given, it is included in the price of the room (i.e., for bed-and-breakfast)
120 sites: *12.18€*	Number of camp sites and cost for 2 people with a car
12.18€ lunch- *16.74/38.05€*	Restaurant: fixed-price menus served at lunch only – mini/maxi price fixed menu (lunch and dinner) or à la carte
rest. *16.74/38.05€*	Lodging where meals are served mini/maxi price fixed menu or à la carte
meal 15.22€	"Family style" meal
reserv	Reservation recommended
⌿	No credit cards accepted
P	Reserved parking for hotel patrons

The prices correspond to the higher rates of the tourist season

Principal sights

BORDEAUX	★★★ Highly recommended
St-Savin	★★ Recommended
St-Jean-Pied-de-Port	★ Interesting
Civaux	Other sight described in this guide.

Seaside resorts ⚓ spas ♨ and winter resorts ❄ are classified according to the quality and range of facilities offered.

Itinerary described in this guide: look up one of the sites in the index at the back of the guide to find the page where the tour is described.

Driving tours

For descriptions of these tours, turn to the Practical Information section following.

40 km
0

1	Poitou: North-east of Poitiers
2	The Saintonge region
3	The Vendée region
4	South of the Loire estuary
5	Bordeaux vineyards
6	The Côte d'Argent south of Arcachon
7	The Basque coast
8	The Basque mountains
9	Béarn

Legend / Map symbols:

- 🖻 Boat trips
- ✪ Outstanding man-made site
- 🏛 Old town
- 🍇 Vineyards
- 🏘 Picturesque village
- **M** Museum, art gallery
- **F** Fresco
- 🎨 Regional specialities
- 🎢 Theme or amusement park
- 🏖 Seaside resort
- ◖ Cliff dwellings
- ♨ Spa (mineral springs)

- ⫴ Roman ruins
- ⛪ Religious building
- 🏰 Château, castle or historic house
- 🚂 Tourist train
- ▲ Outstanding natural site
- ⛬ Fortifications
- ⌒ Cave
- ❀ Garden, park
- ✳ Historic site
- ⚔ Battleground
- ⛟ Sports and recreation area
- ⛰ Panorama
- 🦓 Wildlife park, zoo
- 🦉 Bird sanctuary, aviary

Place names on map:

Luxey, Pissos, Marquèze, Sabres, Courant de Contis, Mimizan-Plage, Courant d'Huchet, Vieux-Boucau-les-Bains, Hossegor, Capbreton, Biarritz, St-Jean-de-Luz, Hendaye, Corniche Basque, Donostia/San Sebastián, la Rhune, Sare, St-Étienne-de-Baïgorry, Orreaga/Roncesvalles (Roncevaux), Ainhoa, Espelette, Bayonne, Tropica Parc, St-Paul-lès-Dax, Salies-de-B., Isturitz et Oxocelhaya, St-Jean-Pied-de-Port, St-Palais, Mauléon-Licharre, Gotein, Iraty, Crevasses d'Holçarté, Gges de Kakouetta, Arette-Pierre-St-Martin, Orthez, Sauveterre-de-B., Morlanne, Lescar, Oloron-Ste-Marie, Lescun, Pau, Morlaàs, Nay, Aste-Béon, Gourette, Col d'Aubisque, Lac d'Artouste, Lourdes, Tarbes

Regions/areas: GOLFE DE GASCOGNE, LANDES, GERS, TARN-ET-GARONNE, HAUTES-PYRÉNÉES, Adour, Agen, Montauban

Numbered zones: 6, 7, 8, 9

40 km

Festivities in Coulon on the Sèvre Niortaise

Practical
Information

Planning your trip

Useful addresses

INTERNET

www.ambafrance-us.org
The French Embassy in the USA has a Web site providing basic information (geography, demographics, history), a news digest and business-related information. It offers special pages for children, and pages devoted to culture, language study and travel, and you can reach other selected French sites (regions, cities, ministries) with a hypertext link.

www.franceguide.com
The French Government Tourist Office / Maison de la France site is packed with practical information and tips for those travelling to France. The home page has a number of links to more specific guidance, for American or Canadian travellers for example, or to the FGTO's London pages.

www.FranceKeys.com
This sight has plenty of practical information for visiting France. It covers all the regions, with links to tourist offices and related sites. Very useful for planning the details of your tour in France!

www.fr-holidaystore.co.uk
The French Travel Centre in London has gone on-line with this service, providing information on all of the regions of France, including updated special travel offers and details on available accommodation.

www.visiteurope.com
The European Travel Commission provides useful information on travelling to and around 27 European countries, and includes links to some commercial booking services (ie vehicle hire), rail schedules, weather reports and more.

FRENCH TOURIST OFFICES

For information, brochures, maps and assistance in planning a trip to France travellers should apply to the official French Tourist Office or Masion de la France in their own country:

Australia – New Zealand
Sydney – Level 22, 25 Bligh Street,
NSW 2000 Sydney
☏ (02) 9231 5244 – Fax: (02) 9221 8682.

Canada
Montreal – 1981 Avenue McGill College, Suite 490,
Montreal PQ H3A 2W9
☏ (514) 876 9881 – Fax: (514) 845 4868.

Eire
Dublin – 10 Suffolk Street, Dublin 2
☏ 15 60 235 235

South Africa
P.O. Box 41022, 2024 Craighall,
☏ 00 27 11 880 80 62, Fax: 00 27 11 770 16 66.

United Kingdom
London – 178 Piccadilly, London WIV OAL
☏ (0891) 244 123 – Fax: (0171) 493 6594.

United States
East Coast – New York – 444 Madison Avenue,
16th Floor, NY 10022-6903,
☏ (212) 838-7800 – Fax: (212) 838-7855.
Mid West – Chicago – 676 North Michigan Avenue,
Suite 3360, Chicago, IL 60611-2819.
☏ (312) 751-7800 – Fax: (312) 337-6339.
West Coast – Los Angeles – 9454 Wilshire Boulevard,
Suite 715, Los Angeles, CA 90212-2967.
☏ (310) 271-6665 – Fax: (310) 276-2835.
Information can also be requested from **France on Call**,
☏ (202) 659-7779.

LOCAL TOURIST OFFICES

Visitors may also contact local Tourist offices for more precise information, to receive brochures and maps. The addresses and telephone numbers of Tourist offices in the larger towns are listed after the symbol **B**, in the *Admission times and charges* section at the end of the guide. Below, the addresses are given for local Tourist offices of the *départements* and *Régions* covered in this guide. The index lists the *département* after each town.

Départments – Address inquiries to the **Comité Départemental du Tourisme (CDT)**:

Charente
27 place Bouillaud
16021 Angoulême
☎ 05 45 69 79 09

Charente Maritime
11 bis, rue des Augustins
BP 1152,
17088 La Rochelle Cedex 02
☎ 05 46 41 43 33

Deux-Sèvres
15 rue Thiers, BP 8510
79025 Niort Cedex 9
☎ 05 49 77 19 70

Maison du tourisme de la Gironde
21, cours de l'Intendance
33000 Bordeaux
☎ 05 56 52 61 40

Landes
4 av. Aristide-Briand, BP 407
40012 Mont-de-Marsan Cedex
☎ 05 58 06 89 89

Loire-Atlantique
2 allée Baco
44000 Nantes
☎ 02 51 72 95 30

Lot-et-Garonne
4, rue André-Chenier, BP 158
47005 Agen Cedex
☎ 05 53 66 14 14

Pyrénées-Atlantiques
Agence touristique du Béarn
22 ter, rue Jean-Jacques-de-Monnaix
64000 Pau
☎ 05 59 30 01 30

Vendée
8, place Napoléon, BP 233
85006 La Roche sur Yon Cedex
☎ 02 51 47 88 22

Vienne
1bis, rue Victor-Hugo, BP 287
86007 Poitiers Cedex
☎ 05 49 37 48 48

Regions – Contact the **Comité régional de tourisme (CRT)**:

CRT Aquitaine
(Bordeaux, Landes, Pyrénées-Atlantiques)
Cité mondiale, 23, parvis des Chartrons
33074 Bordeaux Cedex
☎ 05 56 01 70 00

CRT Pays de la Loire
(Vendée)
2, rue de la Loire, BP 20411
44204 Nantes Cedex 2
☎ 02 40 48 24 20

CRT Poitou-Charentes
62, rue Jean Jaurès
BP 56, 86002 Poitiers Cedex
☎ 05 49 50 10 50

EMBASSIES AND CONSULATES IN FRANCE

Australia	Embassy	4 rue Jean-Rey, 75015 Paris ☎ 01 40 59 33 00 – Fax: 01 40 59 33 10.
Canada	Embassy	35 avenue Montaigne, 75008 Paris ☎ 01 44 43 29 00 – Fax: 01 44 43 29 99.
Eire	Embassy	4 rue Rude, 75016 Paris ☎ 01 44 17 67 00 – Fax: 01 44 17 67 60.
New Zealand	Embassy	7 ter rue Léonard-de-Vinci, 75016 Paris ☎ 01 45 01 43 43 – Fax: 01 45 01 43 44.
South Africa	Embassy	59 quai d'Orsay, 75007 Paris ☎ 01 53 59 23 23 – Fax: 01 53 59 23 33.
UK	Embassy	35 rue du Faubourg St-Honoré, 75008 Paris ☎ 01 44 51 31 00 – Fax: 01 44 51 31 27.
	Consulate	16 rue d'Anjou, 75008 Paris ☎ 01 44 51 31 01 (visas).
USA	Embassy	2 avenue Gabriel, 75008 Paris ☎ 01 43 12 22 22 – Fax: 01 42 66 97 83.
	Consulate	2 rue St-Florentin, 75001 Paris ☎ 01 42 96 14 88.
	Consulate	15 avenue d'Alsace, 67082 Strasbourg ☎ 03 88 35 31 04 – Fax: 03 88 24 06 95.

Travellers with special needs

The sights described in this guide which are easily accessible to people of reduced mobility are indicated in the *Admission times and charges* by the symbol &.

Useful information on transportation, holidaymaking and sports associations for the disabled is available from the *Comité National Français de Liaison pour la Réadaptation des Handicapés* (CNRH), 236 bis rue de Tolbiac, 75013 Paris. Call their international information number ☏ 01 53 80 66 44, or write to request a catalogue of publications. Web-surfers can find information for slow walkers, mature travellers and others with special needs at www.access-able.com and www.handitel.org. For information on museum access for the disabled contact La Direction, *Les Musées de France, Service Accueil des Publics Spécifiques*, 6 rue des Pyramides, 75041 Paris Cedex 1, ☏ 01 40 15 35 88.

The Red Guide France and the **Michelin Camping Caravaning France** indicate hotels and camp sites with facilities suitable for physically handicapped people.

Formalities

Documents

Passport – Nationals of countries within the European Union entering France need only a national identity card. Nationals of other countries must be in possession of a valid national **passport**. In case of loss or theft, report to your embassy or consulate and the local police.

Visa – No **entry visa** is required for Canadian, US or Australian citizens travelling as tourists and staying less than 90 days, except for students planning to study in France. If you think you may need a visa, apply to your local French Consulate.

US citizens should obtain the booklet *Safe Trip Abroad* (US$1), which provides useful information on visa requirements, customs regulations, medical care etc for international travellers. Published by the Government Printing Office, it can be ordered by phone (☏ (202) 512-1800) or consulted on-line (www.access.gpo.gov). General passport information is available by phone toll-free from the Federal Information Center (item 5 on the automated menu), ☏ 800-688-9889. US passport application forms can be downloaded from http://travel.state.gov.

Customs

Apply to the Customs Office (UK) for a leaflet on customs regulations and the full range of duty-free allowances; available from HM Customs and Excise, Dorset House, Stamford Street, London SE1 9PS, ☏ 0171 928 3344. The US Customs Service offers a publication *Know before you go* for US citizens: for the office nearest you, consult the phone book, Federal Government, US Treasury (www.customs.ustreas.gov).

There are no customs formalities for holidaymakers bringing their caravans into France for a stay of less than six months. No customs document is necessary for pleasure boats and outboard motors for a stay of less than six months but the registration certificate should be kept on board. Americans can bring home, tax-free, up to US$ 400 worth of goods (limited quantities of alcohol and tobacco products); Canadians up to CND$ 300; Australians up to AUS$ 400 and New Zealanders up to NZ$ 700.

Persons living in a member state of the European Union are not restricted with regard to purchasing goods for private use, but the recommended allowances for alcoholic beverages and tobacco are as follows:

Spirits (whisky, gin, vodka etc)	10 litres	Cigarettes	800
Fortified wines (vermouth, port etc)	20 litres	Cigarillos	400
Wine (not more than 60 sparkling)	90 litres	Cigars	200
Beer	110 litres	Smoking tobacco	1 kg

Health

First aid, medical advice and chemists' night service rota are available from chemists/drugstores *(pharmacie)* identified by the green cross sign.

It is advisable to take out comprehensive insurance coverage as the recipient of medical treatment in French hospitals or clinics must pay the bill. Nationals of non-EU countries should check with their insurance companies about policy limitations. Reimbursement can then be negotiated with the insurance company according to the policy held.

All prescription drugs should be clearly labelled; it is recommended that you carry a copy of the prescription.

British and Irish citizens should apply to the Department of Health and Social Security for Form E 111, which entitles the holder to urgent treatment for accident or unexpected illness in EU countries. A refund of part of the costs of treatment can be obtained on application in person or by post to the local Social Security Offices *(Caisse Primaire d'Assurance Maladie)*. **Americans** concerned about travel and health can contact the International Association for Medical Assistance to Travelers, which can also provide details of English-speaking doctors in different parts of France: ☎ (716) 754-4883.

The American Hospital of Paris is open 24hr for emergencies as well as consultations, with English-speaking staff, at 63 boulevard Victor-Hugo, 92200 Neuilly sur Seine, ☎ 01 46 41 25 25. Accredited by major insurance companies.
The British Hospital is just outside Paris in Levallois-Perret, 3 rue Barbès, ☎ 01 46 39 22 22.

Seasons

Climate

In the summer months, the Atlantic shore is very popular with French and foreign vacationers, who come to enjoy the vivifying atmosphere of the ocean spiced with the balsam scent of pines, a tonic for the body and the spirit.
Sea breezes cool the sun's ardour and the light is extraordinary: brilliant and bright at its purest, in the summertime a barely perceptible mist softens the outlines of the landscape. Across the pale blue sky trail wisps of cloud like silk scarves in the wind.
Reclining against the slope of the dunes, the warm sand beaches rumble with the breakers; children's voices trill in counterpoint, gay in the open air and sunshine.

In the autumn the crowds and heat subside. When waves batter the coast and rain pounds the shore, the fine weather moves inland. This is the perfect time to visit the vineyards of Bordeaux, busy with the grape harvest.
The light falls obliquely from the heavens, saturating the colours of the deepening season: red vine creeping over an old stone wall, purple grapes heavy and ripe, the brown gloss of chestnuts inside their prickly husks, tender mushrooms below the forest bracken.

Winter is a splendid time of year to discover the rugged isolation of the Pyrenees beneath a white cloak. Whether glimpsed at high speed as your skis cut through fresh powder, or contemplated more sedately as you glide across the valley on a cross-country trail, the landscape is memorable.

Spring is a cool season, heralded by a profusion of flowers and flowering trees. As the equinox approaches, storms whip up cold rains which flood the river valleys. Between the dark masses of mountainous clouds, a piercing yellow light highlights the natural and architectural beauty of the land.

A FEW WEATHER FACTS...

The Atlantic Coast is exceptionally sunny, logging in over 2 000 hours yearly. The brightest days are between May and September; over that period the water warms up to an average 20°C/70°F as it hits the beach. Snow is rare and spring comes early. The central part of the coastal area covered in this book is subject to 20 to 30 spectacular thunder storms annually, blown in by prevailing winds from the west. Around Biarritz, on the Basque Coast, the mountains create a different climate with considerably more rainfall. In the winter months, frequent warm spells (up to 20°C/70°F) give the Basque "micro-climate" an exotic air. In the high mountains, snow may continue to fall well into spring. Climbers and campers will find late July and early September the most clement for enjoying nature in the part of the Pyrenees covered in this guide (August is often stormy). Skiers seeking fresh *néou* (as snow is called by some locals), will find slopes open from December to April.

A. Thuillier/MICHELIN

What to pack

As little as possible! Cleaning and laundry services are available everywhere. Most personal items can be replaced at reasonable cost. Try to pack everything into one suitcase and a tote bag. Porter help may be in short supply, and new purchases will add to the original weight. Take an extra tote bag for packing new purchases, shopping at the open-air market, carrying a picnic, etc. Be sure luggage is clearly labelled and old travel tags removed. Do not pack medication in checked luggage, but keep it with you.

Public holidays

Museums and other monuments may be closed or may vary their hours of admission on the following public holidays:

1 January	New Year's Day *(Jour de l'An)*
	Easter Day and Easter Monday *(Pâques)*
1 May	May Day
8 May	VE Day
Thurs 40 days after Easter	Ascension Day *(Ascension)*
7th Sun-Mon after Easter	Whit Sunday and Monday *(Pentecôte)*
14 July	France's National Day (Bastille Day)
15 August	Assumption *(Assomption)*
1 November	All Saint's Day *(Toussaint)*
11 November	Armistice Day
25 December	Christmas Day *(Noël)*

National museums and art galleries are closed on Tuesdays; municipal museums are generally closed on Mondays. In addition to the usual school holidays at Christmas and in the spring and summer, there are long mid-term breaks (10 days to a fortnight) in February and early November.

Time

France is 1 hr ahead of Greenwich Mean Time (GMT).

When it is **noon in France**, it is

3am	in Los Angeles
6am	in New York
11am	in Dublin
11am	in London
7pm	in Perth
9pm	in Sydney
11pm	in Auckland

R. Corbel/MICHELIN

In France "am" and "pm" are not used but the 24-hour clock is widely applied.

Budget

Currency

There are no restrictions on the amount of currency visitors can take into France. Visitors carrying a lot of cash are advised to complete a currency declaration form on arrival, because there are restrictions on currency export.

NOTES AND COINS

Since 17 February 2002, the euro has become the only currency accepted as a means of payment in France. However, until the end of June 2002, notes and coins in French francs can be exchanged in banks. After that, they will only be accepted by the Banque de France (3 years for coins and 10 years for notes).

BANKS

Banks are open from 9am to noon and 2pm to 4pm and branches are closed either on Monday or Saturday. Banks close early on the day before a bank holiday. A passport is necessary as identification when cashing travellers cheques in banks. Commission charges vary and hotels usually charge more than banks for cashing cheques. One of the most economical ways to use your money in France is by using **ATM machines** to get cash directly from your bank account or to use your credit cards to get cash advances. Be sure to remember your PIN number, you will need it to use cash dispensers and to pay with your card in shops, restaurants, etc. Code pads are numeric; use a telephone pad to translate a letter code into numbers. PIN numbers have 4 digits in France; inquire with the issuing company or bank if the code you usually use is longer. Visa is the most widely accepted credit card, followed by MasterCard; other cards, credit and debit (Diners Club, Plus, Cirrus, etc) are also accepted in some cash machines. American Express is more often accepted in premium establishments. Most places post signs indicating the cards they accept; if you don't see such a sign, and want to pay with a card, ask before ordering or making a selection. Cards are widely accepted in shops, hypermarkets, hotels and restaurants, at tollbooths and in petrol stations. If your card is lost or stolen, call one of the following 24-hour hotlines:

American Express	☎ 01 47 77 72 00	**Visa**	☎ 08 36 69 08 80
Mastercard/Eurocard	☎ 01 45 67 84 84	**Diners Club**	☎ 01 49 06 17 50

You must report any loss or theft of credit cards or travellers' cheques to the local police who will issue you with a certificate (useful proof to show the issuing company).

Prices and tips

Since a service charge is automatically included in the price of meals and accommodation in France, any additional tipping is up to the visitor, generally small change, and generally not more than 5%. Taxi drivers and hairdressers are usually tipped 10-15%.

As a rule, the cost of staying in a hotel, eating in a restaurant or buying goods and services is significantly lower in the French regions than in Paris.

Here are a few indicative prices, based on surveys conducted by French authorities between 1999-2000. Exchange rates change regularly, so you will have to check before you leave for an exact calculation. At press time, the exchange rate for 1€ was: USD 0.92; GBP 0.63; CAD 1.46; AUD 1.89.

Hotel rooms (based on double occupancy) in a city	Euros
1 star (French Tourist boardstandards)	27.44 – 53.36
2 star	53.36 – 76.22
3 star	76.23 – 121.97
4 star	137.21 – 228.69
4 star (luxury)	228.69 – 381.15

Food and entertainment	Euros
Movie ticket	7.62
River cruise	6.1 – 9.91
Dinner cruise	68.61 – 76.23
In a café:	
Expresso coffee	1.83
Café au lait	3.35
Soda	3.35
Beer	3.05
Mineral water	3.05
Ice cream	4.88
Ham sandwhich	3.20
Baguette of bread	0.69
Soda (1 litre in a shop)	2.13
Restaurant meal (3 courses, no wine)	22.87
Big Mac menu meal	5.34
French daily newspaper	0.91
Foreign newspaper	1.52 – 2.29
Compact disc	12.00 – 21.00
Telephone card – 50 units	7.47
Telephone card – 120 units	14.86
Cigarettes (pack of 20)	2.44 – 3.25

Public transportation	Euros
Bus, street car, metro	1.30
Book of ten tickets	9.30
Taxi (5km + tip)	9.91
TGV ticket Paris-Bordeaux 2nd class (one way)	56.10

The overall average yearly salary in France in 1999 was 141,970 French francs (21,643€). The minimum wage per hour was 40.22 French francs (6.13€).

Restaurants usually charge for meals in two ways: a *menu*, that is a fixed price menu with 2 or 3 courses, sometimes a small pitcher of wine, all for a stated price, or *à la carte*, the more expensive way, with each course ordered separately.

Cafés have very different prices, depending on where they are located. The price of a drink or a coffee is cheaper if you stand at the counter *(comptoir)* than if you sit down *(salle)* and sometimes it is even more expensive if you sit outdoors *(terrace)*.

Tourist Pass: 100 sights for 42€

This pass gives unrestricted access to more than 100 historic buildings managed by the *Centre des Monuments Nationaux*. It is valid for one year throughout France as of the date of purchase and is for sale at the entrance to major historic buildings, monuments and museums. With the pass, you can save time by skipping the wait at the ticket window. For a list of all the monuments, plus details on their history, information on travel, and other entertaining features to help you plan your trip, visit the lively web site: www.monuments-france.fr.

Significant discounts are available for senior citizens, students, youth under age 25, teachers, and groups for public transportation, museums and monuments and for some leisure activities such as movies (at certain times of day). Bring student or senior cards with you, and bring along some extra passport-size photos for discount travel cards.

The **International Student Travel Conference** (www.istc.org), global administrator of the International Student and Teacher Identity Cards, is an association of student travel organizations around the world. ISTC members collectively negotiate benefits with airlines, governments, and providers of other goods and services for the student and teacher community, both in their own country and around the world. The non-profit association sells international ID cards for students, youth under age 25 and teachers (who may get discounts on museum entrances, for example). The ISTC is also active in a network of international education and work exchange programmes. The coorporate headquarters address is Herengracht 479, 1017 BS Amsterdam, The Netherlands ☎ 31 20 421 28 00; Fax 31 20 421 28 10.

See the section below on travelling by rail in France for other discounts on transportation.

Transport

Getting there and getting around

BY AIR

It is very easy to arrange air travel to one of Paris' two airports (Roissy-Charles-de-Gaulle to the north, and Orly to the south). Contact airline companies and travel agents for details of package tour flights with a rail or coach link-up as well as Fly-Drive schemes. For example, some packages include a direct link from Roissy airport to the high-speed TGV train which serves the region, stopping in Poitiers, La Rochelle, Bordeaux and as far south as Biarritz, Hendaye and Tarbes.

Alternatively, there are several daily connecting flights from Paris to the regional capital Bordeaux, direct regular flights from London and seasonal flights from a number of destinations outside France, including Montreal, Toronto and Shannon. Information is available from the French Tourist Office in your country *(see Planning your trip)* as well as from travel agents and airline companies.

Visitors arriving in **Paris** who wish to reach the city centre or a train station may use public transportation or reserve space on the **Airport Shuttle** (for Roissy-Charles-de-Gaulle ☎ 01 45 38 55 72, for Orly ☎ 01 43 21 06 78). Air France operates a coach service into town with frequent departures (☎ 01 41 56 89 00). The cost and duration of a taxi ride from the airport to the center of town varies with traffic conditions. From Charles-de-Gaulle: about 1hr, 30.49€; from Orly about 30min, 22.87€. There is an extra charge (posted in the cab) for baggage; the extra charge for airport pick-up is on the meter; drivers are usually given a tip of 10-15% of the fare.

BY SEA (from the UK or Ireland)

There are numerous **cross-Channel services** (passenger and car ferries, hovercraft) from the United Kingdom and Ireland, as well as the rail Shuttle through the Channel Tunnel (**Le Shuttle-Eurotunnel**, ☎ 0990 353-535). To choose the most suitable route between your port of arrival and your destination use the Michelin Tourist and Motoring Atlas France, Michelin map 911 (which gives travel times and mileages) or Michelin maps from the 1:200,000 series (with the yellow cover). For details apply to travel agencies or to:

P & O Stena Line Ferries	Channel House, Channel View Road, Dover CT179JT, ☎ 0990 980 980 or 01304 863 000 (Switchboard), www.p-and-o.com
Hoverspeed	International Hoverport, Marine Parade, Dover, Kent CT17 9TG, b 0990 240 241, Fax 01304 240088, www.hoverspeed.co.uk

Brittany Ferries	Millbay Docks; Plymouth, Devon. PL1 3EW, ☎ 0990 360 360, www.brittany-ferries.com
Portsmouth Commercial Port (and ferry information)	George Byng Way, Portsmouth, Hampshire PO2 8SP, ☎ 01705 297391, Fax 01705 861165
Irish Ferries	50 West Norland Street, Dublin 2, ☎ (353) 16 610 511, www.irishferries.com
Seafrance	Eastern Docks, Dover, Kent, CT16 1JA, ☎ 01304 212696, Fax 01304 240033, www.seafrance.fr

BY RAIL

Eurostar runs via the Channel Tunnel between **London** (Waterloo) and **Paris** (Gare du Nord) in 3hr (bookings and information ☎ 0345 303 030 in the UK; ☎ 1-888-EUROSTAR in the US). In Paris it links to the high-speed rail network (TGV). TGV departures for the Atlantic coast are from the Gare Montparnasse.

Eurailpass, Flexipass, Eurailpass Youth, EurailDrive Pass and **Saverpass** are three of the travel passes which may be purchased by residents of countries outside the European Union. In the US. Contact your travel agent or **Rail Europe** 2100 Central Ave. Boulder, CO, 80301 ☎ 1-800-4-EURAIL or **Europrail International** ☎ 1 888 667 9731. If you are a European resident, you can buy an individual country pass, if you are not a resident of the country where you plan to use it. In the UK, contact Europrail at 179 Piccadilly London W1V OBA ☎ 0990 848 848. Information on schedules can be obtained on web sites for these agencies and the **SNCF**, respectively: www.raileurop.com.us, www.eurail.on.ca, www.sncf.fr. At the SNCF site, you can book ahead, pay with a credit card, and receive your ticket in the mail at home.

There are numerous **discounts** available when you purchase your tickets in France, from 25-50% below the regular rate. These include discounts for using senior cards and youth cards (the nominative cards with a photograph must be purchased – 44 and 41€, respectively), and lower rates for 2-9 people travelling together (no card required, advance purchase necessary). There are a limited number of discount seats available during peak travel times, and the best discounts are available for travel during off-peak periods.

Tickets must be validated *(composter)* by using the orange automatic date-stamping machines at the platform entrance (failure to do so may result in a fine).

The French railway company SNCF operates a telephone information, reservation and prepayment service in English from 7am to 10pm (French time). In France call ☎ 08 36 35 35 39 (when calling from outside France, drop the initial 0).

BY COACH

Regular coach services between London and Paris, connections to other cities:

Eurolines (London), 52 Grosvenor Gardens, Victoria, London SW1W OAU, ☎ 0171 730 8235 Fax 0171 730 8721.

Eurolines (Paris), 28 avenue du Général-de-Gaulle, 93541 Bagnolet, ☎ 01 49 72 51 51.

MOTORING IN FRANCE

The area covered in this guide is easily reached by main motorways and national routes. **Michelin map 911** indicates the main itineraries as well as alternate routes for avoiding heavy traffic during busy holiday periods, and gives estimated travel times. **Michelin map 914** is a detailed atlas of French motorways, indicating tolls, rest areas and services along the route; it includes a table for calculating distances and times. The latest Michelin route-planning service is available on Internet, **www.ViaMichelin.com**. Travellers can calculate a precise route using such options as shortest route, route avoiding toll roads, Michelin-recommended route and gain access to tourist information (hotels, restaurants, attractions). The service is available on a pay-per-route basis or by subscription.

The roads are very busy during the holiday period (particularly weekends in July and August) and, to avoid traffic congestion it is advisable to follow the recommended secondary routes (signposted as *Bison Futé – itinéraires bis*). The motorway network includes rest areas *(aires)* and petrol stations, usually with restaurant and shopping complexes attached, about every 40km/25mi, so that long-distance drivers have no excuse not to stop for a rest every now and then.

DOCUMENTS

Travellers from other European Union countries and North America can drive in France with a valid national or home-state **driving licence**. An **international driving licence** is useful because the information on it appears in nine languages (keep in mind that traffic officers are empowered to fine motorists). A permit is available (US$10) from the National Automobile Club, 1151 East Hillsdale Blvd., Foster City, CA 94404 ☎ 650-294-7000 or nationalautoclub.com; or contact your local branch of the American Automobile Association. For the vehicle, it is necessary to have the registration papers (logbook) and a nationality plate of the approved size.

Certain motoring organisations (AAA, AA, RAC) offer accident **insurance** and breakdown service schemes for members. Check with your current insurance company in regard to coverage while abroad. If you plan to hire a car using your credit card, check with the company, which may provide liability insurance automatically (and thus save you having to pay the cost for optimum coverage).

HIGHWAY CODE

The minimum driving age is 18. Traffic drives on the right. All passengers must wear **seat belts**. Children under the age of 10 must ride in the back seat. Headlights must be switched on in poor visibility and at night; use side-lights only when the vehicle is stationary.

In the case of a **breakdown**, a red warning triangle or hazard warning lights are obligatory. In the absence of stop signs at intersections, cars must **yield to the right**. Traffic on main roads outside built-up areas (priority indicated by a yellow diamond sign) and on roundabouts has right of way. Vehicles must stop when the lights turn red at road junctions and may filter to the right only when indicated by an amber arrow.

The regulations on **drinking and driving** (limited to 0.50g/l) and **speeding** are strictly enforced – usually by an on-the-spot fine and/or confiscation of the vehicle.

Speed limits – Although liable to modification, these are as follows:
– toll motorways *(autoroutes)* 130kph/80mph (110kph/68mph when raining);
– dual carriageways and motorways without tolls 110kph/68mph (100kph/62mph when raining);
– other roads 90kph/56mph (80kph/50mph when raining) and in towns 50kph/31mph;
– outside lane on motorways during daylight, on level ground and with good visibility – minimum speed limit of 80kph/50mph.

Parking Regulations – In town there are zones where parking is either restricted or subject to a fee; tickets should be obtained from the ticket machines (*horodateurs* – small change necessary) and displayed inside the windscreen on the driver's side; failure to display may result in a fine, or towing and impoundment. Other parking areas in town may require you to take a ticket when passing through a barrier. To exit, you must pay the parking fee (usually there is a machine located by the exit – *sortie*) and insert the paid-up card in another machine which will lift the exit gate.

Tolls – In France, most motorway sections are subject to a toll *(péage)*. You can pay in cash or with a credit card (Visa, Mastercard).

CAR RENTAL

There are car rental agencies at airports, railway stations and in all large towns throughout France. European cars have manual transmission; automatic cars are available in larger cities only if an advance reservation is made. Drivers must be over 21; between ages 21-25, drivers are required to pay an extra daily fee; some companies allow drivers under 23 only if the reservation has been made through a travel agent. It is relatively expensive to hire a car in France; Americans in particular will notice the difference and should make arrangements before leaving, take advantage of fly-drive offers, or seek advice from a travel agent, specifying requirements.

Central Reservation in France:

Avis: 08 02 05 05 05

Europcar: 08 25 35 23 52

Budget France: 08 00 10 00 01

Hertz France: 01 39 38 38 38

SIXT-Eurorent: 01 40 65 01 00

National-CITER: 01 45 22 88 40

A Baron's Limousine: 01 45 30 21 21

Worldwide Motorhome Rentals offers fully equipped campervans for rent. You can view them on the company's web pages (mhrww.com) or call (US toll-free) US ☎ 888-519-8969; outside the US ☎ 530-389-8316 or Fax 530-389-8316.

Overseas Motorhome Tours Inc. organises escorted tours and individual rental of recreational vehicles: in the US ☎ 800-322-2127; outside the US ☎ 1-310-543-2590; Internet www.omtinc.com

Petrol (US: gas) – French service stations dispense: *sans plomb 98* (super unleaded 98), *sans plomb 95* (super unleaded 95), *diesel/gazole* (diesel) and *GPL* (LPG). Petrol is considerably more expensive in France than in the USA. Prices are listed on signboards on the motorways; it is usually cheaper to fill up after leaving the motorway; check the large hypermarkets on the outskirts of town.

Where to stay, Where to eat

FINDING A HOTEL

THE GREEN GUIDE is pleased to offer a new feature: lists of selected hotels and restaurants for this region. Turn to the sections bordered in blue for descriptions and prices of typical places to stay and eat with local flair. The key on page 9 explains the symbols and abbreviations used in these sections. We have reported the prices and conditions as we observed them, but of course changes in management and other factors may mean that you will find some discrepancies. Please feel free to keep us informed of any major differences you encounter.

Le Château de St-Loup is ready to welcome you...

Use the **map of Places to stay** below to identify recommended places for overnight stops. For an even greater selection, use **The Red Guide France**, with its famously reliable star-rating system and hundreds of establishments all over France. Book ahead to ensure that you get the accommodation you want, not only in tourist season, but year round, as many towns fill up during trade fairs, arts festivals, etc. Some places require an advance deposit or a reconfirmation. Reconfirming is especially important if you plan to arrive after 6pm.

For further assistance, **Loisirs Accueil** is a booking service that has offices in some French *départements* – contact the tourist offices listed above for further information.

A guide to good-value, family-run hotels, **Logis et Auberges de France**, is available from the French Tourist Office, as are lists of other kinds of accommodation such as hotel-châteaux, bed-and-breakfasts etc.

Relais et châteaux provides information on booking in luxury hotels with character: 15 rue Galvani, 75017 Paris, ☎ 01 45 72 90 00.

Economy Chain Hotels – If you need a place to stop en route, these can be useful, as they are inexpensive (30-45€ for a double room) and generally located near the main road. While breakfast is available, there may not be a restaurant; rooms are small, with a television and bathroom. Central reservation numbers:
– **Akena** ☎ 01 69 84 85 17
– **B&B** ☎ 0 803 00 29 29
– **Etap Hôtel** ☎ 08 36 68 89 00
– **Mister Bed** ☎ 01 46 14 38 00
– **Villages Hôtel** ☎ 03 80 60 92 70

The hotels listed below are slightly more expensive (from 45€), and offer a few more amenities and services. Central reservation numbers:
– **Campanile, Climat de France, Kyriad** ☎ 01 64 62 46 46
– **Ibis** ☎ 0 803 88 22 22

RENTING A COTTAGE, BED AND BREAKFAST

The **Maison des Gîtes de France** is an information service on self-catering accommodation in France. *Gîtes* usually take the form of a cottage or apartment decorated in the local style where visitors can make themselves at home, or bed and breakfast accommodation *(chambres d'hôtes)* which consists of a room and breakfast at a reasonable price.

Contact the Gîtes de France office in Paris: 59 rue St-Lazare, 75439 Paris Cedex 09, ☎ 01 49 70 75 75, or their representative in the UK, **Brittany Ferries** *(address above)*. The Internet site, www.gites-de-france.fr, has a good English version. From the site, you can order catalogues for different regions illustrated with photographs of the properties, as well as specialised catalogues (bed and breakfasts, chalets in ski areas, farm stays, etc). You can also contact the local Tourist offices, which may have lists of available properties and local bed and breakfast establishments.

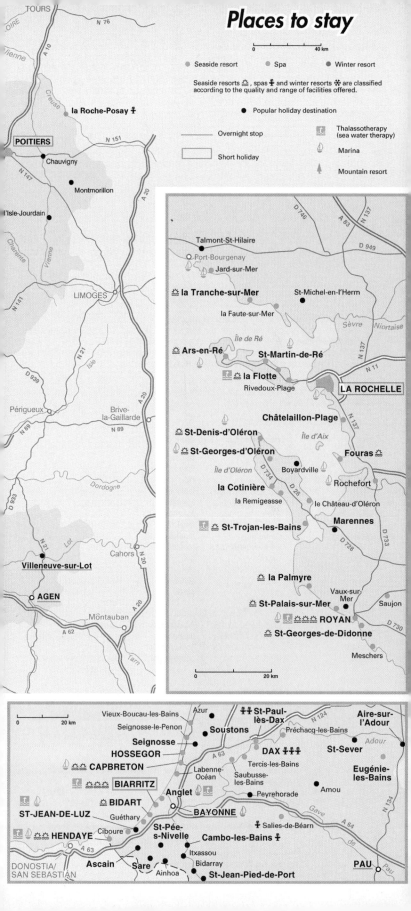

Places to stay

0   40 km

● Seaside resort   ● Spa   ● Winter resort

Seaside resorts ☆, spas ✚ and winter resorts ❄ are classified according to the quality and range of facilities offered.

● Popular holiday destination

Overnight stop

Short holiday

Thalassotherapy (sea water therapy)

Marina

Mountain resort

TOURS

N 76

N 10

Vienne

Creuse

la Roche-Posay ✚

POITIERS

Chauvigny

N 151

N 147

Montmorillon

l'Isle-Jourdain

N 20

Charente

Vienne

LIMOGES

N 141

Isle

N 21

D 939

A 20

Périgueux

Brive-la-Gaillarde

N 89

N 89

Dordogne

D 933

Lot

Villeneuve-sur-Lot

N 21

Cahors

N 20

AGEN

Montauban

A 20

Tarn

A 62

D 746   A 83   N 137

D 949

Talmont-St-Hilaire

Port-Bourgenay

Jard-sur-Mer

☆ la Tranche-sur-Mer   St-Michel-en-l'Herm

la Faute-sur-Mer

Sèvre   Niortaise

Île de Ré

☆ Ars-en-Ré   St-Martin-de-Ré

N 11

☆ la Flotte

Rivedoux-Plage

LA ROCHELLE

N 137

Châtelaillon-Plage

☆ St-Denis-d'Oléron   Île d'Aix

☆ St-Georges-d'Oléron   Fouras ☆

Île d'Oléron   Boyardville

D 734   D 26   Rochefort

la Cotinière

la Remigeasse   le Château-d'Oléron

☆ St-Trojan-les-Bains   Marennes

D 728   D 733

☆ la Palmyre

Vaux-sur-Mer   Saujon

☆ St-Palais-sur-Mer

ROYAN

D 730

☆ St-Georges-de-Didonne

Meschers

0   20 km

0   20 km

Vieux-Boucau-les-Bains   Azur

✚✚ St-Paul-lès-Dax

Aire-sur-l'Adour

N 124

Seignosse-le-Penon

Soustons

Préchacq-les-Bains

Adour

N 124

Seignosse

HOSSEGOR

A 63

DAX ✚✚✚

St-Sever

☆☆ CAPBRETON

Labenne-Océan

Tercis-les-Bains

Eugénie-les-Bains

☆☆☆ BIARRITZ

Saubusse-les-Bains

N 134

Anglet

Peyrehorade   Amou

☆ BIDART

BAYONNE

Gave

St-Pée-s-Nivelle

ST-JEAN-DE-LUZ

Guéthary

✚ Salies-de-Béarn

A 64

☆☆ HENDAYE

Ciboure

Cambo-les-Bains ✚

N 134

DONOSTIA/SAN SEBASTIAN

A 63

Ascain   Sare

Itxassou   Bidarray

Ainhoa

St-Jean-Pied-de-Port

PAU

de   Pau

HOSTELS, CAMPING

To obtain an International Youth Hostel Federation card (there is no age requirement, and there is a "senior card" available too), you should contact the IYHF in your own country for information and membership applications (US ☎ 202 783 6161; UK ☎ 1727 855215; Canada ☎ 613-273 7884; Australia ☎ 61-2-9565-1669) There is a new booking service on the internet (iyhf.org), which you may use to reserve rooms as far as 6 months in advance. There are two main youth hostel associations *(auberges de jeunesse)* in France, the **Ligue Française pour les Auberges de la Jeunesse** (38 boulevard Raspail, 75007 Paris, ☎ 01 45 48 69 84, Fax 01 45 44 57 47) and the **Fédération Unie des Auberges de Jeunesse** (27 rue Pajol, 75018 Paris, ☎ 01 44 89 87 27, Fax 01 44 89 87 10).

There are numerous officially graded **camping sites** with varying standards of facilities throughout the Loire Valley. The **Michelin Camping Caravaning France** guide lists a selection of camp sites. The area is very popular with campers in the summer months, so it is wise to reserve in advance.

FINDING A RESTAURANT

Turn to the pages bordered in blue for descriptions and prices of selected places eat in the different locations covered in this guide. The key on page 9 explains the symbols and abbreviations used in these sections. Use **The Red Guide France**, with its famously reliable star-rating system and hundreds of establishments all over France, for an even greater choice. If you would like to experience a meal in a highly rated restaurant from The Red Guide, be sure to book ahead! In the countryside, restaurants usually serve lunch between noon and 2pm and the evening meal between 7.30-10pm. It is not always easy to find something in-between those two meal times, as the "non-stop" restaurant is still a rarity in small towns in the provinces. However, a hungry traveller can usually get a sandwich in a café, and ordinary hot dishes may be available in a *brasserie*.

Typical places to enjoy local specialities are the **Bars à Vin** (Wine Bars) of the Bordeaux region and the **Cabanes à Huîtres** (oyster huts) around Arcachon. Near the Spanish border, many bars offer **Tapas** to eat with a glass of wine. In the Gers and Lot-et-Garonne departments, foies gras and confits are on almost every restaurant *menu* (fixed price meal) or *carte* (as in *à la carte*).

In French restaurants and cafés, a service charge is included. Tipping is not necessary, but French people often leave the small change from their bill on their table, or about 5% for the waiter in a nice restaurant.

Menu Reader – Regional specialities

agneau	lamb	langouste /	
alose	shad	langoustines	Spiny lobster
anguilles	eels	lapin	Rabbit
boudin blanc	chicken sausage	loukinos	Garlic sausage
boudin noir	blood sausage	magret	Duck fillet
brioche	sweet egg-and-	marrons	Chestnuts
	butter bread	mojettes	White beans
canard	duck	moules	Mussels
cèpes	wild mushrooms	mouton	Mutton
chapon	capon	noix	Walnuts
charcuterie	pork meats	oie	Goose
chèvre	goat	palombe	Wood pigeon
chipirones / seiches	squid	pastis	Flaky rum-flavoured
choux	cabbage		Pastry
confits (canard)	(duck) cooked and	pêche	Peach
	preserved in fat	pibales	Young eels
crevettes	shrimp / prawns	piperade	Spicy tomato Omlette
crudités	raw vegetable salad	poule / poulet	Chicken
éclade	mussels cooked	poule au pot	Chicken stew with
	over pine needles		Vegetables
escargots	snails		
esturgeon	sturgeon	prune	Plum
fèves	broad beans	pruneau	Prune
foie	liver	ravigote	Seasoned white
fromage de brebis	sheep's milk cheese		Sauce
fruits de mer	seafood	salmis	Stew of roast fowl
garbure	hearty vegetable		And game
	and meat soup	tournedos	Fillet steak
haricots	beans	tourteau fromager	Sweet cake made
homard	lobster		With cheese
huître	oyster	tourtière	Flaky pastry with
jambon	ham		Prune filling
Lamproie	lamprey	tripotcha	Mutton sausage
		ttoro	Basque fish stew

well-done, medium, rare, raw = **bien cuit, à point, saignant, cru**

Basic information

Electricity

The electric current is 220 volts. Circular two-pin plugs are the rule. Adapters and converters (for hairdryers, for example) should be bought before you leave home; they are on sale in most airports. If you have a rechargable device (video camera, portable computer, battery recharger), read the instructions carefully or contact the manufacturer or shop. Sometimes these items only require a plug adapter, in other cases you must use a voltage converter as well or risk ruining your appliance.

Post and telephone

Main post offices open Monday to Friday 8am to 7pm, Saturday 8am to noon. Smaller branch post offices generally close at lunchtime between noon and 2pm and at 4pm.

Postage via air mail: UK: letter (20g) 0.46€

North America: letter (20g) 0.67€

Australia and NZ: letter (20g) 0.79€

Stamps are also available from newsagents and *bureaux de tabac*. Stamp collectors should ask for *timbres de collection* in any post office.

Public Telephones – Most public phones in France use pre-paid phone cards *(télécartes)*, rather than coins. Some telephone booths accept credit cards (Visa, Mastercard/Eurocard). *Télécartes* (50 or 120 units) can be bought in post offices, branches of France Télécom, *bureaux de tabac* (cafés that sell cigarettes) and newsagents and can be used to make calls in France and abroad. Calls can be received at phone boxes where the blue bell sign is shown; the phone will not ring, so keep your eye on the little digital screen.

National calls – French telephone numbers have 10 digits. Paris and Paris region numbers begin with 01; 02 in north-west France; 03 in north-east France; 04 in south-east France and Corsica; 05 in south-west France.

International calls – To call France from abroad, dial the country code (33) + 9-digit number (omit the initial 0). When calling abroad from France dial 00, then dial the country code followed by the area code and number of your correspondent.

International dialling codes (00 + code):

Australia . . . . . . ☎ 61	New Zealand . . . ☎ 64	Canada . . . . ☎ 1
United Kingdom . ☎ 44	Eire . . . . ☎ 353	United States . . . ☎ 1

To use your **personal calling card** dial:

AT&T. . . . . ☎ 0-800 99 00 11	Sprint . . . . ☎ 0-800 99 00 87
MCI. . . . . . ☎ 0-800 99 00 19	Canada Direct . . ☎ 0-800 99 00 16

International information, US/Canada: 00 33 12 11
International operator: 00 33 12 + country code
Local directory assistance: 12

Minitel – France Télécom operates a system offering directory enquiries (free of charge up to 3min), travel and entertainment reservations, and other services (cost per minute varies). These small computer-like terminals can be found in some post offices, hotels and France Télécom agencies and in

Emergency numbers:	
Police	17
SAMU (Paramedics)	15
Fire *(Pompiers)*	18

many French homes. 3614 PAGES E is the code for **directory assistance in English** (turn on the unit, dial 3614, hit the *connexion* button when you get the tone, type in "PAGES E", and follow the instructions on the screen).

Conversion Tables

Weights and measures

1 kilogram (kg)	2.2 pounds (lb)	2.2 pounds
1 metric ton (tn)	1.1 tons	1.1 tons

to convert kilograms to pounds, multiply by 2.2

1 litre (l)	2.1 pints (pt)	1.8 pints
1 litre	0.3 gallon (gal)	0.2 gallon

to convert litres to gallons, multiply by 0.26 (US) or 0.22 (UK)

1 hectare (ha)	2.5 acres	2.5 acres
1 square kilometre (km²)	0.4 square miles (sq mi)	0.4 square miles

to convert hectares to acres, multiply by 2.4

1 centimetre (cm)	0.4 inches (in)	0.4 inches
1 metre (m)	3.3 feet (ft) - 39.4 inches - 1.1 yards (yd)	
1 kilometre (km)	0.6 miles (mi)	0.6 miles

to convert metres to feet, multiply by 3.28 . kilometres to miles, multiply by 0.6

Clothing

Women	🇪🇺	🇺🇸	🇬🇧		🇪🇺	🇺🇸	🇬🇧	Men
	35	4	2½		40	7½	7	
	36	5	3½		41	8½	8	
	37	6	4½		42	9½	9	
Shoes	38	7	5½		43	10½	10	**Shoes**
	39	8	6½		44	11½	11	
	40	9	7½		45	12½	12	
	41	10	8½		46	13½	13	
	36	4	8		46	36	36	
	38	6	10		48	38	38	
Dresses &	40	8	12		50	40	40	**Suits**
Suits	42	12	14		52	42	42	
	44	14	16		54	44	44	
	46	16	18		56	46	48	
	36	08	30		37	14½	14,5	
	38	10	32		38	15	15	
Blouses &	40	12	14		39	15½	15½	**Shirts**
sweaters	42	14	36		40	15¾	15¾	
	44	16	38		41	16	16	
	46	18	40		42	16½	16½	

Sizes often vary depending on the designer. These equivalents are given for guidance only.

Speed

kph	10	30	50	70	80	90	100	110	120	130
mph	6	19	31	43	50	56	62	68	75	81

Temperature

Celsius (°C)	0°	5°	10°	15°	20°	25°	30°	40°	60°	80°	100°
Fahrenheit (°F)	32°	41°	50°	59°	68°	77°	86°	104°	140°	176°	212°

To convert Celsius into Fahrenheit, multiply °C by 9, divide by 5, and add 32.
To convert Fahrenheit into Celsius, subtract 32 from °F, multiply by 5, and divide by 9.

Cellular phones in France have numbers which begin with 06. Two-watt (lighter, shorter reach) and eight-watt models are on the market, using the Itinéris (France Télécom) or SFR network. *Mobicartes* are pre-paid phone cards that fit into mobile units. Cell phone rentals (delivery or airport pick-up provided):

Rent a Cell Express   ☏ 01 53 93 78 00, Fax 01 53 93 78 09
A.L.T. Rent A Phone   ☏ 01 48 00 06 06, E-mail altloc@jve.fr

Shopping

Most of the larger shops are open Mondays to Saturdays from 9am to 6.30 or 7.30pm. Smaller, individual shops may close during the lunch hour. Food shops – grocers, wine merchants and bakeries – are generally open from 7am to 6.30 or 7.30pm; some open on Sunday mornings. Many food shops close between noon and 2pm and on Mondays. Bakery and pastry shops sometimes close on Wednesdays. Hypermarkets usually stay open non-stop from 9am until 9pm or later.

People travelling to the USA cannot import plant products or fresh food, including fruit, cheeses and nuts. It is acceptable to carry tinned products or preserves.

RECOVERING VALUE ADDED TAX

There is a Value Added Tax in France *(TVA)* of 19.6% on almost every purchase (some foods and books are subject to a lower rate). However, non-European visitors who spend more than 183€ (figure subject to change) in any one participating store can get the VAT amount refunded. Usually, you fill out a form at the store, showing your passport. Upon leaving the country, you submit all forms to customs for approval (they may want to see the goods, so if possible don't pack them in checked luggage). The refund is usually paid directly into your bank or credit card account, or it can be sent by mail. Big department stores that cater to tourists provide special services to help you; be sure to mention that you plan to seek a refund before you pay for goods (no refund is possible for tax on services). If you are visiting two or more countries within the European Union, you submit the forms only on departure from the last EU country. The refund is worth while for those visitors who would like to buy fashion articles, furniture or other fairly expensive items, but remember, the minimum amount must be spent in a single shop (though not necessarily on the same day).

Discovering the region

Driving tours

Following is a brief description of each of the driving tours shown on the map on page 13.

1 POITOU: NORTH-EAST OF POITIERS – *230km/143mi starting from Poitiers*

The tour begins with a visit to Futuroscope, which has become the symbol of the whole region. East of Poitiers, Chauvigny's ruined castles form the impressive setting of fascinating falconry shows. As a contrast, St-Savin offers the sheer beauty of its 11C frescoes. Aim for La Roche-Posay via the picturesque village of Angles-sur-l'Anglin. Next, as you walk through the centre of Châtellerault in the footsteps of Descartes, take time to admire the Église St-Jacques, once the rendezvous of pilgrims on their way to Santiago de Compostela, and to enjoy the Auto-Moto-Vélo Museum housed in La Manu. Head north to Loudun, birthplace of the first printed newspaper in France, stopping on the way to look at the Romanesque church in Lencloître and the Château de Coussay, which once belonged to Richelieu. Head back to Poitiers via Moncontour.

M. Thiery/MICHELIN

Talmont-sur-Gironde

2 THE SAINTONGE REGION – *210km/130mi starting from Saintes*

On your way to Rochefort, with its rich maritime past, stop at the fairy-tale castle of La Roche-Courbon. South-east of Rochefort, the ramparts of Brouage rise proudly above the surrounding marshland. From Marennes and its famous oysters, make a detour to the picturesque island of Oléron then follow the coastline south through the Forêt de la Coubre, stopping at La Palmyre, reputedly one of the finest zoos in France. Further south, you will find a succession of seaside resorts, St-Palais-sur-Mer, Royan, St-Georges-de-Didonne, Meschers-sur-Gironde and finally, Talmont-sur-Gironde, camped at the end of a peninsula, with its fishermen's huts standing on piles in the foreground.

3 THE VENDÉE REGION – *225km/140mi starting from Fontenay-le-Comte*

The Renaissance town of Fontenay-le-Comte lies between the Marais Poitevin and the Forêt de Mervent-Vouvant, ideal for hiking, riding, biking and climbing. Don't miss the picturesque villages nestling at the heart of the forest. Head north to Le Puy-du-Fou through the rolling hills of Vendée, via Mouilleron-en-Pareds and Pouzauges. Let the spectacular night show at Le Puy-du-Fou take you on an exciting journey back in time before continuing through windmill country to Luçon, Cardinal Richelieu's town. Further south is the dry marsh, an area of the Marais Poitevin where wide open spaces are crisscrossed by canals and dikes. Return to Fontenay-le-Comte after visiting the imposing ruins of the Abbaye de Maillezais and the village of Nieul-sur-l'Autise.

4 SOUTH OF THE LOIRE ESTUARY – *255km/158mi starting from St-Gilles-Croix-de-Vie*

Drive north-west out of the fishing port of St-Gilles to the seaside resort of St-Jean-de-Monts and its vast sandy beaches ideal for a family holiday. Tear yourself away from the beach and continue north-west to Noirmoutier; enjoy the island's old-world charm, indulge in birdwatching and watch the last salt-marsh workers. Follow the coast round the Baie de Bourgneuf to Pornic, a sought-after seaside resort. Drive on to the rocky Pointe de St-Gildas then turn back and continue inland to St-Philbert-de-Grand-Lieu and its lake, via the safari park of La Planète Sauvage. Turn south towards Challans, famous for its ducks, and make a detour to Apremont and its castle before getting back to St-Gilles.

5 BORDEAUX VINEYARDS – *305km/190mi starting from Bordeaux*

Châteaux, vineyards and wine cellars dominate this region traditionally dedicated to wine. Drive south-east to Cadillac, a 13C *bastide* (fortified town), then on to the vineyards of Ste-Croix-du-Mont and Sauternes (in particular the exclusive Château Yquem and Château de Malle). Veering north-east, continue to the picturesque village of Sauveterre-de-Guyenne, the ruins of Blasimon Abbey and on to St-Émilion, a jewel of a town set among hilly vineyards. Nearby are the Romanesque church of Petit-Palais and the Écomusée du Libournais in Montagne. To the north-east, on the River Dordogne, the town of Libourne is the starting point of the journey of Bordeaux wine to every part of the world. Having reached the Gironde estuary, you enter Haut Médoc, an area dotted with famous châteaux Château Margaux, Château Maucaillou vineyards and fine architecture blend to offer you an inspiring visit. Fort Médoc is a reminder that the region was, for a long time, torn between English and French domination...no wonder when you see what was at stake laid out before your eyes: elegant rows of vines producing world famous wines whose names are music to the ear of wine lovers: Château Mouton-Rothschild, Château Lafitte-Rochschild...

6 THE CÔTE D'ARGENT SOUTH OF ARCACHON – *375km/233mi*

This is a region of retrieved marshland, lakes, sandy beaches and pine forests. Climb to the top of Dune du Pilat for a splendid panorama over a vast area. Further south, you can take full advantage of the wealth of sporting facilities on offer between Biscarosse Lake and Mimizan-Plage. Boat trips along Courant de Contis enable visitors to savour landscapes of marshes, pine forests and dunes. Inland, Sabres is the starting point of a tourist train leading to Marquèze and the Écomusée de la Grande Lande; part of the museum is in Luxey to the north-east. Continue your journey to the Château de Cazeneuve then to the old town of Bazas nestling round its cathedral and the Château de Roquetaillade. Change direction and drive south-east to Pissos, renowned for its handicraft activities. Drive north to Belhade, Hostens and Belin-Béliet through ideal hiking country then west to Sanguinet and its lake, where water-based activities abound, before returning to Arcachon.

7 THE BASQUE COAST – *280km/174mi starting from Biarritz*

Follow the coast south to Bidart and Guéthary (why not take a dip in the ocean on the way!) then on to St-Jean-de-Luz and its old town still vibrant with memories of Louis XIV's wedding to the Infanta of Spain. After a short incursion into Spain to visit San Sebastián, return to France and drive inland to La Rhune where a small rack railway beckons you aboard to offer you a splendid panorama. Further east you will encounter the picturesque villages of Sare, Ainhoa and Espelette before driving north to Bayonne along the Route Impériale des Cimes. Beyond Bayonne, you will drive through typical Landes landscapes, making a pause for a relaxing boat trip along Courant d'Huchet. Back to the coast and its picturesque resorts of Vieux-Boucau-les-Bains, Hossegor and Capbreton; continue south along the coast road to return to Biarritz whose striking Virgin's Rock can be seen from afar.

⑧ THE BASQUE MOUNTAINS – *285km/177mi starting from St-Jean-Pied-de-Port*

This mountainous region dotted with small villages and historic places has a lot to offer. It is only natural to start from the capital of Basse-Navarre, the medieval town of St-Jean-Pied-de-Port. From there it's a steady climb through the mountains to the convivial winter sports resort of Iraty, then down into the Crevasses d'Holçarté (narrow gorges) and the grandiose Gorges de Kakouetta. Continue north to see the Gotein calvary, visit Mauléon-Licharre, a former stronghold, and watch a game of pelota in St-Palais. Drive on to the Isturitz and Oxocelhaya caves and veer southwards to St-Étienne-de-Baïgorry, a typical Basque village. Further south is the Vallée des Aldudes and its characteristic small black pigs, then Spain and Roncevaux, once a traditional stopover for pilgrims on their way to Santiago de Compostela.

Basque landscape

⑨ BÉARN – *370km/230mi starting from Pau*

Meadows and cultivated areas alternate with slopes covered with vines and pointed Pyrenean summits. The region may sometimes look austere but it is always welcoming. Having strolled through the old town and visited the castle, leave Pau southwards to Nay, where there is an interesting museum devoted to *bérets* (the local headdress), then drive through the mountains via Col de l'Aubisque, one of the passes on the Tour de France route offering superb views. Beyond are the ski resort of Gourette and the small spa of Eaux-Bonnes. A detour to Pic de la Sagette will enable you to hop on a tourist train leading to Lac d'Artouste. Turn back and continue to the cliffs of Aste-Béon inhabited by vultures. Further on is Lescun surrounded by limestone peaks; drive through Issaux forest to the ski resort of Arette-Pierre-St-Martin. Turn north to Oloron-Ste-Marie, then Sauveterre-de-Béarn and Salies-de-Béarn, another spa. The last part of your journey can take in the old town of Orthez, a former capital of Béarn, the Château de Morlanne, Lescar's cathedral and the Église Ste-Foy in Morlaàs.

Thematic itineraries

Travel itineraries on specific themes have been mapped out to help you discover the regional architectural heritage. You will find brochures in tourist offices, and the routes are generally well-marked and easy to follow:

Route des Abbayes et Monuments du Haut-Poitou – Roman vestiges and Romanesque churches, Gothic architecture in the Plantagenet or angevin style, châteaux and feudal fortresses vie for the visitor's attention over this rich historical itinerary. Information on this route is also available at Ligugé town hall.

Route des Plantagenets – Eleven itineraries in the western part of France trace the great dynasty. The brochure includes a suggested tour passing through La Sauve-Majeur, Blaye, St-Emillion, Bazas, Dax and Bayonne.

Route des Trésors de Saintonge – A tour around the region of Saintes reveals a wealth of Romanesque churches in the Saintonge style, set like jewels in the beautiful green countryside.

Route Historique des Châteaux et Cités au Cœur d'Aquitaine – This tour includes the châteaux of La Brède, Cadillac, Malle, Roquetaillade and Cazeneuve as well as the medieval towns of Loupiac, Ste-Croix-du-Mont and Bazas. Information on this route is also available at the Château de Cazeneuve.

Route Historique sur les Pas des Seigneurs du Béarn et du Pays Basque – This tour visits some of the most picturesque manors, châteaux and towns of Béarn and the Basque Country, steeped in the history of Aquitaine, from the 13C to the 18C. Urtubie, Cambo-les-Bains, Guiche, Sauveterre, Laas, Navarrenx, Oloron-Ste-Marie, Orthez and Pau.

Cheese Lovers' Route – Traditional Pyrenean sheep's cheese is produced in the heart of the Béarn and Basque Country. From St-Jean-de-Luz to the Col d'Aubisque (182km/109mi), 30 stops along the way will give you ample occasion to sample and savour this regional speciality. For detailed information, contact the Syndicat de défense de l'AOC Ossau-Iraty, Maison Baratchartenea, 64120 Ostabat Asne, ☎ 05 59 37 86 61.

To market, to market, to buy a fat... goose liver – Traditional markets known as *marchés au gras* were previously held in winter months only for the sale of ducks and geese, prepared and raw livers. The most picturesque of these markets are now held in Samtan (Gers) on Mondays year-round and in Mirande (Gers) on Mondays from November through March.

Local fairs – Mid-February, in Bazas, is time for the Fête des Bœufs gras du Carnaval, with a parade of ribbon-bedecked cattle through the town.

In early May, lambs hold the centre stage in Pauillac, and traditional shepherding activities are demonstrated (sheepfold, sheepdogs etc).

Late May or early June is cherry time in Itxassou, famous for this succulent fruit.

Get tasty local cheese at the Chabichou and goat cheese festival in Melle, also in July.

July and August, vistors can take a guided tour of the cattle market in Parthenay on Wednesday mornings at 7.30.

In August, ripe melons abound in Sauzé-Vaussais *(Michelin map 72, fold 2)* and Nieul-sur-l'Autise, whereas St-Gilles-Croix-de-Vie celebrates onions.

In September, time for hot vegetable soup at the annual international *garbure* cook-off in Oloron-Ste-Marie.

In November, it's back to Sauzé-Vaussais for the wine and gourmet foods fair.

VINEYARDS AND WINE TOURS

There is no dearth of *caves* (wine cellars) offering *dégustation* (tasting) along the roads from Poitiers down through the Bordeaux region. Specific addresses for the famous Bordeaux wines are listed under Vignoble de Bordeaux in *Admission times and charges*. While some may prefer to contact their travel agent and set off on a coach tour with an expert, others may prefer to travel the by-ways, stopping off at a local wine-grower's *chais* to pick up a bottle to accompany a picnic lunch. A visit to a small proprietor producing local wine, often a family affair generations old, can be as memorable as a tour of one of the great châteaux or distilleries.

A few addresses:

Vins de Bordeaux – Maison du vin de **Bordeaux**, 3, cours du XXX-Juillet, 33075 Bordeaux Cedex, ☎ 05 56 00 22 88.
Maison du tourisme et du vin de Pauillac **(Médoc)**, 33250 Pauillac, ☎ 05 56 59 03 08.
Maison des vins de **Graves**, 61, cours Maréchal-Foch, BP 51, 33720 Podensac, ☎ 05 56 27 09 25.
Maison du vin de **Barsac**, place de l'Église, 33720 Barsac, ☎ 05 56 27 15 44.
Maison du vin des **Premières Côtes de Blaye**, 11, cours Vauban, BP 122, 33390 Blaye, ☎ 05 57 42 91 19.
Maison du vin des **Côtes de Bourg**, place de l'Éperon, 33710 Bourg, ☎ 05 57 94 80 20.
Maison du vin de **Ste-Foy-Bordeaux**, route de Bergerac, 33220 Pineuilh, ☎ 05 57 46 31 71.
Maison du vin de **St-Émilion**, place Pierre-Meyrat, BP 52, 33330 St-Émilion, ☎ 05 57 55 50 55.

The guide *Vignobles et chais en Bordelais – Terroirs de Gironde* gives information on more than 600 establishments; apply to the Comité départemental du tourisme de Gironde *(see Planning your trip)* and the Maison du Vin de Bordeaux *(see BORDEAUX)*.

Vins basques – Cave coopérative des vins d'**Irouleguy** et du Pays basque, 64430 St-Étienne-de-Baïgorry, ☎ 05 59 37 41 33.

Vins béarnais – Cave des producteurs de **Jurançon**, 53, avenue Henri-IV, 64290 Gan, ☎ 05 59 21 57 03.

Cave coopérative **Béarn-Bellocq**, 64270 Bellocq, ☎ 05 59 65 10 71.

Vins gascons – Maison des vins de **Madiran et Pacherenc du Vic-Bilh**, place de l'Église, 65700 Madiran, ☎ 05 62 31 90 67.
Les Vignerons du **Tursan**, 40320 Geaune, ☎ 05 58 44 51 25.

The guide *Restaurants et Vins du Sud-Ouest* is available from the association *Les Vins du Sud-Ouest*, ☎ 05 61 73 87 06.

Vins de l'Agenais – Les Vignerons de **Buzet**, 47160 Buzet-sur-Baïse, ☎ 05 53 84 74 30.
Union interprofessionnelle des vins des **Côtes de Duras**, Maison du vin, 47120 Duras, ☎ 05 53 83 81 88.
Cave de Goulens en **Brulhois**, 47390 Layrac, ☎ 05 53 87 01 65.

Grands crus du Haut Médoc

D. Guittot/PHOTONONSTOP

Armagnac – Bureau national interprofessionnel de l'**armagnac** AOC, 11, place de la Liberté, BP 3, 32800 Eauze, ☎ 05 62 08 11 00.
Maison du Floc de Gascogne, rue des Vignerons, 32800 Eauze, ☎ 05 62 09 85 41.

Cognac *(Charente)* – The main producers of brandy are open for tours and sales.

While many of the wines in the region covered in this guide are celebrated around the world, some lesser-known vintages are worth tasting, too. Their flavour will linger in your memories of the countryside that produces them.

Vins de Mareuil *(Vendée)* – **Maison Mourat**, Route de la Roche, ferme des Ardillers, 85320 Mareuil-sur-Lay, ☎ 02 51 97 20 10.
Domaine des Dames, Daniel Gentreau, Follet, 85320 Rosnay, ☎ 02 51 30 55 39.

Muscadet de Sèvre et Maine, Gros Plant, Muscadet *(Loire-Atlantique)* – **Domaine La Roche Renard**, I. et P. Denis, Les Laures, 44330 Vallet, ☎ 02 40 36 63 65.
Maison des Vins de Nantes, Bellevue, 44690 La Haye-Fouassière, ☎ 02 40 36 90 10.
Domaine des Herbauges, 44830 Bouaye, ☎ 02 40 65 44 92.

Aperitif and after-dinner drinks

Local *aperitifs* and *digestifs* not commonly found elsewhere:

Bise dur, La Chouanette, Rosée des Charentes, Kamok, Liqueur des Vendéens *(Vendée)* – Société H. Vrignaud, 1, Place Richelieu, 85400 Luçon, ☎ 02 51 56 11 48.

Pineau des Charentes – This fortified wine is omnipresent; reds, rosés and golden white varieties are widely available throughout the region.

Trouspinette *(Vendée)* – Maison Mourat, La Ferme des Ardillers, 85320 Mareuil-sur-Lay, ☎ 02 51 97 20 10.

Trinquet vendéen *(Vendée)* – C. et I. Cochain, La Rivière, 85160 St-Jean-de-Monts, ☎ 02 51 58 82 40.

Fine Bretagne *(Loire-Atlantique)* – Distillerie Seguin, 10, Boulevard St-Rémy, 44270 Machecoul, ☎ 02 40 31 40 50.

OENOLOGICAL COURSES

The Bordeaux Tourist Office offers an initiation to oenology, with a wine-tasting programme every Thursday at 4.30pm (also Saturdays at 4.30pm in July and August). Join in the initiation to wine-tasting at the Maison du Vin de St-Émilion daily from 11am to noon, mid July through September, and at the Maison du tourisme et du vin de Pauillac on Wednesdays at 11am, early July to mid-September. The École du Vin du Château Maucaillou (Espace Maucaillou, 33480 Moulis-en-Médoc, ☎ 05 56 58 01 23) teaches tasting techniques in a 2-day course. The château also conducts Médoc vineyard discovery tours and weekends combining châteaux, wine and golf.

OENOLOGICAL FESTIVITIES

The Foire aux Sarments held in mid-July in St-Yzans-de-Médoc (Mairie (town hall) ☎ 05 56 09 05 06) is the occasion to savour beefsteak grilled over charcoal made from aged grape vines (Cabernet-Sauvignon), accompanied by a Médoc wine.
On the third weekend in July, Buzet hosts the Fête des Vins de Buzet en Pays d'Ambret (☎ 05 53 84 74 30).
The Fête des vins de Duras takes place in early August in the courtyard of Duras Castle (Union interprofessionnelle, ☎ 05 53 83 81 88).
In October, an old-fashioned grape harvest is the scene for the festivals of Monfort-en-Chalosse (Domaine de Carcher, ☎ 05 58 98 69 27) and Marcillac (Mairie (town hall) ☎ 05 57 32 41 03).

Equine adventures

Savour the countryside at a gentle pace aboard a **horse-drawn caravan**. Obtain a brochure from the Maison Poitou-Charentes (68-70, rue du Cherche-Midi, 75006 Paris ☎ 01 42 22 83 74) for information on hiring a caravan with bunk beds and kitchen facilities for 2-7 days.
The **Délégation Nationale au Tourisme Équestre** (9, boulevard Macdonald, 75119 Paris, ☎ 01 53 26 15 50; www.eii.fr) will supply general information as well as addresses of local organisations. It is also possible to contact regional associations directly, by writing to any of the following:

Comité Départemental de Tourisme Équestre de Gironde,
153, rue David-Johnston
33000 Bordeaux
☎ 05 56 00 99 28

Comité Départemental de Tourisme Équestre de Charente Maritime,
M-F Pennec,
Lycée Marcel-Dassault
Esplanade des Ports
17300 Rochefort
☎ 05 46 87 53 44

**Association Régionale du Tourisme
Équestre de Poitou-Charentes,**
J-G Mercier,
2, rue du Puits
17330 Villeneuve-la-Comtesse
☎ 05 46 24 05 94

**Comité Départemental de Tourisme
Équestre de Charente,**
boulevard de Bury
16000 Angoulême
☎ 05 45 38 94 48

**Comité Départemental de Tourisme
Équestre des Deux Sèvres,**
J-G Mercier,
2, rue du Puits
17330 Villeneuve-la-Comtesse
☎ 05 46 24 05 94

Activities children will love

South-west France has a lot to offer children from swimming and playing in the sand along the sunny Côte d'Argent, backed by a string of peaceful lakes, to cycling through the Landes Forest, having fun in amusement parks, or visiting zoos, safari parks, aquariums and museums of special interest.

Throughout the Sights section of the guide, your attention is drawn to activities particularly suited to children by the symbol 🐾.

Tourist trains – Several picturesque railways welcome tourists aboard for pleasant rides through fields, woods and marshlands, including a few pulled by steam locomotives. For detailed information, see the following:

Bassin d'ARCACHON: Cap Ferret (Tourist train to Plage de l'Océan)
Les HERBIERS (Chemin de fer de la Vendée)
Île d'OLÉRON: St Trojan-les-Bains (Pointe de Gatseau tourist train)
Parc naturel régional des LANDES DE GASCOGNE: Marquèze (Train de l'Écomusée de la Grande Lande)
MARAIS POITEVIN: Coulon (Le Pibalou)
Haut-OSSAU (Scenic train from La Sagette to Lac d'Artouste)
ROYAN: Saujon (Chemin de fer touristique de la Seudre)
SAINT-ÉMILION (Train des Grands Vignobles)
SAINT-JEAN-DE-LUZ: Le Labourd (Chemin de fer de la Rhune)
SOULAC-SUR-MER (Pointe de Grave scenic railway)

Eco-tourism

RIVER CRUISING

Rivers, estuaries, canals and channels offer numerous opportunities to enjoy pleasant **boat trips** (sometimes aboard crafts of a bygone age), thus slowing down the pace and alleviating the stress of a busy touring holiday.

Crown blue Line,
quai François-Mitterrand
16200 Jarnac
☎ 05 45 3659 98

La Gabare de Gironde,
Office de tourisme, allées Marine
33390 Blaye
☎ 05 57 42 12 09

Union des Bateliers arcachonnais,
Boat trips on the Arcachon lagoon
See Bassin d'ARCACHON

Aliénor,
Boat trips along the Gironde Estuary
See BORDEAUX

Capitaine Croisière,
Ponton de l'Aviron
47300 Villeneuve-sur-Lot
☎ 05 53 49 48 55

Alternatively, **house-boats**, which can be hired for a day, a weekend or a week, offer a peaceful glide along rivers (Charente, Sèvre Niortaise, Lot, Baïse) and canals (Canal latéral à la Garonne).

Crown Blue Line,
47430 Le Mas-d'Agenais
☎ 05 53 89 50 80;
Aquitaine Navigation,
Halte nautique
47160 Buzet-sur-Baïse
☎ 05 53 84 72 50;
quai de la Baïse
47600 Nérac
☎ 05 53 65 66 66

Locaboat Plaisance,
quai de Dunkerque
47000 Agen
☎ 05 53 66 00 74;
Central booking:
☎ 03 86 91 72 72

RAIL-BIKING

Sight-seeing with a difference! How do you fancy pedalling along a disused railway line? It is possible to go for a 10km/6mi ride around St-Gilles-Croix-de-Vie and along the coast. Each small truck can take up to 5 persons (information from the tourist office).

BIRDWATCHING

There are guided tours around the **Réserve naturelle des Marais de Müllembourg**, Fort-Larron, Normoutier-en-l'Île, ☎ 02 51 35 81 16.

NATURE AND THE ENVIRONMENT

Parc interrégional du Marais poitevin: Information centre at the Maison des marais mouillés, 79510 Coulon, ☎ 05 49 35 86 77.

Centres permanents d'initiatives pour l'environnement: these centres organise weekends and longer stays (known as Sépia) to encourage people to become aware of nature and the environment.
Information is available from the **Union nationale des centres permanents d'initiatives pour l'environnement**, 2, rue de Washington, 75008 Paris.

Spas and sea water therapy

Hot springs, mineral waters, mud and algae packs have been used to treat afflictions and relieve stress since Roman times. The various therapeutic properties of the different spas are adapted to the treatment of respiratory ailments, rheumatism, and dermatoses. *Thermalisme* usually refers to medically prescribed, 21-day cures, while *thalassothérapie* sea water facilities serve a more general public, for what the French call *remise en forme* (shaping up). In addition to the medical care provided to the numerous *curistes*, many establishments offer short-term packages aimed at improving the general well-being of guests. You can even sign up for a special stay to quit smoking, lose weight, or increase your stamina. Most spa towns have ample sports facilities, such as tennis courts and golf courses, and many have their own casinos. Do check the details ahead of time, as some spas require a medical check-up before you can have treatments, and accommodation may be scarce at certain times of year.
For general information, write to:

Time to relax

Fédération Thermale et Climatique Française
16, rue de l'Estrapade
75005 Paris ☎ 01 43 25 11 85

Fédération Mer et Santé
8, rue de l'Isly
75008 Paris ☎ 01 44 70 07 57

Chaîne Thermale du Soleil/Maison du Thermalisme
32, avenue de l'Opéra
75002 Paris ☎ 01 44 71 37 00

Maison de la Thalassothérapie
5, rue Denis Poisson
75017 Paris ☎ 01 45 72 38 38

The **Michelin Red Guide France** gives the official opening and closing dates of spas.
Here is a description of just two of the many spas in the region:

Dax is France's leading thermal resort, and one of the largest, specialised in the treatment of rheumatism and arthritis in all forms. Therapy centres around the application of warm mud packs. To obtain brochures on special 6, 9 and 12-day packages offered by the many different establishments in town, as well as information on sports and entertainment in this busy resort, contact the Syndicat d'Initiative, place Thiers, BP 177 40100 Dax, ☎ 05 58 56 86 86, www.ville-de-dax.fr.

La Roche Posay is hidden deep in the quiet countryside, surrounded by gentle valleys and pretty rivers and streams, far from the madding crowd. The spa treats all types of skin problems, using relaxing mineral baths, jet sprays and high-pressure showers. The Mélusine centre (May-mid-October) offers short cures for relaxation and skin care, and the town provides a service for organising business seminars. Write to the local tourist office (postal code 86270), or Société Hydrominérale de la Roche-Posay, 3 rue Henri-Michaux, 75013 Paris, ☎ 01 43 13 10 50, Fax 01 43 13 10 51.

In Hendaye, the **Complexe de Thalassothérapie Serge Blanco** (boulevard de la Mer, 64700 Hendaye, ☎ 05 59 51 35 35, Fax 05 59 51 36 00) is well-known to sports enthusiasts who appreciate the whirlpools, massages and algae packs, as well as the giant jacuzzi, sauna, weight machines and squash courts. The chic establishment, open year-round in a beautiful setting, offers personalised programmes designed to help you slim down, cheer up, and improve your sports performance.

Information can also be obtained directly from the tourist offices of the spa towns indicated on the map.

Sports and outdoor activities

Mountain sports – Play it safe

Safety first is the rule for neophytes and old hands when it comes to exploring the mountains as a climber, skier or hiker. The risk associated with avalanches, mud slides, falling rocks, bad weather, fog, glacially cold waters, the dangers of becoming lost or miscalculating distances, should not be underestimated.

Avalanches occur naturally when the upper layer of snow is unstable, in particular after heavy snowfalls, and may be set off by the passage of numerous skiers or hikers over a precise spot. A scale of risk, from 1 to 5, has been developed and is posted daily at resorts and the base of hiking trails. It is important to consult this *Bulletin Neige et Avalanche* (BNA) before setting off on any expeditions cross-country or *hors-piste*. You can also call toll free ☎ 08 36 68 10 20 *(in French)*.

Lightning storms are often preceded by sudden gusts of wind, and put climbers and hikers in danger. In the event, avoid high ground, and do not move along a ridge top; do not seek shelter under overhanging rocks, isolated trees in otherwise open areas, at the entrance to caves or other openings in the rocks, or in the proximity of metal fences or gates. An automobile is a good refuge.

SKIING

In the western Pyrenees, there are **valley resorts**, with high curving slopes and plateaux and **mountain top resorts**, which are contemporary, purpose-built resorts such as Arette-Pierre-St-Martin and Gourette.
Cross-country skiing is especially good in Iraty, Issarbe and Somport-Candanchu.

WINTER SPORTS RESORTS *(département)*	Number of downhill runs	Km of cross country trails	Other activities	☎ Information activities
Arette-Pierre-St-Martin (64)	19	5	Luge	05 59 66 20 09
Artouste-Fabrèges (64)	13	10	Snowboard and halfpipe	05 59 05 34 00
Gourette (64)	30	20	Halfpipe and slalom; night skiing; off-piste authorised	05 59 05 12 17
Iraty-Soule (64)	–	42		05 59 28 51 29
Issarbe (64)	–	31		05 59 05 82 28
Le Somport-Candanchu (64)	–	34		05 59 34 71 48

These boots were made for walking...

Choosing the right equipment for a rambling expedition is essential, especially in the mountains. Hiking shoes should be flexible, waterproof and have non-slip soles. Always bring a rain jacket or poncho and an extra sweater. Other indispensable items: sun protection (hat, glasses, lotion), drinking water (1-2l per person), something to nibble on between meals (chocolate, cereal bars, banana...), a bag for trash and a first aid kit. Of course, you'll need a good map (and a compass if you plan to leave the main trails). Plan your itinerary well, keeping in mind that while the average walking speed for an adult is 4kph/2mph an hour, you will need time to eat and rest, and children will not keep up the same pace. Leave your itinerary with someone before setting out (innkeeper or fellow camper).
Respect for nature is a cardinal rule and includes the following precautions: don't smoke or light fires in forests, which are particularly vulnerable during the dry summer months; always carry your rubbish out; leave wildflowers as they are (certainly don't dig up the roots) and likewise, walk around, not through, farmers' fields. Close gates behind you.

The Fédération française de la randonnée pédestre publishes "topo-guides" available from its information centre, 14, rue Riquet, 75019 Paris. ☎ 01 44 89 93 90; www.ffrp.asso.fr. Some English-language editions are available. The regional guides describe long-distance trails (GR, for Grande Randonnée and GRP for Grande Randonnée de Pays) and shorter ones (PR – petite randonnée) in detail, distances and approximate times.

CYCLING

Whereas the mountains draw climbers and hikers, the forests, plains, islands, river banks and moors of south-west France are favoured by bicyclists. It is not unusual to see coastal travellers pedalling along with camping gear strapped on back; the relatively flat landscape makes for pleasant riding. The Île de Ré is perfect for a one-day tour.

In the **Haut-Saintonge** area around Saintes, 32 mixed-use trails and 18 mountain-bike tours are marked out. Maps are available in tourist offices.

On Sunday mornings in **Bordeaux** you can rent a bike for the day and pedal around the city with a guide (details at the tourist office).

Some SNCF train stations (Châtellerault, Niort, La Rochelle, Royan, Les Sables-d'Olonne, Valence-d'Agen, Verdon) rent touring and mountain (in French, VTT for *vélo tout terrain*) bikes.

The **Marais Poitevin** is a great place for a ride on the *petite reine* (or little queen, as the French affectionately dub the bicycle), offering cool shaded lanes, shimmering canals and glimpses of Gothic and Romanesque architecture in the calm, sunny countryside. For rentals and information on organised trips, contact the Maison Poitou-Charentes (68-70, rue du Cherche-Midi, 75006 Paris ☎ 01 42 22 83 74).

Other areas particularly suitable for cycling along marked-out tracks include the **Landes**, **Entre-Deux-Mers** and **Médoc** regions. Information and maps available from the Comité départemental du tourisme de Gironde *(see Planning your trip)* and from the Maison du tourisme et du vin de Pauillac, ☎ 05 56 59 03 08.

Tourist offices will provide a list of private rental agencies – in summer it is a good idea to reserve.

For more general information concerning France, contact the **Fédération Française de Cyclotourisme** (12, rue Louis-Bertrand, 94200 Ivry-sur-Seine, ☎ 01 44 16 88 88, www.ffct.org). Mountain-bike enthusiasts, contact the **Fédération Française de Cyclisme** (5, rue de Rome, 93561 Rosny-sous-Bois Cedex, ☎ 01 49 35 69 00, www.ffc.fr) and request the *Guide des centres VTT*.

Swimming and water sports

SWIMMING

Along the Atlantic ocean, it is best to swim from one of the many supervised beaches, where flags (red = beach closed, orange = some danger, green = safe to swim) advise bathers. Along the open coast, where the surf is often high, life guards are mobile and attentive, moving the flags marking out the area under their surveillance as rising and falling tides change the danger zones created by depressions in the sea bed and strong undertow. Sheltered beaches (Bassin d'Arcachon, Les Sables-d'Olonne, Capbreton...) are more appropriate for small children, who will also enjoy the calm, relatively shallow waters of the inland lakes such as the Lac de Lacanau or the Étang de Léon.

SURFING AND WINDSURFING

One swimmer's breaker is another surfer's swell. The same deep underwater chasm *(le Gouf)* which makes Capbreton one of the safest swimming beaches on the coast makes **Hossegor** the uncontested capital of surf in France. International competitions are held in Hossegor, **Biarritz** and **Lacanau** every August. Novice windsurfers may want to test the waters inland on the calmer waters of a lake before hitting the ocean beach. These sports are restricted to certain areas and subject to regulations for the protection of swimmers.

Sand-yachting and its variation **speed sailing** are ideally suited to the vast beaches of the Vendée coast and Côte d'Argent, where large flat areas of sand are left uncovered at low tide. You will find centres in Notre-Dame-

Funboard

de-Monts, Chéray (Oléron), La Faute-sur-Mer, St-Jean-de-Monts, St-Georges-de-Didonne, St-Gilles-Croix-de-Vie, Archachon, La Teste-de-Buch and Hendaye, among others.

General information is available from the **Fédération française de Surf**, BP 28, 30, impasse de la Dighe-Nord, 40150 Hossegor, ☏ 05 58 43 55 88; the **Fédération française de Voile**, 55, avenue Kléber, 75784 Paris Cedex 16, ☏ 01 44 05 81 00, www.ffv.fr; and from the **Fédération française de Char à Voile**, PA de la Vigogne, 62600 Berck-sur-Mer Cedex, ☏ 03 21 84 27 69.

CANOEING – KAYAKING – RAFTING

The region's numerous rivers, canals and lakes offer ample opportunities to enjoy these sports.

For general information, contact the **Fédération Française de Canöe-Kayak** (87, quai de la Marne, Joinville-le-Pont ☏ 01 45 11 08 50, www.ffcanoe.asso.fr) or **AN Rafting**, 144, rue de Rivoli, 75001 Paris, ☏ 01 42 96 63 63.

Sea-kayaks are popular at the Bassin d'Arcachon as well as Fouras *(see Places to Stay map, south of La Rochelle)*. The **Courant d'Huchet** and the **Courant de Contis** are beautiful sights for an initiation.

In the mountains, rapid water sports are practised on the rivers Garonne, Eyre and Adour. Local tourist offices can provide details.

Canyoning is a technique for body-surfing down narrow gorges and over falls, as though on a giant water slide, whereas **hydrospeed** involves swimming down rapids with a kickboard and flippers. These sports require protection: wear a wet suit and a helmet.

AND OTHER WATER SPORTS...

For **water-skiing and motor boating**, enquire at the tourist offices of the larger seaside resorts. The use of jet-skis is restricted in France.

Diving clubs *(clubs de plongée)* are active in St-Gilles-Croix-de-Vie, St-Hilaire-de-Riez, Royan and Les Sables-d'Olonne.

For more information, contact the Fédération française d'études et de sports sous-marins, 24, quai de la Rive-Neuve, 13284 Marseille Cedex 07, ☏ 04 91 33 99 31.

FISHING

Freshwater fishing enthusiasts will revel in the abundance of rivers, streams, marshland canals and lakes.

Fishing regulations are enforced and anglers must be affiliated with an association, thus obtaining a *carte de pêche* (permit). Apply to the **Conseil Supérieur de la Pêche** (134, avenue de Malakoff, 75016 Paris ☏ 01 45 01 20 20), which also supplies a map, *Pêche en France* (Fishing in France). Permits are easily obtained locally, often sold in cafés where you are likely to pick up a few tips from the regulars.

The extensive coastline, the bays, straits and the wide **ocean** itself offer almost limitless fishing options, the only restrictions being to adhere to local and national regulations and not to interfere with the business of professional fishermen. For fishing trips out to sea on fully equipped boats, ask at tourist offices, or have a walk around the marina and strike up a conversation. You can reserve a spot on a fishing boat (equipment provided).

For general information, apply to the **Fédération française des pêcheurs en mer**, Résidence Alliance, centre Jorlis, 64600 Anglet, ☏ 05 59 31 00 73.

On the beaches at low tide, the bucket-and-spade brigades are engaging in the popular French pastime known as *pêche à pied*, digging for shellfish or scooping up shrimp. There are no administrative formalities for this activity, although quantities per fisherman may be limited, and some beaches may be posted off limits.

Underwater fishing is subject to strict regulation.

The *Gîtes de France (see Accommodation, above)* have created a special category, *Gîtes de Pêche*, which identifies accommodation most suitable for anglers who are really hooked.

GOLF

South-west France has many 9 and 18-hole golf courses, mentioned on a map entitled *Golf, les parcours français*, based on the Michelin map of France 989.

For general information, contact the Fédération française de Golf, 68, rue Anatole-France, 92309 Levallois-Perret Cedex, ☏ 01 41 49 77 00, www.ffg.org.

Traditional spectator sports

Certain sports are part of the traditional lifestyle in south-west France, and their heroes are local legends. In addition to major national and international events, there are many local games going on, which will give you a feel for the people and their ways.

Rugby is big in the south-west. An early form of the game was practised in France and Great Britain in the Middle Ages, and folks have been playing rugby as we know it since 1900. Rugby has its own periodical *(Midi Olympique)*; bookstores in the region can track down over 100 titles; there is a shrine known as Notre-Dame-du-Rugby in

Larrivières. There is an ongoing debate between those who favour the 15-person team and those who play with 13 (as in Carcassonne, Lézignan, Limoux). Women's teams mostly play touch rugby, without tackling each other to the ground (*Les Lionnes* in Auch).

More information is available from the **Fédération française de rugby**, 9, rue de Liège, 75009 Paris, Fax 01 45 26 19 19, www.ffr.fr.

An unusual event known as **courses landaises** calls on courageous combatants to step into the arena with very large black cows with very long horns. More acrobatic than a Spanish-style bullfight, these events are also more humane, as the animals are not killed. Evolved from the old practices of running the bulls through the streets, the event became especially popular around 1850 with the introduction of the *écarteur*, the equivalent of a toreador.

Pelota in St-Pée-sur-Nivelle

A calendar of events is available from the **Fédération française de la course landaise**, 1600, avenue du Président-Kennedy, 40282 St-Pierre-du-Mont Cedex, ☏ 05 58 46 50 89.

And of course **Pelote Basque** (called jai alai in Mexico, Havana and Miami, where it is also very popular) is a must-see for visitors to the Basque Country. The most appreciated form is the **grand chistera**, the name of the distinctive curved basket players wear on one hand. Two teams of three players hurl the *pelote* (ball) against the fronton (wall). There are many variations on this game, and an unexpected pleasure is listening to the *chacharia* (announcer) sing out the score.

The standard rules are similar to handball rules, except the court is much larger: 53.7m/176ft long. The *pelote*, hard, wound rubber covered by linen thread and two layers of goatskin, is 5cm/2in in diameter and can travel at 240kph/150mph.

Detailed information from the **Fédération française de pelote basque "Trinquet Moderne"**, BP 816, 64108 Bayonne Cedex, ☏ 05 59 59 22 34.

Suggested reading

Eleanor of Aquitanine

Eleanor of Aquitaine, Queen of France and England, a 12C divorcee, patroness of poets, source of inspiration for chivalry and Courtly Love, ruler of a kingdom that spanned from Scotland to the Pyrenees, mother of 10 children (including Richard the Lion Heart), lived her 82 years as few women in history before or since. The story of her life is a good introduction to regional history, and a fascinating tale:

Eleanor of Aquitaine: A Life, Alison Weir, Ballantine Books, 2000.

Eleanor of Aquitaine, Marion Meade, Penguin Paperbacks, 1992.

Eleanor of Aquitaine: The Mother Queen, Desmond Seward, Dorset Press, 1986.

Eleanor of Aquitaine and the Four Kings, Amy Kelly, Harvard University Press, Paperback edition 1974.

Beloved Enemy: the Passions of Eleanor of Aquitaine: a Novel, Ellen Jones, Simon and Schuster, 1994.

For young readers:

A Proud Taste for Scarlet and Miniver, EL Konigsburg, Atheneum, 1974 (illustrated).

Queen Eleanor: Independent Spirit of the Medieval World, Polly S Brooks, Lippincott, 1983 (illustrated).

Words on wine

French Wines: The Essential Guide to the Wines and Wine Growing Regions of France, Robert Joseph, DK Publishing, 1999. This is a very useful book, in a travel-friendly paperback format, for anyone wanting to buy or taste all sorts of wine, whether during a trip to France (includes maps) or to the corner wine shop.

Grands Vins: The Finest Châteaux of Bordeaux and Their Wines, Clives Coates, University of California Press, 1995. Coates is one of Britain's best-known wine critics, and he has written an extensive survey on the history, geography, grape varieties, and other wine-making idiosyncrasies of the region which produces what many believe to be the world's greatest wines.

The Winemaker's Year: Four Seasons in Bordeaux, Michael Buller, photographs by Michel Guillard, preface by Paul Bocuse, Thames and Hudson, 1991. Lush photographs and a preface by one of France's most celebrated chefs add to the delicious savour of this tome.

Enjoying Wine, Don Hewitson, Elm Tree Books, 1985. Friendly, no-nonsense approach to one of life's great pleasures, with useful explanations and illustrations.

The Winemasters, Nicholas Faith, Hamish and Hamilton, 1978. History and people – two centuries of winemaking in Bordeaux.

The Wines of France, Alexis Lichine, Knopf, 1963. A classic that ages well.

Fiction

The Three Musketeers, by Alexandre Dumas, is a perfect choice. Grosset and Dunlap Junior Library edition (1953, illustrated) is sure to fire the imaginations of young readers, and several film versions are available on video, including Hanna-Barbera's animated feature.

By the River Piedra I Sat Down and Wept, Paulo Coelho, Harper Collins, 1996. A romantic adventure and search for spiritual sustenance on a journey through the French Pyrenees.

History and personal experience

The Basque History of the World, Mark Kurlansky, Penguin (USA) Paperbacks, 2001. This rare book in English on the political, economic, social, and even culinary history of the Basque people is an excellent introduction to this rather mysterious culture. Take a look beyond the popular media focus on separatist terrorists and ponder the saying in the Euskara language: *Garean gareana legez* – Let us be what we are.

The Land of My Fathers: A Son's Return to the Basque Country, Robert Laxalt, Joyce Laxalt (Photographer), University of Nevada Press, 1999. The author, who has written several novels set in the Basque country, here gives a record of the years he spent with his family in the 1960s in a village in the French Basque country. His descriptions of the isolated, beautiful mountain world where the Basques have lived for uncounted centuries complement his wife's photographs and show us Basque market days and festivals, reveal local humour and history, the deep sense of community and pride in the Basque culture and homeland.

The Fronde: A French Revolution, Orest A Ranum, Norton, 1993. Unrest and turbulence in 1648 ended up in a showdown between the monarchy and insurgents in Bordeaux.

The Lost Uplands: Stories of Southwest France, WS Merwin, Knopf, 1992. Three narrative portraits of small-town life in the region, from the pen of an award-winning poet.

A House in the Sunflowers: Summer in Aquitaine, Ruth Silvestre, Allison and Busby, 1990. A British family's search for and discovery of the perfect French holiday home.

Jasmin's Witch, Emmanuel Ladurie, George Braziller, 1987. Popular tradition and legend, magic, witchcraft and sorcery in the Agen region; the story of a beautiful dancing girl and the poet who recounted her downfall.

Calendar of events

Many Regional Tourist Offices publish brochures listing local fêtes, fairs and festivals. Most places hold festivities for France's National Day (14 July) and many organise events on 15 August, also a public holiday.

Traditional festivities, fairs and historical pageants

1 May

Mimizan-Plage . . . . "Fête de la mer" (sea festival).

Weekend of Whitsunday

Vic-Fezensac . . . . "Grandes corridas" bullfights. ☎ 05 62 06 34 90.

June

Le Puy du Fou . . . . "Jacques Maupillier, paysan vendéen" (historical pageant, sound and light show Fri and Sat 10pm, mid-June to July, 10.30pm Aug to early Sept) ☎ 02 51 64 11 11.

Bougon . . . . "Nuit du Solstice", Musée des Tumulus (weekend near 21 June) ☎ 05 49 05 12 13.

St-Jean-de-Luz . . . . "Fête de la Saint-Jean" midsummer festival: high mass, concerts, *chistera*, traditional games, bonfires, ball, *toro de fuego* etc.

Sunday around 14 July

St-Étienne-de-Baïgorry . . . "Force basque" traditional games championship.

14 July

St-Étienne-de-Baïgorry . . . Pageant: Basque wedding feast in the year 1900.

Mid-July to mid-August

Nieul-sur-l'Autise . . . . Imaginary encounters at the abbey (10pm). ☎ 02 51 50 43 00.

Early August

Clisson . . . . Night-time pageant at the château. ☎ 02 40 54 02 95.

Saint-Sever . . . . Historical pageant: "Life in Town, from the Middle Ages to Today" and sound and light show. ☎ 05 58 76 34 64.

1st Sunday in August

Moncrabeau . . . . International lying contest, with the coronation of the "King of Liars" (a Gascon tradition perpetuated by the Academy of Liars, founded in the 18C).

Hagetmau . . . . "Les 5 jours d'Hagetmau": bullfights, "courses landaises", fireworks, music.

1st week in August

Bayonne . . . . "Courses de vaches landaises", bullfights, water games, parades with floats, concerts, balls, *toro de fuego*.

15 August

Arcachon . . . . "Fêtes de la mer" (sea festival).

Biarritz . . . . "Nuit féerique": fireworks. ☎ 05 59 22 37 10.

Mirande . . . . Cycling race, horse races, street games.

St-Étienne-de-Baïgorry . . . Pageant: Basque wedding feast in the year 1900.

Mid-August

Dax . . . . "Feria": bullfights, "concours landais", folk dancing and music, balls, fireworks.

Last but one or last weekend in August

Labastide-d'Armagnac . . . . Historical pageant in period costume. Candlelight dinner under the arcades. ☎ 05 58 44 67 56.

Late August

Bagnères-de-Luchon . . . . . . "Fête des fleurs" (flower festival created in 1888 by Edmond Rostand).

Festivals

Angoulême. . . . . International Comic Strip show (at the end of the month) ☎ 05 45 97 86 50.

Cognac. . . . . International Detective Film Festival (at the end of the month) ☎ 05 45 82 10 71.

Lourdes . . . . Sacred music festival. ☎ 05 62 42 77 40.

Angoulême. . . . . World Music Festival (Wed to Sun) ☎ 05 45 95 43 42.

Melle St-Savinien . . . . Classical music festival (2nd half of May, early June) ☎ 05 49 29 08 23.

St-Gilles-Croix-de-Vie . . . . . International Jazz Festival (Fri to Whitsunday) ☎ 02 51 55 03 66.

Auch . . . . Classical and contemporary music festival. ☎ 05 62 05 20 82.

La Rochelle. . . . . International Film Festival ☎ 05 46 51 54 00.

Pau . . . . "Festival de Pau" (theatre, music, dance). ☎ 01 47 20 95 40.

Parthenay. . . . . International Festival of Games (first 3 weekends of the month) ☎ 05 49 94 24 20.

Saintes. . . . . "Les Académies musicales de l'abbaye aux Dames" ☎ 05 46 97 48 31.

Luz-St-Sauveur . . . . "Altitude" Jazz Festival. ☎ 05 62 92 38 38.

Parthenay and area . . . . . . "Jazz au fil de l'eau" (2nd week of the month) ☎ 05 49 64 18 11.

Arcachon . . . . Not'ambules: street theatre. ☎ 05 57 52 98 98.

Mont-de-Marsan . . . . Flamenco Festival. ☎ 05 58 06 89 89.

Saintes . . . . International folklore festival, "Santons" (2nd and 3rd week of the month) ☎ 05 46 74 47 50.

Andernos-les-Bains . . . . . . Jazz Festival. ☎ 05 56 82 02 95.

La Rochelle . . . . "Les Francofolies", French song festival (around 14 July) ☎ 05 46 28 28 28.

Cirque de Gavarnie. . . . . . . Theatre festival, 1 400m altitude. ☎ 01 45 4911 01.

Oloron-Ste-Marie . . . . "Festival international des Pyrénées": folklore, traditional art and popular traditions. ☎ 05 59 39 37 36.

Cognac. . . . . "Blues Passions" Festival ☎ 05 45 32 17 28.

Confolens. . . . . International folk festival ☎ 05 45 84 00 77.

Marciac . . . . Jazz in Marciac. ☎ 05 62 09 33 33.

Parthenay and area . . . . . . "De bouche à oreille": traditional and world music festival ☎ 05 49 94 90 70.

Uzeste . . . . "Hestejada de las arts d'Uzeste": pop music, theatre, poetry, art exhibits, dance, cinema etc. ☎ 05 56 25 38 46.

St-Palais . . . . "Force basque" traditional games. ☎ 05 59 65 71 15.

Early September
St-Sever . . . .   World music festival ☎ 05 58 06 85 85.

1st half of September
**Anglet, Ascain, Bayonne,
Biarritz, Ciboure,
St-Jean-de-Luz** . . . .   Classical music festival. ☎ 05 59 51 19 95.

October-November
Angoulême . . . .   "Piano en Valois" (1st half of the month)
☎ 05 45 38 61 63.

Sports events

Weekend of Whitsunday
Pau . . . .   Grand Prix automobile, Formula 3000.

May-June
Arcachon . . . .   Jumping International d'Arcachon.

La Rochelle . . . .   International Sailing Week (during the Ascension and
Whitsunday holidays) ☎ 05 46 44 62 44.

Beauvoir-sur-Mer . . . .   "Les Foulées du Gois", foot race against the tide.
☎ 02 51 68 71 13.

July
Arcachon . . . .   "18 heures Arcachon Sud-Ouest": sailing race.

Biarritz . . . .   Biarritz Surf Festival: international longboard
competition.

Biarritz . . . .   Biarritz Golf Cup.

August
Biarritz . . . .   Cesta Punta Golden Gloves championships.

St-Jean-de-Luz . . . .   World Championship Pelote Basque tournament (Tue
and Fri at 9pm).

Soustons . . . .   "Pelote basque grand chistera"; "course landaise".

Noirmoutier . . . .   Historical ships regatta, Bois de la Chaize,
☎ 02 51 39 80 71.

Parthenay . . . .   "Sur les Chemins de St-Jacques" walking and biking
tours with guides (around 15 August)
☎ 02 49 63 13 86.

Ascain . . . .   "Course à la Rhune" foot race up and down the
mountain.

Lacanau . . . .   Lacanau Pro: surfboard competition.

September
Angoulême . . . .   Vintage car rally around the ramparts (around
15 August) ☎ 05 45 94 95 67.

La Rochelle . . . .   "Le Grand Pavois", floating boat show (3rd week of
the month) ☎ 05 46 44 46 39.

Late September
Nogaro . . . .   Grand Prix automobile.

November
Les Sables-d'Olonne . . . . . .   "Vendée Globe" (departure of the solo sailing race, held
every four years since 1988) ☎ 02 51 96 85 85.

Useful French words and phrases

Architectural terms

See the section on architecture in the Introduction

SIGHTS

abbaye	abbey
beffroi	belfry
chapelle	chapel
château	castle
cimetière	cemetery
cloître	cloisters
cour	courtyard
couvent	convent
écluse	lock (canal)
église	church
fontaine	fountain
halle	covered market
jardin	garden
mairie	town hall
maison	house

marché	market
monastère	monastery
moulin	windmill
musée	museum
parc	park
place	square
pont	bridge
port	port/harbour
porte	gate/gateway
quai	quay
remparts	ramparts
rue	street
statue	statue
tour	tower

NATURAL SITES

abîme	chasm
aven	swallow-hole
barrage	dam
belvédère	viewpoint
cascade	waterfall
col	pass
corniche	ledge
côte	coast, hillside
forêt	forest

grotte	cave
lac	lake
plage	beach
rivière	river
ruisseau	stream
signal	beacon
source	spring
vallée	valley

ON THE ROAD

car park	parking
driving licence	permis de conduire
east	Est
garage (for repairs) . .	garage
left	gauche
motorway/highway . .	autoroute
north	Nord
parking meter	horodateur
petrol/gas	essence

petrol/gas station . . .	station essence
right	droite
south	Sud
toll	péage
traffic lights	feu tricolore
tyre	pneu
west	Ouest
wheel clamp	sabot
zebra crossing	passage clouté

TIME

today	aujourd'hui
tomorrow	demain
yesterday	hier
winter	hiver
spring	printemps
summer	été
autumn/fall	automne
week	semaine

Monday	lundi
Tuesday	mardi
Wednesday	mercredi
Thursday	jeudi
Friday	vendredi
Saturday	samedi
Sunday	dimanche

NUMBERS

0 . . . . zéro	**10** . . . . dix	**20** . . . . vingt
1 . . . . un	**11** . . . . onze	**30** . . . . trente
2 . . . . deux	**12** . . . . douze	**40** . . . . quarante
3 . . . . trois	**13** . . . . treize	**50** . . . . cinquante
4 . . . . quatre	**14** . . . . quatorze	**60** . . . . soixante
5 . . . . cinq	**15** . . . . quinze	**70** . . . . soixante-dix
6 . . . . six	**16** . . . . seize	**80** . . . . quatre-vingt
7 . . . . sept	**17** . . . . dix-sept	**90** . . . . quatre-vingt-dix
8 . . . . huit	**18** . . . . dix-huit	**100** . . . . cent
9 . . . . neuf	**19** . . . . dix-neuf	**1000** . . . . mille

SHOPPING

bank	banque
baker's	boulangerie
big	grand
butcher's	boucherie
chemist's	pharmacie
closed	fermé
cough mixture	sirop pour la toux
cough sweets	cachets pour la gorge
entrance	entrée
exit	sortie
fishmonger's	poissonnerie
grocer's	épicerie
newsagent, bookshop	librairie
open	ouvert
post office	poste
push	pousser
pull	tirer
shop	magasin
small	petit
stamps	timbres

FOOD AND DRINK

beef	bœuf
beer	bière
butter	beurre
bread	pain
breakfast	petit-déjeuner
cheese	fromage
chicken	poulet
dessert	dessert
dinner	dîner
fish	poisson
fork	fourchette
fruit	fruits
glass	verre
ice cream	glace
ice cubes	glaçons
ham	jambon
knife	couteau
lamb	agneau
lunch	déjeuner
lettuce salad	salade
meat	viande
mineral water	eau minérale
mixed salad	salade composée
orange juice	jus d'orange
plate	assiette
pork	porc
restaurant	restaurant
red wine	vin rouge
salt	sel
spoon	cuillère
sugar	sucre
vegetables	légumes
water	de l'eau
white wine	vin blanc
yoghurt	yaourt

PERSONAL DOCUMENTS AND TRAVEL

airport	aéroport
credit card	carte de crédit
customs	douane
passport	passeport
platform	voie
railway station	gare
shuttle	navette
suitcase	valise
train/plane ticket	billet de train/d'avion
wallet	portefeuille

CLOTHING

coat	manteau
jumper	pull
raincoat	imperméable
shirt	chemise
shoes	chaussures
socks	chaussettes
stockings	bas
suit	costume
tights	collant
trousers	pantalon

USEFUL PHRASES

goodbye	au revoir
hello/good morning	bonjour
how	comment
excuse me	excusez-moi
thank you	merci
yes/no	oui/non
I am sorry	pardon
why	pourquoi
when	quand
please	s'il vous plaît

Do you speak English? . . . . Parlez-vous anglais?
I don't understand . . . . Je ne comprends pas
Talk slowly . . . . Parlez lentement
Where's...? . . . . Où est...?
When does the... leave? . . . . . . À quelle heure part...?
When does the... arrive? . . . . . . À quelle heure arrive...?
When does the museum open? . . À quelle heure ouvre le musée?
When is the show? . . . . À quelle heure est la représentation?
When is breakfast served? . . . . . À quelle heure sert-on le petit-déjeuner?
What does it cost? . . . . Combien cela coûte?
Where can I buy a newspaper
in English? . . . . Où puis-je acheter un journal en anglais?
Where is the nearest petrol/gas
station? . . . . Où se trouve la station essence la plus proche?
Where can I change
traveller's cheques? . . . . Où puis-je échanger des traveller's cheques?
Where are the toilets? . . . . Où sont les toilettes?
Do you accept credit cards? . . . . Acceptez-vous les cartes de crédit?

Cascades de Kakouetta

Introduction

Landscapes

This guide describes the regions, bordering the Atlantic Coast, which lie between the estuary of the River Loire, to the north, and the barrier of the Pyrenees to the south.

ADMINISTRATIVE REGIONS

- Pays de la Loire
- Centre
- Poitou-Charentes
- Limousin
- Aquitaine
- Midi-Pyrénées

Area covered by this guide

This large and ancient province centred on the town of Poitiers incorporates the Pays de Retz, Vendée and the Marais Poitevin (the Poitou marshlands).

The plain – The limestone plateau between the ancient massifs of the **Vendée** (which are the southern extremity of the Armorican peninsula on which Brittany sits) and Limousin (the region east of Angoulême) describes a crescent stretching from Loudun to Luçon. Almost denuded of trees and gashed with deep valleys, the plain seems to roll away to infinity, its succession of fields, meadows and moors scarcely interrupted by the occasional village.

Certain nuances however are discernible: in the north the plain is actually part of Touraine (the region around Tours); from Thouars to Châtellerault there are outcrops of local chalk, carpeted with thin patches of cultivation and moorland cropped by sheep. Here and there deposits of sand occur, and fields of asparagus can be seen in the middle of pinewoods. On the exposed hillsides bordering the River Thouet and River Vienne, the scattered wine-growers' houses are built of tufa (a hard crystalline chalk with a high mica content). The areas around Chauvigny and Montmorillon (on the Poitou borders), composed of sands and clay, were once a region of infertile heaths or **brandes**. In certain areas this heathland still subsists, supporting flocks of sheep and goats (the goat's cheese of Chauvigny is well known). In other places, where the heath has been cleared, Charollais or Limousin bullocks are raised. Flocks of *pirons* (a variety of goose raised for its skin and *duvet* or down) wander near the farms. West of Clain, continuing as far as Melle and St-Maixent, the Jurassic limestone, lacerated by valleys, has decomposed on the surface into what is locally called **terre de groie** (a compound soil part clay, part gravel, part lime, of proverbial fertility – especially for cereals and fodder plants such as clover and alfalfa).

Le Bocage – The areas of the Vendée and the **Gâtine de Parthenay**, south and west of the River Thouet, have many features in common. This is the region known as *le bocage* – an empire of lush meadows bordered by hedgerows of hawthorn or broom, with sunken lanes leading to smallholdings and farms half-hidden in leafy copses. The breeding of cattle fattened for beef takes pride of place in this patchwork of small fields where the speckled brown Parthenay bullocks graze. The area is dotted with apple orchards and the occasional field of fodder plants grown to feed the cattle. A chain of low, rounded hills forms the backbone of this productive agricultural area, and these are known as *Les Collines Vendéennes* (the Hills of the Vendée).

Le Marais Poitevin

Marshlands and coast – The marsh (Marais) area extends from the schists of the **Pays de Retz** to the limestone cliffs of the **Aunis** – an ancient region centered on La Rochelle. Between these cliffs, which mark the limit of the prehistoric Bay of Biscay (or Golfe de Gascogne as it is known in France), and the sea, salt-marshes transformed into oyster farms glitter in the sun, sheep and cattle graze in the water-meadows, early fruit and vegetables ripen on the alluvial soil and wild duck paddle the canals beneath over-hanging hedgerows alive with smaller birds. The marshland, formed from debris accumulated by rivers and ancient ocean currents, lies sheltered behind the coastal dunes; rocky islets from an earlier epoch thrust through here and there, and that ancient coastline defines the area's inner limit. From north to south the route passes successively through the Breton-Vendée marshland, which includes the marshes of Monts, the marshes of Olonne and of Talmont and the famous **Marais Poitevin**, the Poitou marshlands.

Huge beaches of fine sand lie along the foot of the dunes and on the offshore bars; between Noirmoutier and the mainland, on either side of the causeway known as the Passage du Gois, enormous stretches of mudflat are exposed at low tide. Noirmoutier itself and the more southerly Île d'Yeu (Isle of Yeu) provide yet more contrast: the one flat, peaceful and gentle, the other rocky and savage on its western coast.

Vineyards of the Cognac region

CHARENTES

The region known as the Charentes comprises the two *départements* of Charente and Charente-Maritime, separated by the green and placid valley of the River Charente, which themselves embrace the ancient provinces of **Angoumois** (the Angoulême region), **Aunis** *(see above)* and **Saintonge** (the region around Saintes).

Charente itself, abutting the foothills of the Massif Central, divides into four natural geographic areas: to the west the wine country of Cognac, at the centre the cereal-growing Angoumois, in the north-east the Confolentais with its plateaux, and to the south the Montmorélien, a hilly landscape of mixed farming.

Charente-Maritime, facing the Atlantic, presents a coastline of rocks and dunes and sandy beaches, with a rural interior of forests and plains.

Vineyards – The heart of the Charentes beats in the town of Cognac, the capital of that chalky **champagne** area (the soil is similar to that in the Champagne region, east of Paris) bordering the south bank of the river, which nourishes the fruit from which the world-famous spirit bearing the name of the town is distilled.

The Plain – The limestone plateau which extends from Angoulême to La Rochelle provides a slightly monotonous landscape, only rarely cut by valleys (such as that of the Boutonne), dotted with small towns and an occasional whitewashed hamlet. As in Poitou, the Jurassic bedrock is cloaked with a reddish *terre de groie (see above)* or a fertile alluvium on which cornfields take second place to artificial meadows of clover and alfalfa or fields of sugar-beet grown as fodder.

Coast – The Charentais coast is slightly unusual because, especially towards its centre, alluvial deposits from the River Charente and River Seudre have combined with marine currents to form an area of marshland not unlike that in Poitou. Most of this swampy land has been either reclaimed as **polders** (low-lying lands protected by dykes) on which crops are grown, or transformed – especially near Marennes – into shallow basins in which mussels and oysters are farmed. The distance the tide goes out varies from 2km/1mi to 5km/3mi.

Not far offshore, the low-lying and sandy islands of Oléron and Ré, scattered with pretty white houses, define the outer limit of an inner sea – the **Mer de Pertuis**, so-called because the only way its waters can reach the open sea is via one or other of the straits *(pertuis)* dividing these isles from the mainland.

BORDELAIS

The region known as Le Bordelais, at the heart of the ancient province of **Guyenne** (Aquitaine), centres on the confluence of the River Garonne and River Dordogne. This transitional area between the limestone plains of Charentes to the north and the vast sandy expanse of the Landes to the south is drained by the Garonne and its tributaries towards the zone of subsidence around the estuary.

Agriculture here is dominated by the cultivation of vines.

Gironde estuary – The Gironde is the name given to the great estuarial stretch of water lying between the Garonne-Dordogne convergence and the sea. It is a modest reminder of the marine reaches which covered the Aquitaine basin long ago in the Tertiary era. The northern bank of the estuary is bordered by limestone hills known as the Côtes de Bourg and Côtes de Blaye. On the south bank, where the land on the whole is lower, similar limestone formations have been eroded and then covered by gravels, producing the topsoil in which the famous vines of the Médoc flourish.

Covering the limestone bedrock of the Gironde are deposits washed down by the two great rivers; these deposits, stirred by the action of the tides, have determined the formation of marshes, which are separated from the running water by an alluvial belt, the **palus**.

Some of the marshland has been transformed, in the Dutch manner, into polders *(see above)* where meadows now lie; the rest remains the province of hunters and waterfowl. Artichokes are grown on the *palus*, and certain vines which produce a *palus* wine.

Over the centuries the movement of the water has created a number of elongated islands as well as sandbanks which are revealed at low tide.

Médoc – This world-famous wine-producing area is divided into three separate zones: the region of viticulture proper, a zone of coastal forest, and the *palus (see above)* which punctuates the limestone bluffs of St-Estèphe and Pauillac. Fine red wines come from the first zone: north of St-Seurin-de-Cadourne these are produced mainly by local cooperatives and sold under the simple overall description of Médoc; to the south, from St-Seurin to Blanquefort, lies the district meriting the more distinguished Haut-Médoc appellation.

LANDES

The word *landes* (moors) still conjures up a vision of the more desolate aspect of this part of the coast which existed prior to the 19C, when a remarkable project of arboreal husbandry transformed the area into a huge pine forest.

The Bassin d'Arcachon and the Dune du Pilat

Coast and dunes – The Landes sit on an enormous plain, roughly triangular in shape, covering an area of 14 000km²/5 400sq mi. The side of the triangle runs down the 230km/143mi of coast from the Gironde estuary to the mouth of the Adour, and turns eastwards from the two points to meet at the triangle's apex 100km/62mi inland.

This ruler-straight shoreline, known as the **Côte d'Argent** (Silver Coast), is essentially one vast beach on which the sea deposits sand at an annual rate of 15 to 18m³ per metre of coast/20 to 24cu yd per yard of coast. The sand – especially in those reaches of the strand only reached by the highest equinoctial tides – is then dried and blown inland by the west wind, where it accumulates in dunes. Until the last century these dunes then moved away from the sea at a speed varying between 10m/32ft and 27m/88ft per year. Today, fixed in position by the plantation of shrubs, grasses and forest trees, the dunes form a continuous but static coastal belt 5km/3mi wide. The strip is the longest – and highest – series of dunes in Europe.

Lakes, lagoons and the plain – Most of the watercourses in the region find themselves blocked by the dune barrier, the one exception being the Leyre (known also as the Eyre in its lower reaches) which finds its way directly to the sea via Arcachon Lagoon. Elsewhere the streams have formed lakes, the surfaces of which are 15m/50ft to 18m/60ft above sea level. Most of these lakes intercommunicate; their waters force a passage through to the ocean with difficulty, via turbulent currents popular with water-sports enthusiasts; the Huchet and Contis currents are typical examples.

The lakes and currents are well stocked with fish (trout, tench, carp, eel etc) but the huge areas of water involved make these coastal lakes and lagoons particularly suitable for the use of large-scale boating equipment.

Sands distributed over the inner areas of the Landes originally formed part of material gouged from the Pyrenees by Quaternary Era glaciers; they exist now as a layer of brown sandstone, no more than 50cm/20in thick, known as the **alios**. This bed inhibits the percolation of water and blocks the extension of roots, and this, combined with the poor drainage of the plains because of their negligible slopes, adds to the dampness of

55

the region and the sterility of its soils. Until the middle of the 19C this inner zone was no more than an unhealthy stretch of moorland, transformed into a swamp when the rains came, and supporting only a scanty shepherd population which went about on stilts. Even the sheep were raised more for their manure than for their meat or wool.

Wayward river – Over the centuries the course of the **River Adour** and its outlet to the sea has been altered by the region's shifting sands. Documents reveal that in AD 907 the river left Capbreton to carve a route to the sea via Vieux-Boucau-Port-d'Albret; in 1164 it again channelled a new path, this time near Bayonne, but later returned to Capbreton. A terrible storm in the 14C blocked the river's way and so it once again flowed to Port-d'Albret. Meanwhile, the port at Bayonne was being engulfed by sand. In 1569 Charles IX insisted that the river should be given a fixed estuary, which saved the harbour at Bayonne; nine years later a channel leading through 2km/1mi of dunes beyond Bayonne was opened, and the port at Boucau-Neuf was created.

Consolidation of the dunes – As early as the Middle Ages it was known that mobile sand dunes could be fixed by the use of maritime pines or plants with spreading roots. A number of experiments were made in the Landes but it was **Nicolas Brémontier** (1738-1809), an engineer from the Roads and Bridges Department, who perfected the process and started the gigantic task here in 1788. First he constructed a dyke designed to check the movement of the sand at its starting point, then, about 70m/230ft from the high-water mark, he planted a palisade of stakes against which the sand could pile up. Adding to the height of the palisade as the accumulated sand rose higher, he progressively formed an artificial coastal dune 10m/33ft to 12m/39ft high, which acted as a barrier. He fixed the surface sand by sowing **marram grass**, a variety of grass with a thick network of rapidly spreading roots. He then turned his attention to the problem of the inland dunes.

Brémontier mixed the seeds of maritime pines with gorse and broom seeds, sowing them beneath brushwood which temporarily held back the sand. After four years the broom had grown into bushes nearly 2.5m/7ft high. These sheltered the slower-growing pines, which eventually outgrew the bushes, and, as they died and rotted, provided fertilizer for the young trees. By 1867 the work was almost complete: 3 000ha/7 500 acres of coastal dunes were carpeted with marram grass and 80 000ha/198 000 acres of inland dunes were planted with pine trees.

Cleaning up the interior – At the beginning of the 19C the inner part of the Landes area was still a fever-swamp unfit for cultivation; it was badly drained and resisted all attempts to establish an agricultural presence. Under the Second Empire, however, an engineer named **Chambrelent** found the answer: he systematically broke up the unfertile layer of *alios (see above)* and then drew up a scheme of drainage, clearance and reforestation. The results justified the large-scale planting of maritime pines, cork-oaks and ilex trees: the Landes *département* soon became one of the richest in France as the many products from pine trees brought large returns.

The forest under threat – For maritime pines the greatest danger, which in a dry climate can never be entirely eliminated, is fire, especially when allied with wind. Today the pine forest covers nearly 1 000 000ha/2 350 000 acres in the Landes, and to preserve it a special corps of forest firefighters has been created. Numerous observation posts linked by telephone and radio ensure the rapid detection of an outbreak of fire. Air assistance can be called up. Everything possible has been done to facilitate the firefighters' access in all weathers and with the least delay. Commercial developments, access for traffic and especially camping are strictly controlled.

AGENAIS

Agenais is a transitional region lying between the southern part of Périgord, Bas-Quercy (Lower Quercy, to the east) and the Landes. This fertile area is lent a certain unity by the valley of the River Garonne.

In the damp northern sector herds of dairy cows graze in the pastures covering the clays; further east, pinewoods and plantations of oak and chestnut appear. In the area around Fumel, on the River Lot, a number of small metallurgical works exploit the local sands rich in iron ore.

Pays des Serres – This area stretches as far as the southern part of the Lot *département*. Unlike nearby Quercy which has retained a variety of crops, this region of long, narrow hills tends to specialize. On the muddier plateaux of Tournon-d'Agenais wheat is the most important crop; the hillsides are used for the cultivation of vines.

Lot Valley – The Lot Valley is one immense orchard punctuated by nurseries and fields of tobacco. Fresh peas, green beans and the melons of Villeneuve-sur-Lot are among the renowned local products.

Valley of the Garonne – The alluvial soils and mild climate here allow more delicate crops, most of them grown on terraces, to flourish; each town and village has its speciality. Agen, for example, is famous for its onions and its prunes: hand-picked, specially graded fresh plums, grown on grafted trees, are subsequently dried either naturally or in a slow oven to produce the **pruneaux d'Agen**. The use of grafted plum trees here dates back to the Crusades. In the 16C the monks of Clairac, near Tonneins, were the first to foresee the commercial possibilities of the plum, and 200 years later the market had grown to such an extent that it had to be government-controlled. The plum variety used almost universally in the region today is the *Robe-Sergent* (Red Victoria plum). Marmande is famous for its tomatoes and pumpkins; Ste-Marie produces peaches and cherries. Since the 18C even poplar trees have been pressed into service: plantations on land subject to flooding provide wood used in carpentry and the manufacture of paper.

GASCOGNE

The Aquitaine basin is part of a series of French sedimentary beds which resulted from the silting up of an ancient ocean depth; what distinguishes Gascogne (Gascony), the region lying between the Pyrenees and the River Garonne, is the upper covering provided by enormous masses of debris washed down by the rivers after the erosion of the mountains during the Tertiary Era.

The most common formation in Gascony is known as the **molasse** – layers of sand frequently cemented into a soft yellow sandstone penetrated by discontinuous marl and limestone beds. This geological structure has resulted in a hilly landscape of mixed topography.

From an agricultural point of view the soils here vary between **terreforts**, which are clayey and heavy to work, and **boulebènes** – lighter and slightly muddy, but less fertile and more suitable for grazing and cattle-breeding.

The hills of Gascony – The rivers, all tributaries of the Garonne, fan out northwards from the foothills of the mountains and cut through the hills of Armagnac in thin swathes. Those emerging from the major Pyrenean valleys – the Neste d'Aure and the Gave de Pau (Aure and Pau torrents) for instance – are already discharging the deposits they carry, and this material, mixed with the detritus from ancient glacial moraines, has produced a soil that is relatively poor. As a result there is a succession of moors between the high **Plateau de Lannemezan** and Pont-Long, north of Pau, via the Ger Plateau on the western side of Tarbes.

In the hills themselves, careful watering has led to the establishment of market gardens specializing in such exotic produce as strawberries and melons.

Vines in this region form only a part of the traditional polyculture; the part played by such *appellation contrôlée* wines as the Jurançon and Madiran whites and reds, and VDQS *(vins délimités de qualité supérieure)* from Béarn and Tursan, remains limited.

Adour country – The great curving sweep of the River Adour – northwards from its source, then west and finally back towards the south – creates a major demarcation line on the hydrographic chart of the region; the convergence towards Bayonne of all the rivers within this arc is evidence of a continuous sinking of the earth's crust beneath the ocean, which has persisted since the end of the Secondary Era.

Within the area encompassed by the Adour is a hilly landscape cut through by the tributaries of the river. The lower slopes of the valleys are terraced as they drop towards the cultivated alluvial strips flanking these streams.

THE PYRENEES

The customary division of this mountain range into three large natural areas succeeding one another from west to east is justified by major differences in structure, climate and vegetation. The distinction is underlined by the traditions and language of the inhabitants *(the Central Pyrenees and the Mediterranean section of the chain are described in The Green Guide Languedoc-Roussillon-Tarn-Gorges)*

Le Pic du Midi d'Ossan

Formation of the chain – The remarkable view from the town of Pau of the Pyrenean mountains rising above the hills of the Béarn district presents a seemingly endless series of finely serrated crests – a mountain barrier revealing at that distance neither individual peaks, apart from Pic du Midi d'Ossau, nor saddles.

The barrier itself, stretching 400km/248mi from the Atlantic to the Mediterranean, is relatively narrow (30km/19mi to 40km/25mi on the French side of the frontier) yet also massive and continuous: the average height of the Pyrenees is 1 008m/just over 3 300ft.

History of the range – Approximately 250 million years ago a Hercynian (Paleozoic) mountain mass similar to the Massif Central or the Ardennes stood on the site occupied by the Pyrenees today; however, whereas the central and northern heights experienced a relatively tranquil existence, this chain between the Atlantic and the Mediterranean was sited in a particularly unstable zone. Already vigorously folded, and then partially levelled by erosion, the Hercynian block was submerged about 200 million years ago beneath a continental sea and covered by Secondary Era sedimentary deposits, before being totally resurrected – and literally shaken from top to bottom – by the Alpine folding, the earliest spasms of which occurred here.

Under the enormous pressure of this mountain-building movement the most recent beds, still comparatively pliant, folded without breaking but the rigid ancient platform cracked, broke up and became dislocated. Hot springs burst through near the fractures; mineral deposits formed and metal-bearing ores appeared.

During the geological eons that passed while this was occurring, the mountain mass, now tortured and misshapen, was ceaselessly worn down by erosion, and the material torn from it washed out by rivers across the plains below.

Central Pyrenees

The overall structure of the Pyrenean region is characterized by the juxtaposition of large geological masses arranged longitudinally. Starting from the Upper Garonne, the relief encompasses:

– the rises known as the Petites Pyrénées, of only medium height but remarkable for the alignment of limestone crests pleated in a fashion typical of the Jurassic period;

– the real foothills, formations of the Secondary Era (either Cretaceous or Jurassic), with folded beds more violently distorted;

– the **Axial Zone**, the true spine of the Pyrenees along which granitic extrusions, recognizable by sharply defined peaks chiselled by glacial erosion, thrust through the Primary sediments: the Balaïtous, the Néouvielle and Maladetta massifs, the Luchon Pyrenees. The summits however are not made up entirely of granite, since patches of extremely hard schist and limestone exist which are even more resistant to erosion;

– the southern Secondary Era sediments, under-thrust to a height of more than 3 000m/9 840ft at Monte Perdido, which are to be found largely on the Spanish side of the frontier. Two masterpieces of mountain scenery stand out among this limestone relief: in Spain the canyon of the Ordesa Valley (a National Park); in France the lower part of the Gavarnie amphitheatre, with its gigantic platforms of horizontal strata piled one upon the other.

Valleys – The inner part of the chain lacks a channel, parallel to the backbone of the range, which could link up the many transversal valleys. This makes internal communications difficult, a problem exacerbated in the Central Pyrenees by the fact that most passes are impracticable in winter. Each of these valleys was therefore isolated for much of the time, and this led to a survival of socially autonomous lifestyles of the kind still to be found in such *petit pays* districts as the Couserans, the Quatre

Vallées (Four Valleys) region, and the Pays Toy. The valleys are nevertheless far from being inhospitable; despite being hemmed in, they seem no more than a hilly extension of the plains of Lower Aquitaine – with the additional advantage of a sheltered climate.

Glaciers – A hundred centuries ago the ancient glaciers thrust their abrasive tongues across the mountain landscape, gouging out the terrain as far as the present sites of Lourdes and Montréjeau. Since then these giant ice-floes have shrunk to negligible proportions (less than $10km^2/4sq$ mi for the Pyrenees, compared with $400km^2/155sq$ mi in just the French part of the Alps). There is only one whole glacier, complete with tongue and terminal moraine, in the entire range: the Ossoue, on the eastern slopes of the Vignemale.

Many of the most dramatic and appealing features to be found at the heart of the Pyrenees were formed by the old glaciers: hanging valleys, amphitheatres, canyons transformed into pastoral sweeps, jagged crests and scatters of huge boulders, lakes (over 500 in the French Pyrenees), cascades, bluffs, sudden morainic platforms and powerful waterfalls, some of which are harnessed for the production of hydroelectric power.

Summits – The frontier between France and Spain is marked by the peaks of Balaïtous (3 146m/10 321ft) and Vignemale (3 298m/10 820ft), though the greatest heights of the Pyrenees are located on the Spanish side of the border: the impressive massifs of the Maladetta (3 404m/11 168ft) and Posets (3 371m/11 059ft). The French side nevertheless boasts Pic du Midi d'Ossau (2 884m/9 462ft), which owes its majestic silhouette to the extrusion of volcanic rocks, and Pic du Midi de Bigorre (2 865m/9 400ft), notable also for the way it towers over the plain below. The Massif de Néouvielle (3 192m/10 472ft at Pic Long) includes an extraordinary water tower, the contents of which are now almost totally reserved for the hydroelectric installations in the valleys of the Pau and Upper Neste torrents.

Picturesque Pyrenees – The Cauterets Valley perfectly illustrates those traditional and well-loved aspects of the Pyrenees which have inspired so many artists: steep-sided, narrow valleys opening up in the higher reaches of their rivers into huge upland pastures, gently sculptured, jewelled with lakes and webbed with torrents both turbulent and limpid. Such attractions, added to the benefits of the hot springs, the individuality of local customs and the exoticism of nearby Spain, appeal to romantic natures. Despite the progressive abandonment of temporary dwellings (mountain refuges, summer sheepfolds etc), of upland tracks and some of the highest pastoral slopes, the Central Pyrenees retain – at least in the Axial Zone – that friendly and characteristic image of mountains that have been in some way humanized.

Atlantic Pyrenees

This part of the range is characterized geographically by the disappearance of the Axial Zone, which has led to a confusion of the general relief, there being no longer a continuous spine or backbone to act as a "natural" frontier.

It is among the calcareous beds covering the eastern extremity of the Axial Zone that the most noticeable examples of geomorphological disturbance occur. These are the twisted contortions of the 2 504m/8 213ft Pic d'Anie and the savage gashes of the Kakouetta and Holcarte gorges. The subterranean levels of these fissured limestones riddled with potholes have provided an immense field of exploration and study for speleologists (cave scientists).

The slopes of these Lower Pyrenees are abundantly wooded and relatively difficult to cross (the Forest of Iraty for example).

Nearer the ocean a more placid topography characterizes the Basque Country, typified by La Rhune, Mont Ursava (at Cambo-les-Bains) and the mountains surrounding St-Jean-Pied-de-Port. The landscape between the Adour estuary and Spain mainly comprises hills sculpted from a heterogeneous mass of marine sediments.

Basque Pyrenees – The charm and cohesion of this region derives mainly from its oceanic climate with plenty of humidity, and the colourful language and civilization of the Basque people, so closely interwoven with those in the neighbouring Spanish provinces of Guipuzcoa and Navarra. Trans-Pyrenean traffic is largely concentrated on the coastal route but the inland passages remain very popular with tourists and locals who have used them ever since the era of the great pilgrimages to Santiago de Compostela in Spain.

Coast – The dunes and pinewoods of the Landes region stretch beyond the mouth of the River Adour, as far as Pointe de St-Martin near Biarritz.

Further south however the coastline bites into the Pyrenean folds, and the rocks – sedimentary beds violently arched over, foliated into thin laminated layers – form the low, slanting cliffs responsible for the picturesque appearance of the Basque Corniche.

Pyrenean flora and fauna

Flora

There are three main types of vegetation in the Pyrenees, associated with the different geographic zones. To the west, the climate is affected by the Atlantic; the central Pyrenees is a continental-mountain zone; on the far eastern end of the range, the Mediterranean clime prevails. The diversity of species also depends on altitude, as in other mountainous areas. Below 800m/2 625ft, in the foothills, the forest is mostly common oak, typical of Atlantic regions. As the hills rise to 1 700m/5 580ft, the mountain sides are covered with beech on the lower slopes, and pine higher up, where the undergrowth is thick. From this level up to 2 400m/7 874ft, a robust species of hard pine (*pinus uncinata* – it proliferates in the rocky soil around the Cirque de Gavarnie) joins birch and *serbus domestica*, a fruit-bearing tree resembling mountain ash. At this limit, the forest grows sparse, rhododendrons and alpine meadows strewn with wild flowers predominate. From here up to 2 800m/9 186ft, few trees subsist, apart from the dwarf willow; other multicoloured vegetation hugs the ground. Beyond this altitude, the wintry landscape is one of rocks covered in the barest layer of moss and lichen, growth which resists the long months spent under snow.

There is an extraordinary wealth of native species of plants, flowers which are found nowhere else on earth. Some of them can be traced back to the Tertiary Era, when the climate was subtropical, such as ramondia, a small plant with deep violet blossoms and fuzzy leaves. Countless species flourish in the mountainous, sub-alpine and alpine zones. Among the loveliest and best known, the lily of the Pyrenees, long-leafed saxifrage, blue Pyrenees thistle, campion, sisymbrium, Welsh poppies (blown in, no doubt, by the western wind), wild iris (especially around the Cirque de Gavarnie), and a profusion of others. These delightful and rare plants flower in June and July, as well as in August at high altitudes.

Fauna

Mountain species each find their home in the different altitude zones. Among the protected species, the brown bear, now unfortunately a rare sight, lives in the mountainous clime. In the beech and pine woods, the last of the lynx roam (it is uncertain how many of them survive in the wild). The isards (local name for the indigenous chamois) prefer the grassy meadows and rocky outcroppings of the alpine altitudes, where these graceful antelopes bound effortlessly across the steep mountain flank. Beyond 1 500m/4 921ft, the river banks provide shelter for muskrat; the local species is known as desman, and these rodents grow to about 25cm/10in. The lakes and streams of the Pyrenees had been fished out, but recent efforts to reintroduce species have been successful, and trout and salmon again swim the waters. An amphibian of the uridela order, resembling a newt with a yellow underside and flattened tail, known as the Pyrenean euprocte, likes to hide under flat stones in rivers and ponds (10-20cm/3-8in). Soaring and gliding above the land-bound species, many birds of prey can be observed: the royal eagle, flying in splendid solitude; griffon vultures, gathered together; the rare bearded vulture (Gypaetus barbatus), the largest bird of prey in Europe, also known as a lammergeier. The wood grouse is found in the underbrush, where it feeds on grains, berries and pine buds. During mating season, it parades its love joyfully and noisily. Marmots come out in the early morning to start their daily routine of eating, napping, playing and keeping watch for predators.

Observing mountain animals

It is unusual to encounter wild animals casually, because they prefer to keep well away from the human species. However, you can increase your chances by using a few simple techniques. Firstly, walk as quietly as possible, avoid snapping branches, keep your voice low. In relative silence, animals are less likely to run away, and you may be able to hear tell-tale sounds such as rustling in the underbrush, or even an animal's cry. Through careful observation, you may discover tracks in the snow or on the ground, remains of a meal (nut shells, pine cones or berries which have been nibbled), or droppings, which tell naturalists a good deal about an animal's habits. Certain times of day or periods of the year are more propitious: many animals are more easily spotted at dusk or dawn, while spring mating season encourages males to wander farther afield, and even close up to paths used by people. In the winter, most mountain animals hibernate, and reappear with the vernal melt.

Traditional economic activities

FISHING AND THE FRUITS OF THE SEA

Since the western part of the region enjoys a favoured situation beside the sea, fishing is naturally one of its principal commercial assets.

Deep-sea fishing – Modern trawlers are ideally suited to fishing on the high seas – a branch of the industry which supplies most of Europe's fresh fish and which concentrates its activities at the limit of the continental shelf, where the depth is often 500m/1 640ft or more. Sole, bream and hake landed by these trawlers play an important part in the economy of La Rochelle, Les Sables d'Olonne, the Île d'Yeu, St-Gilles and other ports in the northern coastal section.

Fishing for the huge **tuna fish** takes place from June to October, from boats equipped with dragnets and live bait (sardines, anchovies etc). The great white Atlantic tuna, known locally as *germon*, is fished at the beginning of the season between Portugal and the Azores, and the fleets then follow its migration north from the Bay of Biscay as far as the south-west of Ireland. Tuna is the main catch brought back to St-Jean-de-Luz.

Fishing along the coast

Coastal fishing – Though coastal fishing is more limited in its scope than deep-sea fishing, it nevertheless supplies a particular demand – for varieties of fish and seafood which are especially prized when they are absolutely fresh. Small trawlers, motor-boats and local fishing smacks bring in sole, whiting, mullet, mackerel, skate etc, according to the season and the locality. To fish **sardines**, fishermen use "turning" nets – seines from 200m/656ft to 300m/984ft long. The catch is landed daily and sold immediately at quayside auctions. The increasing rarity of sardine banks off the Vendée coast has, however, driven the fleets further towards the coast of Morocco, where ships with deep-freeze compartments have to be used.

Recreational fishing uses lines, cords, fixed nets, seine nets from the beach, or regionally typical **carrelets** (suspended nets manoeuvred via pulleys from a landing stage). Carrelets remain popular, particularly in the Gironde estuary, although a certain picturesque quality may weigh more in their favour than any particular effectiveness. In the spring, when fish swarm upriver to spawn, the catches of shad and lamprey in the Gironde are at their most plentiful. The eels return at the same time; their tiny **pibales** (elvers) are fished from the shore, thousands at a time, with fine-meshed shrimping nets.

Crustaceans – Lobsters, crabs and crayfish are caught – in wicker pots or hoop nets – mainly in the cold waters off the rocky coasts of the Vendée and the Île d'Yeu. Langoustines (crayfish) are fished further out by the trawlers. Fishermen from Royan and La Cotinière seek out shrimps and prawns on the banks off the Gironde estuary.

Salt marshes – From the 11C to the 18C the marshes, bordering almost the entire Poitou coast, were one of the principal economic assets of that area, especially in the Aunis and Saintonge regions. The salt trade played an important part then in both sea and river traffic. Merchants sailing to northern Europe carried salt as far as the Hanseatic ports, where it was used to preserve fish. Then the receding sea withdrew further still; the marshes silted up and transformed themselves into *gâts* (fever swamps). Today the only salt pans still worked are on Noirmoutier Island and the Isle of Ré, with a few more among the Breton-Vendée marshes. The rest have been turned into pastureland, market gardens, nature reserves or *claires* (basins) for fattening oysters.

The working of salt flats is a delicate operation. The marsh is divided into a grid, squared off with small *bossis* (banks) of earth bearing a large proportion of clay. Sea water, brought by the rising tide, is carried into the grid via narrow canals or *étiers*, allowed to settle, and then concentrated in a series of reservoirs that become shallower and shallower. The water in the final pans, known as *œillets*, is no more than 5cm/2in deep. It is here, once the liquid evaporates, that the salt crystallizes.

From May to September the *paludier* (salt-worker) "draws" with the help of a large rake (known as a *las* or *rabale*) the grey salt deposit from the bottom of the pan after skimming the white salt off the surface with a flat shovel. The harvest is then assembled in *mulons* (small heaps) at the side of the pan – often protected against bad weather today by plastic sheeting – to be stocked later in the local *salorges* (special salt stores, usually built of wood).

Oysters

The Marennes-Oléron basin, which extends from the River Charente to the mouth of the Gironde, is among the most important oyster-farming regions in France: the Charente-Maritime *département* alone supplies almost half the national market in these epicurean delicacies. Brittany is the other big oyster-producing area.

History and biology – The two main varieties, the flat oyster *(plates)* and the concave or deep-shelled oyster *(creuses)*, live in their natural state, respectively, on sandbanks or in beds attached to undersea rocks. The **flat oyster** is hermaphrodite and viviparous (the young are produced live and do not have to be hatched). This variety has been known in the region since Gallo-Roman times, and has been gathered or dredged since then; it was a delicacy on the table of Louis XIV, who was a great oyster-lover. In 1920, however, the species was almost entirely destroyed by a disease, and flat oysters can only be found now – in very small quantities – in the region of Marennes.

The fleshier, richer **deep-shelled oyster**, with a taste that is less delicate and very different, is unisexual and oviparous (the young are hatched from eggs) as well as being less sensitive to changes in the weather. The variety was introduced into the area accidentally in 1868: a ship sheltering from a storm stayed too long in the Gironde on its way from Portugal to England with a cargo of these oysters; the cargo was in danger of going bad and the oysters had to be thrown into the sea. The survivors, having scattered, then imposed themselves on the majority of local farms.

When disease struck again in 1971, these *portugaises* were in turn supplanted by *japonaises (Crassostrea Gigas)* – oysters bred in the Pacific and imported from Japan or Canada (British Columbia).

Exploitation – Ostreiculture (oyster breeding) in France remains very much a cottage industry – frequently a family affair – and still a fairly uncertain business: apart from the risk of disease, oyster farms can be destroyed by pollution, silting up, excess salinity, storms, an unusually cold spell or degeneration of the oysters – which can also be attacked by crabs, starfish or even winkles.

The **nassain** (young seed oysters or spats), drifting this way and that with the currents, become attached in summer to **collectors** – lime-washed tiles, slates, wooden stakes or stones according to the region; these are then transported to the first oyster park. After a year or two the oysters are prised off the collectors – a technique known as **détroquage** – and placed in a second park. They remain a further year or two here, usually in special *pochons* (containers) placed on tables. In the Marennes-Oléron basin the oysters receive a final treatment to mature and refine them, giving them their characteristic pale greenish-blue hue, in fattening pools known as **claires** full of microscopic blue algae. Oysters sold as **spéciales** have spent longer in the *claires*, and are less densely distributed in them, than the ordinary **fines de claires**.

Gathering mussels

M. Thiery/MICHELIN

Mussels

The mussel is a bivalve with a blue-black shell, and in its wild state lives in colonies on rocks assaulted by the sea. It has been farmed since the 13C and is reared professionally along the coast of the province of Aunis – separated (except in Aiguillon Bay) from the oysters, since the two shellfish are biologically incompatible. The centres of mussel production today are the coast near Brouage, the Isle of Oléron (Boyardville Bay) and the Anse de Fouras to the south of the province; Aiguillon Bay to the north of it.

Sea snail

Scallop

Periwinkle

Treasures from the sea

Starfish

Donacidae

Clam

Razor shell clam

Limpet

Cockle

Knotted wrack

Mussels

Mytiliculture – This is the French term for mussel breeding, including their fattening and beautifying for the market. The mussels attach themselves to **bouchots** (stakes) driven into the mud or silt in long lines or arranged in grids, where they fatten and increase in size. The arrangement of the *bouchots* varies from district to district and is subject to strict control. In the Breton Straits the *bouchots à nassain*, for the very young mussels, are well off-shore, and those where the shellfish grow to commercial size much nearer the coast. The *boucholeurs* visit their mussel beds in small, flat-bottomed boats or, if the tide is low, on their *accons* – flat wooden crates which they slide across the mud with a hefty kick from their boot.

Gastronomically, mussels serve as the base for the preparation of a regional delicacy known as *mouclade*.

AGRICULTURE

Poitou, the Charentes and the region around Bordeaux all rely heavily on agriculture – crops on the limestone plains, vines on the valley slopes. In the Landes, the forest overshadows everything.

Mixed farming – Mixed agriculture is still the norm in these lands where tenant farming (with a generous percentage of the crop being given to the landlord), although rapidly disappearing, still exists and the average property rarely exceeds 50ha/125 acres.

Cereals (wheat, maize, oats) in the small farms grow side by side with meadows of clover, alfalfa and other **fodder plants**. There exist also a number of slightly less common crops: in the coastal regions, for example, with their humid atmosphere warmed by the ocean, **early fruit and vegetables** flourish; on the islands (with the exception of the Île d'Yeu) and in the rich alluvial soil of the marshlands, it is easy to grow new potatoes, artichokes, carrots and peas. The melons known as Charentais also grow in this same area and in recent years these have been so successful that they have spread as far as the Rhône Valley, where they have threatened to supplant the Cantaloupe melon.

Market gardens abound in the lower parts of the Vienne, Thouet and Garonne valleys and those of their tributaries. The Garonne basin, in addition, specializes in tomatoes, various fruits and even tobacco. **Tobacco**, largely a family business, is grown in small fields in the region around Bazas and on the alluvial soil flooring the valleys of the Dordogne, the Lot and the Garonne, where the principal centres are Marmande and Tonneins.

The pines of the Landes – The huge forest covering the Landes consists mainly of maritime pines, although parasol varieties occur here and there. The maritime pine, with its tall bole ringed by tufts of needles, is not a beautiful tree though it does have a certain elegance – and it grows quickly; it has also brought prosperity to what was once a poor and desolate region.

A. Thuillier/MICHELIN

Resin harvesting in the Landes forest

Among other uses it has been since ancient times the base of a traditional activity: **gemmage** – resin harvesting. Formerly, the *gemmeur* (gum collector) periodically tapped the tree with the aid of a tool known as a *hapchot*. From the wounds made by this the resin bled into small earthenware cups (called *cramponnés* because they were clamped to the trees). Every few weeks the resin was collected, packed into barrels and sent to distilling plants. Today this practice has largely been superseded by the use of sulphuric acid, which activates the process and has the advantage that it does far less damage to the tree. Today the region serves as a processing centre for turpentine, pitch, transparent wrapping material and other solids.

Even when they are very old, the pines remain useful; after they have been "bled dry" of their resin, they are felled and sent to factories which transform them into parquet flooring, crates and wood-fibre boards (especially compressed woodchip sheeting). Important installations producing paper, wood pulp and pine cellulose exist in the region (especially at Facturen which alone contributes half of the country's cellulose production).

LIVESTOCK

Cattle – Cattle are reared throughout the region, for their meat or for their milk. Fattening, particularly of the distinctive white Charolais breed, takes place in the fields of the Pays de Retz, the Gâtine de Parthenay, the *bocages* of the Vendée, and on the polders of the marshlands. Bressuire and Parthenay, important cattle markets, handle thousands

Ducks from the Gers region

of tawny Parthenay cattle and an increasing number of Charolais. Eastwards, towards the Massif Central, the chesnut-coated Limousin breed and again Charolais predominate.

Between Poitiers and La Rochelle, and again between the Vendée and the Charentes, lie regions in which French breeds – Black-and-Whites and Normans – supply milk to numerous cooperatives; this area produces cheese, long-life milk and the famous *beurre des Charentes*, a rich, creamy butter.

Sheep, goats and horses – Sheep, which originally appeared indigenously on the heaths and pastureland of the region, are increasingly important in these otherwise ill-favoured areas. The zones particularly suited to the flocks are the eastern reaches of Poitou, in the Berry district, and also the Gâtine de Parthenay (home of the very tender Charmoise lamb). Goat rearing has considerably increased in the southern parts of Deux-Sèvres and Vienne, within the framework of a dairy cooperative which produces 50% of all goat-milk products in France. **Chabichou**, the celebrated goat's cheese, is a traditional speciality of the region. Horse rearing has been in decline since the increase in motorization; breeding racehorses, however, remains a thriving business, especially in the Vendée. The Poitou **baudet** (donkey) and the Mellois mule, on the other hand, have become rare to the point where measures have been taken to preserve them from extinction.

Poultry – From Clisson to Mont-de-Marsan, the farmyards are still full of poultry: Poitou geese, Bressuire and Barbezieux hens, old-fashioned white ducks from Challans. Specialized poultry production is particularly important in the northern part of Deux-Sèvres and in the Vendée.

East and south of the Landes forests is a region of crops (mainly maize) and poultry farming (yellow, corn-fed chickens; geese, ducks, turkeys) with a flourishing preserved-foods industry which includes in particular a choice variety of *foie gras* (prepared duck and goose livers).

WINES AND SPIRITS

The area both to the north and to the south of the Gironde is known throughout the world for its fine wines, fortified wines, cognacs and armagnacs, which have long been exported and play a major role in the local economy.

Wines of Bordeaux

The world-famous Bordeaux vineyards, 105km/65mi from north to south and 130km/81mi from west to east, cover an area of approximately 105 000ha/405sq mi. The region, widely considered the best in the world for fine wines, contains over 8 000 wine-producing *châteaux* (which can mean an estate or simply a property, and not necessarily something resembling a castle) which between them produce wines with 53 different controlled *appellations* under six main "family" headings. Added to these are the *Crémant de Bordeaux*, a sparkling wine, and the local **digestif** spirit called *Fine de Bordeaux*. Production breaks down into approximately 75% red wines and 25% white, at an output of some 600 million bottles per year; 40% of the wine is exported to Great Britain, Belgium, Germany and the Netherlands.

Red wines – According to a local saying, "all the edges are rounded off in the bottle" – and red wines do indeed have a remarkable ability to improve with age. The wines of the region include the elegant wines of the Médoc – the great reds – the delicate, slightly spicy and vigorous Graves to which they have a family resemblance, and the wines of St-Émilion with their strength of character.

The Pomerol district is renowned for warm, deep red wines with an affinity both to those from St-Émilion and the Médoc, while the lesser-known Fronsacs – coarse when first bottled but refining with age – are firm in flavour with a lot of body. Further downstream, the vineyards of Bourg and Blaye are known for their *grands ordinaires* – admirable wines both white and red. Production is similarly diversified in the Premières Côtes de Bordeaux region on the east bank of the Garonne.

White wines – The range of white wine available is equally delectable. Pride of place must go to the great wines of Sauternes and of neighbouring Barsac, which produce the best sweet white wines in the world, pressed from grapes just beginning to feel the effects of the famous noble mould. Less well-known but also of note are the whites of Ste-Croix-du-Mont and Loupiac, on the other side of the Garonne.

At the opposite pole, in the matter of taste, are the dry white Graves – wines of distinction which, for many, typify the whites of Bordeaux: clean-tasting, lightly fruity, vigorous.

The lightly fragranced products of the Cérons vineyards, ranging from quite dry to slightly luscious, are a link between the best wines of the Graves district and the great Sauternes.

Among the *Premières Côtes de Bordeaux*, the town of Cadillac produces mellow, velvety white wines that are agreeably light. Finally, the huge area known as Entre-Deux-Mers (between two seas: the Atlantic and the Mediterranean), with its wine producers' cooperatives, is a very important supplier of dry white wines and reds which are marketed as *grands ordinaires*.

Appellations – The term "appellation d'origine contrôlée" (AOC) on a wine label is a certification of the wine's supervised origins, carrying with it an implication – though not necessarily a guarantee – of quality.

The Médoc, thanks to the variety of its *terroirs* (soils), is classed into eight zones of *appellation contrôlée*: Médoc and Haut-Médoc, and more specifically St-Estèphe, Pauillac, St-Julien, Moulis, Listrac and Margaux.

Serving Bordeaux wines – The red wines of Bordeaux should not be drunk too young; the whites, on the other hand – especially the dry whites – are at their best relatively soon after bottling.

Wines of Gascogne

The region, situated north-east of the Landes and extending south to the Gers and the Pyrenees, produces palatable red wines such as the spicy Madiran and dry or sweet white wines such as the Pacherenc.

Wines of the Agenais

Buzet is a light red wine which becomes full-bodied with age. The Côtes de Duras, in the north of the Lot-et-Garonne *département*, are light, fruity red wines and refreshing white wines. As for the Côtes du Marmandais, north of Marmande, they are mainly full-bodied fruity red wines.

Wines of Béarn

The Béarn region *(see BÉARN)* produces wines of note including the famous Jurançon, a heady wine grown on the left bank of the Gave de Pau, and the Rosé du Béarn, once exported to northern Europe, as far as Hamburg.

Wines of the Basque country

They consist mainly in mountain red wines under the *appellation* Irouléguy.
Yellow or green Izzara is a liqueur distilled from mountain plants.

Muscadet

This well-known dry white wine which forms, with the Gros Plant and Côteaux d'Ancenis, part of the **Vins de Nantes** group, was accorded *appellation d'origine contrôlée* status in 1936. The vineyards producing the wines of this group stretch away south of the Loire.

Muscadet is made from the Melon grape, which came originally from Burgundy. The vines were imported and planted in the Nantes area after the terrible winter of 1709 because of their resistance to frost.

There are three *appellations*, corresponding to three different regions: the Muscadet de Sèvre-et-Maine, which accounts for the major part of the production, the Muscadet des Côteaux de la Loire (which comes from around Ancenis) and plain Muscadet (from the neighbourhood of St-Philbert-de-Grand-Lieu). All of them yield wines that are light and dry, with an alcoholic content limited to 12%. Served cold, Muscadet is a marvellous accompaniment to fish and seafood.

The **Gros Plant du Pays Nantais** has been classed as a VDQS (*vin délimité de qualité supérieure* – a superior wine) since 1954. It is made from the Folle-Blanche grapes grown in the Charentes since the 16C. Being a light wine (11%) it complements seafood in general and shellfish in particular.

Cognac

Cognac, famous for centuries throughout the world, is a distillation of white wines produced in the region of the Cognac *appellation* (essentially the Charentes *département*). A good cognac should taste like the very essence of fresh grapes, strong and heady. More than 80% of the production is exported; Britain and the United States alone accounting for 40% of those sales.

A Charentais Pot Still

History – The distillation of wine to make spirits, practised in the region since the 16C, became generalized in the early 17C. The local vintners at first distilled just the wines that did not travel well but later realised that the process could help turnover, reduce excise duties and facilitate storage (between seven and ten barrels of wine are used to make one barrel of cognac). The taste for the resulting *eau-de-vie* (spirit) spread and it began to be exported, like the wines before it, to the countries in the north of Europe as an adjunct to the salt trade.

Much of the wine trade at that time was in the hands of the English and the Dutch – who, learning that the people of Charentes burned their wine, dubbed the result *brandewijn* (burnt wine). From this the English coined the word brandy, which has been used in the Anglo-Saxon world ever since. In France the spirit took the name of the town where it was first commercialized, Cognac.

From Cognac the barges and tenders laden with barrels sailed down the River Charente to Tonnay-Charente and La Rochelle, where the cargo was transferred to full-rigged merchantmen bound either for northern Europe or for the colonies – where the fire-water accompanied the baubles and beads used to pacify and bargain with the natives. Ruined by the devastating outbreak of phylloxera (American aphids) in the 19C, the Cognac vineyards were replanted by the burghers of Cognac, who had themselves escaped ruin because of the huge stocks they held in store ageing. English merchants and traders played an important part in the promotion of brandy; the names of several famous Cognac brands still have an Anglo-Saxon ring about them.

The vineyards – Almost 90 000ha/222 400 acres are planted with vine, most of which being the variety Ugni Blanc (incorrectly termed St-Émilion des Charentes in the region). The vineyards are planted in an area of temperate climate – humid in winter, sunny in summer – and chalky soil similar to that found in the Champagne region, east of Paris. Cognac of maximum finesse, Grande Champagne cognac, is produced from vines at the centre of this region, the area of chalkiest soil; the other five classed *crus* or growths – producing more full-bodied and highly flavoured spirit – radiate outwards from it.

THE COGNAC VINEYARDS

Appellations
- Grande Champagne
- Petite Champagne
- Borderies
- Fins Bois
- Bons Bois
- Bois Ordinaires

Development of Cognac – In short, distilling is a means of concentrating the strength and flavour of any alcoholic drink by removing most of the water content. The technique stems from the fact that alcohol in chemical terms is more volatile than water: it boils at a lower temperature. All the alcohol and most of the aromatic elements in a heated wine will therefore be driven off as vapour long before the water boils. If this vapour is collected and condensed, the resulting liquid will contain virtually all the alcohol, certain other volatile elements – known as the congenerics – and very little water.

The system of distilling first came west with the Arabs in the 14C (the Arabic term *al embic* is the root of the French *alambic* – a still – and *al kohol* is the root of alcohol). For cognac the process is completed in two stages: the Charentais pot still, made of beaten copper, yields first (after about 8hr) a liquid containing 25-35% alcohol, the **brouillis**, which is passed back into the still after undesirable elements in the congenerics have been drawn off; the second distillate then emerges (after about 12hr) at a maximum strength of 72%.

The process itself is as follows: vapours compressed in the still head pass into the swan neck which then passes through the wine heater; this cools the vapours and warms the wine already in there, which will refill the boiler; finally the pipe from the swan neck leads the vapours to the worm – the coiled copper tubing of the cooling tank – where they condense into liquid.

The brandy, fiery but colourless when it leaves the still, is only faintly flavoured; all its character is derived from the maturing process, in barrels left in the darkness of the producer's well-aired *chais* (stores). Here the pale oak of these barrels, brought from the hills of the Limousin, stimulates the oxidization of the spirit, adds tannin and activates the amber coloration. The incredible amount of evaporation from the barrels is equivalent to the loss of 12 million bottles of spirit every year.

The last step before the cognac appears in bottles is taken by the merchants and shippers who put their name on the label: the spirit is diluted with distilled water to the accepted legal strength for the market, cut and blended with brandies of different age, from different *crus*, and sugar and caramel are added to obtain the required colour, until a consistent quality is arrived at with characteristics recognizable as typical of a particular brand.

There are several different categories of cognac, classed according to the length of time they have spent maturing in the oak casks.

The three-star label signifies a brandy of normal quality, between five and nine years of age. The acronyms VO (Very Old) and VSOP (Very Special Old Pale) apply to cognacs aged on average between 12 and 20 years. The terms Vieille Réserve, Grande Réserve, Royal, Vieux, XO, Napoleon, Extra etc are used to distinguish cognacs 20 to 40 years old or even more. The words Fine Champagne on the label identify a cognac that is a blend of the Grande and Petite Champagne growths.

Armagnac

Armagnac is very different from cognac both in style and in the technique used to make it. This spirit should be velvety smooth, dry and with a pungent smell; it is considered to have less finesse than cognac.

The region legally permitted to sell its products under the name "Armagnac" extends over a great stretch of land (35 000ha/ 35sq mi), roughly triangular in shape, which is divided into three sub-zones: **Haut-Armagnac** (Upper Armagnac, the hilly region of Auch) in the east; **Ténarèze** (around Condom) in the centre; and **Bas-Armagnac** (Lower Armagnac, the Eauze region) in the west. Armagnac from Ténarèze is fuller and richer while that from Bas-Armagnac is fruitier. Only white wines made from 10 approved varieties of vine may be distilled to make the spirit, and their common characteristic is a strong, fixed level of acidity. The most popular of these grapes are the Ugni Blanc and the Folle-Blanche (known as Gros Plant in the Nantes area).

It is distilled in a sort of double boiler, at a much lower temperature than cognac, resulting in a stronger flavour and scent which, combined with the effect of the sappy black oak casks in which it is stored, adds character (and it matures faster).

Each brand of Armagnac has, as for cognac, its expert *maître de chai*, the Master Blender who creates the finished product with its particular identity.

Fortified Wines and Aperitifs

Floc – Floc is the old Gascon word for flower. Floc de Gascogne – a fortified wine between 16º and 18º, about the strength of port or sherry – is drunk chilled as an aperitif, either red or white. Made from selected wines grown in the region of the Armagnac *appellation,* it results from a mixture of these wines with Armagnac at more than 52º. The aperitif is aged in oak barrels.

Pousse-rapière – Rapier Thrust is another aperitif, invented in the 16C at Château Monluc, near the town of Condom, by Marshal Blaise de Monluc, army commander and man of letters. It is made from Armagnac mixed with fruit. Add it to dry sparkling wine for an excellent cocktail!

Pineau des Charentes – This is a fortified aperitif wine, classified *appellation d'origine contrôlée* and produced in the same area as Cognac; it is made in both red and rosé forms, and it should be served chilled.

The aperitif was created by accident in the 16C, when a grower ran a quantity of grape must into a barrel which inadvertently still had some cognac left in the bottom. He was agreeably surprised, some years later, to discover in the barrel a strong wine that was smooth, heady and deliciously fruity.

Pineau is produced from the same growths as Cognac. The musts utilised before the *mutage* (the addition of Cognac) should have an alcoholic content of 10%. After the *mutage* the strength of the drink should be at least 16.5%. The blend is then transferred to oak casks and kept for several months in dark stores.

When it has sufficiently matured, it is submitted to an official Commission of Tasters who will decide whether or not it merits the *appellation* Pineau des Charentes.

Pineau sells very well in France and is exported to Belgium, Canada, Germany, Britain, Luxembourg and the United States.

Prehistory

The Quaternary Era began about 2 million years ago. It was during this period that glaciers developed (the Günz, Mindel, Riss and Würm glacial stages), spreading over the highest mountains. However, the most significative event of the period was the appearance of the first humans in Europe, and more particularly in the Pyrenees.

Archaeology and scientific methods of dating have made it possible to classify various phases of evolution – Paleolithic (Old Stone Age), Mesolithic (Middle Stone Age), Neolithic (New Stone Age) – which can themselves be subdivided into different periods. *See table below.*

Lower Paleolithic – The Lower Paleolithic period is represented in the Pyrenees by **Tautavel man**, who came to light when the remains of a human skull were discovered in a layer of ancient sediment in the **Caune de l'Arago** in 1971 and 1979.

Tautavel man belongs to the *Homo erectus* genus, which inhabited Roussillon 450 000 years ago. He was between 20 and 25 years old and was able to stand upright, about 1.65m/5ft 6in tall. He had a flat, receding forehead, prominent cheekbones, and rectangular eye sockets beneath a thick projecting brow. Since no trace of any hearth has been found, it is assumed that this intrepid hunter, who had not mastered the use of fire, ate his meat raw.

THE STONE AGE

PERIOD	HOMINID EVOLUTION	STAGE OF CIVILISATION	SITES	FAUNA	CLIMATE
1 500 MEGALITH AGE		Dolmens and tumulus			
NEOLITHIC		Points and arrows Polished stone choppers			Warm
7 500 **MESOLITHIC**		Painted stones			
AZILIAN 10 000		Carved Venus figures Needles Burins		Reindeer	
MAGDALENIAN SOLUTREAN	Cro-Magnon		Lespugue Brassempouy	Mammoths, Bears, Cave Hyena, Woolly	Würm Glacial
UPPER PALEOLITHIC		Harpoons Convex side scrapers Spears	Gargas Aurignac	Rhinoceros, Hippopotamus	Period
AURIGNACIAN PERIGORDIAN	**Homo sapiens**	Bone tools Cave paintings and engravings			
35 000 MOUSTERIAN					
MIDDLE PALEOLITHIC		Oval flints Blades, Disks,			Warm
LEVALOISIAN 150 000		Arrows, Scrapers, Biface flint tools		Mammoth Elephant	
TAYACIAN	**Neanderthal Man**			Appearance of Mammoth Ox, Lion	
ACHEULIAN		Handaxes in flint or quartzite Awls Scrapers Saws			Riss Glacial Period
LOWER PALEOLITHIC				Aurochs/Bison, Rhinoceros, Tiger	Warm
CLACTONIAN	Montmaurin Man	Handaxes, shaped on both sides ("bifaces")	Montmaurin	Hippopotamus, Rhinoceros Big Bear	Mindel Glacial Period
ABBEVILLIAN					Warm
	Java Man *Pithecanthropus erectus*				Günz Glacial Period
2 million					
	Lucy (Ethiopia) *Australopithecus afarensis*				
3 million years ago	**Homo erectus**				

R. Corbel/MICHELIN

The first hunters who came to live in the Caune d'Arago used it for several purposes: as a look-out to keep track of the movements of animals which had come to drink from the Verdouble, as a temporary place to set up camp and dismember their prey, and as a workshop for manufacturing tools.

Palynology (the analysis of fossilised pollen grains) has helped to determine the specific characteristics of flora and fauna from different prehistoric periods. Although the alternation of climates produced changes (from grassy steppes to deciduous forests), Mediterranean plant species (pines, oaks, walnut trees, plane trees, wild vines, etc) have always been present. There was much game in the area: large herbivores included various types of deer and mountain goats, prairie rhinoceros, bison, musk ox and an ancient species of wild sheep. Carnivores (bears, wolves, dogs, polar foxes, cave lions, wild cats) were hunted for their fur. Small game comprised rodents (hares, voles, beavers, field mice) and birds still to be found today (golden eagles, lammergeyer vultures, pigeons, rock partridges, red-billed choughs).

The tools found are in general quite small (scrapers, notched tools). The largest tools found are pebbles, measuring on average 6-10cm/2-4in, made into choppers, or flat two or poly-sided implements of varying degrees of sharpness. These early humans used material they found nearby such as quartz or schist, and more rarely limestone, flint and jasper.

Middle Paleolithic – The presence of numerous Mousterian deposits is evidence that Neanderthal man was present in the Pyrenees. Taller than *homo erectus*, he had a well-developed skull (1 700cm^3/103cu in). He was forced to adapt to the climatic conditions of the Würm glacial period.

Neanderthal man produced more sophisticated, specialised tools. He fashioned numerous double-sided implements, stone knives with curved edges, chisels, scrapers, pointed tools and all kinds of notched implements. His evolution is also evident in the construction of vast dwelling and burial places.

Upper Paleolithic – With the advent of *homo sapiens*, there was now a significant human presence in the Pyrenees. During the Aurignacian period, stone implements were supplemented with bone and horn. The appearance of long thin wooden spears with metal tips (assegais), awls and spatulas pointed to a technical evolution which progressed still further during the Solutrean and Magdalenian periods. Towards the end of the last Würm glacial period (Würm IV), a transformation in landscape and fauna occurred, with boar and deer predominating from now on. Humans both hunted and fished. However, the most revolutionary change was the birth of art. Sculpted human figures (the Aurignacian "Venuses") and cave paintings are of exceptional archaeological interest. The animals, painted in red or black, on the walls of **Niaux** cave look strikingly realistic.

Mesolithic Age – At the end of the Ice Age, the historical landscape of the Pyrenees became established. The Mesolithic Age is, in fact, an intermediary phase during which a multitude of civilizations appeared. During the Azilian culture (named after the **Mas d'Azil** cave), which began at the end of the Upper Paleolithic period, the harpoon became an increasingly important weapon. Art, on the other hand, was restricted to enigmatic pebbles with symbolic markings.

Neolithic Age – The Neolithic Age is characterised by polished (as opposed to chipped) stone tools and the use of earthenware. This evolution was accompanied by a decisive change in economy and life style. However, in the eastern Pyrenees and the Ariège, evolution appears to have been slower, for it has been recorded that the local post-Paleolithic population, who were joined by groups from outside the Pyrenees, remained static; they continued to live in caves and earthenware came into use only sometime later.

Further north, valuable ethnological information was discovered in the Font-Juvénal shelter, between the River Aude and the Montagne Noire. As early as the fourth millennium, agriculture and cattle-rearing had become a means of subsistence, with wheat and barley being cultivated. At the same time, habitations were adapted to meet increasingly elaborate domestic requirements, a fact borne out by the discovery of flat hearths for cooking, air vents to raise the combustion temperature, supporting structures (posts and slabs) and silos for storage.

In the Narbonne region, rural communities with specialised activities, using very elaborate implements, started to barter and trade with each other. Megalithic constructions (dolmens and tumili) were introduced to the Pyrenees from the western zone during the third millennium. The middle mountain slopes were the most densely populated. Activities included stock-rearing, and, increasingly, the making of weapons (arrows, axes and knives). Jewellery (necklaces and bracelets) and earthenware (bowls and vases) became more widespread. In the Catalan region, the Megalithic culture lasted until the Bronze Age.

Historical table and notes

The Roman conquest

72 BC	Foundation of Lugdunum Convenarum (St-Bertrand-de-Comminges), religious capital of the population south of the River Garonne, by Pompey.
56	Aquitaine conquered by Crassus, Caesar's lieutenant.

Invasions, the rise of the Carolingian Empire and the Hundred Years War

2C-4C AD	Introduction of Christianity in Gaul. St Hilaire elected Bishop of Poitiers.
276	Germanic invasion.
5C	Visigoth kingdom in Aquitaine: continuation of the Latin culture and written Roman law.
End 6C	The Vascons, Basque mountain people from the south, repulsed by the Visigoths, settle in the flat country – Gascogne (Gascony).
507	Defeat of Alaric II, King of the Visigoths, by Clovis at Vouillé (north of Poitiers).
732	The Arab advance into Europe halted by Charles Martel at Moussais-la-Bataille.
778	Kingdom of Aquitaine created by Charlemagne.
801	Barcelona taken from the Arabs by Charlemagne and Spanish Marches organized.
820	Start of the Norman incursions. Destruction of Saintes, Angoulême (c 850) and Bordeaux.
c 950	Beginning of pilgrimages to Santiago de Compostela.
1058	Union of the duchies of Aquitaine and Gascogne. The south-west under the hegemony of the Comtes (Comtes of Poitiers and Angoulême).
1137	Marriage of Eleanor of Aquitaine to Louis, son of the French king.

Eleanor of Aquitaine (c1122-1204) and the Plantagenet Territories

The marriage in 1137 of Eleanor, the only daughter of **William of Aquitaine**, to Louis, the French *dauphin*, brought with it a dowry which included the duchies of Guyenne, Gascogne, Périgord, Limousin, Poitou, Angoumois and Saintonge, plus suzerainty over the Auvergne and the Comté of Toulouse. Her husband was crowned Louis VII the same year. Fifteen years later, in 1152, the marriage ended in divorce; Eleanor retained all the lands of her dowry.

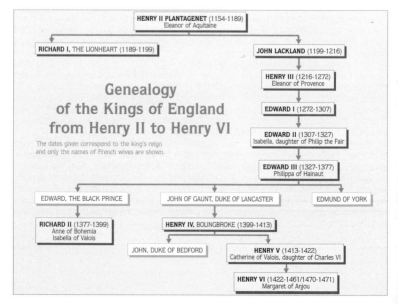

Genealogy of the Kings of England from Henry II to Henry VI

The dates given correspond to the king's reign and only the names of French wives are shown.

- **HENRY II PLANTAGENET** (1154-1189) — Eleanor of Aquitaine
  - **RICHARD I, THE LIONHEART** (1189-1199)
  - **JOHN LACKLAND** (1199-1216)
    - **HENRY III** (1216-1272) — Eleanor of Provence
      - **EDWARD I** (1272-1307)
        - **EDWARD II** (1307-1327) — Isabella, daughter of Philip the Fair
          - **EDWARD III** (1327-1377) — Philippa of Hainaut
            - EDWARD, THE BLACK PRINCE
              - **RICHARD II** (1377-1399) — Anne of Bohemia, Isabella of Valois
            - JOHN OF GAUNT, DUKE OF LANCASTER
              - **HENRY IV**, BOLINGBROKE (1399-1413)
                - JOHN, DUKE OF BEDFORD
                - **HENRY V** (1413-1422) — Catherine of Valois, daughter of Charles VI
                  - **HENRY VI** (1422-1461/1470-1471) — Margaret of Anjou
            - EDMUND OF YORK

Eleanor's subsequent marriage to **Henry Plantagenet** in 1154 was a political disaster for the Capetian dynasty: the combined possessions of the bride and groom, extending from the English Channel to the Pyrenees, were as vast as those of the French crown. Henry's crowning as Henry II of England finally upset the fragile international equilibrium; the resulting Anglo-French struggle lasted on and off for 300 years.

Later, separating from her second husband, Eleanor left London for Poitiers where she held a brilliant court. From 1173 her various intrigues – she supported her son Richard the Lionheart in the fight against his father, Henry, for example – resulted in her being imprisoned in London by her husband, and she was only released on his death 15 years later in 1189. She took up her plotting again, this time against her youngest son, John (Lackland), and Philippe Auguste, King of France.

Eleanor spent her later life peacefully at her castle on the Isle of Oléron and finished her days at Fontevraud Abbey, where she is buried, together with her husband Henry Plantagenet *(for further details of her life, see Eleanor of Aquitaine).*

Eleanor of Aquitaine

1224	Poitou attached to the French crown.
1345	Start of the Hundred Years War in Aquitaine.
1356	The French King, Jean le Bon, captured by the English at the Battle of Poitiers and taken prisoner by the Black Prince.
1360	Treaty of Brétigny: the duchies of Aquitaine, Aunis, Saintonge and Angoulême become possessions of the English crown.
1369	Jean de Berry installed as Governor of Poitou.
1380	Restriction of the English presence in the south-west to Bordeaux and Bayonne, thanks to the formidable Constable Du Guesclin (who had chased the *grandes compagnies* – bands of terrorizing mercenaries and brigands – into Spain).

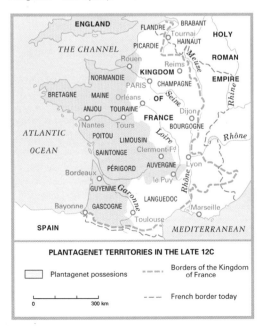

PLANTAGENET TERRITORIES IN THE LATE 12C

Plantagenet possesions — Borders of the Kingdom of France

- - - French border today

0   300 km

1422	Charles VII proclaimed King in Poitiers.
1450-1500	Dismantling of English Gascony; re-attachment of the Comtés of Armagnac and Comminges to the French crown.
1453	Final battle of the Hundred Years War, won by the Bureau brothers at Castillon-la-Bataille. Progressive abandonment of France by the English.

From the Renaissance to the Revolution, an era marked by the Wars of Religion

1484	The Albrets – Kings of Navarre – become all-powerful in the Gascon Pyrenees.
1494	Birth of François I in Cognac.
1515	Accession of François I. Battle of Marignano: victory for François over the Swiss and the Italians; northern Italy becomes French.
1533-34	The doctrine of the Reformation preached by Calvin in Saintonge, Angoumois and Poitiers (in 1558, from Basle in Switzerland, Calvin tells his fellow Protestants of the Confession of La Rochelle, a sign of the town's early conversion to the principles of Reformation).
1539	The administration of justice reshaped by the Edict of Villiers-Cotteret, which imposed French as the official language of the judiciary, instead of Latin or the Langue d'Oc.
1555	Jeanne d'Albret crowned Queen of Navarre (reigned until 1572).

Richelieu during the siege of La Rochelle
(H. Motte)

B. Kaufmann/MICHELIN

1562	Beginning of the Wars of Religion.
1569	Victory for the Duc d'Anjou over the Protestants in the battles of Jarnac and Moncontour. Poitiers under siege from Protestants.
1570-71	Imposition of the Protestant faith on Béarn by Jeanne d'Albret. Bloody rivalry between her lieutenant, Montgomery, and his Catholic adversary, Blaise de Monluc.
1579	An attempt made, with les grands jours de Poitiers, to end religious discord in the region.
1589	Accession of Henri IV, the son of Jeanne d'Albret.
1598	End of the Wars of Religion. Protestants granted freedom of worship, and 100 safe places (among them La Rochelle) in which to practise it, through Henri IV's promulgation of the Edict of Nantes.
1608	The future Cardinal Richelieu created Bishop of Luçon.
1627-28	Siege of La Rochelle and eventual submission to Richelieu.
1659-60	Treaty of the Pyrenees. Marriage of Louis XIV and the Infanta Maria Teresa at St-Jean-de-Luz.
1685	Revocation of the Edict of Nantes by Louis XIV. Persecution of Protestants in Béarn by the King's Dragoons (Dragonades). Evacuation of many Huguenots from the country.
18C	A decisive impetus to the country's economic development brought during the era of the Intendants (stewards or governors): the Comte de Blossac in Poitiers, Reverseaux in Saintes, Tourny in Bordeaux.
1789-99	The French Revolution and the end of the Ancien Régime (execution of Louis XVI in January 1793); establishment of the Convention.
1793-95	The Vendée War.
1794	Deportation of priests aboard the hulks of Rochefort.

The Vendée War (1793-95)

By early 1793 a combination of the execution of Louis XVI, years of resentment over the religious issue capped by the rounding up and persecution of priests, the imposition of arbitrary taxes and the Convention's decision to conscript 300 000 men triggered an insurrection and a wave of riots in the west of France.

In Maine, Normandy and Brittany where the rebels were known as the *chouans* and were fairly loosely dispersed, operating in a guerrilla fashion, the authorities did regain control; in the territories south of the River Loire, however, where fewer troops were available and communications were more difficult, the government collapsed. In this area, collectively known as the **Vendée Militaire**, the rebels were able to form the Catholic and Royal Army. Their strongholds were in the Gâtine, the *bocage* and the marshes – difficult country to penetrate, crisscrossed with hedgerows and perfect for ambushes, and in the Retz district, around Grand-Lieu Lake.

Led at first by royalists of peasant stock such as **Cathelineau**, a pedlar, and the game-keeper **Stofflet**, the peasants themselves soon called on their gentlemen (local nobles, estate stewards, priests) for help: these included **Gigost d'Elbée**, the Marquis of Bonchamps, Sapinaud, the Chevalier de **Charette**, **La Rochejaquelein** and **Lescure** among others. They also sought help – with limited success – from the British.

These so-called brigands, armed at first only with pitchforks and scythes and later with guns taken from the Republicans, worked in cells grouped parish by parish, each wearing a cloak bearing the insignia of a Sacred Heart surmounted by a Cross; their flag was white (hence the royalists' nickname, the **Whites**; republicans were known as **Blues**), covered with fleurs-de-lis, and often inscribed with the motto *Long live Louis XVI*. Their tactics were based on surprise: the good shots, hidden in the hedgerows, would silently surround an enemy patrol and pick off half of them, after which the ambushers would hurl themselves into the attack. If the resistance was too robust, the whole troop would melt away into the depths of the *bocage* – which was bitterly referred to by the Republican general, **Kléber**, as "the labyrinth".

From the spring of 1793 superior Republican troops led by generals Westermann, Kléber and Marceau were deployed in the area. Battles were won by both sides until the winter of 1794 when the Republicans got the upper hand; thousands of Whites were shot or guillotined, while the Blue "**Infernal Columns**" devastated the entire province. Following more battles and treaties the tired rebels eventually submitted to the Revolution through the diplomacy of the astute Republican General Lazare **Hoche**. Stofflet and Charette were finally captured and subsequently shot, the latter with the cry "Long live the King!" on his lips.

From the First to the Second Empire

1804	Consecration of Napoleon I as Emperor of the French, and founding of the town of Napoleon-Vendée (today La Roche-sur-Yon).
1806	The continental blockade, designed to ruin England by denying the country its economic outlets on mainland Europe, also severely reduced activity in the ports along the Atlantic Coast of France.
1815	Embarkation of the deposed Napoléon for the Isle of Aix.
1822	Plot by the Four Sergeants of La Rochelle to overthrow the Restoration government.
1832	Attempts by the Duchesse de Berry to provoke another Vendée uprising, this time against Louis-Philippe.
1845	Birth of the town of Arcachon.
1852-70	The Second Empire – a period of splendour for the Basque coast and country and the spas in the region.
1855	Opening of the Poitiers-La Rochelle railway link.
1860	Opening of the Eaux-Bonnes to Bagnères-de-Bigorre Thermal Cure route.
1867	The topography of the Landes revolutionized by the extensive planting of pines.
1868	Appearance of the Portuguese oyster in the Gironde.

From the Third Republic to the present day

1870	Installation in Tours and then in Bordeaux of a delegation from the National Defence government, headed by Gambetta.
1876	Phylloxera crisis in the vineyards.
1905	A law separating the Church from the State pushed through by Émile Combes, Mayor of Pons, and Georges Clemenceau, a Deputy in the National Assembly.

1914	President Poincaré, the government and both chambers of the Assembly moved temporarily to Bordeaux before the first German offensive in the First World War.
1929	Death of Clemenceau at St-Vincent-sur-Jard.
1939	End of the Spanish Civil War. Seizure of the Spanish gold reserves (lodged in Mont-de-Marsan) by the Fascist victors; 500 000 refugees flood into the south-west of France.
1940	Refuge again taken in Bordeaux by the authorities of the Third Republic after the German advance southward following the breakthrough at Sedan during the Second World War.
1945	German forces still entrenched in the Atlantic pockets (among them Royan) besieged by Free French soldiers and members of the Resistance.
1951	Death of Marshal Pétain on the Isle of Yeu.
1954	Inauguration of the oil wells of Parentis.
1966	Oléron becomes the first French island to be linked to the mainland via a bridge.
1988	Completion of the bridge leading to the Isle of Ré.
1990	Opening of the new high-speed Paris-Bordeaux rail link, with the train à grande vitesse (TGV) atlantique making the journey in less than 3hr.
1996	President Mitterrand is buried in his native village of Jarnac.
1997	The Cirque de Gavarnie is added to UNESCO's World Heritage list. 1998 The mint in Pessac begins production of euro coins.
1999 December	– a terrible storm uproots trees and damages buildings across the south-west.

Architecture and Art

ABC OF ARCHITECTURE

Religious architecture

CHAUVIGNY - Ground plan of St-Pierre (11C-12C)

Bay: the transverse section of the nave between two pillars

Ambulatory: extension of the side aisles around the choir allowing the faithful to file past the relics

Nave

Pillar

Apsidal chapel

Apse: the rounded east end of the chancel of the church; the exterior is known as the chevet

Porch

Transept crossing

Apsidal or axial chapel. In churches not dedicated to the Virgin, this chapel in the axis of the monument is often dedicated to her.

Narthex: a vestibule of the church

Side aisle

Arm of the transept, which may or may not project

Chancel: almost always facing east

ANGOULÊME - Cross-section of the transept of the Cathédrale St-Pierre (12C)

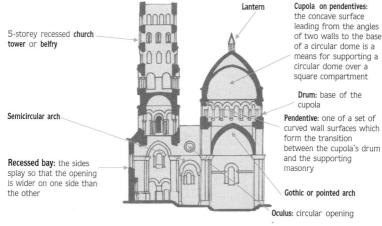

Lantern

5-storey recessed church tower or **belfry**

Cupola on pendentives: the concave surface leading from the angles of two walls to the base of a circular dome is a means for supporting a circular dome over a square compartment

Drum: base of the cupola

Semicircular arch

Pendentive: one of a set of curved wall surfaces which form the transition between the cupola's drum and the supporting masonry

Recessed bay: the sides splay so that the opening is wider on one side than the other

Gothic or pointed arch

Oculus: circular opening

AULNAY - South portal of St-Pierre (12C)

Intrados: the inner surface of an arch or vault

Arch mouldings: concentric arches covering the embrasure of a bay; the set of arch mouldings forms the **archivolt**

Abacus: the uppermost section of the capital

Historiated capital: decorated with scenes depicting figures

Jambshaft: a small shafts with a capital and a base, forming the jamb of the door and supporting the arch

Base: the base of a column includes the plinth and the torus

Shaft: between the base and the capital

PETIT-PALAIS - The Église St-Pierre (end 12C)

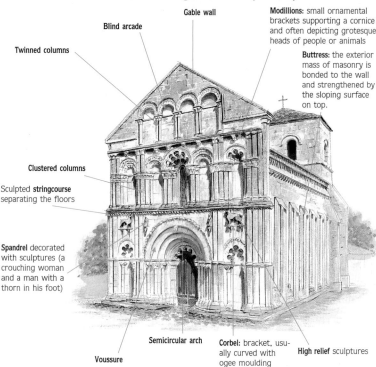

Gable wall

Blind arcade

Twinned columns

Modillions: small ornamental brackets supporting a cornice and often depicting grotesque heads of people or animals

Buttress: the exterior mass of masonry is bonded to the wall and strengthened by the sloping surface on top.

Clustered columns

Sculpted **stringcourse** separating the floors

Spandrel decorated with sculptures (a crouching woman and a man with a thorn in his foot)

Semicircular arch

Corbel: bracket, usually curved with ogee moulding

High relief sculptures

Voussure

POITIERS - Façade of Notre-Dame-la-Grande (12C)

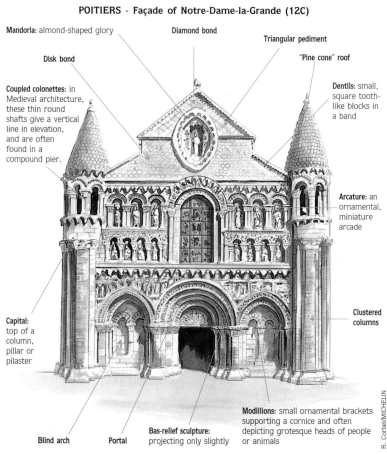

Mandorla: almond-shaped glory

Diamond bond

Triangular pediment

Disk bond

"Pine cone" roof

Coupled colonettes: in Medieval architecture, these thin round shafts give a vertical line in elevation, and are often found in a compound pier.

Dentils: small, square tooth-like blocks in a band

Arcature: an ornamental, miniature arcade

Clustered columns

Capital: top of a column, pillar or pilaster

Blind arch

Portal

Bas-relief sculpture: projecting only slightly

Modillions: small ornamental brackets supporting a cornice and often depicting grotesque heads of people or animals

R. Corbel/MICHELIN

SAINTES - Belfry of the Église de l'Abbaye aux Dames (12C)

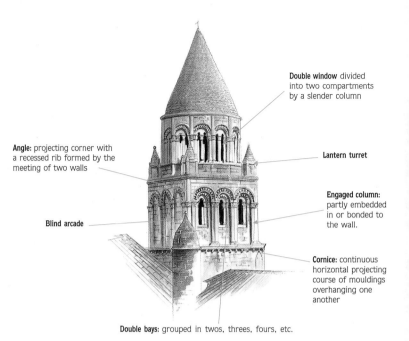

Double window divided into two compartments by a slender column

Angle: projecting corner with a recessed rib formed by the meeting of two walls

Lantern turret

Engaged column: partly embedded in or bonded to the wall.

Blind arcade

Cornice: continuous horizontal projecting course of mouldings overhanging one another

Double bays: grouped in twos, threes, fours, etc.

Military architecture

ROQUETAILLADE - Château neuf (14C - restored 19C)

Keep

Watch-tower: small construction used as a lookout post at the top of a tower.

Crenel

Polygonal turret enclosing the spiral stairs leading to the different floors

Merlon

Curtain wall: section of wall between two towers. Here the windows were added in the 16C.

Circular angle tower

Loophole: cruciform loophole for shooting the cross-bow

Fixed bridge

Entrance gateway

Bartizan (added in 19C)

Coursed masonry: made of varying size stones arranged in courses

Dry moat

R. Corbel/MICHELIN

79

Civil architecture

Château de MALLE (17C)

"Imperial" style **dome**: slightly bulbous in shape

Dormer window console decorated with a scroll

Dormer window

Low pitched **upper slope** of mansard roof

Mansard roof also known as a "broken roof"

Crest finial: ornament terminating the point of a spire, pinnacle, etc., in ceramic or metal

Lower slope of mansard roof

Projecting **pavilion**

Wing on the same line as the main portion of the building

Tourelle

Curved pediment sculpted in bas-relief

Transom: horizontal element of window tracery

Mullion: vertical element of window tracery

Main building: main body of a manor house or château

Ionic **pilaster**

BORDEAUX - Palais de la Bourse (18C)

Flame ornament: decorative feature in the form of a vase capped with a flame, characteristic of classical architecture.

Triangular pediment sculpted with an **allegory**

Œil-de-bœuf (round or oval aperture)

Trophy: a sculpted composition of arms and armour

Dentils: small, square tooth-like blocks in a band

Architrave: lower part of the entablature, set on the top (abacus) of the columns

Ionic **capital**

Bay with window panes

Cartouche: ornamental tablet around an empty space intended for an inscription

Column with "drum" segments hewn against the stratum of the stone: separated from the wall by a small space

Transom: a horizontal member above a window or door

Colossal order: order of columns and pilasters that extend more than one storey

Rusticated course. Rustication is texturing on the facing of cut stone

Groovings: cut into the façade to simulate or accentuate the stone-work pattern

BORDEAUX - Staircase of the Grand Théâtre (end 18C)

Rose: decoration consisting of a centre or bud surrounded by leaves

Lunette: a crescent-shaped or semi-circular area on a wall or vaulted ceiling, framed by an arch or a vault

Decorative Panel

Fluted pilaster (shallow rectangular pillar attached to the face of the wall)

Caryatid: statue of female figure used as a support

Arch stone or **voussoir** **with crosettes:** the upper edge extends horizontally to make a strong bond with the surrounding masonry

Festoon: decorative motif in the form of a garland of stylised leaves, fruit or flowers.

Loggia

Landing

Double flight with diverging steps

Tiled landing

Sculpted banisters

Fliers: all of equal width

Central flight

ARCACHON. Winter house - Villa Trocadéro (end 19C)

Overhanging lightweight trussed rafter. The truss usually triangular, constitutes a rigid framework.

Gableboard or **bargeboard:** in metal or wood, it hangs from the projecting end of the roof, covering the gables

Crest finial

Oeil-de-boeuf (round or oval aperture)

Acroter: ornament on a pedestal at the corners or peak of a roof

Joist: horizontal piece of wood supporting a ceiling

Balustrade with cross-bars

Overhanging gallery

Stone balcony

Vertical bond alternating two colours of plastering

Bow-window: a glass window in a protruding bay

Strut or **bracket**

R. Corbel/MICHELIN

81

Art and architecture

Gallo-Roman era

Despite the institutionalized vandalisms of the 19C, many examples still remain of the arts which flourished in the Roman colony of Aquitaine, the capitals of which were Bordeaux, Poitiers and Saintes. The ruins of amphitheatres, theatres, temples and bathhouses, and votive arches scattered throughout these areas offer a broad view of Gallo-Roman civilization.

Romanesque period (11C-12C)

After the turbulent period of the early Middle Ages, marked by conflicts between the great feudal houses, the year AD 1000 saw a renewal of faith exemplified in the Crusades and the great pilgrimages. In the south-west of France the important religious sanctuaries were all built along the routes leading to Santiago de Compostela in Spain *(see the Way of St James)*.

Façade of Notre-Dame-la-Grande, Poitiers

Church Design – In Poitou, Romanesque churches generally comprised a high, barrel-vaulted central nave, buttressed by side aisles which were scarcely less tall. Light entered through the window bays of these aisles.

In Angoumois and Saintonge (the regions around Angoulême and Saintes) the wide, single nave was sometimes barrel-vaulted, sometimes topped by a **line of domes** showing influence from the Périgord region.

West fronts – The façades were characterized by arcades or tiers of blind arcades. Arcading at the upper level was nevertheless typical more in Angoumois and Saintonge, whereas churches in Poitou were often distinguished by a tripartite division vertically, with large arcades separated by columnar buttresses (Notre-Dame-la-Grande in Poitiers is an exception). The west front was usually surmounted by a triangular pediment and flanked by columns or groups of columns sometimes crowned by pierced lanterns with conical roofs. These roofs, and often those of the church belfries, would be covered by overlapping tiles. The façade itself was normally decorated with statues and low-relief sculptures, intended to deliver a message. Notre-Dame-la-Grande in Poitiers is one of the most successful examples of these façade-screens; the story told by the statuary is a page from the Bible and is easily understood.

In Angoumois the west fronts are generally more sober, although that of St-Pierre in Angoulême is famous for its depiction, through 70 different characters, of the Last Judgement.

East ends – Churches with an ambulatory at their east end and radiating chapels buttressed by columns are common in Poitou: St-Hilaire, in Melle, is typical. Certain east ends in Saintonge, on the other hand, were built to a simpler design, like the church at Rioux, with a five-faced apse and columnar buttresses; the bays separating the columns have archivolts at the middle level, decorated with a row of blind arcades and miniature columns above. The whole is topped by an elegant frieze running beneath a cornice with carved, double-scroll brackets.

Sculpture – The use of sculpture – on façades, east ends, corbels, arches, consoles and capitals – was facilitated by the nature of the local limestone, which is relatively easy to work; Romanesque edifices are notable for the abundance, variety and finesse of the religious ornamentation. On these surfaces foliage, acanthus leaves in the antique style and pre-Romanesque plaited stonework rival in complexity the bestiary of oriental monsters, biblical illustrations, legends of the saints and scenes of everyday life.

The lavish embellishment of the west front of Notre-Dame-la-Grande in Poitiers stands out in the area; in the Saintonge such sumptuousness in the sculpture is regarded as normal. Whilst the richness of the overall decoration can be almost overwhelming, it is also worth looking closely at the wonderful individual details.

Fresoes and mural paintings – A fresco (from the Italian word *fresco* meaning fresh) is a wall or ceiling painting executed on a surface of freshly applied, still-damp plaster, into which the design is incorporated before the plaster dries. The number of colours that can be used is limited, since only pigments made from natural earths and iron oxides suit the technique – allowing the artist yellow to red, and green, violet and cobalt blue.

The most extraordinary murals of the Poitou School are found in St-Savin, where the compositions are remarkable as much for the beauty of the colours, the harmony of the design and the perfection of the technique as for their lively content.

From Romanesque to Gothic: the Plantagenet Style

In the west of France the Plantagenet style, also known as **Angevin**, marked the transition between Romanesque and Gothic styles; artistically its highest point was at the beginning of the 13C – and by the end of that century it was no more.

Angevin vaulting – In normal Gothic vaulting all the keys are situated at approximately the same height. Plantagenet architecture, however, is characterized by steeply recessed quadripartite vaulting – probably derived from an earlier use of the dome – in which the keystones of the diagonals are higher than the stringer or transverse keys by as much as 3m/10ft.

At the end of the 12C these Angevin vaults became lighter as the number of ribs increased and arched more gracefully, springing from slender circular columns. The early 13C saw the style at its finest, the tall, slim pillars supporting an airy tracery of lierne vaulting.

Examples of the style can be seen in Vendée, Poitou (Poitiers Cathedral, Airvault, St-Jouin-de-Marnes south-east of Thouars), Saintonge and as far away as the region around the Upper Garonne.

Gothic period (12C-15C) – Apart from its appearance in the Plantagenet style, which nevertheless retains many elements of the Romanesque, Gothic art raised scarcely an echo in the west and south-west of France; such examples as there are tend to be Southern Gothic, the style of the Mediterranean, characterized by a single, very wide nave and no transept. Certain English influences are evident in the square, Flamboyant towers of a few 14C and 15C churches in Saintonge (St-Eutrope in Saintes, Marennes).

Renaissance period

The Renaissance did not take hold in France overnight, but rather the traditions of the Gothic style were slow to disappear. The arrival of a score of Neapolitan artists, however, brought from Italy by Charles VIII at the end of 1495, did breathe new life into the French architectural establishment of the time.

S. Sauvignier/MICHELIN

Château d'Oiron

Civil architecture – The Renaissance style was brought to the west by members of the court of François I who were natives of Saintonge or Angoumois and had been influenced by the architecture of the Loire Valley. The François I Wing of the Château d'Oiron, for example, displays a characteristic series of basket-handled arches, whereas the Château de la Rochefoucauld, with its celebrated courtyard surrounded by a three-tiered gallery, is reminiscent of an Italian *palazzo*.

Extensive use of decorative arabesques and grotesqueries – along with a deep nod in the direction of antiquity – distinguishes the châteaux of Dampierre-sur-Boutonne and Oiron: the roofs are tall, with all the slopes on each side at the same angle; the inclusion of splendid staircases accounts for the projecting façades of the central blocks.

Similar features can be found in other châteaux of the region – the old royal Castle in Cognac, for instance (guard-room and gallery) – or in such Renaissance mansions as the Hôtel Fumé in Poitiers and the Hôtel Saint-Simon in Angoulême.

Classical period

The accession of the Bourbon dynasty in 1589, following the era of stagnation which characterized French art and architecture towards the end of the Renaissance, heralded a radical shift in direction: the period of material prosperity which coincided with the reign of Henri IV fired artists eager for change with new ideas, new interpretations of classical, antique themes. Classical art held sway in France from 1589 to 1789.

Classical fortifications – From the 16C onwards fortifications were constructed above all to protect frontier towns, and consisted of curtain walls and bastions surmounted by platforms from which cannon could be fired. Overhanging turrets allowed the defenders to survey the surrounding ditches and keep watch over the terrain beyond. The acknowledged master of fortifications was **Sebastien le Prestre de Vauban** (1633-1707). Developing the ideas of his predecessors – military engineers employed by the king – he evolved a system based on the use of massive bastions complemented by ravelins or demilunes, the whole being protected by very deep defensive ditches. Vauban's designs are notable for the way he made use of natural obstacles, used only local materials, and added aesthetic value to the functional works he produced, incorporating monumental stone entrance gates, often adorned with sculpture. His talent can be admired at Blaye, where the citadel protecting the entrance to the port of Bordeaux is part of a complex defence system; further south, Bayonne and Navarrenx (south of Orthez) are also examples of the genius of this great military architect.

Basque religious architecture in the 17C

Most of the churches in the Basque country were renovated during the period of the Council of Trent (1545-63), which generated a movement within the Catholic clergy and laity for widespread religious renewal and reform that yielded substantial results in the 17C, even affecting religious architecture. In this region, the belfry is a particularly distinguishing element. Around La Soule, a distinctive form of **belfry-calvary** is common, such as the one in Gotein. The flattened belfry rises up like a wall, with three pointed gables, each crowned with a cross. The shape symbolises the Holy Trinity, whereas the crosses recall Jesus and the two thieves crucified. In lower Navarre and Labourd, the belfry-wall is rounded, resembling the fronton of a pelota court. Certain churches have massive, tiered **belfry-porches**. Often the porch, whatever its dimensions, is surmounted by a room used to hold town council meetings or catechism classes.

In the northern Basque regions of Labourde and Basse Navarre, the inner disposition is characteristic: a wide nave is surrounded by two or three tiers of **galleries**, which are in theory reserved for men. The pulpit is integrated into the lower gallery. The main altar often is monumental **baroque** in style, a profusion of gilding, sculpture, curls and wreaths typical of the Catholic baroque churches all over Europe.

In the cemeteries, the oldest and most remarkable tombstones – some dating from before the 16C – are known as **discoidal tombstones**: atop a plinth, a round, flat stone is often carved with a swastika figure, or *cruz gammata*, believed to have been a symbol of solar power and movement, possibly of Hindu origin. The exact source of the design remains a subject of speculation and debate, along with the many other unique aspects of Basque culture.

1830-1930: Architecture on the Atlantic coast

19C Eclecticism – In the 19C, European architecture was characterised by a penchant for eclecticism, bringing styles from the past (Antique, Romanesque, Gothic, Renaissance and Classical) back into fashion, and borrowing largely from foreign architectural styles, especially those of the Far East. Such buildings are found from the Gironde to the Basque country, along the shore and in spa towns in the Pyrenees. Some of them are highly original, many are luxurious villas, lending their image to the reputation of certain resorts.

In the Bordeaux area, neo-Classicism has prevailed (early 19C), as evidenced in the châteaux of local wine-growers. But some odd mixtures can be found here as well, as at the Château Lanessan *(see p 172)* where the Spanish Renaissance meets Dutch tradition, or the Cos d'Estourel, rising pagoda-like from the vines.

The popular Arcachon lagoon inspired a miscellaneous building boom in the 19C, as holiday homes owned by families from Bordeaux went up in styles ranging from the Algerian villa to the Swiss chalet, the Basque house to the English cottage. Around Cap Ferret and in the Ville d'Hiver section of town, so successfully promoted by the Pereire brothers, these hideaways still surprise the passer-by.

Biarritz became a fashionable seaside resort thanks, in part, to Napoléon III and his neo-Classical Villa Eugénie. Luxury beach houses in a hodgepodge of styles were built right up to the 1930s: the Villa de la Roche-Ronde is neo-Medieval (towers and look-outs); the Boulard château (1870-71) neo-Renaissance; the Françon Villa adopts the Old England look. In Hendaye, the Château d'Abbadia imitates Gothic architecture, while the interior is Moorish in inspiration, a style also in play at the Casino de la Plage.

Art Deco – This 20C style is most evident along the Basque coast: the town casino, the Maritime Museum (1932-35) and the interior decoration of private homes in Biarritz; the Atrium Casino (1928) and the Splendid Hotel (1932) in Dax; the Leïhora Villa (1926-28) in Ciboure. Like the Art Nouveau movement which preceded it, Art Deco draws from classical motifs, but they are reduced to geometric stylizations, and the noodle, whiplash, tapeworm, and cigarette-smoke style lines of Art Nouveau give way to the straight and pure. Architects used wrought iron, glass (creating luminous rooms within buildings) and ceramics to express these colourful designs.

During the 1920s and 1930s, villas built in Hossegor, in the Landes region, were inspired by rural houses of the Basque country and a neo-regional style developed, which combined timber-framing, typical brick bond from the Landes, overhanging roofs, projecting load-bearing walls and white roughcast façades characteristic of the area with Art Deco ornamentation.

Medieval town planning

Military architecture

From the 9C to the 12C the weakness and remoteness of the central power in medieval France contributed to the establishment of powerful dukedoms and counties. When the enforced feudalism began to crumble, one of the results was a generalized increase in the scattering of new strongpoints. The south-west and in particular the former Aquitaine, which had been disputed for three centuries by two different crowns, became peppered with fortresses. Outside the towns where, through the consolidation of existing Gallo-Roman protective enclosures, defence could usually be assured, crude new strongholds proliferated in the open countryside a surrounding ditch, a palisade, a wooden tower (later built of stone) rising on a hillock which were enough to provide at least basic refuge.

Keeps – Rectangular keeps built of stone made their appearance in the early 11C. Their role initially was purely defensive: the stonework was not particularly thick, there were no loopholes with a field of fire. The ground-floor level, which was dark, served as a store. The keep could only be entered at first-floor level, via either a ladder or a retractable footbridge. This design (illustrated by the keep at Bassoues), which persisted until the 14C, explains why the spiral stone staircases of so many of these structures only started at the higher level.
Before the Hundred Years War there was a 13C-14C Gascon variant of the keep known as a **salle** – a fortified dwelling flanked by one or two rectangular towers, set along the diagonal if there were two. Again, only the upper storeys were inhabited and provided with windows.

Castles of brick – Certain castles in the Béarn district bear the trademark of **Sicard de Lordat**, a military engineer employed by Gaston Fébus, the 14C overlord of Béarn. For reasons of economy they were built of brick rather than massive stonework. The single square tower astride a polygonal defensive perimeter served both as a keep and as a gateway. The living quarters and the barracks were built against the inside of the curtain wall.

Fortified churches – Fortress-churches occupy a special place in the history of French military architecture, and are numerous in the south-west.
Two types of machicolation were employed in their construction: the classic variety supported by corbels, and another in the form of arches curving between the buttresses (as at Beaumont-de-Lomagne). They appeared for the first time in France in the late 12C, in the Langue d'Oc country.
The churches were traditionally places of asylum, refuges for the hunted, with their robust architecture and their belfries which could be used as watchtowers; moreover the Truce of God ordered by the Vatican Council in the 10C and 11C stipulated a "zone of inviolability", extending for 30 paces around each church, in which refugees might not be touched. The Council's orders forbade the waging of war on certain days of the week and during Advent, Lent and Easter week. Violation of the Truce was punished with excommunication.
Examples of these fortified churches still exist in the Upper Pyrenees, in the valleys once subject to cross-frontier raids from Aragon; the best-known are Luz Church, enclosed within a crenellated curtain wall, and Sentein Church, which has three towers.

New Towns of the Middle Ages

Medieval urban development in south-western France has left only three sites still substantial enough today to be called towns: Montauban (south-east of Agen), founded by the Comte de Toulouse in 1144; the lower part of Carcassonne (1247), built on the west bank of the Aude by St Louis to shelter the homeless after the town was sacked; and **Libourne** (east of Bordeaux), named after Sir Roger Leyburn, Seneschal to Edward I of England (1270) *(for details of Montauban and Carcassone, see The Green Guide Languedoc - Roussillon - Tarn Gorges)*. Aquitaine, however, at first strewn with *sauvetés* and *castelnaux* (refuges and fortified towns), was above all characterized by an abundance of *bastides* – those new towns, half urban, half rural and characterised by a geometric ground plan, which remain today even at their largest no more important than a county seat.

Sauvetés and Castelnaux (11C and 12C) – The **Sauveté** (Sauvetat, Sauveterre etc) usually arose as the result of an ecclesiastical initiative. Prelates, abbots or dignitaries of a military Order of Chivalry would found the village or hamlet; the inhabitants would clear, prepare and cultivate their lands; a host or overseer, installed perhaps in a small manor house, would supervise the work. These rural townships also provided sanctuary for fugitives. In a similar fashion, the **castelnau** (Châteauneuf, Castets etc) originated with the dependencies built by a seigneur around his château. Auvillar (south-west of Agen), Mugron and Pau were once *castelnaux*. In Gascony the name Castelnau is completed by the name of the local fief: Castelnau-Magnoac, Castelnau-Barbarens etc.

Bastides (1220-c1350) – The *bastide* was an entirely new concept, a true purpose-built and efficiently planned place where people could live. By the middle of the 14C something like 300 *bastides* had been created between Périgord and the Pyrenees. In Gascony and Guyenne these new towns were so numerous that it suggests that at one time they were the most important form of collective habitation in the region. Although not all of them were fully developed, and despite their relative lack of importance today – some have disappeared altogether – the *bastides* in their time were a genuine response to demographic, financial and economic needs as well as to military and political imperatives. The construction of many *bastides* arose from a contract of *paréage*. Such contracts, frequently drawn up between the king and a local seigneur or between an abbot and a lay seigneur, could also permit two neighbouring seigneurs to detail the rights and powers of each over territories they might hold in common; or they could stipulate that a less powerful seigneur would enjoy the protection of his stronger neighbour in return for a fixed proportion of the former's revenues. The contracts also affected the inhabitants of the *bastide*, establishing their status, outlining the allotment of building plots, specifying the taxes to be paid. To encourage people to move into the *bastide*, new arrivals were granted – among other privileges – the right of asylum and exemption from any military service due to the seigneur. The immigrants were free to bequeath property to their inheritors and dispose of their other possessions as they wished. Penalties, on the other hand, could be imposed on those who were slow to build.

Place names of the *bastides* followed three different principles: they could evoke the settlement's status – Villefranche (Free Town); they could carry the name of the founder – Montréjeau (Mount Royal), Beaumarché, Hastingues (Hastings); or they could suggest a symbolic twinning with some famous foreign city – Valence (after Valencia in Spain), Fleurance (Florence), Cologne, Tournay etc.

These settlements were fairly rigidly planned, based on the model of a right-angled grid, either square or rectangular (with the exception of Fourcès, a rare circular *bastide*). Variations on this plan were due either to the lay of the land or to considerations of

SOME BASTIDES IN GUYENNE

::: : Founded by the French   ::: : Founded by the English

0   20 km

Miramont-de-Guyenne
Castillonnès
St-Étienne-de-Londres
Villeréal
St-Pastour
Marmande
Monclar
Monflanquin
Laparade
Villeneuve-s-Lot
Lagruère
Tournon-d'Agenais
St-Sardos
Damazan
Nicole
AGEN
GARONNE
Puymirol
Vianne
Baïse
Lamontjoie
Caudecoste

defence. The use of professional surveyors at the planning stage is evident in the rectilinear layout of the streets, always meeting each other at right-angles to form a symmetrical pattern of equal-area lots. Those moving in were allowed so much on which they could build, so much for a garden, and – outside the built-up area but not too far away – an allotment which they could cultivate. The road system was ahead of its time: the principal streets were usually 8m/26ft wide, a generous size when none of the buildings had more than two floors.

In the centre of the grid was the main (and only) square, normally closed to traffic and reserved for markets; many of the central, covered market places still stand today. The square was effectively an open lot islanded among the regular ranks of buildings; the four streets framing it passed from the open air to the *couverts*, and then out again on the far side, retaining their continuity and frequently their street names. The **couverts**, most of them unfortunately now truncated or lost altogether, were covered passages surrounding the square running beneath either stone-built arcades or projecting upper storeys supported by wooden pillars.

Bastide Churches – The proliferation of *bastides* from the 13C onwards led to the construction of many new churches. They were built either close to the market square or out on the periphery of the grid, on the specified lot assigned for church and cemetery; here, therefore, the Languedoc single-nave-no-transept style was particularly suitable. Churches in Gascony share a family likeness, with their belfry-porches (Mirande, Marciac) and their wide, dark naves lit mainly through the clerestory windows of a cramped apse.

The Way of St James

Pilgrim routes to Santiago de Compostela

History and legend – St James the Great, beheaded in Jerusalem in the year AD 44, was the first Apostle martyred for his beliefs; according to legend, his body and head

were transported to north-western Spain in a stone boat and buried on the coast of Galicia. On the site of his tomb, miraculously rediscovered in the early 9C, a church was built, and around it grew the town of Compostela. When the Moors were driven from Spain St James (San Tiago in Spanish) became the patron saint of Christians: in the year 844, it is said, at the height of a decisive battle at Clavijo in Rioja, he appeared on a white charger and vanquished the enemy – a manifestation which earned him the nickname of *Matamore* (Moor-slayer).

The Pilgrimage – Soon after the building of the church to St James, the faithful from far and wide began flocking to the site to venerate the relics. They travelled from hostel to hostel visiting churches, abbeys and holy places along a number of well-defined routes. Throughout the Middle Ages this traffic grew to such an extent that the church of Santiago in Compostela became a shrine equal in importance to Jerusalem itself or Rome.

The first French pilgrimage was led by the bishop of Le Puy in the year 951. Subsequently millions of **Jacquets**, Jacquots or Jacobites (*Jacques* in French means James) set out from Paris, Tours, Le Puy, Vézelay and Arles, which developed into assembly points for pilgrims from all over Europe.

Pilgrims to Santiago wore a uniform of a heavy cape, an 8ft stave with a gourd attached to carry water, stout sandals and a broad-brimmed felt hat, turned up at the front and marked with three or four **scallop shells**, the badge of the saint, which identified the pilgrim's destination. The shells, found in great banks along the Galician coast and still called *coquilles St-Jacques* (St James' shells) in France today, were also used as a receptacle to collect alms. A scrip or pouch, a bowl and a small metal box for papers, passes etc completed the equipment. The network of hostels and hospices where pilgrims could find food and shelter for a night, or receive attention if they were sick, was organized by the Benedictine monks of Cluny, the Premonstratensians and other orders; the Knights Templars and the Hospitallers of St John with their commanderies policed the routes, marked with carved mileposts or cairns; everything was done to ensure the pilgrims' welfare, both spiritually and temporally.

There was even a *Pilgrims' Guide*, the first tourist guide ever written, which was produced in Latin in c 1135, probably by Aymeri Picaud, a monk from Parthenay-le-

Vieux. This outlined local customs, gave advice on the climate and weather conditions to be expected, spiced the more mundane information with comments on the morals, customs, and mentality of the inhabitants of each region, and listed the most interesting routes, towns, and the sights on the way – the pilgrim in those days was in no hurry and frequently made detours which took weeks or months to complete, to visit a sanctuary or shrine (*Le Guide du Pèlerin de St-Jacques-de-Compostelle*, edited by Jeanne Vielliard (Vrin, Paris) is a translation into French of the 12C Latin handbook).

The main routes all converged in the Basse-Navarre district before crossing the Pyrenees. The most important junction was at Ostabat; St-Jean-Pied-de-Port was the last halt before the climb towards the frontier. The pilgrims reached Roncesvalles by a mountain route which was once part of the Roman road linking Bordeaux with Astorga via the Valcarlos gap. The bell of the monastery at Ibañeta pass would toll when it was foggy – or sometimes for much of the night – to signal the right direction to those pilgrims who might have got lost or lagged behind.

With the passage of time, however, the faith that fired people to set out on pilgrimages began to wane; false pilgrims seeking gain by trickery and robbery, and known as *coquillards*, increased; the Wars of Religion, when Christians fought among themselves, reduced the faithful even more. In the late 16C, when Francis Drake attacked Corunna, the relics were removed from the cathedral to a place of safety, after which the pilgrimage was virtually abandoned. By the 18C anyone wishing to make the journey to Santiago de Compostela was obliged to provide the authorities, when requested, with a letter of introduction from their parish priest and other documents certified to be true by a police official or signed by the pilgrim's local bishop.

The Basque Country

The landscape of the Basque Country (Pays Basque) presents a dramatic contrast with that of Bordeaux and the moors to the north. Suddenly, there are mountains all around and the cliffs and rugged rocks along the coast are a complete contrast to the long, level strands of the Landes. The Basque hinterland consists of green valleys adorned with traditional white houses. The Basque Country is one of the most distinctive regions in France.

The geology of the Basque region seems somewhat chaotic, marked by the last collapse of the folds of the Pyrenees. The valleys are full of winding roads making communications between them difficult. One 17C chronicler described it as "very bumpy country". This partly explains the former division of the country into small states, each with its separate identity. The seven Basque provinces nevertheless share a unique linguistic and cultural heritage, on both the French and Spanish sides of the Pyrenees. Their common motto, in the Basque language, is *Zaspiak-bat* – Seven-in-One. This guide describes the three provinces on the northern side of the border, those in the French sector of the Basque Country: **Le Labourd**, **La Basse Navarre** (Lower Navarre) and **La Soule**.

Spanish or French name and its Basque equivalent

Bayonne/Baiona
Biarritz/Miarritze
Bilbao/Bilbo
Hasparren/Hazparne
Mauléon/Maule
Pamplona/Iruña
St-Jean-de-Luz/Donibane-Lohizun

St-Étienne-de-Baïgorry/Baigorri
St-Jean-Pied-de-Port/Donibane-Garazi
St-Palais/Donapaleu
San Sebastián/Donostia
Tardets-Sorholus/Atharratze-Sorholüze
Ustaritz/Uztaritze

Mysterious origins – The origin of the Basque people and their common tongue has always been an enigma. All that is known for certain is that they were driven out of the Ebro Valley in Spain by the Visigoths and founded the kingdom of Vasconia in the western Pyrenees. The Vascons of the plain then intermarried with the local peoples of Aquitaine and became Gascons. Those who remained in the mountains fiercely safeguarded their own traditions and their language, **Euskara**, which binds the race together.

Basque autonomy and nationalism – In the 9C, Inigo Arista founded the Basque dynasty and became king of Pamplona. Two centuries later, Sancha the Great ascended to the throne of Pamplona and reunited the Basques on either side of the Pyrenees. This is where the history of the Basque Country begins, intimately linked to that of both Spain and France. Before the French Revolution, the French Basque provinces held on to their political autonomy. Leaders from each village met to discuss territorial matters, after which each province would hold an assembly. Royal emissaries regularly consulted these assemblies before making political decisions.

The French Revolution in 1789 brought an end to these special rights and the three French Basque provinces joined Béarn to form the Basses-Pyrénées *département*.

At the end of the 19C, the Spanish Basques were quick to join the great nationalist movement which was spreading throughout Europe. In 1895, **Sabino Arana Goiri** (1865-1903) founded the **partido nacionalista vasco** (Basque Nationalist Party) in Bilbao. His aim was to reunite the seven Basque provinces in France and Spain and form one confederate state which he first called Euskeria, changing it in 1896 to **Euskadi**, the name still used today by the Basque Separatist Movement. In 1894, Arana designed the **Ikurrina** – a red flag with two green and white crosses. Autonomy was granted to the three Spanish Basque provinces on 11 October 1936, in exchange for republican support against Franco's followers during the Spanish Civil War. In 1937, however, the new Basque government was suppressed in Guernica, and Franco's regime set out to repress and persecute Basque culture. This was the beginning of the ETA (*Euskadi Ta Askatasuna* meaning Basque country and liberty), the underground armed separatist movement. After Franco's death, the Spanish Basque Country gained greater autonomy and in 1978 became Euskadi.

Basque houses – The traditional houses in Labourd, perhaps the most attractive in the Basque Country, have inspired the design of many suburban villas and holiday homes. The exposed wooden framework, usually painted a reddish-brown, contrasts with the original walls of cob (compressed loam, clay or chalk reinforced with straw) coated with whitewashed rough cast. Houses are east-facing and are sheltered from rain, brought by the westerly winds from the Atlantic, by a huge overhanging tiled roof.

The houses in Basse (Lower) Navarre have a stone framework and semicircular balconies. The darker, slate roofs found in La Soule are an indication of the region's proximity to the Béarn region. Basque houses all share the characteristic white finish, and many proudly carry over their front doors the date of their construction or their owner's name. Nowhere else is the family so closely connected with the home.

The Basques go to the Americas

Unable to partake in their father's estate, the non-eldest children left to seek their fortune elsewhere, emigrating in particular to the Americas, especially Latin America (Argentina, Uruguay, Paraguay, then Chile, Colombia and Mexico). During the 19C, the French Basque Country sent 90 000 of its children across the Atlantic where they raised animals, exported wool, cut wood and traded in timber, just as they had done in their homeland. Having made their fortune, the **Americanuaks** returned to their native country or encouraged their descendants to join them.

From the turn of the century until 1960, the Basques emigrated to the United States, and more especially, California. Most of them were shepherds from Basse Navarre. With the help of an immigration agency, they went to tend sheep in the Rocky Mountains, where they had to endure far harsher weather conditions than they had known in the Basque Country. Some remained, totalling 43 140 in 1980. Although they are now a part of American society, they have been careful to keep up their old traditions.

Before the French Revolution, furniture, the right to use common land, church rights (the place occupied in church determined one's social status) and burial rights were attached to the house, which was a veritable economic and social entity passed down from generation to generation. The master of the household, the **etcheko jaun**, had ultimate authority and his main concern was to safeguard the family inheritance. The house was left to the son or daughter designated by the father as the eldest child.

A Basque trilogy: Town Hall/Church/Pelota Court – The town hall, the church and the *pelote* court are the three focal points of Basque community life. They are all centred around the main square at the heart of village life. The **Basque church** plays a fundamental role, and the village is symbolically constructed around it. Many worshippers attend daily church services, usually celebrated in the Basque language.

The traditional game of *pelote basque*, played against a high, orange-coloured wall or **fronton**, is very popular among the men and boys all over the region. One version, known as *le grand chistera* (the name of the long wicker scoop strapped to one arm), is the most frequently played in official competitions and tourist exhibitions. The ball is flung against the fronton wall and caught up immediately or after a single rebound, and flung back. In professional games, it is not uncommon for the hard ball, covered with goatskin, to travel at speeds of 240kph/150mph!

A more recent variation, *la cesta punta*, has gained fans. This is the jai alai (*jai alai* comes from the Basque for merry festival) played in Latin America, against three walls (front, left and back). Points are marked by hitting the ball between vertical lines marked on the left wall. Spectators sit on the open side, with the front wall to their right, the left wall in front of them, and the back wall on their left.

Yet there are older, subtler variations, which some traditionalists prefer, including *yokogarbi* (with a small glove) and barehanded pelota.

Basque tombstone

Different games are played by teams of three or two, or one-on-one. In the *pasaka* game, players face each other across a net, as in tennis, and wear gloves. And in any and every small village in the Basque Country, wherever you see a fronton, there will always be boys with their *palas* (wooden rackets) passing the time.

La force basque – If you attend a local fair, you may witness competitions between the men of neighbouring villages. There are eight established tests of strength, performed by teams of 12; each team member has his own special prowess. Among the feats they perform: spinning a 350kg/770lb wagon around with one hand, chopping or sawing tree trunks at top speed, running a race with a sack weighing 80kg/176lb slung across the shoulders – all concluding with a great game of tug-of-war between the teams.

Folklore – The Basque people, typically silent and serious by nature, express themselves in their dancing, singing and communal activities. The young men – most of the traditional dances do not include female partners – travel from village to village for local festivities. In the evening, as they return home, their rallying cries echo from mountain to mountain.

The dances are numerous and complex. They are generally accompanied by a *tchirulä* (three-holed ocarina or flute) and a *ttun-ttun* (small drum) or a stringed tambourine, though an accordion, cornet or clarinet are sometimes used. The famous Basque leaps (danced by men only) have many different steps. The striking contrast between the stillness of the torso accompanied by an expressionless face, and the incredibly agile leg movements, is common to all of them.

The **Fandango**, a dance described as "both chaste and passionate", refers to man's eternal pursuit of his female ideal. The movements of the woman's arms and the upper part of her body harmonise with alternating rhythms representing invitation and flight. For the celebrated "Wineglass Dance", the fleet-footed men from La Soule wear dazzling costumes. The *zamalzain* (a dancer who appears, in a wicker frame, as both a horse and its rider) and the other dancers perform complicated steps around a glass of wine placed on the ground. Each of the dancers stand on the glass for a fraction of a second, without breaking it or spilling a drop of its contents.

Basque songs are haunting melodies with lyrics inspired by everyday life (in much the same way as the American Blues). French Basques sometimes sing *Guernikako Arbola* (The Tree of Guernica), the sacred song of the Spanish Basques which has practically become their national anthem. In it, the Oak of Guernica – the Basque village devastated by Fascist air raids during the Spanish Civil War and immortalised by Picasso – symbolises *fueros*, or local freedom.

Basque dance

Regional specialities

Visitors to the Atlantic Coast region of France have a rich variety of choice local products to feast on. All along the coast itself good, fresh seafood is available whereas inland, in Poitou and the Charentes, the "simple, honest and direct, even rustic" cuisine – according to the great chef Curnonsky (1872-1956) – is based on fine, fresh ingredients and careful preparation. In the Bordeaux region the accent is naturally on wines and wine sauces.

Hors-d'œuvres – For lovers of seafood the obvious starter must be oysters from Arcachon or Marennes, or perhaps mussels from Aiguillon; *pibales* (elvers) from the Gironde, either grilled or *à la ravigote* (with a highly seasoned white sauce) are a delicious alternative.

Those who prefer *charcuterie* might like to try the famous Bayonne ham or that from Poitou, or such Basque specialities as **loukinkos** (miniature garlic sausages) and **tripotcha**, a mutton boudin or blood sausage not unlike a small black pudding. Gourmets will also delight in the rich *foies gras* (prepared goose and duck livers) of Gers and the Landes.

Espelette peppers
and Basque *charcuterie*

A glass of chilled Pineau des Charentes may be taken as an aperitif or savoured with *foie gras*, whereas a chilled white wine such as a Graves or an Entre-Deux-Mers served at 8º to 10ºC is a delightful accompaniment to oysters, fish, crustaceans and other shellfish.

Fish dishes – This area favoured with an abundance of water – both fresh and salt – offers the choice of sole or turbot from the *pertuis* (straits), fresh sardines from Royan or Les Sables d'Olonne, or stuffed carp in the Poitou fashion or **chipirones** – tiny cuttlefish, stuffed or cooked in a casserole.

Near Bordeaux choice fish is caught in the Gironde estuary: shad, smelt, salmon, sturgeon, eels and lamprey.

Meat, poultry and vegetables – The quality of meat in the region, whether it be a *chevreau* (young goat), Charmoise mutton or lamb from Pauillac, is invariably excellent. Many dishes around Bordeaux are served with a wine sauce; tender steaks accompanied by this sauce will be described on the menu as *à la Bordelaise*.

The superb quality of vegetables grown in Charentes help form the base for the delicious *pot-au-feu* (beef stew) known locally as **le farci**; the luscious local broad beans, haricots, peas and Chinese cabbage can equally well be cooked *à la crème* (with cream) or with *beurre de Surgères* (a butter sauce).

Seafood platter

Poultry specialities include *poule-au-pot* (chicken stew), Poitou goose with chestnuts, Challans duck and green peas, Barbezieux capon or chicken, and wood-pigeon *salmi* (casserole or ragout). Duck, if it is not conserved in its own fat (the delicious *confit de canard*), may be roasted or served as a *magret* (slices of breast).

Red wines from Médoc or Graves, served cool (cellar temperature) are an ideal complement to poultry, white meat and light dishes, while those from St-Émilion, Pomerol or Fronsac, served at room temperature, are wonderful accompaniments to game, red meat, mushrooms and cheese.

Cheese – In Poitou, Vendée and Charentes it is quite normal to start off the dessert course with cheeses, for the local varieties are essentially unsalted cottage cheeses made from curdled milk or cream which can be taken with sugar if desired; they include **Caillebote d'Aunis**, a crustless sheep's cheese (sometimes made with goats' or cows' milk), and **Jonchée niortaise**, a goats' cheese served on a rush platter. Equally delicious is the Poitou **Chabichou**, another strongly-flavoured goats' cheese. The sheep's cheeses of the Basque Country and Béarn remain characteristic local products. A traditional way to finish up a meal in the Basque Country is with a slice of cheese topped with cherry preserves from Itxassou.

Fruit and dessert – Delicious Charentais melon is served in the summer months as a dessert, as are peaches and plums from the valley of the Garonne, or succulent prunes steeped in Armagnac. Baked desserts include Poitou cheesecake *(tourteau fromager)*, macaroons from St-Émilion, Charentais gâteau, and *clafoutis* (dark cherries baked in a sweet batter). Sweetmeats include Poitiers *nougâtines*, chocolate *marguerites* and *duchesses* from Angoulême, and angelica-based sweets from Niort.

The exquisite dessert wines of Sauternes, Barsac, Ste-Croix-du-Mont and Loupiac, served very cold (5ºC), are the perfect accompaniment to sweet dishes; a fine cognac makes an excellent digestive.

A FEW RECIPES

A rare treat

Authorities on Bordelais cooking agree that a genuine **entrecôte bordelaise** is hard to find. First of all, it must be grilled over two different sorts of dried clippings *(sarments)* from the Bordeaux vineyards. Begin with Cabernet Sauvignon branches, which burn at a high temperature, for searing the meat. Grill the steak on both sides until the juice begins to appear on the surface. As the juice rises, toss on a bunch of twigs from Merlot vines, which add a subtle smoky flavour. Top off the steak with fresh chopped shallots.

The ideal side dish is a generous helping of the wild mushrooms known as *cèpes*, sprinkled with finely chopped garlic and parsley. The traditional preparation of the *Boletus edulis* mushroom is an exact science. Lightly grill the mushrooms to remove excess moisture, separate the cap from the stem, make a small cut in each cap with the point of a knife, then poach the caps in peanut oil (this releases the tannin).

Nowadays, the steak is usually served with a wine-based sauce, although this was most likely the invention of 19C Parisian chefs. Oh yes, the culinary historians tell us that the *entrecôte* steak was introduced to France by the English in the late 18C. Previous to that, the vintners and winegrowers of Bordeaux made their special dish with the meat of vineyard rodents who had grown plump and tasty amid the rows of ripening grapes.

A la basquaise

Chicken and tuna dishes frequently listed on menus as "in the Basque style". The term does not appear in French cookbooks before the early 20C. It seems to be a catchall for chicken or fish cooked in a thick, orange-red sauce mainly consisting of tomatoes and red peppers. Cooks seeking more precision will whip up a **piperade**, which makes excellent use of the moderately hot, thin red peppers that festoon villages around Espelette (dried ground peppers can be purchased in the region and substituted for fresh ones with success, or use any fresh chilli peppers).

Skin four large sweet red, yellow and green peppers; remove the cores and cut the peppers into strips. Heat 60ml/1/4 cup of olive oil in a heavy pan; sauté a sliced onion until it is tender. Add the pepper strips, four large peeled tomatoes (cut into chunks), chopped garlic to taste, one half of a hot pepper, a bay leaf and a sprig of thyme. Cook this aromatic mixture over a low flame for at least 30 minutes, or until it reaches the desired thickness, stirring regularly. Salt to taste. *Piperade* is especially good added to an omelette as it begins to set. Mix it in gently with the eggs, the fold the omelette over while it is still a bit runny.

A surely walk along la pointe du Devin, île de Noirmoutier

Sights

Agen sprawls across the fertile plain between the River Garonne and the Ermitage Hills. The modern, well-planned town boasts wide avenues and the impressive green expanse of Esplanade du Gravier. The busy centre, at the intersection of Boulevard de la République and Boulevard Carnot, includes the nearby pedestrian precinct. Midway between Bordeaux and Toulouse, Agen is an economic centre for the Middle Garonne region. Its practical location has made it an important centre for early fruit and vegetables, especially peaches, Chasselas (white) grapes and plums. **Pruneaux d'Agen**, the best-known prunes in France, are dried from local plums. They are often steeped in brandy.

HISTORICAL NOTES

Artists and scholars – Leading lights of the Renaissance were particularly prominent in Agen. **Matteo Bandello** (1485-1561), monk, diplomat and courtier, banished from Milan by papal decree after the publication of his scandalous stories in the style of Boccaccio, found peace and tranquillity as an exile on the banks of the Garonne. He later became Bishop of Agen.
Julius Caesar Scaligero (1484-1558), born in Padua but settled in Agen, brought fame to his adopted home with his sparkling personality, extensive learning and influence on many literary figures. His tenth son, Joseph Justus Scaligero (1540-1609), born in Agen, was an eminent philologist, humanist and Protestant philosopher.

OLD TOWN *2hr*

Start from place Dr-Pierre-Esquirol.

Place Docteur-Pierre-Esquirol – The square, named after a former Mayor of Agen, is surrounded by the town hall (the office of the provincial governor in the 17C), Ducourneau Theatre, built at the beginning of the 20C, and the Fine Arts Museum.

Rue Beauville – The street is lined with restored medieval houses. Note, in particular the fine timber-framed building with corbels at no 1.

A. Thuillier/MICHELIN

Old-fashioned prune box

Turn right onto rue Richard-Cœur-de-Lion.

At the intersection with rue Moncorny there is another half-timbered house (tobacconist shop).

Rue Garonne leads to place des Laitiers.

Place des Laitiers – This square, with its arcades and shops, lies at the heart of the oldest part of the town.

Cross boulevard de la République and turn left onto rue Puits-du-Saumon.

Maison du Sénéchal – The upper storey of this 14C steward's house has fine Gothic windows. On the ground floor, various items from the Fine Arts Museum (sarcophagi, 17C busts, the bell from the old town hall) are on display behind a glass door.

Rue des Cornières – Half-timbered houses (nos 13, 17 and 19) and stone houses built over arcades make this busy shopping street very picturesque.

Turn right onto rue Floirac then follow rue des Cornières to place de la cathédrale.

Cathédrale St-Caprais – This former collegiate church, founded in the 11C, was granted the status of cathedral in 1802. Its most remarkable feature is the 12C east end, which comprises an apse flanked by three radiating chapels each pierced by semicircular arched windows with scrolled corbels in the form of carved human and animal heads.
The interior, restored in the 19C, is decorated with frescoes which depict the patron saints of Agen.
There is an excellent view of the east end from place Raspail.

Return to rue des Cornières then take rue Banabéra on the left.

On the corner of rue Jacquard is a charming timber-framed house.

Cross boulevard de la République in the direction of the covered market which you then leave on the left before reaching rue Montesquieu.

Eating out

BUDGET

Restaurant Oasis – *46 r. Molinier* – ☎ *05 53 66 89 33* – *closed evenings, Sun and holidays* – *reserv. recommended* – *10/22€*. In this little restaurant situated on a shopping street, you can choose between the small modern room and the one decorated in shades of the south. The menu is deliberately limited – savoury quiches, *plat du jour* and pastries. Tea salon in the afternoon. Friendly welcome and prices.

La Bohème – *14 r. E.-Sentini* – ☎ *05 53 68 31 00* – *closed 10-24 Feb, 1-19 Sep, Fri evening, Sat lunch from Sep to May and Sun* – *22.11/28.97€*. This restaurant situated on a pedestrian street downtown presents a well-mixed cultural cocktail. Refined decor with a Scandinavian soul, classic cuisine subtly inspired by regional recipes and a West Indies menu in memory of the balmy islands where the owner used to live.

MODERATE

Mariottat – *25 r. L.-Vivent* – ☎ *05 53 77 99 77* – *closed Feb school holidays, Sat lunch, Sun evening and Mon* – *16.77/47.26€*. This old 19C mansion, with its sculptured door pediment and slate roof, exudes character. Climb the handsome stone steps to reach the solemn dining rooms. Pleasant terrace under the trees. Appetizing cuisine prepared from fresh ingredients.

Les Saveurs – *11 r. Molinier* – ☎ *05 53 48 03 32* – *closed Sun evening and Mon* – ✝ – *22.71€*. This young establishment used to be a pizzeria. The decor – white walls, red bricks and paintings – is agreeable. Prepared with quality ingredients, the food is influenced by the flavours of Basque cuisine. Very gracious reception.

Where to stay

MODERATE

Régina Hôtel – *139 bd Carnot* – ☎ *05 53 47 07 97* – ✝ 🅿 – *24 rooms: 27.44/36.59€* – ☕ *4.42€*. Successful renovations have given this central hotel all the niceties of modern comfort. Pretty colours provide each room with a personal touch; many of them are spacious and all have double-glazed windows. Have a look at the pretty Breton fresco adorning the hall.

MID-RANGE

Atlantic Hôtel – *133 av. J.-Jaurès* – *E of Agen via N 113* – ☎ *05 53 96 16 56* – *closed 22 Dec to 2 Jan* – 🅿 – *44 rooms: 41.16/51.83€* – ☕ *5.49€*. This hotel built in the 1970s behind a petrol station is a short distance from the city centre. Don't let the surroundings daunt you – the rooms are pleasant and the more recent ones are modern and sizable. Breakfast by the pool.

On the town

La Péniche "Les Copains d'abord" – *Quai de Dunkerque* – ☎ *05 53 48 10 81* – *Wed-Thu and Sun 7pm-3am, Fri-Sat 7pm-5am*. This original bar-discotheque has set up shop on a barge. Congenial bartenders maintain a buddy ambience well appreciated by sportspeople. At weekends, the place is packed.

Place Jasmin – *Pl. Jasmin*. Noisy with conversation and the clinking of glasses and cutlery, this square houses a multitude of bars and *brasseries* whose terraces draw a healthy local population in the summer months. Don't miss the Bodega and its Thursday evening Latino music concerts.

Saint-Barth – *132 quai Baudin* – ☎ *05 53 66 33 31* – *Wed-Sat from 11pm*. Its central location and solid reputation make this little discotheque a very popular destination, especially at weekends.

Florida – *95 bd Carnot* – ☎ *05 53 47 59 54* – *www.le-florida.org* – *Tue-Sun 9am-7pm* – *closed Christmas and New Year's day*. In 1993, this former 1930s music hall became a music centre devoted to amplified music. From rappers to jazz musicians to electronic music buffs – a broad range of artists are invited to play here. In addition to its rehearsal rooms, the Florida offers a multimedia zone (with internet access) and a bar.

Sports and recreation

Canoë-Kayak club de l'Agenais – *Quai du Canal* – ☎ *05 53 66 25 99* – *daily 9am-noon, 2pm-6pm, Sat-Sun by prior arrangement*. This club rents kayaks and organizes water trips. Open to all, including novices, it also offers beginners' lessons.

Poney-club de l'Agenais – *Darel* – *47480 Pont-du-Casse* – ☎ *05 53 96 90 33* – *Mon-Sat 8am-noon, 2pm-7pm* – *closed national holidays*. Located on the Agen heights, this centre organizes lessons and horse or pony rides in a wooded area.

Locaboat Plaisance – *Quai de Dunkerque* – ☎ *05 53 66 00 74* – *www.locaboat.com* – *late Mar to early Nov: Mon, Fri-Sat 8am-noon, 1:30pm-7pm, Sun, Tue-Thu 9am-noon, 2pm-6pm.* Discover the region through its rivers and canals by hiring a boat or a barge at the marina.

Take a break

Colonial Café – *10 av. du Gén.-de-Gaulle* – ☎ *05 53 48 28 10* – *Mon-Wed 8am-1am, Thu-Sat 8am-2am* – *closed public holidays.* A former Agen rugbyman, Gérald Mayout, runs this friendly bar. Modern and bright, it attracts a clientele of all ages who especially appreciate the big bay windows overlooking the avenue du Général-de-Gaulle.

Confiserie P. Boisson – *20 r. Grande-Horloge* – ☎ *05 53 66 20 61* – *pierre.boissonsarl@free.fr* – *Mon-Sat 9am-12:30pm, 2pm-7:30pm, Sun and national holidays: groups by prior arrangement.* The Boisson family has been manufacturing delightful confectionery from the prunes for which Agen is famous since 1835. Its first hit dates from 1876, when a pastry cook's boy was inspired to stuff prunes with filling. A free slide show tells the history of this illustrious lineage. Samplings.

Le Central Café – *82 bd de la République* – ☎ *05 53 48 09 55* – *Mon-Thu 10am-1am, Fri-Sat 10am-2am, Sun 3pm-1am.* Former stamping ground of the militia, today this bar is one of the hip haunts of the city, frequented by the nurses (whose school is nearby) and yuppies of Agen. Frequent concerts (rock, salsa) and theme evenings.

Rue Montesquieu – Note the picturesque 13C-14C church, **Notre-Dame-du-Bourg**, with its brick and stone construction and belfry-wall. **Hôtel Escouloubre** at no 12 dates from the 18C.

Place Armand-Fallières – The *préfecture*, the 18C former bishop's palace, stands next to the imposing 19C law courts in this shady square. The 18C Hôtel Lacépède on the north side houses the public library.

Turn left onto rue Palissy, right onto rue Louis-Vivent then follow rue Richard-Cœur-de-Lion opposite.

Église des Jacobins – The only remains of a convent founded by the Dominicans in the 13C. The vast, brick Gothic building has two identical naves separated by circular pillars and a flat chevet.

Rue Beauville on the right leads back to place Dr-Pierre-Esquirol.

STROLL ALONG THE GARONNE

The banks of the River Garonne and of the canal offer relaxing walks.

Esplanade du Gravier – Plane trees and lawns on either side of a circular pond make this the most popular walk along the Garonne. The footbridge provides a good view of the river, town and bridge-canal.

On the right is the **Pont Canal**, a 500m/547yd long bridge with 25 arches, which carries the Canal Latéral across the Garonne.

The **stone bridge** on the left was commissioned by Napoleon when he stayed in Agen.

ADDITIONAL SIGHT

★★ Musée des Beaux-Arts ⊘ – The Fine Arts Museum is made up of elegant 16C and 17C mansions – Vaurs, Vergès, Monluc and Estrades – which, though their interiors have been reorganised to make room for the exhibits, have largely retained their original façades.

Medieval archaeology – Romanesque and Gothic capitals carved with leaves and fantastic animals adorn the walls of one of the rooms. The main exhibit is the **tomb of Étienne de Dufort** and his wife. Note also the 16C Brussels tapestry titled *The Month of March*, and various funerary stones.

Gallo-Roman archaeology – Among the mosaics, amphorae and small bronzes of this section stands the museum's finest exhibit, the **Vénus de Mas**. This 1C BC Greek marble statue, discovered near Mas d'Agenais in the 19C, is noted for its elegant contours, perfect proportions and the graceful flow of its draperies.

War and hunting – In a neighbouring room, which features an impressive Renaissance chimney-piece, are exhibits based on the themes of *War* and *Hunting*. The ancient weapons on display include a 16C hunting dagger with a scabbard decorated with a Dance of Death. The 17C tapestry, *The Stag Hunt*, is after a cartoon by Van Orley, and the 15C marble profile of a woman is attributed to Mino da Fiesole.

Nearby stands a large bronze Minotaur by a local artist, François-Xavier Lalanne.

Prehistoric and mineral collections – The cellars of Hôtel de Vaurs, once used as the local prison (note the chains and shackles still fixed to the walls), today house the museum's prehistoric collections, ranging from the most primitive stone implements, to more sophisticated stones from the Neolithic period, as well as a collection of minerals.

Paintings and decorative arts – A fine spiral staircase leads to the upper floors which house a collection of 16C and 17C French and foreign canvases. Most notable among them are *The Temptation of St Anthony* by Teniers the Elder and *Portrait of a Man* by Philippe de Champaigne. Also on view are displays of porcelain and 14C-19C **ceramics**, both French and foreign, including dishes by Bernard Palissy. On the same floor is a striking series of **cameos** (porcelain cameos set in glass), on religious, historical and mythological themes, by Boudon de Saint-Amans (1774-1856). He was a local artist, also responsible for unique examples of earthenware designed to rival products from English porcelain factories.

The 18C paintings feature portraits by Greuze and a fine canvas, *The Dying Page* by Tiepolo. The highlight of this section, however, is a **series by Goya** which includes an expressive *Self Portrait*, showing a keen, lively expression under rather heavy features, *The Climb of a Hot-Air Balloon* and a small, almost surrealist picture *(Caprice)*, showing a donkey, a bull and an elephant flying over a group of terror-stricken human beings bathed in a strange, mystical light.

Impressionism – Fine collection displayed on the first and second floors. French painting in the 19C is represented by Corot with his masterpiece, **L'Étang de Ville-d'Avray**, Courbet and Isabey, a collection of pre-Impressionists (numerous views by Boudin) and Impressionists (Lebourg, Caillebotte, Sisley, Guillaumin and Lebasque). *Head of a Romanian Peasant Woman* was the work of the Romanian artist Grigoresco. The 20C is ushered in by a Picabia, *On the Banks of the Loing*, unusual for its Impressionist flavour.

Docteur-Esquirol Room – This room houses paintings, furniture and Asiatic figurines. The paintings include two fine portraits by Clouet; and a fine *Head of a Child* by Greuze.

A dedicated potter

Bernard Palissy (1510-90), born locally, wrote technical and philosophical treatises, though he is better known as a glassblower and potter. He worked with endless determination and at great personal sacrifice (he allegedly burnt his own furniture to fuel his furnaces) and rediscovered the art of enamelling. He created a type of pottery halfway between Italian faience and glazed earthenware. His rustic bowls, decorated with fruit, plants and animals in coloured relief were extremely successful.

EXCURSION

Moirax – *9km/5.6mi S*. The **church**★, which belonged to a priory of the Cluniac order founded in the 11C, is a fine example of 12C Romanesque architecture. The long edifice is surmounted by a conical pinnacle and a campanile over the west front. The most interesting decorative motifs are those adorning the east end and the apsidal chapels. Inside, the forward part of the chancel is no doubt the most original: square at the base, it is octagonal higher up and is topped by a cupola. The capitals are decorated with foliage and figures (note Daniel in the lions' den, near the crossing on the left, and the original sin on the right). The statue of the Virgin Mary in the chancel, the stalls and the walnut panels in the aisles were carved by Jean Tournier (late 17C).

AINHOA★

Population 599

Michelin map 342: C-5 or 234 fold 33 – 8km/5mi SW of Cambo-les-Bains

Ainhoa, a typical Basque village, grew up around a walled redoubt founded in the late 12C by monks of the Premonstratensian order as a staging post on the pilgrims' route to Santiago de Compostela. This brotherhood from northern France combined evangelism and parish duties with a contemplative life. The road D 20, which passes through the village, is one of the oldest pilgrimage and trade routes to Spain in the Nive-Nivelle region.

★ **Main Street** – The picturesque main street is lined with 17C and 18C houses, their overhanging roofs, often asymmetric, covered with very old tiles. The sunlit façades are freshly whitewashed each year for the Feast of St John, the shutters and half-timbering painted and the main beams sometimes embellished with inscriptions. The vast porches, known as lorios, decorating the front of houses, have retained the metal rings used to tie mules long ago, when Ainhoa was a stopover for merchants on their way to Spain.

Church – This traditional Basque church is notable for its two-tiered galleries, wooden ceiling and gilded woodwork in its chancel.
The war memorial at the entrance to the cemetery bears the characteristic disk motif of Basque headstones.

BED AND BOARD IN AINHOA

Ithurria – ☎ *05 59 29 92 11 – closed 5 Nov to 6 Apr and Wed except Jul-Aug – reserv. required Sun – 27.44/41.92€.* This pretty Basque house across from the fronton dates from the 17C. Snug interior with woodwork, tiles, fireplace and stone walls. After having enjoyed a good meal, you can have a nap in the garden by the pool. The rather traditional rooms are comfortable.

Hôtel Oppoca – ☎ *05 59 29 90 72 – closed 15 Nov to 15 Dec, Sun evening and Mon except Jul-Aug –* 🅿 *– 12 rooms: 41.16/48.78€ –* ☕ *5.34€ – restaurant 14.48/26.68€.* On the place du fronton, there's an old Basque auberge from the 17C a stone's throw from the church. The rooms are classic and well kept; those in the back are quieter. Regional-style dining room and small terrace amid greenery and flowers.

Notre-Dame-de-l'Aubépine ⓥ – *Take the street to the left of the town hall and follow the red and white markers of the GR rambling path – allow 2hr round trip.* This rocky path, which lies along the GR10, is a Way of the Cross *(general view from Ainhoa)* leading to Notre-Dame-de-l'Aubépine, a tiny chapel perched on the side of Mont Ereby. Basque pilgrims flock here every year on Whit Monday. It offers a beautiful panoramic view of the harbour of St-Jean-de-Luz and Socoa and the Spanish villages in the foothills of the lofty Navarrese mountains.

Île d'AIX★

Population 199
Michelin map 324: C-3 or 233 fold 14

Île d'Aix (the final x is not pronounced) is a small island in the Atlantic, only 133ha/329 acres in area. It has a mild climate and clear skies which, combined with its attractive layout and impressive fortifications, make it an interesting place to visit. As the boat approaches Île d'Aix, sandy beaches and magnificent cliffs appear along the coast. Inland, pine trees, ilex and tamarisk, flourishing in the mild climate, give the landscape an almost Mediterranean air.
Motor traffic is restricted to service vehicles, which means that the island can only be explored on foot, by bike or barouche.

Access ⓥ – The island is accessible by boat, from **Pointe de la Fumée** and, during the high season, from La Rochelle, Île d'Oléron and Île de Ré. The direct route *(25min)* offers interesting views northwards along the coast up to La Rochelle and out towards Île de Ré; westwards to the offshore forts of Enet and Boyard and to Île d'Oléron. Boats land at the jetty at Pointe Ste-Catherine, below Fort de la Rade citadel.

Call of Destiny – Memories of Napoleon at the time of his downfall are an important part of this solitary island, still steeped in the past.
It was on Île d'Aix that **Napoleon Bonaparte** last stood on French soil. In July 1815, the frigate which was supposed to take the exiled Emperor to America was anchored off Fort Enet.

Ainhoa – Basque houses

E. Baret

Meanwhile a potentially threatening British naval force was cruising in the Antioche Straits, blocking the frigate's exit to the open sea.

The following day, Napoleon landed on Île d'Aix and visited the fortifications, to wild acclaim from the islanders and the garrison of 1 500 sailors (he had previously inspected the stronghold in 1808, at the height of his power). On his return to the ship, he learnt what options lay open to his guards. If combat with the British could be avoided, they would sail past to the ocean,

and if not, they would discuss terms. Negotiations lasted three days, during which time the Emperor's envoys were assured (falsely) that he would be permitted to seek asylum in England. Finally, escape appearing impossible, Napoleon accepted the advice of his officers and decided to surrender himself to the magnanimity of his adversaries.

On 12 July, Napoleon had gone ashore, again to stay with the garrison commander, and on 14 July he wrote his now-famous letter *(see Musée Napoléon below)* to the Prince Regent in London. The next day he donned the green uniform of a colonel in the Imperial Guard – the uniform he had worn at the Battle of Austerlitz – and embarked on a brig which was met by an admiral's barge. The barge then took him to the warship *Bellerophon*, where he was taken aboard. This was to be his last sad voyage, carrying him to exile on another mall island, St Helena, where he was to end his days.

THE VILLAGE

Wide streets intersecting at right angles, and a double line of fortifications separated by deep dykes, give the impression of a large town. However, the small church and single-storey whitewashed cottages surrounded by hollyhocks, reveal it as a small village where the sight of a motorised vehicle is still a rarity. From here, visitors can tour the island on foot *(2hr 30min)* or enjoy a **horse-drawn carriage ride** Ⓥ.

Place d'Austerlitz – At the mainland end of Pointe Ste-Catherine, a gate with a drawbridge leads to this pleasant open space, once the parade ground, with its shady walks between rows of fine cypress trees. Just beyond the drawbridge, on the right, stands the arcaded harbour office.

Fort de la Rade – This citadel overlooking the harbour was originally designed in 1699 by Vauban, the brilliant military architect. Work on the five bastions and ring of fortifications was completed in 1702 but 55 years later, most of it was destroyed by the British. The island's strategic importance was again recognised in 1793 by the powerful State Security Committee, although it was not until 1810 that Napoleon gave the order for rebuilding to start. Work was completed in 1837. The fort today is an isle within an island, completely surrounded by a wide, water-filled moat and a circle of anti-siege defences. There are two lighthouses on the fort. The jetty below provides a view of the massive Fort Boyard (3km/1.75mi away), rising straight up out of the sea.

Église St-Martin – This was once the church of a priory occupied by Benedictine monks from Cluny. All that remains today are the transept, apse and apsidal chapel. The 11C crypt has fine columns with foliate capitals.

FORT LIÉDOT

During the 19C, Île d'Aix became a prison, and a variety of lodgers were accommodated within the walls of Fort Liédot, on the northern coast, including Russian prisoners from the Crimean War and the First World War, Prussian prisoners from the War of 1870 and convicts whose boat had foundered on the rocks on the way to Devil's Island. More recently Ben Bella, one of the leaders of Algeria's outlawed National Liberation Frónt (FLN), was detained here for seven years, along with his colleagues, during the Algerian War in the late 1950s and early 1960s.

Getting around

Bicylce hire – It is easy to find bikes for hire at the port or in the village (you may want to compare prices). You can hire a trailer for carrying small children along with you.

Horse-drawn carriage rides – ♿ Apr-Sep. Look for the carriages on place d'Austerlitz, where the horses wait patiently in the shade for customers. ☎ 05 46 84 07 18.

Swimming

Beaches on the island (most pleasant at high tide) do not have life guards. On the western side, there are long sandy beaches (from Anse de la Croix to La Batterie de Jamblet). There is a small beach on the eastern shore (Anse du Saillant), and nice little coves to the north-east (Les Sables Jaunes, Baby Plage) where oak trees provide shade.

Specialities

Oysters – These are sold by the basket *(une bourriche d'huîtres)* from oyster shacks at the north-eastern end of the village or from some shops in the centre (in season only, naturally).

Nacre – *Pl. de l'Église – 17123 Île d'Aix* – ☎ *05 46 84 66 17*. This shops sells items made with mother-of-pearl, and you can watch the craftsman at work.

ADDITIONAL SIGHTS

Musée Napoléonien ⊙ – The museum (part of the Gourgaud Foundation) is installed in the house which was built on Napoleon's orders in 1808, and where he took refuge in July 1815. It is one of the few buildings on the island with an upper storey, surmounted by the imperial eagle. Two Classical columns frame the entrance. Baron Gourgaud, great-grandson of the Emperor's aide-de-camp, bought the building in 1925 and left it to the nation.

The 10 rooms contain memorabilia of Bonaparte, his family and his entourage – weapons, works of art, clothes, furniture, documents, and portraits by Isabey, Gros, Appiani and others. In the garden stands an oak tree which was grafted to an elm by Napoleon himself in 1808, and a Classical-style bust of the Emperor which once served as a ship's figurehead.

Napoleon's room on the first floor is particularly evocative, as nothing in it has been changed since the days when he stood outside on the balcony, watching the manoeuvres of the British fleet through his telescope. It was in this room that he composed the famous letter to the Prince Regent in London:

"Faced with the factions dividing my country and with the enmity of the great powers of Europe, I have ended my political career and I come, like Themistocles, to seat myself at the table of the British people. I place myself under the protection of their laws and the indulgence which I crave from your Royal Highness as the most powerful, the most steadfast and the most generous of my enemies."

General Gourgaud was entrusted with delivering the letter to London, but he was refused permission to land at Plymouth. Napoleon made the General a gift of the document, and a facsimile of the Emperor's rough draft of the letter is on view in the museum.

Musée Africain ⊙ – This museum (another part of the Gourgaud Foundation) is housed in a former army barracks. It displays ethnographic and zoological items collected by Baron Gourgaud in Africa between 1913 and 1931.

Slides are used to illustrate interesting examples of African fauna. The white dromedary ridden by Napoleon during the Egyptian campaign was later taken to the Jardin des Plantes in Paris and stuffed after its death. It was transferred to Île d'Aix in 1933.

The village of Angles, built above the River Anglin, is built on terraces beneath the ruins of a castle. Like England, its names derives from Angles, a warlike tribe from Germania which invaded Britain in the 5C. In the 9C, Charlemagne dispatched the descendants of these northern peoples southwards, to settle on the banks of a tributary of the River Gartempe, the Angla, which subsequently became the Anglin. The inhabitants of Angles are called Anglais, also the French for English.

Ruins above the village

Les jours d'Angles, a highly prized form of drawn-thread embroidery, is still made in the village today.

Archaeological excavations carried out in neighbouring rock shelters have unearthed important carvings dating from the Magdalenian (Late Paleolithic) Era.

A cardinal sin – Like the proverbial victim "hoisted on his own petard", **Cardinal Balue**, a native of Angles born in 1421, was condemned by Louis XI to be locked up in a *fillette*, a small, uncomfortable type of iron cage allegedly designed by the cardinal himself.

Balue came from a modest family but rapidly gained wealth and power, rising through the ranks of King's Chaplain, Financial Steward, Secretary of State to finally become Bishop of Evreux. Subsequently, he became Bishop of Angers, after which he was made Cardinal. Foolishly, Balue betrayed the King's confidence and sold state secrets to the Duke of Burgundy. Once discovered, he was sentenced to prison for treason. Eleven years later he was freed at the request of the Pope, emigrated to Rome, and lived another 11 years, showered with honours.

Le Relais du Lyon d'Or – *rte de Vicq* – ☎ *05 49 48 32 53* – *closed Jan-Feb, Tue lunch and Mon* – *16.77/28.97€*. A country-style dining room with exposed beams and fireplace in this 15C house is where you'll settle in for a copious meal. After dessert, if so inspired, you can visit the exhibitions in the atelier or take a short course in decorative painting before retiring in one of the pretty bedrooms.

SIGHTS

★**Site** – There is a splendid **view**★ of the village from the south-eastern end of the bluff where the castle stands, beside a roadside cross and a small Romanesque chapel. Beyond a breach in the cliff are what remains of the walls and towers of the old castle. To the north, on another promontory, the Romanesque belfry of the upper church rises above the roof tops, and at the foot of the escarpment, the River Anglin, with its reeds and water-lilies, winds peacefully between two rows of poplars. Beyond the turning wheel of an ancient water mill, a stone bridge leads to the Sainte-Croix quarter, where the former abbey church has a fine 13C doorway.

★**Castle ruins** ⓥ – Angles Castle, an important stronghold in the Middle Ages due to its commanding position and the strength of its defences, was abandoned in the 18C. The Revolution (1789) added to its downfall as local builders were allowed to use the place as a stone quarry.

ANGOULÊME★★

Population 43 171
Michelin map 324: K-6 or 233 folds 29, 30

From route N 141, north-west of the town, there is a fine view of Angoulême and its impressive **site**★ above the River Charente.

Like many towns with a long history, Angoulême is divided into an upper town known as *le Plateau*, built on a promontory and ringed by ramparts, and a lower town, which includes most of the outlying areas.

Every year in January, a festival, created in 1974, crowns Angoulême as the world capital of the comic strip *(bande dessinée)*, a form of graphic art celebrated in the **Centre national de la bande dessinée et de l'image**, which includes a museum and a multimedia library.

Marguerite d'Angoulême – Marguerite de Valois, François I's sister, also known as **Marguerite des Marguerites**, was born in the town in 1492 and spent much of her youth here. She was a woman of great culture and learning – her *Heptameron*, a collection of stories in the style of Boccaccio, won her a permanent place in French literature. She was, however, also famous for her fêtes and parties, and was very influential in court life.

Her name lives on in two kinds of local confectionery: *marguerites* (a chocolate confection) and *duchesses*.

The two Balzacs – The author **Guez de Balzac** (1597-1654), who was born in Angoulême, returned to the town to indulge his moody temperament and vanity. A rigorous stylist, he was dubbed "the man who restored the French language". The other writer, **Honoré de Balzac** (1799-1850), the genius who wrote *La Comédie Humaine* (The Human Comedy), was adopted by Angoulême and described the town in his famous work *Les Illusions Perdues* (Lost Illusions).

★★UPPER TOWN

It is possible to walk right round the fortifications in an anti-clockwise direction. Start this walk from place des Halles and aim for the northern section of the ramparts to admire the view.

North Ramparts – Here there are impressive views over the river bridge, the suburb of St-Cybard, the valley of the River Charente and the industries dotted along it. In 1806, General Resnier (1728-1811), born in Angoulême, launched

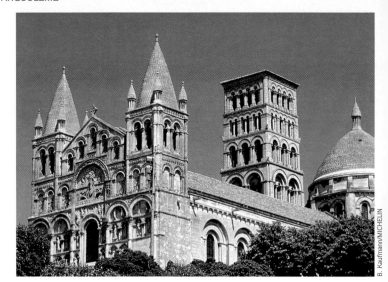

Cathédrale St-Pierre

himself from the top of the Ladent Tower in a flying machine which he invented himself, and thereby became the first man to achieve a non-powered flight. However, since he broke his leg on landing, the General abandoned plans to exploit his invention which, it is said, was intended for a future airborne invasion of England by the Imperial Army. A plaque commemorates General Resnier and his attempt.

Retrace your steps along rue du Chat and follow rue de Genève on the left.

Hôtel de ville – *See Sights.*

Walk along rue de la Cloche-Verte.

Note the Hôtel St-Simon at no 15, with its fine Renaissance courtyard.

Hôtel St-Simon – FRAC Poitou-Charentes – *See Sights.*

Continue straight on along rue St-André.

In **square St-André**, note the mural entitled Souvenir of the 20C, after an original drawing by Yslaire. Further on, the imposing neo-Classical façade of the law courts dominates the tree-lined place du Murier.

Turn right onto rue Taillefer.

Step inside St-André Church to admire the fine furniture, the carved wooden pulpit and Baroque altarpieces.

Turn immediately left onto rue du Soleil.

Note the interesting Louis XVI façade overlooking the courtyard of no 17.

Walk along rue Vauban on the right then turn left to reach rue de Turenne.

No 15 has a Louis XIII doorway; opposite is the doorway of the former Carmelite convent (1739).

Continue along the Beaulieu rampart.

Place Beaulieu – This esplanade is at the end of the promontory, where a school has replaced the old Benedictine abbey. It offers views of the St-Ausone district and the church of the same name, built in the 19C by Paul Abadie (1812-84), one of the architects responsible for the Sacré-Cœur Basilica in Paris. Beyond, the confluence of the River Charente and River Anguienne can be seen. Immediately below is a small park which is a popular place to stroll.

Walk along rue de Beaulieu.

No 79 boasts an imposing façade flanked with three square turrets and decorated with an Ionic colonnade (1783). On the corner of rue de Beaulieu and rue Guérin stands the Chapelle des Cordeliers.

Ancienne chapelle des Cordeliers – This chapel was once a convent church belonging to the Franciscan friars. In 1556, one of the monks, André Thevet, brought the first samples of tobacco – which he called Angoulême grass – back from Brazil. He was followed by the lexicographer Jean Nicot, after whom the poisonous alkaloid nicotine is named.

Eating out

Tour des Valois – *7 r. Massillon - ☎ 05 45 95 23 64 – closed 14-22 Feb, 16 Aug to 6 Sep, Sun evening and Mon lunch – 10.37/33.23€.* A very popular address with the locals. In a 15C house a few steps from the markets, the auberge atmosphere, exposed beams and chimney contribute to its renown. The interesting menu tips its beret to the cuisine of the south-west.

Preuve par Trois – *5 r. Ludovic-Trarieux – ☎ 05 45 90 07 97 – closed Sun – 15.24€.* A boutique for bargain-hunters and gourmands in the heart of the old city. Simple, light and convivial cuisine for lunch; scones, home-made pastries and tea at teatime – just what you need before setting off to explore their little second-hand shop.

La Chouc' – *16 pl. du Palet – ☎ 05 45 95 18 13 – closed Aug, Christmas, New Year's day, holidays, Sat lunch, Sun and Mon – 23/31€.* Lest the name mislead you, there's no *choucroute*, or sauerkraut, to be found in this small, discrete restaurant on a square. Instead, you'll find food fresh from the market place, simple and well prepared. Service swift but not rushed. A must.

Where to stay

La Templerie Bed and Breakfast – *Denat – 16430 Champniers – 9.5km/6mi N of Angoulême. Take N 10 dir. Poitiers then D 105 to Balzac – ☎ 05 45 68 73 89 – 5 rooms: 35.06/39.64€.* You will be lodged in the old utility rooms of this magnificent vineyard farm. Not to worry – every room is very pleasant and colourful. Two of the ground-floor bedrooms look out on the pool. Self-catering cottage for six.

Hostellerie du Moulin du Maine Brun – *16290 Asnières-sur-Nouère – 10km/6mi NW of Angoulême on N 141 then D 120 – ☎ 05 45 90 83 00 – closed 16 Oct to 14 Apr – ▣ – 18 rooms: 70.13/114.34€ – ☖ 9.91€ – restaurant 17.53/33.54€.* If you dream of sleeping in Louis XIII, Louis XV or Empire surroundings, the rooms of this distinctive mill on the banks of a charming River Charantaise are the answer to your prayers. A pretty terrace and pool overlook the peaceful countryside. On site the Cognac distillery and cellars can be visited.

Domaine du Chatelard Bed and Breakfast – *Le-Got-de-Dirac – 16410 Dirac – 8km/5.4mi SE of Angoulême dir. Périgueux then side road – ☎ 05 45 60 29 45 – 5 rooms: 72.41/129.58€ – meals 34.30€.* Between Périgueux and Angoulême, this lakeside château is an island of tranquillity set in a property of 90ha. Run by an English couple, its lovely, stylish and comfortable rooms are perfectly suited to the dignified calm of the surroundings. A charming sojourn.

Going out

Le Tire-Bouchon – *18 r. de la Cloche-Verte – ☎ 05 45 95 00 12 – summer: Tue-Fri noon-3pm, 5pm-2am, Sat 5pm-2am; rest of the year: Tue-Sun noon-3pm, 5pm-2am.* This hospitable wine bar entirely decorated with second-hand finds offers fruity wines to be savoured with fresh cuisine. Good cheer is served by the delightful proprietors at no extra cost. A fine place to unwind.

Sports and recreation

CAM'S Ski Nautique (Water-Skiing) – *Quai du Halage – ☎ 05 45 92 76 22 – Apr-May, mid-Sep to Oct: Sat-Sun noon-8pm; mid-Jun to mid-Sep: Tue-Sun noon-8pm – closed Nov-Mar.* You have before you the perfect address for your no-risk, no-wipe-out introduction to water-skiing. Be you 6 or 86 years old, the friendly staff will dispel your last hesitations and put you on skis for an unforgettable experience. Why resist?

Base Nautique Éric Tabarly – *Plan d'eau de la Grande Prairie – 16710 St-Yrieix-sur-Charente – ☎ 05 45 68 42 46 – cvac16002@oreka.com – daily 8am-10pm – closed late Nov to end of Mar.* This 25ha lake run by the dynamic French Sailing School is the stage for two exceptional yearly events: the magnificent 14 August fireworks display and, especially, the Active Summer which lasts two months. During this period the lake becomes a theatre where a multitude of free concerts and other activities take place. In the meantime, you can enjoy canoeing and sailing while your children safely play in the water and swim under supervision.

Moulin du Got – 🖼 – *Moulin du Got – 16410 Dirac* – ☎ *05 45 61 52 72; 06 82 06 32 84 – Sep to Jun: Wed, Sat, Sun 9am-7pm; Jul to Aug: Mon-Fri 9am-7pm – closed beginning to mid-Aug*. This riding club, established in a superb mill, puts the accent on developing an autonomous and responsible relationship between child and horse. Courses of one day or one week take place in a family atmosphere and include rides in the woods, lunch and snack. The sort of children's holiday life-long memories are made of.

Take a break

Café Chaud – *1 r. Ludovic-Trarieux* – ☎ *05 45 38 26 32 – Tue-Thu noon-2am, Fri-Sat noon-3am, Sun 5pm-2am*. New music fans have settled into this café dedicated to hip-hop and bringing together different musical styles and eras. The intimate decor of wood and stone and the balcony make it one of the most enjoyable haunts in the city.

Chez Paul – *8 pl. Francis-Louvel* – ☎ *05 45 90 04 61 – daily 7am-2am*. A stream runs through the inner courtyard of this sizable café. In the background, a *trompe-l'œil* fresco turns a banal stone wall into a country landscape. In the winter, a faux garden set up on the first floor overlooks this surprising scenery.

Letuffe – *10 pl. Francis-Louvel* – ☎ *05 45 95 00 54 – Mon-Sat 9am-noon, 2pm-7pm – closed holidays*. Founded in 1873, this renowned establishment has opened the doors of its confectionery atelier to visitors. Specialities include cognac and pineau-flavoured chocolates as well as the famous *duchesses of Angoulême*, nougatines with praline filling.

M.R Galerie – *38 r. de Genève* – ☎ *05 45 92 90 14 – Tue-Sat 10am-7:30pm – closed for one week in Feb*. At the back of a modern art gallery, in a charming little flower-filled courtyard decorated with bits of polished glass, you can savour a few moments of refreshing serenity a few steps from the most animated street of Angoulême.

Now the hospital chapel, it has an elegant Gothic belfry with a projecting side supported on two small squinches. The nave contains the tomb of Guez de Balzac *(see above)*, who was buried here in 1654.

Continue along rue de Beaulieu then turn right onto rue du Minage leading to the cathedral and town hall district.

* **Cathédrale St-Pierre** – *See Sights*.

Musée municipal des Beaux-Arts – *See Sights*.

Walk towards the southern section of the ramparts to admire the view.

South Ramparts – From here the view is of the Anguienne Valley with its tree-covered slopes.

Walk along the tree-lined place de New-York to the town hall and enter the St-Martial shopping district via rue Marengo.

SIGHTS

The cathedral façade

* **Cathédrale St-Pierre** – Built in the 12C, the cathedral was partially destroyed by the Calvinists in 1562, and restored in 1634, followed by a more complete restoration started by Abadie in 1866.

** **Façade** – The impressive façade, decorated in the Poitiers style, is an enormous sculpted tableau in which 70 characters, statues and bas-relief sculptures, portray the Last Judgement. The ensemble is presided over by a glorious Christ in Majesty surrounded by angels, saints set in medallions and symbols of the Evangelists. Both the archivolts and friezes above and around the side doors are decorated with intricately carved foliage, animals and figures. On the lintel of the first blind doorway, on the right, are strange scenes of combat based on episodes from *La Chanson de Roland* (Song of Roland).

The tall tower with six diminishing storeys which rises above the far end of the north transept was partly restored by Abadie.

Interior – The inside has several striking features. Domes resting on pendentives represent an extremely bold concept, and in the north transept, a huge chapel sits beneath the Abadie tower, its supporting columns embellished with remarkable capitals. Also of note is the Romanesque bas-relief in the nave depicting a Madonna and Child, and the 18C organ loft.

In the chancel, the capitals with floral decoration originate from the 9C cathedral built by Grimoald de Mussidan.

★ **Musée municipal des Beaux-Arts** ⓥ – The Fine Arts Museum, housed in the 12C former Bishops' Palace rebuilt in the 15C and 16C, is best known for the quality and wealth of its exhibits from the South Pacific region and Africa (ritual statues from the Congo, masks and Kota reliquaries) and for the famous **Casque d'Agris★** (Agris' Helmet) on the upper floor, a masterpiece of 4C BC Celtic goldsmith's work. In addition, there are collections of medieval treasures (capitals, crosses, sculptures), ceramics (mainly regional) and 18C and 19C French paintings *(on the ground floor)*, as well as a wide selection of 17C and 18C Italian and Flemish paintings, and French works and sculptures by local artists *(on the upper floor)*.

Musée de la Société Archéologique ⓥ – This museum devoted to the work of the local archaeological society displays, indoors and outside in a garden, examples of prehistoric finds in the neighbourhood, along with Gallo-Roman mosaics, lapidary collections from Roman times to the 18C, and various regional antiquities (weapons, pottery, trinkets, enamels from the Limousin area).

Hôtel de Ville ⓥ – Abadie built this Gothic-Renaissance town hall on the site of the old castle which was the seat of the Comtes d'Angoulême. All that remains of the castle today is the so-called polygonal tower – a 13C and 14C keep from which a fine **panorama** can be enjoyed – and the 15C round tower where Marguerite d'Angoulême was born.

Hôtel St-Simon – FRAC Poitou-Charentes ⓥ – This is the regional centre of the Poitou-Charentes Contemporary Art Collection, which consists of works representing recent international artistic output.

F. Bourgeon – Travellers in the wind

★ **Le Centre national de la bande dessinée et de l'image (CNBDI)★** ⓥ – *Entrance: rue de Bordeaux. Alternatively, a stairway leads up from avenue de Cognac.*

The Comic Strip Centre, housed in a group of turn-of-the-century industrial buildings which the architect Roland Castro remodelled with resolutely modernistic elements, is as inventive as the works on display.

Inside, the **Médiathèque** *(1st floor)* houses almost all of French comic strip production since 1946. Since 1982, all comic strips published in France have been legally registered here for reasons of copyright. A very large media bank (video cassettes, comic strip books, magazines etc) can be freely consulted.

In the **museum**, rich collections of original drawings are displayed in rotation. Rooms on the ground floor pay tribute to the great masters of the comic strip (through one or several plates or original illustrations or an illuminated screen with a commentary). Videos retrace significant moments in the history of the comic strip. Among comic strip pioneers are the Swiss Töpffer (mid-19C), Christophe (*La Famille Fenouillard*, 1889), Pinchon (*Bécassine*, 1905), Forton (*Les Pieds Nickelés*, 1908) and Alain St Ogen (*Zig et Puce*, 1925). Innumerable later talents represented include the Belgians, Hergé (*Tintin*, 1929) and Franquin (*Gaston Lagaffe*, 1957), the Americans, Raymond (*Flash Gordon*, 1934) and Schulz (*Peanuts*, 1950), and the French artists Goscinny and Uderzo (*Astérix*, 1959). A host of contemporary creators include Gotlib, Claire Bretécher, Reiser, Bourgeon, Wolinski, Loustal, Bilal, Baudoin, Tardi and Teule.

Musée du Papier "Le Nil" ⓥ – The former Bardou-Le-Nil paper mill, which specialised in the production of cigarette papers, operated here on the banks of the River Charente until 1970. It has since been converted into a museum devoted to the industry which made the region prosperous.

One of the six metal-vaned waterwheels which powered the machinery until the end of the 19C, when they were replaced by electrical energy, is on view, together with an exhibition detailing the different stages in the industrial production of paper and cardboard. The raw material – first rags, then wood and waste paper – is turned into a paste and subsequently into a continuous sheet by a machine invented by Nicolas Robert in 1799. Once dried, the sheet undergoes numerous other treatments before the final product is obtained.

Two other exhibitions – one devoted to industry in Charente, from the earliest times to the present day, the other following the history of the paper trade world-wide – give a comprehensive survey of papermaking.

Rooms on the 3rd floor also have displays of contemporary art.

▶▶ **Grottes du Quéroy** ⓥ★ *(16km/10mi E via D 699 and D 412)* – Labyrinth of impressive caves.

ARCACHON ♨♨

Population 11 454
Michelin map 335: D-7 or 234 fold 6

Arcachon is a seaside resort built on a lagoon and reputed for its oyster farms. It consists of four separate districts renowned for their beauty, tranquillity and vitality. The Winter Resort was for decades the favourite haunt of celebrities from Alexandre Dumas to Jean Cocteau and Marilyn Monroe. Today, several festivals bring life to the town: Festival Jeunes Solistes (classical music) in April; parachuting competition in June; Not'Ambules (street festival) and Les 18 heures d'Arcachon (sailing competition) in July; Fêtes de la Mer (blessing of boats, music in the evening) in August; Festival du cinéma au féminin (cinema festival) in September.

Birth of Arcachon – In 1841, a new branch line extended the railway from Bordeaux to La Teste, a favourite bathing place for holidaymakers from the famous wine capital. In 1845, a deep-water landing-stage was constructed 5km/3mi north of La Teste and the two towns were linked by a road across the salt-marshes. Villas were subsequently built along the road, and Arcachon was born.

In 1852, the **Pereire brothers**, Émile and Isaac, founded a railway company, Compagnie des Chemins de Fer du Midi, and took over the Bordeaux-La Teste line which they extended to Arcachon. At the beginning of the 1860s, they purchased forest land from the State. To make the line and land profitable, they started building facilities to attract clients – a station, a Chinese-style dining room, a luxury hotel, a Moorish casino and several mansions. The plans for the first buildings were mainly the work of Paul Régnault assisted by the young Gustave Eiffel. Already a summer resort popular for sea bathing, the town also became a winter resort in 1866, attracting tuberculosis patients. It was not until after 1935 that Arcachon became a popular seaside and tourist resort as well as a health resort.

Fishing in Arcachon – Arcachon is considered to be a pioneer port in the history of sea fishing. It was here that the *Turbot*, **the first steam-operated trawler in the world** (with a paddle wheel), put to sea in 1837. In 1865, Arcachon saw the first French steamers with propellers and iron hulls. At the turn of the last century, it was the second largest fishing port in France after Boulogne-sur-Mer. In the same spirit of innovation, the first motorised trawler in France, the **Victoria**, was commissioned in 1927. Commercial fishing in Arcachon declined in the 1950s, as the trawlers left for the more profitable Breton ports, and fishing in Arcachon returned to traditional methods.

Every year, 2 000t of fine quality fish – sole, bass, hake, mullet, turbot and squid – fetching high market prices, are unloaded onto the Arcachon jetties (do not miss the unloading of the catch which often takes place around 6.45am). The fleet which fishes in the **Bay of Biscay** is made up of traditional fishing smacks and catamarans with nets. In the lagoon itself, apart from holidaymakers and locals who gather clams, cockles and winkles at low tide, traditional methods are still used, with nets of various gauge held in different ways – the *jagude* – three increasingly smaller-gauged nets one inside the other; the *loup* – a horn-shaped net for fishing sea bass; the *palet* – similar to the *loup* but with a spiral base; the *balai* – bunches of broom used to trap prawns; *esquirey* – a term in local patois meaning landing net; the *trahine* – a seine-net, one end of which is drawn along the beach and the other out to sea; and the *foëne* – a two-pronged fishing spear for catching eels.

Plage Péreire

STAYING IN ARCACHON

The **Summer Resort** stretches along the seafront between Jetée de la Chapelle and Jetée d'Eyrac, attracting tourists to its terrace cafés, casino and nautical events (sailing regattas, speedboat races). The **Autumn Resort** is the maritime quarter with its large marina and busy fishing port animated by a regular stream of trawlers. The unloading of fresh fish early in the morning is a sight not to be missed.
The **Winter Resort**★ ⊘, further inland and more sheltered from the sea breezes, is a quiet, pine-shaded area whose broad avenues are lined with handsome late-19C and early-20C villas. The green expanse of its Moorish park lying above the town centre makes it Archachon's most peaceful district.

To the west, Pereire Park with its large sports complex (bowling, swimming pool, tennis courts, golf course and riding centre) and avenues lined with wealthy mansions forms the **Spring Resort**. Mineral water from the **Abatilles** spring which once supplied a local spa, is now bottled for sale. Pereire beach is lined by a shaded pedestrianised alleyway. The southern end, known as Les Arbousiers, is the surfing enthusiasts' favourite spot.

★ THE SEA FRONT

The pleasant promenade along the tamarisk-shaded boulevard Gounouilhou and boulevard Veyrier-Montagnères, by Jetée Thiers, overlooks Arcachon's fine, sandy beaches. To the east can be seen the white façade of the **Palatium** conference centre, part of the neo-Renaissance Château Deganne, which also houses the casino. The jetty offers a general **view**★ of the resort and the lagoon.

Église Notre-Dame – This 19C church is located along Jetée de la Chapelle, just beyond the Sailors' Cross. Inside, **Chapelle des Marins**, adorned with numerous thanksgiving offerings, houses the revered statue of Our Lady of Arcachon.

★ **Boulevard de la Mer** – This charming seaside walk, bordered by pine trees growing in the sandy ground, skirts Pereire Park and offers fine views of the Cap Ferret peninsula.

★ THE WINTER RESORT 2hr

From place du 8-Mai, take the lift up to the edge of the grounds of the Moorish Casino which overlooks the Summer Resort below.

As a result of a real estate project inaugurated by the Pereire brothers in 1860, the Winter Resort is a sort of city park, crisscrossed with winding avenues, sometimes skirting the dunes, sometimes following their contours, and protecting it from the sea winds. This picturesque neighbourhood, planted with pine trees and filled with the fragrance of balsam, considered beneficial for tuberculosis patients, turned Arcachon into a popular resort. In 1863, the Emperor Napoleon III visited the Winter Resort, and for decades, it remained a meeting place for famous politicians, authors and artists of the time.

Today, there is a strong movement towards consolidating and renovating this highly original and charmingly outdated architectural heritage, characterised by the sculpted wood of its gables, balconies and external staircases.

Below are some suggestions for places to visit on foot.

Parc Mauresque – Featuring numerous exotic species, the park offers an excellent **view** of the town and the Arcachon lagoon. Many of the original buildings, including the Moorish Casino, destroyed by fire in 1977, and inspired by the Alhambra in Grenada and the mosque in Cordoba, have now disappeared.

Observatoire Ste-Cécile – This metal-framed observatory by Gustave Eiffel can be reached by a footbridge over Allée Pasteur. The platform affords a **view** of the Winter Resort, Arcachon and the lagoon *(to be avoided if you suffer from vertigo)*.

Villas – Even though there is a variety of styles (Swiss and Basque chalets, English cottages, Moorish villas, neo-Gothic manors and colonial-style houses), villas usually follow the same design. A raised first floor above a semi-basement service floor

Eating out

BUDGET

Le Bayonne – *9 cours Lamarque* – ☎ *05 56 83 33 82* – *closed 21 Oct to 29 Mar, Sun evening and Mon from Apr to Jun* – *12.20/30.49€*. Right near the shore in an animated neighbourhood, here's a traditional restaurant with a warm welcome. Regional cuisine at very reasonable prices. A few simple but well-kept rooms.

Restaurant Le Grand Bleu – *30 bd de la Plage* – ☎ *05 56 54 92 92* – *closed Sun evening and Mon* – *13.57/19.82€*. Yearning for a plate of seafood, bouillabaisse, paella or another ample, ocean-flavoured dish? This address between beach and wharf is for you. The blue and white setting and jolly reception are most pleasant.

Le Bistrot – *3 av. du Gén.-de-Gaulle* – *33260 La Teste* – *4km/2.4mi S of Arcachon* – ☎ *05 57 15 11 11* – *closed Sun evening* – *13.72/16.01€*. The great popularity of this address is no surprise. The decor – yellow walls, decorative objects, fruit and flower prints – is welcoming, the service efficient and affable, and delightful sycamores preside over the terrace. Dishes with a regional accent.

MODERATE

Le Patio – *10 bd de la Plage* – ☎ *05 56 83 02 72* – *closed 15-28 Feb, 15-30 Nov, Tue except evenings in summer and Mon lunch from 10 Jul to early Sep* – *25.92€*. Near the marina, this is a traditional restaurant where you can dine on the patio under the stars. If the coolness of the evening doesn't suit you, the sparkling colours of the dining room will. Classic cuisine.

Cap Pereire – La Réserve du Parc – *1 av. du Parc-Pereire* – ☎ *05 56 83 24 01* – *33.54/45.73€*. Come here to indulge in the seafood platter you've been craving. Far from the crowds, with a view of the sea, this restaurant next to the peaceful Parc Pereire is just the thing.

Where to stay

BUDGET

Hôtel Orange Marine – *35 bd Chanzy* – ☎ *05 57 52 00 80* – *21 rooms: 38.11/64.03€* – ☐ *5.79€*. Here's a little address where you needn't spend a fortune. A stone's throw from the fishing docks, the rooms are sober and impeccably maintained. Ask for a seaside room, unless you prefer one overlooking the pretty patio where diners are seated in the summer.

MODERATE

Hôtel Les Mimosas – *77 bis av. de la République* – ☎ *05 56 83 45 86* – *closed 31 Dec to 1 Mar* – ▣ – *21 rooms: 48.78/60.98€* – ☐ *5.34€*. From the outside, this villa looks like an old bourgeois residence. Albeit rather modest, the small rooms are cool and clean. Even in the summer, prices are relatively reasonable for this seaside resort town.

On the town

Casino d'Arcachon – *163 bd de la Plage* – ☎ *05 56 83 41 44* – *arcachon@europe.casinos.com* – *Fri-Sat noon-4am, Sun-Thu noon-3am; Jul to Aug: daily noon-4am*. This casino has a traditional games room and 80 slot machines. A restaurant, bars and the discotheque (Le Scotch-Club) also await you, with their frequent cocktail hours and theme evenings.

La Feria – *9 r. Jehenne* – ☎ *05 57 52 22 15* – *Jul-Aug: daily 10pm-3am; off-season: Tue-Sun 10pm-2am*. Booming music constantly fills this bar room where you can sing, party or kiss your bachelorhood goodbye... At weekends, a DJ turns the heat up. Costume party nearly every month. Sangria is the house special.

Quartier du Moulleau – *Av. N.-D.-des-Passes*. The lion's share of Arcachon nightlife is concentrated in the chic Moulleau district. Summertime, numerous bars, restaurants and deluxe shops (open late) attract a very healthy crowd.

Sports and leisure

L'Étrier d'Arcachon – *25 av. Pierre-Frondaie* – ☎ *05 56 83 21 79* – *winter: daily 9am-7pm; rest of the year: 9am-9pm*. This handsome horseback riding school organizes lessons, courses and outings in the woods or on the beach (from October to the end of May). It has a covered manège, three outdoor arenas and a club house with terrace.

Le Fronton – *14 av. du Parc* – ☎ *05 56 83 17 87* – *open daytime every day; wall: 9am-11pm*. This pelota Basque fronton was built in the Parc des Abatilles in 1932. Each Saturday evening in July and August, *chistera* matches are held here. Note the excellence of the Arcachon players of this discipline – they hold several Champion of France titles in *grand chistera* (one of the forms of the sport).

Tennis Club d'Arcachon – *Av. du Parc* – ☎ *05 57 72 09 50* – *tcarcachon@aol.com* – *off-season: daily 9am-12:30pm, 2pm-8pm; summer: 8am-8:30pm*. This splendid tennis club boasts 12 hard courts (two are covered) and 10 paved courts. Modern club house with bar.

Centre nautique Pierre-Malet – *Quai de Goslar-BP 82* – ☎ *05 56 22 36 83* – *www.port-arcachon.com* – *office: Mon-Fri 9am-noon, 2pm-5pm, Sat-Sun 9am-7pm*. In addition to courses and sailboat rentals, the Centre Pierre-Mallet proposes various water activities, including sea kayaking, rowing and diving.

Dingo Vélos – *1 r. Grenier* – ☎ *05 56 83 44 09 or 05 56 66 37 57 or 06 87 27 39 86* – *dingovelos@aol.com* – *Apr to Jun, Sep: daily 9:30am-6:30pm; Jul to Aug: 9am-midnight*. In addition to traditional bicycles (mountain and road), this bicycle rental shop offers some pretty strange steeds – tandems or bikes with three or even five seats, whence the name Dingo – rhymes with tango and loosely translates as zany. Dinghy, catamaran, windsurfing board, canoe, pedal boat and small craft rentals.

Union des Bateliers Arcachonnais – *76 bd de la plage* – ☎ *05 57 72 28 28* – *www.bateliers-arcachon.asso.fr* – *Jun to Sep: hourly 9am-noon, 2pm-6pm; Jul to Aug: hourly 9am-2pm, half-hourly 2pm-7pm; Oct, Apr, May: 9am-noon, 2:30pm-5:30pm; Nov to Mar: daily except Tue and Thu 9am-noon, 2:30pm-5:30pm*. Les Bateliers are ocean-going professionals from the fields of fishing and oyster farming. Come on board ship for a trip around Île aux Oiseaux (Bird Island), rod-and-line fishing, a visit to the oyster beds or a jaunt towards Cap Ferrat or Andernos. *Pinasse* (the traditional crafts of oyster-breeders) rentals.

Take a break

Au Cornet d'Amour – *Av. N.-D.-des-Passes* – ☎ *05 56 54 52 16* – *summer: daily 9am-1am; off-season: 2pm-7:30pm* – *closed Jan*. The biggest home-made ice cream shop of the Arcachon Basin, the 'Love Cone' has 70 different flavours of ice cream and sherbet and makes its own cones. Have a seat and savour their iced desserts, such as the *marmite nougatine* with 16 ice creams (for 8), or the *pinasse en nougatine*, filled with 30 scoops (for 15).

Café de la Plage – *1 bd Veyrier-Montagnères* – ☎ *05 56 22 52 94* – *daily 8am-2am; mid-Jun to mid-Sep: daily 8am-3am*. This century-old bar lies in an ideal location on the Arcachon beach, near the casino and *palais des congrès* (convention hall). One comes here to be seen and to sip whisky on the terrace; there's no better place to do it – their drinks menu features no fewer than 90 different brands. Jazz concerts every fortnight; excellent musical ambience in the evening.

contains the reception rooms and veranda-lined living room. The bedrooms are on the first floor. The opulent villa roofs emerge from the vegetation, mainly tall Atlantic pines, interspersed with oaks, maples, black locust (robinia), Japanese ornamental cherry trees, nettle trees, plane and lime trees. When in bloom, mimosas, catalpas and magnolias offer a vibrant display of colour amid the dark green foliage of the pines.

Allée Rebsomen – Villa Theresa (no 4, now Hôtel Sémiramis).

Allée Corrigan – **Villa Walkyrie** (no 12), Hôtel de la Forêt, **Villa Vincenette** (bow window with beautiful leaded glass).

Allée Dr-F.-Lalesque – Villas l'Oasis, Carmen and **Navarra**.
On the corner of rue Velpeau and allée Marie-Christine – **Villa Maraquita** (no 8).

Allée du Moulin-Rouge – **Villa Toledo** (no 7, fine, carved-wood staircase).

Allée Faust – Villas Athéna, Fragonard, Coulaine, **Graigcrostan** (no 6), Faust and Siebel.

Allée Brémontier – **Villas Brémontier** (no 1, turret and balcony), Glenstrae (no 4) and Sylvabelle (no 9).

Allée du Dr-Festal – Villas **Trocadéro** (no 6, finely carved balcony – *see illustration in the Introduction: Architecture and art*) and Monaco.

Allée Pasteur – Villas Montesquieu and Myriam.
On the corner of Allée Pasteur and Allée Alexandre-Dumas – Villa A.-Dumas (no 7).

ADDITIONAL SIGHT

Aquarium and museum ⊙ – 🖻 In the aquarium on the mezzanine floor, 30 glass tanks display marine life found in the lagoon and the nearer reaches of the ocean beyond.
The museum upstairs boasts a special section devoted to oyster farming, and collections of birds, fish, reptiles and invertebrates native to the region. Another section displays finds from local archaeological digs.

Bassin d'ARCACHON★

Michelin map 335: D-6 or 234 fold 6

The Bassin d'Arcachon (Arcachon lagoon), a vast triangular-shaped inlet, is the only major indentation along the Côte d'Argent (Silver Coast). It is almost cut off from the sea by the narrow promontory of Cap Ferret, which leaves an exit channel barely 3km/1.8mi wide.

Several small rivers flow into the bay, the most important being the Eyre which irrigates the Parc Régional des Landes de Gascogne. At low tide *crassats* appear (silty sandbanks full of underwater vegetation) surrounded by secondary channels called *esteys*.

The inlet extends over an area of 25 000ha/almost 100sq mi, four-fifths of which is exposed at low tide. The 9 500ha/23 475 acres which remain above water at high tide contain dykes enclosing the fish reservoirs of Audenge and Le Teich, and include the low, almost treeless relief of Île aux Oiseaux (Bird Island).

The 80km/50mi of shoreline enclosing the lagoon, flat to the east and south and bordered by wooded dunes on either side of the entrance channel, includes a number of small oyster ports and attractive bathing resorts among the pine trees and mimosa. The region's prosperity is based on oyster farming, pine plantations (sawmills, paper mills), fishing and tourism (note the many weekend cottages, holiday homes and camp sites). With an annual production of 18 000t, the Arcachon lagoon is one of the major European centres for oyster production (almost 1 800ha/4 447 acres of the lagoon's surface). It is the main breeding centre and supplies seed oysters or spats to other oyster beds in Brittany, Normandy, Languedoc and the Netherlands.

Oyster Country – The famous oysters from Arcachon lagoon have long been a delicacy. The Roman poets, Ausonius and Apollinaris Sindonius, and later, Rabelais, praised their excellent gastronomic qualities in their writing. Over-exploitation of their natural beds, however, exhausted the supply, until the naturalist Victor Coste stepped in and started developing oyster-farming or ostreiculture in 1859. Until 1920, the flat oyster from Arcachon, or *gravette (ostrea edulis)*, was the most intensely cultivated in the lagoon, followed by the Portuguese deep-shelled oyster *(crassostrea angulata)*. In the same year, a disease struck the flat oyster beds, but left the Portuguese oysters untouched. The latter were then closely observed and became the predominant species until 1970, when disease struck again and they were replaced by a Japanese variety *(crassostrea gigas)*.

The oyster cycle lasts for about four years. It starts in July when the oyster spats are gathered in collectors consisting of sand and lime-washed semicircular tiles which are then put in wooden cages or baskets, and strategically placed along the canal. The following spring, the oysters are prised off the collectors and placed in beds sealed off with wire netting which protects them from their predator, the crab. After 18 months, the oysters are detached from the cultch to be fattened for another year in pools of water rich in plankton. During this period, they are repeatedly turned, to give them a uniform shape. Having reached maturity, the oysters are sorted, and left in degorging tanks to rid them of their impurities. They are washed for a last time and then packed up in small wooden crates and delivered.

The Pinasse, emblem of the lagoon – The brightly coloured streamlined fishing smack called the *pinasse* is the symbol of the Arcachon lagoon. It was originally made of pinewood (hence its name) and pegged together. Nowadays, it is made of iroko (African wood), locust or walnut and assembled with rivets. Formerly used for coastal fishing, the *pinasse* was adopted by the lagoon's oyster farmers in the 19C. Since it is flat-bottomed, it can be easily pulled aground and pass through even very shallow channels. It is generally motor-driven and 9m-10m/30ft-33ft long; the *pinasotte*, a smaller version, is 6m-7m/20ft-23ft long with either sails or oars.

Few of these fishing smacks are produced nowadays (only two *pinassayres*, the yards which make these boats, are still in operation in the lagoon). However, because of their similarity to Venetian gondolas and Mediterranean caiques, they are highly prized and looked after with great care. The old smacks are refurbished, cosseted and raced in the lagoon during regattas, to the admiration of boating enthusiasts.

BOAT TRIPS

Tours of the lagoon, or fishing trips and oyster-bed tours are available at several locations.

Île aux Oiseaux – This small flat island covered with dwarf vegetation used to be a birds' paradise until oyster-breeders took possession of the surrounding mud flats.

The Banc d'Arguin Nature Reserve ⊙ – Banc d'Arguin is a small, sandy island at the mouth of the channels, constantly changing shape as the Atlantic changes mood. It was made a nature reserve in 1972 and is visited from March to August by a large colony of Cabot's sterns (4 500 mating couples) and oyster-catchers. In winter, the curlew, bar-tailed godwit, red-backed sandpiper, grey plover, seagull and black-headed gull live here in great numbers.

FROM CAP FERRET TO DUNE DU PILAT

76km/47mi – allow one day

Although the roads cited in the itinerary below offer few glimpses of the water, you are never far from a stretch of shore or a small jetty giving at least a partial view of the great lagoon.

Cap Ferret – The long thin promontory of Cap Ferret runs north-south at the entrance to Arcachon lagoon, sheltering narrow straits leading into the basin. The area has been developed into a seaside resort, with hotels and holiday villas scattered among the pines. It is also an oyster-farming centre, with the most accessible oyster beds in the lagoon.

Lighthouse ⊙ – This landmark (rebuilt in 1947) is 52m/171ft high, with a revolving lantern which can be seen 50km/31mi out to sea. From the platform (258 steps)

Chapel entrance, Villa Algérienne

there is a fine **panorama**★ embracing the whole of the peninsula, the lagoon, the straits, the open sea and Pilat Dune.

Plage de l'océan ⊙ – A narrow-gauge railway service operates between Bélisaire landing-stage (eastern side) and this splendid beach on the ocean side of the promontory.

Drive out of Cap Ferret along avenue de la Vigne towards Bordeaux.

The road runs through wooded dunes dotted with villas. The smell of the sea mingles with the scent of pine trees.

Villa Algérienne – *4km/2.5mi N.* This site, named after a building in the Moorish style which was demolished in 1965, offers a good view of the lagoon and Bird Island. The oriental influence remains in a chapel, built about 150 years ago, looking out across the sea.

Eating out

MODERATE

La Côte du Sud – *4 av. du Figuier – 33115 Pyla-sur-Mer –* ☎ *05 56 83 25 00 – closed 12 Nov to 31 Jan – 16.77/25.15€.* Fish and seafood enthusiasts, this pleasant restaurant near the ocean is for you. The colourful dining room ends on a terrace with a view of the deep. Comfortable rooms with an exotic touch.

Pinasse Café – *2 bis av. de l'Océan – 33970 Cap-Ferret –* ☎ *05 56 03 77 87 – closed 1 Oct to 15 Mar, except Sat-Sun and November school holidays – 19.82€.* Here's an original, laid-back bistro. The wood-panelled walls are decorated with paintings of boats and drawings of fish – not surprising, considering its situation overlooking the basin and the oyster-breeding pools. Home-made regional cuisine.

L'Escalumade – *8 r. Pierre-Dignac – au port de Larros – 33470 Gujan-Mestras –* ☎ *05 56 66 02 30 – closed 15 days in the beginning of Jan, 14 Oct to 5 Nov, Sun evening and Mon except 1 Jun to 31 Aug – 20.43/44.21€.* A delicious, unassuming seafood meal. The charm of this cool, tranquil oyster-breeders' cabin cum restaurant is enhanced by its wood furnishings and bay windows. The oysters come directly from the oyster ponds below the terrace. Shellfish prepared with care.

Where to stay

BUDGET

Les Tilleuls Bed and Breakfast – *17 bis r. des Écoles – 33380 Mios –* ☎ *05 56 26 67 85 – gitemios@club-internet.fr – closed Nov to Apr –* ☒ *– 4 rooms: 35.06/59.46€ – meals 15.24€.* Quite a pleasing blend of red brick and wood in these entirely renovated barns and stables far from the madding Arcachon Basin crowd. Tastefully decorated rooms with period furniture. Ask the owner to cook you a traditional meal.

MODERATE

Hôtel des Pins – *R. des Fauvettes – 33970 Cap-Ferret –* ☎ *05 56 60 60 11 – closed 16 Nov to 31 Mar – 14 rooms: 51.07/68.60€ –* ☂ *6.10€ – restaurant 18.29€.* An early-20C regional-style house with a white wood veranda that doubles as a dining room and terrace in the summer. The rooms, with their painted wood panelling, are bright. Pretty, flower-decked terrace.

On the town

Surf Café – *7 r. Camille-Pelletan – 33260 La Teste-de-Buch –* ☎ *05 57 52 88 34 – summer: Tue, Fri and Sat 6pm-2am; rest of the year: Fri-Sun 6pm-2am.* Located in a futuristic building, this big, striking bar is original indeed with its surfing atelier interior where drinks are served on a boat-shaped counter. Concerts (reggae, rock...) twice a week. Young crowd.

Sports

Aéro-club du Bassin d'Arcachon – *Aérodrome de Villemarie – 33260 La Teste-de-Buch –* ☎ *05 56 54 71 13 – www.acba-fr.com – reception: daily 9am-noon, 2pm-6pm; aero club: summer 8am-10pm.* This aero club organizes first flights and introductions to air acrobatics as well as piloting lessons. One can also find parachuting and hang-gliding clubs at the Aérodrome de Villemarie.

École Pyla parapente – *Maison forestière Gaillouneys – 33115 Pyla-sur-Mer –* ☎ *05 56 22 15 02 – beginning May to end Sep: daily 1pm-7pm.* Located near the 118m-high Dune de Pilat, this school offers para-gliding and delta plane flights. Expect to pay 61€ per adventure.

Parks, Zoos, Attractions

Aqualand de Gujan-Mestras – ⬚ – *R. des Grands-Lacs, Parc de Loisirs de la Hume – 33470 Gujan-Mestras –* ☎ *05 56 66 39 39 – early Jun to early Sep: daily 10am-7pm.* This water park has an impressive array of different slides, a mini-park for the little ones and a pool with waves. An area just for relaxing, a bar, an ice-cream parlour, a crêperie and a fast-food restaurant are also at your disposal.

Le Jardin des Papillons – ⬚ – *16 r. du Port – 33470 Le Teich –* ☎ *05 57 52 33 53 – www.lejardindespapillons.com – early Apr to early Jul: daily 11am-6pm; early Jul to early Aug: daily 10am-7pm; early Aug to end Sep: daily 2pm-5pm – closed end Sep to early Apr.* The biggest collection of exotic butterflies and moths in France! Enter into a fairyland of a tropical garden, where hundreds of brightly coloured butterflies fly about in total freedom, fluttering over waterfalls, tropical plants and... you. Free parking, playground and picnic ground.

Zooland Park – 🖼 – *D 112 – rte de Cazaux – 33260 La Teste-de-Buch – ☎ 05 56 54 71 44 – Apr to Sep: daily 10am-7pm; Oct to Mar: Sat-Sun, national and school holidays: 2pm-6pm.* This zoo is under the patronage of the football player Jean-Pierre Papin. It houses around 50 big cats and has the largest bear enclosure in Europe. If you visit between May and September, your children will be able to satisfy their budding nurturing instincts by giving young lambs the milk bottle.

Les Viviers d'Aquitaine – *62 Digue-est des Ostréiculteurs – 33260 La Teste-de-Buch – ☎ 05 57 52 56 60 – daily 8am-noon, 3pm-7pm.* Take a veritable gastronomic stroll among the different pools along this oyster-breeders' dike with a superb view of the La Teste port and its picturesque cabins. You can buy oysters, clams, mussels, winkles, whelks, crabs, prawns or crayfish to eat in or take home.

Oyster-breeding villages – Le Canon, Le Four, Les Jacquets, L'Herbe…Oyster-breeding villages alternate with beaches along the edge of the Bassin d'Arcachon; crates and lime-washed tiles lie in front of their wooden huts (those of L'Herbe, one of the most picturesque villages, are always freshly painted).

D 106 wends its way between the edge of the forest and the shore of the lagoon.

Arès – Arès was originally an oyster port; it now also harbours pleasure boats and is a seaside resort. A Romanesque church stands on the town's central square. Inside, the carved capitals of the columns are illuminated by modern stained-glass windows. The round tower (restored) on the water-front was once part of a windmill.

From Arès to Biganos, the road passes through a landscape of endless pine forests, linking the towns and villages along the lagoon's eastern shore.

Andernos-les-Bains – This sheltered site at the far end of the lagoon has been inhabited by man since prehistoric times. Today, the town is one of the major local resorts, very popular in summer, with beaches stretching for over 4km/2mi and a casino.
Opposite the beach and next to the small church of St-Éloi, with its 11C apse, lie traces of a 4C Gallo-Roman basilica.
The jetty offers extensive views over the lagoon, the town's oyster port, the beaches and the marina.

Lanton – The restored Romanesque church (12C apse and nave walls) incorporates an oven-vaulted, raised apse of a restrained and cohesive design. Framing the central bay, twinned columns support capitals decorated with pine cones and herons *(left)* and stylised leaf motifs *(right)*.

Audenge – The town, an oyster-farming centre, is also known for its fish reservoirs (a system of locks which encloses the catch at low tide).

Beyond Biganos take D 3^{E12} to join D 650. Opposite the junction is the impressive smoking bulk of the Cellulose du Pin paper mill, visible for miles around.

The route crosses the inner end of the marshy Eyre delta *(bridge over the river)* and follows the lagoon's southern shore, which remains pleasantly leafy all the way to the outskirts of Le Teich.

★ **Parc Ornithologique du Teich** – 🖼 The **nature reserve** Ⓥ covers a surface area of 120ha/300 acres in the Eyre delta, including 80ha/200 acres of water used in the past for fish breeding and now linked to Arcachon lagoon via a system of locks. The reserve promotes the preservation of species of wild fowl threatened with extinction, and encourages the public to discover European bird species.

Bird sanctuary

A traditional stopover in the spring and autumn for tens of thousands of migratory birds (such as the spoonbill, greylag goose and black-headed gull), the meadows and dikes along the Eytre and around the old fish tanks also shelter numerous birds in the winter including teal, dunlin and cormorant. There are also nesting species such as a colony of herons consisting of more than 1 000 couples of common heron, little egret and cattle egret. In summer, the rare bluethroat rewards patient visitors with his pure song and vibrant colours.
The rich, varied vegetation will delight botany enthusiasts: wild berries (arbutus, brambles) highly appreciated by the frugivorous species; water irises, rushes and oaks planted to consolidate the dikes, as well as tamarisk and alders used by ducks and moorhens to build their nests.

Low-tide fishing

At low tide, the Archachon lagoon offers the possibility of fishing for shellfish and other seafood.

Cockles and **clams** can be gathered by just scraping the surface of the sand to a depth of 4cm/2in. Clams are easier to locate as two small holes in the sand indicate their presence. They can be found in large numbers near the Arquin sandbank and on the mudflats uncovered at low tide. It is advisable to leave them to sweat in salt water for a few hours before eating them.

Winkles can be gathered by hand on the mudflats. In order to eat them as an appetizer before a meal, it is necessary to plunge them for a few minutes in boiling water.

Wild **mussels**, found near the oyster beds, can be dislodged with a knife.

Green crabs also abound on the beaches at low tide; they can be caught with a net and cooked in seasoned boiling water.

Fishing for **shrimps** is done with the help of a net.

As for gathering **razor-shells**, it is real fun. They can be detected by the key-shaped mark they leave on the sand; place two or three grains of coarse salt on this mark to trick them into coming up to the surface as they believe the high tide is returning. Razor-shells are not a refined kind of seafood but they make an excellent bait for line fishing.

Gathering oysters, even wild ones, is strictly forbidden.

Fishing for cockles and clams is on the other hand allowed but restricted to 2kg/4lb per person at every tide. Shell-gathering is sometimes forbidden for health reasons (in case of excessive heat for instance). Be careful when walking on mudflats as there is always a risk of getting bogged down.

The reserve is divided into four parks: Les Artigues, La Moulette, Causseyre and Claude Quancard.

🚶 The visitor is given a choice of tours on foot, all well marked and equipped with look-outs: the short tour (2.4km/1.5mi), the long tour (3.6km/2mi) and the complete tour (6km/3.6mi). *We recommend that you rent binoculars.*

Gujan-Mestras – This busy town with its six oyster farms is the oyster capital of the Arcachon area. It is extremely picturesque with tile-roofed cabins, canals crowded with fishing smacks, oyster-purging tanks and waterfront kiosks where oysters can be sampled, ordered and dispatched to family or friends.

Parc ornithologique du Teich – Stork

In the port of Larros, at the **Maison de l'Huître** Ⓥ, an exhibition and film explain the different stages of oyster-farming, from preparation of the collectors to consumption. A *pinasses* yard (local fishing smacks) and oyster-packaging unit are visible.

You can then sample and compare oysters in fishermen's huts in the heart of the port of Larros.

Parc de Loisirs de la Hume – Ⓒ The park, at the intersection of N 250 and D 652, offers a range of leisure facilities including a "**medieval**" **miniature golf** Ⓥ; **Aqualand** Ⓥ, a water park; and **La Coccinelle** Ⓥ, a menagerie for younger visitors, where they can feed lambs, kids and calves themselves.

La Teste-de-Buch – La Teste was once the capital of the former kingdom of the Buch family and is now part of one of the biggest municipalities (18 000ha/44 500 acres) in France. Settled by the Boli or Boians before the Roman colonisation, it was later developed by the English and subsequently became an important oyster port. Today the municipality includes the ancient forest of La Teste, Cazaux and its lake *(south)*, and the resorts of Pyla-sur-Mer and Pilat-Plage with its famous dune *(south-west)*.

Note, near the tourist office in place Jean-Hameau, the façade of the 18C **Maison Lalanne**, adorned with representations of an anchor, rigging and the heads of the owner's children.

Dune du Pilat

⌂⌂ **Arcachon** – *See ARCACHON.*

The road passes through the neighbouring resort of Moulleau and then Pyla-sur-Mer and Pilat-Plage, where hotels and villas are scattered beneath the pines, before climbing in a series of hairpin bends towards the famous dune.

★★ **Dune du Pilat** – This colossal sand dune, at 114m/374ft the highest in Europe, is 2.7km/over 1.5mi long and 500m/550yd wide. Created by the combined action of wind, waves and the land itself, the dune is still constantly changing. The west face slopes gently towards the Atlantic rollers, whereas the hollowed landward side to the east drops sharply to the woodland pines below.

To reach the summit, either scale the flank of the dune (a fairly difficult ascent) or climb the 154-step staircase *(in summer only)*. From the top, the **panorama**★★ over the ocean and the forests of the Landes – the finest of all views over the Silver Coast – is breathtaking, especially at sunset.

AUBETERRE-SUR-DRONNE★

Population 365
Michelin map 324: L-8 or 233 folds 40, 41

Aubeterre is a very old village, one of the finest in France, with steep, narrow streets, huddled in a semicircle at the foot of its castle, high above the green pastureland of the Dronne Valley. The village stands out against a line of white chalk cliffs, which give Aubeterre its name (*alba terra* in Latin meaning white land).

The village is centred around place Trarieux, a quiet square containing a bust of Ludovic Trarieux, native of Aubeterre and founder of *La Ligue pour la Défense des Droits de l'Homme et du Citoyen* (the League for the Defence of Human Rights). From here, visitors can climb up to Église St-Jacques, or walk down to the monolithic church.

CHURCHES

★★**Monolithic Church** ⊘ – The church, dedicated to St John, is one of a rare type which has been hewn from a single, solid block of rock. Another example of a monolithic church is to be found in St-Émilion near Bordeaux. A passageway lined with funerary recesses leads to a vast rocky cavern, whose crude materials and stark interior make it a captivating and impressive sight. The 5C or 6C baptismal font, carved in the form of a Greek cross, indicates the existence of a previous church, at the time when baptism by immersion was practised. The crypt would have housed worshipers of Mithras, the ancient Persian deity. The main rival of early Christianity, this cult, characterised by the sacrifice of a bull whose blood was used to baptise worshipers, was spread throughout Gaul by the soldiers of the Roman empire.

Work on the church probably began in the 12C, to house the relics of the Holy Sepulchre from Jerusalem, brought back from the Crusades by Pierre II de Castillon, owner of the nearby castle. Used as a saltpetre works during the Revolution, it was the local cemetery until 1865.

The 12C nave, which runs parallel to the cliff, is 20m/69ft high. A small spring still filters up through the single side-aisle. Its waters were no doubt considered beneficial and venerated by the early pilgrims. The apse houses a solid rock reliquary of monumental size set aside when the church was hewn. It used to enclose the shrine containing the relics of the Holy Sepulchre. At the opposite end of the nave is the original 6C chapel, turned into a necropolis in the 12C when the church was refurbished. A series of tombs have been hollowed out of the rock.

In the upper part of the nave, a gallery with a suspended ambulatory affords an interesting view of this once primitive place

Monolithic church

of worship. In former times, a castle stood above the church, linked by a hidden staircase still visible today, providing the lords of the castle with easy access to the gallery, from which they could spy on the congregation and attend religious services.

Église St-Jacques – This former Benedictine abbey church has a Romanesque west front enhanced by arcading delicately carved with geometric motifs in Moorish style. Note in particular the interesting frieze on the left of the central doorway, which depicts the various tasks to be performed throughout the year.

Below the church, a machicolated tower guards the residential quarters of the chapter.

Église St-Pierre d'AULNAY ★★

Michelin map 322: G-3 or 233 fold 17

Église St-Pierre-de-la-Tour, standing on the borders of Poitou and the Saintonge, along the age-old pilgrims' route to Santiago de Compostela, rises in solitary state among the dark cypresses of an ancient cemetery *(on the side of D 950, NW of the village)*.

★★ CHURCH

The rare harmony of the composition, the abundant and ornate yet restrained decoration, and the warm patina of old stone combine to make this 12C church a masterpiece of regional Romanesque architecture.

The best overall view of the church is from the far end of the cemetery, just to the left of the west front.

West front – The west front is crowned with small lanterns. In its centre stands a porch of broken arches flanked by blind arcades forming funerary niches. The Crucifixion of St Peter is carved on the tympanum of the northern arcade. On the southern tympanum, Christ in Majesty is seen with two figures presumably representing St Peter and St Paul.

The receding arches behind the archivolt are carved with graceful sculptures illustrating the favourite themes of the Poitou image makers – 1st arch *(below)*, angels worshipping the Lamb of God; 2nd arch, Virtues exterminating Vices; 3rd arch, the Wise *(left)* and Foolish Virgins; on the 4th arch, Signs of the Zodiac and Labours of the Months. The central blind bay on the upper level of the façade once framed a statue of the Emperor Constantine on a horse.

St-Pierre d'Aulnay

121

Transept – The square belfry-tower, which stands over the transept crossing, served as a landmark for pilgrims and other travellers. The arching over the **south transept doorway** features rows of superbly carved figures and animals. The carvings are as follows.

Outer arch: mythological characters and creatures – the musical ass, a goat, a deer, an owl, and a mermaid.

3rd arch: the Old Men of the Apocalypse – 31 here instead of the usual 24 – each holding a phial of perfume and a musical instrument. The intrados (underside) of the arch is carved with kneeling atlantes (male figures used as pillars).

2nd arch: the Disciples of Christ and the Apostles (seated atlantes adorn the intrados).

Inner arch: animals (centaurs, griffins) and foliage of Eastern inspiration in light relief. A tall opening above the porch features a central arch adorned with four fine sculptures of the Virtues conquering the Vices.

East end – On each side of the axial window, strange, Eastern-style wreaths of foliage encircle enigmatic figures.

Interior – The nave is roofed with broken-barrel vaulting and buttressed by tall aisles. Note the unusually deep openings, narrower on the north side than on the south, and the massive pillars cut by two layers of capitals.

A handsome dome on pendentives crowns the inside of the transept crossing, its ribs radiating from a circular opening through which bells in the tower above can be rung.

The capitals in the church, especially those in the transept, are exceptionally fine with carvings of tiny eared elephants *(south transept, by the entrance to the aisle)*, Samson, sleeping, being bound by Delilah while a Philistine cuts his hair with enormous scissors *(north-west pillar, transept crossing)* and imps pulling the beard of a poor man *(north transept, entrance to the aisle)*.

Cemetery – The burial ground, strewn with tombstones in the form of sarcophagi, still has its 15C **hosanna cross**, complete with lectern from which the priest read the lessons on Palm Sunday, and the canopied statues of Saints Peter, Paul, James and John.

BAYONNE★★

Conurbation 178 965
Michelin map 342: D-4 or 234 fold 29

Bayonne lies near the coast on the boundary between the Landes and the Basque country, where the River Nive joins the Adour.

The heart of this lively and interesting town combines good shopping facilities with picturesque old streets, ramparts and quays on the south bank of the Adour. The main ramparts extend from the 16C Château Vieux (Old Castle) to the Spanish Gate. **Parc de Mousserolles**, on the eastern side of the town known as Petit Bayonne, is a pleasant place for a stroll, with children's playgrounds and a small lake. The citadel overlooking the suburb of St-Esprit, on the northern bank of the river, was built by Vauban.

At the beginning of August, **traditional festivities★** – bullfights, fairs and folklore activities – go on day and night. "For six days, boys and girls frolic from the Nive to the Adour", as a popular song tells it.

HISTORICAL NOTES

In the 12C, Bayonne was part of the dowry of **Eleanor of Aquitaine**. When Eleanor's second husband, Henry Plantagenet, assumed the crown of England in 1154, Bayonne became English, and remained so for three centuries.

During the Hundred Years War, a naval force from Bayonne served with the English fleet. The port was bursting with merchandise and the town flourished. However, after the city fell to the French in 1451, the integration of Bayonne into the Kingdom of France brought heavy penalties. A war indemnity had to be paid and the English market, which had made the town prosperous, was lost.

The French Kings encroached on local freedom more than their English counterparts, and laws and legal documents which they decreed, from then on, had to be written in French and not in Gascon. This created deep-rooted resentment among the inhabitants of Bayonne. In the 16C, Charles IX decided to re-open the port, which in the meantime had silted up. The direct channel to the sea was completed in 1578 and trading began again.

Zenith – The prosperity of Bayonne reached its peak in the 18C. The Chamber of Commerce was founded in 1726. Trade with Spain, Holland and the West Indies together with cod-fishing off Newfoundland and local shipbuilding, gave the port as much business as it could handle.

Bayonne was declared a free port in 1784, and this trebled its traffic. In the same year, it was included in the famous series by the painter Joseph Vernet, *Great Ports of France*. The spoils of war on the high seas were considerable, and affluent citizens commissioned many privateers. The Ministers of Louis XIV – Seignelay, the eldest son of Colbert, and Pontchartrain – officially decreed a system of dividing the spoils: one-tenth was to go to the Admiral of France, two-thirds to the ship-owners, and what was left to the crew. A sum was also set aside for widows, orphans and ransoms to release prisoners from the Barbary pirates.

The town's Corporation of Ironworkers and Armourers is well known: their members invented the **bayonet** – named after Bayonne and first used by the French infantry in 1703.

Eating out

BUDGET

Le Bayonnais – *38 quai des Corsaires* – ☎ *05 59 25 61 19* – *closed 1-15 May, 1-7 Aug, Nov, Mon-Tue* – *14.94€*. With a name like Le Bayonnais, this restaurant on the docks of the Nive has no choice but to serve native cooking, and the owner does just that, concocting local dishes with great care. Photos and posters tip their beret to Basque sports. Our kind of address.

MODERATE

Itsaski – *43 quai Jauréguiberry* – ☎ *05 59 46 13 96* – *closed Sun evening and Tue* – *19.06€*. This restaurant open on the docks of the Nive is often packed. The dining room with its boat-like interior design is a hit, as is the seafood-rich cuisine. The terrace looks out on the Petit Bayonne.

El Asador – *19 r. Vieille-Boucherie* – ☎ *05 59 59 08 57* – *closed 17-30 Jun, 3 wks in Dec, Sun evening and Mon* – *26.22/39.63€*. The grilled specialities *à la plancha* of this little restaurant transport one to the Spanish Basque country. The owner, who prepares local dishes with passion and talent, is quite proud of the freshness of her fish and prawns. Images of San Sebastian in the 1930s on the walls.

Where to stay

BUDGET

M. et Mme Ladeuix Bed and Breakfast – *26 av. Salvador-Allende* – *40220 Tarnos* – *5km/3mi N of Bayonne via N 10* – ☎ *05 59 64 13 95* – ⌷ – *5 rooms: 38/46€*. Silence lovers, this place is for you. A park with oaks, chestnuts, mimosas, banana trees, pears, maples... A vast lawn with a pool, a pen where ewes graze near the rabbit hutches and chicken cages... The rooms are simple but comfortable. Self-catering cottage for four.

MODERATE

Grand Hôtel – *21 r. Thiers* – ☎ *05 59 59 62 00* – *closed Feb, Sat-Sun from Oct to Apr* – ⌷ – *54 rooms: 76.22/108.24€* – ⌷ *9.15€* – *restaurant 21.34/27.44€*. Close by the cathedral, this traditional hotel proposes rooms with a slightly passé charm. Ask for one on the far side – they're quieter. Small, luminous dining room under a glass roof.

On the town

Le Petit Bayonne – *Le Petit-Bayonne*. Right where the River Nive meets the Adour, the Petit Bayonne is the quarter where the city's young folk gather – the beating heart of local nightlife. As soon as the weather warms up, so does the general party atmosphere, thanks to the bars and restaurants crowding the neighbourhood. Between rue des Cordeliers, rue Pannecau and rue des Tonneliers, there are a good 30 establishments. Among them, you may want to try the Txalupa (26, rue des Cordeliers) and the Killarney Pub (35, rue des Cordeliers).

Chai Ramina – *11 r. Poissonnerie* – ☎ *05 59 59 33 01* – *Tue-Thu 10am-8pm, Fri-Sat until 2am*. Ramina, a former rugby champion, found a new calling 25 years ago when he became the hub of his pub, a buddies' bar where native Bayonnais come horse around like kids. If whisky outshines other potions here, blame the menu – there are 300 varieties to choose from!

Killarney Pub – *33 r. des Cordeliers* – ☎ *05 59 25 75 51* – *Mon-Sat 4pm-2am*. This is one of the rare bars in the Petit Bayonne quarter with a more mature clientele. Beer is the forte of this long pub with wood furnishings and parquet. Occasional blues or French pop concerts.

Showtime

Arènes de Bayonne – *Av. Alfred-Bouland* – ☎ *05 59 46 61 00 or 05 53 25 48 19* – *daily 9:30am-12:30pm, 3pm-6:30pm*. From bull fighting to pop concerts, a large variety of shows are organized in the Bayonne arenas.

La Luna Negra – *R. des Augustins* – ☎ *05 59 25 78 05* – *Tue-Sat 7pm-2am* – *closed Sep*. Art in all its manifestations is the star of this dynamic café-theatre that offers a different show every evening: plays, songfests, cabarets, one-man shows, jazz, blues or rock concerts, story-telling sessions and readings of great literary works... Painting and photography exhibitions are also organized regularly.

Théâtre de Bayonne – *Pl. de la Liberté* – ☎ *05 59 59 07 27* – *snbayonne@wanadoo.fr* – *information/reservations: Tue-Fri 1pm-6pm, Sat 10am-1pm, 3pm-6pm* – *closed mid to late Aug, public holidays*. This is the national theatre of Bayonne and the Sud Aquitain. All sorts of performances are put on here – plays, dance, opera... They hold a yearly festival called Jazz in the Ramparts in mid-July.

Shopping

M. Leoncini – *37 r. Vieille-Boucherie* – ☎ *05 59 59 18 20* – *Mon-Fri 10am-noon, 4pm-6:30pm, Sat 10am-noon*. Mr Leoncini is one of the last craftsmen to continue the *makila*-making tradition. A *makila* is a Basque cane used for hiking and defence made of medlar wood, sculpted while still green, that contains a long, sharp blade.

Marché des Halles – *Quai Cdt-Roquebert* – *Mon-Sat 8am-1pm*. Located on the banks of the Nive, this traditional market delights the senses with its vivid colours and heady aromas.

Maison Montauzer – *17 r. de la Salie* – ☎ *05 59 59 07 68* – *Tue-Sat 7am-12:30pm, 3:30pm-7:30pm and Sun 7:30am-12:30pm* – *closed public holidays*. Among this delicatessen's specialities, their Ibaïona ham comes from pigs raised exclusively on Basque country grains. In accordance with tradition, it is dried 15 to 18 months outside, where it soaks up the flavours of the four seasons.

Pierre Ibaïalde – *41 r. des Cordeliers* – ☎ *05 59 25 65 30* – *pierre.ibaialde@wanadoo.fr* – *summer: Mon-Sat 10am-12:30pm, 2am-7pm; rest of the year: Tue-Sat 9am-12:30pm, 2pm-6pm*. After having visited this cottage-style canning factory, you'll know Bayonne ham from A to Z. Pierre Ibaïalde will explain each step of the ham-making process and will invite you to taste his products, ham and foie gras.

Chocolat Cazenave – *19 r. du Port-Neuf* – ☎ *05 59 59 03 16* – *school holidays: Mon-Sat 9am-noon, 2pm-7pm; general hours: Tue-Sat 9am-noon, 2pm-7pm* – *closed 3 weeks in Oct*. Early in the 17C, Bayonne was the first French city to produce chocolate. Of the numerous *chocolatiers* who set up shop in rue du Port-Neuf, only two remain: Cazenave (since 1854) and Daranatz (since 1930).

Sports and leisure

L'Aviron Bayonnais – *Garage de la Nive* – ☎ *05 59 63 33 15* – *www.aviron-bayonnais.asso.fr* – *office hours: Mon-Fri 9am-noon, 2pm-7pm, Sat 9am-noon* – *closed public holidays*. The ancient fortifications of Vauban are the setting for this distinctive tennis club, founded in 1922. If you don't care to come and play on one of the 12 courts, it's worthwhile just to come and watch. Two important tournaments take place at Easter and during the first fortnight of August.

Trinquet Moderne – *60 av. Dubrocq* – ☎ *05 59 59 05 22* – *daily from 9am*. Many bare-handed pelota matches take place between the glass walls of this covered *trinquet* (court). The French are among the finest players of this discipline internationally.

Trinquet St-André – *2 r. du Jeu-de-Paume* – ☎ *05 59 59 18 69* – *Mon-Sat 8:30am-10pm*. This 17C *trinquet* is among the oldest in France. The Basques come here for a game of *pala* before reconnoitring at the bar. Bare-handed matches are held from the first Thursday of October to the last Thursday of June. Wooden palettes are let for 20.12€ per hour (for four players).

Le Bayonne – *Allée Boufflers* – ☎ *06 80 74 21 51* – *www.perso.wanadoo.fr/david.ravel* – *all year by prior arrangement* – *closed from beginning to mid-Jan*. Embark on this boat for a scholarly visit of the River Adour and its tributaries. From geology to flora, from economics to fauna, every aspect of this rich region is revealed.

OLD TOWN *3 hr*

★ **Cathédrale Ste-Marie** – St Mary's Cathedral was built between the 13C and the 16C in the characteristic style of churches built in northern France. Initially, there was only one south tower. The north tower and both steeples were added in the 19C.

A 13C sculpted knocker, known as a sanctuary ring, is fixed to the north door, leading to the transept. Any fugitive criminal who seized the knocker was assured of sanctuary within the church.

Inside, the windows in the nave incorporate fine examples of Renaissance stained glass. In the second chapel on the right (dedicated to St Jerome), a splendid window dating from 1531 depicts *The Canaanite's Prayer*. In the sixth chapel, a commemorative plaque (1926) recalls the Miracle of Bayonne (a celestial apparition in 1451), when English Bayonne was under siege. According to legend, a great white cross surmounted by a crown appeared in the sky, and then the crown turned into a fleur-de-lis, the emblem of France. The townsfolk interpreted this as a sign from God that He wished them to be French, and so discarded the banners and pennants bearing the red cross of St George in favour of those bearing the white cross of France. The following day, Bayonne surrendered.

The harmonious lines and beautiful proportions within the cathedral can best be appreciated from the centre of the three-tiered nave, with its ribbed vaulting, triforium and clerestory windows.

Proceed to the ambulatory where the architecture is reminiscent of the Champagne region; the ribbed vaulting of the five radiating apsidal chapels was decorated by Steinheil at the end of the 19C.

★ **Cloisters** ⊙ – *Entrance from place Louis-Pasteur.* The three galleries which remain form a fine 14C Gothic ensemble, with attractive twinned bays. A number of ancient funerary stones can be seen.

From the south gallery, there is a fine view of the Cathedral and its windows, celebrated for their vast dimensions and unusual design.

Leave via the west door, turn right and then left onto rue de la Monnaie; continue as far as rue du Port-Neuf.

At the junction with rue Orbe, an attractive half-timbered house stands on the left.

Along the River Nive

Rue du Port-Neuf – This charming pedestrian precinct is lined with low arcades, beneath which famous pastry shops and confectioners tempt passers-by with mouth-watering displays of chocolates. The art of chocolate-making was brought to Bayonne in the 17C by Jews whose ancestors had been banished from Spain and Portugal.

Place de la Liberté – This is a busy square at the western end of Pont Mayou; the bridge crosses the River Nive at the northern end of the old town. The town hall, the local administrative offices and the theatre, all under the same roof, stand at one end of the square. The town's motto *nunquam polluta* (never spoilt) is engraved on the marble paving.

Walk along quai Dubourdieu then across Pont Marengo.

Petit Bayonne – This is the town's popular district; the narrow streets covered with graffiti are lined with small bars which come to life in the evening. The Musée Bonnat and Musée Basque are located in this area *(see below)*.

Cross back via Pont Pannecau.

Unfaithful or loose women used to be thrown over the bridge in an iron cage! The bridge leads to rue Poissonnerie; note the fine timber-framed house on the left.

Walk to the end of rue Poissonnerie then turn left onto rue d'Espagne and right onto rue Tour-de-Sault skirting the ramparts.

Botanical Gardens – Overlooking the ramparts is a Japanese-style botanical garden with over 1 000 perennials.

The shady lawns below are an ideal place to stroll.

ADDITIONAL SIGHTS

★★★ **Musée Bonnat** ⊙ – A chronological tour of the museum's works of art begins on the second floor, where the Primitive and Old Master paintings hang. Among those dating from the 14C and 15C, are a *Head of Christ Dead* from the Venetian School and a *Virgin and Child with Pomegranate* attributed to the School of Botticelli.

The carefully lit Rubens Room contains canvases showing *Apollo and Daphne* and *The Triumph of Venus*.

The 17C and 18C artists represented include Vouet *(Roman Charity)* and Tiepolo (study for the royal palace in Madrid). From the Spanish and English schools from the 17C to the early 19C, there are works by Ribera *(Woman Tearing Out Her Hair)*, Murillo *(San Salvador de Horta and the Inquisitor of Aragon)*, Goya *(Portrait of Don Francisco de Borja)*, Constable *(Hampstead Heath)* and Hoppner *(Head of a Woman)*. 19C French painting is represented by *The Oath of the Horati* (School of David), several works by Ingres including *The Bather, Study of a naked young Man* by Flandrin... and, on the first floor, paintings by Delacroix, Géricault, Degas, Puvis de Chavannes and Bonnat – the artist who assembled this superb collection during his long lifetime (1833-1922) and left it to his native town. His works are exhibited in a gallery surrounding the ground floor terrace (late 19C-early 20C wrought-iron balconies).

The museum's Drawings Department houses a selection by the Grand Masters, French and foreign; the display alternates various works from the collection. There is an archaeological display in the basement.

*** **Musée Basque et de l'histoire de Bayonne** Ⓥ – The newly re-opened museum, which was created in 1924, has a vast collection of objects, pictures and books which relate to the history and people of the Basque country and the western region of the Pyrenees. The **Maison Dagourette** houses the permanent collection, whereas the **Château-Neuf** site is used for temporary exhibits. The curatorial approach has been to enliven the ethnographic displays with music and images, creating a space, which is playful and dynamic as well as informative.

The exhibits are centred around the themes of work on the farm (shepherding, traditional crafts and cheese-making); architecture and interior furnishings; boats, shipping and other economic activities; games, sports, arts and music and religious traditions. The library and documentation centre is especially useful to scholars and researchers interested in the Basque country.

EXCURSIONS

* **Croix de Mouguerre** – *10km/6mi E. Exit Bayonne via D 312 – road to Bidache. Turn right and follow the mountain road through Mouguerre, then right again to the Crucifix.* This French national monument commemorates battles fought by the troops of Maréchal Soult against the invading English, Spanish and Portuguese troops, commanded by Wellington in 1813-14. There is a **panoramic view**★ of the Landes region, Bayonne, the Basque coast and the Pyrenees.

* **Route Impériale des Cimes** (Napoleon I's Scenic Highway) – *From Bayonne to Hasparren, 25km/15mi. Leave Bayonne to the SE by D 936. At the far end of St-Pierre-d'Irube turn right on D 22.*

  Napoleon I had this winding route carved out through the mountains, as part of a strategic link between Bayonne and St-Jean-Pied-de-Port. The **view**★ opens out on the Basque coastline and the summits of the Pyrenees nearest the sea – La Rhune, the jagged crest of Les Trois Couronnes and Le Jaizkibel, which at this distance looks like a steeply contoured island. As the road approaches **Hasparren** the Basque Pyrenees of the upper Nive basin stretch from La Rhune to L'Artzamendi.

BAZAS★

Population 4 379 – Michelin map 335: J-8 or 234 fold 15

Bazas stands encircled by decaying Gothic ramparts on a narrow promontory forming a prow above the Beuve Valley. The town is the capital of this region of fertile hills and has been the seat, since the 5C, of a bishopric (the title of which, since 1937, has belonged to the archbishop of Bordeaux).

The 4C Latin poet **Ausonius**, born in Burdigala (Bordeaux), stayed here several times. Recent excavations have brought to light foundations of the ancient *oppidum* (settlement), which date back to the 7C BC.

Place de la Cathédrale – This lovely square is lined with 16C and 17C houses. No 3 is decorated with astrological symbols (serious looking faces of the moon and the sun, oriental astrologer wearing a pointed hat...).

* **Cathédrale St-Jean** Ⓥ – The cathedral dates from the 13C-14C and was built on the model of the great Gothic sanctuaries of northern France. The blood of John the Baptist was venerated here. The west front is of an attractive and cohesive design, despite the differences in style between the three storeys. The first dates from the 13C, the second from the 16C, and the top storey, from the 18C.

Doorways – Their tympana and coving still have fine 13C sculptures which the locals saved from Protestant vandals by paying the sum of 10 000 *écus*. The central doorway shows the Last Judgement and the story of John the Baptist, and the side doors, the Virgin and St Peter.

Interior – The long, narrow nave, devoid of a transept, gives a striking impression of grandeur.

In the chancel, the Louis XV-style high altar in different coloured marbles is somewhat mannered. The axial chapel contains paintings by François Lemoyne (18C).

Jardin du Chapitre – This garden is a haven of peace located over the ramparts, on the right side of the cathedral. There is a fine view of the Beuve Valley.

Return to the cathedral and turn left (before the town hall) onto rue Théophile-Servière then walk along the Maurice-Lapierre ramp.

Promenade de la Brèche – Enjoy the walk under the lime trees, beneath the old ramparts covered with moss and ivy.

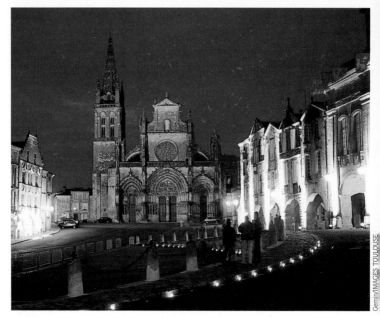

Bazas by night

EXCURSIONS

★ **Collégiale d'Uzeste** ⊘ – *11km/7mi W by D 110*. The collegiate church in the village of Uzeste is somewhat of a rival to Bazas Cathedral. **Pope Clement V** played a major part in building the church. He raised it to a collegiate church in 1312, and named it in his will as the site for his tomb.

Outside, note the arrangement of the east end and the belfry, the latter completed only in the 16C.

Enter the church by the south door, with its tympanum decorated with a fine Coronation of the Virgin. Behind the altar, holding a crucifix, thought to date from the 15C, lies the white marble figure of Clement V which was damaged by the Protestants. In the axial chapel is a 13C figure of the Virgin which was venerated by Pope Clement (born Bertrand de Got, in Villandrault) in his youth and, in the neighbouring chapel, a 14C funerary effigy.

Château de Villandraut ⊘ – *13km/8mi W along D 110 then D 3*. This striking example of Gothic castle architecture was built for Pope Clement V, who often stayed here. A fairly large area was for residential use, which was characteristic of medieval castles in Italy and the Middle East. The south side is more spectacular due to the alignment of its four large towers, the one on the right having been levelled in 1592 on the orders of the Parliament of Bordeaux.

Note the central postern, where channels for the portcullis and the store for the bludgeons can still be seen and which gives access to the interior courtyard.

★★ **Château de Roquetaillade** ⊘ – *11km7mi NW by D 3 and D 223 (right)*. This imposing medieval castle was built in 1306 by Cardinal Gaillard de la Mothe, a nephew of Pope Clement, and is part of an ensemble made up of two forts from the 12C and 14C within a single set of walls. Six enormous round towers, crenellated and pierced with arrow slits, surround a rectangular main body. Two of them flank the entrance. In the courtyard, there stands a powerful square keep and turret. The twinned and trefoil bays are characteristic of the castles owned by Pope Clement.

The castle was restored by Viollet-le-Duc in the late 19C.

The park contains one-hundred-year-old trees and a small **farm** ⊘ evoking 19C rural life.

★★ **Château de Cazeneuve** ⊘ – *10km/6mi SW by D 9*. The château rises on a rocky spur not far from Ciron Gorge. The original 11C encampment was superseded by a castle which became the stronghold of the lords of Albret in the 14C. It was handed over in 1572 to Henri III of Navarre, the future Henri IV of France. The castle was converted into a residential château in the 17C, and nowadays still belongs to descendants of the Albrets.

The only trace of the former town of Cazeneuve is a triumphal arch. Beyond this former entrance is the castle's south front, flanked by two square towers linked by a stone balustrade, and overlooking a dry moat. The gateway with its broken pediment leads through to the main courtyard, which is surrounded by two-storey medieval buildings, crowned with balustrades.

DINNER AT THE FARM...

Ferme-auberge Aux Repas Fermiers de Haoun Barrade – *34430 Cudos – 5km/3mi S of Bazas via D 932 dir. Mont-de-Marsan –* ☎ *05 56 25 44 55 – open 10 Jul to 1 Sep; lunch Sat-Sun and public holidays –* 🍽 *– 13/22.75€.* Plain and simple ambience in the countryside for discovering products made by farmers belonging to this co-op. Duck, kid, chicken, rabbit and young boar transformed into *rillettes*, *gibelotte*, or *blanquette au vin blanc* or *en civet*, are served here with the best local wines.

... BREAKFAST AT THE CHÂTEAU

Château d'Arbieu Bed and Breakfast – *D 655 –* ☎ *05 56 25 11 18 – arbieu@wanadoo.fr – closed Feb school holidays – 4 rooms: 80/95€.* A rocky road through the country leads to this 19C château with a vast park. Its spacious, regal rooms are graced with numerous handsome period pieces. Unwind in the reading room, or with a game of billiards or baby-foot.

Inside, the tour leads through the Consistorial Chamber to the ground floor gallery, which its Spanish leather smoking chairs (the smoker sat astride the chair and took his tobacco from a special compartment in the top of the chair back). On the first floor, Queen Margot's drawing room, entirely decorated in the Louis XV style, is adjacent to the Bedchamber of Louis XVI which contains memorabilia of Delphine de Sabran, beloved of Châteaubriand. At the end of the gallery is the 17C chapel, followed by the Bedchamber of Queen Margot and the Bed chamber of King Henri IV. This room, hung in dark red cloth, still has Henri IV's original four-poster bed (restored in the 18C). The tour ends with the dining room (beautiful faience soup tureen from Montpellier) and the kitchen with its Provençal bread box and kneading trough.

The grounds are planted with bamboos, sequoias, North American redwoods and parasol pines.

Château de Cazeneuve – Henri IV bedchamber

Le BÉARN★★

Michelin map 342: J-5 – 16 to K-8 or 234 folds 35, 39, 42, 43 and 47

Béarn, the largest of the formerly independent Pyrenees States, is crossed diagonally by Gave de Pau and Gave d'Oléron. Meadows and ploughed fields rise in terraces on either side of these fast-flowing streams, whereas orchards and vines flourish on the lower slopes of the long ridges above, mainly covered in moors.

In the southern part of the region, the Pyrenees rise to the dramatic heights of Pic du Midi d'Ossau (alt 2 884m/9 462ft) and Pic d'Anie (alt 2 504m/8 215ft). The route to the pass, Col d'Aubisque (alt 1 709m/5 610ft), linking Béarn to the Bigorre region through the mountains, is the most picturesque in the area.

The Béarnais people – The people of Béarn are used to an isolated existence. But unlike the Basques, they are very communicative. They often converse in a variant of the old Gascon tongue. Despite their apparent brusqueness, the people of Béarn are both courteous and witty.

Traditional Béarn can be seen most clearly during the 15 August procession at Laruns, in the Vallée d'Ossau. The men wear red jackets, waistcoats with wide lapels, knee breeches, gaiters and berets. The women are dressed in black or brown wide, pleated skirts, partly covered by a small lace apron. They also wear an embroidered shawl and a silk-lined, scarlet hood which falls to the shoulders. A white traditional *bonnette* crowns the women's plaited hair. Only "heiresses" can wear a red skirt and the family gold jewellery.

Young men and women dance the Ossau *Branle* (swing or shake) to the music of the three-hole *fluto* (a flageolet like the Basque *txirulä*) and tambourines – both played by the same musician.

In spite of its name, *sauce béarnaise* is not a local culinary speciality; it was invented in 1830 in the kitchens of the Pavillon Henri IV in St-Germain-en-Laye, near Paris. However... there is a connection: good King Henri IV was a native of Béarn!

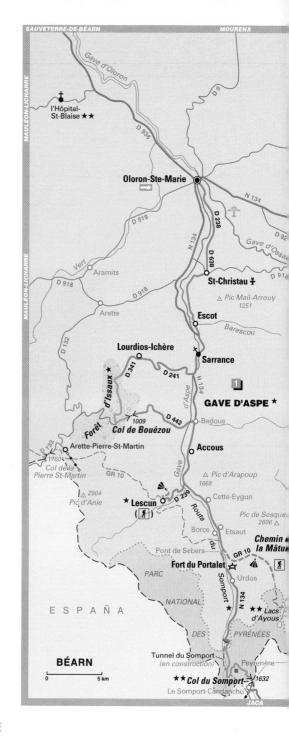

★GAVE D'ASPE

1 From Oloron-Ste-Marie to Col du Somport

66km/41mi – 3hr

Today, despite improvements to the roads and the opening in 1928 of a trans-Pyrenean railway (currently not operating south of Bedous), the glaciated valley of the Gave d'Aspe – narrowing into wild gorges, opening out sometimes into fertile basins – retains all the harshness of its mountain heritage. The villages here make no concession to being picturesque or charming. The occasional bear (these days protected by the

National Parks authority) still roams the lonely forests. The population of the long valley now numbers less than 5 000. However, the Somport Tunnel linking Pau and Zaragossa should bring considerable changes and breathe new life into this area.

One of its famous emigrants was Pierre Laclède (1729-78), who was born in Bedous and later founded the city of St Louis, Missouri.

Oloron-Ste-Marie – *See OLORON-STE-MARIE.*

Leave Oloron to the SE via rue d'Aspe.

The road, following the east bank of the Aspe, crosses a rural valley planted with maize and wheat, divided occasionally by windbreaks of poplar trees. Ahead, Pic Mail-Arrouy (alt 1 251m/4 100ft) appears to block any passage south.

Eating out

MODERATE

La Pimparela – *plateau d'Ipère - 64490 Osse-en-Aspe* – ☎ *05 59 34 52 23* – ☒ – *reserv. required off-season* – *9.15/22.87€*. Perched above the Aspe valley, this authentic mountain stable is set amid fields covered with *pimparelas* (daisies). A delightful array of home-made products to savour on the terrace or in the charming dining room featuring floral bouquets and blue-tinted wood.

Auberge Chez Lazare – *64800 Nay* – *3km/1.8mi SW of Nay via D 36 and D 287* – ☎ *05 59 61 05 26* – *closed Sun evening* – *11.43/21.34€*. An agreeable family auberge in the middle of the countryside – at the crack of dawn you're sure to hear the neighbour's cock crowing. Simple rooms. Several fixed-price, regional menus. Order ahead to try the menu based on the *poule au pot*, a traditional favourite.

Auberge Bellevue – *55 r. Bourguet* – *64440 Laruns* – *6km/3.6mi W of Eaux-Bonnes via D 918 and D 934* – ☎ *05 59 05 31 58* – *closed 5 Jan to 20 Feb, Tue evening and Wed* – *11.89/28.97€*. A nice little family auberge in a chalet. Once you've settled in on the terrace, you'll be loath to leave – the regional cuisine is flavoursome and the view of the mountains is lovely.

Where to stay

MODERATE

La Ferme aux Sangliers Bed and Breakfast – *Micalet* – *64570 Issor* – *10km/6mi W of St-Christau via D 918 to Asasp, then N 134 and D 918 dir. Arette* – ☎ *05 59 34 43 96* – ☒ – *reserv. required* – *5 rooms: 36.58/48.78€* – *meals 13.71€*. Tastefully restored with the original farm in mind, this isolated house is remarkably situated facing the Pyrenees. Pretty rooms with a blend of stones and exposed beams. Try the home-made products, notably the *civet de sanglier* made from boar raised in the park.

Chez Rolande Augareils Bed and Breakfast – *6 pl. Cazenave* – *64260 Buzy* – *4km/2.4mi N of Arudy via D 920* – ☎ *05 59 21 01 01* – *rolande.augareils@wanadoo.fr* – *closed Oct to Easter* – ☒ – *5 rooms: 37.35/45.73€* – *meals 15.24/24.39€*. Behind its wrought-iron fence, this is a lovely house with a courtyard and flower-filled windows. Charming rooms with family furniture and lacework, but without heating. You'll be invited to share real Bearnaise cuisine with your hospitable hosts.

MID-RANGE

Hôtel Au Bon Coin – *rte des Thermes* – *64660 Lurbe-St-Christau* – ☎ *05 59 34 40 12* – *closed Sun evening and Mon from 10 Oct to 30 Mar* – ▯ – *18 rooms: 42.69/65.55€* – ☒ *6.86€* – *restaurant 13.72/44.21€*. This long edifice surrounded by trees faces the countryside. The rooms are modern and comfortable; half of them have a view of the mountains. Meals are served in the rustic dining room or on the veranda. Garden with a pool across the way.

Kangaroo Zoo

Zoo d'Asson – Parc aux Kangourous – ▣ – *Chemin Nay – 64800 Asson* – ☎ *05 59 71 03 34* – *daily 8am-dusk*. This 35-year-old zoo is home for 60 kangaroos of five distinct species, including the two-coloured wallaby and the big red and grey Australian kangaroo. Some 400 other mammals, such as the lion tamarin and the blue-headed monkey, live in the park.

St-Christau – The air in this small spa is fresh and cool. The waters are rich in iron and copper and the cure centre, standing in a 60ha/148 acre park, specialises in treating troubles of the mucous membranes.

Escot – This was the first Aspe village, strikingly perched on a terrace at the mouth of Vallée du Barescou. In accordance with the local *for*, the Viscount of Béarn had to exchange hostages with representatives of the valley before setting foot in Escot. Louis IX, on a pilgrimage to Notre-Dame-de-Sarrance, indicated that he was leaving his own kingdom by ordering his sword-bearer to lower his blade.

Sarrance – Sarrance, a place of local pilgrimage was visited by both Louis XI (1461) and Marguerite d'Angoulême (Queen of Navarre), who wrote part of her book of tales, *Heptameron*, here. The **church**, rebuilt in 1609, has a very Baroque octagonal belfry-porch with concave sides surmounted by a lantern. Inside, are 15C wooden panels with naïve carving. The **cloisters** of the former 17C monastery have a slate roof supported by 14 small transverse gables.

At Bedous, a pronounced humpback rise affords an unexpected view of the valley's central basin and its seven villages. In the background the crests of Arapoup are visible and, to the right in the distance, the first summits of the Lescun cirque (Pic de Burcq).

The road again enters a narrow gorge.

Turn right to Lescun.

* **Lescun** – Lescun is a favourite village with mountain lovers, owing to the surrounding cirque with its needle-sharp limestone peaks.

 To admire the full **panorama****, park in the car park behind Hôtel du Pic d'Anie and walk to the viewpoint *(30min round trip on foot)*. Follow the GR10 footpath as far as the church.

Lescun

Beyond a public wash-house with a crucifix, the footpath winds around a hillock. From here, looking back, there is a fine view of Pic d'Anie to the right and, to the left, Le Billare and Dec de Lhurs.

The **Route du Somport*** *(N 134)* continues to climb the valley, which is now an almost continuous succession of gorges and narrow passes. The villages, built in pairs on opposite sides of the valley, seem to be watching over one another (Eygun and Cette, Etsaut and Borce).

Chemin de la Mâture – *From Pont de Sebers – 3hr round trip on foot along the GR10 footpath. This route is not for those who suffer from vertigo. The path, completely exposed to sun and wind, twists above sheer drops with no railings or other protection.*

18C naval engineers carved out this passage, often blasted from the solid rock, to provide wood cutters with access to the trees in Le Pacq Woods. The timber was then transported along this route down to Vallée d'Apse. When the river was high, the logs were tied into rafts and floated down to the naval shipyards in Bayonne. From the pathway there are views of the upper part of Portalet Fort.

Turn back after reaching the meadows of the upper basin.

Fort du Portalet – This stronghold is perched on a sheer cliff above the river in one of the narrowest, most steep-sided sections of the valley. It was built in the early 19C, and later used for the internment of prominent anti-Nazis during the Occupation (1941-45). From the road, the walled ramps leading to the casemates commanding the road to Urdos can be seen.

Leaving the gorge, the peaks marking the Spanish border appear as a jagged crest cut through by Pas d'Aspe. The scene is dominated by Pico de la Garganta (2 636m/8 660ft), which is usually flecked with snow.

Beyond Urdos, on the left, is Arnousse Viaduct.

** **Col du Somport** – At an altitude of 1 632m/5 351ft, this pass (the only one in the Central Pyrenees accessible the whole year round) has been famous since the passage of the Roman legions. Until the 12C, it was used by pilgrims on the way to Santiago de Compostela. An important staging post at the time was St Christine's Hospice (now demolished) on the southern slopes of the range.

The high ground behind the restaurant affords an impressive view of the Aragon Pyrenees on the far side of the border.

The blue hues of this distant panorama form an attractive contrast with the green of the forests and the reddish tones of the rocks in the foreground.

Le tunnel du Somport

This rail tunnel, linking Forges d'Abel to Canfranc in Spain, was inaugurated in 1928. The tunnel, nearly 8km/5mi long, was designed to take trains from Pau, in France, through Vallée d'Aspe, and into Spain. Unfortunately, this technical feat (in particular the spiral tunnel after Arnousse viaduct) did not meet with the commercial success anticipated. As it was not linked to any main road routes, the railway proved uneconomical and after the collapse of a bridge in 1970, the SNCF (French railways) decided to close the line and the tunnel. The French and Spanish governments have recently completed a road tunnel between Peyrenère and Canfranc, parallel to the disused rail tunnel, providing a trans-Pyrenean link between Pau and Zaragossa.

★★ LE HAUT OSSAU *See Le Haut OSSAU.*

★ FRANGE DES PYRÉNÉES

2 Round tour from Pau

79km/49mi – about 4hr 30min

Leave Pau to the SW via the suburb of Jurançon; N 134 follows the valley of the River Nez. At Gan turn left on D 24.

Notre-Dame-de-Piétat – Opposite the 17C pilgrims' chapel, at the end of the esplanade, there is a roadside crucifix. Behind this is a viewing table providing a **panorama**★ of the Gave de Pau Valley and its many villages. Pic du Midi de Bigorre is visible in the distance *(southeast)*, beyond the line of wooded foothills, along with the Vignemale, Grand Gabizos and Caperan de Sesques *(south)*.

Continue to D 37 and turn right along the valley.

Between Pardies-Piétat and Nay the road passes through several pretty Béarn villages whose splendid houses have gateways decorated with piers surmounted by stone urns.

Nay – Nay (pronounced to rhyme with "high") is a *bastide* typical of the Béarn region.

The **Musée du Béret** ⊙, situated at the entrance of the village, relates the history of the genuine beret from Béarn and illustrates the various stages of its manufacture.

In the main square, the **Maison Carrée**, also called Maison de Jeanne d'Albret, was built in the Renaissance period. The inner Florentine-style courtyard shows three classical forms of architecture and is a unique example of this style in south-west France.

Asson – *3km/1.8mi W of the village (towards Bruges) a road branches off to the Jardin Exotique.* This one-time agricultural show place, now converted into a **zoo** ⊙ ⌂, is home to a raucous and colourful collection of parrots, parakeets, pink Cuban flamingos, emus, lorikeets, chimpanzees and gibbons, as well as a colony of lemurs from Madagascar.

The road continues through a series of villages with flower-filled gardens. Fields of maize make way for orchards, and these in turn are succeeded by trellised vines. As the road drops down finally to the Lower Ossau Valley, the stone belfry of **Louvie-Juzon church**, with its distinctive outline of an inverted chalice, comes slowly into view.

Turn right onto N 134 beyond Louvie-Juzon.

Arudy – Industrially, this is the most developed town in Lower Ossau, due to the surrounding marble quarries and the various factories (components for aircraft landing gear, cold lamination) built on the outskirts.

Maison d'Ossau ⊙, a 17C house near the east end of the church, contains displays on prehistoric life in the Pyrenees (diagrams, charts and exhibits from excavations illustrate the evolution of tools and implements) in its basement. The former residential rooms on the ground floor include an exhibit on the flora, fauna and geology of Vallée d'Ossau.

Displays on the attic floor are devoted to the history of the valley and the life of the local shepherds.

To return to Pau, follow D 920 to Buzy then turn right onto D 34 which leads back to N 134.

★★★ ROUTE DE L'AUBISQUE

③ Round tour from Eaux-Bonnes

107km/66mi – allow one day

As a rule, Col d'Aubisque (Aubisque Pass) is blocked by snow from November to June. The cliff road beyond Col de l'Aubisque is very narrow which makes it difficult for vehicles to pass one another. Consequently, traffic alternates every 2hr.

Eaux-Bonnes – This spa, nestling in the wooded Vallée du Valentin, offers thermal cures initially developed by the great doctor from Béarn, Théophile de Bordeu, to treat respiratory disorders. The "promenades" laid out in the 19C in the wooded foothills of the Gourzy, are witness to the refined appreciation of nature and the creature comforts of the times.
The esplanade in Darralde Gardens, bordered by mansions typical of Second Empire spas, is the hub of local activity.

Turn left to Aas.

Aas – In this village typical of the Ossau region, with its steep, narrow streets, some of the locals still use the whistling language once used by shepherds to communicate with one another throughout the valley, at distances of up to 2 500m/7 000ft. A similar language is also used on Gomera Island in the Canaries, the villages of the Görele Valley in Turkey and by the Maztec and Zapatec Indians in Mexico.

The road crosses the River Valentin *(note the waterfall)* and starts the long haul up the side of the mountain, offering splendid views of the Pic de Ger massif, especially in the early morning and at dusk when the play of colours can be superb.

✳ **Gourette** – Gourette is a popular winter sports resort, which owes its existence to Henri Sallanave, a native of Pau, who pioneered downhill skiing in the Pyrenees in 1903. Although international skiing championships had been held here yearly since 1908, the resort was not opened until 1930. Apartment blocks nestle in an cirque scarred by the rugged strata of Pic du Ger (alt 2 613m/7 316ft) and the rocky jagged formation of Pène Médaa, which is an impressive **site**★ in the limestone mountains of the Pyrenees.

★ **Pène Blanque** – *1hr 30min round trip using the gondola lift which rises from Gourette.* The upper platform of the **gondola** (the cable-cars ride up the longest single-span hoist in Europe) is in the northern cirque of Pène Blanque, at the foot of Pic de Ger and not far from a group of small mountain lakes. From here, there is a fine **view**★ of Gourette and the road winding up to Col d'Aubisque.
🚶 A difficult footpath, zigzagging between Pic de Ger and Géougue d'Arre, leads to a pass *(allow an extra 2hr round trip for this excursion)* from which there is an interesting view of the border peaks of the **Balaïtous**. Below is a lake and Vallée d'Artouste.
Cows and horses graze freely in the pastures along the roadside. Not far beyond Gourette, from a corner of the Crêtes Blanches (White Crests), a splendid panorama unfolds from Grand Gabizos to Pic de Sesques. In the distance, Pic du Midi de Bigorre can be seen, and the mast of its television transmitter is clearly visible in good weather.

Col de l'Aubisque under snow

The Tour de France bicycle race

Every year the cyclists in the Tour de France take on this awe-inspiring challenge through the passes of the Pyrenees, bringing glory to a few and disappointment to the rest. Aubisque, Tourmalet, Aspin, Soulor are synonymous not only with pulled muscles, violent summer storms, steep inclines and extremely narrow roads, but also with huge crowds from all over France and Spain cheering on the leader in the yellow jersey.

The Pyrenees joined the Tour in 1910, with a segment from Perpignan to Bayonne, and a stopover in Luchon. In 1918, Envalira Pass was included, at an altitude of 2 407m/8 063ft. In the 1960s, the Tour went through the newly established winter sports resorts of Superbagnères, La Mongie, Luz-Ardiden, Hautacam and Val-Louron etc. The 1990s, with the five consecutive victories of the unbeatable Spanish cyclist, Indurain, will no doubt go down in the history of the Tour for ever more.

★★ Col d'Aubisque – The pass is at an altitude of 1 709m/5 608ft. Sports enthusiasts will recognise it from the annual Tour de France bicycle race. The south knoll *(TV relay – 15min on foot from the car park)* affords a striking view of the whole Gourette cirque, and an immense **panorama★★** from Pic de Gers to Pic de Montaigu *(due east, in the distance)* with nine major peaks in between.

Beyond the pass, the road *(D 918)*, carved into the mountainside, offers views of the Vallée de Ferrières and, in the distance, the Béarn plain. After that, the **Corniche des Pyrénées** skirts Cirque du Litor at a height of almost 300m/1 000ft. This is one of the most impressive sections of the drive, along a road which was one of the boldest feats of 19C engineering.

★ Col du Soulor – The pass lies at an altitude of 1 474m/4 740ft. Here, grass-covered peaks with spiky tips form the foreground to an enormous mountain landscape. Once more, beyond Vallée d'Azun, the summits between Pic du Midi de Bigorre and, further to the left, Pic de Montaigu, rise into view.

Turn left onto D 126.

Asson – *See* 2 *above.*

In the distance, after crossing the bridge to Louvie-Juzon, the great mass of Pic du Midi d'Ossau comes into view.

Beyond Louvie-Juzon, turn left onto D 934.

The road enters the **Vallée du Gave d'Ossau★★**.

Bielle – This former county seat, split in two by a tributary of Gave d'Ossau, retains a certain sleepy dignity. Several 16C town houses can be seen in the south bank district, between the main road and the church; on the north bank stands a castle built by the Marquis de Laborde (1724-94), a banker during the time of Louis XV and the Duc de Choiseul.

Follow D 294 to Bilhères.

Bilhères – *Drive right through the village.* This is a scattered village containing several houses with 16C and 17C decorative elements – embellished keystones, for example, in the arched doorways.

★ Plateau de Bénou – Above Bilhères the view opens out southwards as far as Pic de Ger. The chapel of Notre-Dame-de-Houndaas *(rest stop facilities)*, shaded by two lime trees, appears in a **site★** which is kept fresh by running water from several main springs. The road then runs into the pastureland of the Bénou basin where large flocks of sheep graze in summer.

Return to Bielle and drive upriver towards Laruns.

Aste-Béon – *On the right bank of the Ossau Torrent.* On the way into Béon village, there is a wildlife centre called **Falaise aux Vautours** ○, (Vulture's Cliff) ◎. Lying at the foot of a limestone cliff are nesting grounds for a large colony of tawny vultures. They are protected along with the other inhabitants of the Ossau Nature Reserve (bearded vultures, Egyptian vultures, black and royal kites, peregrine falcons and kestrels), living in natural surroundings conducive to their reproduction.

The exhibit, divided into 12 sections, offers an insight into the lifestyles of these birds of prey. Of particular interest is the three-dimensional model of the cliff with a panoramic screen projecting images of the vultures' seasonal behaviour patterns, from the courting display, nest-building, hatching of the solitary egg, to the feeding and flying away of their young. There are other displays on cattle farming, tales and legends from Vallée d'Ossau and the fauna and flora of the Pyrenees.

Drive back to Eaux-Bonnes along D 918.

Sites de BÉTHARRAM★

Michelin map 342: K-6 or 234 fold 39

The Bétharram caves and sanctuary are located near the former *bastide* of Lestelle-Bétharram, founded in 1335 by Gaston de Foix. Several beautiful Renaissance and 18C houses still line the streets laid out at right angles to each other. The sanctuary, an age-old place of pilgrimage, used to enjoy considerable popularity.

SANCTUAIRE DE BÉTHARRAM

The Bétharram Sanctuary, which dates back to the 15C, consists of vast monastic buildings which now house the congregation of the Sacred Heart of Jesus and its college, a 17C chapel and a Way of the Cross. Beyond the chapel, towards the monastic buildings, an old ivy-covered **bridge** bears the date 1687.

Chapelle-Notre-Dame – The chapel, seen from the road bridge, has an austere Classical façade (1661) of grey marble. The interior and furnishings are Baroque in style. On the left as you go in, behind a screen, is a 14C polychrome wood statue of the Madonna Nursing her Child, formerly worshipped at the high altar; on the right, an 18C Scourging at the Pillar and, at the high altar, a plaster statue of Notre-Dame-de-Bétharram (1845).

Against the chevet *(access through a door to the left of the chancel)*, the **chapelle St-Michel-Garicoïts** ⓥ (1926), contains the shrine of the Basque priest (1797-1863) who restored the sanctuary and calvary and founded the congregation of the Sacred Heart of Jesus.

The hill, overlooking Chapelle de Notre-Dame, is dotted with 14 chapels from the 19C, marking the Stations of the Cross. Note especially the eight bas-relief sculptures by Alexandre Renoir (1845). The site affords a panoramic view of the surrounding hills and plain.

★GROTTES DE BÉTHARRAM ⓥ

2.5km/1.5mi from the southern exit of Lestelle-Bétharram on D 152

The caves were discovered in 1819 by local shepherds and explored the same year by naturalists from Pau. A more systematic exploration, begun in 1888 by three speleologists, also from Pau, took 10 years and unearthed 5 200m/over 3mi, of underground galleries. In 1898, the caves were brought to the attention of Léon Ross, a painter from St Malo in Brittany, who had settled in Bigorre. It took him four years to prepare the caves for the first regular stream of tourists. In 1919, he finished excavating the exit tunnel.

Tour – The underground tour covers 2.8km/more than 1.5mi, and leads through five tiers of galleries, hollowed out of the limestone mountain by the river (which later flows into Gave de Pau). The upper level is the largest, comprising huge interconnected chambers. Their most interesting feature is their porous roof, which has led to the formation of beautiful stalactites in the *Salle des Lustres* (Chandelier Room), and a stalagmite column. This process is very slow, 1cm/0.4in every century in our temperate climate. The collapsed pot hole into which the subterranean stream finally plunges is 80m/262ft deep and contains scattered boulders and curious Romanesque cloisters. The old river bed is a deep and narrow fissure containing different examples of erosion. The lowest galleries are on the same level as the river which visitors follow by boat over a short distance. A miniature train takes them through a tunnel and back into daylight.

NEAR THE CAVES

Hôtel du Vieux Logis – *rte de Lestelle- Bétharram – 64800 Lestelle-Bétharram* – ☏ *05 59 71 94 87 – closed 28 Jan to 8 Mar, 25 Oct to 3 Nov, Sunday evening and Mon off-season* – 🅿 *– 40 rooms: 32.01/45.73€ –* ☕ *6.86€ – restaurant 16.77/36.59€.* This old farm near the caves of Bétharram features two rustic dining rooms with a warm ambience. Functional, well-equipped rooms are to be found in a recent wing, but your children may prefer one of the five amusing chalets located in the vast park. Excellent reception.

Biarritz stands on the borders of the Basque Country, and is the most fashionable and most frequented seaside resort in south-west France. The setting is magnificent, with Atlantic rollers breaking against rocks and reefs, impressive cliffs, a small port, and superb bathing beaches.

The town's international status has been enhanced by nine easily accessible golf courses, two casinos and numerous sports facilities in the town itself.

Empress Eugénie's town – At the beginning of the 19C Biarritz was but a small, whale-fishing harbour. The people of Bayonne, when they started coming here to enjoy the sea, made the 5km/3mi journey on donkeys or mules. Then Spanish nobility from the far side of the border discovered its charms, and from 1838 onwards, the Countess of Montijo and her daughter Eugénie made a habit of coming each year. When Eugénie became Empress of France, she persuaded her husband, Napoleon III, to accompany her on her annual visit to the Basque coast. The Emperor was also captivated by the area. Their first trip together was in 1854. The following year, he had a house built and named it Villa Eugénie (today Hôtel du Palais). Suddenly, Biarritz was famous.

The charm of the town and its growing reputation for discreet luxury, drew the rich, famous and aristocratic from all over Europe. Villas overlooking the sea testify to the growing attractiveness of this seaside resort, whose illustrious list of visitors is hard to rival.

In 1956, while he was filming *The sun also rises*, the American script-writer Peter Viertel had a go at the Atlantic waves with a surfing board he ordered from California. The new sport took Biarritz by surprise and became a craze overnight!

VIPs in Biarritz

Since the beginning of the 19C, Biarritz has been a holiday resort for many of the rich and famous, starting, of course, with Napoleon III and Eugénie, who commissioned the neo-Classical Villa Eugénie. Kings, queens and aristocrats from all over the world came to sun themselves in Biarritz, including Edward VII, then Prince of Wales. At the turn of the last century, two casinos were built, providing Sarah Bernhardt and Lucien Guitry with the opportunity to perform for a very fashionable audience. The 1920s saw celebrities such as Rostand, Ravel, Stravinsky, Loti, Cocteau, and Hemingway. After the Second World War, the Marquis of Cuevas gave sumptuous parties, whereas the Duke and Duchess of Windsor came here to rest and relax. It was not unusual to run into some of the great film stars of the 50s and 60s, such as Frank Sinatra, Rita Hayworth and Gary Cooper.

BEACHES

Biarritz owes much of its charm to its hydrangea-lined garden promenades, which follow the contours of the cliffs, over the rocks and along the three main beaches, which have become an international meeting place for surfers and a focal point for local entertainment both day and night.

Grande Plage – Overlooked by the Municipal Casino, the Grande Plage is the largest and most fashionable of Biarritz's beaches. In former times, only the most daring of bathers would swim here, which led to its now-forgotten nickname of *Plage des Fous* (Madman's Beach). To the north, it becomes Plage Miramar.

Plage du Port-Vieux – Sheltered by two overhanging cliffs, it is a small family beach and a local favourite.

Plage de la Côte des Basques – Lying at the foot of a cliff which periodically has to be shored up against landslides, this is the most exposed and best surfing beach in Biarritz, because of its long reach; it owes its name to a traditional trip to the coast held on the first Sunday after the 15 August every year, which brought Basques from the inland provinces to the seaside.

STROLL THROUGH THE TOWN

★ Rocher de la Vierge – The Virgin's Rock, crowned with a statue of the Virgin Mary, is Biarritz's main landmark. It is surrounded by reefs and joined to the shore by a footbridge rendered impassable in rough weather by the breaking waves. It was Napoleon III who had the idea of hollowing out the rock and linking it to the cliff by a wooden bridge which has since been replaced by a metal one built by Gustave Eiffel.

A gently sloping footpath shaded by tamarisks leads to Rocher du Basta and Grande Plage.

Eating out

BUDGET

La Goélette – *4 r. du Port-Vieux* – ☎ *05 59 24 84 65* – *closed 15 Nov to 15 Dec and Wed off-season* – *11.43/18.29€*. Take a break from shopping and treat yourself to this pleasant restaurant-*salon de thé* surrounded by boutiques. The decor is inspired by the nearby sea – blue and white tones, fishing nets, and marine miscellany. Cuisine with an accent on fish and salads.

Tikia – *1 pl. Ste-Eugénie* – ☎ *05 59 24 46 09* – *11.89/18.29€*. Tikia means small in Basque. It's true that there's not much space here, but it is a nice place to linger. Pretty decor of the boat cabin ilk, with varnished wood panelling on the walls, porthole-shaped mirrors and marine knick-knacks. Giant brochettes on the menu.

Bar Jean – *5 r. des Halles* – ☎ *05 59 24 80 38* – *closed 1 Jan to 6 Feb, Tue-Wed off-season* – *13/33€*. True Spanish flavour is served in this authentic tapas bar near the Biarritz market place. Popular, very animated atmosphere; Hispanic decor with coloured tiles, arcades, posters starring bulls and a charming patio. Basque and Spanish specialities include tapas, naturally.

MODERATE

Comme à la Maison – *14 av. de Verdun* – ☎ *05 59 22 58 04* – *closed Sun-Mon off-season* – 🍴 – *15.24/22.87€*. Old stones, beams, antiques and second-hand finds set the tone for this inviting restaurant. Traditional dishes and salads served on novel tables made of old sewing-machine bases.

La Pizzeria des Arceaux – *20-24 av. Édouard-VII* – ☎ *05 59 24 11 47* – *closed 10-24 Jun, 4-25 Nov and Mon* – *17.53/27.44€*. The ambience in this pizzeria just a stone's throw from city hall is particularly nice. Beneath tile frescos and mirrors, the pizzas are devoured by a young, hip Biarritz crowd. For an appetite stimulant, have a look at the dessert table as you come in.

Le Bistroye – *6 r. Jean-Bart* – ☎ *05 59 22 01 02* – *closed 1-15 May, 22 Dec to 8 Jan, Wed evening and Sun* – *19.82/27.44€*. Imposing beams, posters and paintings celebrating Spain and the Basque country, and a handsome fireplace with ceramic decorations: *voilà* the decor of this pleasant, Hispanic-flavoured restaurant. Tapas and local dishes on the menu.

Chez Albert – *on the Port des Pêcheurs* – ☎ *05 59 24 43 84* – *closed 6 Jan to 10 Feb, 1-15 Dec and Wed except Jul-Aug* – *26.68€*. There's a friendly, bistro-style ambience Chez Albert. Opening onto the Port des Pêcheurs (Fisherman's Wharf), the rustic dining room with blue and white Basque tablecloths continues onto a parasol-covered terrace. Simple seafood cuisine.

La Tantina de la Playa – *Plage du Centre* – *64210 Bidart* – *6km/3.6mi S of Biarritz via N 10* – ☎ *05 59 26 53 56* – *closed 12 Nov to 12 Dec, Sun evening and Mon except Jul-Aug* – *25.92/36.59€*. Beach, waves and surfers: these three elements characterizing the Basque coast provide the entertainment for those who dine here. Relaxed atmosphere and maritime decor in the large panoramic room with its oilcloth tablecloths. Fish of the day presented on a slate menu.

Where to stay

BUDGET

Hôtel Gardenia – *19 av. Carnot* – ☎ *05 59 24 10 46 6* – *closed 15 Nov to 1 Jan* – *19 rooms: 38.11/51.83€* – 🍴 *5.34€*. This central hotel with a pink facade has the charm of a private home. Its quiet, attractively decorated rooms are regularly smartened up. The reception and salon have just been refurbished. Reasonable prices considering the location.

Hôtel Atalaye – *6 r. des Goëlands, Plateau de l'Atalaye* – ☎ *05 59 24 06 76* – *24 rooms: 42.69/60.22€* – 🍴 *5.34€*. This imposing turn-of-the-century villa owes its name to the superb Atalaye plateau overlooking the Atlantic ocean. Plain, clean rooms – ask for one on the seaside. Free parking nearby.

Maison Berreterrenea Bed and Breakfast – *Quartier Arrauntz* – *64480 Ustaritz* – *11km/6.6mi SE of Biarritz via D 932, Arrauntz exit* – ☎ *05 59 93 05 13* – *bereter.nicole@wanadoo.fr* – 🍴 – *3 rooms: 40/47€*. Facing a cider apple orchard, this 17C Basque house dominates the Nive Valley. Simple and well-renovated with its white walls and mountain stones, it has regained its dignity of yore. Sober rooms with beams and old doors.

MODERATE

Hôtel Maïtagaria – *34 av. Carnot* – ☎ *05 59 24 26 65* – *17 rooms: 51.83/54.88€* – 🍴 *5.34€*. A warm, personal reception in this little hotel near the garden, just 500m/545yd from the beach. The rooms, of varying sizes, are bright and functional and were recently renovated. Pocket garden blossoming in the back.

Le Petit Hôtel – *11 r. Gardères* – ☎ *05 59 24 87 00* – *petit.hotel@wanadoo.fr* – *12 rooms: 56.41/76.22€* – ☐ *4.57€*. This appealing little hotel is the ideal home base for discovering the city by foot or taking a sunbath on the beach. Its very well soundproofed rooms have been renovated in tones of blue or yellow; all have Internet access.

On the town

Bar Jean – *5 r. des Halles* – ☎ *05 59 24 80 38* – *summer: daily 10am-4pm, 7pm-2am; off-season: Thu-Mon 10am-4pm, 7pm-2am* – *closed Jan*. This very popular tapas bar has a clientele of regulars who wouldn't go elsewhere for love or money. Some come for a tête-à-tête nibble, others to chat with the amiable owners at the bar counter. Spanish music and ambience.

Casino de Biarritz – *1 av. Édouard-VII* – ☎ *05 59 22 77 77* – *www.lucienbarriere.com* – *Sun-Thu 10am-3am, Fri-Sat until 4am*. Located on the Grande Plage, this enormous casino has a table games room (roulette, Black Jack) and 180 slot machines as well as Le Café de la Plage *brasserie*, Le Baccara restaurant, Le Flamingo discotheque, a show room (theatre, dance) and a ballroom.

L'Impérial (Hôtel du Palais) – *1 av. de l'Impératrice* – ☎ *05 59 41 64 00* – *daily 9am-midnight* – *closed Feb*. La Villa Eugénie, the scene of Napoleon III's love affair with the Empress Eugénie, became the majestic Hôtel du Palais in 1893. In the Impérial, its chic bar facing the sea, you can graciously sip a glass of champagne while dreaming of bygone opulence. A pianist makes the ambience complete from 8 to 11 every evening.

Le Caveau – *4 r. Gambetta* – ☎ *05 59 24 16 17* – *daily 10:30pm-5am*. The hippest bar-discotheque of the area, where you can rub elbows with superb creatures of both sexes as well as the inevitable stars on holiday. The trendy multitude comes to party as well as to be seen, *naturellement*.

Lodge – *1 r. du Port-Vieux* – ☎ *05 59 24 73 78* – *summer: daily 9am-2am; off-season: Wed-Mon 9am-2am* – *closed Jan to Mar*. This highly charming bar, decorated with care, also has an artistic calling: paintings and sculptures are frequently exhibited here. And should you happen to fall in love with a piece of original furniture, be advised that it's for sale too. The ambience owes its peaceful quality to the low-key conversation between artists who spend time here. Menu with a regional bent.

Irish Pub – *10 av. Victor-Hugo* – ☎ *05 59 24 66 06* – *summer: daily 5pm-3am; rest of the year: 5pm-2am*. This roomy bar, half saloon, half pub, decorated with musical instruments and lanterns, is a lovely spot where one can have a chat without raising one's voice or paying through the nose. The bar room has a giant screen used for broadcasting sports events. Weekly concert and frequent theme evenings.

La Santa Maria – *Espl. du Port-Vieux* – ☎ *05 59 24 92 25* – *Apr-Jun, Oct: daily 10am-2am; Jul-Sep: daily 9am-3am*. The splendid view of the Rocher de la Vierge and the Port Vieux beach is not the least asset of this little bar perched on a boulder. A terrace, a few stools and a counter in a cave make this a pleasant, unpretentious spot where you can sample tapas while listening to the little orchestra.

Showtime

Gare du Midi – *21 bis av. du Mar.-Foch* – ☎ *05 59 22 37 10* – *www.biarritz.tm.fr* – *open performance evenings; ticket office run by the Office du Tourisme: daily 10am-6pm*. This is the city's main theatre, with 1 400 seats. Many different kinds of performances are held here: plays, pop concerts, ballets...

Shopping

Cazaux et fils – *10 r. Broquedis* – ☎ *05 59 22 36 03* – *Mon-Sat 10am-12:30pm, 3pm-7pm, public holidays by appointment*. The Cazaux family has been committed to ceramic pottery craftsmanship since the 18C. Jean-Marie Cazaux is happy to talk about his profession, describing it as 'austere and solitary'. The boutique also offers personalized creations every step can be undertaken according to the customer's wishes, from extracting the clay to hand-painting the finishing touches.

Fabrique de chistéras Gonzalez – *6 allée des Liserons – 64600 Anglet – ☎ 05 59 03 85 04 – Mon-Fri 9am-noon, 2pm-7pm, Sat 9am-noon; visits: 5pm – closed public holidays – adults 3.05€*. Since 1887, the Gonzalez manufacture produces hand-made baskets *(cestas)*, those wicker scoops that prolong the protective pelota glove. In one hour, you'll learn everything there is to know about the history and manufacture of pelotas and *cestas*.

Chocolats Henriet – *Pl. Clemenceau – ☎ 05 59 24 24 15 – daily 9am-7pm*. Established after the Second World War, Henriet is the local guiding light in chocolates and confectionery, featuring *calichous* (Échiré butter and fresh cream caramels), and *rochers de Biarritz* (bitter chocolate, orange rinds, almonds). Serge Couzigou, *maître chocolatier* responsible for the creation of the Musée du Chocolat (located 4 avenue de la Marne), has been running it for the past 20 years.

Maison Arostéguy – *5 av. Victor-Hugo – ☎ 05 59 24 00 52 – www.maison-arosteguy.com – Mon-Sat 9:30am-1pm, 3pm-8pm*. Founded in 1875, this famous Biarritz grocery store (formerly the Epicerie du Progrès) has kept its original walls, shelves and facade. Here's where you can acquire a variety of specialities and products difficult to find elsewhere: rare bottles of Bordeaux, prestigious Armagnacs, Basque products, flavoured teas and spices.

Sports

Biarritztarrak (Fronton Mur à Gauche) – *42 av. du Mar.-Foch – ☎ 05 59 22 15 72 – daily 9am-midnight – closed 1 week early Nov*. In July and August, pelota Basque galas (bare-handed, leather paleta and small *cesta*) are held Tuesday and Friday nights from 9pm on. When matches are not being played, you can try your hand at the *pala* (wood racket).

Euskal-Jaï Fernand Pujol – *R. Cino-del-duca – ☎ 05 59 23 91 09 – open match days*. This pelota Basque school organizes *cesta punta* competitions nearly every Wednesday and Saturday from June to September.

Hippodrome des Fleurs – *Av. du lac Marion – ☎ 05 59 43 91 56 – open racing days*. Horse races have been held here on July and August evenings for over 50 years. This trotters' hippodrome has an 800m/872yd cindered track with sharp bends.

Jeff Hakman Surf School – *Quai de la Grande-Plage – ☎ 05 59 22 03 12 or 06 08 74 51 28 – Jun-Sep: Mon-Sat 10am-7pm; Jul-Aug: daily 2:30pm-6pm; Oct-May: Mon-Sat 10am-noon, 2pm-7pm, Sun 2:30pm-6pm – closed Jan-Feb*. This school offers surf and bodyboard lessons and courses and rents suits and flippers to practice in.

Parc des Sports d'Aguilera – *R. Cino-del-duca – ☎ 05 59 01 64 64 – www.bopb.com – Mon-Fri 8am-7pm, Sat 9am-noon*. This sizable sports complex is equipped for a whole panoply of sports disciplines. It includes the Biarritz Olympique rugby stadium (where Serge Bianco played), tennis courts, an athletics track, a Basque pelota court...

Piscine municipale – *Bd du Gén.-de-Gaulle – ☎ 05 59 22 52 52 – schedule varies depending on the school calendar*. Located on the shore, this municipal complex features heated sea-water pools as well as a jacuzzi, a hammam and a sauna.

Sea-water therapy

Thermes Marins – *80 r. de Madrid – ☎ 05 59 23 01 22 – www.thermesmarins-biarritz.com – Apr-Oct: Mon-Fri 8:30am-12:30pm, 2:30pm-6:30pm, Sat 8:30am-12:30pm, Sun 10am-noon, 4pm-7pm; Nov-Mar: Mon-Fri 9am-noon, 2:30pm-6:30pm, Sat 8:30am-12:30pm, Sun 10am-noon, 4pm-7pm – closed early to late Jan – half-day formula: 62.5€. Entrance fee only: 11.43€*. This spa featuring a leisure pool and jacuzzi proposes various treatments: affusion or underwater showers, seaweed treatment booths, massages, sea-air bath booths...

Plateau de l'Atalaye – This open stretch of ground lies between Basta Rock and the promontory bearing the town's last remaining *atalaye* or watchtower from which smoke signals were sent to fishermen when whales were sighted. Charming fishing village below.

"La Perspective" – This fine promenade overlooking Plage des Basques offers a splendid **view★★** south towards the last of the Basque summits – La Rhune, Les Trois Couronnes and the Jaizkibel massif.

Pointe St-Martin ⊘ – The gardens and, in particular, the **lighthouse**, towering 73m/240ft above the sea, offer an excellent **view★** of the town and the Basque Pyrenees.

BIARRITZ

Villas – *A guided tour of the town's villas is organised by the tourist office in July and August.* The small fishing port of Biarritz suddenly became extremely fashionable during the second half of the 19C and many sumptuous villas were built in the eclectic style of the period. Thus, Villa Belza, standing on a rocky spur at the extremity of the Côte des Basques and built in 1880 for Marie-Belza Dubreuil, became a Russian cabaret during the roaring 20s. Villa La Roche Ronde (avenue de l'Impératrice), on the other hand, was built by Alphonse Bertrand in neo-Gothic style, complete with crenellated roof and bartizan. Château Javalquinto is another neo-Gothic building designed by its owner, the Duke of Osuna; it now houses the tourist office. By contrast, Villa Etchepherdia, situated near the lighthouse of Pointe St-Martin, is more in line with the local architectural style, since it is modelled on a farm from the Basque country.

ADDITIONAL SIGHTS

★ Musée de la Mer ⓥ – 📷 This marine museum and scientific research centre stands opposite Rocher de la Vierge, with its back to Atalaye Plateau. It exhibits a wide range of marine life, the human activity connected with it, and a general presentation of the close relationship between Biarritz and the ocean throughout the centuries. In the basement a series of **aquariums** display the remarkable wealth and variety of the ocean fauna in the Bay of Biscay.

On the first level, **Salle de Folin** is named after the pioneer of oceanography in the Bay of Biscay, and contains an exhibit on the history of the museum, founded in 1935. The **cetacean gallery**, mainly consisting of a presentation on whaling, has animal skeletons and models of animals caught or washed ashore along the coast (finback and killer whales, dolphins etc). Models of boats and navigational instruments complete the section devoted to fishing methods.

The second level contains further information on the resort, including conservation of the coastline, a study of the ocean around Biarritz, and an underwater display of seals and sharks in their natural habitat.

The terrace affords a **panoramic view** of the coast from the Landes to Cape Machichaco in Spain. The seals' acrobatics – especially at feeding time *(10.30am and 5pm)* – is wonderful entertainment for young children.

The ornithological gallery at the end of the tour offers a complete display of all the sedentary and migratory species to be found along the coast and in the Pyrenees. The birdsong of 40 different species resonates in an aviary equipped with an interactive system.

Musée du Chocolat ⓥ – 📷 Let yourself be guided by the delicious smell round this interesting museum devoted to chocolate making and...eating!

EXCURSIONS

Anglet – The town links Biarritz and Bayonne and its success as a resort and tourist centre followed that of Biarritz during the Second Empire. The site, however, is geographically closer to the countryside of the Silver Coast north of the Adour estuary with its long straight strands bordered by dunes, and a flat hinterland planted with pines. The Olympic skating rink at La Barre, the swimming pool and tennis courts at El Hogar, the marina and Atlanthal Complex (a cure centre specialising in sea-water

Seafront

therapy) are busy centres of activity. However, Anglet is also known for its excellent facilities for outdoor sports such as surfing, horse riding and golf.

Just off Plage de la Chambre d'Amour (the main beach), steps lead to the cave in which it is said that two lovers, caught unawares by the rising tide, were trapped and died. Each summer an International Festival of Humorous Drawings is held in Anglet. The festival was founded in 1979 and features amateur as well as professional artists (see Calendar of events).

Bidart – 6km/3.7mi S. The small resort of Bidart, halfway between Biarritz and St-Jean-de-Luz, is built at the highest point on the Basque coastline, on the edge of a cliff. From Chapelle Ste-Madeleine (accessible from rue de la Madeleine), the clifftop **view★** looks over the Jaizkibel (a promontory closing off the Fontarabia natural harbour), the Trois Couronnes and La Rhune.

The charming Place centrale (main square) is framed by the church, the pelota (jai alai) fronton and the town hall. Local pelota matches and competitions are always watched by enthusiastic crowds.

The church is typically Basque in style with its belfry-porch, fine wooden ceiling, and enormous, brightly coloured 17C altarpiece. The mezzanine galleries were reserved for the men attending services; women sat below.

Rue de la Grande-Plage and promenade de la Mer lead steeply down to the beach.

Guéthary – 8.5km/5.3mi S. Originally a traditional fishing port on a small inlet along the Basque coast, Guéthary is now a seaside resort with well-to-do Labourd-style villas nestled in spacious grounds. The view from the terrace above the beach stretches north-east as far as Biarritz.

Beyond N 10, on Elizalda hill, the **church** ⊘ houses a 17C Crucifixion, a 17C Pietà and a statue of Monsignor Mugabure (1850-1910), who was born and bred in the region and became the first archbishop of Tokyo.

BISCAROSSE

Population 9 281
Michelin map 335: E-8 or 234 folds 9 and 13

Once famous for its high-flying pioneers and now the paradise of surfers, Biscarosse is located along the Atlantic coast, just south of the Bassin d'Arcachon. Its name refers to the dunes which abound in the area. As part of a vast project to prevent them from shifting and consolidate them, 3 000ha/7 413 acres of coastal dunes were covered with a plant which retains the sand and another 8 000ha/19 768 acres of inland dunes were planted with maritime pines. Today, the resort includes three distinct sites: Biscarosse-Plage on the coast, Biscarosse-Bourg inland and Étang de Biscarosse et de Parentis, of several lakes along this stretch of coastline.

Where to stay

BUDGET

Camping de la Rive – *10km/6mi NE of Biscarosse via D 652, rte de Sanguinet, on the banks of l'Etang de Cazaux –* ☎ *05 58 78 12 33 – larive@wanadoo.fr – open Apr to Oct – reserv. required – 640 sites: 27.29€.* Leave your cares at the gate when you settle into this campground under the pines. You can take a dip in the lake or in one of the pretty round pools with slides. Open-air theatre; children's club. Mobile homes and bungalows.

Hôtel Les Vagues – *99 r. des Iris –* ☎ *05 58 83 98 10 – closed end Oct to end Mar –* 🅿 *– 29 rooms: 29.73/83.85€ – restaurant 16.01€.* A good address for those who would rather avoid the bustle of centre city. Located in a residential neighbourhood, this establishment is being renovated bit by bit; the rooms are basic, some have a balcony. Very pleasant terrace and garden in the shade of pine trees.

Hôtel La Caravelle – *5314 rte des Lacs – 40600 Ispe – 6km/3.6mi N of Biscarosse via D 652 and D 305 –* ☎ *05 58 09 82 67 –* 🅿 *– 15 rooms: 60.98€ –* ☲ *6.10€ – restaurant 13.72/38.11€.* In a calm setting ideal for unwinding, this hotel touches the water and has a mooring dock for private boats. The rooms are furnished with painted bamboo fittings. Veranda dining room with terrace on the lake.

STAYING IN BISCAROSSE

⌂ **Biscarosse-Plage** – Ideal for those who enjoy huge rollers… and exciting surfing possibilities! Fishing is a less strenuous alternative.

Étang de Biscarosse et de Parentis – This magnificent stretch of water, also known as the Southern Lake covers an area of 3 600ha/8 900 acres. There is only one beach with a marina and games for children.

Étang de Cazaux et de Sanguinet – This body of water, also known as the Northern Lake, is linked with its neighbour by a canal. It offers sailing and various water sports. From Biscarosse to Navarrosse the road runs through a pine forest, ideal for hiking, cycling and horse riding.

SIGHT

Musée Historique de l'Hydraviation ⊙ – The Seaplane and Flying Boat Museum is housed in four pavilions which trace the evolution of these flying machines, at the height of their usefulness between the wars, when concrete runways did not exist and landing gear was unable to support the weight of ever-larger aircraft. Numerous documents, models and original parts (engines, propellers etc) tell the story of water-borne aircraft, the pioneers who designed them, the inauguration of an airmail service, the Biscarosse seaplane base, the first long-distance flights, and the evolution of larger and larger civil planes (reconstitution of the cock-pit of a cruiser plane) and military craft. There is an 18min film *(in French, afternoons only)* on the giant flying boats' brief hour of glory.

Opposite the museum, seaplanes and flying boats can be viewed in a huge glass hangar. It is also possible to visit a laboratory in which the remnants of aircraft shot down during the war are protected by electrolysis against corrosion.

EXCURSIONS

Sanguinet – *13km/8mi NE (E of the Étang de Cazaux).* The interesting **Archaeological Museum** ⊙ in the village displays finds from local digs and excavations in and around the lake. The dugout canoes from the Iron Age made out of a single piece of pine are well worth taking in.

Parentis-en-Born – *9km/5.6mi SE (E of the Étang de Biscarosse)*. The name of this small town is familiar in France today, thanks to the oil wells which have sprouted up there. Esso REP's **Musée du Pétrole** ⊙ examines some of the technical aspects and problems involved in prospecting and processing black gold.

BLAYE

Population 4 666
Michelin map 335: H-4 or 233 folds 37, 38 local maps in Introduction
(Wines of Bordeaux) and Vignoble de BORDEAUX

Blaye (pronounced Bly) is situated on the eastern bank of the Gironde, 43km/27mi downstream from Bordeaux, and is known mainly for its citadel, its Côtes de Blaye wines and its port. The port includes a deep-water landing-stage and an extended dock basin, at right angles to the Gironde, used by coastal steamers and sailing ships. Fishing boats land lampreys and shad in the spring.
The Gironde estuary is also a natural reserve of sturgeon which is now a protected species and the local caviar therefore comes from sturgeon farms.

★ CITADEL *1hr 15min*

Access is either on foot via Porte Dauphine to the south, or by car through Porte Royale to the east. Both gateways are decorated with shields carrying fleur-de-lis, both protected by ravelins in the curtain wall.
The citadel, built by Vauban in 1689 and still partly inhabited, is a real town within a town, very lively in season thanks to the local craftsmen.
The landward side, which is 45m/148ft above the river, is defended by bastions, themselves protected by a dyke.

Château des Rudel – This medieval castle is triangular in shape, and has a romantic history. It was the birthplace of the 12C troubadour **Geoffroy** (or **Jaufré**) **Rudel**, who fell poetically in love with "a distant princess", Melisande of Tripoli, without ever seeing her. According to legend, he sailed across the sea to join her, fell ill on the voyage, and died on arrival in the arms of his beloved.
Only two towers of the castle still stand. However, the bridge, which led to the entrance, and the foundations of the walls are also visible. In the middle of the courtyard, the coping around the ancient well can be seen, grooved by the constant rubbing of the chain or rope which lowered the bucket. From the top of the tower, Tour des Rondes, there is a good **view** of the town, the Gironde estuary and the surrounding countryside *(viewing table)*.

Tour de l'Aiguillette – From the side of the tower, which rises at the north-western end of the citadel, there is a fine **view★** of the estuary, studded with islets as far as the open sea.

Take the pathway on the western side of the citadel.

Place d'Armes – From the esplanade on the edge of the cliff overlooking the Gironde there is another view of the estuary and the islands. Near place d'Armes (the old parade ground) there stands a former monastery belonging to the mendicant order of Minims, complete with its chapel and cloisters.

Pavillon de la Place – *Closed for repairs*. At the citadel's centre is the house, once used by the Captain of the Guard, where the Duchesse de Berry was held captive. It is now the **Musée d'Histoire et d'Art du Pays Blayais**, devoted to the history of Blaye.

The Citadel

Château de BONAGUIL★★

Michelin map 336: I-2 or 235 fold 9

This majestic fortress, just on the edge of Périgord Noir and Quercy, is one of the most perfect examples of military architecture from the late 15C and 16C. Its uniqueness is that although it appears to be the traditional defensive stronghold, able to hold off any attack its design was also a response to the development of firearms, such as the cannon and the harquebus.

Also, Bonaguil, which was built neither as a lookout post nor as a fortress, but as a secure place of refuge, pioneered from 1480 to 1520 the use of firearms essentially for defensive purposes. This, after all, is what forts were designed for.

A stronger character – It was a strange quirk of character that made Bérenger de Roquefeuil proclaim himself the "noble, magnificent and most powerful lord of the baronies of Roquefeuil, Blanquefort, Castelnau, Combret, Roquefère, Count of Naut". He belonged to one of the oldest families of Languedoc and was a brutal and vindictive man who, in his determination to be obeyed, did not hesitate to use force. But the extortion and other outrages he perpetrated incited revolt. In response, Bérenger transformed Bonaguil Castle, which had been built in the 13C, into an impregnable fortress from which he would be able to observe and quell any signs of uprising without delay. It took him nearly 40 years to build his fortified eagle's eyrie, which seemed an anachronism when compared with the châteaux being erected by his contemporaries for a life of ease at Montal, Assier and along the Loire. However, his castle was never attacked and stayed intact until the eve of the Revolution. Although demolished during the Revolution, in the prevailing urge to destroy all signs of the old feudal system, this colossus (notwithstanding its mutations), still evokes the absolute power it once represented.

This masterpiece of military architecture, while still keeping the traditional defences against attack by escalade or sapping, was also designed to make use of artillery and other new battle equipment.

Château ⊙ – *1hr 30min*. After passing through the outer wall, the visitor comes to the **barbican**. This was an enormous bastion on its own with a separate garrison, powder store, armouries and escape route. The barbican formed part of the 350m/380yd-long first line of defence whose embrasures were designed for cross-firing. The second line of defence consisted of five towers including the **Grosse Tour**, which is among the strongest round towers ever to have been built in France. It is 35m/115ft high and crowned with corbels. The upper storeys served as living quarters, whereas the lower contained weapons, such as muskets, culverins and harquebuses.

Overlooking both lines of defence, the keep **(donjon)** with its cant walls, served not only as a watchtower but also as a command post. It was shaped like a vessel, with its prow – the most vulnerable point – turned towards the north. It was the last bastion of defence. Inside, a room houses arms and objects found during excavation of the moats.

Equipped with a well sunk through the rock, outbuildings (including the **baking house**) in which provisions could be stored, monumental chimneys, drainage systems, dry internal ditches and vaulted tunnels enabling the troops to move about quickly, the castle garrison of about 100 men could easily withstand a siege provided they were not betrayed or starved out.

EXCURSIONS

Bonaguil stands at the heart of an area rich in *bastides* and strongholds which bear witness to the troubled history of Aquitaine. Two of these *bastides* are worth a detour.

Monflanquin – *28km/17mi W via D 124*. The distinctive tiled roofs of this venerable bastide, founded in the 13C by Alphonse de Poitiers, are clustered together on a hill dominated by the slender silhouette of the church. Narrow, steeply sloping streets, sometimes spanned by covered passages known as *pontets*, climb up to the attractive place des Arcades covered market, where the four *cornières*, gateways to the *bastide's* main square, are still in place. The 15C fortified façade of the Southern Gothic style church, with its brick vaulting, has been restored.

A street encircling the upper town provides a pleasant walk with panoramic **views**★ of the surrounding

---

FOUR SEASONS FARM

Ferme-auberge Les 4 Saisons – *47500 St-Front-sur-Lémance – 3.5km/2mi N of Château de Bonaguil, take dir. St-Front – ☎ 05 53 40 69 88 – closed Sun evening and Wed – ⬛ – 13.72/27.44€*. Take a detour and discover this inn deep in the countryside. You'll love the farm-raised poultry, foie gras and terrines produced on site, while your children will enjoy getting to know the farm animals in their pen.

Château de BONAGUIL

- Underground entrance
- Boulevard
- Baking house
- Seigneurial living quarters
- Boulevard
- Chicane
- Well
- DONJON
- Outbuildings
- Inner Courtyard
- Tour carrée and Oratory
- Main Courtyard
- Salle d'armes
- Esplanade
- Grosse Tour
- Draw-bridge
- Moat
- Barbican
- Moat
- P
- N
- D 158, VILLAGE DE BONAGUIL

FORT DE BONAGUIL

0   20 m

- 1st line of defence
- 2nd line of defence

P   VILLAGE DE BONAGUIL

countryside and the River Lède, tributary of the Lot. To the north-east, overlooking a crest line, the Château de Biron stands out clearly on the horizon.

Villeréal – *13km/8mi N of Monflanquin via D 676.*
This *bastide* founded by Alfonse de Poitiers, the brother of St Louis, has kept its original right-angled grid plan, corbelled houses and overhanging roofs. In the centre of the *bastide*, the two-storied 14C markets are supported by oak pillars. *Cornières* (corner gateways typically found on the central square of a *bastide*) stand on the main square. The fortified 13C **church** dominates the *bastide* with its slender silhouette, combining charm and severity. The high façade is framed by two towers crowned with pinnacle turrets connected by a crenellated watch-path; the left-hand tower is pierced with arrow slits.
A lake with water sports facilities lies at the foot of the village.

BORDEAUX★★★

Conurbation 753 931
Michelin map 71 fold 9 or 234 folds 2,3,6 and 7

Bordeaux, built 98km/61mi upriver at the first bridging point of the tidal River Garonne, is the regional capital of Aquitaine and one of the most important ports in Europe. The elegant city boasts a wealth of Classical architecture which contrasts with the small store houses lining the narrow cobbled streets of some districts.

As a trade centre, the town is renowned not only for the export of the world-famous **Bordeaux wines** and spirits distilled in the south-west of France but also for its farming, food-processing and timber connections, and for its place in the high-tech world of aeronautics, electronics and chemicals. Bordeaux is also part of a powerful communications network which was further enhanced by the completion of the TGV high-speed rail link with Paris at the end of 1990. The development of international exhibition sites and the construction of such projects as the World Trade Centre and the staging of international exhibitions testify to the spirit of enterprise which has made Bordeaux an important junction between Northern Europe and the Iberian peninsula.

HISTORICAL NOTES

Dukes of Aquitaine – Bordeaux (or Burdigala before it was colonised and developed under the Romans) was built on a choice site repeatedly attacked by Visigoths, Normans, Saracens and Moors. It was Good King Dagobert who, in the 7C, regained the town and the surrounding territory for the Frankish empire and the Merovingian dynasty, creating a Duchy of Aquitaine with Bordeaux as its capital. One of these dukes of Aquitaine was the legendary **Huon of Bordeaux**, who is said to have killed one of the sons of Charlemagne, without knowing who he was. Exiled by the Emperor, Huon was subsequently involved in a number of adventures before he eventually married the daughter of the Emir of Babylon. A celebrated 13C *chanson de geste* (a long epic poem featuring a single hero) was based on an embroidered version of this amorous exploit. According to the myth, the hero's pardon depended on Huon going to Babylon, cutting off the Emir's beard and bringing it back, together with four of the potentate's molars, to Charlemagne. The task was successfully accomplished with the help of Oberon, that same King of the Fairies used by Shakespeare 300 years later in *A Midsummer Night's Dream*.

GIRAUDON

Eleanor of Aquitaine

Eleanor's Dowry – In 1137, Louis, son of the French king, married **Eleanor of Aquitaine**, the only daughter of another duke of Aquitaine, William. The bride's dowry comprised the Duchy of Guyenne, the regions of Périgord, Poitou, Limousin, Angoumois, Saintonge and Gascony – practically the whole of south-western France – together with the suzerainty of the Auvergne and the Comté de Toulouse. The marriage, solemnised in Bordeaux Cathedral, was not a success. Louis, who became King Louis VII, was a religious man and an ascetic, contrary to his queen, who was frivolous and enjoyed the good things in life. After 15 years of unhappy marriage, Louis returned from the Crusades and obtained a divorce (1152) through the Council of Beaugency. The settlement gave Eleanor her freedom, and she retained the whole of her dowry. Two years later, she married **Henry Plantagenet**, Duke of Normandy, Count of Anjou, ruler of Maine and Touraine.

Politically, this marriage was a disaster for the Capetians. Henry and Eleanor's combined territories covered an area as vast as that ruled by the King of France. When, barely two months after the marriage, Henry succeeded to the throne of England and became Henry II, the resulting imbalance proved too much for the French. The conflict it provoked lasted, intermittently, for three centuries.

Black Prince's territory (14C) – Bordeaux was known as the capital of **Guyenne** (an old English corruption of the word Aquitaine, which remained in use until the French Revolution). Under English rule the town had the right to choose its own mayor and its councillors or *jurats*, and throughout the Hundred Years War, trade continued to flourish in the port. Wine was still exported to England, and the Bordelais (the people of Bordeaux) cheerfully sold arms to belligerents on both sides. At the same time, nobles and *jurats* built themselves substantial stone houses, known as *taules* or *hostaux*, and the son of the English king, Edward III, known as the Black Prince, possibly because of his dark armour, established his headquarters and held court here.

The Claret connection

It was the Romans who introduced viticulture to the Bordeaux region. The red wine, christened claret by the English occupiers, was much appreciated by the Plantagenets – 1 000 casks were set aside for the coronation celebrations. The grape at that time was a sacred fruit (the punishment for thieves was the loss of an ear) and the quality of the wines even then was all-important. Six sworn tasters testified to its excellence or otherwise, and no innkeeper dared broach a barrel before it had been submitted for their approval. Merchants who adulterated the wine were severely punished, and so were coopers whose casks proved to be defective.

The Black Prince was one of the most talented military leaders of his time and one of the most savage plunderers. From his Bordeaux base, he sallied forth for one campaign after another, terrifying in turn the people of the Languedoc, Limousin, Auvergne, Berry and Poitou regions. A victim of dropsy, however, the heir to the English throne died before having reigned anywhere but in Bordeaux.

In 1453, Bordeaux and the whole of Guyenne was retaken by the French Royal Army, and the Hundred Years War was over.

Bordeaux and the Intendants – These high-ranking provincial representatives of the French Crown, or stewards, first appointed by Richelieu during the reign of Louis XIV in the 17C, were made an effective instrument of central government by Jean-Baptiste Colbert (1619-83), the King's Secretary of State, Controller-General of Finances and Superintendent of Buildings. In the 18C the Intendants' broad vision of a spacious, well-planned city to replace the tangle of medieval streets in Bordeaux brought them into conflict with the short-sighted and penny pinching representatives of the local population, but they succeeded in their aims. The work of Claude Boucher, the Marquis of Tourny, Dupré and St Maur turned a maze of narrow, twisted and stinking lanes surrounded by swamps into one of the most beautiful towns in France. Grandiose urban concepts such as Tourny's avenues, the Bordeaux quays, the Stock Exchange complex and monuments such as the Customs House, the City Hall and the Grand Theatre date from this period. Once the new Bordeaux was established, its position on the Atlantic seaboard was exploited to the full, and it soon became the leading port in France.

Trade boom – The Empire period (early 19C) was a bleak time for the city, as the maritime trade on which it depended was badly affected by the Continental Blockade. The Restoration, however, revived the fortunes of the people of Bordeaux. The great stone bridge and the huge Quinconces Esplanade, dating from this era, were both projects which the Intendants had no time to complete.

Under the Second Empire, the city's role as a trade centre continued to develop, largely because of improved communications and the drainage of the Landes marshes to the south.

In 1870, during the siege of Paris, in 1914 before the German offensive and again in 1940, the French government fled south to take refuge in Bordeaux – dramas which earned the town the nickname of the Tragic Capital. After the Second World War, Bordeaux once again found the dynamic spirit of enterprise that its shipbuilders, financiers and merchants had enjoyed in the 18C.

The port

Bordeaux stands strategically upriver of the Gironde estuary, just 98km/61mi from the coast, and commands the shortest land link between the Atlantic Ocean and the Mediterranean Sea, via the valley of the River Garonne and the Midi Canal (240km/149mi long) which includes Naurouze Pass. The city's importance as a port dates back to the blossoming of the wine trade during the English domination, when the exportation of claret began. This was markedly increased in the 18C by a heavy traffic in colonial products from the French West Indies.

More recently, the activity of the inner-city docks has declined in favour of the new container terminal downstream at Le Verdon where the Gironde meets the ocean.

Bordeaux's west bank, which is being redeveloped, is reserved for ocean liners, large sailing ships and naval craft.

The liners – about 20 a year, mostly cruise boats or special wine excursion steamers – dock in **Port de la Lune** (Moon Port), so-called because it flanks a crescent formed by the river. A marina has been built at the river's edge near the suspension bridge.

Eating out

BUDGET

La Table du Pain – 6 pl. du Petit-Parlement – ☎ 05 56 81 01 00 – closed Christmas and New Year's Day – 10.67€. This very successful restaurant genre originated in Belgium. The dining room – blond stone walls, old shelves and waxed pine furnishings – is quite inviting. The menu proposes a wide selection of sandwiches, toasts and salads.

Lou Magret – 62 r. St-Rémi – ☎ 05 56 44 77 94 – closed 7-21 Jul, Sun and holidays – 10.82/16.77€. If overwhelmed by the choice of restaurants in this street, try this pleasant establishment whose speciality is canard de Chalosse, duck served grilled or with a delicious sauce. No-frills decor and outdoor terrace.

Le Bistro du Musée – 37 pl. Pey-Berland – ☎ 05 56 52 99 69 – bistrodumusee.com – closed Aug, 23 Dec to 2 Jan, Sat lunch and Sun – 15.09/27.44€. This bistro with a pretty green wood entrance makes a promising impression from the start. Thoughtful decor with exposed stone walls, oak parquet, moleskin seats and wine paraphernalia. South-west cuisine and a fine Bordeaux wine menu.

Bar Cave de la Monnaie – r. Porte-la-Monnaie – ☎ 05 56 31 12 33 – closed Sun – 6.86€ lunch – 28.97€. This very young wine bar decorated with photos of old Bordeaux bistros has an original flair. Customers choose their dishes first (omelettes or salads), then they draw their glass of Bordeaux from one of four taps in the wall. Affordable prices.

Café des 4 Sœurs – 6 bis cours du 30-Juillet – ☎ 05 56 81 52 26 – closed Feb school holidays, public holidays and Sun except the first Sun of the month – 13€ lunch – 15/25€. Close by the Grand Théâtre, this café founded in 1841 is charming indeed with its stucco, mirrors, mosaic and red velvet wall seats. Choose an omelette aux cêpes, a jambon piperade, a morue basquaise or some chipirons frais à l'encre with a glass of wine.

MODERATE

Chez Mémère – 11 r. de la Devise – ☎ 05 56 81 88 20 – 9.15€ lunch – 19.06/28.97€. Under the vaulted ceiling of this 16C workshop, discover the flavour and ambience of a fine meal chez mémère (at granny's): garbure landaise (soup), agneau de Pauillac, encornets frais aux piments d'Espelette... and, at the end of the week, la sanguette, a sort of black pudding made of poultry blood.

Café Régent – 46 pl. Gambetta – ☎ 05 56 44 16 20 – 21.34€. A Parisian brasserie in all its splendour, featuring wood furnishings, mirrors, black leather wall seats and red velvet chairs. Enjoyable atmosphere if you don't mind a crowd. Daily specials on the slate menu.

Café Louis – 2 pl. de la Comédie – ☎ 05 56 44 07 00 – 22.87/33.54€. Intelligent renovations have given new life to this ex-brasserie of the Grand Théâtre de Bordeaux, built in the 18C. The interior design – gilded pilasters, high ceiling with frescos and crystal chandeliers – is based on glory past. Pleasant terrace under the arcades. Traditional menu.

Where to stay

BUDGET

Hôtel Clemenceau – 4 cours Georges-Clemenceau – ☎ 05 56 52 98 98 – clemenceau@hotel-bordeaux.com – closed 15 days late Dec – 45 rooms: 25.92/45.73€ – ☒ 3.81€. Those who enjoy discovering the city by foot will appreciate this hotel established in an 18C building. Simple, air-conditioned rooms. Nice view of the roofs of Bordeaux from the breakfast room.

Hôtel Acanthe – 12 r. St-Rémi – ☎ 05 56 81 66 58 – info@acanthe-hotel-bordeaux.com – closed 23-30 Dec – reserv. required – 20 rooms: 27.44/47.26€ – ☒ 4.88€. A central location and very reasonable prices are the strong points of this recently renovated hotel. The bright rooms are big enough and well sound-proofed, and the reception is agreeable.

Hôtel Opéra – 35 r. de l'Esprit-des-Lois – ☎ 05 56 81 41 27 – closed 24 Dec to 2 Jan – 27 rooms: 32.01/48.78€ – ☒ 5.34€. Near the Grand Théâtre and allées de Tourny, lies this modest little family hotel. The reception is courteous and the rooms are functional. Those on the street are well sound-proofed. Good value for the euro.

Hôtel Notre-Dame – 36 r. Notre-Dame – ☎ 05 56 52 88 24 – 21 rooms: 35.83/44.21€ – ☒ 4.88€. An unpretentious little family hotel in an 18C house just behind quai des Chatrons. Rooms small but well-kept; reasonable prices.

MODERATE

Hôtel Presse – *6 r. de la Porte-Dijeaux* – ☎ *05 56 48 53 88* – *closed 25 Dec to 2 Jan* – *27 rooms: 44.97/76.22€* – ☑ *6.86€*. In the pedestrian shopping quarter of the old city, this is a nice little hotel despite the rather difficult access by automobile. Superb stairway with crimson carpets. Modern, functional, yet cosy rooms.

Hôtel Continental – *10 r. Montesquieu* – ☎ *05 56 52 66 00* – *50 rooms: 50.31/88.42€* – ☑ *6.10€*. In the old city, here's a venerable 18C mansion with a fine staircase in the hall. Breakfast room under a glass roof. Modern rooms with waxed wood furnishings.

On the town

Baud & Millet – *19 r. Huguerie* – ☎ *05 56 79 05 77* – *www.baudetmillet.com* – *Mon-Sat 11:30am-midnight*. If you fancy a good glass of wine and a tasty bit of cheese, come on a gastronomic expedition through this little restaurant's wine menu, featuring no fewer than 950 vintages from 48 different countries.

Bodega Bodega – *4 r. des Piliers-de-Tutelle.* – ☎ *05 56 01 24 24* – *Mon-Sat noon-2:30pm, 7pm-2am, Sun 7pm-2am*. The exuberance of the Spanish music and the range of flavours as you savour a variety of tapas will transport you to Castille, at least for the evening.

Calle Ocho – *24 r. des Piliers-de-Tutelle* – ☎ *05 56 48 08 68* – *Mon-Sat 5pm-2am*. This bar is all the rage – everybody comes here to party and dance the salsa. If the peanuts at the bar don't satisfy your hunger, try the house speciality, the *mojito*.

Chez Brunet – *9 r. de Condé* – ☎ *05 56 51 35 50* – *Tue-Sat 10am-2pm, 5pm-10pm* – *closed 2nd and 3rd weeks of Aug*. A charming woman runs this little restaurant where you can discover one of the region's specialities – oysters with grilled sausages.

Chez Ducon – *20 allées de Tourny* – ☎ *05 56 81 61 61* – *Mon-Sat noon-2pm, 5pm-midnight*. The Bordeaux bourgeoisie is quite fond of this *brasserie* located on the broad, chic allées de Tourny. Evenings are livened up by a jazz orchestra or pianist.

H36 Bassin à Flot n°1 – *1 r. de Gironde* – ☎ *05 56 50 40 60* – *www.h36.fr* – *Mon noon-2:30pm, Tue-Fri noon-2:30pm, 8pm-2am, Sat 8pm-2am* – *closed 1 and 8 May*. In remembrance of the heroic era of Marxism-Leninism, this big bar-restaurant set up in a former metallurgic plant is equipped with corresponding furnishings of rust-coloured metal. A DJ presides over weekend nights; concerts and record promotions take place here in collaboration with Sony. House specialities: vodka and cocktails.

Le Rétro – *13 pl. Stalingrad* – ☎ *05 56 86 57 16* – *daily 11pm-5am*. This discotheque has become a veritable local institution over the years. Theme evenings are its speciality.

Place de la Victoire – *Pl. Victoire*. This is where the Bordeaux youth comes to play! The dozen bars and cafés on this square are a never ceasing source of concerts and theme evenings. Among them, you might try El Bodegon, known for its ambience, or Le Plana, where every student worthy of the name must be seen.

Quai Paludate – *Quai Paludate*. Guided by a solid partying instinct, scores of night owls come to roost in one of the bars or discotheques along the quay. It can be so crowded in the wee hours that if you don't use your elbows, you may wind up in the water! Check out Le Comptoir du Jazz (jazz and blues concerts) and La Distillerie, specialized in whisky.

Showtime

L'Onyx – *11 r. Fernand-Philippart* – ☎ *05 56 44 26 12* – *office: 6pm-8pm performance evenings; Nov-May: Thu-Sat and 1st Mon of the month* – *closed Jul-Sep*. The oldest café-theatre of the city, L'Onyx is a requisite stop for discovering local culture.

La Boîte à Jouer – *50 r. Lombard* – ☎ *05 56 50 37 37 (reserv.)* – *ticket office: Wed-Sat 8pm; performances 8:30pm* – *closed Jul-Sep*. This theatre has two small rooms (60 and 45 seats) where lesser regional, national or international troupes specialized in contemporary or musical theatre perform.

Le Thelonius – *18 r. Bourbon* – ☎ *05 56 11 00 50* – *depending on shows*. Thelonious Monk, high priest of be-bop, would have appreciated this jazz bar where amateur and professional musicians take turns playing to the delight of the crowd.

Opéra de Bordeaux-Grand théâtre – *Pl. de la Comédie – BP 95 – ☎ 05 56 00 85 95 – www.opera-bordeaux.com – ticket office: Tue-Sat 11am-6pm; performances variable – see program – closed public holidays.* The Grand Théâtre de Bordeaux is one of the most handsome of France its architectural assets are a showpiece for its impressive cultural wealth. Henri Tomasi's Sampiero Corso (1956), Jean-Michel Damase's Colombe (1961) and the French adaptation of Benjamin Britten's Gloriana (1967) are among the significant performances that were first staged here. Symphonies, operas and ballets are performed here under excellent acoustic conditions.

Théâtre Fémina – *20 r. de Grassi – ☎ 05 56 79 06 69 – depending on shows.* With 1 100 seats, this handsome edifice sets the stage for plays, comedies, operettas, dance and concerts.

Théâtre du Port-de-la-Lune – *Sq. Jean-Vauthier – ☎ 05 56 91 98 00 – Tue-Sat 1pm-7pm – closed mid-Jul to mid-Aug.* This theatre's repertoire includes classic and contemporary drama staged by the Centre Dramatique National Bordeaux Aquitaine.

Shopping

Librairie Mollat – *15 r. Vital-Carles – ☎ 05 56 56 40 40 – www.mollat.com – Mon-Sat 9:30am-7pm.* France's first independent bookstore is still a veritable regional institution.

Baillardran Canelés – *Galerie des Grands-Hommes – ☎ 05 56 79 05 89 – Mon-Sat 8:30am-7:30pm.* Located in the Grands-Hommes market, this boutique makes delicious *canelés*, the small brown Bordelais cakes, irresistibly delicate and caramelised, that take on the shape of the ribbed *(canelé)* cake tins they're baked in. Crisp outside, they're soft and spongy inside.

Cadio-Badie – *26 allées de Tourny – ☎ 05 56 44 24 22 – Mon 9am-noon, 2pm-7pm, Tue-Sat 9am-7pm.* You can't help but be charmed by the old-fashioned style of this appealing boutique founded in 1826. Their *truffes* and Armagnac-flavoured *bouchons bordelais* are worth a special trip.

Chocolaterie Saunion – *56 cours Georges-Clemenceau – ☎ 05 56 48 05 75 – Mon 2pm-7:15pm, Tue-Sat 9:15am-12:30pm, 1:30pm-7:15pm.* One of the most illustrious chocolate confectioners of Bordeaux – a must.

Conseil Interprofessionnel des Vins de Bordeaux – *1 cours du XXX-Juillet – ☎ 05 56 00 22 88 – www.vins-bordeaux.fr – mid-Oct to end Mar: Mon-Fri 10am-5:15pm; Jun to mid-Oct: Mon-Fri 9:30am-5:30pm, Sat-Sun 9:30am-3pm.* This is where you'll find ample information about Bordeaux wines and vineyards – workshops, tastings... Several different wine cellars are to be found around this centre, including La Vinothèque Bordeaux (8 cours du XXX-Juillet), L'intendant (2 allées de Tourny) and Bordeaux Magnum (3 rue Gobineau).

Darricau – *7 pl. Gambetta – ☎ 05 56 44 21 49 – www.darricau.com – Mon-Fri 10am-7pm, Sat 10am-1pm, 2pm-7pm – closed the week of 14 Jul and public holidays.* Since the turn of the last century, this *chocolatier* pampers the city with the irresistible *pavé Gambetta* (praline with raisins soaked in wine), Bordeaux bottle-shaped chocolates *(confits de sauterne or de médoc)*, *la cadichonne* (crunchy vanilla) and *niniches* (soft caramel with dark chocolate).

Sports

Centre de Voile de Bordeaux-Lac – *Bd du Parc des Expositions – 33520 Bruges – ☎ 05 57 10 60 35 – Mon-Fri 9am-noon, 2pm-6:30pm.* This sailing centre organizes boat and wind-surfing courses for young and old alike.

Up up and away

Aéro-Lune – *Quai de Queyries -6ZA Queyries – ☎ 05 56 40 20 22 – Mon-Thu 11am-8pm, Fri 11am-midnight, Sat 9am-midnight, Sun 9am-8pm – closed Nov-Mar.* Imagine floating gently up to the sky under this big yellow hot-air balloon for a view of the city at 150m/492ft above ground. Some 30m/98ft high and 22m/72ft wide, the aerostat can carry up to 30 adults. Three flights per hour.

Take a break

Café Brun – *45 r. St-Rémi – ☎ 05 56 52 20 49 – daily 5pm-2am.* Why Brun? Because the ceiling of this neighbourhood bistro has taken on a nicotine-brown colour due to the innumerable cigarettes puffed herein. The owner, who introduces himself as being a hard-working, modest sort, likes to play jazz, blues and salsa to keep the friendly atmosphere at its peak.

La Comtesse – *26 r. du Parlement St-Pierre* – ☎ *05 56 51 03 07* – *Mon-Sat 6pm-2am*. Tranquil atmosphere in this minuscule café where the decor – all chandeliers and mirrors – reminds one of a château where the owner just might be the countess. A few artists join the mainly bourgeois clientele. Terrace on the little street.

Le Lucifer – *35 r. de Pessac* – ☎ *05 56 99 09 02* – *Mon-Fri 11am-2am, Sat 6pm-2am, Sun 9pm-2am*. Beer buffs are sure to be impressed by the selection proposed here – over 250 different kinds, including 12 on draught. Le Lucifer, far from diabolical, enjoys a calm ambience nurtured by a clientele of regulars.

The Connemara – *18 cours d'Albret* – ☎ *05 56 52 82 57* – *daily 11:30am-2am – closed Christmas*. Everything in this pub is Irish – the beer (9 on tap), whiskies (40 odd), salmon, and even the waiters! The inevitable dart boards complete the Emerald Isle decor and music (occasionally live).

★★ VIEUX BORDEAUX

Situated between the Chartrons and St-Michel districts, the old town, which includes some 5 000 buildings dating from the 18C, is currently undergoing large-scale restoration in an effort to return the city's ancient stonework to its original splendour.

1 From the Quinconces to the Chartrons

At the centre of this area is the triangle formed by the intersection of cours Clemenceau, cours de l'Intendance and allées de Tourny.

Esplanade des Quinconces – The sheer size (about 126 000m²/150 700sq yd) of this rectangular esplanade is very impressive. It was laid out during the Restoration (early 19C) on the site of the old Château Trompette.

The **Monument aux Girondins** with its bronze statuary was erected between 1894 and 1902, in honour of the *députés* from Bordeaux who fell under the guillotine in 1792, and of the Republican spirit. The huge work (65m/214ft long, 44m/145ft wide, and 50m/165ft high) is bursting with allegory: Liberty Breaking Her Chains atop the central column; various vices (Ignorance, Deceit etc) and virtues (Labour, Public Education, etc) on the Republique **fountain**★ facing the Grand Théâtre; Fraternity, Abundance and Happiness on the Concorde **fountain**★ opposite, to name but a few. The sea-shell shaped Triumphal Chariots are drawn by chimerical beasts with the forequarters of a horse and the tail end of a fish or reptile.
Statues of the writers Montesquieu and Montaigne (1858) preside over the Esplanade. Between the Esplanade and the waterfront stand two rostral columns (ship figureheads), decorated with figures representing Commerce and Navigation.

Place de la Comédie – The square, together with place de Tourny and place Gambetta, encloses the heart of one of the city's finest urban developments.

Monument to the Girondins

J. Malbure/MICHELIN

** **Grand Théâtre** – The recently restored Grand Théâtre is among the most beautiful in France, and is a potent symbol of the richness of both French architecture and French cultural ideas at the time.

The building was designed by the architect Victor Louis (1731-1802) and erected between 1773 and 1780 on the site of a Gallo-Roman temple. From the outside, it is distinguished by its Classically inspired peristyle, surmounted by a balustrade supporting 12 statues representing graces and muses.

Rue Mautrec, opposite the theatre leads to place du Chapelet; take passage Sarget on the left and turn right onto cours de l'Intendance.

Cours de l'Intendance – Cours de l'Intendance is the main street for high-fashion and luxury goods stores. From no 57, along rue Vital-Carles, there is a fine view of the towers of Bordeaux Cathedral. No 57 itself, the house where the artist Goya lived and died (1828), is now a Spanish cultural centre.

Place Gambetta – This square was formerly known as place Dauphine. All the houses were built in the Louis XV style (with arcades at street level and mansard roofs), giving a pleasing architectural unity. An attractive English garden has been laid out at the centre of the square which, during the Revolution, was the site of the scaffold.

Set back slightly is **Porte Dijeaux**, one of the town gates, which dates from 1748, and leads to the shopping street of the same name.

Walk along rue du Palais-Gallien.

The Chartrons district, in the northern sector of the city centre, lies between cours de Verdun and quai des Chartrons, and is bordered by cours Portal to the north. The name stems from a former Carthusian monastery founded here in the late 14C. The area reached its heyday in the 18C when it became fashionable for members of Bordeaux's high society to build their mansions here. Today, the heart of the district, which is being restored to its former glory, has become the centre of the city's antique trade.

Palais Gallien ⓥ – *Rue du Dr-Albert*. All that remains of this Roman amphitheatre which could seat 15 000 spectators are a few rows and arcades overgrown with weeds.

Jardin public – This 18C French-style garden was turned into an English-style park during the reign of Napoleon III. Palm trees and magnolias provide shade among colourful flower beds.

Cours Xavier-Arnozan – Formerly known simply as *le pavé* (the cobbled street), this avenue reflects the wealth of the great merchant and wine-growing families of the 1770s, who had their sumptuous town houses built conveniently close to but sufficiently removed from the noisy bustle of the port. Such private projects, independent of any overall town planning, nevertheless combined to form an architectural ensemble of remarkable unity. The three-storey Classical façades have arches at ground level. Above, squinches support magnificent **balconies**★ with ornamental wrought-iron railings.

During the 19C, small houses, known as *échoppes*, with tall narrow doors and carved window frames imitating those of middle-class residences, were erected in the vicinity of the town centre to satisfy popular demand.

La Cité Mondiale

Inaugurated in 1992, this complex located in quai des Chartrons, was designed by the local architect Michel Petuaud-Letang. Its harmonious curved structural glass façade includes a round tower. Until 1995, Cité Mondiale was given over to wines and spirits. Nowadays, it has become a business and conference centre with shops and restaurants.

---

② Round Trip starting from La Bourse

This stroll will lead you through a network of picturesque narrow streets extending between the St-Pierre and St-Michel districts.

** **Place de la Bourse** – Now named after the Stock Exchange (La Bourse), this magnificent square was formerly called place Royale and was the work of the architect Jacques Jules Gabriel (1667-1742) – Premier Architecte du Roi – and his son Jacques-Ange (1698-1782).

The eastern side gives onto the symmetrical façades lining the quays, whereas to the north rises the Stock Exchange itself. The southern side is graced by the former

Place de la Bourse

Hôtel des Fermes (tax assessors) whose upper floors have triangular pediments supported by columns – also used on the western pavilion.
Three Graces Fountain stands in the centre.

Continue, via rue F.-Philippart, to place du Parlement.

Note the majesty of the façades and the variety of their sculpted decoration combining to form one of the most splendid architectural examples of the Louis XV style.

★ **Place du Parlement** – Parliament Square, was once a royal market. This pleasant quadrangle of Louis XV buildings is arranged around a central courtyard paved with old cobblestones *(restored)*. A Second Empire fountain is set in the centre of the square. Many of the houses are very fine, some with ground-floor arcades, delicate fanlights and mask decorations. They are surmounted by open-work balustrades.

Take rue du Parlement-St-Pierre to place St-Pierre.

Many 18C houses in the St-Pierre district have been gradually restored. The 14C-15C church of St Peter was altered substantially in the 19C. On Thursdays, the square is livened up by a market of organic produce where one can enjoy a delicious healthy meal in convivial surroundings.

Follow rue des Argentiers.

The house at no 14, known as **Maison de l'Angelot**, dates from c 1750. The carved ornamentation of the façade includes a haut-relief of a child, and keystones in the Louis XV rough-cast style known as *rocaille*.

Continue to place du Palais.

The square owes its name to the old Palais de l'Ombrière, which was built by the dukes of Guyenne in the 10C, rebuilt in the 13C, used subsequently by the kings of England (who were also dukes of Aquitaine) and which finally, under Louis XI, became the seat of the Bordeaux Parliament in 1462. The Palace was demolished in 1800 to make way for the present rue du Palais.

Porte Cailhau ⊘ – The name of this triumphal arch derives either from the Cailhau family, who were members of the Bordeaux nobility, or from the *cailloux* (pebbles) washed up around its base by the Garonne and used as ballast by ships. The arch is built on the site of an ancient city gate, east of the old Palais de l'Ombrière, and was completed in 1495, which was the year of the Battle of Fournoue, won by Charles VIII, and to whom the monument is dedicated. This might explain the juxtaposition of the decorative and defensive elements (conical roofs, windows surmounted by interlaced arches and crenellated parapets).
Inside, on three different levels, an exhibit retraces the history of old Bordeaux, outlines the important stages of urban expansion and reveals plans for the future (videos). The top floor, under the rafters, offers an unusual **view** across the quays of the Garonne to the stone bridge.

Follow rue Ausone, cross cours d'Alsace-et-Lorraine and fork right; turn right onto rue de la Rousselle.

Pont de pierre

This street is lined with the shops in which the city's wine merchants, grain and salted meat sellers once plied their trade. The buildings are characterised by tall ground floors surmounted by low-ceilinged mezzanines. No 25 was the town house of the 16C philosopher-essayist Montaigne.

Turn left onto rue Neuve and continue to the cul-de-sac (right).

Still preserved in the city is a 14C wall, pierced with two windows surrounded with stone tracery. Through the porch to the right, stands the city's **oldest house**, where Montesquieu's wife, **Jeanne de Lartigue**, lived, its arches crowned with stone busts.

On the other side of cours Victor-Hugo there is a view of **Porte des Salinières** (Salt Sellers' Gate), formerly Porte de Bourgogne (Burgundy Gate).

Take rue de la Fusterie, opposite, to place Duburg and Basilique St-Michel.

Tour St-Michel ⓥ – The people of Bordeaux are justly proud of this late-15C hexagonal Gothic belfry, which stands apart from the basilica. At 114m/374ft tall, it is the highest tower in all of southern France (the tallest tower in the country belongs to Strasbourg Cathedral: 142m/468ft). The tower easily dwarfs the cathedral's Pey-Berland Tower, also a separate structure, a mere 50m/164ft high. Beneath the slender spire and superbly decorated facades lies a circular crypt.

Take rue Camille-Sauvageau.

Église Ste-Croix ⓥ – *Closed Sunday afternoon.* Built in the 12C and 13C and considerably restored during the 19C, this church has a Romanesque west front typical of the Saintonge region; The north tower is modern. The arches of the blind windows surrounding the main doorway are decorated with interesting carvings depicting Greed and Lust.

Walk to place de la Victoire (a favourite haunt of elderly people in the afternoon and of students in the evening) via place Léon-Duguit and place des Capucins.

Porte d'Aquitaine – This imposing 18C triumphal arch, erected in the centre of place de la Victoire, is surmounted by a triangular pediment bearing the royal arms and those of the city.

Follow the pedestrianised rue Ste-Catherine and turn right onto cours Victor-Hugo.

★Porte de la Grosse-Cloche – The 15C arched gateway (Great Bell Gate) with its three round turrets and conical roofs, is another source of local pride. The clocks date from 1592 (inside) and 1772 (outside);

La Grosse-Cloche

the bell was cast in 1775. The gateway stands on the site of an older structure, Porte St Éloi (St Eligius' Gateway), which was one of the entrances to the 13C walled town. When it existed, this belfry had the joyous task of ringing out the news that the grape harvest was to begin.

Follow the narrow rue St-James, which passes through the gateway, cross place Lafargue to rue du Pas-St-Georges and continue to place C.-Jullian. Turn left and continue to rue Ste-Catherine.

Rue Ste-Catherine – Further along the street a number of houses are built over ground-floor arcades, with wide semicircular bays opening at first-floor level. At the junction with rue de la Porte-Dijeaux note the Galeries Bordelaises *(opposite)*, a covered passageway and shopping arcade built by Gabriel-Joseph Durand in 1833.

Rue St-Rémi, on the right, leads back to place de la Bourse.

QUARTIER DES QUINCONCES

** **Grand Théâtre** Ⓥ – Inside the theatre, the coffered ceiling of the foyer is supported by 16 columns. Beneath the dome at the far end, a handsome staircase rises in a single flight then divides into two (an arrangement copied by Garnier when he designed the Paris Opera House; *see Introduction: Art and architecture).*
The panelled auditorium with its 12 gilded columns, provides a splendid interior with perfect acoustics. From the centre of the ceiling, painted by Roganeau after the primitive frescoes of Claude Robin, hangs a chandelier glittering with 14 000 drops of Bohemian crystal.

* **Église Notre-Dame** Ⓥ – This church, dedicated to the Virgin, was formerly a Dominican chapel. It was built between 1684 and 1707 by the engineer Michel Duplessy. The **façade**, in typical baroque style, is organised around a projecting central block comprising two superimposed orders surmounted by a triangular pediment. The wide entablature, decorated with a frieze of acanthus leaves, helps to emphasise the different masses, whereas pilasters, engaged columns and carved ornamentation animate the surface to give an interesting play of light and shade.
The name of the square – place du Chapelet – derives from the bas-relief above the entrance to the church, which depicts the Virgin presenting the rosary *(chapelet)* to St Dominic.
The stonework in the **interior** is especially impressive, including barrel vaulting, pierced by the lunettes of the clerestory windows for the nave, groin vaulting in the side aisles, and an organ loft extended on each side by gracefully curving balconies. The quality and design of the wrought-iron work – in particular the gates around the chancel – provide a fitting complement to the architecture. **Cloisters** dating from the 17C adjoin the wall on the right side of the church.

QUARTIER DE LA BOURSE

Musée des Douanes Ⓥ – The Customs Museum, which recounts the history of the Customs Department in France, is housed in a large hall with fine vaulting *(restored)*. On the right-hand side, the history of the customs administration is followed chronologically with the help of documents, uniforms, an old Customs Director's office, professional equipment, and prints and paintings including a portrait of St Matthew, the patron saint of customs officers (the Apostle had been employed as a tax collector and customs officer).
On the opposite side, different themes are presented – arms, customs in the cinema, in literature and in comic strips, customs activities (seizure of drugs, the arrest of counterfeiters), and the life of a customs brigade (*The Customs Inspectors' Hut, Afternoon* by Claude Monet). The tour ends with a display on the customs officer's latest weapon – the computer.

* **Basilique St-Michel** Ⓥ – The construction of St Michael's Basilica began in 1350, and lasted for two centuries, during which time the original design was much modified. The side chapels were added after 1475.
The generous dimensions of the restored basilica are impressive. Inside, the two-storey elevation is emphasised by high arcades, topped with tall clerestory windows, and wide side aisles. The lines of the flattened east end are barely affected by the three small chapels.
In the first chapel off the south aisle, stands a statue of St Ursula sheltering 1 000 virgins beneath her cloak. The modern stained-glass windows, behind the high altar, are by Max Ingrand. The moulded coving of the north transept doorway frames a tympanum decorated with an allegorical scene representing Original Sin *(left)* and Adam and Eve being expelled from the Garden of Eden *(right)*. The organ loft and pulpit date from the 18C. The latter, mahogany with marble panels, is surmounted by a statue of St Michael slaying the dragon.

QUARTIER PEY-BERLAND

Cathédrale St-André, with its famous tower, stands in the middle of place Pey-Berland, which is flanked by the city's most important museums. On the first Sunday of every month, the town centre is closed to traffic (bikes can be hired on place des Quinconces) and admission to museums is free.

★ **Cathédrale St-André** ⓥ – This cathedral, devoted to St Andrew, is the most impressive of all the religious buildings in Bordeaux.

The 11C-12C nave was altered in the 13C and again in the 15C. The rayonnant Gothic chancel and the transept were rebuilt in the 14C and 15C. Later, when the roof of the nave threatened to collapse, the building was strengthened by buttresses and flying buttresses, added at irregular intervals.

Approach the cathedral from the north and circle it to the left (clockwise).

★ **Porte Royale** – This 13C entrance to the right of the north doorway is renowned for its sculptures, inspired by the outstanding statuary adorning religious buildings in île-de-France (the region surrounding Paris, where Gothic architecture originated). Most remarkable are the Twelve Apostles in the entrance bay and, on the tympanum, the fine Gothic *Last Judgement.*

North Doorway – The 14C sculptures here are partially hidden by a wooden porch.

East End – The exterior is distinguished by its fine proportions and by its elevation: the two-tiered flying buttresses soar over the side aisles. Between the supports separating the axial chapel from the one on the left, note the statues of St Thomas, patron saint of architects, holding his square, and Mary Magdalene, in 15C costume, with her jar of sweet-smelling ointment.

South Transept Doorway – This entrance to the cathedral is below a pediment pierced by an oculus and three rose windows. The upper part, embellished with trefoil arcades, also boasts an elegant rose window set within a square. The west front, destroyed in the 18C and then rebuilt, remains unadorned.

Interior – The impressive nave features late-Gothic upper parts, resting on 12C bases. Note the lierne and tierceron vaulting over the first three bays. The pulpit, fashioned from mahogany and coloured marble, is 18C. The different height of the **chancel**★, also Gothic, contrasts with the nave and is accentuated by the slenderness of the tall arches, above which a blind triforium is illuminated by Flamboyant clerestory windows. An ambulatory with side chapels encircles the chancel.

Enter the ambulatory from the southern side.

Against the fourth pillar to the right of the chancel, there is a charming early-16C sculpture group depicting St Anne and the Virgin. The axial chapel closes off the 17C choir stalls. Opposite, a fine 17C door of carved wood separates the chancel from the nave.

On the inner face of the west front is the **Renaissance organ loft**. Below it two bas-relief sculptures trace the development of Renaissance sculpture. The group on the right shows Christ, harried by pagan deities from Hell, descending into Limbo, whereas that on the left shows the Resurrection, with the Saviour mounted upon an eagle, like Jupiter.

★ **Pey-Berland Tower** ⓥ – The tower, crowned with a belfry and lavishly decorated, was built in the 15C on the orders of Archbishop Pey-Berland. It has always stood separate from the main body of the cathedral, beyond the east end. The steeple, truncated by a hurricane in the 18C, now supports a copper figure of the Virgin. From the top *(229 steps up a narrow spiral staircase; beware of low door lintels)* there is a panoramic **view**★★ of the town and its steeples.

It is worth standing back a little (to the south), for an overall view of the twin spires above the north transept of the cathedral and, in the foreground, the massive, square, terraced towers flanking the south transept.

Centre Jean-Moulin ⓥ – This museum, devoted to the Resistance and deportation under the German occupation, presents a panorama of the Second World War. Jean Moulin, the most famous of France's Resistance heroes, became President of the clandestine National Resistance Council after a secret visit to General de Gaulle in Britain. Subsequently betrayed, he was caught by the Gestapo, tortured and murdered in 1943.

On the ground floor, the Centre displays Resistance pamphlets, secret communications, underground newspapers, illegal radio transmitters and other items – particularly relating to Jean Moulin – which developed as a result of the Nazi occupation. The first floor concentrates on the spread of Nazi tyranny and the deportations which followed – photographs of concentration camps, prisoners' uniforms, various scale models, and a series of moving canvases by Jean-Jacques Morvan on the theme of Night and Fog *(Nuit et Brouillard)*. The displays on the second floor are devoted to the men of the Free French Forces and their exploits, and include the boat *S'ils-te-Mordent* (If They Bite You) which, crammed with volunteers, linked the Brittany fishing port of Carantec with England. There is also a reconstruction of Jean Moulin's secret office.

Hôtel de Ville ⓥ – The City Hall is installed in the former bishop's palace, built in the 18C for Archbishop Ferdinand Maximilian de Meriadek, Prince of Rohan. The building marks the introduction of neo-Classicism to France.

The **main courtyard** is separated from the street by an arcaded gateway. The opposite side is bounded by the façade of the palace, its rather solemn lines enlivened by a projecting central section and corner pavilions.

Inside, the most notable features are the state staircase, the salons with their fine 18C panelling, and a banqueting hall decorated in *grisailles* by Lacour.

★★ **Musée des Beaux-Arts** ⓥ – The Fine Arts Museum bordering the gardens of City Hall displays a fine collection of 15C to 20C paintings in the north and south galleries. The **south wing** houses paintings from the Italian Renaissance (Titian's *Tarquin and Lucretia*), 17C French works, such as Vouet's *David Holding the Head of Goliath* directly inspired by Caravaggio, works from the 17C Dutch School, such as Ter Brugghen's *The Lute Player*, the captivating *Oak Struck by Lightning*, by Van Goyen, and paintings from the 17C Flemish School including the admirable *Wedding Dance*, painted in a popular rustic style by Jan I (Velvet) Brueghel. The 18C and early 19C are represented, among others, by the graceful *Portrait of Princess Louise of Orange-Nassau* by Tischenbein, Chardin's *Still Life* and four paintings by the local artist Pierre Lacour, who was the museum's first curator in 1811.

The **north wing** is given over to modern and contemporary works. The Romantic School is represented by Delacroix' famous *Ruins of Missolonghi*, whereas *The Forest of Fontainebleau* by Diaz de la Peña (born in Bordeaux) is an illustration of work by the Barbizon School, the first school to paint in the open air. The second half of the 19C is introduced by the outrageous *Rollas* by Henri Gervex, a nude refused by the 1878 Salon, followed by Henri Martin's *Chacun sa Chimère*, a large canvas inspired by the symbolist movement. A side room has a collection of interesting works by Odilon Redon, including one of his famous *Apollo's Chariot* series (1909) and the *Mystical Horseman* (charcoal outlined with pastel). From the 20C, there is the impressive *Église Notre-Dame à Bordeaux* by the Austrian Expressionist Kokoschka, the sinuous, tormented *Homme Bleu sur la Route* by Soutine and the extremely beautiful *Portrait of Bevilacqua* (1905), outlined in blue, by Matisse. Recent acquisitions include *Entrée du bassin à flot à Bordeaux* (1912) by the local artist, André Lothe, who incorporates Cubist concepts into figurative painting. The last room is dedicated to contemporary works.

The **Galerie des Beaux-Arts** in nearby place du Colonel-Raynal holds temporary art exhibits.

★ **Musée des Arts Décoratifs** ⓥ – The Lalande mansion which houses the Museum of Decorative Arts was designed by Laclotte in 1779. It has tall slate roofs and dormer windows.

A tour of the right wing begins with the Jeanvrot Collection (items relating to the lives of the last kings of France), presented in a setting furnished in 19C fashion, and continues through rooms of elegant woodwork and fine furniture, such as the Compagnie room, containing an 18C terracotta statue symbolising America (on the chimney-piece), and a marble bust of Montesquieu signed by Jean Baptiste Lemoyne. In the dining room is a display of local faience decorated with a pewter glaze, and a collection of fine 18C porcelain. Next door, the Guestier room typifies an elegant bourgeois lifestyle, displaying carved furniture and bronze statues by Barye. The two antechambers with their blue and white panelling are evocative of 18C, town life style in Bordeaux. The central staircase, embellished with a fine wrought-iron balustrade, leads to the first floor rooms, the first two of which are dedicated to French and foreign ceramics. The Jonquille lounge is decorated with a magnificent Venetian glass candelabra and splendid 18C decanters and flasks. The second floor houses an exhibit of faience from south-western France. Ornamental ironwork, enamel inlay and pre-18C collections of the locksmith's craft are displayed on the attic floor.

★★ **Musée d'Aquitaine** ⓥ – *20 cours Pasteur*. This regional museum, housed in the former Literature and Science Faculty and laid out on two levels, traces the life of Aquitaine Man from prehistoric times to the present day.

Collections in the **prehistory section** contain precious relics of arts and crafts practised by the hunters of the Stone Age. These include the famous Venus with a Horn (20 000 BC) from the Great Grotto in Laussel, and bison from the Cap Blanc grotto (Middle Magdalenian Age). A display of axes unearthed in the Médoc region illustrates the variety of tools fashioned by the metallurgists of the Bronze Age (4 000-2 700 BC). Iron Age spoils include funerary items (urns, jewellery, weapons) discovered in the Gironde burial grounds or Pyrenees tumuli, and the prestigious **Tayac Treasure** – a quantity of gold artefacts comprising coins, small ingots and a remarkable torque (necklace or collar) which dates from the 2C BC.

In the **Gallo-Roman section**, aspects of day-to-day religious and economic life in the Aquitaine provincial capital are illustrated through ceramics, glassware, mosaics, fragments of cornices and bas-relief sculptures. Of particular note are a grey Pyrenean marble altar, an imperious **statue of Hercules** in bronze, and the **Garonne Treasure** which comprises 4 000 orichalque (bronze alloy) coins bearing the effigies of emperors from Claudius to Antoninus Pius.

Early Christian times and the Middle Ages are illustrated by grey marble and limestone sarcophagi and mosaics, including a 4C representation of *The Holy Sepulchre*. Excavations and public works in the city have uncovered significant pieces, which have been added to the collections – Romanesque capitals from St Andrew's Cathedral and a Flamboyant Gothic rose window from the Carmelite monastery.

Bordeaux's golden age (18C) saw the development of grandiose urban projects and the building of splendid mansions which were luxuriously furnished (superb Bordeaux cabinet from Gayon Château, fine glassware and ceramics). Several displays focus on country life and farming in former times. The accent is always placed on the natural resources of Aquitaine, which embraces the rural landscape of Béarn, the Landes (moors) of Gascony, the Gironde and its vineyards, and of course Arcachon and its oyster farming.

Beyond the rooms dotted with quotations from famous writers, several rooms evoke **19C Bordeaux** (the port, the town, colonial trade) and the modern region of Aquitaine (20C).

Musée Goupil ⊙ – The museum's important collections of photographs, etchings and copperplates illustrate 19C picture-reproduction techniques, used by Goupil & Co to introduce to a wide public the work of ancient and contemporary masters (Rodin, Degas, Toulouse-Lautrec etc)

QUARTIER DES CHARTRONS

★ **Musée d'Art Contemporain** ⊙ – *Entrance at 7 rue Ferrère*. The former **Lainé warehouse**★★, built in 1824 for storing goods imported from the French colonies, has been successfully remodelled into a Museum of Contemporary Art. It houses the collections of the Centre d'Arts Plastiques Contemporains de Bordeaux (CAPC), which are particularly strong on works from the 1960s and 1970s. These are displayed thematically and alternately.

Inside, a tall, twin-aisled central section runs the length of the building. It is flanked by side aisles, each separated into three storeys, and the components are rhythmically linked by great, semicircular arches. The huge amount of space available allows even the largest exhibits to be mounted here, accommodating individual works of great dimension. The sober character of the original structure of the building (grey limestone, pale-red brick and wood) was further accentuated during its conversion by the use of severe black metal.

The museum also functions as a cultural centre with conferences and debates, guided tours on a particular artist or aspect of contemporary art, children's workshops and film projections.

Musée des Chartrons ⊙ – *41 rue Borie, just N of cours de Verdun (take rue Notre-Dame)*. This small museum, which traces the history of the maritime wine trade, occupies part of a lavishly appointed wine-merchant's home. Built in c 1720 for an Irish dealer called Francis Burke, it is the only house in the district to have its storerooms and bottling plant above street level. An elegant staircase with a wrought-iron balustrade leads to the *plancher* (literally floor – the name customarily used in wine cellars to designate the sector where bottles are packed). Here the evolution of bottling, labelling and packaging techniques is illustrated alongside developments in the wine trade. Many different types of bottles, flasks, jars, stencils and lithographed labels are on view.

Vinorama ⊙ – *12 cours de Médoc*. Thirteen tableaux with costumed figures recount the history, production and commercialisation of Bordeaux wines from antiquity to the present day. The tour ends with a wine-tasting session including a vintage wine from 1850, a modern wine and wine drunk in Roman times (addition of honey and spices).

★★ **Croiseur Colbert** ⊙ – *The tour of the ship consists of three signposted circuits, with green and yellow markers for the forecastle deck and the first deck, red markers for control room and engine room, and blue markers for the castle and bridge. The two last sections include steep steps and are not recommended for the less agile.*

The *Colbert* has been berthed in Port de la Lune near cours de la Martinique since 1993, casting its imposing triangular silhouette onto the waters of the River Garonne. This anti-aircraft warship was launched in 1959 and carried out its first mission in Toulon as the Mediterranean Squadron's flagship. She was then converted into a missile-launcher and served during the 1970s in the Atlantic Squadron in

Brest. Although she performed few military operations, she went on some memorable missions, including the rescue of victims of the Agadir earthquake in March 1960, repatriation of Maréchal Liautey's ashes in 1961, General de Gaulle's trips to South America in 1964 and Quebec in 1967 and Operation Salamander (summer 1990 in the Gulf War). The exhibits vary according to the circuit chosen – weapons' room (Masurca and Exocet systems), the engine room, the control rooms, the two officers' quarters, the crew's galley, a medical centre (operating room, dentist), post office and many other facilities designed for daily life on board a warship in the second half of the 20C. The cabins belonging to the different members of the crew can also be viewed, including the Admiral's cabin (green/yellow circuit) with its chimney piece, where famous guests such as Général de Gaulle were entertained. From the decks, fore and aft, the pad for helicopters and other war machinery is visible.

Meriadeck District

Named in honour of Prince Ferdinand Maximilien de Rohan, Archbishop of Bordeaux in the 18C, this ultra-modern complex is the administrative centre of the Aquitaine region.

The area includes offices, administrative buildings, apartment blocks, a shopping centre, an ice-skating rink and the municipal library. Esplanade Charles-de-Gaulle is an example of the formal gardens and ponds here. Suspended footbridges lead to roads bordering the complex. Some of the cubed and rounded concrete and glass buildings are encased in metal super-structures. The most distinctive are the **Caisse d'Épargne** building with its superposed curved and rectangular forms, the mirror-walled **Bibliothèque** (Library), the **Hôtel de Région** with its harmonious, vertically lined façade made of concrete, and the **Hôtel des Impôts** (Tax Office) which is a gleaming mass of metal.

ADDITIONAL SIGHTS

▶▶ **Musée d'Histoire Naturelle** ⓥ (Natural History Museum); **Basilique St-Suerin** ⓥ – 11C crypt; **Site paléochrétien** ⓥ – Paleo-Christian site.

EXCURSIONS

★ Vignoble de Bordeaux – *See Vignoble de BORDEAUX.*

★ Établissement Monétaire de Pessac – *Southern suburbs of Bordeaux. Follow the signs to Parc Industriel de Pessac. At the roundabout turn right on avenue Archimède leading to Voie-Romaine (Roman Way).*
This concrete fortress, in which coins and medals are struck, has housed the country's Mint since 1973 – (notes are made in Chamalières, Puy-de-Dôme). The hall contains an exhibit of coins and medals. A 350m/400yd-long upper gallery gives a good view of the whole process from delivery, melting and laminating of the metal ingots to cutting, finishing and conditioning of the coins. The 180 000 rough coins, called blanks, produced per hour, are given a preliminary check, then turned into coins at the rate of 250 per minute. The Ministry of Finance thus produces 4 million copper and silver coins a day, not only for France but also for several foreign countries (Israel, Lebanon, Cyprus, French-speaking Africa). The first French Euro was coined here in March 1998.

Ancien Prieuré de Cayac – *At the southern exit of Gradignan via N 10.* This priory was built in the 13C and restored in the 17C. It used to be on the road to Santiago de Compostela.

Vignoble de BORDEAUX★

Michelin map 335: F-3 – H-5 and 1-5 – K-8, 233 folds 37
and 38 or 234 folds 2, 3, 4, 8 and 11

For some, Bordeaux may be the capital of Aquitaine, but for wine-lovers, it is synonymous with the world-famous wines. Numerous **guided tours** Ⓥ of the vineyards (Vignoble de Bordeaux) are available.

The Bordeaux wine-producing region covers 135 000ha/520sq mi in the valleys of the River Garonne and River Dordogne in the *département* of Gironde; it includes several distinct areas each producing characterictic wines: Côtes-de-Bordeaux, Entre-Deux-Mers, Sauternais, St-Émilion and Médoc.

CÔTES-DE-BORDEAUX

1 Round tour from Bordeaux *105km/65mi – allow one day*

Drive out of town along D 113 and D 10 which follow the River Garonne SE of Bordeaux.

Château de Langoiran Ⓥ – All that remains of the 13C castle is a ruined outer wall and an imposing circular keep among luxurious vegetation.

Rions – This small fortified town is entered via the 14C Porte du Lhyan, which has kept all its original defensive features – machicolations, guard-rooms on either side, grooves guiding the portcullis, and an *assommoir* (a platform from which objects could be dropped on attackers) etc.

Cadillac – The town, originally a *bastide* founded in 1280, is situated on the north bank of the Garonne, and is known for its sweet white wines. The remains of the 14C town walls are still visible. The austere **château** Ⓥ (built between 1589 and 1620 for the Duc d'Épernon then devastated during the Revolution and later rebuilt) stands inside its own defensive walls with bastions at the corners. Inside, there are enormous rooms with coffered ceilings and monumental, richly carved and decorated marble fireplaces. The 17C tapestries relating the history of Henri III were woven in the huge vaulted basement.

★ **Ste-Croix-du-Mont** – The village is noted for its strange **caves**★ hollowed out from a thick fossilised oyster bed laid down by the ocean in the Tertiary Era. One of these has been turned into a **cave de dégustation** Ⓥ (tasting cellars). There are also splendid **views**★ stretching towards the distant Pyrenees.

St-Macaire – This small, medieval town of dark, narrow streets, perched on a rock above the river, still has the original 12C walls, with their 15C machicolations and three gates.

St-Sauveur Ⓥ is a huge, imposing church with an unusual trefoil-shaped Romanesque apse. Other features include the 13C murals near the chancel, the Gothic nave and polygonal belfry, and the 13C porch crowned by a Flamboyant Gothic rose window. A 13C priory and its cloisters stand nearby.

Verdelais – Basilique Notre-Dame Ⓥ, is an important place of pilgrimage. Worshippers come to venerate the 14C wooden statue of the Virgin, said to prevent drowning and heal paralytics.

Château de Cadillac

A. Thuillier/MICHELIN

Eating out

BUDGET

Le Lion d'Or – *pl. de la République – 33460 Arcins – 6km/3.6mi NW of Margaux via D 2 –* ☎ *05 56 58 96 79 – closed Jul, 23 Dec to 1 Jan, Sun-Mon – reserv. required – 10.37€.* Bistro ambience in this restaurant, with its wall seats and big mirrors reflecting the Châteaux de Bordelais wine racks. The generous and well-prepared fare is quite popular, especially because the prices are so reasonable.

Auberge de Savoie – *1 pl. Trémoille – 33460 Margaux –* ☎ *05 57 88 31 76 – closed Spring school holidays, Mon evening off-season, Sat lunch in season, Sun and public holidays –* ✏ *– 12.96/34.30€.* A very friendly reception awaits you in this handsome 19C stone house near the tourist office. Two colourful, pleasant dining rooms. When the weather is agreeable, you may prefer the nice terrace in the back. Well-prepared cuisine at affordable prices.

MODERATE

Ferme-auberge Château Guittot-Fellonneau – *33460 Macau – 6km/3.6mi SE of Margaux via D 2 and D 211 –* ☎ *05 57 88 47 81 – closed Feb school holidays and 16 Aug to 5 Sep – 18/37€.* In this wine-producing property in Médoc, the alchemy of the grape is combined with the science of good cookery. On a shady terrace overlooking the vineyards, let yourself be tempted by the pleasures of an authentic south-west repast, featuring *rillettes*, *confits*, *foie gras*... prepared by the proprietor herself.

Le Flore – *1 Petit-Champ-du-Bourg – 33540 Coirac – 7.5km/4.5mi W of Sauveterre-de-Guyenne via D 671 then D 228 after St-Brice –* ☎ *05 56 71 57 47 – closed Wed and Sun evenings and Mon – 15.09€ lunch – 18.14/29.73€.* Whether you choose the shaded terrace or the big, flower-filled dining room of this little house, prepare yourself for a first-rate meal, prepared by a very creative young chef. Affable and professional, his wife will gladly help you choose from among the subtly flavoured dishes.

Le St-Julien – *11 r. St-Julien – 33250 St-Julien-Beychevelle – 4km/2.4mi S of Pauillac via D 2 –* ☎ *05 56 59 63 87 – closed Feb, Sun and Tue evenings and Wed from Nov to Mar – 25.15/53.36€.* This restaurant used to be the village bakery. Built in 1850, it has exposed beams and stonework in the dining room. The chef, a native son of Pauillac, concocts an elaborate regional cuisine.

Where to stay

BUDGET

La Lézardière Bed and Breakfast – *Boimier-Gabouriaud – 33540 St-Martin-de-Lerm – 8km/4.2mi SE of Sauveterre-de-Guyenne via D 670, D 230 and D 129 –* ☎ *05 56 71 30 12 – closed 13 Nov to 22 Mar –* ✏ *– 4 rooms: 36/48€ – meals 16€.* Colourful rooms have been nicely fitted out on the upper level of this 17C smallholding overlooking the valley of the Dropt. *Table d'hôte* in the upper barn. Room with documents about wine and the region behind the cribs where the cattle used to eat. Pool and one big self-catering cottage.

Chassagnol Bed and Breakfast – *33410 Ste-Croix-du-Mont – at Peyrat on D 10 –* ☎ *05 56 62 00 58 –* ✏ *– 3 rooms: 38.11€.* A very nice stop for wine enthusiasts is this large 19C house set in the heart of the Ste-Croix-du-Mont vineyards. A few period pieces in the spacious bedrooms. The garden and terrace with a barbecue are quite popular.

Château du Broustaret Bed and Breakfast – *La Greche – 33410 Rions – 6km/3.6mi N of Cadillac via D 11 toward Targon then D 120 –* ☎ *05 56 62 96 97 – closed Nov to Easter school holidays –* ✏ *– 5 rooms: 40/45€.* Hospitality is a 25-year-old tradition in this winery amid the Premières Côtes de Bordeaux grape vines. Woods and fields surround this noble house and its simple, comfortable rooms. A tranquil halt, perfect for discovering the vineyards.

Domaine de Carrat Bed and Breakfast – *rte de Ste-Hélène – 33480 Castelnau-de-Médoc – 1km/0.6mi SW of Castelnau-de-Médoc –* ☎ *05 56 58 24 80 – closed Christmas –* ✏ *– 4 rooms: 41.16/53.35€.* Surrounded by a pine and deciduous forest, this majestic, red-shuttered house used to accommodate the stables of the neighbouring château. Considerate reception and very cosy rooms. You'll enter via the splendid paved porchway that horse-drawn carriages used to pass through.

Château Cap Léon Veyrin Bed and Breakfast – *33480 Listrac-Médoc – 4km/2.4mi from Listrac via D 5*^{E2} *–* ☎ *05 56 58 07 28 – closed Christmas to New Year's day –* ✏ *– 5 rooms: 41,16€.* The same family has been running this long residence situated in the heart of a 20ha winery since 1810. The Louis XV-style rooms are endowed with lovely bathrooms. The breakfast room opening onto the *chai* is superb.

Le Manoir de James Bed and Breakfast – *rte de Ste-Colombe* – *33580 St-Ferme* – *☎ 05 56 61 69 75* – *midubois@wanadoo.fr* – *closed 15 Dec to 15 Jan* – *✉* – *3 rooms: 46/55€*. In the 19C, the addition of handsome towers topped with pointed roofs gave this 17C farm its present noble appearance. A verdant setting, rooms with fireplaces, Gironde tiles in blond shades gracing the front entrance, a warm welcome and the pool combine to ensure a lovely stay.

MODERATE

Château le Foulon Bed and Breakfast – *33480 Castelnau-de-Médoc* – *☎ 05 56 58 20 18* – *closed 15 Dec to 2 Jan* – *4 rooms: 76.22€ ✉*. This château dating from 1840 is the perfect starting point for your discovery tour of the great vintages of the Médoc. The rooms, furnished with antiques, have preserved their spacious feel. All overlook the park and the swans gliding on its waterway.

The painter **Henri de Toulouse-Lautrec** (1864-1901) is buried in the cemetery of this small town.

Drive along D 117.

After Verdelais, the road crosses the vine-covered hills of a district known for its sweet white wines affected by the noble mould which concentrates the grape juice by dehydration. Here, the châteaux are hidden among clumps of trees. There are views of Ste-Croix (in the foreground), the valley of the Garonne and the distant forests of the Landes.

Loupiac – Loupiac, famous for its white wines, is set in picturesque surroundings. The town already existed in Roman times and is said to have been home to the Latin poet Ausonius.

Beyond Langoiron, turn right onto D 20 to enter Entre-Deux-Mers country.

St-Genès-de-Lombaud – The church in this village, halfway up a valley slope, is a place of pilgrimage venerating the Black Virgin. It is built on a site thought to have been occupied by a Roman villa. The west front, with its belfry-gable, is pierced by a Romanesque doorway beneath coving carved with animals and small human figures, most of them comic. There are Romanesque capitals in the nave and, on the north side, carved stonework which was probably once part of a domestic altar.

To return to Bordeaux, continue along D 20, then turn left onto D 14 which joins D 113.

ENTRE-DEUX-MERS

2 Round tour from Bordeaux *55km/34mi – 4hr*

The pleasing, gentle slopes of the Entre-Deux-Mers region, carpeted with vineyards, fields rich in summer with ripening corn, and an occasional copse, undulate between the valleys of the Dordogne and the Garonne.

Leave Bordeaux to the E via D 936, then turn right on D 115.

Sadirac – The town is an important pottery centre, where craftsmen mainly work with the local blue clay. The heyday of this traditional activity was in the 18C, and fine examples can be seen in **La Maison de la Poterie** – **Musée de la Céramique Sadicacaise** ⊙. This local museum, on the site of a former workshop built in 1830 (the original furnace can be seen at the far end of the gallery), displays examples of local work dating from the 14C to the 18C (ceramics used domestically and in sugar refining), along with models of furnaces from other periods. Production today, from the three remaining workshops, concentrates on garden pottery, building materials, and the recreation of traditional designs.
The **Ferme-parc Oh ! Légumes Oubliés** ⊙ is a farm devoted to preserving "forgotten" varieties of vegetables and plants, offering a tour of its orchard and kitchen gardens.

D 115^{E8} and D 671 lead to Créon.

Créon – Once a *bastide* (13C arcaded square), the capital of Entre-Deux-Mers is an important agricultural market. The surrounding area has so many valleys that it has been nicknamed Little Switzerland.

La Sauve – There are two interesting churches in this village built on the former site of a large forest cleared by monks. The **old abbey★** ⊙ was founded in 1079 by St Gérard and was once very powerful (dependencies stretched from Spain to England). The Romanesque and Gothic ensemble was, however abandoned in the 16C, though re-inhabited by monks in the 17C until the time of the Revolution; the vaulting collapsed in 1809. The 12C-13C abbey church has magnificent **capitals★**

carved with scenes from the Old and the New Testaments, and 13C ruined cloisters. **St-Pierre** is late 12C. The west front, with its belfry-wall and buttresses, presents an austere grandeur. Between the bays of the flat east end stand 13C statues of St Michael, St James, the Virgin and St Peter.

Église de Castelvieil – The church is distinguished by a superb **Romanesque doorway**★ in the Saintonge style, with lavishly carved capitals and covings. Scenes illustrated include the labours of the months *(first cove, starting from the top)*, the combat between the Virtues and the Vices *(second cove)* and human figures linked by a rope, symbolising the community of the faithful *(third cove)*.

The capitals include the Holy Women at the Tomb, and the beheading of John the Baptist, on the right, and the Seven Deadly Sins *(the first capital on the extreme left represents Lust)*, on the left.

Sauveterre-de-Guyenne – This is a typical *bastide*, created in 1281, with four fortified gates and a vast central square.

Ancienne Abbaye de Blasimon – Nestling in the hollow of a valley are the ruins of an old Benedictine abbey which was once encircled by fortified walls (a tower still remains). The 12C-13C church has both Romanesque and Gothic elements (rounded and pointed arches) and a 16C open-work belfry-gable. The coving of the main doorway is carved with fine

Doorway of the Castelvieil church

hunting scenes etc. Only a few arcades (with Romanesque capitals) remain from the **cloisters**, together with a section of the chapter-house.

Rauzan – Rauzan, one of the market towns of Entre-Deux-Mers, has kept the romantic ruins of a **château** , built between the 12C and the 15C. Perched on the lip of a valley, the castle was protected by fortified walls with merlons, and has a seigniorial dwelling pierced by mullion windows and a majestic circular keep 30m/98ft high. From the top of the keep there is a fine view of the surrounding countryside. On the far side of the valley – at the bottom of which nestles a charming old wash-house – stands the village **church** with its three splendid 13C doorways, and a belfry-gable in a style more typically found in the Pyrenees.

Follow D 128 to Daignac.

Daignac – This is a picturesque village, spanning a ravine carved out by a stream called Le Canedone. Downstream of the old bridge are the ruins of a 13C mill.

Return to Bordeaux along D 936.

SAUTERNES AND BARSAC

③ Round tour from Barsac *30km/19mi – allow 2hr*

Small in size, but highly reputed for its white wines, this wine-growing area is limited by the lower valley of the Ciron, near its confluence with the Garonne. The *terroir* – the land producing a given *appellation* – covers the five municipalities of Sauternes, Barsac, Preignac, Bommes and Fargues. The vines grow on the valley slopes, in walled vineyards, generally planted in rows at right angles to the river. Only three grape varieties are used – Sauvignon, Muscadelle and Sémillon.

The original feature of this part of the Bordeaux region is the harvesting method used. The grapes, once ripened, are not picked right away. They are left on the branch so that they can be affected by **noble mould** or *botrytis*, a fungus peculiar to the district which increases the sugar content of the fruit. The overripe or candied grapes are then picked, one by one, and transported to the press with infinite care. A local guild, the Commanderie du Bontemps de Sauternes et Barsac, whose headquarters are in Château de Malle *(see below)*, participates in numerous events designed to promote the wines of the district, most of which are exported.

Barsac – The **church** , a curious building dating from the late 16C and early 17C, has three aisles of equal height, and vaults demonstrating the survival of the Gothic style in the Classical period. The furnishings – gallery, altars, reredos, and confessionals – are in the Louis XV style, and the sacristies are wood-panelled or stuccoed.

Budos – The village of Budos, a little outside the actual Sauternes area, has preserved the **ruins** of an early-14C feudal castle built by a nephew of Pope Clement. The sloping approach to the old esplanade passes through a fortified gateway crowned by a square, crenellated tower. The massive strength of the curtain wall and towers, shored up with timber, is best appreciated from inside the moat protecting the west façade.

Sauternes – This is a typical wine-growers' village. A little way to the south is the 17C **Château Filhot**.

Château Yquem – The château is the home of the most prestigious Sauternes in the world. Its wines have been famous since the 16C.

Château de Malle – Château d'Yquem stands unique as the sole *premier grand cru* (or classified first quality) of the Sauternes-Barsac region. Immediately below it, are the fine 11 *premiers crus* and 13 *deuxièmes crus* – the Château de Malle being classed among the latter.

Entrance gates, adorned with superb wrought-iron work, lead into the property. The attractive château and gardens were created at the beginning of the 17C by

Vineyards of the Sauternes region – Château Yquem

an ancestor of the present owner. The château itself is charming, with a layout similar to that of some of the isolated manor houses in the Gironde. The outbuildings house the wine-stores or cellars.

The interior of the château, resplendent with fine period furniture, boasts a collection of 17C *trompe-l'œil* silhouettes which is unique in France. They were used in former times as part of the setting of the small rockwork theatre set up in the gardens.

Italian-style terraced gardens are embellished with 17C carvings and statues depicting mythological themes, hunting or grape-harvest scenes.

Beyond the gardens, the vineyard – the only example of its kind in the Gironde – extends over two different *terroirs:* Sauternes (white wine) and Graves (red wine).

Return to Barsac via D 8^{E4} to Preignac, and N 113 leading N.

ST-ÉMILION

④ Round tour from St-Émilion *52km/32mi – 6hr*

It is best to visit the wine country in autumn, when a soft golden light bathes the contours of the landscape and the bronze rows of vines are alive with the fever of the grape harvest, usually the second fortnight in September. The picturesque landscape of neatly planted slopes crowned by the châteaux set in groves of trees, with glimpses, here and there of the valleys of the River Dordogne and River Isle, can nevertheless be appreciated at any time of the year.

★★ St-Émilion – *See St-ÉMILION.*

Leave St-Émilion via D 122 heading N.

Just before the village of St-Georges, its fine Louis XVI château can be seen on the right, crowned with a balustrade and *pots-à-feu* (classical urns from which stone flames leap).

St-Georges – This small 11C Romanesque church has a square tower wider at the top than at the base, and a curved apse with modillions carved with saucy subjects, treated in an almost Cubist style.

Montagne – The Romanesque church in this small town has three polygonal apses, topped by a square tower containing a strong room. From the terrace, beside the church, there is a view of St-Émilion and the Dordogne Valley.

The **Écomusée du Libournais** ⓥ nearby, offers visitors a trip into the rural world of the past. There are two museums, presenting the traditional activities and social background of local wine growers in Libourne in the late 19C and the early 20C. Temporary exhibitions explain present-day wine-growing techniques.

Continue along D 122 – 2km/1mi beyond Lussac turn left into D 21 and continue for 4.5km/3mi.

Petit-Palais – The late-12C church with its delightful Romanesque façade★ in the Saintonge style is surrounded by its cemetery. The scale is small, but perfectly proportioned, and the decorations are carved with a rare delicacy in a profusion of motifs.

The elevation presents three tiers of arches and blind arcades of different designs, some of them multi-lobed in the Arabic style. The archivolt of the central doorway is carved with a series of animals chasing one another and, in the corners, two amusing figures of a woman, and of a man pulling a thorn from his foot. The entrance is flanked by two blind doorways, which give a false impression of the interior which in fact only has a nave and no side aisles. A disparity between the two blind bays at the extremities of the façade's second tier, one multi-lobed, the other plain, is another particularity of this fascinating building.

Return to D 17 and turn S.

Castillon-la-Bataille – Castillon was the site of a famous battle, in 1453, which put an end to the English domination of Aquitaine. The English troops led by General Talbot were decimated by a French army under the command of the Bureau brothers (14C-15C brothers who modernised French artillery, which was instrumental in defeating the English on this occasion).

The town is built on a hillock overlooking the north bank of the Dordogne. The surrounding slopes produce a wine called Côtes de Castillon, classed as a Bordeaux Supérieur.

La Bataille de Castillon – *Château-de-la-Brande – 33350 Castillon-la-Bataille – ☎ 05 57 40 14 53 – from mid-Jul to mid-Aug: shows: daily 10pm; phone hours: daily 8am-noon, 2pm-6pm.* An open-air performance relives the famous Battle of Castillon, the final battle of the Hundred Years War that witnessed the defeat of General Talbot's English troops in 1453, allowing Charles VII and the French Kingdom to conquer the Aquitaine anew.

Return to St-Émilion via D 130 to St-étienne-de-Lisse and D 245.

★ HAUT MÉDOC

5 Round tour from Bordeaux *125km/78mi – allow one day*

Leave Bordeaux to the NW via N 215. In Eysines turn right on D 2 and continue for about 15km/9mi.

The Upper-Médoc district, with its exceptional natural conditions and fine-wine tradition dating back to the time of Louis XIV, is true château country and the origin of many wines classed as *grands crus*, which are carefully kept in wine stores or **chais**.

The Médoc is particularly attractive during the autumn, when the skies are a veiled blue, and the yellowing leaves of the vines temper the excitement of the grape-picking with a hint of melancholy.

A number of different wine stores welcome visitors, the most interesting are described below.

Château Siran ⊘ – *At Labarde.* A visit to the wine stores is followed by a tour of some of the rooms inside the château, which once belonged to the Comtes de Toulouse-Lautrec, ancestors of the 19C painter. A reception room is furnished with fine pieces, and there is a collection of dessert plates richly decorated with hunting

Wine-growing in Médoc

Although the gravel deposited in the past by the Gironde estuary has not produced very fertile soil, at least it has the advantage of storing heat during the day and releasing it slowly at night, thus minimising spring frosts. Médoc vines are pruned down very close to the ground to take advantage of this. Also, the steep-sided valleys, known as *jailles*, at right angles to the Gironde estuary facilitate the run-off of excess water, offering growers a variety of exposures. The climate also helps – while the water mass in the estuary tends to keep the temperature mild, the pine forest of the Landes acts as a screen, sheltering the Médoc from Atlantic breezes.

The Médoc supplies 8% of the appellation wines of Bordeaux. They are exclusively red and are made principally from the Cabernet grape producing a wine which is light, has a nice bouquet, is elegant, even a little astringent, and a delight to a discerning palate. The most highly rated are Château Lafite, Château Margaux, Château Latour and Château Mouton.

scenes, marriage scenes etc. A painting in the style of Caravaggio, *The Young Bacchus*, hangs above the staircase leading to the first floor. The dining hall – named the Décaris Room, after the artist who depicted wine-related subjects in his paintings – displays interesting glazed earthenware decorated with twining vine motifs. Note also the engravings signed by Rubens, Velasquez, Boucher and Daumier.

Château Margaux – The wine from this estate is one of the five wines of Bordeaux classed as a *premier grand cru classé*, one of the aristocrats of the Médoc. The **vineyards** which produce it cover an area of 85ha/210 acres including rows of extremely old and valued vines, which are gnarled and twisted.

Visitors are shown the **wine stores** Ⓥ, various wine-making installations and an interesting collection of old wine bottles.

The château itself is a finely proportioned building. It was constructed in 1802 by an architect named Combes and comprises a basement, two storeys and an attic. The informal appearance of the English-style gardens contrast with the formal lines of the building.

Beyond Margaux, route D 2 follows the contour of the hillside rising above the *palus* (the alluvial soil at the foot of the valley).

At Arcins turn left to Grand-Poujeaux. From here, turn right on D 5 towards Lamarque.

Château Maucaillou – This estate offers a visit to the stores followed by a tour of the **Musée des Arts et Métiers de la Vigne et du Vin** Ⓥ, a museum which illustrates wine-making methods, ancient and modern, on this estate.

Rejoin D 2 and continue N. At Cussac-le-Vieux turn right.

Fort Médoc Ⓥ – This fort, designed by Vauban in 1689 to prevent the English fleet from penetrating the Gironde and approaching Bordeaux, could pepper the estuary with cannon fire, adding to the defences of Fort Pâté and the citadel of Blaye on the far side. Beyond a gateway, Porte Royale with its pediment carved with a sun (the emblem of Louis XIV, the Sun King), lies the courtyard and the main features of the fort – guard-room, powder magazine, bakery and gun emplacements etc. Beyond the courtyard, a bastion offers interesting views of the Gironde and over to Blaye and beyond, the vine-covered slopes.

Continuing N along D 2, a lane on the left leads to Château Lanessan.

Château Lanessan Ⓥ – The château, standing on a ridge in the middle of a 400ha/988-acre estate, overlooks woods and meadows as well as vines. It was built in 1878 by Abel Duphot, and displays a strange marriage of styles – a mixture of Spanish Renaissance and what looks like traditional Dutch, with stepped gables and tall, monumental stone chimneys. The outbuildings house the **Musée du Cheval** which includes an interesting collection of horse-drawn vehicles dating from 1900, including a 15-seat stage-coach. A collection of saddles, harnesses, bits and stirrups is on view in the tack room. The feeding troughs in the stables are made of marble. The wine stores, which date from 1887, can also be visited.

Château Beychevelle Ⓥ – This is a delightful white manor house, rebuilt in 1757. The pediment is decorated with garlands of palm leaves. The name of Beychevelle (allegedly derived from *baisse-voile* meaning lower sail) is a reminder of a ship's salute, customary in the 17C when vessels passed the property. It belonged then to the Duc d'Éperon, Grand Amiral de France, who exacted a toll from masters navigating the Gironde. The view of the estuary remains very attractive today.

St-Julien-Beychevelle – This is one of the better-known names of the Médoc. The region includes such famous châteaux as Lagrange, Léoville, Beaucaillou, Talbot – after the English general who lost at Castillon-la-Bataille – and Gruaud-Larose (its proprietor, it is said, used to hoist upon the château tower a different coloured flag to signal the quality – excellent or otherwise – of each year's vintage).

Pauillac – Pauillac is a riverside town, a port with fine quays equipped to accommodate cruise liners. It is known above all, however, as a major centre of the wine trade, honoured by such famous vineyards as Château Lafite Rothschild, Château Latour and Château Mouton Rothschild. There is also a wine cooperative, La Rose Pauillac, the oldest in the Médoc.

★ **Château Mouton Rothschild** Ⓥ – At the heart of the vineyards above Pauillac rises Château Mouton Rothschild, one of the most exalted names of the Médoc. Its wine was classed *premier cru* in 1973. The **wine stores** are open to the public.

The superbly furnished reception hall of the château is embellished with paintings and sculptures on the theme of wine and vineyards. The banqueting hall beyond is hung with a magnificent 16C tapestry illustrating the grape harvest. Also on view is an interesting collection of wine labels commissioned from Braque, Dali,

HAUT-MÉDOC

0   5 km

● Vineyards producing first-quality vintages

★★★BORDEAUX

Masson, Carzou, Villon and other modern artists. The tour finishes at the main wine store, where the barrels containing the most recent vintage are stored, and the cellars in which bottles of the precious wine, thousands upon thousands, ageing and aged, are racked.

Another series of very old cellars has been converted into a **museum**★★. It contains an extraordinary selection of paintings, sculptures, tapestries, ceramics and glasswork, celebrating wine and its production. It includes precious stones and a dazzling collection of 16C and 17C gold plate. Among the contemporary pieces, note the fine work by the American sculptor Lippold.

Château Lafite Rothschild ⓥ – This is perhaps the most famous of the *premier grands crus* of the Médoc. Among the treasured bottles of wine stored in the château's impregnable cellars are some known as *Comète* vintage, commemorating a celestial phenomenon of 1811. The name Lafite corresponds to the Gascon term *la hite* (originally derived from the Latin *petra ficta* meaning carved stone), and was used initially because the château was built on a small rise. The terrace on which it stands is planted with fine cedar trees and bordered by an elegant Louis XIV balustrade. It has belonged to the Rothschild family since the Second Empire (1868).

Château Mouton Rothschild storehouse

Beyond Château Lafite Rothschild, on the right-hand side of D 2, the silhouette of **Château Cos d'Estournel** appears, reminiscent of 19C Indian-style pagodas. The main door is from the Sultan of Zanzibar's palace. In fact, the founder of the château exported his wine as far as India and had this exotic mansion constructed as a reminder of his far-off business dealings.

Turn right (D 2) to St-Estèphe.

St-Estèphe – This little town, clustered around its church, rises like an island in a sea of vines. From the small port on the Gironde, east of the town, the view includes the slopes around Blaye, formerly the banks of the estuary.

Follow minor roads W.

Vertheuil – The 11C **Romanesque church**, modified in the 15C, is a former abbey church whose importance can be seen in its two belfries, three aisles, and a chancel with an ambulatory and radiating chapels. On the north wall are the remains of a handsome Romanesque doorway with covings, decorated with figures (peasants pruning vines and the Old Men of the Apocalypse).
The interior, with its 15C ribbed vaulting and aisles almost as tall as the nave, is reminiscent of the Poitou style. In the chancel, where the vaulting is reinforced by radiating ribs, are stalls carved with scenes from monastic life, and a suspended gallery, both dating from the 15C. The unusual ambulatory is roofed with a series of transverse barrel vaults. In the nave stands a 15C font, carved from a single stone block.
Impressive 18C buildings remain in the grounds of the old abbey, along with traces of its Gothic cloisters. The village is overlooked by the *(restored)* 12C keep of a ruined castle.

Turn S along D 104.

Moulis-en-Médoc – The **Romanesque church** here was slightly altered during the Gothic period, the south apsidal chapel being replaced by a round turret enclosing a spiral stairway that led to a belfry with a strongroom. At the angles of the transept crossing, the columns supporting the church tower had to be reinforced at one time, thereby reducing the width of the supporting arches. The remarkable apse has carved modillions and blind arcades on the outside, and blind arcades in the interior, their capitals naively carved with historiated cats and birds. The fourth on the left (Tobias carrying the fish whose venom will cure his father's blindness) is especially noteworthy. The *bénitier* (stoup) outside the church, built into the façade, was reserved – according to local history – for lepers. Recent archaeological digs have unearthed the foundations of a 4C-5C place of worship and several Merovingian sarcophagi.
The Grand-Poujeaux vineyards have made wines from Moulis famous.

Castelnau-de-Médoc – Three features of particular interest distinguish the church in Castelnau – a stained-glass Renaissance window portraying the Crucifixion, a wood carving dating from 1736 representing Pentecost, and a 14C alabaster bas-relief of the Holy Trinity, which hangs above the font.

Return to Bordeaux via D 1.

Tumulus de BOUGON★★

Michelin map 322: F-6 or 233 fold 6 – NE of La Mothe-St-Héray

This important Megalithic site, parts of which date back to c 4700 BC, lies hidden in a wood near Bougon, a village known today for its goat's cheese.

Megalithic Necropolis – The site comprises five tumuli or barrows (ancient burial mounds) predating the Egyptian pyramids by 2 000 years. These barrows, circular or rectangular in shape, built with stones and earth, are one of the oldest examples of funerary architecture in the world, and were the work of Neolithic tribes living in the neighbourhood; of their dwellings, very little remains.

TOUR ⊙

Museum

This elegant, ultra-modern metal and glass peristyle, built on limestone, encompasses the ruins of a Cistercian priory. Start here for a walk through prehistory, from the creation of the universe to the necropolis of Bougon.
The modern-style exhibition retraces human, technological, geological and climatic evolution from the very beginning of man's existence. Partial, life-size reconstructions give a more true-to-life idea of a primitive world which is still the basis of our society – dwellings from the Çatalhüyük village in Anatolia (one grotto is painted with huge vultures carrying off tiny men), a dwelling made with branches and rushes from Charavines in Isère, a chamber with a megalithic passage grave from Gavrinis (Morbihan) and lastly an exhibition room dedicated to the Tumuli of Bougon where offerings and skulls – one cut into three pieces – lie in a reconstructed funerary chamber.
There is a 12C **chapel** on the way from the museum to the Neolithic site.

The Neolithic site

The site is accessed via a footpath lined with interesting reconstructions such as a sun and lunar calendar (based on Stonehenge in England), and the erection of a megalithic flagstone. There is also a botanical garden.

Tumulus A – This circular construction, the first to be discovered in modern times (1840), dates from c 4000 BC. The funerary chamber, one of the largest known (7.8m/27ft long), is roofed with a single stone slab weighing 90t. A smaller slab, standing vertically, divides the chamber in two. As well as the 220 skeletons seen here, the tumulus also yielded a rich collection of funerary objects.

Tumulus FO

S. Sauvignier/MICHELIN

Tumulus B – The shape of this barrow is elongated. The interior revealed two funerary vaults at the east end and two passage graves at the west. Shards of pottery discovered here have been dated to the middle of the fifth millennium BC, which makes this the oldest monument on the site.

Tumulus C – This circular mound, 5m/17ft high, dates from 3500 BC. It shelters a small passage grave and also has a rectangular platform which may have been used for religious ceremonies. A 35m/115ft long wall runs between Tumulus C and Tumulus E. It appears to have been designed to separate the sanctuary into two separate zones.

Tumulus E – The barrow contains an east-facing passage which leads to two chambers where bones and funerary objects dating from 4000 to 3500 BC were found. These are the oldest-known passage graves in the centre-west of France.

Tumulus F – This, the longest enclosure (80m/262ft), encompasses two more barrows. F2, to the north, dates from 3500 BC and has a passage grave of the type known here as *angoumoisin* (in the Angoulême style). The passageway leads to a rectangular chamber. FO to the south dates from c 4700 BC.

Château de La BRÈDE★

Michelin map 335: H-6 or 234 fold 7

In the Graves region, bordering the moors of Gironde, the austere lines of the Château de la Brède are reflected in the waters of its wide moat. The fortified castle appears to be an island in a lake. There has been no change to the property since the days when the angular-faced, but kindly figure of **Baron Montesquieu** (1689-1755), the writer and philosopher, could be seen pacing around the outer edge of the moat. Château de La Brède (*brède* in the local dialect means bush or thorn) still belongs to his descendants today.

A country gentleman – Charles de Secondat, future Baron of Labrède and Montesquieu, was born within these castle walls in 1689. As a sign of family humility he was carried to the baptismal font by a beggar.

Montesquieu's kinsmen were Bordeaux magistrates and he himself – mediocre by his own admission in that profession – eventually became President of the Bordeaux Parliament. Like Montaigne, he had a passionate love of the countryside, withdrawing frequently to his castle, which he described as "the most peaceful and beautiful rural retreat that I know". Here, he looked after his business affairs (he exported a lot of wine to England), supervised the cultivation of his vines with his steward – conversing with his staff in the local dialect – and visited his cellars.

Montesquieu, who was by nature easygoing and even-tempered, found relaxation (again like Montaigne) in scholarship and the intellectual life. "Learning, for me," he said, "is the supreme remedy against world-weariness. I never suffered a disappointment that could not be dispelled by an hour's reading." Two of his best-known works, *Thoughts on the Rise and Fall of the Romans* and *The Spirit of the Law* were written at the castle. Every year, the Baron spent the winter in Paris, where he was welcomed by the intellectual elite of the Académie Française, to which he himself was elected in 1727. It was in the capital that he died, quite suddenly, of an attack of fever, on 10 February 1755.

TOUR ⊘ *30min*

Château – A wide avenue, laid out by Montesquieu, skirts the moat and leads, indirectly, to the austere 12C-15C Gothic castle. The original interior courtyard was converted into a terrace during the Renaissance by levelling one section of the outer wall.

Small bridges which link two ancient fortifications, their doorways surmounted by Latin inscriptions, cross the moat and lead to the vestibule supported by six spiral columns. From the vestibule, which contains the Baron's travelling chests, visitors pass into the salon adorned with family portraits and a fine 16C cabinet.

Montesquieu's own simple **sanctuary** remains exactly as it was when he was alive. A sculpted bust of the writer, his cane and various mementoes are among the items on view. A worn mark visible on one side of the chimney-piece was the result of Montesquieu's shoe repeatedly rubbing against it – he used to sit by the fire here and write with his papers in his lap. Notice the **library**, which has panelled barrel-vaulting.

Park – Montesquieu took a great interest in the grounds of his castle. He once wrote to Abbot Guasco: "It will give me such pleasure to bring you to my Labrède estate, where you will find a castle – Gothic it must be said, but set in a charming landscape, which I modelled around ideas I found in England. Here, Nature is in its night-gown, just getting out of bed."

Château de La Brèche

BRESSUIRE

Population 17 799

Michelin map 322: D-3 or 232 folds 43 and 44

Bressuire is the chief town of the Vendée *bocage* – a patchwork of farmlands criss-crossed with hedges and woods south of the River Loire. It is an important agricultural market, as attested by the huge dimensions of place Notre-Dame, the size of the covered food market, and the cattle market in which large local sales are held every Tuesday.

The low houses, roofed with their convex tiles, cling to the hillside on the banks of the River Dolo.

Ravages of war – The Vendée Wars (1793-96) raged as the result of an anti-revolutionary insurrection involving Royalist-Catholic forces in south-western districts of the Loire. Bressuire, at that time, was under the sovereignty of the Royalist **Marquis de Lescure**, the Saint of Poitou and Lord of Clisson. The town consequently became the headquarters of the Royalist forces. As a result it was set ablaze and attacked, on 14 March 1794, by the Infernal Columns of General Grignon – a former cattle merchant who kept a scrupulous tally of the number of Royalists killed by his men and who prided himself on the fact that 200 were massacred in a single day on the outskirts of Bressuire.

Where to Stay

BUDGET

Hôtel de la Boule d'Or – *15 pl. Émile-Zola* – ☎ *05 49 65 02 18 – closed Aug, 26 Dec to 10 Jan, Sun evening and Mon lunch* – 🅿 – *20 rooms: 35.06/44.21€ – 🛏 4.57€ – restaurant 10.52/30.49€.* Not far from the train station, this hotel could be a stopover for limited budget travellers. Its outmoded rooms are of varying sizes; some are a bit more comfortable than others. Several fixed-price menus are proposed in the restaurant.

Château de Cirières Bed and Breakfast – *79140 Cirières – 11km/6.6mi W of Bressuire via D 960bis then D 150 dir. Bretignolles* – ☎ *05 49 80 53 08 – closed Oct to Apr* – 🚭 – *3 rooms: 47.26/54.88€.* In the bosom of the wooded countryside, this elegant 19C château sits amid an 18ha park, a verdant setting for its peaceful rooms. Hunting pictures and pretty view from the breakfast room. Fishing lake.

SIGHTS

Église Notre-Dame – The architecture of this church resembles that of sanctuaries in the Loire Valley. The single, very wide nave with Gothic vaulting but with doorways and capitals still in Romanesque style is characteristic of the 13C Plantagenet (Angevin) style. In addition, the huge quadrangular chancel in Flamboyant Gothic style appears also to show an Angevin influence, despite the fact that it dates from the late 15C.

The tower, conceived as a whole in the 16C, achieves a harmonious marriage between Gothic and Renaissance styles – the latter manifesting itself in the upper part. Crowned with a dome and lantern, it rises above the town and surrounding farmlands to a height of 56m/184ft.

Musée Municipal ⓥ – This small museum, devoted to the history and culture of the region, is housed in a former granary. It stands near the town hall (built in the early 19C on the site of a Franciscan monastery) in an attractive square. Inside, in a typically regional setting, the displays include collections of local faïence, and mementoes of the Vendée Wars.

Château ⓥ – On the western side of the town stands the castle, now partly in ruins, which was once the headquarters of the powerful Barony of Beaumont-Bressuire. It comprises two separate walls punctuated by 48 semicircular towers. The outer wall, dating from the 13C, has a circumference of c 700m/770yd. Following it around on the left for just over 92m/100yd, the visitor is rewarded with a romantic view of curtain walls and crumbling towers. The inner wall dates back to the 11C. A postern leads into the main courtyard.

The ruined 15C domestic quarters, which were burned down during the Revolution, have since been replaced with a Troubadour-style building.

There is a fine view of the castle and its curtain walls from the bridge across the River Dolo *(on the road to Cholet)*.

BROUAGE★

Population 498
Michelin map 324: D-4 or 233 fold 14

The ramparts and turrets of Brouage, still extremely well-preserved, despite constant assault from the sea winds, soar above the desolate marshland around them.

Memories of lost love and lost wars haunt the old walled town now sunk into silence. Brouage stands as a stoic memorial to the friendship between France and Quebec, flags flapping in the ocean breeze.

Emplacement de la maison
de Samuel de Champlain . B
Escalier Mancini . . . . D
Ancienne Tonnellerie. . . . . . F
Courtine de la Mer . . . . G

HISTORICAL NOTES

Grandeur and decadence – In medieval times Brouage played an important commercial role. The town, sheltered by Île d'Oléron at the inner end of "the finest haven in France", was the salt capital of Europe. Some 8 000ha/19 768 acres of salt-marshes provided the precious mineral which was to be refined and sent abroad – particularly to Flanders and Germany.

At some time between 1567 and 1570, **Samuel de Champlain** was born into a Protestant family living in Brouage. The boy became an expert navigator and, on the orders of King Henri IV, sailed away to colonise parts of Canada. In 1608, he left Honfleur in Normandy and discovered Quebec, opening up the fur trade in beaver and mink. A monument marks the place in Brouage where he was born.

During the siege of La Rochelle in 1628, Brouage became the arsenal of the royal army, and Cardinal Richelieu instructed the Picardy engineer, Pierre d'Argencourt, to rebuild the fortifications. By the time the work was finished 10 years later, Champlain's birthplace, with a garrison of 6 000 men, was the most impregnable stronghold on the Atlantic coast.

At the end of the 17C, Brouage entered a period of decline. The founding of Rochefort and the re-establishment of La Rochelle as a military base, removed most of the military reasons for its existence. Vauban, nevertheless undertook to reinforce the ramparts once more. However, the haven silted up, the salterns degenerated into rot-marshes which bred fever, and the garrison was reduced.

Love affairs and Affairs of State – In 1659, the 21-year-old Louis XIV was in love with **Marie Mancini**, the raven-haired niece of Richelieu's successor, Cardinal Jules Mazarin. The young couple wanted to marry, but their dreams were thwarted. The Cardinal had decided that, for "reasons of State", the King must marry the Infanta of Spain to guarantee the peace brought by the Treaty of the Pyrenees, recently signed by the two countries. Marie Mancini was sent to La Rochelle, where she heard, with despair, of the forthcoming marriage. From September to December that year, she withdrew to Brouage, where another of her uncles was Governor, "because solitude is the only solace for my broken dreams". Mazarin subsequently allowed her to return to Paris.

Six months later, after the royal marriage in St-Jean-de-Luz, Louis contrived to absent himself from the official cortège, returning to the capital, and then rode to Brouage, where he occupied the room in which Marie had stayed, pacing the ramparts, as he too sighed for the love he had lost.

Racine was inspired by this melancholy episode to write his tragedy *Bérénice*.

★★ RAMPARTS

◉ The Brouage Tourist Office organises guided tours of Pierre d'Argencourt's ramparts; constructed between 1630 and 1640; they are a perfect example of the art of fortification before the Vauban era. They describe an exact square measuring four times 400m/440yd, and are protected by seven massive bastions, each equipped with gracefully corbelled turrets. The walls, 13m/43ft high, are topped by a brick parapet pierced with apertures for cannon fire. Two gateways, Porte Royale and Porte de Hiers, allow access to the enclave. The western rampart is additionally protected by a ravelin detached from the curtain wall.

Though most of the houses in Brouage, including the Governor's mansion where Marie Mancini and Louis XIV stayed at different times, have disappeared, the military dependencies have better resisted the erosions of time.

The fortifications are well preserved

M. Thiery/MICHELIN

Watch-path – It is possible to walk almost entirely around the town's circumference along the top of the old ramparts, now carpeted with grass. From here the neat rectilinear layout of the plan is apparent, and there is a good view across the marshes to Île d'Aix and Île d'Oléron.

Porte Royale – Located in the northern **Bastion Royal**, this gateway once opened onto the quays. On the right-hand wall of the vaulted passage, leading out, ancient graffiti showing different types of ships can be seen. The outside of the gateway is surmounted by a pediment with the armorial bearings – partly worn away – of France and Navarre. On the left of the gateway there are traces of ironwork between the stone blocks which helped to strengthen the walls.

Forges Royales – The old blacksmiths' forges back onto Bastion Royal. In the middle of the one occupied today by the tourist office, an imposing furnace chimney can still be seen. Left of the forge, **Escalier Mancini** is the stone stairway that was used by the King's beloved each time she climbed to the ramparts to dream her solitary dreams. Parallel to the steps is a ramp which was used to hoist up cannons. To the left are the **hangars de la Porte Royale**, a row of one-time sheds, workshops and stalls, today converted into shops. The Governor's mansion lay just to the south.

▶▶ **Église St-Pierre**; **Halle aux Vivres** – restored food market; **Ancienne Tonnellerie** – old cooper's workshop; **Poudrière de La Brèche** – old powder magazine; **Port Souterrain** – underground harbour.

CAMBO-LES-BAINS‡

Population 4 416
Michelin map 342: D-4 or 234 fold 33

Haut Cambo, the upper residential district of this small spa, has a number of hotels and villas on the edge of a plateau overlooking the River Nive, whereas Bas Cambo, the lower town, is an old Basque village nestling in a wide curve of the river. At one time Cambo was the navigable limit for barges bringing cargoes inland from Bayonne. Further upstream, the thermal cure centre, built in 1927 in neo-Classical style with Art deco mosaics and wrought-iron work, is active once again.

It is the exceptionally mild climate – plus a visit by the well-known poet and writer, Edmond Rostand (1868-1918) – which made Cambo a fashionable cure resort at the turn of the last century. Arriving for the first time in the autumn of 1900, Rostand at once fell in love with Cambo and decided to live here permanently. He built a huge villa with beautiful gardens *(now open to the public)* overlooking the Bayonne road. Rostand was inspired by his walks in the Basque countryside around Cambo to write *Chantecler*, the successor to his *Cyrano de Bergerac*.

★ **Arnaga** ⊘ – This spacious **villa** in the Labourdes Basque style was built under Rostand's supervision between 1903 and 1906. It stands on a promontory which the writer turned into French-style formal gardens. "It was here", said the Comtesse de Noailles, herself a poet, "that his spirit returned to Nature itself, to the tortoise-shell and jasper-coloured mountains and to the placid waters of the long, quiet Nive." The spacious house, with its great Basque roof, decorative painting and wooden balconies, contains Rostand memorabilia – furniture, documents, the original costume designs for *Chantecler*, and portraits of Rostand and Rosemonde Gérard by Pascau and Caro.

Eating out

Venta Burkaitz – *Col des Veaux – 64250 Itxassou – from Itxassou, take Pas de Roland, then Artzmandi* – ☎ *05 59 29 82 55 – closed Jan to mid-Mar, evenings and Wed –* 🍽 *– 13.72/35.06€*. On the Spanish side of the mountain range, a venta with two dining rooms. The more authentic has a traditional counter where you can have a before-dinner drink or buy liquor and conserves; the second offers a pretty view of the valley from the veranda. Plentiful local cuisine.

Domaine Xixtaberri – *4km/2.4mi E of Cambo-les-Bains via D 10 –* ☎ *05 59 29 22 66 – closed Jan, Mon-Tue and lunchtime – reserv. recommended – 22€*. It's a steep drive to this house but you'll be rewarded by a splendid view of the Basque coast and the Pyrenees. Basque specialities to savour under the arbour or in the pleasing dining room with classic art on the walls. Comfortable rooms, decorated with a personal touch.

Where to stay

Hôtel Chez Tante Ursule – *Quartier Bas-Cambo – 2km/1.2mi N of Cambo –* ☎ *05 59 29 78 23 – closed 15 Feb to 15 Mar and Tue –* 🅿 *– 17 rooms: 26.68/45.73€ –* 🍴 *5.34€ – restaurant 13.72/30.49€*. A small, discrete hotel across from the fronton, well-placed for watching a game of Basque pelota. Very well-kept, classic rooms – ask for one in the more modern annex. Traditional fare in the dining room under the wooden ceiling.

Soubeleta Bed and Breakfast – *64250 Itxassou –* ☎ *05 59 29 78 64 –* 🍽 *– 5 rooms: 36.59/48.78€*. Perched above the town, this imposing 17C edifice's *tourelle* and finely sculpted granite frame are still intact. The spacious rooms are decorated with family furniture; two have marble fireplaces.

Domaine Silencenia Bed and Breakfast – *64250 Louhossoa – 10km/6mi SE of Cambo dir. St-Jean-Pied-de-Port –* ☎ *05 59 93 35 60 – domaine. de.silencenia@wanadoo.fr –* 🍽 *– 5 rooms: 50/55€ – meals 20€*. A sweet quietude permeates this fine 18C house where a true *art de vivre* prevails. Each room echoes one of the owner's passions – rugby, fishing, wine and good food… The kitchen honours local cuisine.

★ MONTAGNES D'ITXASSOU

15km/9mi S via D 918 – 3hr

The road climbs out of the last farmlands of the Lower Nive.

★ **Itxassou** – The hamlet's cottages are set in clusters among cherry orchards, which supply the main ingredient of the famous local cherry jam. The rustic-looking **church**★, standing alone near the River Nive, has three tiers of galleries adorned with statues and turned balusters, an 18C gilt wood altarpiece and a fine pulpit with decorations picked out in gold.

N of the village, take the road to the gliding field (terrain de vol à voile).

Mont Urzumu – From the viewing table, near a statue of the Virgin, there is a remarkable **panorama** of the Basque Pyrenees and the coast from Pointe Ste-Barbe to Bayonne.

The narrow minor road runs along the west bank of the Nive.

Pas de Roland – Park where the road widens, just beyond the parapet with a roadside crucifix. Beyond the crucifix, there is a view down to Pas de Roland, a rock with a large aperture said to have been formed by a kick from Roland's mount when he was being pursued by the Vascons. *A path leads to the site.*

Turn right at Laxia; the road becomes very narrow, and climbs steeply with hairpin bends.

★ **Artzamendi** – From next to the telecommunications station, there is a **panorama**★ extending northward towards the lower valley of the Nive, the Nivelle basin and its upland pastures, and southward, beyond the border, to the slopes above the Bidassoa Valley.

CELLES-SUR-BELLE

Population 3 480
Michelin map 322: E-7 or 233 fold 6

The small town of Celles grew up in the shadow of the tall, imposing belfry of an old Augustinian abbey built on a terrace above the valley of the River Belle.

SIGHTS

Église Notre-Dame – This former abbey church is the site of a pilgrimage to the Virgin known as the *Septembresche*, which takes place on the first Sunday of each September. King Louis XI was a regular worshipper here. The church was destroyed by the Huguenots in 1568, but rebuilt a century later, in 15C style, by the architect **François Leduc**. He was known as François the Tuscan because of his taste for Tuscan architecture.

The Romanesque main **doorway**★ of the original abbey church, visible inside the narthex, is most unusual. Its multi-lobed arching, decorated with grimacing masks, betrays an Eastern influence which can be seen throughout France on the pilgrims' route to Santiago de Compostela.

Inside, the church is striking for the luminosity of the nave and aisles, and for the purity of line seen in the pillars soaring towards the high, curved vaulting.

The 17C statue of Notre-Dame-de-Celles, stands at the far end of the chancel.

Abbaye ⏱ – *Access to the abbey is via the main doorway below the church.*

Three of the presiding abbots here left their mark on history – Geoffrey d'Estissac, Cardinal de La Rochefoucauld, who was Louis XIII's prime minister, and the famous minister Talleyrand.

The monastic buildings and their dependencies were, like the church, the work of Leduc. The attractive main façade (85m/279ft long) features Ionic columns resting against scrolled buttresses. The right wing of the building was unfortunately never completed. Inside, there is a fine staircase, the old refectory, kitchen and a cloister gallery, all dating from the 17C. The ruins of the old parish church of St-Hilaire (St Hilary), with its 12C crypt, can be seen in the abbey grounds.

> **The Abbey Hostel**
>
> **Hostellerie de l'Abbaye** – *1 pl. Epoux-Laurant* - ☎ *05 49 32 93 32 - closed during Feb holidays and Sun evening from 15 Oct to 31 Mar - 10.67/34.30€.* Situated next to the church, this venerable house is more picturesque seen from the courtyard than from the street. The terrace there is used when fine weather prevails; wintertime the traditional cuisine is served in a pleasant, colourful dining room. Several fixed-price menus. Simple rooms.

EXCURSIONS

Maison du Protestantisme Poitevin – *11km/6.6mi N.* The exhibit centre focusing on Protestantism in Poitou is located in two temples, as Protestant churches are known in France.

Beaussais – The **temple** ⏱, a former 12C Catholic church with a Romanesque oven-vaulted chancel, now houses a small museum. Panels and displays at the entrance relate to the activities of Protestants in the 20C, while those in the nave trace the history of the movement in France, with special emphasis on Poitou. A Huguenot footpath links Beaussais to La Couarde *(4km/2mi, details from the museum)*.

Take D 10 N to La Couarde.

La Couarde – This section of the **Maison du Protestantisme Poitevin** ⏱ is housed in a church built in 1904. The showcases and displays concentrate on the period known as the Desert, the period of resistance and repression which followed the revocation of the Edict of Nantes in 1685. Among the exhibits are *méreaux*, tokens used by Huguenots at that time to identify themselves as members of the faithful. There is a reconstruction of a Desert Assembly (a meeting or service held in secret) with a collapsible pulpit which could be quickly dismantled and hidden. There are video films in French.

Logis de la CHABOTTERIE★★

Michelin map 316: H-6 or 232 fold 40

It is in the woods of La Chabotterie that the Vendée War ended with the capture of the Royalist leader, Charrette (1796).

TOUR OF THE MANOR ⊘

A new type of construction appeared in Vendée in 1560 known as the *logis clos*, so-called because the fortified courtyard enclosed the seignorial manor and its attendant outbuildings. This typical configuration was found in Vendée until the 18C.

The refined atmosphere of the 18C century – a mixture of country ways and gracious living typical of the rural society of the time in Bas-Poitou – has been brought to life again through careful restoration of the manor house to which Charette was brought after his capture, thus putting an end to the Vendée War.

Salles historiques – They feature authentic period pieces in a reconstructed dining room (table laid for a meal, hallmarked chairs, cut-crystal chandelier), bedroom (canopied bed made of fabric from Nantes, 1783), and study (17C and 18C Aubusson tapestries).

Salle des maquettes – It contains scale models of many traditional houses of the Vendée region.

Parcours spectacle – *The atmosphere of this place may be oppressive to children and particularly sensitive persons.* In the modern building, visitors walk through rooms illustrating great moments in local history, including the main episodes of the Vendée War.

Walled garden – It is divided into flower beds where lovely roses are tended, and a vegetable plot, where the flowers can also be unexpectedly spectacular.

Croix de Charette – This granite cross can be reached from La Chabotterie *(30min on foot there and back)*.

⚑ Erected in 1911 in La Chabotterie Woods, the cross marks the place where the Royalist leader was captured.

EXCURSIONS

Château du Bois-Chevalier ⊘ – *20km/12mi W.* The central body of this Louis XIV château is crowned by a dome and flanked by six wings with high French roofs; the ensemble is reflected in the waters alongside. Charrette stayed here during the Vendée War.

In Charrette's footsteps *45km/28mi round tour – allow 3hr*

From Logis de la Chabotterie, rejoin D 18 and turn right; cross D 763 and continue to La Copechagnière, turn left onto D 86 to Les Brouzils then right onto D 7 towards Les Essarts.

Roads D 7 then D 6 (towards Belleville-sur-Vie) run close to the edge of **Grasla Forest** where Charrette and his troops sought refuge on 11 January 1794. A commemorative cross stands at the entrance of an unusual village hidden at the heart of the forest.

Refuge de Grasla ⊘ – In 1793, many inhabitants of the surrounding parishes, fleeing the Blues (Republican army) sought refuge in Grasla Forest. Some 2 000 of them built a village of wooden huts in order to survive.

Continue along D 6. In St-Denis-la-Chevasse, turn right onto D 39 to Les Lucs-sur-Boulogne.

Les Lucs-sur-Boulogne – On 28 February 1794, one of General Cordelier's Infernal Columns slaughtered many of the inhabitants of Grand-Luc, and, on 5 March, parishioners of Petit-Luc who had sought refuge in the church. This, however, was not the only place where the Republican Infernal Columns held sway, and the memorial inaugurated in May 1993 was erected to the memory of all their victims.

The historiated stained-glass windows of **Église St-Pierre**, built in 1902, tell of the 1794 massacres *(a tape recorder can be turned on next to the organ)*.

In the middle of the roundabout on the way out of the town on the road to Belleville-sur-Vie, is a commemorative monument **(Vendée 93)** and carillon.

Drive NE out of Les Lucs along D 18. After crossing the River Boulogne, turn right onto a minor road leading to a vast parking area.

★ **Le Chemin de la Mémoire des Lucs** ⊘ – Dedicated to the memory of the martyrs and victims of the Reign of Terror, in the spirit of historical and spiritual commemoration, the memorial in Les Lucs is a contemporary creation, an architectural

This canopied bed is known as a *lit à la duchesse*

and landscaped ensemble leading from the banks of the Boulogne to the hilltop chapel. Many historical landmarks lie along the **Allée de l'Histoire** recalling the major events in the Vendée War from March to December 1793.

In the foreground stands the **Memorial de Vendée**, of intentionally sober architecture. The corridor of memory, divided into four rooms, evokes the end of the insurrection and the destruction of Vendée through reconstructed scenes and symbolic objects (monstrance, Sacred Heart tapestry, a peasant's scythe upturned for use as a weapon). The crypt, its floor covered with dozens of steles, perpetuates the memory of all the unknown victims.

On the other side of the footbridge over the Boulogne, stands a blackened wall, symbolising the mass burning of villages.

A path leads to the **Chapelle Notre-Dame-du-Petit-Luc**, built in 1867 on the remains of the former church which was burned to the ground.

Rejoin D 18 and turn right towards St-Sulpice-le-Verdon to return to Logis de la Chabotterie.

CHARROUX★

Population 1 320
Michelin map 322: I-8 or 233 fold 19

Charroux, which lies 50km/31mi south of Poitiers in a valley on the east bank of the Charente, grew up around a Benedictine abbey dedicated to the Holy Saviour, on the way to Santiago de Compostela. A 15C wooden market is still standing in the main square.

HISTORICAL NOTES

Holy relics, a source of wealth – The success of Holy Saviour Abbey was assured from the start because the original monks were under the patronage of Charlemagne himself. Ecclesiastical Councils were held here from time to time, one of which, in 989, laid the foundations for the Truce of God. The abbey church was consecrated by Pope Urban II in 1096.

The abbey, the guardian of priceless relics (flesh and blood of Jesus Christ, parts of the True Cross), attracted impressive numbers of pilgrims; at one time 25 000 of the faithful would visit it each June. Wealthy pilgrims enriched the treasury with gifts of money and magnificent works of art. Eventually the abbey had possessions as far away as England.

Decline – The Wars of Religion in the 16C put an end to this prosperity, and the abbey was sacked. In 1762, its function was suppressed altogether and by the beginning of the 19C, over half of the buildings had been demolished.

The preservation of what remained is the work of Mérimée, Inspector-General of Historic Monuments under the Second Empire. Excavations and restoration work carried out between 1946 and 1953 have exposed the ground plan of the abbey church and revealed the crypt. The cloisters have been restored. Building works in the chapter-house led to the discovery of sarcophagi containing a fine collection of funerary items.

★ABBAYE ST-SAUVEUR

Abbey church – The ground plan here allied the traditional Latin cross outline with the circular design of the Holy Sepulchre Church in Jerusalem. The church comprises a narthex, a nave, a transept with side chapels, and an apse with radiating chapels. In the centre of the transept crossing was a circular sanctuary surrounded by three concentric aisles, positioned above a crypt. It was surmounted by a tall tower (still standing). The building as a whole, which was 126m/413ft long, suggested certain early Middle Eastern churches.

Polygonal tower

🎧 In the tourist office, you can see a scale model of the abbey as it must have appeared in its former glory. Price 0.76 €.

The church was built in the Poitou Romanesque style with the exception of the west front which was Gothic. Several elements from this façade are incorporated in the walls of a nearby house.

The polygonal **tower**★★ dates from the 11C and was in the exact centre of the church. It stands like a gigantic canopy above the rotunda sheltering the high altar, which itself surmounts the crypt in which the sacred relics were displayed. The first two storeys of the tower, now empty, were actually inside the church. The upper part was probably crowned by a spire.

Cloisters – The cloisters – today open to the sky and extensively plundered – were reconstructed in the 15C under the direction of Abbot Chaperon, whose heraldic arms, three hoods, are reproduced on the capitals of the columns in the chapter-house.

Chapter-house – The large, impressive building houses a number of excellent 13C **sculptures**★★ which once adorned the main doorway of the west front. These include Christ in Judgement, originally on the tympanum, and several figures decorating the arches – kings, prophets, former abbots of Charroux, and the delightful statuettes of the Wise and Foolish Virgins so often seen in the Poitou region. These works are attributed to the sculptor who worked on the doorways of Poitiers Cathedral.

★**Treasury** – The treasury houses a fine collection of Romanesque pastoral staffs and pieces by Gothic goldsmiths and silversmiths, discovered in the abbots' tombs excavated beneath the chapter-house. Two magnificently worked silver-gilt reliquaries stand out among the gold and silver plate – one, dating from the 13C, is particularly remarkable: two angels hold a box which contained the relics.

Thermes de CHASSENON★

Michelin map 324: O-4 or 233 fold 21 – 5.5km/3mi NW of Rochechouart

In 1958, a remarkable Gallo-Roman site was discovered in the Charente and Limousin area. It seems that Chassenon was a health resort in Roman times and was eventually abandoned in the 6C.

Cassanomagus or **Cassinomagus** – The etymological origin of this term remains a debatable point. For some, Cassanomagus is composed of the Celtic words *cassanos* (oak) and *magos* (market). Another interpretation gives Cassinomagus, from *Cassinus* (a man's name) and *magos*. Either way, both names are related to the Gauls. Even though its role before the Roman Conquest remains unknown, it is certain that the Romans were familiar with a site located at an important road junction, possibly endowed with thermal springs. For a long time, it was even thought that a large town was built here and what we see today was a Roman governor's palace.

Chassenon had one or several temples, a theatre, a forum and thermal baths.

The rise and fall – The sanctuary reached its peak in the 2C. It is easy to imagine the grandiose style of these richly ornate marble baths, decorated with sumptuous works of art. Its decline began in the late 3C, accelerated by the spread of Christianity. Defaced statues found in the gutter and sewers testify to the exhaustive destruction of all pagan symbols. The barbarian invasions also contributed to the ruin of the building, which was later partly converted into a foundry after making alterations to the ovens. For a while, it was even used to make sarcophagi out of local stone. It would appear, however, that certain medical practices associated with continuing local paganism lasted up until the 6C, when the miraculous healings performed by St Junien made the old Gallo-Roman sanctuary redundant.

The thermal baths – Traces of a high curtain wall and a few remnants of the temple and theatre can still be seen but nothing of the forum, which is still buried. Only the thermal baths have survived intact. These baths were unusual, not only because they had two sets of everything, but also because they were used for healing. The people who came here were mainly pilgrims with health problems, who observed a specific religious ritual (the temple was 230m/760ft away). When people came to the thermal baths, they entered through a doorway in the eastern façade (the side opposite the present pathway). They then went into the changing room before going through to another heated room, where they may have paid or been checked – the exact use remains unknown. After that, they went through to the large central room, and into the *tepidarium* (warm room), where the skin was thoroughly scraped with a curved metal instrument called a *strigile*; the *caldarium* (hot room) contained the steam room and boiling hot baths designed to make the bather sweat profusely, and the *frigidarium* (cold room) was used for taking a cold plunge after leaving the *tepidarium*. The *palestra* next to the southern *frigidarium* was used for all types of physical activities, including swimming. The baths would almost certainly have had additional rooms adapted to specific therapies.

TOUR ⓥ

The building, whose walls are still 5m/16.5ft high, had three floors. The south wing, better preserved, was the mirror image of the north wing. Two aqueducts provided the building with a constant flow of water and a drainage system.

The tour starts with the north wing: follow the cart track (where the fuel was off-loaded) along the foot of the high walls, into the dark, vaulted underground chambers which seem to have been built to carry water. The zigzag passageways connecting the chambers were designed for maximum decantation. Items collected during the excavations are displayed in one of the passageways.

The service or boiler rooms were located on the intermediate level. Note the ingenious underground heating system using a hypocaust, or hollow space under the floor. The coal-fired furnaces could be heated to more than 300°C/570°F. The resulting heat was routed to the hypocaust, a layer of tiles laid in a bed of clay mortar, and radiating flues distributed the heat into the room above. The temperature of about 20°C/68°F to 25°C/77°F was obtained in the rooms above the hypocaust.

The ground floor in the south wing has remained relatively intact, and the visitor can easily imagine what the rooms were like when they were full of bathers. The southern cold room and several other rooms lead into the largest room in the very heart of the baths. Several hypotheses have been put forward concerning the function of this 232m²/763sq ft room, with its six windows and six doors – a place of worship, a waiting hall, a physician's surgery or a room dedicated to the god of healing.

The tour ends with a visit to the warm and cold rooms in the north wing.

CHÂTELLERAULT
Population 34 126
Michelin map 322: J-4 or 232 fold 47 – 35km/22mi NE of Poitiers

The city, which has developed on the banks of the River Vienne, at the upper limit of its navigable reach, owes its name to Ayraud, Vicomte de Poitou, who built a château on the site in the 10C.

The growth of the modest local metal-working trade from the 13C onwards led to the establishment of a cutlery industry in the city in the 18C. Later (1820), the metallurgy business expanded into an arsenal and arms manufacture. The latter, which operated until 1968, played an important role in the economic success of Châtellerault.

STROLL THROUGH THE TOWN *allow 2hr*

This walk is pleasant in good weather. Start from the tourist office on boulevard de Blossac and enter the pedestrianised district. Follow rue Bourbon on the right.

Maison Descartes – The philosopher Descartes spent several years of his childhood in this 16C family home, currently undergoing restoration.

Eating Out

BUDGET

Petite Auberge – *14 r. Cognet* – ☎ *05 49 21 72 85* – *closed 1-13 Aug, 24 Dec to 2 Jan, Sun and Mon* – *11.43/21.34€*. A modest but pleasant address without pretence in a narrow street of the old city. Rustic setting with visible beams and stones. Traditional cuisine.

La Gourmandine – *8 pl. Notre-Dame* – ☎ *05 49 21 05 85* – *www.la-gourmandine.com* – *closed 1-6 Jan, 1-25 Aug and Sun evening* – *15€ lunch* – *21/33€*. This 17C post house near the River Vienne has resumed its calling of yore. The modern decor, with its exposed stones, mouldings and painted decorations, is inspired by years past. As for the innovative cuisine, contented wayfarers leave the dining room well pleased to have tarried there.

La Grillade – *r. Chédeville – 86530 Naintré – 9km/5.4mi S of Châtellerault dir. Poitiers via N 10* – ☎ *05 49 90 03 42* – *closed Sun evening* – *14.03/30.18€*. Beyond the city, on the road to Futuroscope, this cottage-like restaurant serves meat grilled in the fireplace in front of customers as well as other simple dishes. No frills in the round dining room with exposed frame and beams.

Where to Stay

BUDGET

Grand Hôtel Moderne – *74 bd Blossac* – ☎ *05 49 93 33 00* – ◘ – *21 rooms: 60.98/114.34€* – ☕ *7.93€* – *restaurant 13.11/18.29€*. Next to the city hall, this rather elegant little building has old-fashioned pediments. The architecture dates from the early 20C, but the decor is much newer and the rooms are spruced up regularly. Have a meal they take pride in their cuisine.

Église St-Jacques – *Walk along the pedestrianised rue Bourbon to a small square then turn right to reach the church.* The west front and the two neo-Romanesque towers of this former priory church dedicated to St James date only from the 19C, but the transept and the east end with its buttress-columns were built in the 12C-13C.
The nave has quadripartite vaulting in the Anjou Gothic style whereas the south side chapel has lierne and tierceron vaulting with historiated keystones.
A 17C statue of St James in polychrome wood stands in the northern arm of the transept. The figure is dressed as a pilgrim on his way to Santiago Compostela, a reminder that Châtellerault was one of the stages on the pilgrims' route (Santiago means St James).
A **carillon** of 52 bells is housed in the north tower.

Go past the Misée Municipal to the Henri IV Bridge.

Pont Henri-IV – The bridge (144m/472ft long and 21m/69ft wide) was built between 1575 and 1611 by Charles Androuet du Cerceau, a member of a famous family of architects. Two massive slate-roofed towers, once linked by a central block, protected the entrance to the west end – a wise precaution so soon after the Wars of Religion. In the middle of the bridge, on the upstream side, two anchors hanging from a cross are a reminder of the time when inland river transport was a thriving business. It disappeared in the mid-19C.

Walk across the bridge then upriver along an avenue shaded by plane trees until you reach the Manu.

La Manu – This former weapons' foundry, set in shady grounds on the left bank of the River Vienne has been restored and now combines culture, teaching and leisure activities.

Musée Auto Moto Vélo – *See additional sights.*

Saint James (*Jacques* to the French)

Comme deux tours – In 1994, the artist Jean-Luc Vilmouth added a platform and a spiral staircase to a couple of high factory chimneys so that people could climb up and admire the town and its surroundings.

It is possible to walk to the Envigne Canal.

Canal de l'Envigne – Situated on the west bank of the River Vienne and framed by the skating rink and a park planted with cedar trees and sequoias, the canal offers water-sport activities.

ADDITIONAL SIGHTS

Musée Municipal ⊘ – *Rue Sully*. The museum stands at the far end of a splendid courtyard, in Hôtel Sully, a mansion built in the 17C by Androuet du Cerceau. Collections of weapons, knives, 17C to 19C porcelain and earthenware are on view, together with carved wooden chair backs, sculptures, paintings and other works of art. One room is devoted to Rudolph Salis (1851-97) who was born in Châtellerault and later founded the famous Parisian cabaret, Le Chat Noir. Menus and wine lists from the cabaret are on display with posters and a number of metal shadowgraph silhouettes representing an army on the march. The silhouettes were projected onto a screen, producing an effect rather like a primitive animated cartoon. Salis himself added a spoken commentary, and one of his shadow theatre shows was an entire Napoleonic saga.

Local history from prehistoric times to the present day is traced in another department, including an archaeological display of the Gallo-Roman site of Vieux-Poitiers, prints and engravings of Châtellerault, bills from coaching inns including lodging for the traveller's horse.

Documents, photos and explanatory tableaux in a section on the Acadians follow their odyssey to the New World and back, and examine the economic and cultural role played by Acadia today (New Brunswick and Nova Scotia).

Regional headdresses, bonnets, shawls and christening robes from the 18C to the early 20C can also be seen. The considerable skill of the local linen workers is reflected in the variety of shapes and the richness of the embroidery.

Musée Auto Moto Vélo ⊘ – ⌧ This interactive museum, covering a surface area of 4 300m²/46 300sq ft, retraces the very early beginnings of the motor vehicle and its subsequent popularisation through a series of gleaming motor cars. The motorbike collection is remarkable.

CHAUVIGNY★

Population 6 665
Michelin map 322: J-5 or 233 fold 9 – 23km/14mi E of Poitiers

The battlements of Chauvigny rise in the valley of the River Vienne. It developed as a trade and industrial centre specialising in the manufacture of porcelain. Traditional quarrying of local freestone – a fine-grained limestone with regular cleavage – has also remained important.

★UPPER TOWN

The upper town *(ville haute)*, standing on a spur, is surmounted in turn by the jagged ruins of forts and castles dominated by the elegant belfry of St Peter's.

Château baronnial – This 11C baronial castle, built when the bishops of Poitiers were also the lords of Chauvigny, comprises both an upper part – with an enormous keep – and a lower part surrounded by ramparts, revealing traces of the Château Neuf (New Castle) ruins.

Falcony show ⊘ – The castle precinct lends itself perfectly to demonstrations of birds of prey in flight (eagles, falcons, vultures).

Château d'Harcourt – The castle originally belonged to the earls of Châtellerault, who built it between the 13C and 15C, on the crest of the promontory. Massive ramparts with a fortified entrance gate still exist.

★ **Église St-Pierre** – The construction of this former collegiate church, founded by the lords of Chauvigny, started in the 11C with the apse and was completed in the following century by the erection of the nave. The style is Romanesque, and the building material a fine grey stone. There are two different levels of open-work in the square belfry. The east end, richly decorated with sculptures, is notable for the pleasing proportions of the apse and chapels.

The interior of the church has unfortunately suffered from over-enthusiastic 19C repainting.

Chauvigny – Capitals in Église St-Pierre

The capitals of the columns, supporting the broken-barrel vaults in the nave, are decorated with palm leaf designs. The **capitals in the chancel**★★ are particularly interesting, embracing a fascinating selection of biblical, evangelical and mythical scenes – the Annunciation, the Adoration of the Magi, the Weighing of the Souls, the Arrival of the Shepherds, the Temptation and other religious subjects alternate with an extraordinary phantasmagoria of winged monsters, sphinxes, sirens and demons subjecting resigned humans to the worst possible torments.

★ **Donjon Gouzon** – *Just north of the church.* This keep is all that remains of a castle acquired in the late 13C by the Gouzon family and subsequently (around 1335) bought by Bishop Fort of Aux. The square keep was originally supported by rectangular buttresses, which were later surmounted by rounded buttresses.

Espace d'Archéologie Industrielle ⊙ – A local archaeological exhibition was set up in the keep after its restoration in 1988. A glass lift, encased in the spiral staircase of the tower with its transparent dome, leads up to the exhibition rooms (computer and video displays). The terrace at the top of the keep commands a fine view of the surrounding countryside.

Musée de Chauvigny ⊙ – This typical example of local traditional architecture houses a display on objects relating to life in Chauvigny in bygone days and an archaeology room (1C ceramics).

▶▶ Église Notre-Dame – 14C fresco; **St-Pierre-les-Églises** ⊙ (2km/1mi south) – pre-Romanesque church with 9C-10C frescoes.

EXCURSIONS

★ **Château de Toufflou** ⊙ – *6km/3.6mi NW.* The warm, ochre-coloured stone of this château with its terraces overlooking the River Vienne helps to form a unified whole, despite the juxtaposition of four different architectural styles.
The oldest part of Touffou Castle is the massive keep, which was formed during the Renaissance by twinning two older keeps dating from the 11C and 12C. At each of the outer corners the buttresses are crowned by elegant turrets. Four huge round towers were added in the 14C: Tour St-Georges, with finely sculpted openings, Tour St-Jean, Tour de l'Hostellerie, restored in 1938, and Tour de la Chapelle with its prison cells.
The Renaissance wing, linking Tour St-Georges with the keep, was added c 1560. It is adorned with mullioned windows and dormers; the triangular pediments carry a series of 17 different coats of arms, representing the genealogy of the Chasteignier family.
Terraces and a hanging garden precede the château. The main features inside are François I's Chamber (also known as the Four Seasons Room), which is embellished with fine frescoes illustrating work in the fields throughout the year, the chapel, the guard-room and its cells, the bakery and kitchen.

Archigny – *13km/8mi N.* The name of this village is inextricably linked with the story of the Acadians – early-17C emigrants from the Poitou region who settled in the eastern part of French Canada.

MEDIEVAL MENU

Les Choucas – *21 r. des Puys* – ☎ *05 49 46 36 42* – *closed 15-30 Nov and Wed from Sep to Apr* – *10.98€ lunch* – *15.24/26.67€*. Across from the keep, this small restaurant is set in a medieval house. Hungry travellers will not regret sampling the fare at the ground-level bar-crêpe eatery or the upper-level restaurant with its casement windows, fireplace and wooden beams. Regional cuisine or medieval menu to be ordered ahead.

SLEEP IN THE SHADOW OF THE CASTLE

La Veaudepierre Bed and Breakfast – *8 r. du Berry* – ☎ *05 49 46 30 81* – *laveaudepierre@club-internet.fr* – *closed 1 Nov to Easter except during school holidays* ⊠ – *5 rooms: 32/47€*. Dominated by the castle ruins, this beautiful and distinguished 18C house is charming indeed. The collection of old instruments appeals to music lovers, and all visitors appreciate the view and the refined decor. Access to the city heights up nearby stairways.

Acadia, corresponding roughly to the present-day Canadian provinces of Nova Scotia and New Brunswick, was ceded to the British in 1713. After the Treaty of Paris at the end of the Seven Years War (1763), the British government in Canada colonised the area and, in 1773 and 1774, forcibly repatriated the 10 000 French living there to make room for English immigrants.

Returning to Poitou, the dispossessed Acadians settled south-east of Châtellerault on fallow land given to them by the Marquis de Pérusse des Cars.

La Ligne Acadienne, the Acadian Line, was the name given to a series of similar farms established on the heath between Archigny and La Puye: 58 clay and brushwood houses on rubble foundations, which the ex-colonists hoped eventually to own. Some, impatient because the charter they awaited was delayed, moved to Nantes and later to French Louisiana. Those that remained received their title deeds only in 1793.

Today, 34 of these houses are still standing. Each year on 15 August, in the hamlet known as **Huit-Maisons** (Eight Houses), descendants of the Poitou Acadians organise a fête to commemorate this period in their history.

Ferme acadienne des Huit-Maisons ⊙ – An old Acadian farm at Huit-Maisons *(6km/3mi E of Archigny, signposted)* has been converted into a museum. Here, under the same roof, visitors can see living quarters with furniture of the period, a cow shed containing agricultural implements, and the barn, where documents relating to the history of the Acadians and their return to Poitou are on display.

Civaux – *15km/9mi S.* The number of rare archaeological treasures found around Civaux confirms the importance of this modest village in relation to the spread of Christianity in the Poitou region.

★ **Nécropole Mérovingienne** – This ancient burial ground dates from Merovingian times (AD c 500-750) when the Frankish dynasty founded by Clovis reigned over Gaul and Germany.

The origin of the burial ground remains a mystery. It is thought that the graves might have been those of warriors who fell in a battle between Clovis and Alaric, the King of the Visigoths, or perhaps they were the tombs of penitents who had expressed a wish to be buried on the site of their conversion.

A ruined chapel, dedicated to St Catherine, had been remodelled several times since the Romanesque period.

Musée Archéologique ⊙ – This small museum not far from the cemetery contains exhibits from Merovingian and Gallo-Roman times (stelae, tombstones, ceramics, funerary items). Of special interest are the reconstructions of various types of grave discovered in the necropolis – both with and without coffins, directly in the earth or surrounded by a drystone frame, in sarcophagi or in simple cairns.

Église St-Gervais et St-Protais – The church was built on the site of a Roman temple, the ruins of which still contain a loggia converted into a baptistery.

The apse, which dates from the 4C, has a stone belfry adorned with two tiers of blind arcades. In the barrel-vaulted nave (10C), the cylindrical columns are topped by **historiated capitals** embodying themes which reflect fears of hell and damnation. Sealed into the south wall of the apse is a 4C funerary stone engraved with the Greek letters Alpha and Omega on either side of a chrisma (a monogram formed from the first two letters of the Greek word for Christ).

Clisson stands on a picturesque **site**★ at the junction of the River Moine and the Sèvre Nantaise. In 1794, the Infernal Columns of the Republicans attacked the town and set it ablaze so savagely that, by the end of the Revolution, virtually every inhabitant had fled. In the early years of the 19C, Clisson rose phoenix-like from its ashes, largely owing to the enthusiasm of the Cacault brothers, who were natives of nearby Nantes, and the sculptor, Frédéric Lemot. They had spent some time in Italy, and under the influence the restored town was progressively Italianised. Today, houses in Clisson itself and a number of watermills and small factories in the neighbourhood (recognisable by their brick-dressed, rounded-arch windows) are evidence of that architectural trend, the first examples of which appeared in Garenne-Lemot park *(see below)*.

OLD TOWN

Château d'Olivier de Clisson Ⓥ – The ruins rise impressively above the Sèvre Nantaise. The castle, located on the border of the Duchy of Brittany, was designed to repel attacks from both Anjou and Poitou. The first overlords were the Sires of Clisson, among them the famous Constable, Olivier de Clisson (1336-1407). In 1420 the castle was confiscated by the Duc de Bretagne.

An earlier castle had been built in the 11C and 12C. This was enclosed within a polygonal structure flanked by towers in the 13C. A keep, also polygonal, was added in the 14C (a section of wall topped by machicolations still exists). The kitchens, the chapel and the lords' living quarters also date from the 14C.

The Duc de Bretagne, François II, modernised the fortifications in the 15C with the addition of a second enclave, which included a prison and a huge gateway. This new entrance was protected by a drawbridge, replacing the ancient barbican. Finally, fearing an attack by the Catholic League, the overlords strengthened the defences still further in the 16C by building three new bastions.

In the middle of the central courtyard stands a well into which, in 1794, the Republicans flung 18 citizens of Clisson who had sought refuge in the castle.

Bridges – From the viaduct carrying route N 149 across the Moine, there is an attractive view of the castle, the river with its green banks, and the 15C Pont St-Antoine (St Anthony's Bridge). From the second bridge, spanning the Sèvre, there is an equally picturesque vista of the river with the awe-inspiring castle towering overhead.

Les Halles – The covered market originated in the 15C, though the fine timber framework was fashioned from oak in the 17C and 18C.

★DOMAINE DE LA GARENNE-LEMOT

Access via N 149

In 1805, Frédéric Lemot purchased Bois de la Garenne, a wood just south-east of Clisson, and employed the architect Mathurin Crucy to carry out a number of projects in the Italian style.

Park Ⓥ – Scattered throughout the park are statues and follies in the style of classical antiquity (a Temple of Vesta imitating the one in Tivoli in Italy, an oratory, a military monument and a tomb), the Grotto of Héloïse, two rocks engraved with poems and, notably, a charming rocky site on the banks of the Sèvre known as the Baths of Diana.

Clisson – Villa Lemot

A. Thiery/MICHELIN

ONE FOR LUNCH, ONE FOR DINNER?

La Bonne Auberge – *1 r. O.-de-Clisson – ☎ 02 40 54 01 90 – closed 15-28 Feb, 10 – 31 Aug, Sun evening, Tue lunch and Mon all day – 28.97/68.60€*. A nice restaurant a little off the beaten track for transient gourmets. In a very pleasant and luminous decor, the series of rooms continues back to a veranda that opens onto the garden. Indulge in the lobster *millefeuille*, the baked perch or the veal kidney.

La Gétignière – *3 r. de la Navette – 44190 Gétigné – 3km/1.8mi SE of Clisson; take N 149 towards Cholet – ☎ 02 40 36 05 37 – closed 16 Aug to 9 Sep, Sun and Tue evenings, and Wed – 17.53/50.31€*. In a small street in the heart of Gétigné, this restaurant run by a young couple succeeds in being both unprentious and refined. Dapper dining room renovated in a contemporary style, with plenty of room between the tables and an innovative, modern cuisine. Interesting lunch menu.

Villa Lemot ⓥ – This villa was built in neo-Classical style and fronted by a semicircular colonnade, recalling the famous Bernini columns in front of St Peter's in Rome. It is used as a venue for art exhibitions. The terrace behind the villa offers a **view** over the town, the castle, the River Sèvre and the Temple of Friendship, a columned building in which the remains of Frédéric Lemot lie.

Maison du Jardinier (Gardener's House) ⓥ – *To the right on entering the park*. The building, with its dovecote tower, is an imitation of an Italian country house, and served as a model for a number of others in the area. Inside, there is a scale model of the park, a video display and a permanent exhibition on Italian architecture in Clisson.

THE MUSCADET AND SÈVRE ET MAINE REGION

Round trip of 65km/40mi – 4hr

Clisson is one of the gateways to the vineyards of the Sèvre-et-Maine region *(see Introduction, Wines and Spirits)* which produces the popular Muscadet wine and the lesser-known Gros Plant white wine. The wine-growing estates are built on the slopes on either side of the green and fertile valley of the winding Sèvre Nantaise.

Leave Clisson by D 763 then N 149 towards Nantes.

Le Pallet – This is the birthplace of **Pierre Abélard** (1079-1142), a scholastic philosopher, dialectician and theologian, whose genius profoundly influenced the thinking of his time. He is also famous for his tragic love affair with Héloïse, niece of the cruel Fulbert.

Musée du Vignoble Nantais ⓥ – The museum, housed in a large modern-style glass building, is devoted to wine-growing in the Nantes area.
After a presentation on the different areas of production, there is a display of the wine-grower's work: grafting methods, grape-picking, pressing, wine-making and marketing. Tools and machinery used in former times (pruning shears and knives, copper-sulphate sprayers, carts and tractors), include a monumental 18C long barrel **winepress**. The final section is dedicated to cooperage (tools and scales to weigh barrels) as well as local crafts and folk traditions.

Leave Le Pallet eastwards on the road which runs along the River Sanguèse.

Mouzillon – The wine festival, *La Nuit du Muscadet*, is celebrated here in early July. South of the church is a **Gallo-Roman bridge** across the River Sanguèse.

Leave Mouzillon N via D 763.

Vallet – This wine-growers' town is considered to be the Muscadet capital.

Leave Vallet on D 37 NW

Château de la Noë de Bel-Air ⓥ – This elegant château, rising above the vineyards, destroyed during the Revolution and rebuilt in 1836, now has an enormous loggia with Tuscan columns facing onto the park. The use of bricks in the orangery and outbuildings is characteristic of the houses in Clisson.

Continue along D 37.

Les Moulins du Pé – From the top of one of these disused mills, there is a captivating **view** of the vineyards and marshlands of the Goulaine region.

Return to and continue along D 37.

Le Loroux-Bottereau – During the insurrection of 1793, the inhabitants of the town formed an elite corps, incurring the anger of Turreau, who destroyed the town in 1794.

Église St-Jean-Baptiste ⓥ – The church has two 12C frescoes telling the legend of St Gilles. The vine-covered slopes can be admired from the belfry.

Leave Le Loroux-Bottereau SE, via D 7.

Marais de Goulaine – This green stretch of marshland covering 1 500ha/3 700 acres is crisscrossed with little canals, bordered with reeds. Nature enthusiasts can explore the marshes by **boat** ⓥ or on foot along the canal paths. By road, Butte de la Roche near the legendary **Pont de l'Ouen** (bridge), offers a fine view.

Turn right on D 74.

Château de Goulaine ⓥ – The château, surrounded by vineyards, was built between 1480 and 1495 by Christophe de Goulaine, Groom of the Bedchamber to Louis XII and François I.

Remains from the military past include a machicolated tower and a small castle in front of a bridge spanning the moat. This handsome residence consists of a 15C Gothic main building made of limestone tufa from the Saumur region, and two wings added in the early 17C.

Interior – A spiral staircase leads to the first floor, which opens into the **grand salon** (monumental Renaissance chimney-piece), the **salon bleu**, the **salon gris** (remarkable panelling and interesting mythological scenes on the piers).

Butterfly aviary – 😊 An enormous greenhouse next to the curtain wall of the castle contains exotic butterflies in among tropical flowers and shrubs.

Return via D 74. At Haute-Goulaine, follow D105 S. On reaching Vertou, turn left and take D 59 towards Clisson. In 500m/550yd turn left onto D 359.

La Haye-Fouassière – The village probably derives its name from a kind of flat cake, *fouace*, which is a local speciality. The **Maison des Vins de Nantes** ⓥ, next to the water tower, is the headquarters of the Nantes wine-growers' association which provides information on local wines and runs wine-tasting sessions.

Leave La Haye-Fouassière to the S, crossing the River Sèvre Nantaise on D 74, then turn left on D 76 following the river.

Monnières – The village church dates from the 12C and 15C but the interesting stained-glass windows are modern, with wine and the vine providing the main decorative themes.

D 76 leads back to Clisson.

COGNAC

Population 19 534
Michelin map 324: I-5 or 233 fold 28 – 28km/17mi SE of Saintes

Cognac, the birthplace of François I and cradle of the fine brandy which bears its name, is a peaceful little town. The buildings around its famous cellars and stores have been darkened over the years by the microscopic fungi which thrive on the alcohol fumes. **Place François I**, a busy square with an ornamental fountain, links the old part of Cognac, huddled on the slope above the River Charente, with the sprawling modern town. Not far from here, at no 10 place Jean-Monnet (named after one of the founders of Europe), is the **Cognathèque**.

Royal childhood – The literary and artistic House of Valois-Angoulême held court in the town from the late 14C until the accession of **François I** in 1515. It was here that François, the son of Charles of Angoulême and Louise of Savoy, was born "about ten hours after midday on the 12th day of September", in 1494. Part of his youth was spent in the Valois château near the River Charente, where he lived a carefree life with his sister Marguerite d'Angoulême and Charles' two illegitimate daughters, Madeleine and Souveraine.

THE OLD TOWN

Porte St-Jacques and Rue Grande – The restored 15C gateway, flanked by two round towers with machicolations, once commanded a bridge which has since disappeared. However, it still leads to rue Grande, originally the main street in Cognac. On the left, at the foot of the hill, is a Renaissance fountain. The winding street is typically medieval, lined with 15C houses with their projecting, half-timbered upper floors (note in particular the *Maison de la Lieutenance*).

Eating Out

La Boîte à Sel – *68 av. Victor-Hugo* – ☎ *05 45 32 07 68* – *closed 23 Dec to 8 Jan and Mon* – *11.43/47€*. This former grocery store in a shopping street close by place François-1er has preserved picturesque details like the shelves line with bottles, a small old-fashioned counter and wooden floor covered with throw rugs. Local cuisine.

Taverne du Coq d'Or – *Pl. François-1eer* – ☎ *05 45 82 02 56* – *12.04/37.96€*. Opened in 1908, this is Cognac's oldest restaurant. It has been recently renovated in a very successful evocation of the 1920s style with lots of pizzazz. From noon to midnight, the bistro menu includes oysters, sauerkraut etc.

Le Parc – *Parc François-1er, follow signs to the base de plein air* – ☎ *05 45 82 34 78* – *closed Mon evening from Nov to Mar* – *10.67€ lunch* – *17.99/31.25€*. You will find this odd little chalet amid the trees of the banks of the River Charente close to the François-1er Park. As soon as weather permits, you can enjoy the lovely terrace that leads to the garden… and, a bit further, the mooring bridge. Traditional cuisine and ice-cream bar.

Les Pigeons Blancs – *110 r. J.-Brisson* – ☎ *05 45 82 16 36* – *closed 1-15 Jan, Sun evening and Mon lunch* – *27.14/45.58€*. This 17C post house was made into a restaurant in 1973. Located in a garden outside the city, it has the feel of a comfortable old home. Local customers appreciate the reception and the fare. Pleasant terrace and a few rooms.

Where to stay

Hôtel Résidence – *25 av. Victor-Hugo* – ☎ *05 45 36 62 40* – 🅿 – *20 rooms: 36.59/48.78€* – 🍽 *5.34€*. The sober façade with its exposed stones stands out against the colours of the hotel's interior decoration scheme. Salon in tones of green and garnet, modern breakfast room in pink and fuchsia and functional rooms in brightly coloured prints.

L'Échassier – *quartier l'Échassier, 72 r. Bellevue* – ☎ *05 45 35 01 09* – 🅿 – *22 rooms: 68.60/77.75€* – 🍽 *8.38€* – *restaurant 20.58/53.36€*. Two buildings on either side of a garden. The recent villa features cosy modern rooms. The restaurant resides in the old stables of the Château de l'Yeuse (19C). Contemporary interior. Terrace beneath linden trees; classic yet inventive cuisine.

Stepping Out

La Maison Blanche – *2 imp. des Moulins* – ☎ *05 45 36 51 17* – *discotheque: Tue-Thu, Sun 11pm-4am, Fri-Sat 11pm-5am; bar and canoe rentals: Jul-Aug: Tue-Sun noon-9pm*. During the day, it's a small terrace on the banks of the Charente. At night, this establishment with a style of its own is transformed into a bar-discotheque popular among the 30-40 crowd. You'll only be able to order cognac, but there's no limit to the kinds of music and dance both inside and outdoors, in the small garden.

Sit back and relax

Saint-John – *Parc François-1er* – *open daily in season 10am-11:30pm*. This large café, situated in the very heart of the forest on the banks of the Charente, features Cognac's loveliest terrace.

Festival du film policier de Cognac – This festival of detective films takes place at the end of March, and draws film-makers and fans from around the world. There are awards for full length and short films and TV films. Retrospectives and other special events are organised, and there is also an award for the best detective book.

Festival blues passion – The leading blues festival in France, this event sets the beat in town at the end of July.

Rue de l'Isle-d'Or – This street is lined with 17C town houses with fine façades *(restored)*.

Rue Saulnier – In contrast to rue Grande, rue Saulnier is bordered by aristocratic Renaissance buildings. Its name recalls one of the traditional activities of Cognac – the salt trade. The street, which was very wide for the period, has retained its irregular cobblestone surface and its handsome 16C and 17C houses. At the far end is a Renaissance house with a shop. **Rue du Palais, rue H.-Germain, rue Magdelaine** and Maison de la Salamandre are also of interest.

Église St-Léger ⊘ – This 12C church has been extensively remodelled. The most interesting part is the Romanesque west front, pierced in the 15C with a large Flamboyant Gothic rose-window. The archivolt of the doorway below is adorned with carvings representing the Signs of the Zodiac and the Labours of the Months. The vast nave dates from the 12C. In the south transept hangs a fine 17C Assumption of the Virgin.
On the right-hand side of the doorway, 18C cloisters lead to the library.

Couvent des Récollets – This restored convent houses exhibitions and the headquarters of several charities. Note the beautiful hall with its ribbed vaulting and the covered well in the middle of the cloisters.

Parc François-Iᵉʳ – The park, bordered to the west by the River Charente, was part of the former castle grounds, prolonged by a thicket of tall trees. So dense was the growth that Louise of Savoy used to call it her *dedalus* or maze. It is mainly planted with ordinary oaks and holm oaks.

WINE CELLARS AND STORES

The cellars and wine stores *(chais)* spread out along the riverside quays, near the port and in the suburbs.

Camus ⊘ – *29 rue Marguerite-de-Navarre*. The tour offered by this cognac trading company, founded in 1863, concentrates on the history of cognac, its distillation, ageing and blending. Visitors are conducted through the cooper's shop and wine stores before watching the bottling process.

Hennessy ⊘ – After 12 years' service with Louis XV's Irish Brigade, Captain Richard Hennessy, wearying of army life in 1760, discovered the Charente region and settled in Cognac.
Attracted by the taste of the delicious elixir distilled here, he sent several casks to his relatives in Ireland and, in 1765, founded a trading company which was an immediate success. The Captain's descendants still head the company today.

Quais Hennessy – The stores of this company are located on both banks of the River Charente. A modern white-stone building, standing on the right bank, was designed by Wilmotte, who has used the three symbols of Cognac: copper (for the still), oak (for the casks) and glass (for the bottles). As an introduction to the world of Cognac, visitors are first taken across the river by boat and led into the wine stores where the various stages of brandy making are realistically explained with the help of special effects involving sounds and smells: double distillation, manufacture of oak casks, maturing and blending of the different brandies. After watching a film and being shown round an exhibition, visitors can take part in a tasting session and enjoy Cognac on the rocks.

Martell ⊘ – The oldest of all the Cognac distilleries owes its name to Jean Martell, native of Jersey, who settled in the town in 1715. The tour includes the semi-automated bottling process, and the stores and cellars where the brandy is left to age for six to eight years in oak barrels – this wood is preferred because of the slight tannin content which gives Cognac its beautiful colour, and the fine grain which limits evaporation of the alcohol. In the blending room which follows, brandies of different origins are mixed to ensure consistently high quality. Access to the tasting room is limited to brandy specialists and creators of blends such as the highly renowned Cordon Bleu. Three rooms have been recently restored in the house of this famous entrepreneur in order to recreate his life and work in the early 18C.
Before going back to the hall for a tasting session, the visitor is invited to take a look at the most prestigious wine stores, known as *purgatoire* (purgatory) and *paradis* (heaven) in which some of the brandies have been ageing in demi-johns for over 100 years.

Otard – *See Ancien Château below.*

Prince Hubert de Polignac ⊘ – *4km/2mi SE along N 141. Drive towards Angoulême and leave by the first exit; pass beneath the main road and follow signs for Z.A.* This cooperative, set up in 1949, brings together a number of local growers. A tour can be made of the different facilities in Pavillon du Laubaret.

Cognac – Ageing spirits, Hennessy distillery

Rémy Martin ⓥ – *4km/2mi SW along D 732. Drive towards Pons then turn left onto D 47 to Merpins*. This firm, founded in 1724, creates its cognac exclusively from the elite Grande Champagne and Petite Champagne vintages. A **miniature train** takes visitors on a tour of the plant. It goes through the cooper's shop (the largest in Europe), where the coopers can be seen at work on the casks, and then travels through part of the vineyard and various cellars used for stocking and ageing the spirit. Two different commentaries *(in French)*, illustrated with slides, punctuate the journey.

Pineau des Charentes consists of fresh grape juice to which Cognac has been added.
Fine Champagne is a brandy distilled exclusively from Grande and Petite Champagne vintages.
The abbreviation V.S.O.P. means Very Superior Old Pale.

ADDITIONAL SIGHTS

Ancien Château ⓥ – This 15C and 16C château recalls the memory of the Valois family and François I, who was born here. It became the property of the Comte d'Artois (the future Charles X) under Louis XVI and was sequestrated by the Republicans during the Revolution. Since 1795 it has been used as a wine store by the firm **Otard**, which was originally founded by an old Scottish family.
The façade overlooking the Charente has a fine balcony, known as the King's Balcony, the supports of which are sculpted with salamanders, the emblem of François I.
Inside the old château, it is possible to visit Helmet Hall, where Richard the Lionheart married his son Philip to Amélie de Cognac. The room contains a magnificent chimney-piece surmounted by a helmet, the work of Jean le Bon. In one corner are traces of the Lusignan family's original 13C feudal castle. The huge rooms, with their ribbed vaulting (including the Guard-room) are extremely elegant. The tour ends with a visit to the wine stores.

Musée de Cognac ⓥ – This municipal museum is housed in Hôtel Dupuy d'Angeac, in the grounds of the town hall.

Ground Floor (Local arts and crafts) – The displays here cover the history and civilisation of the Cognac area from the earliest times to the present through maps, plans, prints and photographs; headdresses, bonnets and traditional costumes; glasswork from the collection of Claude Bouiher (who invented a bottle-moulding machine in 1897); fine glazed earthenware, and fossils (mainly shellfish) found in the region's Secondary limestone formations. A section devoted to archaeology contains prehistoric stone artefacts such as ceramics and a Neolithic dugout canoe (made from a single piece of wood), pottery, statuettes, and bracelets from the Gallo-Roman period.
There is also a reconstruction of the interior of a rural house, evoking the life of a local wine-grower c 1875.

Basement (Cognac Ethnology Gallery) – The first display is a documentary illustration of the history of brandy. In the next six rooms, tools and machines recreate vine-growing and winemaking, distillation, the brandy and Pineau des Charentes trade, related crafts, cooperage and saddlery. Another room is devoted to traditional agriculture.

First Floor (Fine Arts) – This section houses paintings, sculpture, furniture and *objets d'art*, both French and foreign, from the 15C to the 19C.

On the landing, are interesting works in molten glass by Émile Gallé (1846-1904), one of the main pioneers of Art Nouveau.

The period paintings originate from countries which were clients of the Cognac brandy trade. Particularly noteworthy are two works from the 16C Antwerp School – *Lot and his Daughters* by Jan Massys, and *Adam and Eve* by Frans Floris. One room on this floor has a display of contemporary paintings.

EXCURSIONS

Gensac-la-Pallue – *9km/5mi SE via N 141, then D 49*. Before arriving at Gensac, route D 49 skirts the *pallue* or marshland from which the small town derives its name. The interesting 12C **church** has a Romanesque west front decorated with haut-relief sculptures of the Virgin (left) and St Martin (right), the patron saint of the church, both being carried heavenwards by angels. The Romanesque nave, with its four domes supported by pendentives, leads to a Gothic chancel.

Les Borderies *35km/22mi round tour – about 2hr*

Drive W out of Cognac along the road to Saintes. At the roundabout, drive to Javrezac then follow D 401.

Richemont – The church and the castle ruins rise, half-hidden, among the trees crowning a spur. The **church** ⊘ is built on the site of an ancient stronghold (its loopholes and arrow slits are still visible) and contains a delightful pre-Romanesque crypt (10C).

Continue N beyond Richemont towards l'Épine. Turn right onto D 731 then, 1km/0.6mi further on, turn right again onto D 85 to Cherves.

Château-Chesnel – This curious residence was built between 1610 and 1625 by Charles Roch-Chesnel. Architecturally, the château seems to hesitate between the Renaissance style and 17C Classicism, whereas nevertheless retaining a strong flavour of medieval military architecture – for example, in the deep dry moats around it. The central block and the towers at each corner are crowned with a castellated parapet. The complex as a whole forms a huge square, surrounded by large agricultural buildings.

Continue along D 85. Shortly after Vignolles, turn left onto D 120.

Migron, Écomusée du Cognac ⊘ – *2km/1mi N; follow the signs*. This little craft museum located among vineyards, is dedicated to brandy making.

A home distillery has been reconstructed, where the old-fashioned pot still, or *alembic* stands nearby the ever-vigilant moonshiner's bed. As he slept with one eye open, alcohol vapours rose while the fermenting liquid boiled; trapped and recondensed, the powerful distillate could be bottled and sold. Also on view are winepresses, one of which required treading feet, a cooper's workshop, vine-growers' tools and examples of the huge copper stills used in the trade today. This area has been making Pineau des Charentes (a fortified wine made from brandy and grape-must) and Vieux Cognac since 1850.

Drive S out of Migron along D 131. In Burie, take D 731 to return to Cognac.

Fins Bois vineyard

M. Thiery/MICHELIN

Vignoble des Fins Bois

40km/25mi round tour – about 2hr

Drive NE out of Cognac along D 24. In Ste-Sévère, take the direction of Les Buges and continue along D 24.

Macqueville – This peaceful village, in the heart of the Fins Bois vineyards, north-east of Cognac, has modern distilleries devoted exclusively in the production of cognac. The white houses, with their tiled roofs, have Empire-style porches and closed courtyards. A façade with decorated gable and pepper-pot turret is all that remains of the former 11C **Château de Bouchereau**. In the shady square, **Église St-Étienne** (St Stephen's) is a charming example of the Romanesque art which flourished in the ancient province of Saintonge during the 12C. The north transept is replaced by a bell-tower with radiating chapels, the east end is flattened, and the north doorway has a carved archivolt. Equally characteristic are the semicircular blind arcades of the walls and the amusing modillions on the cornices. Inside, recessed pillars with elegant capitals support the Gothic vaulting of the wide nave. The ribbed transept crossing is magnificent.

Leave Macqueville eastwards along D 227.

Neuvicq-le-Château – This is another village of picturesque low houses with tiled roofs. The château, which overlooks a small valley and gave the village its name, incorporates a 15C main block with a charming staircase-tower, and a 17C pavilion crowned by a tall, steep, typically French roof. Today, it houses the post office.

Leave Neuvicq-le-Château southwards along D 23. In Sigogne, take D 15 to return to Cognac.

CONFOLENS

Population 2 855
Michelin map 324: N-3 or 233 fold 20

Confolens lies in a pleasant setting on the border between the regions of Limousin and Angoumois, at the junction or confluence of the River Vienne and River Goire, hence its name.
It was the home of a disciple of Louis Pasteur, **Doctor Émile Roux** (1853-1933), who discovered how to treat diphtheria in 1894.
Confolens is also known for its International Folklore Festival, held every August.

★ LE VIEUX CONFOLENS (Old Town) *1hr 30min*

Start from place de l'Hôtel-de-Ville (parking) and follow rue de la Ferrandie to the left.

★ **Pont-Vieux** – The bridge was probably built in the 12C and modernised in the early 19C. For a long time it looked like a fortress, with its three towers – one in the centre and one on either bank. The tower on the west bank had a drawbridge, making it possible to cut off all access to the town, until it was replaced by an arch in the 18C. The curving span is a particularly pleasant place to stroll.
It leads to the Fontorse district (named after an elegant ornamental fountain), the old town's busy suburb.

Turn right on rue E.-Roux, then, at place de la Liberté, turn left on rue des Buttes. Half way up the street, a passageway leads to a fortified gatehouse.

Porte de ville – On the other side of the gatehouse, once the obligatory passageway for those seeking to enter the town, is a façade pierced by two Romanesque clerestory windows, no doubt built in the late 11C. The wartime residence of the local overlord, it contained a courtroom and prison and was an integral part of the fortifications surrounding the town on the east bank of the River Vienne.
Go back through the gateway and take rue des Buttes to the 11C **keep**, which stands on what used to be the moat. In former times, travellers arriving from the south-east went through a doorway here, traces of which can still be seen at the base of the keep and on the lower tower opposite.
Plan d'Olivet nearby, a public garden, offers an attractive **view** of the rooftops of the town.

Go back down towards the centre via rue du Vieux-Château, then take rue Pinaguet.

Rue Pinaguet – The street is lined with medieval houses (one of them, very tall, has a tower with a spiral staircase inside).
On the corner of rue Bournadour, another tower juts out, with a square half-timbered upper section.

Go back as far as the crossroads and turn left on rue Fontaine-de-Pommeau.

Église St-Maxime – Restored in the 19C, this church has an octagonal Gothic Troubadour tower surmounted by a spire with crockets. At its east end there is an attractive half-timbered house.

Take rue de la Côte.

Le Manoir – Rue de la Côte leads to a manor house with high gables and decorative carved finials.
It was built in the 16C by the Comte de Confolens.

From the bridge over the River Goire, take rue du Soleil.

The Pont-Vieux ("old bridge")
Seen from the Pont-Neuf ("new bridge")

Rue du Soleil – This was the main street until the 19C. It is lined with tall houses backing onto hanging gardens and grounds which are not visible from the street. On the left, is **rue des Francs-Maçons**, a staircase-street so narrow that the eaves of facing houses nearly cover it. Just beyond is the **Maison du Duc d'Épernon★**, used by the Duke of Épernon as a meeting point for the conspirators who helped Marie de Medicis to escape in 1619. The house dates from the 15C and 16C. It has three half-timbered upper storeys set back from the ground floor and sealed with cob (compressed loam, clay or chalk, reinforced with straw).

Return to place de l'Hôtel-de-Ville.

ADDITIONAL SIGHTS

Église St-Barthélemy – This interesting Romanesque church, located on the river bank opposite, has a square belfry with an almost flat roof with Roman tiles. The wide horizontal band (known as a string-course) above the doorway arch, set in an extremely sober façade, is decorated with primitive sculptures, including a halo-crowned Lamb of God, held by two angels, and a number of fantastic beasts resembling centaurs with monstrous heads. Inside, three 15C chapels with ribbed vaulting line the north side of the nave. In the central chapel, the ribs of the vaulting come together in a beautiful hanging keystone.

VALLÉE DE LA VIENNE

Round trip of 75km/47mi – allow 4hr

Leave Confolens by the north along the east bank of the Vienne (D 952).

St Germain-de-Confolens – St Germain-de-Confolens, once the site of an important feudal castle, is located in a picturesque setting at the junction of the River Vienne and River Issoire. Perched on a mound overlooking the valley of the River Issoire are the ivy covered ruins of the huge towers of Château de St-Germain, at the foot of which is a tiny Romanesque chapel.

From the terrace near the church, the view opens over the valley.

Drive SE out of St-Germain along D 952 then turn left onto D 82.

Lesterps – *8.5km/6mi east along D 30. Pronounced Laytair.*

Église St-Pierre – The remains of an abbey founded in the early 11C are preceded by an impressive grey granite **belfry-porch★**. Above the porch with its three bays, decorated with rather coarse capitals, is a massive belfry. Inside, the narrow side aisles contrast with the wide barrel-vaulted nave which houses the remains of the old chancel and 12C capitals.

Leave Lesterps S along D 29 then D 30.

Brigueuil – This historical burg perched on a hill still has many of its medieval fortifications ramparts with seven towers and two gatehouses. Near the Romanesque church (additions made in the 14C and 15C) are the remains of an old castle (11C truncated keep) and a manor house rebuilt in the 16C. There are also several other historical houses, a graveyard lantern, and in nearby Boulonie, a strange Romanesque mausoleum, said to be the tomb of Saint George.

Drive W along D 165; in Saulgond, turn left onto D 193.

Château de Rochebrune ⊘ – Built on a basalt rock, on the border of Poitou and Limousin, the castle is flanked with towers reflecting in the still water of the moat. In the 16C, its owner, the governor of Guyenne, Marshall Blaise de Monluc, led a pitiless fight against the Protestant community.

One enters the main courtyard, past the outbuildings covered with curved tiles and across a small stone bridge spanning the moat. The four 11C-13C round towers are linked by three buildings. The arms of Marshall de Monluc are carved above the doors. The apartments are furnished in Renaissance and Empire style and contain numerous mementoes of the Napoleonic period.

Continue along D 193, cross the River Vienne then turn right onto D 160.

Thermes de Chassenon – *See Thermes de CHASSENON.*

Continue W along D 29. In Chabanais, take N 141 on the left then turn right onto D 370 2km/1.2mi further on.

Exideuil – The 16C Château de la Chétardie overlooks the town and the river. Built as a priory in 1200, **Église St-André** has a flattened chevet and ovolo mouldings over the porch. The broken-barrel-vaulted nave with its recessed pillars is invitingly simple. It houses three stone tombs and a 13C baptismal font in the middle of the baptistery.

Return to Confolens via D 370 then D 16.

Phare de CORDOUAN★★

Michelin map 324: C-6 or 233 fold 25 – off the coast near Royan

Cordouan watches over the approaches to the Gironde estuary, which are frequently rough and at the mercy of dangerous currents. The architecture of this lighthouse is as captivating as its isolated setting; the rocky outcrop on which it stands was once part of Pointe de Grave, but was separated from the mainland and reduced to an islet during the 16C and 17C. Today, the ancient land link is revealed only at exceptionally low tide.

A feat of engineering – In the 14C the Black Prince had an octagonal tower built on the promontory, at the top of which a hermit was to keep a fire blazing at all times. A chapel and a few small cottages were added around the base of the tower. At the end of the 16C, however, the main structure was in danger of collapsing so Maréchal de Matignon, governor of Guyenne, called in the architect-engineer **Louis de Foix**, who had just finished diverting the River Adour, a huge undertaking in those times. De Foix arrived with a work force of more than 200 men and built a sort of belvedere surmounted by domes and lanterns and surrounded by a protective platform on the rocky base. In 1788 the engineer Teulère remodelled the upper part of the structure in the Louis XVI style; its sobriety forms a vivid contrast with the richness and flamboyance of the lower levels.

Cordouan lighthouse

J.-D. Sudres/PHOTONONSTOP

Access ⊘ – The lighthouse can be reached either from Royan or Pointe de Grave, where there is a museum devoted to it.

Tour ⊘ – The Renaissance architecture of the lower storeys separated from the upper Classical portion by a balustrade, makes the 66m/216ft lighthouse a bold and majestic presence.

A postern leads into the circular bastion which protects the building from the fury of the seas and contains the lighthouse-keepers' quarters. On the ground floor of the tower itself a monumental doorway provides access to the vestibule from which 301 steps lead up to the modern lantern (with a flashing light). On the first floor, surrounded by an outside gallery, is the King's Apartment. There is a **chapel** on the second floor, also circled by a gallery, and crowned with an elegant dome. The bust above the entrance door is of Louis de Foix.

The **Musée du Phare de Cordouan** is located on Pointe de Grave (see SOULAC-SUR-MER).

This village, pleasantly situated in the green valley of the River Boutonne, is known for its Renaissance château, built in an ideal setting on a tiny island in the river. Since 1981, Dampierre has also become famous as a breeding centre for the celebrated *baudets* (donkeys) of Poitou.

SIGHTS

Château Ⓥ – Of the four wings originally framing the inner courtyard, only the living quarters remain. The building is flanked by two massive towers designed to defend the building from attack. From the courtyard itself, the château seems less forbidding. The most impressive feature is a two-tiered Renaissance **gallery★** of basket-handle arches, with its two levels separated by a frieze of carved foliage. The upper gallery features a coffered ceiling whose 93 sections are carved with crests (a swan pierced by an arrow, the emblem of Claude of France, wife of François I), insignia (Catherine de' Medici and Henri II), and allegorical scenes and symbols (a labyrinth and a cherub astride a chimera etc). These are often bordered by scrolls bearing Latin mottoes. An interpretation and explanation of these decorations was proposed by Fulcanelli in his alchemical work, *Les Demeures Philosophales*, in 1931.

Among the furnishings on view in the apartments are fine Flemish tapestries and a superb Italian ebony cabinet (16C). In the guard-room, above the chimney-piece, reads the inscription: *Estre, se cognestre et non parestre* (To be is to know oneself rather than be known).

There are two exhibitions in the castle reception area – *Art and Alchemy* (which analyses details of the coffered ceiling) and *Dali's Horses* (paintings inspired by the ceiling).

Maison du Baudet de Poitou Ⓥ – *At La Tillauderie, 5km/3mi NE on D 127 towards Chizé.*

⌖ The **baudet du Poitou**, an unusually large donkey, reddish-brown in colour with a long, woolly coat, has been bred in this region for centuries. Crossing a mare with the male ass of this breed produces a hybrid, sterile mule known as a *mule Poitevine* which is particularly suited to carrying heavy loads over difficult terrain. Most were bred in St-Martin-les-Melle, near the town of Melle, and were in great demand until the beginning of this century, when they were replaced by more modern methods of transport.

Display panels and video in the small museum illustrate the history of the Baudet and the efforts being made to preserve the breed. Nearby, she-asses from Portugal and local Baudets can be seen grazing peacefully together. The centre's robust, mule-producing stallion may also be seen in the stables.

S. Sauviquier/MICHELIN

Poitou donkey

Population 19 515
Michelin map 335: E-12 or 234 fold 26

Dax, the most popular spa in France, is reputed for its hot mud treatments. The maceration of silt from the River Adour in water from the hot springs encourages the development of vegetable and mineral algae. The mud is particularly effective in treating rheumatic complaints.

The town, built on the edge of the Landes pine forest, is also an important commercial centre. Riverside walks, colourful public gardens, interesting churches, and even bullfights, combine to make the town an enjoyable stopping place for tourists.

HISTORICAL NOTES

A lake village, with houses on stilts, once stood on the site where Dax is built today. However, alluvia from the Adour gradually silted up the lake and the village developed on dry land.

After the Romans settled in the region, the hot springs of Aqua Tarbellicae, named after the first tribe to inhabit the area, became famous. When Emperor Augustus brought his daughter Julia here to treat her rheumatism, the town received favours from Rome and consequently prospered.

After celebration of the marriage between Louis XIV and Maria Teresa in St-Jean-de-Luz, the King and his bride stopped at Dax on their way home to Paris. The townsfolk set up a triumphal arch at the entrance to the town as a sign of welcome. The painting on the arch of a dolphin emerging from the water, and an inscription in Latin, were a pun on the words dolphin and *dauphin* (identical in French) in the hopes that the couple's stay in Dax would bear fruit.

TOWN CENTRE

Cathédrale Notre-Dame – The Romanesque cathedral was built in the 11C on the site of a very ancient chapel. It was destroyed in 1295 after the English laid siege to Dax. The Gothic building which replaced it in the 14C collapsed in 1645. The present cathedral was built in the Classical style – a fine 13C Gothic doorway still remains in the north transept. The embrasures of the double doorway are decorated with 12 columns supporting large statues of the Apostles; a statue of Christ adorns the pier. Both the tympanum and archivolt are richly embellished.

Fontaine Chaude (Hot Fountain) – The spring at the centre of town is the main attraction in Dax. Its waters, of meteoric origin, and tapped since Roman times, gush forth at a temperature of 64°C/147°F into a huge basin surrounded by arcades. Nearby is the statue of **Borda**, an 18C marine engineer born in Dax *(see box below)*.

Banks of the Adour – The **riverside walks** are a pleasure to discover. Upstream from the bridge, on the south side, is **Parc Théodore-Denis**, where Gallo-Roman ramparts provide a shady walk under a row of plane trees. In the centre of the park, the arenas are the site of the Feria de Dax, a festival held in August every year. Downstream is **Jardin de la Potinière**, leading down into the heart of the thermal district, whereas just beyond is the *Trou des Pauvres* or paupers' hole, once a public bath. Further west lies the Bois de Boulogne, a vast open space offering pleasant walks *(6km/3.7mi through the woods)*.

ADDITIONAL SIGHTS

Musée de Borda ⊘ – The museum is housed in a 17C mansion and contains collections of Gallo-Roman and medieval archaeology (statuettes and 1C bronzes discovered in Dax), 18C to 20C paintings, memorabilia belonging to the scholar Jean-Charles de Borda and the Minister of French Colonies, Milliès-Lacroix. One room is devoted to regional folklore, and another to breeds of cattle from the Landes region.

A Great Seaman

Jean-Charles de Borda was born in Dax in 1733. He was a marine engineer, mathematician, surveyor and all-round seaman, worthy of being the namesake of ships serving in the Navy school until the beginning of the 20C. Borda made great progress in nautical calculation and observations. He was part of a mission directed by the Constituent Assembly, which included Méchain and Delambre, charged with establishing the metric system and measuring the meridian arch between Dunkirk and Barcelona. The museum is named after him and his statue stands in place Thiers.

Eating out

BUDGET

Auberge des Pins – *86 av. F.-Planté* – ☎ *05 58 74 22 46* – *closed 16 Dec to 14 Jan, Mon and Sat evenings from Oct to Apr and Sun evening year round* – *15.24/28.20€*. Located in a Basque house in a residential neighbourhood, here's a small family auberge with a warm welcome. Take a seat in the dining room with a fireplace, in the brighter veranda or on the terrace. A few simple, clean rooms.

Ferme-auberge de Thoumiou – *Chemin de Thoumiou* – *40180 St-Pandelon* – *4km/2.4mi S of Dax via D 29* – ☎ *05 58 98 73 41* – *closed Jan-Feb, open Fri evening to Sun lunch from Oct to May, daily except Sun evening and Wed from Jun to Sep* – ⊠ – *reserv. recommended* – *11.50/25.50€*. Flavourful, simple and authentic, the cooking prepared in this farm reminds one of grandmother's kitchen. Give your tastebuds a treat in the dining room located in the roomy former stables under a wood frame ceiling. Access for travellers with special needs.

MODERATE

Les Champs de l'Adour – *5 r. Morancy* – ☎ *05 58 56 92 81* – *closed Christmas and New Year's day, Sun, Mon and Tue evenings* – *19.82€*. Near the cathedral, a great little address that we were tempted to keep to ourselves. The dining room's decor is an attractive blend of old (19C stone walls) and new (handsome furniture in rounded forms). Fare fresh from the market place.

Le Moulin de Poustagnacq – *40990 St-Paul-lès-Dax* – *6km/3.6mi E of Dax via D 459* – ☎ *05 58 91 31 03* – *closed Sun evening and Mon* – *20.58/45.73€*. You'll be enchanted with this old mill on a lake surrounded by peaceful woods. Part of the building has been converted into a restaurant; the surprising dining room decor has white stucco arches. Appetizing, sometimes original cuisine.

Le Cabanon et Grange aux Canards – *1129 av. des Landes* – *40140 Magescq* – *15km/9mi NW of Dax via D 16* – ☎ *05 58 47 71 51* – *closed 20 Sep to 20 Oct, Sun evening except 14 Jul to 15 Aug and Mon* – *21.34/53.36€*. On the edge of the forest in a typical half-timbered Landaise house, here's a rustic restaurant under wooden beams. Well-prepared regional cuisine with a spotlight on duck and other delicacies that the Landes are famous for.

Where to stay

BUDGET

Capcazal de Pachiou Bed and Breakfast – *606 rte de Pachiou* – *40350 Mimbaste* – *12km/7.5mi SE of Dax via D 947 and D 16* – ☎ *05 58 55 30 54* – ⊠ – *4 rooms: 38.25/56.61€*. You won't want to leave this 17C house where remnants of the past have maintained their authenticity throughout the centuries. Sculpted wood fireplaces, antique furniture and canopied beds in the bedrooms, together with a warm, generous welcome and real family cooking.

MODERATE

Grand Hôtel Mercure Splendid – *cours de Verdun* – ☎ *05 58 56 70 70* – *closed 2 Jan to 24 Feb* – *155 rooms: 70.13/109.76€* – ⌧ *9.15€* – *restaurant 19.82/28.97€*. Ambience Belle Epoque in this resort hotel near the River Adour. Built in 1930, the very spacious rooms have been given every modern comfort while preserving their original character. Vast dining room entirely restored in the Art Deco style. Garden with pool under the trees.

Hôtel Calicéo – *r. du Centre-Aéré, at the Lac de Christus* – *40990 St-Paul-lès-Dax* – ☎ *05 58 90 66 00* – 🅿 – *48 rooms: 68.60/90.71€* – ⌧ *7.62€* – *restaurant 13.72/13.72€*. Recharge your batteries in this modern hotel facing the Lac de Christus. Aquatic fitness facilities open to the public feature round pools with currents and fountains, a heart-training room, hammams and saunas. The rooms are furnished in the style of the 1940s, as is the dining room.

On the town

Casino de Dax – *8 r. Eugène-Milliès-Lacroix* – ☎ *05 58 58 77 77* – *Mon-Thu, Sun 11am-3am, Fri-Sat 11am-4am*. This brand-new casino (July 1999) has a traditional games room, a bar and a restaurant. Slot machines in mint condition.

El Meson – *18 pl. Camille-Bouvet* – ☎ *05 58 74 64 26* – *daily noon-2pm, 7pm-2am except Sat lunch, Sun and Mon lunch* – *closed mid-Aug to Sep*. From the tapas to the wine, from the music to the aperitifs, everything in this bar-restaurant evokes the festive spirit of Spain.

Pub 29 – *29 av. Georges-Clemenceau –* ☎ *05 58 90 83 53 – Mon, Wed-Fri 6pm-2am, Sat-Sun 3pm-2am; Jul-Aug: from 6pm.* This eclectic bar is located above an Italian restaurant. It has eight billiards tables (monthly play-offs), a giant screen where sports events are broadcast and a central bar counter. Karaoke Friday nights.

Casino César Palace – *R. du Centre-Aéré-Lac de Christus – 40990 St-Paul-lès-Dax –* ☎ *05 58 91 52 72 – manager.cesar.palace@freesbee.fr – daily: casino: 11am-4am; bowling: 5pm-2am, Wed-Sat 3pm-2am, Sun 2pm-2am.* This complex is comprised of a casino, bowling alleys, two restaurants, two bars, a hotel and a very popular discotheque open weekends only. Big terrace overlooking the Lac de Christus.

Showtime

Arènes de Dax – *Parc Théodore-Denis – open performance days.* The arenas were built in 1913 and enlarged in 1932 to their current 8 000-seat capacity. Visit them to discover the *patio de caballos*, the *chapelle des matadors* (where bullfighters gather their forces before battle) and the infirmary. Corridas are organized in Dax each summer around 15 August and in the second half of September.

L'Atrium – *Cours du Mar.-Foch –* ☎ *05 58 90 99 09 – ticket office managed by the Régie Municipale des Fêtes et des Spectacles.* The Atrium's performance hall was built of what was left of the 1928 Dax casino, now in ruins. But what ruins! The ceiling, inside walls and stage border are sumptuous. Many concerts, plays and ballets are performed here.

Régie Municipale des Fêtes – *Pl. de la Fontaine-Chaude –* ☎ *05 58 90 99 09 – Sep to mid-Jul: Mon-Fri 9:30am-noon, 1:30pm-5:30pm; mid-Jul to late Sep: Mon-Sat 10am-6:30pm.* The Régie is where you'll find tickets for most of the shows and festivities organized throughout the city – bullfights, *courses landaises*, pop concerts and performances at the Atrium.

El Cortijo – *Rte du Clédon et de Constantine – 40990 Mées –* ☎ *05 58 97 50 90 – www.elcortijo1@libertysurf.fr – daily 11am-midnight on request.* Helena Gayral, female torero on horseback, will greet you and show you around her arenas, covered riding ring and stables near the Dax city gates. She offers theme days and evenings (horse shows, bullfighting shows and flamenco) with or without meals; reservations required.

Sports and leisure

Parc municipal des Sports – *Bd des Sports –* ☎ *05 58 74 12 29 – daily 8am-9pm.* This big sports complex includes the US Dax rugby pitch, a Jaï Alaï court, a fronton, football fields, an athletics track and a sports room. Basque pelota matches are held every Wednesday from June to September: 5:30pm at the fronton; 8pm at the Jaï Alaï.

Adour Plaisance – *Quai du 28ᵉ-Bataillon-des-Chasseurs –* ☎ *05 58 74 87 07 – Mar to mid-Nov: 10am-noon, 2pm-6:30pm; short cruise: Mon-Sat 2pm-6:30pm; long cruise with lunch: Mon-Sat 10am-6pm, Sun 10am-7pm.* Explore the meanders of the Adour, a 335km/208mi-long river that begins in the Pyrenees near the peak of the Midi de Bigorre, crosses Tarbes and Dax, and finally ends up in the Atlantic Ocean near Bayonne, on board La Hire. Your cruise will take half a day if you go to Saubusse, the whole day if you prefer to travel all the way to Port-de-Lanne.

Calicéa – *R. du Centre-Aéré – 40990 St-Paul-lès-Dax –* ☎ *05 58 90 66 66 – www.caliceo.com – Mon-Thu 10am-10pm, Fri-Sat 10am-11pm, Sun 10am-8pm.* This fitness centre features three mineral water pools, jacuzzis, whirlpools, hydrojets, geysers and a fast water river, but that's not all! A heart-training room, hammams and saunas, a bar and a restaurant complete this comprehensive complex.

Take a break

A. Cazelle – *6 r. de la Fontaine-Chaude –* ☎ *05 58 74 26 25 – Mon-Sat 8:30am-12:15pm, 2pm-7:15pm.* Since 1906, the Cazelle family has devoted itself entirely to making Dax madeleines. Prepared fresh each morning, they are 100% natural.

Charly's Bar – *Cours Julia-Augusta –* ☎ *05 58 90 29 44 – Tue-Sun 4pm-2am.* This hip bar occupies several storeys. There are billiards tables on the first floor, a mellow bar on the ground floor and a night bar underneath. Artistic decor. Theme evenings frequent wintertime.

La Tourtière – *12 r. St-Vincent* – ☎ *05 58 74 00 75* – *Mon-Fri 8am-7:30pm, Sat 8am-8pm, Sun 8am-noon.* Among the many sinful house specialities, note the *tourtière* (a light flaky pastry with apples or prunes, flavoured with Armagnac), the *nid d'abeille* (cream cake), the *pastis pyrénéen* (an aniseed-flavoured brioche) and the peach soufflé.

Roger Junca – *22 bis pl. de la Fontaine-Chaude* – ☎ *05 58 90 01 43* – *rogerjunca@wanadoo-fr* – *Mon-Sat 7:30am-12:30pm, 2:30pm-7:30pm, Sun 7:30am-1pm* – *closed 2 weeks in Feb.* Roger Junca has personified the traditional know-how of Landes gastronomy since 1949. Today, he delivers goods directly from his canning factory to homes all over France and has an on-site boutique specialized in *foie gras*, *confits* and *salaisons*.

Sax y Rock Café – *5 av. Eugène-Milliès-Lacroix* – ☎ *05 58 56 21 82* – *Mon-Sat 11:30am-2am; Jul-Aug: 9am-2am.* Saxophone and rock'n'roll are the icons of this trendy Dax bar with a bent for beer. Jazz concerts Mondays from October to March and rock concerts once or twice a month. Summertime, most of the customers are tourists from far and near who appreciate the convivial atmosphere.

Crypte Archéologique ⓥ – Recent archaeological digs, opposite the museum, have uncovered the podium of a 2C Gallo-Roman temple.

Parc du Sarrat ⓥ – *Rue du Sel Gemme.* The park contains a house designed by the American architect Frank Lloyd Wright. The façade, consisting entirely of plate glass, brings nature right into the house. The park is arranged in theme gardens with a wide variety of vegetation, interspersed with winding canals – a French garden, leading to a pond surrounded by magnolias, a little Japanese garden, a watercress bed, a vegetable plot, etc.

Musée de l'Aviation Légère de l'Armée de Terre (ALAT) ⓥ – *Dax Aerodrome is due S of the town. Take D 6 in the direction of Peyrehorade, then D 106 and turn right on avenue de l'Aerodrome.*
Created in 1954, ALAT is a descendent of the balloon corps which first appeared in the French Army in 1794 and the captive balloon units used in the First World War. ALAT had a high profile in Algeria during air operations, reconnaissance and rescue missions. In 1977, this air force subdivision was restructured into helicopter combat regiments. The museum houses an historical gallery with collections of documents, memorabilia, uniforms, etc. A hangar contains about 30 aeroplanes and helicopters, including a Hitler UH 12 A which is of particular interest as it was flown to Indo-China by Valérie André, the first woman General in the French Army.

EXCURSIONS

Église de St-Paul-lès-Dax – *North of the town centre, take the road to Bayonne, then follow the signposts.* The 11C bas-relief sculptures decorating the exterior of the east end of the church are of particular interest. From left to right, the early Romanesque naive works depict the Holy Women at the Tomb, the Holy Trinity *(on one of the buttresses)*, a trio of fantastic beasts, the Last Supper; the Kiss of Judas, the Crucifixion, Samson riding a lion *(also on a buttress)*, St Veronica, a dragon and an allegory of Heaven.

Dax – Fontaine chaude

Berceau de St Vincent de Paul (St Vincent de Paul's birthplace) – *4km/2.5mi NE. Leave Dax by N 124.*

Buildings owned by the charitable and educational institutions founded by the saint are grouped around a modern neo-Byzantine style church. The complex was built in 1864 to honour Monsieur Vincent.

On the approximate site of the saint's birthplace, on the left of the square, is an old house built with surviving relics of the original cottage, which can be visited. Inside are numerous mementoes relating to Monsieur Vincent. Outside, the ancient oak tree was already standing when Vincent de Paul was a child here.

Notre-Dame de Buglose – *9km/5mi. Leave Dax along N 124 to the N and turn left onto D 27.* Above the altar of the Romanesque-style basilica is a polychrome stone Virgin discovered in 1620. The church tower houses a carillon of 60 bells.

A lane leads to a spring and the small chapel (now enveloped within a larger, modern chapel) built on the site on which the statue was found.

Préchacq-les-Bains – *16km/10mi NE. Leave Dax by N 124 heading E and at Pontonx-sur-l'Adour turn right on D 10, then right again.* The small spa, once used by the writer Montaigne, stands among oak woods on the south bank of the Adour, and like Dax, specialises in the treatment of rheumatism and respiratory complaints. In the gardens beyond the thermal treatment centre, pools of plant and mineral-containing mud can be seen.

A Great Saint

In 1581, **Vincent de Paul** was born in a hamlet not far from Dax. From a poor peasant family, he worked as a shepherd from an early age. In 1595, the intelligent child was sent to one of the Franciscan schools in Dax.

Five years later he was ordained a priest at Château-l'Évêque. He was appointed parish priest at Châtillon-les-Dombes, where he founded the first Brotherhood of Charity. In 1625, he created an organisation, known as the Lazarists, to teach and help the poor, and eight years later, with Louise de Marillac, founded the Sisters of Charity who succoured the sick.

Throughout his apostolic ministry, "Monsieur Vincent" fought to combat the terrible poverty of the times. When Louis XIII appointed him Chaplain-General to the galleys, he lavished consolation and spiritual help on the convict-slaves. Horrified by the filth of the existing hospitals, he founded Le Bicêtre, La Salpêtrière, La Pitié and Les Enfants-Trouvés (a foundling hospital) in Paris, as well as a hospital for convicts in Marseille.

It was Saint Vincent de Paul who attended Louis XIII on his deathbed. At the request of the Regent, Anne of Austria, he sat on the Council of Conscience and helped to reform the Catholic Church. During the *Fronde* (the French civil war which raged between 1648 and 1653), he tried to restore peace, organised food supplies for towns threatened with famine, and set up soup kitchens and public employment centres.

This forerunner of modern welfare services died in 1660, at the age of 79. He was canonised in 1737.

DONOSTIA/SAN SEBASTIÁN★★
Pais Vasco (Guipúzcoa)
Population 176 019 Michelin map 442: C 23

★★★ **The resort and its setting** – San Sebastiàn – Donostia in Basque – long known as the Pearl of Cantabria, stretches between Monte Urgull and Monte Igueldo alongside its scalop-shaped bay, the Concha. The islet of Santa Clara partly closes off the bay.

For information on visiting San Sebastiàn, see the Green Guide Spain.

ESPELETTE★

Population 1 661
Michelin map 342: D-4 or 234 fold 33

This village dates from medieval times, and remains a sprawling collection of Basque-style red and white houses lining narrow, winding streets. Espelette specialises in growing a regional variety of red pepper but there is also a brisk local trade in a breed of pony called a **pottock** (a Pottock Fair is held in late January) which live in herds, in a semi-wild state, on the uninhabited slopes of the mountains along the Spanish border. Once used in the mines because of their docile nature and diminutive stature, these animals are now perfectly suited to pony trekking.

Red hot

Espelette peppers – In autumn, the façades of the houses in Espelette are draped with garlands of dark red peppers drying in the sun. The peppers were brought to the Basque country from America and Spain in the 17C and very quickly became the favourite local condiment. Baked in the oven and ground into a powder they were initially used in chocolate (Bayonne was the first town to make chocolate in France). They soon replaced ordinary pepper in local dishes such as Poulet Basquaise (chicken with ratatouille), Tripotxa (veal sausage), Axua (veal cutlets) etc. Today, Espelette peppers are an all-purpose remedy – used as a foot bath, they are said to cure colds and bronchitis! The Espelette Pepper Fair is held on the last Sunday in October. Festivities start with the blessing of the red peppers, followed by processions through the streets. At the end of the day, nominations are made for the *Chevaliers du Piment d'Espelette* (Knights of the Espelette Pepper).

BASQUE HOSPITALITY...

La Ferme de Pinodiéta Bed and Breakfast – *Rte d'Ainhoa - 64250 Souraide - 3km/1.8mi W of Espelette via D 20 - ☎ 05 59 93 87 31 - closed 5 Nov to 1 Mar - ⊠ - 5 rooms: 30.50/38.50€*. This is a simple and authentic farm. Plain, quiet rooms overlooking the countryside, family furniture, a garden... What more could one need? Should you care to go for a ramble, the jovial owner will be happy to point you in the right direction.

Hôtel Euzkadi – *Karrika Neagusia - ☎ 05 59 93 91 88 - closed 1 Nov to 20 Dec, Mon-Tue off-season - ⊠ - 32 rooms: 42.69€ - ⊑ 5.79€ - restaurant 13.72/25.92€*. You can't miss this typical Basque establishment – the red facade certainly catches the eye! Come taste regional cuisine in a rustic setting spiced up with garlands of Espelette peppers. Ask for a room on the far side.

Église – The church contains a gilt-wood reredos; in the nearby cemetery you will find 17C and 18C discoidal headstones unique to the Basque culture (perhaps a remnant of an ancient cult of sun worship).

Ancien Château ⊙ – The town hall, housed in a former 11C castle destroyed and rebuilt several times, holds a permanent exhibition on red pepper.

FONTENAY-LE-COMTE

Population 17 792
Michelin map 316: L-9 or 233 fold 4

Fontenay lies in a sheltered spot on the banks of Vendée River, bordering the plain, the *bocage* (farmlands criss crossed with hedgerows) and the Poitou marshlands. Its limestone houses, sometimes coated with rough cast, sprawl between two thoroughfares perpendicular to the river. Place Viète, now the centre of the town, occupies the site of a bastion which was part of the old curtain wall. To the east, particularly in the areas around Église Notre-Dame and Église St-Jean (beyond Rue des Loges), is the Old Town. The modern part of Fontenay extends southwest of the line traced by Rue Clemenceau and Rue de la République.

In the Middle Ages and during the Renaissance Fontenay, the capital of Lower Poitou, was a fortified town accustomed to violent attacks. In 1372, a local heroine, Jeanne de Clisson, defended it against Bertrand du Guesclin, one of the generals responsible for ousting the English from France. At the end of the 16C, Fontenay was disputed by the Protestants and Papists (Catholics). Two centuries later, the Republicans twice fought the Royalists in the Vendée region, beneath its walls.

A fountain of fine minds – In the 16C, Fontenay (the name is derived from the Quatre-Tias fountain – *see below*) was a centre of Renaissance exuberance.

In 1520, the young **Rabelais** knocked at the gates of the Franciscans' headquarters, which stood on the site of the present town hall. He had left the Franciscans of Angers and hoped to study Greek literature under Friar Pierre Amy, a precursor of the Reformation. Amy put him in touch (by letter) with the Hellenist scholar Guillaume Budé (1467-1540), a humanist whose later *Correspondance* with Rabelais and others became an important document in the literary history of the period.

In Fontenay Rabelais and his friends would meet at the home of **André Tiraqueau** (1480-1558), a learned legal writer, proud father of 30 children and author of a treatise on matrimonial laws for which Rabelais composed an epigraph in Greek verse. In 1523, however, Rabelais was constrained to seek refuge with the Benedictines in Maillezais after his Father Superior discovered books in favour of the Reformation among Rabelais' belongings.

In the second half of the century, other Fontenay humanists found fame, including Barnabé Brisson, Head of the Paris Parliament, who was hanged in 1591 during the disputes concerning the Catholic League, and **François Viète** (1540-1603), the brilliant mathematician who invented algebra. The poet and strict magistrate **Nicolas Rapin** (c1540-1608) was another major local figure. During the *Grands Jours* of Poitiers, he took part in a poetry competition, the theme of which was to be a flea frolicking on the snow-white bosom of Mademoiselle de Roches, a noted Poitou bluestocking. Rapin won the prize with his piece *La Puce* (The Flea), which was followed by *L'Anti-Puce*. Later, in Paris, he was one of the chief instigators of *La Satire Ménippée* (a political pamphlet directed against the Catholic League and published in 1594) before retiring to his country residence, Château de Terre-Neuve *(see below)*.

TOWN WALK

Église Notre-Dame – The church is marked by a slender, elegant 15C **belfry★** which was remodelled in 1700 by the architect François Leduc. The 82m/270ft tower, crowned by a spire decorated with crockets, is similar to that of Luçon cathedral. The main doorway is Flamboyant Gothic, with a large stone filigree opening replacing the tympanum. Wise Virgins with upright lamps and Foolish Virgins with their lamps upside down are carved in the coving. A delicate 19C Madonna adorns the pier niche.

A Louis XVI pulpit is among the features worth noting inside the church. Others include the Brisson chapel and the apsidal chapels, dating from the time of François I, which are now partly concealed by the outsized 18C altarpiece.

The small 9C **crypt**, discovered by chance in the 19C, is a rare and important example of early architecture in the Lower Poitou region. Roman mortar was used for the groin vaulting. The capitals of the supporting pillars are in the Byzantine style.

Rue du Pont-aux-Chèvres – A number of interesting old houses can be seen in this street. The former Benedictine priory at no 3 has a staircase tower. At no 6, the Villeneuve-Esclapon mansion is adorned with a monumental Louis XIII entrance surmounted by a Laocoon (an antique sculpture group representing Laocoon, the priest of Apollo, strangled with his two sons by serpents. The original is in the Vatican). The figures are flanked by statues of Hercules and Diana. No 9 boasts a fine balustraded staircase. The property belonged in the 16C and 17C to the Bishops of Maillezais. No 14 is a splendid example of a Renaissance private house, though recently deprived of its left wing. It belonged once to André Rivaudeau, mayor of Fontenay in the late 16C and author of the tragedy *Aman*, which inspired Racine to compose *Esther*.

Place Belliard – The statue in the quiet square represents General Belliard (1769-1832) who saved the life of Napoleon Bonaparte at Arcole by shielding him with his own body. The General was born at no 11.

Five interesting houses (three of them with arcades), flanking one side of the square, were built by the architect Jean Morisson

Place Bellard, a quiet square in a quiet town

M. Thierry/MICHELIN

during the reign of Henri IV. Morisson himself lived at no 16 – the pediment is crowned by a statue of the architect holding a pair of compasses, the emblem of his profession. His personal motto, *Peu et Paix* (roughly equivalent to "Less is More") is carved above the first-floor bay.

Fontaine des Quatre-Tias – In the local dialect, the word *tias* means pipes. The fountain, built in 1542 by the architect Lienard de Réau, bears the Latin inscription *Fontanacum Felicium Ingeniorum Fons et Scaturigo* (The Fountain and Source of Fine Minds) – a motto bestowed on the town by François I. The King's coat of arms, complete with emblematic salamander, is engraved on the pediment. The fountain is also inscribed with the names of famous magistrates who have sat on the bench in Fontenay, including Nicolas Rapin.

Rue des Loges – In the 18C, this street, flanked by quaintly named lanes and alleys – rue du Lamproie (Lamprey Lane), rue de la Grue (Crane Street), and rue de la Pie (Magpie Alley) – was the town's main street. Today rue des Loges is a pedestrian shopping precinct, still bordered by a number of houses with fine old façades. Among these are the house at no 26 with wrought-iron balconies and carved human faces, no 85, with an impressive late 16C doorway of carved stone, and no 94, a medieval building with projecting upper floors. On the corner of rue St-Nicolas stands a carefully restored early 16C half-timbered house.

ADDITIONAL SIGHTS

Musée Vendéen Ⓥ – *East side of place Viète*. The ground and first floors of this regional museum contain collections of archaeology (Gallo-Roman glassware from local tombs), ornithology (stuffed birds) and ethnography (furniture from the south of Vendée).

The second floor is given over to the history of the town and to artists with Vendée connections, including the painters Paul Baudry *(Diana Surprised)*, August Lepère *(The Squall* – a storm at sea – and *Views of the St-Jean-de-Monts Dunes)* and Charles Milcendeau *(View of the Wet Marsh, The Embroideresses, The Spinning-Wheel)*. Also on view are sketches by Lepère which served as a basis for engravings.

A small modern art department includes works by Émile Lahner (*The Kitchen, The Egyptian Woman* and highly coloured abstracts dating from 1959 and 1960). A huge sculpture, by the brothers Jan and Jol **Martel**, represents *An Olonne Woman Wearing a Shawl.*

Château de Terre-Neuve Ⓥ – *Take rue Rabelais west out of place Viète and turn first left on rue Barnabé-Brisson to the château.*

Jean Morisson, who built the houses in place Belliard, was also the architect of this country retreat commissioned by his friend Nicolas Rapin at the end of the 16C. It was here that Rapin wrote his well-known work, *Plaisirs du Gentilhomme Champestre* (The Pleasures of a Country Gentleman). The archaeologist and engraver Octave de Rochebrune restored the château in c 1850, adding to the decoration and collecting a number of works of art which generally lent the property a fine Renaissance air tempered by Classical influences. The building comprises two main blocks at right angles to one another, with turreted bartizans at each corner. The façade is adorned with Italian Renaissance muses in terracotta, and a porch, which was originally part of another château.

The **interior★** has a number of remarkable features – Louis XIV woodwork from Chambord Château on the Loire, a door from François I's study, fine Louis XV and Louis XVI furniture, 17C and 18C paintings and a handsome chimney piece, designed by Philibert Delorme, with carvings evoking the symbolic system devised by the Renaissance alchemists. Weapons, costumes, mortars, keys and a collection of carved ivory pieces are on display. The Renaissance decoration of the dining hall includes a monumental doorway with a splendid frame, an imposing chimney piece supported by two griffins, and a coffered ceiling of carved stone.

> ### BY THE CANALS
> ### OF THE GREEN VENICE
>
> **L'Auberge de la Rivière** – *r. Fouarne – 85770 Velluire – 11km/6.6mi SW of Fontenay-le-Comte. Take D 938ter and D 68 –* ☎ *02 51 52 32 15 – closed 1 Jan to 1 Mar, Sun evening from Oct to Jun and Mon except evenings from Jul to Sep – 30.49/38.11€.* In this pretty Virginia creeper-clad house on the water you can savour seafood and river fish while enjoying the coolness of the canals of Venice the Green. Country-style house with waxed wooden furniture. A few big, well-kept rooms.

★ FORÊT DE MERVENT-VOUVANT

55km/34mi round tour from Fontenay-le-Comte – allow 4hr

This National Forest lies at the junction of the Vendée plain and the mixed woodland, farmland and pasture known as **le bocage**. It covers 5 000ha/20 sq mi of a granite plateau carpeted with clays and sand, and gashed by deep, steep-sided valleys. Three of these have been flooded to form a 130ha/320 acre reservoir enclosed within four separate dams.

In the 12C the forest belonged to the house of Lusignan which owned both the Château de Mervent and the Château de Vouvant. The forest was annexed to the royal domain in 1674 and then assigned to the Comte d'Artois in 1778 on a grace-and-favour basis (it would return to the Crown on the death of the family's last surviving male heir). Following the French Revolution, it became the property of the State.

The deep and dark, close-packed thickets of conifers and oak once harboured packs of wolves; today wild boar and deer still roam the forest.

Numerous well-marked footpaths, cycle tracks and bridle paths cross the area.

Drive north along D 938ter towards la Châtaigneraie; 1.5km/0.9mi beyond Pissotte, take a one-way road on the right.

★ Barrage de Mervent – The approach to Mervent Dam is marked by a stone sculpture representing a Siren, the work of the Martel Brothers (20C). The 130m/426ft long dam plugs the valley of the Vendée, retaining a volume of 8 500 000m³/11 330 000 cu yd and supplying water to the southern half of the Vendée *département* and several neighbouring towns.

From the dam there is an attractive and picturesque view of the reservoir, curving among the wooded slopes upstream.

Below the barrage is a water purification plant and power station.

Continue along the one-way road, turn left onto D 65.

Parc Zoologique du Gros Roc – This zoo, set on the hills over-looking the Vendée and planted with many different species of tree, is home to a huge variety of animals from all five continents. The park extends over 5ha/12 acres.

Continue along D 65 then turn left onto D 116.

Mervent – The small town is perched on a rocky spur in the thick of the woodland. In the Middle Ages the castle (on the site of the present town hall) was the seat of the Lusignan family; nothing remains of it today. From the town hall gardens near the church square there is a fine **view★** down over the reservoir with its beach (swimming, pedal boats, etc.) on the eastern shore behind Mervent dam.

Follow D 99 then turn right onto D 99ᴬ.

Grotte du Père Montfort – Louis-Marie Grignion de Montfort, a humble and devout Catholic preacher from Brittany who was later canonised, sought refuge for meditation in the forest around 1715, while on a mission to convert Protestants; the cavern in which he found shelter subsequently became a place of pilgrimage. The footpath leading to it starts behind a wayside shrine on road D99ᴬ, where cars may be parked.

The grotto opens onto the slope of a valley above the River Mère. From there the path descends to La Maison du Curé, where another priest retired in seclusion. The choice then is either to return directly to the shrine or to walk on *(15min)* to Pierre-Brune, turning right onto a track following the west bank of the Mère.

Pierre-Brune – This picturesque site faces a steep, rocky slope near a small dam; a hotel, restaurants and an **amusement park** Ⓥ especially suitable for small children, with a playground and a miniature train known as the Tortillard.

Continue along D 99ᴬ, then turn left; 2km/1.2mi further on, turn left again towards D 938ᵀᴱᴿ (right). When you reach Alouette, turn right onto D 30.

★ **Vouvant** – *See VOUVANT.*

Leave Vouvant along D 31 to the south-east towards Foussais-Payré; 5km/3mi further on, turn right onto D 65 towards Mervent.

La Jamonière – The **Musée des Amis de la Forêt** Ⓥ contains leaflets, books, exhibitions, videos etc. on the forest, its flora and fauna, and the traditional local activities.

Continue in a southwest direction along D 65 to Quillères.

Château de la Citardière – The château, partly hidden behind a belt of ancient trees, has a fine 17C façade reflected in a wide moat. A restaurant now occupies the interior.

Leave Quillères by D 99 and continue south-east.

Foussais-Payré – A number of fine Renaissance houses and a 17C covered market distinguish this small town renowned for its annual folklore festivals. Note a fine corner house dated 1552 to the right of the church.

Church – The entrance and west front feature a remarkable collection of religious scenes carved in the 11C by Giraud Audebert, a monk from the Abbey of St-Jean-d'Angély. The archivolt of the doorway illustrates, from left to right, Chastity overpowering Lust, strolling players, apostles, Christ between the symbols of the Evangelists, then more apostles and strolling players and lastly supernatural animals including a siren symbolising the attraction of sin.

Two blind arcades framing the central doorway are carved with a scene from Christ's Passion (on the left), a fairly rare example of Romanesque art in the Poitou region, featuring the Deposition and, above, an angel's wings between the moon and the sun covered with a dark veil; on the right, one can see the Supper at Simon's and, in the upper part, Christ appearing to Mary Magdalene.

Drive south-west out of Foussais-Payré along D 49 towards Fontenay-le-Comte.

Parc Animalier de Pagnolle Ⓥ – 🎫 More than 1 000 animals can be seen in this wide, flower-filled area – among them 260 varieties of bird, ranging from the tiniest species to the ostrich.

Continue along D 49 which leads back to Fontenay-le-Comte.

Le FUTUROSCOPE★★★

At Jaunay-Clan 10km/6mi north of Poitiers
Michelin map 322: I-4 and 232 fold 46 or 233 fold 8

This modern, original complex was constructed in 1987 on the outskirts of Poitiers, between the River Clan and the A 10 ("Aquitaine") motorway. In a futurist decor, designed by the French architect **Denis Laming**, the Futuroscope has successfully combined work, pleasure and learning, under the banner of a common theme: communication.
To accommodate visitors wishing to stay overnight, hotels have been built within walking distance of the Futuroscope.

★★ LE PARC EUROPÉEN DE L'IMAGE ⊘
(EUROPEAN PARK OF THE MOVING IMAGE)

The 70ha/173-acre park introduces the public to the realities of modern technology and the changes brought about by an image-dominated society. Paths fan out from a shop-lined square (tourist information, souvenirs and gifts, etc.) to the various attractions scattered throughout the grounds. The visitor is immediately plunged into a modernistic architectural universe of glass and steel. Every building is a work of art, integrated into a thoughtfully landscaped park, providing both force and movement. A play area and an attractive footbridge spanning two man-made lakes contribute to the overall harmony. Most films shown on the site are renewed every year.

Culture, Science and Technology

★ **Le Pavillon du Futuroscope** – This building, erected in 1986 on a hill and combining two volumes – a crystal and a sphere – was the starting point for the park's neo-Futuristic architectural design. Symbolic of major transformations in the world today, it houses various temporary exhibitions and a **hologram** display covering 400m²/478 sq yd.

Cinéma Haute Résolution – *350 seats*. The Pavillon de la Communication was erected in 1989. Strips ripple across the white surface of the building which houses the high resolution room (24 to 60 pictures per second) where spectators can follow the Adventures of Mister Barnes.

★★ **Pavillon de la Vienne** – This pavilion was built in 1994. Water streams down its glass façade into a pool spanned by a footbridge. giving access to the building.

Le Mur Vidéo (Video Wall) – *192 seats*. This wall of computer-generated images consists of **850 video monitors** forming a **162m²/532 sq ft screen**. Spectators are caught up in a whirlwind of images which carry them into the technological realms of the Futuroscope.

Cybernetics

Cyber Avenue – This underground space covering some 800m²/957 sq yd proposes a great number of video games (charge) which require suppleness and a great deal of anticipation. Spread over two levels, Cyber Avenue is the favourite haunt of young

Futuristic architecture

Eating out

BUDGET

Le Roller – *Téléport 3 – bd René-Descartes – 86961 Futuroscope-Chasseneuil – ☎ 05 49 49 09 09 – roller@cyberscope.fr – 7.17€ lunch. – 13.72/22.87€.* If you're in a mood to continue your adventure after visiting the park, go spend the evening in this shrine to the 60s. Three-storied circular dining room, vintage cars, dance floor, pink or green booths, service on roller skates, acrobatic rock…and, in your plate, plentiful and varied fare.

St-Fortunat – *4 r. Bangoura-Moridé – 86170 Neuville-de-Poitou – 10km/6mi W of the Futuroscope on D 62 – ☎ 05 49 54 56 74 – closed 5-26 Jan, 16-30 Aug, Sun and Tue evenings, Mon all day – 14.94/28.20€.* This is a favourite haunt of hearty eaters – you can partake of fine fare here without going broke. During a visit to the Futuroscope, don't hesitate: drive a few more kilometres to discover this generous little restaurant.

Where to stay

BUDGET

La Ferme du Château Bed and Breakfast – *Martigny – 86170 Avanton – 3km/1.8mi W of the Futuroscope towards Avanton – ☎ 05 49 51 04 57 – annie.arrondeau@libertysurf.fr – ✉ – 3 rms: 35/45€.* Don't expect to sleep in the château! Here the rooms with rustic furnishings have been constructed in stylishly renovated old outbuildings. Summertime, breakfast is served in the vast garden. Nice pool. A pleasant stop not far from the Futuroscope.

MODERATE

Château de Labarom Bed and Breakfast – *86380 Cheneché – 15km/9mi NW of the Futuroscope. Take Neuville and Lencloître, then D 15 – ☎ 05 49 51 24 22 – chateau.de.labarom@wanadoo.fr – closed 1 Nov to 30 Mar – ✉ – 3 rms: 53.50/69€.* You'll feel as though you were in a time warp when you stay in this 16C château surrounded by a big park. The floorboards crack, the furniture has a venerable patina, the rooms are spacious and the reception quite gracious. Don't miss the imposing registered dovecote with its 2 800 nesting niches.

people. always out to test the latest interactive creation. A bar and a boutique specialising in multimedia communication.

Cyber media – Virtual games are gouped in an area covering 800m^2. Surfing on the Internet is free and there are workshops for children and adults.

Special Effects

*** **Imagic** – *600 seats*. An unusual magician learns the hard way that cloning can lead to difficulties. Using a machine designed by himself, he has to take into consideration the action of a rival who tries to eliminate him. Sensational special effects (images floating in the air, appearing and disappearing) contribute to the success of this show in which many actors take part (Roland Blanche, Darry Cowl).

For your eyes only

* **Kinémax** – *420 seats*. One of the park's original buildings, it is now its architectural point of reference. A cluster of giant rock crystals point their mirrors skywards, the many facets of the glass walls reflecting the whims of the weather and the changing colours of the seasons. Inside the building, a **600m^2/2 000 sq ft Imax screen**, seven-storeys high and as wide as a tennis court, transports the audience right into the heart of the picture.

** **Omnimax** – *351 seats*. The doors of this transparent half-sunken cube lead into a cinema with a **900m^2/3 000 sq ft hemispherical Imax screen** covering the entire human range of vision – 180 degrees. The spectator is bathed in an ocean of images produced by a fish-eye lens in a projection room beneath the seats.

** **Tapis magique** (Magic Carpet) – *246 seats*. The building's anthracite tubes sparkle and shimmer in the lake below. The audience is whisked away on a magic carpet – a feat achieved by the double Imax screens, one **vertical, measuring 672m^2/2 210 sq ft**, and the other **horizontal, measuring 748m^2/2 460 sq ft**. The latter, 25m/100ft beneath a glass floor under the spectators' feet, projects a series of fantastic images which create the illusion of flight.

The 360 degrees – *Standing room for 450.* **Nine screens** cover the walls of this enormous room. From the centre of the circle, each spectator can choose which picture to watch from amongst the 9 electronically synchronised images projected on to the 272m²/894 sq ft screen. The process was developed and installed by the American firm Iwerks.

3-D Imagery

Le cinéma en relief (3-D Cinema) – *420 seats.* The spectators, wearing special glasses, have the impression that they are actually part of the film, an effect created by two slightly staggered images (Iwerks technology).

*** **Imax 3-D** – *578 seats.* A gigantic test pattern, featuring a sphere poised on the edge of a concave wall, symbolises depth of vision. Behind the façade is a **600m²/700 sq yd flat screen**. Wearing polarizing glasses, the audience lives through the intrepid adventures of the film's hero as though they were part of the picture.

** **Solido** – *295 seats.* Wearing liquid-crystal glasses, spectators see an Omnivax image on a **900m²/1 062 sq yd screen**. The illusion is so complete that audience members reach out to grab objects which seem to be moving towards them.

Défi d'Atlantis – *100 seats.* This simulator which makes the spectators' seats move in perfect synchronisation with the picture brings to life the mystery of Atlantis.

Le Solido

Sensational experiences

** **Cinéma Dynamique** – *45 seats.*
This tiered building houses a moving cinema. The audience, seated on long benches mounted on **hydraulic jacks**, is given one final warning before being thrust into a world of virtual reality at the dizzy speed of 60 frames per minute. Enjoy your trip.

** **Astratour** – *80 seats.* The same techniques as Cinéma Dynamique.

Le Simulateur (Simulator) – *192 seats.* In front of a **330m²/1 085 sq ft screen**, the audience lives through the film as though it were true life. The seats move in perfect synchronisation with the picture.

Interactive Voyages

Ciné-Jeu – *192 seats.* Holding a bat fitted with red and green reflectors, each player acts as the game unfolds, by aiming at images shown on a large 18m²/22 sq yd video screen.

Outside Attractions

Gyrotour – A gigantic wheel which looks like a film spool spirals up a 45m/148ft high pylon. It continues to turn at the top, providing the visitor with a panoramic **view** of the spectacular grounds below.

** **The Lake and the Alphanumeric Theatre** – On the lake located in the middle of the park, fountains dance to the rhythm of music throughout the day.

At night, lights, laser beams, projections on water screens and fireworks join the show for a fairy-like display.

Le Monde des Enfants (Children's World) – This playground, surrounded by pools of water, has open-air attractions (giant slides and water games), as well as a games and hands-on room (interactive games, virtual reality, video adaptations, musical house). Tokens are required for most of the games.

Les Paysages d'Europe (European landscapes) – Aboard a cable-tracted boat, travel through the different regions of Europe. Clever use of mirrors creates multi-dimensional effects for each miniature landscape.

213

FUTUROLOGY INSTITUTE

SECONDARY
SCHOOL
AND
UNIVERSITY

N

★ LE 360°

GYROTOUR ★

Planète
Burger

CINÉMA HAUTE
RÉSOLUTION

SOLIDO ★★

THÉÂTRE
ALPHANUMÉRIQUE

IMAGES
STUDIO

Festival
Pizza

IMAX
3D DYNAMIQUE

★★ LAC
AUX IMAGES

★ KINÉMAX

le Cristal

l'Entr'acte

la Vienne

CINÉMA
DYNAMIQUE ★★

CINÉMA
EN RELIEF

PAVILLON
DU FUTUROSCOPE ★

GARE TGV
FUTUROSCOPE

OMNIMAX ★★

N 10

CHÂTELLERAULT

POITIERS

215

OUTSIDE THE PARK

Outside the actual park, the Futuroscope has a number of industrial and educational centres focused on advanced technology and communication.

L'Aire de la Formation (Education Complex) – This complex, in keeping with the park's architectural style, houses educational and research units.

Lycée Pilote Innovant Universitaire – The classrooms of this innovative high school cum university for students from age 15 to post-graduate level, are housed in a vast triangular building, encased in a metal frame, designed by the architect Denis Laming.

C.N.E.D. – Centre National d'Enseignement à Distance – The National Distance Learning Centre is housed in a building with a glass façade slanted towards the sky.

E.N.S.M.A. – École Nationale Supérieure de Mécanique et d'Aéro-Technique – This National Academy trains engineers in the fields of aeronautics and space technology.

Institut International de Prospective – This building, reminiscent of a flying saucer, is used for conferences and seminars on futurology.

Le Téléport – About fifty companies (creators of images, software, etc.) use this state-of-the-art communication space.

Le Palais des Congrès – This new conference centre, constructed in the same architectural style as the rest of the Futuroscope, has replaced the original building located inside the park.

HAGETMAU

Population 4 403
Michelin map 336: H-13 or 234 fold 26

Imposing public buildings (colleges, a covered market) in 1950s style testify to the post-war prosperity of Hagetmau, an agricultural trade centre and a major chair-manufacturing base.

The discovery of numerous prehistoric remains indicate very ancient and very large settlements at various times. In 778, Charlemagne founded the Abbaye de St-Girons which was destroyed in 1569 by the Protestants.

Crypte de St-Girons ⊙ – This crypt, which was a halt on the pilgrims' road to Compostela *(see Introduction, The Way of St James)*, is all that remains of an abbey built to house the relics of St-Girons, the 4C evangelist who preached the Gospel in the Chalosse region. The ceiling of the crypt rests on four central marble columns and eight recessed columns around the walls. The tomb of the saint lay between the marble columns. Scenes carved on the 12C **capitals★** represent his battle against the forces of evil and the dangers surrounding his missionary activities.

Other capitals in the crypt show the deliverance of St Peter – an angel cuts the captive's bonds with the tip of his lance – and the parable of the rich man.

EXCURSIONS

Brassempouy – *12km/7mi W. Leave Hagetmau to the south-west via the road to Orthez; after 2.5km/1.5mi turn right on D 2. Just before St-Cricq turn left on D 21.* This small Chalosse village, the main street of which appears to be straddled by the stone tower of the Romanesque-Gothic church, is among the world's most important prehistoric sites. On a limestone hillside west of the village is **La Grotte du Pape** ⊙, where the first works of art ever created by man were discovered at the end of the 19C. They include the earliest known representation of a human face, carved c 23 000 years BC – the celebrated 3.6cm/1 inch ivory carving known as the **Vénus de Brassempouy** or Figurine à la Capuche (Lady with the Cowl), now exhibited in the Musée des antiquités Nationales in St-Germain-en-Laye. Though many important discoveries had been made over the preceding hundred years, huge archeological tracts still remained largely intact when excavations were resumed in 1982.

Musée de la Préhistoire ⊙ – The museum displays some of the prehistoric discoveries made in the Chalosse district (a millstone, polished axe-heads) along with items found at Brassempouy since excavations were resumed (tools, bones and the remains of animals which had been eaten). Period documents recall the original 19C excavations. An exhibition of prehistoric female statuary includes reproductions of the world's most famous statuettes and copies of nine figurines discovered at Brassempouy.

Samadet – *10km/6mi E along D 2*. The hey-day of this small town was from 1732 to 1811 when its *faïences* (glazed earthenwares) were known throughout the world. The factories here were able to produce both deep and strong tones using the *grand feu* technique (high-temperature firing) and more delicate colours using the gentler *petit feu*. The **Musée de la Faïencerie** ⓥ, in the old abbot's house, contains rare and beautiful collections of celebrated Samadet wares; there are items decorated with roses, carnations, butterflies, and dishes in green monochrome with grotesques and chinoiseries. An 18C bourgeois interior, 18C costumes, various workshops and reconstructions of the Royal *faïencerie* are also of interest.

HENDAYE⌂⌂

Population 12 596
Michelin map 342: B-4 or 234 fold 33

Hendaye is a border town lying on the east bank of the Bidasoa river, which forms the Franco-Spanish border at that point. The town comprises three separate districts: Hendaye-Gare, Hendaye-Ville and Hendaye-Plage, corresponding to the area around the railway station, the town proper, and the sea-front.

SIGHTS

Hendaye-Plage – The resort benefits from uninterrupted views over the open sea and a climate which encourages luxuriant vegetation: magnolias, palm trees, tamarisk, oleanders, eucalyptus and mimosa line the avenues and shade the gardens everywhere. An unusual Moorish-style building houses a bustling shopping arcade with cafés and restaurants; it also marks the beginning of the GR 10 rambling path. From the beach, the coastal view to the northeast is marked by the rock outcrops known as Les Deux Jumeaux (Twins), just off Pointe de Ste-Anne. In the other direction Cabo Higuer (Cape Fig Tree) marks the mouth of the Bidassoa. A cycle track links the beach to the town centre via Chingoudy Bay.

Baie de Chingoudy – At high tide the sharply curving estuary turns into a semicircular lake which offers a wide variety of watersports.

Église St-Vincent – This large Basque-style church has been rearranged inside, enabling the visitor to study fragments of reredos and polychrome statues in detail. On the right is an unusual Romanesque baptismal font installed in a 17C niche with a pediment, embellished by a Basque cross. In the organ loft, the decoration of the beautiful gilded instrument portrays the Annunciation. In the Chapelle du St-Sacrement, note the 13C **crucifix★**.

L'Île des Faisans (Pheasant Island)

This river isle downstream from the Spanish frontier post at the Béhobie bridge is today no more than a wooded strip increasingly threatened by the current; no trace remains of the important historical role it once played. In 1463 Louis XI met Henry IV, the King of Castile, on its banks; in 1526 François I, held prisoner in Spain after the battle of Pavia, was exchanged here for his two sons. Since the island was deemed suitable for occasions in which royal and diplomatic etiquette were involved, it was used again in 1615 as "neutral" ground on which two royal brides-to-be could officially be introduced into their new countries: they were Elizabeth, the sister of Louis XIII chosen as the wife of the Infante of Spain (the future Philip IV), and Anne of Austria, the Infante's sister, chosen for Louis XIII himself.
The **Treaty of the Pyrenees** was signed on Pheasant Island in 1659. A commemorative stone recalls the event.
In the spring of 1660 the island was the scene of feverish preparations. The painter Velasquez (who died soon afterwards of a chill caught during the work) decorated the pavilion in which the marriage contract, provided for in the Treaty of the Pyrenees, was to be signed by Louis XIV and Maria Theresa, the daughter of Philip IV of Spain. As each delegation wished to remain on its own soil – protocol in fact forbade the King of Spain to leave his own territory – the building on the mid-stream islet was divided inside by an imaginary frontier line.

Les Deux Jumeaux – "Twin Rocks"

POINTE STE-ANNE

Leave Hendaye by D 912 towards St-Jean-de-Luz (the cliffroad). Turn left and follow the signs "Domaine d'Abbadia".

Domaine d'Abbadia – The protected area of Domaine d'Abbadia on Ste-Anne headland has the geographical features typical of the Basque coastline; its gorse and heather-covered meadows go right up to the grey cliffs overlooking the sea. The path along the cliff edge provides an excellent view of the two famous "Jumeaux" rock formations to the west. Abbadia is an interesting lookout post for migratory birds such as the grey plover, Montagu's harrier, little bustard and kite.

Return to D 912 and turn left to enter the park of the castle.

★★ **Château d'Antoine Abbadie** ⊘ – The château was built in the 19C by the explorer and astronomer **Antoine d'Abbadie** (1810-1897) on plans by Viollet-le-Duc. Modelled on the medieval fortress, it has crenellated towers and pepper-pots which were previously used as an astronomical observatory.
The park contains exotic plants and trees.
The decoration and furniture, designed by Viollet-le-Duc, illustrate the life and taste of Antoine Abbadie. The polychrome ornamentation of the chapel, which is repeated throughout the castle, is reminiscent of Basque churches. The dining-room walls are lined with buffalo hides of a tawny colour which blends perfectly with the dark green of the seats. The French-style ceilings are decorated with Amharic inscriptions (Abbadie studied this language in Ethiopia). The **Grand Salon**★, housed in a round tower, is painted in deep blue as a background for the initials of Antoine and his wife Virginie. In all the rooms there are verse and mottoes in English, in Basque and in Amharic, illustrating Abbadie's personality (his motto was "Better to be than to seem"). From the large library which Abbadie created for the Observatory of the Science Academy, one walks down to the observatory where one can still see the telescope used by priests until 1975 to establish the position of the stars in the sky.

EXCURSION

Biriatou – *5km/3mi SE. Leave Hendaye via rue de Béhobie, N 111.*
Beyond Béhobie the road follows the course of the Bidasoa before twisting up towards this tiny village, where it ends beside a parking area. The small square with its pelota court, adjoining inn and the church at the top of a flight of steps makes a charming ensemble. The view here embraces the wooded mountains, the frontier river below and the first few miles of Spain on the far side.

In memory of Loti

Pierre Loti was called up as Commander of the warship *Javelot*, assigned to protect the harbour entrance, and spent much of his time in the Bidassoa Estuary; he died in Hendaye on 10 June 1923 in a modest traditional Basque house. The house is closed to the public.

Eating out

BUDGET

Marco Polo – *2 bd de la Mer – Résidence La Croisière –* ☎ *05 59 20 64 82 – closed 7-27 Jan, evenings Nov to Mar except Sat – 13/25€.* You'll think you're on a cruise ship in this restaurant with its blond wood, handrails and copper objects. From the large bay windows, you can contemplate the Baie d'Hendaye, the Estuaire de la Bidassoa, the sea and…Spain. Menu with a spotlight on fish.

MODERATE

Bakéa – *64700 Biriatou – 4km/2.4mi S of Hendaye. Take N 121 and D 258 –* ☎ *05 59 20 76 36 – closed late Jan to early Mar, Sun evening and Mon from Oct to Easter – 22,87/32,78€.* The shady terrace with its view over the Bidassoa valley is the perfect spot to dine when the weather's fine. Stone walls, beams and fireplace in the alpine-style dining room. The chef's activities in the kitchen are designed to delight your tastebuds. A few rooms.

Where to stay

EXPENSIVE

Serge Blanco – *bd de la Mer –* ☎ *05 59 51 35 35 – closed 16-30 Dec –* 🅿 *– 90 rooms: 90,71/204,28€ –* ⎔ *8,38€ – restaurant 28,97/38,11€.* This sea-water therapy resort is the place to go to pamper your body and mind. The functional rooms have balconies and big bay windows overlooking the sea or the courtyard. The cuisine is adapted to your needs and desires – gastronomic, dietetic or simply grilled dishes in the summer.

Les HERBIERS

Michelin map 316: J-6 or 232 fold 42

This little town, standing on a bluff overlooking the River Grande Maine with its grassy banks, is the ideal starting point of a drive through windmill country. The manufacture of clothes and shoes remains the traditional economic activity of Les Herbiers.

Windmill country – In the past the Vendée hills offered both strategic and tactical advantages to armies. The Romans built a road linking the crests, and a temple crowned Mont Mercure. For centuries the heights were dotted with countless windmills which turned every time the sea winds blew – sometimes throughout the night – grinding wheat and rye from the fertile plains nearby. During the Revolution, however, local Royalist supporters used their mills as a kind of rural semaphore system, altering the position of sails and vanes to telegraph information concerning the movements of the enemy. As a result, many were burned down by Republican troops. Mechanisation in the 19C put any surviving windmills out of business. Many mills are again being restored to working order.

A typical example is stone-built, cylindrical in shape, and topped by a movable, conical roof or "cap" covered with shingles (this type is known as a tower mill because of its fixed, tower-like base). Four sails are fixed to the revolving roof to which a *guivre* is frequently attached (a long pole reaching to the ground), to help turn the sails to face the prevailing wind. The wooden sails are either covered with canvas (hemp in earlier times) or made of wooden slats articulated using the Berton System, invented in 1848.

SIGHTS

Church – It has an impressive belfry-porch with a Flamboyant doorway framed by St Peter and St Paul.

Chemin de Fer de la Vendée ⊙ – In season, this quaint train runs on an old line linking Les Herbiers and Mortagne-sur-Sèvre. It is an original way of peacefully exploring 22km/14mi of Vendée farmland, with a stop at Les Épesses station.

Gare des Épesses – *3km/2mi E along D 11.* Les Épesses railway station, on the Herbiers-Mortagne line, is typical of the architecture of early 20C country stations.

Musée de l'Histoire des Chemins de Fer en Vendée – In this little station museum, posters, exhibits and documents trace the short but eventful history of the railways.

★ROUTE DES MOULINS

Round trip 90km/56mi – allow a full day

Leave Les Herbiers going west via N 160 towards La Roche-sur-Yon.

Eating out

Auberge du Mont Mercure – *near the church – 85700 St-Michel-Mont-Mercure – ☎ 02 51 57 20 26 – closed during Feb school holidays, 11-23 Sep, Tue evening and Wed – 11.89/27.44€.* This family auberge at the top of the village is a warm, down-to-earth address. With handsome wooden beams overhead, enjoy the chef's good food prepared from fresh produce. Reasonable prices; children's menu.

Where to stay

La Métairie du Bourg Bed and Breakfast – *5km/3mi NE of Les Herbiers. Take D 755, D 11 and a side road – ☎ 02 51 67 23 97 – ▱ – 3 rms: 38.11/45.73€.* In this typical cattle farm of the Vendée you will be given a large, well-cared-for bedroom. Bons vivants will enjoy the warm welcome and generous breakfasts. Good value.

Forêt des Bois-Verts – This little wood and lake is a popular spot for picnics and walks in fine weather.

Return via N 160 for 4km/2mi then go left.

Abbaye de Notre-Dame-de-la-Grainetière ⊘ – The Abbey, devoted to Our Lady of the Corn Chandlers, was build on the edge of Soubise Forest in 1130 by Benedictine monks from the Monastery of Fontdouce, near Saintes. With the help of the local overlords, the monks became sufficiently powerful in the 13C to build the fortifications which enabled them to resist the English when they laid siege to the abbey in 1372. In the 15C, however, the monks' power waned, becoming even weaker during the Wars of Religion. Revolutionary uprisings and the Vendée Wars finally destroyed the abbey at the end of the 18C. Subsequently used for farming and as a quarry, it underwent restoration in 1963. In 1978, a Benedictine priory was established in the abbey.

Only the west end of cloisters remain, with an ambulatory of fine twinned columns. Opposite, the 12C chapter house still has its original vaults resting on granite pillars. Three apsidioles are all that remain of the abbey-church. The southwest tower, or Tour de l'Abbaye with its one arrow slit, is the only part of the fortifications still standing.

Return to the crossroads and turn right, then right again 500m/547yd further on.

Mouchamps – This village, situated above the Petit-Lay Valley, is the birhtplace of Commandant Guilbaud who, in 1928, was lost in the arctic aboard his seaplace, *Latham 47*, as he was attempting to rescue the airship *Italia*. Since the 17C, Mouchamps has been a Protestant enclave in a Catholic area: until recently, Catholic houses were singled out by a white cross above the door.

Leave Mouchamps towards the northwest along D 13.

Château du Parc-Soubise – The estate once belonged to the powerful Rohan-Soubise family; the 16C-17C castle was burnt down in 1794 (during the Revolution) and 200 women, children and old people perished; the roof alone has been restored. Situated near a 28ha/69-acre lake surrounded by ancient oak trees, the edifice has retained memories of Henri IV who stayed there in 1589 and tried to seduce his cousin, Anne de Rohan. When he asked her the way to her bedroom, she is said to have replied: "through the chapel, your Majesty!"

Return to Mouchamps and continue eastwards along D 13.

Tombe de Clemenceau – Following the Petit-Lay Valley, the road leads to the 16C manor of **Le Colombier**, which belonged to the Clemenceau family. At the end of the road, walk through the doorway opening onto an alleyway. Below, on the way down to the Petit-Lay, you can see the graves of Clemenceau and his father beside a cedar tree.

Return to D 13 and drive towards Pouzauges.

Église du Boupère – This curious 13C church, fortified in the 15C. Its façade is surrounded by buttresses pierced with arrow slits and loopholes and two bartizans linked by a crenellated watchpath. The sides were defended by gatehouses.

Continue along D 13 then turn left onto D 960.

Pouzauges – *See POUZAUGES.*

Leave Pouzauges north-west via D 752 in the direction of les Herbiers.

★ **Moulins du Terrier-Marteau** – *See POUZAUGES.*

Go back along D 752 in the direction of les Herbiers.

The road winds back down into the small valley separating Pouzauges from St-Michel-Mont-Mercure.

★ **St-Michel-Mont-Mercure** – The granite houses of this town, the highest in the Vendée hills, are clustered around a church dedicated to St Michael (who was often associated with high places), built on a site previously venerated by worshippers of Mercury, the protector of travellers.

The **church**, dating only from 1898, is 47m/154ft high. It is surmounted by a huge copper statue of the saint, itself 9m/30ft tall. Church and statue can be seen in the distance from viewpoints for miles around. From the top of the **belfry** ⊙ *(194 steps)* a broad **panorama**★★ stretching as far as the ocean can be admired. At this height, the complex pattern of the surrounding farmland appears almost like a continuous forest. The crest-line of the hills is clearly visible, bordered to the south by the trees of Bois de la Folie, near Pouzauges, and to the north by Mont des Alouettes, not far from Les Herbiers.

Leave St-Michel-Mont-Mercure north-west via D 755 in the direction of Les Herbiers.

Moulin des Justices ⊙ – This mill, built at the end of the 19C, owes its name to the fact that it is perched on top of a bluff, 275m/900ft above sea level, from which justice was administered in former times. The mill, which still grinds organic flour, has a shingle roof which can be rotated using an inside winch. The width of the sails, made of wooden slats articulated using the Berton System, can be varied.

Return to St-Michel and follow D 752 on the left.

After St-Michel, D 752 winds its way through the valley, past a hill with a windmill without sails (Moulin des Landes) to Les Épesses with its two churches standing side by side.

Mallièvre – This old weaving centre is built on a granite outcrop overlooking Vallée de la Sèvre Nantaise. The village can be toured on foot by taking the **Sentier Génovette**, punctuated with water fountains and information points.

Mont des Alouettes – Windmill and chapel

Maison de l'Eau ⊘ – This exhibition on water greets the visitor with a fluorescent water-clock, followed by the **Couloir du Néant** or Passage of Nothingness, which tells the story of the big bang and the creation of water. Through various displays and educational games, the visitor is invited to learn all about this precious liquid, from the first rainfall 4.4 billion years ago, to the current problem of conservation. One of the rooms is also dedicated to local history and the region's many water-powered cloth mills.

Leave Mallièvre, going back over the River Sèvre Nantaise, then turn right on D 72 towards St-Malo-du-Bois.

★★ **Puy du Fou** – *See Le PUY DU FOU.*

Go north along D 27 and take the Cholet road.

★ **Mont des Alouettes** – This 231m/758ft high hill marks the northwestern limit of the Vendée hills. The name is derived from the bronze skylarks *(alouettes)* which decorated the helmets of Gallic warriors when they enlisted in the Roman legions based in the area. In 1793, the seven mills on these moors were among those most frequently used to send signals by the "Whites" or Royalists. Subsequently, all were set afire by the Republicans. After many ups and downs, one of them was started up again in 1989.

The mills are all typical of the region, with their rough-hewn oak *guivres* or tails and shingled conical roofs. One of them is dedicated to the Vendée writer Jean Yole. Another **mill** ⊘, nearby, with its canvas-covered sails, still grinds corn. The small granite chapel in the Troubadour neo-Gothic style was started in 1823 in honour of the royalist Catholic Army. The windows and other finishings were only added in 1968.

The wide-reaching **view**★★ encompasses Nantes, the Atlantic Ocean and, towards Pouzauges, the chain of hills dominated by the church of St-Michel-Mont-Mercure. It is from here, too, that the impressive, almost mysterious effect of the surrounding farmland, with its intricate mixture of copse and spinney and hedgerow, is most strongly felt.

Continue on N 160 to return to Les Herbiers.

Hossegor is a pleasant seaside resort bordered by Boudigau Canal, which separates the town from neighbouring Capbreton. Thanks to the efforts of successive generations of local architects, writers and painters since the beginning of the century, this choice natural site wooded with pines, cork-oak and arbutus has been carefully developed into a holiday centre complete with parks, gardens, hotels, a casino and a golf course.

THE RESORT

The climate, influenced by the coast, the lake and the forest, is temperate, the humidity ideal, making the town an invigorating place to vacation.
Some way off-shore is the famous Gouf de Capbreton, an undersea canyon 3 000m/ 9 800ft deep and over 60km/37mi long. The huge groundswell produced by this submarine phenomenon has made Hossegor a playground for surfing enthusiasts and each summer, in the second half of August, the "Hossegor Rip Curl Pro", a World Championship for professional surfers, is held here.

★ **Le Lac** – Where once the River Ardour flowed, there is now a long salt-water lake, ringed by the pine forest and villas in the local style. Linked directly to the ocean by Boudigau Canal (constructed in the last century), the lake is subject to the movement of the tides.
Lac d'Hossegor is ideal for water sports. Its beaches, with their gently lapping waters, are perfect for small children, while Plage du Rey, on the east bank, offers a wide choice of rental equipment and lessons for windsurfing, yachting, kayaking, sailing, etc.

Capbreton – Separated from Hossegor by Boudigau canal, the town was an important **port** up until the diversion of the River Adour. Decline soon followed but today, its attractive apartment buildings, large marina and sandy beach, have turned it into a prosperous **seaside resort**. The jetty, known locally as *l'estacade*, is a popular vantage point for contemplating the coast, the Pyrenees and the mouth of the canal. Capbreton is also known for its **"gouf"** or swallow-hole – a phenomenon of underwater topography which is invisible from the surface, but which was well-known to local fishermen centuries before it was scientifically identified. It is the main geomorphologic trait of the continental shelf in the Bay of Biscay. The swallow-hole is an east-west chasm running for over 60km/37mi from the exit of the harbour. It is 3-10km/2-6mi wide and up to 3 000m/nearly 10 000ft deep. Various hypotheses have been put forward to explain its existence but none has been conclusively proved – that it is the result of a complex process of underwater fluvial erosion, a fracture linked to buckling of the Pyrenees, or a canyon gouged out by the River Adour during the great glaciations of the Quaternary Age when sea levels lowered.

The Écomusée de la Pêche et de la Mer ⓥ – ⓘ Located above the municipal casino, this museum focuses on marine geology and the history of the fishing industry around Capbreton and the Landes coast. Note the skeleton of an Arctic whale beached near Le Penon in 1988. The terrace provides a **panoramic view** of the surrounding area.

ⓘ **La pinède des Singes** ⓥ *(8km south via D 652, N 10 and D 126)* is a wooded area where monkeys from Java roam freely.

EXCURSION

North of Hossegor

38km/24mi itinerary from Hossegor to Vieux-Boucau-les-Bains.

leave Hossegor north along D 152.

The road leads to **Le Penon**, a seaside resort which combines waterfront apartments and villas set among the forest pines.

Turn right onto D 89 then left just before Seignosse.

The road overlooks Étang Noir before running north towards Étang Blanc.

Étang Blanc – This delightful "white pool" is bordered by fishermen's huts and circled by a narrow road looping through the charming countryside and along the inviting shore.

Continue north along D 189 which veers east after Gaillou-de-Pountaout and passes between Étang Blanc and Étang Hardy. Turn left onto D 652 towards Soustons.

Eating out

MODERATE

Sporting Grill – *119 av. Maurice-Martin – Sporting Casino – ☎ 05 58 41 99 99 – 22,87€.* This typical 1930s edifice on the banks of the canal is registered. Its woodwork and copper evoke the colonial and Art Deco styles. Grilled meat and fish on the menu; tranquil terrace.

Le Hittau – *R. Nouaou – 40230 St-Vincent-de-Tyrosse – 12km/7.5mi E of Hossegor via D 33 – ☎ 05 58 77 11 85 – closed Feb, Mon except evenings in Jul-Aug and Sun evening Sep to Jun – 21,34/60,98€.* In a flower-filled garden, this half-timbered, white-walled former sheepfold is now a restaurant. Genteel Landaise ambience. Dining room with wooden frame ceiling and Louis XIII-style furnishings; traditional cuisine.

Where to stay

BUDGET

Le Bosquet Bed and Breakfast – *4 r. du Hazan (rte de St-Vincent-de-Tyrosse) – 40230 Tosse – 10km/6mi E of Hossegor. Take D 33 and D 652 – ☎ 05 58 43 03 40 – ⊟ – 3 rooms: 36/40€.* Open your bedroom's French doors – the pine and oak park is yours for the enjoying. This low, modern house near Hossegor is hospitable and discrete, as are its owners. Basque dining room in the winter or terrace with barbecue when the weather is amenable.

MODERATE

Les Hortensias du Lac – *Av. du Tour-du-Lac – ☎ 05 58 43 99 00 – closed 12 Nov to 29 Mar – 🅿 – 11 rooms: 103,67/131,11€ – ☕ 10,67€ – restaurant 37,35/44,97€.* A well-deserved rest awaits you in this house by the lake, only 500m from the sea. Its white facade and rounded windows overlook the peaceful waters. Functional rooms with white stuccoed walls and blond wood furnishings. A few duplexes for family holidays.

Tyboni Bed and Breakfast – *1831 rte de Capbreton – 40150 Angresse – 3km/1.8mi E of Hossegor via D 33 – ☎ 05 58 43 98 75 – ⊟ – 3 rooms: 58€.* In the park, by the side of the pool near the lake, sit back and let your thoughts wander freely to the melody of birdsong and the wind in the pines. The warm welcome makes you feel at home. Full kitchen at guests' disposal.

On the town

Casino Barrière d'Hossegor – *119 av. Maurice-Martin – ☎ 05 58 41 99 99 – Jul-Aug: daily until 5am; rest of the year: Sun-Thu 10am-3am, Fri-Sat until 4am.* Built in 1923, this edifice is a chef-d'œuvre of Basco-landaise architecture. In 1998, the Barrière Group made it over into a games complex with a casino (50 slot machines), tennis courts, mini-golf, pool, fronton, discotheque and restaurant.

Place des Landais – *Pl. des Landais.* This square by the sea is the focal point of local nightlife – natives come from far and near to have fun here. Surfers are especially well-represented; this is where their conquest of the waves begins. Between the bistros, bodegas, Basque bars, ice-cream parlours, restaurants and wine bars (like the Lou Balou) there's something for everyone.

Lou Traouc – *Rte de Vieux-Boucau – 40150 Seignosse – ☎ 05 58 43 31 85/05 58 43 22 39 – Jul-Aug: daily from 11pm; rest of the year: Fri-Sat from 11pm – closed Oct-Mar.* It's not surprising that this is the hottest discotheque of the region – the light shows, big bay windows and outdoor pool make it a place of myriad pleasures. As many as 1,200 night owls can alight here.

Surf shop

Rip Curl – *407 av. de la Tuilerie – ☎ 05 58 41 78 00 – Mon-Fri 10am-1pm, 2pm-6pm.* This is the factory store of Rip Curl, manufacturer of surfboards, swimsuits and surfing accessories. The company organizes world surfing championships here every year. Another shop is to be found on Avenue du Touring-Club-de-France.

Sports and recreation

Parc municipal des sports Jaï Alaï – *Av. Maurice-Martin – ☎ 05 58 74 19 40 – tournaments: Jul-Aug.* Pala corta and cesta punta matches are played at this covered Jaï Alaï fronton neighbouring the Sporting Casino. Grosse pala and grand chistera matches are played at the Casino's fronton outdoors.

Hossegor Surf Club – *22 imp. de la digue nord* – ☎ *05 58 43 80 52* – *www.hossegorsurfclub.com – contact: Mon-Fri 9am-12:30pm; school holidays 9am-12:30pm, 2pm-5pm; Jul-Aug: daily*. Located next to the Fédération Française de Surf, this club proposes surf and bodyboard courses.

Yacht Club Landais – *2987 av. du Touring-Club-de-France* – ☎ *05 58 43 96 48* – *Jul-Aug: daily 9:30am-noon, 2pm-6:30pm; mid-Mar to mid-Nov: Mon-Sat 10am-noon, 2pm-5:30pm – closed Jan-Feb*. This yacht club, which organizes courses and private lessons, also rents boats, windsurf boards and canoes.

Atlantic Park – 🔅 – *Av. de la Grande-Plage – 40150 Seignosse* – ☎ *05 58 43 15 30 – www.seignosse.com – May-Sep: 11am-6pm – closed Oct to late Apr*. Water games enthusiasts will have a ball in this park where games and slides have been installed for the wee ones, and whirlpools for their chaperones. Bar and fast food on site.

Take a break

Hôtel-Bar-Restaurant du Rond Point – *866 av. du Touring-Club-de-France* – ☎ *05 58 43 53 11 – daily 7:30am-10pm*. Built in 1876, l'Hôtel du Rond Point was one of Hossegor's first buildings. It has been inhabited by the Vergez family, oyster breeders since 1904. Joël, great-grandson of the first proprietor, continues to sell oysters that you can sample in a bar which virtually hasn't changed since its creation. You can find postcards featuring the Vergez patriarch in his boat throughout the city.

Le Tilt – *366 av. du Touring-Club-de-France* – ☎ *05 58 41 71 34 – daily 7pm-3am*. Nestled in a cellar, this little night bar is run by two women, one of whom sings Brazilian airs while the other seems to know the bar business inside and out. This delightful combination sets the pace for Hossegorian nightlife year round. Mature clientele.

Marcot' – *Av. du Touring-Club-de-France* – ☎ *05 58 43 52 15 – summer: daily 8am-1am; rest of the year: Tue-Sun 8am-8pm*. Established in 1927, this pastry shop-*salon de thé* sets the tearoom standard. Cakes, ice creams, chocolates – everything you taste here is made on site.

Rock Food – *Pl. des Landais* – ☎ *05 58 43 43 27 – rolandcalaudi@hotmail.com* – *Apr-Oct: 10:30am-2am; Nov-Mar: Thu-Sun 10:30am-2am*. Roland used to work for Club Med. Microphone in hand, he's unbeatable for getting things moving. He's proved it many times while animating the Hossegor world surfing championships and he proves it nightly in his bar. The pros know it too; they reconnoitre there to discuss 'spots', 'swells' and 'tubes'...

★**Étang de Soustons** – The figure-8 shape of this 730ha/1 800-acre lake, fringed by reeds and surrounded by dense pine woods, makes it impossible to see the whole of it at once. All parts of the lake, however, are easily accessible through the woods.

🚶 *30min round trip on foot*. To reach it from Soustons, follow allée des Soupirs *(left of the church)* and then avenue du Lac as far as the landing stage, banked with flowers. Take the GR 8 signposted rambling path, to Pointe des Vergnes, to enjoy the view. Continue along the south bank, which goes round the urban development zone "ZAC des Pêcheurs". A pine forest leads to a picnic area on the water's edge.

Leave Soustons west along D 652 and turn right onto a minor road just beyond the bridge spanning the Vieux-Boucau channel; Tropica Parc is 5km/3mi further on.

Tropica Parc – 🔅 This open-air, tropical garden, with exotic touches such as Balinese houses and Indonesian bicycles, contains various species of Asian plants and a number of aviaries. The air is full of birdsong and the scent of patchouli, orchids and heliotrope, and spices such as cacao and turmeric, which can be admired in glasshouses. Further on, flower beds filled with aromatic plants keep company with animal enclosures containing donkeys, dwarf zebus, etc.

Return to D 652 and turn right to Vieux-Boucau-les-Bains.

Vieux-Boucau-les-Bains – The town was renamed Vieux-Boucau (Old Estuary in the local dialect) and almost abandoned in 1578, when the course of the River Adour was deviated. Today, Vieux-Boucau-les-Bains has been revived by the construction of Port d'Albret, a large tourist resort built on a 50ha/120 acre lagoon among the sand and pines. The waters of the lake are renewed each day by a dam with tide-activated locks. An **esplanade** joins Vieux-Boucau to Port-Albret, a charming spot for an evening stroll, when lights on the water sparkle and flow.

Grottes d'ISTURITZ et OXOCELHAYA★★

These two prehistoric **caves** are located between St-Palais and Hasparren; they can be reached from the village of St-Martin-d'Aberoue *(turn left down Rampe des Grottes)*. The caves, one above the other, correspond to two different levels, each long-abandoned, of the subterranean course of the River Aberoue. A single visit encompasses both.

HOME COOKING

Chez Onésime – *64640 St-Esteben - 4km/2.4mi S of the Grottes d'Isturitz and d'Oxocelhaya. Take D 251 and D 14 - ☎ 05 59 29 65 51 – closed Mar, Sun evening and Wed except 15 Jul to 30 Aug - 28,97/38,11€.* A small family restaurant at the village entrance. Rustic dining room in brick. A few regional specialities with a less expensive fixed-price menu in the summer.

Grotte d'Oxocelhaya

Tour

Grotte d'Isturitz – It is through this upper cave that visitors penetrate the lime-stone stronghold of the mountain. It is mainly of scientific interest: traces of occupation by Paleolithic Man from the Mousterian period to the Magdalenian have been discovered, showing an exceptional continuity. Excavations have revealed semi-rounded staffs incised with curvilinear ornamentation, and a number of carvings, examples of which are on display in the local museum.

Grotte d'Oxocelhaya – The second stage of the tour, in the lower cave, reveals a fascinating series of chambers richly decorated with natural rock concretions: stalactites, stalagmites, columns, discs, translucent draperies and a glittering petrified cascade.

JARNAC

Jarnac stands on the north bank of the River Charente, in a pleasant wooded site on the edge of the "Grande Champagne" district, not far from Cognac; the local economy is based on the distillation and shipping of brandies.

The town of Jarnac is now linked with the name of **François Mitterrand** (1916-1996) former President of France who chose to be buried in his home town in Grand's Maisons cemetery to the west of the town.

Jarnac Thrust

In 1547 Gui Chabot, Baron de Jarnac, having been insulted by La Chataigneraie (a close friend of Henri II and one of the finest swordsmen in Europe), challenged him to a duel. The encounter, organised as a "single combat" affair subject to the will of God, took place on 10 July at St-Germain-en-Laye near Paris, in the presence of the King, the Queen, Diane de Poitiers and the entire Court. Jarnac, on the point of losing, vanquished his opponent with a thrust that was within the rules but entirely unexpected, severing La Chataigneraie's hamstring. The term **coup de Jarnac** (Jarnac thrust) has been used to describe this type of attack ever since – but with an added sense of treacherousness which may seem unfair, in the circumstances, to the memory of the battling Chabot.

SIGHTS

Donation François-Mitterrand –
The museum, known as the Orangerie
Cultural Centre, is housed in an former
brandy store on the banks of Charente
River. The library contains the
complete collection of speeches given
by François Mitterrand during his
fourteen years as French president.
The *département* of Charente was the
fourth to receive a donation from the
former President; the inauguration
was held in March 1995. The vast
glassed-in building contains some of
the many works of art (ceramics,
engravings, paintings, sculptures,
etc.) presented to François Mitterand
during his presidency by people from
all over the world. Peruse the *Livre
d'Or*, where visitors leave their
comments, on the way out.

Church – This former abbey church
dating from the 11C has a square
tower adorned with blind arcades. The
upper level is pierced by two bays with
small columns. In the 13C crypt the
remains of mural paintings can be seen.

Bassac Abbey

M. Thiery/MICHELIN

Maison Courvoisier – *Place du Château*. A small **museum** (entrance near the
bridge) traces the history of spirit distillation and the different stages in the
production and refinement of Cognac. The silhouette of Napoleon I on the bottles
of the Courvoisier brand recalls that Emmanuel Courvoisier, the founder of the
company, supplied the Emperor himself, and that in 1869 the firm was appointed
purveyor to the Court of Napoleon III by Royal decree. A visit to one of the brandy
chais (storehouses) includes a slide show projected onto a sphere.

Maison Louis Royer – *Quai de la Charmille*. An entrance hall with beautiful inlaid
work leads into the *Espace Voyage*, an original exhibit on the various stages in the
production of cognac, from the vineyard to exportation throughout the world. After
this imaginative introduction, the tour continues through the *chais de vieillissement*,
redolent with the aroma of ageing brandy. A temporary exhibit and reconstructed
workrooms bring to life the various trades associated with the production of brandy.

EXCURSION

Abbaye de Bassac – *7km/4.3mi
E*. Bassac Abbey, founded soon
after the year 1000 by Benedictine
monks, was abandoned at the time
of the Revolution and returned to
religious life in 1947 by the
Missionary Brothers of St Theresa
of the Infant Jesus. A number of
important relics were preserved
here, including the Holy Bonds said
to have been used to tie up Christ
during the ritual Flagellation.

★ **Abbey Church** – In the 15C, the
interesting façade in the
Saintonge Romanesque style was
given special defences, including a
gable pierced with arrow slits and
flanked by watch towers. During

the Revolution, an anonymous patriot inscribed the words of Robespierre on the
wall: *The people of France recognise the Supreme Being and the immortality of the soul*.
Inside, the single nave with its convex vaulting and flattened east end, testifies to
the far-reaching influence of the Angevin Gothic style.
On the southern side, there is a 17C painted panel representing the Entombment.
The enormous monks' chancel was remodelled in the early 18C. The 40 delicately
carved stalls, the monumental eagle lectern, the high-altar reredos and two small
altarpieces backing the choir screen are all the work of Benedictine fathers helped
by local craftsmen. This sober and elegant decoration perfectly complements the
medieval architecture of the sanctuary.

Monastery buildings ⓥ – These were rebuilt in the 17C and 18C. A majestic doorway framed by Ionic columns, followed by a long passageway with diagonal vaulting, leads to the old cloisters.

The cloister galleries were demolished in 1820 (marks where the charges were rammed in are still visible) but the monastic buildings still exist, surmounted by attractive dormer windows with pediments. The ground floor contains the kitchens, the calefactory, a balustraded staircase in the south wing, and the old chapter-house, nowadays used as a chapel (fine 17C vaulting and modern – 1954 – stained-glass windows). There is a small garden and terrace in front of the façade overlooking the Charente River.

LACANAU-OCÉAN

Population 3 142
Michelin map 335: D-4 or 233 fold 36 or 234 fold 2 – 55km/34mi from Bordeaux

Built along the ocean front, where huge rollers come crashing on the shore, Lacanau is a picturesque resort lying at the foot of a large expanse of sand dunes, carpeted with sea pines, long exploited for timber and resin. The geometrically arranged plantations, rising and falling over sandy valleys, offer a pleasant contrast to the wide sandy beaches extending over a distance of 20km/12.4mi. It is the ideal place for cycling and surfing enthusiasts.

EXCURSIONS

Streams prevented from reaching the sea by a long line of dunes eventually formed a string of lakes linked by canals.

★ **Lac de Lacanau** – This lake, a popular spot for family holidays, covers an area of 2 000ha/5 000 acres. Its 8km/5mi length teems with freshwater fish, including eels, pike and perch. It offers every imaginable water sport – swimming, sailing, windsurfing, water-skiing, canoeing and kayaking *(boats available for hire)*. The lake can also be toured on foot or by bicycle.

Étang de Cousseau – ⓥ *Allow half a day; bring drinking water and mosquito repellent.* Access to the lake, a natural reserve, is via a footpath through Lacanau Forest or along paved bicycle paths *(leave your bike in the areas indicated at the entrance to the park as they are not allowed in the park itself)*. Bordered on the

Eating out

BUDGET

Le Squale – *Pl. du Gén.-de-Gaulle* – ☎ *05 56 26 33 70 – closed Sep to late May – 17/30€.* Like a giant fish market, this picturesque self-service restaurant will gratify seafood aficionados. Each morning, its fishing nets are emptied in front of you before their content ends up on the menu. Don't be put off by the crowd – help yourself directly at the panoramic kitchen.

Where to stay

BUDGET

Camping Talaris – *33680 Moutchic – 3.5km/2.2mi E of Lacanau via D 6* – ☎ *05 56 03 04 15 – talaris.vacances@wanadoo.fr – open 31 Mar to 15 Sep – reserv. recommended – 200 sites: 29.73€.* A pleasant campground with shaded sites and pool. Tennis courts and bike rentals. Children's playground. If you don't have a tent, you can rent a mobile home.

EXPENSIVE

Hôtel du Golf – *Domaine Ardilouse* – ☎ *05 56 03 92 92* – 🅿 *– 50 rooms: 79.27/91.47€ –* 🍽 *10.67€ – restaurant 22.87/27.44€.* Just 4km/2.4mi from the shore, this hotel bordering on a golf course is surrounded by a pine forest, guaranteeing a most relaxing sojourn. Contemporary, functional rooms. Dining room with terrace opening onto nature.

Hôtel Aplus – *Rte de Baganais* – ☎ *05 56 03 91 00 – closed Dec to Feb* – 🅿 *– 57 rooms: 79.27/94.52€ –* 🍽 *8.38€ – restaurant 21.34€.* Come alone, with your family or even with your horse for a stay in the hotel or an apartment (mount stays elsewhere). This modern resort in the middle of the pine forest has it all. Quiet rooms with balconies. Indoor and outdoor pools and fitness room.

western side by waves of undulating dunes, the lake becomes inaccessible marshland on its eastern edge. Information on the fauna (wild boar, a local species of cow, migratory birds, reptiles, insects etc), flora (pines, cane apples, holm oaks, royal ferns, water lilies etc), and on tapping trees for resin, is displayed along the trail.

Maubuisson – A wooden building houses the **Musée des Arts et Traditions Populaires des Landes** ⊘, a museum focusing on local life in and around the forest. Note, in particular, the reconstructions of a resin tapper's cabin and of a traditional interior of the Medoc area.

Lac d'Hourtin-Carcans – This vast, secluded and unspoiled lake, 19km/12mi long and about 3.5km/2mi wide, covers an area of more than 6 000ha/14 800 acres. It is like an inland sea set in a landscape of moors and forests, fringed by marshes in the north and in some parts of the east, most of which is covered in sand. Dunes, sometimes up to 60m/197ft high, line the west bank.

Bombannes – This 200ha/500-acre **open-air recreation centre** among the pines provides facilities for many different sports and leisure activities, including boating, tennis, swimming, gymnastics, archery and other games. There is also a cultural centre and picnic areas. From the northern beach, a pleasant view extends over a large part of the lake.

⌂ **Hourtin** – The village, a popular departure point for travels through the network of lakes, lagoons and canals in the south-west suitable for canoeing, is also a base for pleasure boats, following the development of a lakeside marina.

Parc naturel régional des
LANDES DE GASCOGNE★

Michelin maps 335: E-6 to H-10 or 234 folds 14, 15, 18 and 19

The area was once a marine depression, subsequently filled with fine sands – quite distinct from those on the coast – during the Quaternary Era; the vast tract is poorly drained and below the surface is a hard impermeable layer, further reducing its fertility. Development of the region since the Second Empire has concentrated on the extension of the forest at the expense of the barren *lannes* (the Landes of olden times). The great mantle of pines and deciduous forests that carpet the land so thickly between the Gironde Landes and the River Adour do give way eventually to a variety of other landscapes throughout the old Gascon province. Part of this territory has now been given special protection as the Parc naturel régional des Landes de Gascogne (Landes of Gascony Regional Nature Park).

This regional park, regrouping 40 municipalities of the Landes and Gironde *départements*, and covering 301 500ha/745 037 acres in the heart of the mountain forests of Gascony, stretches from the far east of the Arcachon basin to the Val de l'Eyre, including the valleys of the Grande and Petite Leyre rivers in the south (fishing, canoeing, kayaking) and the wooded areas of the Grande-Leyre (signposted tracks, bicycle routes, footpaths and bridle paths). The considerable 330km/206mi of tracks make a pleasant, tranquil trip around the park by bicycle, with accommodation in *gîtes* along the way.

The park was designed for the protection of wildlife and its environment: permission was given for the restoration of several churches along the route of Santiago de Compostela, the creation of the **Écomusée de la Grande Lande★** (an open-air museum including the sites of Marquèze, Luxey, Moustey), the **Parc Ornithologique du Teich** *(see Bassin d'ARCACHON)*, as well as reserves, study centres, etc.

Houses and huts of the Landes region

An integral part of the landscape are the whitewash roughcast houses typical of the Landes region. They are usually built in glades, inherited from the former *airial*, or forest clearing. They are built on one level and only have an attic with a skylight in the tiled roof. A wide canopy, supported by wooden pillars, the *estantade*, protects the front of the house.

Small huts once used by resin tappers to store their tools can still be seen along the forest roads. These low, rectangular, rather basic huts are made of Landes pine (planks assembled horizontally) and covered with a gently sloping tiled roof. Two huts are often joined together.

Eating out

BUDGET

Le Haut-Landais – *Pl. des Platanes – 40410 Moustey – ☎ 05 58 07 77 85 – hautlandais@yahoo.com – closed Mon to Fri off-season except during school holidays and Mon from 30 Mar to 15 Sep – 14/30€.* On the village square, this auberge has been welcoming travellers since the 17C. Dutch-born but Landais by adoption, the owner will tempt you with specialities from both places: *aiguillettes de canard*, *palombes rôties*, *harengs 'petite vierge'* and the *'Port d'Amsterdam'* plate. Two self-catering cottages.

Café de Pissos – *In the village – 40410 Pissos – ☎ 05 58 08 90 16 – closed 12 Nov to 3 Dec, Tue evening and Wed except Jul-Aug – 15.24/36.59€.* Century-old plane trees shelter the terrace of this family auberge in the middle of town which also serves as the villagers' local watering hole. Simple regional cuisine. A few basic rooms.

MODERATE

Ferme-auberge du Jardin de Violette – *Manoir des Jourets – 40120 Lencouacq – ☎ 05 58 93 03 90 – closed Sun evening, Mon-Tue – ⊟ – reserv. required – 18.50€.* Within nicely renovated old stables in the heart of the Landais Forest, discover the flavour of little-known vegetables fresh from the garden. Chinese artichokes, golden purslane or parsnips, Violette's mother has a knack for cooking them to accompany poultry from the farm. Home-made Armagnac and aperitif. One self-catering cottage available.

Where to stay

BUDGET

Mme Boschetti Bed and Breakfast – *46 rte de Badet – 33770 Salles – 8km/5mi NW of Belin-Béliet dir. Arcachon – ☎ 05 56 88 47 24 – ⊟ – 4 rooms: 28.97€ – ⊆ 4.57€ – meals 13.72€.* A calm setting and low prices are the main assets of this square 1905 house on the edge of the Gironde Landes. Spacious rooms furnished in the 1970s style. Bourgeois-style dining room.

Les Arbousiers Bed and Breakfast – *Le Gaille – 40630 Sabres – 7.5km/4.5mi W of Sabres via D 44 – ☎ 05 58 07 52 52 – ⊟ – 6 rooms: 34/43€ – meals 14€.* This typical Landaise house with its handsome wooden frame is simple and elegant. Set in a clearing of the pine forest, the reception is also simple and the rooms plain yet inviting. Ask the owner to talk about birds – they're her passion.

Chez M. et Mme Clément Bed and Breakfast – *1 r. du Stade – 33830 Belin-Béliet – ☎ 05 56 88 13 17 – ⊟ – 5 rooms: 39/46€ – ⊆ 5.50€.* A handsome 19C bourgeois house in a park graced by venerable old trees. The refined decor features oak woodwork, waxed parquets and marble fireplaces; the rooms are bright and most open onto nature. One self-catering cottage.

TOUR THROUGH THE HEART OF THE LANDES DE GASCOGNE

127km/79mi – allow all day

This route goes through the great Landes Forest, crossed by the Grande and Petite Leyre rivers, with its areas of regeneration, its glades, its hunting grounds and typical low houses. The **Écomusée de la Grande Lande**★, comprising three separate sites near the villages of Sabres, Luxey and Moustey in the heart of the Parc naturel régional des Landes de Gascogne evokes the daily life and traditional activities of the region in the 18C and 19C. The whole region is ideally suited to outdoor tourism and can be explored on horseback, by foot or by bicycle: a bicycle path goes from Hostens to Mios.

Belin-Béliet – Eleanor of Aquitaine was born in this village in 1123. A bas-relief in her memory stands on the site of the castle built by the dukes of Aquitaine *(access via rue Ste-Quitterie; follow signpost to Hôtel Aliénor)*. To the north of town is the **Centre d'Animation du Graoux**, which offers courses about the environment and outdoor sports activities.

Leave Belin-Béliat eastwards via D 110. At Joué, turn right along D 110ES to Moustey via Peyrin and Biganon.

Moustey – Two churches made of ferrous rock known locally as *garluche* stand side by side on the town's main square. A walled-up doorway in the south wall was originally used by *cagots* (outcasts). Église Notre-Dame, to the south, houses the **Musée du Patrimoine Religieux et des Croyances Populaires** ⊙ devoted to local religious heritage and popular beliefs.

Take N134 S to Pissos.

PARC NATUREL RÉGIONAL DES LANDES DE GASCOGNE

🚶	Rambling trail starts	🚂	Tourist train
🏇	Riding centre	🚵	Off-road bike trail
🛶	Canoe-Kayak	🚲	Cycle path
M	Écomusée de la Grande-Lande	♿	Bird reserve

Pissos – The church, just outside the village, has a belfry with a shingle roof. Route de Sore, which runs through an old Landes inn, leads to the **Airial artisanal** in which contemporary art, regional gourmet specialities and crafts are exhibited (ceramics, wood and copper crafts, fabrics and jewellery). Opposite the centre an old shepherd's fold has been transformed into a **glass-blowers' workshop**.

Take D 34 S. At Commensacq, D 626 right leads to Labouheyre. As you enter the town there is a former stopping place on the pilgrimage route to Santiago de Compostela. A road to the left, by the church (follow the signs for the gendarmerie), leads to Solferino. It crosses the Parc de Peyre (forest cabins and a riding centre).

231

Solferino – In 1857, Napoleon III bought some 7 000ha/16 800 acres of marshland. After draining it, he set up an experimental area with model farms. A village was created in 1863.
The train for Marquèze leaves from **Sabres** station.

Marquèze ⓥ – *Access only by train from Sabres. The train runs for almost 5km/3mi through the forest and then leaves visitors in the Marquèze clearing*. This sector of the Écomusée covers almost 70ha/173 acres in the protected region of the Vallées de l'Eyre and comprises a delightful collection of traditional buildings – some original, others reconstructions on their former site – from the 30 or so structures which stood here when the clearing was occupied by three families.
The **airial**, for centuries an oasis in the bleak moorland and subsequently a glade in the pines which replaced the moorland, is a sort of huge esplanade, mainly planted with oak trees, where the houses and farm buildings were grouped. It is here that the master's house *(marquèze)*, dating from 1824, stands. It combines stout beams, cob walls and a three-pitched roof, and, like the other buildings, has no foundations, relying on sound timber construction for its stability.
Nearby, the more modest house with less massive beams was where the servants **(brassiers)** were lodged. Beyond is the tenant farmer's house with its barns, pigsties, beehives and chicken runs.
A path beneath the trees leads to the miller's house (1834) and the **mill** itself, with its two separate millstones for grinding the smaller and the larger varieties of grain. The woodland walk ends at the **charbonnières** (charcoal burners), where old trees were burnt very slowly to produce charcoal, before returning to the *airial* where an information centre presents a selection of documents, maps, models and an illustrated commentary *(in French)* on the museum and the agricultural and pastoral life of the region. A nearby sheepfold contains a flock of grazing sheep; they were once used to clear the moorland for agricultural use and enrich it with their droppings.
On the other side of the railway, between an aviary and an ancient well, there is a second big house, known as Le Mineur, which was transferred from another *airial*, and an exhibition explaining the old pastoral farming system. In the **model orchard** over 1 600 species of fruit trees native to the Grande Lande are tended; they include varieties of apple, plum, cherry, medlar and quince.

Back in time in Marquèze

The Écomusée de la Grande Lande organises several events aiming at reviving 19C traditions from the Landes region.
La Maillade, which takes place on 1 May, is the festival of spring: Maypoles, decorated with flowers are planted in order to honour a young lady or a friend.
Mid-May is the time for **shearing sheep**. Their wool will then be carded, spun and knitted.
Haymaking takes place during the first half of June: hay is cut in the fields and saved to feed cattle in winter.
The biggest laundry of the year; known as the *bugade*, takes place in the middle of June. Ash replaces washing powder. The washing is rinsed in the river.
The 24 June is the **feast of St John** and midsummer's night. Large wooden crosses are burnt in the hope of securing good crops.
Finally, throughout the fine season (from the end of March to October), it is possible to watch craftsmen at work: tapping of pine trees, kneading and cooking bread, grinding rye, ploughing with oxen etc.
Information – ☎ *05 58 08 31 31.*

Return to Sabres or go left via D 315 in the direction of Luxey.

Luxey – The **Jacques and Louis Vidal Resinous Products Workshop** ⓥ illustrates the traditional local industry based on resin products which dates from the beginning of the Industrial Revolution; the workshop operated commercially from 1859 to 1954. Visitors may follow every stage from the arrival of the tapped pine-tree sap to the final storage of refined turpentine.

D651 leads to Belhade via Sore and Argelouse.

Belhade – In the Gascon dialect, this town's name means beautiful fairy. It has a church with a belfry-wall and a doorway with attractive sculpted columns. To the west, on the left, there is a view of the Château de Belhade with round crenellated towers.

Hostens – Between 1933 and 1963, lignite was excavated out of open quarries. The quarries were then flooded by the rising water table, forming the lakes of Lamothe and Bousquey. The **Domaine départemental d'Hostens**, a leisure park covering 500ha/1 200 acres, has been developed on the site. A nature trail guides visitors through the park.

Return to Belin-Bélietvia via D 3 and N 10.

Abbaye de LIGUGÉ

Michelin map 322: H-5 or 233 fold 8 – 8km/5mi S of Poitiers

Ligugé claims the title of the Oldest Monastery in the West. After more than three centuries of interruption, monastic life here on the west bank of the River Clain was resumed in 1853 by Benedictine monks from Solesmes.

Under the sign of St Martin – In the year AD 361 a soldier, born in what is now Hungary, established a monkish cell here in the ruins of a Gallo-Roman villa in the Clain Valley; this was the man who later became St Martin, the patron saint of France.

Martin was a young officer in the Roman army when he encountered a beggar numb with the cold one day at the gates of Amiens; he at once took off his cloak, sliced it in two with his sword and gave half to the shivering pauper. Subsequently, having seen in a dream Christ Himself wrapped in the shared cape, he had himself baptised.

Martin became a disciple of Hilaire (Hilary), the Bishop of Poitiers, and spent almost 10 years here at Ligugé. His burning faith and profound sense of charity were soon spoken of throughout the region, and in the year 370 the inhabitants of Tours entreated him to become their bishop. Not far from Tours, he founded the monastery of Marmoutier.

St Martin died at Candes, on the banks of the Loire, in 397. The monks of Ligugé and those of Marmoutier disagreed over who was to have charge of the body, but the men of Tours had their way by placing the corpse in a boat and rowing silently away after nightfall while their rivals slept. It was then that the miracle occurred: although it was November, as the vessel neared the town leaves appeared on the trees, flowers blossomed and birds sang. The warm autumn days of Indian summer are known in France as l'été de la St Martin.

TOUR

Excavations – The digs here, which were started in 1953 in front of and beneath the nave of the present St Martin's Church, have revealed an exceptional series of pre-Romanesque structures which incorporate the remains of a Gallo-Roman villa, an early basilica (discovered in 1956) dating from before the year AD 370, a 4C martyrium (votive chapel), a 6C church and a 7C basilica.

Some noteworthy features include:

– On the left, the wall of one room of the Gallo-Roman villa, with a floor made of a kind of concrete. On the right is an arcade of the martyrium, which succeeded this room.

– The south transept of the 7C basilica, which forms the foundation of the present belfry; a vault dating from AD 1000; a 4C Ionic capital (reused); a model and plans of the original buildings.

– Beneath the present nave, the crypt of the 7C basilica. Behind this is the apse of the primitive basilica built by Martin in the 4C.

– The southern apsidal chapel of this same 7C basilica. The ornamental tiling, enamelled segments in geometric patterns, is the oldest of its kind in France.

Église St-Martin – Today this is the parish church of Ligugé. It was rebuilt in the early 16C by Geoffroy d'Estissac, at that time Prior of Ligugé.

The **west front** and its belfry, both in the Flamboyant Gothic style, are extremely elegant. On one leaf of the carved Renaissance doors St Martin is depicted dividing his cloak.

Monastery – A number of ancient features are included within the monastery as a whole. A round tower in the outer wall is known as the Rabelais Tower because the celebrated story-teller spent a lot of time here between 1524 and 1527, when he was working as secretary to Geoffroy d'Estissac.

A community of 40 Benedictine monks inhabits the monastery today. The site so impressed the writer **J-K Huysmans** (1848-1907) that he stayed here as an oblate – a lay person attached to a religious community in order to benefit from its spiritual support – in 1901. The painters Rouault and Forain and the poet Louis Le Cardonnel were received at the same time. The poet Paul Claudel, brother of the sculptress Camille Claudel, was also a postulant here.

In the **galerie d'émaux** ⓥ there is an exhibition of the enamelwork from the studio here which has made this monastery famous throughout the world.

The visit ends with a tour of the small **museum** ⓥ in which the monastic history and geography of the area is illustrated.

LUÇON

This charming episcopal town on the borders of the Poitou marshlands and the plain was once a seaport; more recently it has become an important trading and agricultural centre.

Richelieu – On 21 December 1608, in the cathedral here, a pale-faced young man accepted the homage of a handful of canons: Armand du Plessis de Richelieu, aged only 23, was taking over "the ugliest bishopric in France, a mud-caked backwater" – as he himself described it to a friend soon after his arrival.

He was hardly exaggerating: the town had been ruined by the Wars of Religion and by illness and fever brought on by the damp of the surrounding marshes. Such fevers forced

Richelieu by Philippe de Champaigne

the young bishop to retire from time to time to his 16C country château, for the Bishop's residence, which had been deserted for 30 years, had not a single fireplace in working order. Richelieu refused to be discouraged, however, and persevered with his mission, restructuring the See and its clergy, restoring the cathedral and residence, and founding a seminary. He was also responsible for the creation of a town bearing his name south-west of Tours, near the River Loire.

At the same time the man who was later to play an important role as State Adviser to Louis XIII was enhancing his prospects by intensive study of history and theology; by cultivating friendships with diplomats and such influential figures as Father Joseph (who subsequently became Richelieu's mentor on matters of foreign policy), Cardinal de Bérulle (a major force during the Catholic renaissance in the 17C) and the Abbot of St-Cyran (whom he was to have imprisoned, many years later, at Vincennes).

SIGHTS

Cathédrale Notre-Dame – This former abbey church became a cathedral in 1317. As well as Richelieu, the See counts at least one other celebrated bishop on its roll: Nicolas Colbert, the brother of the Minister, who governed the bishopric from 1661 to 1671. The church, built of fine honey-coloured limestone, is largely in the Gothic style, although the northern arm of the transept dates back to Romanesque times. The west front was entirely remodelled in the late 17C under the supervision of the architect François Leduc. The overall balance and strictly Classical layout of this façade (superimposed antique orders, scrolled decoration etc) contrast vividly with the slender, tapered Gothic spire which was rebuilt in 1828 and rises to a height of 85m/279ft. The façade as a whole serves today as a belfry-porch.

The well-proportioned nave and chancel date from the Gothic period; the latter is adorned with ornamental woodwork and a rich 18C canopy. Richelieu himself is said to have preached from a pulpit, delicately

> **CROWNED BEEF**
>
> **Bœuf Couronné** – *2km/1.2mi N of Luçon on the La Roche-sur-Yon road -* ☎ *02 51 56 11 32 - closed mid-Sep to early Oct, Sun evening and Mon - 11.13/25.61€. During a visit to this little city in Vendée, you may choose to dine in this no-pretence restaurant. Be it in the veranda or the contemporary style dining room, a classic cuisine is proposed. A few simple rooms.*

painted with fruit and flowers, in the north aisle. In the south transept is a 16C *Deposition (restored)* from the Florentine School. The 19C organ in the gallery is by Cavaillé-Coll.

Évêché (Episcopal Palace) – South of the cathedral is the 16C façade of the old bishops' residence. Entrance – via the **cloisters** – is through a doorway surmounted by a Gothic arch framing the armorial bearings of Louis, Cardinal de Bourbon, who was Bishop of Luçon from 1524 to 1527. Galleries juxtaposing both Gothic and Renaissance elements were added in the 16C. The western side, formerly the chapter-house library, is pierced by Renaissance windows.

▶▶ Jardin Dumaine★.

LUSIGNAN

Population 2 749
Michelin map 322: G-6 or 233 fold 7

This small Poitou town lies along the crest of a promontory overlooking on one side the valley of the River Vonne, on the other a vale in which a business district has been built flanking the main road to Poitiers.

Mélusine the fairy – A long time ago, according to legend, Raimondin, the young Comte du Poitou, accidentally killed his uncle with a hunting spear while the two men were grappling with an enraged wild boar. Wandering distraught in Coulombiers Forest, not far from Lusignan, Raimondin saw a spring suddenly well up at the foot of a bluff on top of which appeared the filmy white silhouettes of three enchanting female figures. One of them was the fairy Mélusine, whom the young noble determined to make his bride.

Despite her mortal marriage Mélusine retained her magic powers; with a wave of her wand, she conjured up dream palaces. In this way she created not only Lusignan Castle, on the spot where she met Raimondin, but also the fortresses of Pouzauges, Tiffauges, Mervent, Vouvant, Parthenay and Châteaumur. Yet the fairy bride hid a shameful secret from her past. Having murdered her own father, she was condemned to be transformed, every Saturday night, into a creature with the head and torso of a woman, while below her navel she was an odious serpent. Nobody should see her in this form.

One fine Saturday, however, consumed by jealousy at Mélusine's repeated absences, Raimondin burst through the door of the room where she bathed. Stupefied, he discovered his wife's changed and writhing body as she combed her long golden tresses. Mélusine at once dived out of the window, assumed the form of a giant snake, and slithered sinuously three times around the town and the castle before hurtling down onto the gatehouse tower of the château, and vanishing into thin air.

SIGHTS

Castle ruins – The fortress, built at the extremity of the promontory overlooking the steep-sided Vonne Valley, belonged originally to the Lusignan family, whose members, at one time, ruled over Jerusalem and Cyprus.

All that remains of the castle today is a group of buildings occupied by a museum, along with subterranean chambers and the foundations of several towers which were once part of the surrounding fortifications. In the 18C the castle grounds were transformed into the Promenade de Blossac, named after the steward. An avenue of lime trees surrounded by flower gardens now leads to a terrace from which there is an attractive **view** of the Vonne Valley, spanned by a 432m/475yd viaduct.

Church ○ – *Apply to the tourist office*. This fine example of Poitou Romanesque architecture with particularly impressive proportions was built by the Lusignan family in the 11C. The recumbent statue in the south aisle is Gothic. The high altar stands above a crypt with triple barrel vaulting. Outside, a porch added to the southern elevation in the 15C faces an interesting house with half-timbered, projecting upper storeys which dates from the same period.

MAILLEZAIS★

Population 934
Michelin map 316: L-9 or 233 folds 4 and 5 – Local map see MARAIS POITEVIN

A little way outside this Poitou village, on the edge of the flat immensity of the marshlands which make up the Marais Poitevin, stand the imposing ruins of Maillezais Abbey.

The abbey was founded by Guillaume Fier-à-Bras, Comte de Poitou, at the end of the 10C. At that time the limestone rise on which it is built was washed by the Atlantic surf – part of the enormous Gulf of Poitou, since silted up and sealed in to become the Marais Poitevin wetlands. The abbey, dedicated to St Peter, was first inhabited by monks of the Benedictine order, who honoured here the arms of St Rigomer. In the 13C it was sacked by Geoffroi la Grand-Dent, a member of the Lusignan family who claimed to be the son of Mélusine, and who was subsequently used by Rabelais as a model for the boisterous and brave giant **Pantagruel** in his novel of the same name.

In 1317 the French pope John XXII elevated Maillezais to the status of a bishopric but allowed the monks to remain in the abbey. During the Wars of Religion most of the buildings were destroyed and the Bishop of Luçon, Richelieu, ordered the episcopal seat to be transferred to La Rochelle.

TWO HUMANISTS

Geoffroy d'Estissac – Between 1518 and 1542 the Bishop of Maillezais was Geoffroy d'Estissac, a Périgord man who seemed to collect livings as a hobby: he was Abbot of Celles-sur-Belle, of St-Liguaire near Niort, of Cadouin in Périgord, Prior of Ligugé and Hermanault, near Fontenay-le-Comte, and Dean of St-Hilaire de Poitiers.

Geoffroy was a great builder, constantly altering and improving the establishments for which he was responsible; it was he who started the construction of the castle at Coulonges-sur-l'Autize, decorative elements of which were subsequently transferred to the Château de Terre-Neuve at Fontenay-le-Comte.

The erudite and liberal bishop welcomed Rabelais to Maillezais when the young monk was expelled from Fontenay in 1523, and for three years employed him as secretary. Rabelais followed him to several other ecclesiastical residences in the Poitou region. Later, from Rome, he sent d'Estissac the first seeds of the green vegetable which became known as *Salade Romaine* (Cos Lettuce).

Agrippa d'Aubigné – The writer Agrippa d'Aubigné (1552-1630) was born in the Saintonge region and later became a close friend of Henri IV; he was the grandfather of Mme de Maintenon *(for her biographical sketch, see NIORT)*. An ardent Protestant, he was condemned to death four different times for his religious views. A scholar as much as a poet, he wrote among many other works a Huguenot *chanson de geste* entitled *Les Tragiques* (Tragedies).

From 1584 to 1619 Aubigné spent much of his time either in his fort at Doignon, near Maillé south of Maillezais, or within the abbey itself, where he was host to Protestant troops fortifying the outer walls.

★ ABBAYE DE MAILLEZAIS ⓥ *45min*

Much of the fortified wall built around the monastery on Aubigné's orders is still standing. The work transformed the abbey into a true fortress: on the left of the entrance a bastion shaped like the prow of a ship faces the Marais wetlands. It was surmounted by a bartizan watchtower, and because the prow pointed due south, it also served as a giant sundial.

Abbey church – Building of the church began in the early 11C, though only the narthex and the wall of the north aisle remain from this period. The narthex was flanked by two square towers, following a pattern established in Normandy where abbey churches were distinguished by tower strong points on either side of the west front. The façade of the church here was later incorporated into the fortified wall built by Aubigné.

The three tall, crowned openings piercing the existing aisle wall reveal that the nave was altered in the 13C. The aisles were originally topped by galleries – again as in Norman abbeys.

The transept, of which only part of the northern arm remains, was a 14C Gothic addition. It is possible to climb to the top of one of the truncated turrets flanking its gable, from which there is a good general view of the ruins, the village and the marshes. The outlines of the huge chancel, which was rebuilt in the 16C by Geoffroy d'Estissac, can still be made out.

Monastery – Most of the monastic buildings date from the 14C. The foundations of the old cloisters have been uncovered, along with sections of the paving, a 12C storeroom, a *lavabo* where the monks washed their hands before entering the refectory, a well and a number of abbots' or bishops' tombstones.

Proud ruins

CANAL-SIDE PLEASURES

La Grange aux Roseaux – *39-41 r. Grand Port –* ☎ *02 51 00 77 54 – closed Jan and Mon-Fri lunch off-season except school holidays – 12/20€.* Next to the abbey landing-stage, have a seat in the arbour under the weeping willows and try a *farci* or other regional speciality. If the weather isn't compliant, you can take refuge near the big fireplace.

Mme Bonnet Bed and Breakfast – *69 r. de l'Abbaye –* ☎ *02 51 87 23 00 –* ✉ *– 5 rooms: 59.46€.* Such charming accommodation! This beautiful, well-designed 19C house has an Italian-style orangerie that leads to a park featuring ancient yews. Fresh-water sailors have direct access to the wetlands canals from the orchard and the rowboat is there for the taking.

One wing of the monastery still stands and includes the ancient salt cellar (basement); the octagonal kitchen, now housing an exhibition of items discovered during the excavations – scrolled modillions, capitals etc – and the refectories (ground floor); the guests' dorter (dormitory) and infirmary with its large central fireplace (first floor).

A **boat trip** ⓥ *(pedestrian access from the parking area of the abbey)* along the canals of Green Venice, as this part of the Marais Poitevin is known locally, is an excellent complement to the tour of the abbey (interesting views of the abbey).

Nieul-sur-l'Autise – *8km/5mi NE.* This village grew around an old abbey founded in 1068; in the 13C monks began to drain the neighbouring marshes. The abbey was secularised in 1715 and soon abandoned. The Romanesque abbey church in Poitou style was restored in the 19C and features a richly carved west front. The square **cloisters**★ ⓥ are original and have Romanesque galleries offering good views.

The **Maison de la Meunerie** ⓥ is a restored old watermill now housing a museum: the mill workings and domestic rooms of the miller and his family are on view.

Le MARAIS BRETON-VENDÉEN★

Michelin map 316: E-6 to F-7 or 232 folds 26, 27, 38 and 39
NW of the Vendée

This coastal marshland stretches from Bourgneuf to St-Gilles-Croix-de-Vie. In times past, the coastline was dotted with islands (Bouin, Beauvoir, Monts, and Riez) which acted as damns, slowly silting up the gulf.

North of the Beauvoir hills, the Machecoul wetlands are separated from the former island of Bouin by the Dain saltwater canal. To the south, wetlands known as Monts and Challans are divided by the Perrier Canal. The whole area covers more than 20 000ha/49 500 acres.

Like the Marais Poitevin, these salt-marshes have been drained over the centuries as canals and saltwater channels were dug out first by 17C monks, then by Dutch engineers.

Today, the open expanse seen from above is a patchwork of green fields, preferred grazing ground for local species of horses, cows and sheep. The old salt flats have mostly been transformed into pastureland or dammed and flooded for commercial fishing purposes (raising eel and mullet).

On higher ground (hillocks known as *mottes*), there are still a few remaining **bourrines**, the traditional marshlander's dwelling; a low house made of straw and mud, thatched with reeds. The region's trademark windmills are found on the highest points, in the company of little villages; many of these sites were once islands. On the canals, boatmen pole their flat-bottomed **yoles** among the waterfowl.

★ FROM GRAND ÉTIER TO ÉTIER DU DAIN

1 Round trip from Challans *105km/63mi – allow 6hr*

Challans – This farm town is the region's main economic centre. Renowned for the ducks raised here, in demand by the greatest chefs, Challans has diversified production by increasing black chicken stock as well.

In season, during the **Four Thursdays Fair**, the whole village dons an air of the early 1900s, and by-gone traditions are brought back to life: the duck market, a schoolroom, folk dancing, games, cycle races, and more.

Leave Challans to the NW on D 948 towards Beauvoir-sur-Mer.

Sallertaine – In the 11C, this town was still an island, when monks from Marmoutier (near Tours) founded a priory here, building a Romanesque church with a cupola. The novelist René Bazin (1853-1932) chose Sallertaine for the setting of *La terre qui meurt*, proclaiming his attachment to the land and ancestral values. In summer, the Île aux Artisans (a crafts centre) is the starting point for a canoe trip through the marsh.

Leave Sallertaine NW towards St-Urbain.

Moulin de Rairé ⓥ – Standing tall above the marshland, this tower windmill has been catching the breeze since its construction in the 16C. The rotating cap can be adjusted from inside the mill, and the white canvas sails use the Berton system. Along the road, you soon cross over the Grand Étier – *étier* means "tide channel or marsh creek".

La Bourrine à Rosalie ⓥ – This typical marshlander's house has a reed roof, a common room with a raised bed (in case of flooding), and a "reception room" for entertaining special guests.

Carry on along D 199, then take D 82 on the right.

Salle panoramique ⓥ – A lift installed in a **water tower** makes it possible to reach a vast terrace at 70m/230ft above sea level, where a lovely **view★** opens all round: to the east, the wetlands bordered by the hedgerows around Challans; to the north, the Bourgneuf Bay and the bridge to Noirmoutier Island; to the west and south, the forest of Côte des Monts.

Continue along D 82.

Notre-Dame-de-Monts – This seaside resort is a regional landsailing centre. A bike trail leads to La Barre-de-Monts through a sweet-smelling pine forest.

Pont d'Yeu – On the south side of town, a wooden staircase has been built in the dunes to provide access to the beach at Pont d'Yeu. When the tidal reach is strongest, the sea withdraws to reveal 3km/1.8mi of rocky strand, quickly invaded by alert fishermen *(as soon as the tide turns, return to the beach without delay)*. This tidal flat may be all that remains of an isthmus which once connected Île d'Yeu to the continent, during the Ices Ages of the Quaternary Era.

Leave Notre-Dame-de-Monts to the N by a little road running parallel to D 38.

The picturesque **Route de la Rive** traces the border between the **Pays des Monts Forest** and the first glimmerings of the marsh. Many paths lead from the forest to the ocean, through the sea oats waving atop the dunes.

Pey de la Blet – At 41m/135ft, this is the highest point of the former island of Monts. The site has been attractively planted in pine and green oak, making it a pleasant walk to the **scenic overlook**.

Fromentine – This modest seaside resort is nestled between the ocean and the forest. Gateway to the islands, it is the point of departure for boats to Île d'Yeu (regular departures from the jetty) and for Île de Noirmoutier (by the bridge).

Go to the centre of Barre-de-Monts and take the road in front of the church.

* **Écomusée de Daviaud** ⓥ – Set up in a late-19C sharehold farm, the **centre de découverte du Marais breton-vendéen** is a living museum of local architecture and the traditional marshlander lifestyle. It creates the opportunity to imagine the isolated and hard life of the old-timers.

In a typical *bourrine* sod house, an animated model describes the different construction methods and the way the old farms were organised; the salt store, located next to the marsh where salt was collected, displays an exhibit on that process. The Écomusée is in a whitewashed building made of clay and straw, with a reed roof, once used as a barn and stable and now featuring presentations on the local environment and wildlife (geomorphology, fauna, flora, migratory birds). A bit further on, a reconstitution of the inside of an ordinary dwelling at the turn of the 20C gives a good idea of the austere lives led there.

You can try your own hand at some of the marshlanders' special skills, by manoeuvring a yole down the canal, or vaulting over a stream with a long pole.

Continue until you reach D 51, then turn left.

Beauvoir-sur-Mer – This village used to be on the shore, and the site of an 11C castle which was laid to siege by Henri IV in 1588, then destroyed one year later. The church, **St-Philibert**, also dates from the 11C; the bulky bell-tower rises in contrast to the elegant doorway.

Take D 948 W out of Beauvoir-sur-Mer.

** **Passage du Gois** – *See Île de NOIRMOUTIER.*

Head back towards Beauvoir-sur-Mer, and turn left after 2km/1mi.

Le Marais breton-vendéen – Saltwater canal

S. Sauvignier/MICHELIN

Eating out

MODERATE

La Pitchounette – *48 r. Bonne-Brise – 85230 St-Gervais – 3km/1.8mi SE of Beauvoir on D 938 –* ☎ *02 51 68 68 88 – closed 15 days in Jan, 8 days in Jun, 15 days in Sep, Tue lunch and Mon except Jul-Aug – 9.15€ lunch – 15.24/29.73€.* Pull up a chair inside this little white house with blue shutters on the way in to St-Gervais. Thought has been given to the lighting and decorative knick-knacks, resulting in a cosy atmosphere. The baroque decor is very original and quite enticing; unfortunately the terrace is rather noisy.

Gîte du Tourne-Pierre – *85300 Challans – 3km/1.8mi – take the D69 SW of Challans –* ☎ *02 51 68 14 78 – closed 5-27 Mar, 5-27 Oct, Fri off-season, Sat lunch and Sun evening – reservations required – 29.73/56.41€.* A bit off the beaten track, this low house is quite pleasant. Nature is right outside the dining room and the decor is carefully thought out – harbingers of a deeply satisfying meal. The owner, also the cook, makes everything herself, from the cherry teasers to the *eau-de-vie*…

Where to stay

BUDGET

Le Pas de l'Île Bed and Breakfast – *Le Pas-de-l'Île – 85230 St-Gervais – 4km/2.4mi SE of Beauvoir – take D 948, D 59 and a secondary road –* ☎ *02 51 68 78 51 – closed Nov 1 to Easter –* ⊘ *– 3 rooms: 35/40€.* This pretty little house has a strong regional flavour: around a square courtyard, its ground-level rooms are independent and decorated with antiques. You can take a stroll through the wetlands just behind the house or enjoy foie gras made from home-raised ducks.

Antiquité – *14 r. Gallieni – 85300 Challans –* ☎ *02 51 68 02 84 –* 🅿 *–* 16 rooms: *39.64/60.98€ –* ☑ *5.34€.* A modern house built in the local style. The furniture unearthed in antique shops gives each room its own personality. All rooms overlook the courtyard; those in the wing are particularly agreeable.

Époids – The oyster beds of **Port-du-Bec**, situated in the bay of Bourgneuf, have been contributing to the local economy since the 1950s. South of the Bouin polders, related activities have developed, including fish hatcheries, shellfish breeding and algae farms. When the tide is low and the channel known as the Étier du Dain empties out, a veritable forest of wooden piles and foot bridges is revealed, an unusual landscape which gave the wharf the nickname of **port chinois**.

At Époids, take D 51^A, then turn left on D 758.

Bouin – Once an island encircled by the ocean and the Dain tidal channel, this town suffered repeated flooding up until 1940, when a sturdy dike, 14km/8.4mi-long, was built to protect the charming streets and oyster beds of Bouin.
From town, it is a short trip to either the port of Champs *(3km/1.8mi W on D 21^A)* or Brochets *(4km/2mi N on D 21).*

Leave Bouin SE on D 21, after 2km/1mi, turn right on D 59.

Châteauneuf – The bell in the church tower was made in 1487.

Le Petit Moulin ⊘ – Since 1703, when it was erected to replace a wooden mill, this restored tower mill has been grinding grain. The cap can be turned from inside to face the sails to the wind, and the Berton system of adjustable vanes increases efficiency.

Leave Châteauneuf on D 28 NE.

Abbaye de l'Île-Chauvet ⊘ – The abbey was founded around 1130 by Benedictine monks beckoned by the lord of La Garnache. The site was then a deserted island. The building was damaged during the Hundred Years War, and abandoned by the monks in 1588, in the heat of the religious wars ravaging France. In 1680, the abbey came back to life when members of the Camaldolite order moved in; they lived there until 1778. The French Revolution finally closed the book on the abbey's history.
Among the vestiges, admire the pointed arch of the doorway, its covings and decorative interlaced patterns.
Nothing is left of the Camaldolite buildings. In the Benedictine wing, the dormitory and its impressive 13C roof beams are open to visitors. The pilgrims' hostel stands next to it.

Before arriving in Bois-de-Céné, take D 21 straight ahead.

La Garnache – Once a fortified medieval refuge in the hands of powerful feudal lords who possessed much of the surrounding land, La Garanche stands at the north-eastern border of the Marais.

Château ⊘ – The once-proud edifice was long left to sleep beneath a thick cover of vines, as if the fortified walls had finally renounced their vocation. First erected in the 12C, it was renovated in the 13C and 15C, before Louis XIII ordered it razed in 1622; the Vendée Wars finished the task. Time has left the ramparts and two hollow towers erect, and the base of the square keep still marks the ground.

Musée Passé et Traditions ⊘ – This museum offers a reconstitution of a peasant dwelling, with its common and reception rooms. There is also a collection of headdresses and clothing, farm tools, and a dairy.

Leave Garnache on D 75 W.

The road is bordered by pine groves.

At Mollin, D 58 goes back to Challans.

FROM THE SHORE TO THE FIRST HEDGEROWS

[2] **Round trip from Challans** *60km/36mi – allow 3hr*

Challans – *See above.*

Leave Challans on D 753 W.

St-Jean-de-Monts – A popular seaside resort (casino, golf, high-rise buildings along the promenade), the big sand beach at St-Jean is part of the long stretch reaching from Fromentine to Sion, 26km/15.6mi interrupted only by the rocky Pont d'Yeu tidal flat.
The town centre is sheltered by wooded dunes; the church was reconstructed in 1935, with due respect for its 14C charms, and the shingled belfry is 17C.

Take the coast road S (D 123).

Sion-sur-l'Océan – One of the main attractions of this spot is the shrimp fishing – don't forget your bucket!

* **Corniche vendéenne** – South of Sion, the coast road overlooks rocks sculpted by the sea into shapes reminiscent of ancient ruins; a set of five clustered together are known as **les Cinq Pineaux**. The rocky cliff face is pierced by tidal inlets and creeks. At the far end of a promontory, a plaintive wail made be heard rising from the **Trou du Diable** (Devil's Hole). When the incoming tide is strong, the sea booms into this cove and the spray seems to explode from the rocky ground of the cliff top.
The corniche ends at Grosse Terre Point; take the steps near the lighthouse to reach the bottom of the cliff. At low tide, a rake and bucket can turn up fresh shellfish for dinner; more contemplative souls will enjoy studying the minute life found in the tidal pools.

The road continues along the Corniche de Boisvinet, lined with Belle Epoque villas. From the scenic overlook, take in the view of Pointe de la Garenne and the entrance to the port.

S. Sauvignier/MICHELIN

Port du Bec

⌂ **St-Gilles-Croix-de-Vie** – *see ST-GILLES-CROIX-DE-VIE.*

Leave St-Gilles-Croix-de-Vie via D 38ᴮ N towards Perrier.

To the right, the marshlands stretch all the way to the horizon.

⌂ **St-Hilaire-de-Riez** – This village, looks out over the Vie Valley; the **church** ⓥ was rebuilt in the 19C (three 17C polychrome altarpieces).

Go back to D 38B. At Pissot, go straight on via D 59 towards Perrier.

Bourrine du Bois Juquaud ⓥ – Tucked away in a grove, this typical marsh-lander's property has been faithfully restored part and parcel.

In the farmyard, or *tcheraïe*, are several small buildings: the *bourrine* with early-20C furnishings and adjacent bread oven; the barn; shelters for keeping the wheelbarrow and the firewood dry; the chicken coop; the dairy. The vegetable garden is in the farmyard too.

Continue along the country lane, then turn left on D 69 towards Soullans.

Musée Milcendeau-Jeay-Yole ⓥ – The museum is devoted to two artists with roots in the Marais Breton-Vendéen, the painter Charles Milcendeau (1872-1919) and the author Jean Yole. The house, in a pleasant shady grove, was purchased by Milcendeau in 1905. A student of Gustave Moreau, the young artist used sketching and pastel techniques. Influenced by Spanish styles, as the decoration of his studio illustrates, he was inspired by the daily lives of marshlanders. Indeed, the portraits and domestic scenes he painted are like an ethnological record. An audio-visual presentation provides further information.

Also a native son of Soullans, Léopold Robert (1878-1956), alia Jean Yole, a doctor and Senator representing Vendée, was the author of novels and essays on the subject of the upheavals in rural society.

From Soullans, D 69 towards Challans runs along a wooded area; a menhir (Pierre Levée) testifies to prehistoric inhabitants.

Le MARAIS POITEVIN★★

Michelin map 316: H-6 to L9 and 324 D-2 to G-2 or 233 folds 2 to 5

Since 1975 the Poitou Marshlands have been a conservation area extending over three *départements*. Under the clear, luminous skies, meadows are bordered by poplar and willow trees; the black boats of the marshlanders glide along innumerable watercourses. This lush landscape is a popular holiday destination.

The region is divided into **Dry Marsh**, nearer the sea, where the Atlantic winds blow, and **Wet Marsh**, further inland, bounded on the north by the limestone plain of the Vendée and southwards by the hills of Aunis.

The marshland epic – Aiguillon Bay, an Atlantic inlet which is gradually silting up, is all that remains of the vast gulf which stretched in ancient times from the limestone plain in the north to the hills of the Aunis. The gulf, which penetrated inland as far as Niort, was scattered with rocky islets (now towns such as Maillezais, Marans and St-Michel-en-l'Herm). The former shoreline is apparent in the remains of cliffs, laid out along Moricq, Luçon, Velluire, Fontaines and Benet to the north, and Mauzé-sur-le-Mignon, Nuaillé-d'Aunis and Esnandes to the south.

Eels

Abundant in both the Marais Poitevin and the Marais Breton-Vendéen, the European eel *(Anguilla anguilla)* remains for some 10 years in fresh water, where it acquires its characteristic silver colour, before swimming down estuaries and across the Atlantic Ocean, a journey of about 6 000km/3 728mi, in order to breed at great depths in the Sargasso Sea (near Bermuda).

The larvae then migrate back across the Atlantic and reach the coasts of Europe between seven and nine months later. Upon their arrival, the transparent young eels swim up estuaries and rivers between November and March. While they are growing, they are called yellow eels.

Eels are caught with wicker hoop nets or with a *vermée*, a piece of rope on which worms have been tied and which is hung from a long rod. As eels do not like light, fishing is usually done at night.

M. Dewynter/MICHELIN

Little by little the rivers Lay, Vendée, Autise and Sèvre Niortaise discharged their alluvium into the gulf, while at the same time sea currents were piling up a clay-like silt known locally as **bri**, and as a consequence the marine inlet was transformed into a huge salt-marsh.

Drainage work began in the 13C when monks from the neighbouring abbeys dredged out the Canal des Cinq-Abbés (Five Abbots' Canal) which drained the northern part of the swamp.

The work, interrupted by wars, was resumed under Henri IV by an engineer from Bergen-op-Zoom in Holland, leading to the progressive colonisation of the marshlands. Around Aiguillon Bay itself Dutch-style polders protected by dikes were reclaimed from the sea between the 16C and the 19C.

The Marais today – The marshes, extending on either side of the River Sèvre Niortaise, cover an area of 80 000ha/198 000 acres.

The general configuration of the Marais includes a network of embankments or dikes, known locally as *bots*, along the top of which run roads and tracks and below which are the principal channels *(contrebots)*. When the rivers draining into the marshes are in spate, excess water surges into subsidiary channels *(achenaux)*, which divert the flow again into *rigoles* and finally *conches*, marked by lines of small trees. Between these waterways the land, which is extremely fertile, is used both for crops and for grazing.

Fauna – The marshes attract a multitude of birds, some of them migratory birds, looking for food, for a place to rest or nest, for the simple reason that it is situated on the migration route between Northern Europe, Siberia or Canada and the Spanish or African coasts.

Various species can be observed, depending on the season: gulls, seagulls and terns, wild ducks, shelducks, barnacle geese and wild geese, large waders such as herons, egrets, spoonbills and storks, and above all **sandpipers** (small wading birds) such as plovers, redshanks, oystercatchers, stilts, avocets, lapwings etc.

The furry snout of the **nutria** (Myocastor coypus), a large, reddish-brown rodent which proliferates in the Wet Marsh, can often be seen skimming along the water. The discreet **common or Eurasian otter** *(lutra lutra)* with its sleek brown coat is more difficult to spot, as it rarely comes out of its burrow in the day time. You can see where it has been on the banks, however, by its droppings, with their pungent odour of fish. Due to pollution and sometimes sudden changes in its habitat, the otter has difficulty in finding food (mainly fish) and therefore in surviving.

Traditions – The marshlanders lived in low, whitewashed houses grouped in villages either on limestone islets or on the dikes, where there was no risk of flooding. Each householder owned some kind of cabin in an isolated spot. Most houses were flanked by a *cale* – a miniature creek in which boats could be moored. Boats were the normal means of transport, manoeuvred either with a *pigouille* (a hooked pole or gaff) or a short oar called a *pelle*. There were two types of boat: the slim, lightweight *yoles* used for going to church, to market or to school and the larger, more heavily built *plates* taking the place of vans or trucks, delivering farm produce or ferrying horses and cows.

The marshlanders delivered their milk to local cooperatives, which produced much-praised butter, returning the whey for the fattening of pigs. Fishing brought in mullet, perch, carp, crayfish and eels. Hunting for waterfowl and other game birds (duck, plover, snipe) was restricted to the winter months.

Ecological threat – The increase in cereal growing during the last few years is gradually causing the marsh to dry up and the use of fertilisers and pesticides is threatening the entire ecosystem. Plans have therefore been put forward for a return to traditional agriculture.

★★THE MARAIS MOUILLÉ

The Wet Marsh, sometimes called **Venise Verte** (Green Venice), is the more picturesque, particularly east of the Autise, on either side of the Sèvre; it covers 15 000ha/37 000 acres. A profusion of alders, lofty ash trees, willows and poplars of the species known as Poitou Whites lines the banks, and overhangs the labyrinth of narrow channels parcelling the rich fields in which herds of Friesians, Normans and locally-bred cattle graze. The plots under cultivation produce an abundant harvest of artichokes, onions, garlic, melons, courgettes, broad beans and the delicious haricots, usually white, known as *mojettes.*

In summer, the relatively cool Wet Marsh offers charming pastoral landscapes; however, it reveals its specificity during the February and March floods: visitors can then appreciate how difficult the marshlanders' life was in the past. At that time, the Wet Marsh reveals the unusual sight of its flooded meadows and roads *(proceed with care; traffic is sometimes interrupted).*

Boat trips

The best way to really experience the Wet Marsh, to appreciate its poetry, its silences and its uniqueness, is to go by boat. The vessels, mirrored in the still water, glide in summer beneath a dense vault of foliage filtering the bright light through shades of grey-green to jade.

Suggestion – The expansion of tourism in the area has led to the creation of many landing-stages. For your first exploration of this maze of waterways, it would be better to rent a flat-bottomed boat (the traditional wooden one has unfortunately been replaced by a plastic one), steered by a guide. Prices (indicated per person) vary according to the starting point: the most tourist-oriented spots do not necessarily offer the most interesting trips.

The following round trips depict a few small harbours nestling at the heart of the marsh.

MARAIS POITEVIN

- Dry marsh
- Wet marsh
- ☂ Boat trip departure point
- Marais Poitevin interregional park boundaries

1 The eastern part of Green Venice

30km round trip – about 2hr 30min

★ **Coulon** – This small town is the capital of the Wet Marsh and the main departure point for **boat trips** ⓥ through this attractive canal country, locally known as Green Venice. The marshlands can also be explored by **miniature train** ⓥ which leaves from Coulon.

Below the bridge across the River Sèvre Niortaise, the river flows peacefully between quays lined with boatmen's houses. Going back along the jetties on the right bank, **place de la Coutume** recalls the customs duties on transported goods which boatmen had to pay to go up the Sèvre Niortaise.

Église – This initially Romanesque church later remodelled in the Gothic style (west and south doors), is one of very few in France to have a preacher's pulpit outside; this one is shaped like a small canopied tower.

Aquarium ⓥ – Both tropical fish and river fish, including a *silure*, a kind of catfish and the largest freshwater fish in the world – weighing more than 20kg/44lbs – can be seen in the aquarium overlooking the church square.

A slide show provides excellent coverage of the Poitou marshlands whose flora and fauna change with the seasons.

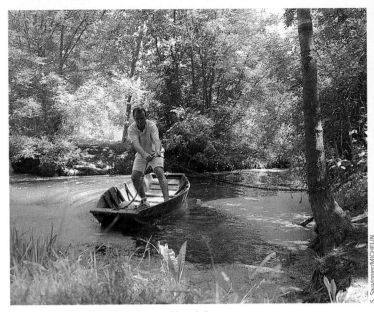

Heave-ho!

Maison des Marais Mouillés ⓥ – The museum, housed in the old customs house, has various exhibits on life in the marshes over the centuries. The main room on the ground floor is reserved for temporary exhibitions on the Poitou marshes. The first floor includes a reconstruction of the interior of a typical 19C marshlander's house and the **Maraiscope**, a simulated model based on audio-visual aids, of the main stages in the formation of the Wet Marsh. A nature room illustrates the environment (fauna and flora) and the traditional activities of the marshlanders, such as eel fishing and dike building. The visit ends with a presentation of local boat building *(balai)* and objects from the Bronze Age found during excavations of various sites around Coulon.

On leaving Coulon, drive W along D 123. At the end of the village, take rue du Port-de-Brouillac (dairy) towards Grand Coin. At the end of the road, turn left and cross the canal. Immediately after the bridge, turn left again.

The Grand Coin dam offers a good example of **boat transfer** technique. The road skirts the canal lined with poplars and weeping willows providing shade for anglers. After crossing a small bridge, one discovers a sturdy Poitou farmhouse with remarkable stone bond.

At the end of the canal, turn right onto D 123 towards Irleau.

Ash trees mark the beginning of the Wet Marsh; planted to consolidate the banks, they owe their unusual aspect to the way they are trimmed every five or seven years. The right bank of the Sèvre Niortaise offers striking views of charming cabins (some of them are only accessible by boat). The course of the river is punctuated by *conches* and *rigoles* and its gradient suddenly drops at the **Sotterie lock** from 30cm per km (1ft per 0.6mi) to less than 5cm (2in); the flow of water, considerably slowed down, floods the marsh.

Beyond the Pont d'Irleau, follow the first road on the left. Turn right at the end of the road. At the crossroads, continue straight on then turn left onto D 102.

Le Vanneau – This boatmen's village has a well-equipped **harbour★**: the remarkable **view** embraces a pastoral setting (landing-stage, characteristic footpath, line of willows). The main *conche* penetrates into the Wet Marsh beyond a screen of poplars.

Rue de Gémond (right) then rue des Vergers (left) lead to D 102: turn left towards Sansais; 200m/219yd further on, take a small road on the right (bike tour no 1 markings).

There has been a change of scenery: cereal crops enclosed by hedges have replaced the woods.

At the end of the road, turn left (unsurfaced road), then right (surfaced road): 200m/219yd further on, turn left.

Surrounded by greenery once more, visitors can cross a bridge to appreciate the beauty and charm of the site.

Turn right at the next intersection and, a little way further on, cross a small bridge. Turn right at the crossroads.

Trees suddenly give way to cultivated fields: on the left, a blue silo adds a touch of colour to the austere landscape.

At the crossroads, drive straight ahead and join D 115. Turn left as you leave St-Georges-de-Rex, then, at the Chausse intersection, turn left again onto D 3 towards Sansais. 400m/437yd further on, take V 8 on the left.

Amuré – The old cemetery (15C Hosanna cross and graves raised on piles) is 300m/328yd away from the new cemetery where two megaliths are said to have healing powers.

Continue eastwards along D 3 to Sansais; after 1.7km/1mi, turn left onto a minor unsurfaced road (Bike tour no 3 markings); 900m/0.5mi further on, turn left onto the surfaced road.

At a place called Vollette, look for a fine example of a traditional Poitou farmhouse, turned into a *gîte rural.*

At the crossroads, follow D 102 on the right and turn left 400m/437yd further on; at the next intersection (700m/765yd), turn left and stop following the bike tour markings.

From Pont de la Chaume du Château, one re-enters the Wet Marsh. This section of road may be closed during flooding or when wild ducks cross the area *(morning and evening).*

Follow the surfaced road. After 2.2km/1.3mi, the road is closed by a wooden gate; turn right, cross a small bridge and turn left 600m/0.5mi further on.

La Garette – This former boatmen's hamlet is characteristic of the area with its rows of houses built without foundation, which open onto a *conche* on one side and onto the road on the other. The high street *(closed to traffic)*, lined with small landing-stages, extends as far as the Vieille Sèvre *(see below).*

From the parking area, follow the street which climbs to D 1; turn left at the crossroads.

The road goes through the eastern part of La Garette and crosses the Vieille Sèvre: from the bridge, there is a fine view of the river and its banks. Road D 1, which takes you back to Coulon, marks the border between the wet area *(on the left)* and the dry area *(on the right).*

② Between Sèvre Niortaise and Autize

50km/31mi round tour – allow 3hr

★ **Maillezais** – *See MAILLEZAIS.*

Drive S out of Maillezais along D 15. In Croix-de-Maillé, turn right onto D 25 and continue to the bridge N of Maillé. Leave the car and follow the towpath on the right.

Aqueduc de Maillé – *1km/0.6mi there and back.*

🚶 Set in pastoral surroundings, this hydraulic complex enables the Canal de Vix (Dry Marsh) to cross that of La Jeune Autise (Wet Marsh).

Maillé – This old village is at the centre of many legends as testify the characters (acrobats, athletes carrying lions) which decorate the recessed arches of the **Romanesque doorway** of the Église Notre-Dame. Conveniently situated along the shaded banks of the Canal du Bourneau, the landing-stage nestles under a group of willow trees. Beyond the lock-bridge, it is possible to take a trip to the Île de la Chatte.

Take the road signposted Dognon, Millé opposite the church.

Agrippa d'Aubigné's keep (where *Les Tragiques* were printed in 1616, *see MAILLEZAIS*) used to stand in **Fort Dognon**. The road crosses a small bridge offering an extended view of the marsh. Strange white-plastic rafts can be seen along the *conches*: they are meant to trap the proliferating nutrias.

1.3km/0.8mi beyond the Millé farm, a footpath starts in a bend (the path is closed off by means of a chain: no vehicles allowed)

★ **Sentier du bateau à chaîne** – *600m/656yd there and back. Follow the marked itinerary Entre Sèvre et Autizes.*

🚶 This unusual itinerary offers the discovery of the hidden side of the marsh (fauna and flora). The narrow path runs alongside a *conche* through thick vegetation which can slow one down considerably. It leads to one of the last **bateaux à chaîne** (flat-bottomed boats propelled by pulling on a chain) in the area, which can be used (with care) to cross a *conche*.

Continue along the same road. At the crossroads, turn left onto D 25[B]. Cross the River Sèvre then turn left as you come off the Pont du Sablon.

Port d'Arçais

The itinerary follows the left bank of the Sèvre Niortaise and offers fine views of the Île de la Chatte *(see above)* and its fishermen's cabins. A picnic area is available near the lock of the Rabatière Canal.

At the intersection of the Croix-des-Mary bridge, carry straight on towards Damvix. At the next crossroads, turn left and cross over the lock.

Several bridges in succession make it possible to reach the right bank of the Sèvre Niortaise across the Bazoin locks, an important intersection of waterways.

Damvix – This small marshland village in a pleasant location on the Sèvre Niortaise contains a number of low cottages linked by footbridges which span the narrow canals.

Cross the Sèvre Niortaise and follow D 104 towards Arçais; 200m further on, turn right onto a minor road (Camping des Conches) which runs across a bridge. Beware: the itinerary leading to the village of la Rivière through the Marais Sauvage follows an unsurfaced road only suitable in dry weather; in rainy weather, go to Arçais by the direct route.

*Le Marais sauvage – A few planks of wood across a *conche* followed by *(take the left-hand road)* the dam of La Garette *(fine view)* give access to the Marais Sauvage *(turn right at the fork)*. This conservation area covering 1 600ha/3 954 acres is crisscrossed by 100km/62mi of waterways forming a real maze.
The village of **la Rivière**, with its fine traditional houses, stands on the edge of the marsh. To the north, the road which joins D 101 offers a striking contrast between the wooded marsh (on the left) and the vast expanse of rolling fields (on the right); **Monfaucon** to the south has a fine landing-stage.

Arçais – Set up in the bend of a reach, the **Grand-Port**** consists of a large paved dock; the landing-stage faces a typical wooden cabin. At each end of the harbour, two wooden cranes have been left as a reminder of the time when trunks of poplars travelling along the waterways were hoisted onto the quayside. There are remarkable farmhouses along the Minet reach in the northern district of **la Garenne**.

From the Grand-Port, follow D 102 towards Damvix. At Les Bourdettes, cross the dam then the lock and take the Chemin de la Foulée on the right.

The itinerary follows the right bank of the Sèvre Niortaise to the Village de la Sèvre. When you reach a typical footbridge, take the road on the left leading to Mazeau harbour (landing-stage after the bridge).

Drive NW out of Le Mazeau along D 68 towards Maillezais; 1km/0.6mi beyond St-Sigismond, at La Ragée, turn left towards Anchais. At the end of the road, turn left onto the path leading to Port d'Anchais.

L'Espace Marais ⊘ – A vast barn houses reconstructions illustrating former marshland crafts. In addition, there is a maze, an aquarium (regional fish) and the devil's garden (containing poisonous plants).

Return to the Quatre Chemins crossroads and drive N; beyond Moulin de Bouteline, D 68 takes you back to Maillezais.

Eating out

BUDGET

Theddy-Moules – *72 r. du 14-Juillet – 17230 Charron – 10km/6mi W of Marans on D 105 – ☎ 05 46 01 51 29 – closed Oct-Apr – reservations recommended – 12.96/21.34€.* You'll have your meal under a wooden lean-to built against the house of this native shellfish farmer. A very popular address among the locals who gather here to savour the famous *moules* (mussels) *à la Theddy*, cooked in cream and Pineau. Fresh produce for sale.

MODERATE

Le Central – *pl. de l'Église – 79510 Coulon – 11km/6.5mi W of Niort via D 9 and D 1 – ☎ 05 49 35 90 20 – closed 28 Jan to 14 Feb, 1-18 Oct, Sun evening and Mon – 15.09/32.01€.* Would you prefer your meal under the patio parasols or in the pretty dining room? It's up to you… A friendly welcome in this old auberge by the church where you can savour tasty cuisine chosen from several set-price menus.

Les Mangeux de Lumas – *access by foot in summer – 79270 La Garette – 12 km/7.2mi W of Niort on D 9 and D 1 – ☎ 05 49 35 93 42 – closed Jan 4-19, Mon evening and Tues except Jul-Aug – 15.24/38.11€.* In a pretty little village, this ancient farm opens its petite terrace on the waterway at the stroke of dawn. In the winter, you'll be nice and warm in its country-style dining room. Accent on regional cuisine.

Where to stay

BUDGET

Camping La Savinière – *85360 La Tranche-sur-Mer – 1.5km/1mi NW of La Tranche via D 105 rte des Sables-d'Olonne – ☎ 02 51 27 42 70 – open 31 Mar to Sep – ⊘ – reservation required – 106 sites: 14.79€.* At the foot of the dunes, this campground in the forest is 900m/981yd from the beach. Very well groomed; some of its facilities are shared with the day camp next door. Pool, half-court, bar-crêpe eatery and bungalow rentals.

Mr. and Mme Ardouin Bed and Breakfast – *Basse-Brenée – 85580 St-Michel-en-l'Herm – ☎ 02 51 30 24 09 – michel.ardouin@free.fr – ⊘ – 3 rooms: 27.50/38.50€.* This 1766 farm in the heart of the marshlands couldn't be more isolated. Its no-nonsense rooms all open onto the countryside, where birds of all feathers abound. The ground level room with kitchenette and terrace is particularly pleasant.

Le Logis d'Elpénor Bed and Breakfast – *5 r. de la Rivière – 85770 Le Gué-de-Velluire – 10 km/6mi SE of Chaillé-les-Marais on D 25 – ☎ 02 51 52 59 10 – closed Dec-Jan – 5 rooms: 44.21/50.31€ – meals 18.29€.* This is our kind of address! On the bank of the river, this enchanting 18C house in a private garden is a delightful place to stay. Its large rooms are nicely furnished with period pieces. Don't miss the home-baked *brioche* for breakfast – it's heavenly!

La Closeraie Bed and Breakfast – *21 r. de la Paix – 85450 Champagné-les-Marais – ☎ 02 51 56 54 54 – closed 31 Dec to 15 Feb – 5 rooms: 45/59€ – meals 15/20€.* The well-kept, ground-level rooms of this 19C abode are grouped around an enclosed garden. The furniture is pleasingly traditional; a kitchen with a fireplace is at your disposal. Breakfasts, sale of regional products, theme weekends. Pool.

MODERATE

Hôtel Au Marais – *Quai L.-Tardy – 79510 Coulon – 11km/6.6mi W of Niort via D 9 and D 1 – ☎ 05 49 35 90 43 – closed 25 Dec to 7 Feb – 18 rooms: 50.31/70.13€ – ☲ 6.86€.* Right next to the quay, these two august houses are the perfect starting point for discovering the Poitevin marshlands – just a few steps down and you're at the edge of the River Sèvre… Sunny bedrooms, modern and well cared for.

★ THE MARAIS DESSÉCHÉ

The **Dry Marsh** presents a very different aspect. A territory of wide open spaces crossed by canals and dikes, it produces wheat, barley and various types of bean despite the fact that the black earth of the *bri* needs constant fertilising. The pastureland has been given over to the rearing of salt-pasture sheep and cattle. Around Aiguillon Bay, which is slowly silting up, there are mussel beds *(bouchots)* particularly near Esnandes and Charron.

③ Marais du Petit Poitou

60km/37mi round tour – allow 3hr

Marans – This is the market town of the Dry Marsh, and noted for its grain storage (silos). The small port, linked to the ocean by a canal, harbours a boatyard. Lock gates maintain the level of the tidal basin, where a number of coasters and pleasure craft are moored. It is possible to have a panoramic view of the marsh from the **tower** of Notre-Dame Church.

Drive N out of Marans along N 137 towards Luçon. In Sableau, turn right onto D 25^A then left in Vouillé onto D 25.

Shortly after La Groie *(2km/1.2mi further on)*, note on the left a dike, known as a *bot*, on the edge of the marsh. The road then skirts the striking cliffs of the Village de l'An VII (a former limestone island) once pounded by the waves.

Chaillé-les-Marais – Built on what is now just a limestone bluff, the town commands the plain which was once under water. It is the centre of the Dry Marsh sector known as Petit Poitou, the first in the province to be drained and dried. From the viewpoint (place de l'Église), there is a fine view of the marsh and of the former islands of Aisne and Sableau to the left.

Return to N 137 and turn right (rue de l'An VII) towards Luçon, then left 900m/0.5mi beyond the tourist office.

Maison du Petit Poitou ⓥ – The former house of the dike master offers comprehensive information on the drying out of marshes, their flora and fauna, and the activities of its inhabitants. Outside, animals whose traditional habitat is the Marais – local donkeys, goats, cows and Marans chickens – roam about.

Continue along N 137 towards Luçon; 700m/0.4mi further on, cross Pont de la Coube and turn immediately left onto D 10.

The road skirts the picturesque **Canal du Clain** offering an interesting view of the Chaillé cliffs. The canal is lined with sparse farmhouses, damp meadows on the left and cereal crops on the right.

Turn right onto D 25 at Ste-Radegonde-des-Noyers crossroads. As you leave Champagné-les-Marais, turn left before the bridge onto the chemin Sud du canal.

The **Canal de Champagné**, one of the favourite haunts of anglers, crosses cultivated fields. The typical fauna (herons) and flora (thistles, reeds) of the Dry Marsh can be seen on either side of the road.

Turn left at the end of the long straight section of road, then continue straight ahead at the next crossroads (3km/1.9mi).

The road skirts round the Marais Fou. A belfry and a water tower emerging from a vast expanse of fields on the right. Further on, the view embraces the small **Port de l'Épine** where a few fishing boats are moored and, beyond, a farmhouse surrounded by umbrella pines (rare in this area).

Follow D 10^A on the right then, 1.1km/0.7mi further on, turn left onto a minor road which crosses the Canal de Vienne; continue for another 100m/110yd and turn right.

At the crossroads, stop in front of the warehouse to look at the *bac à râteau*, once used to dredge the silted-up canals. This cleaning-up process was undertaken every seven or eight years in wintertime and festivities were organised for the occasion. The road crosses several locks including the picturesque Grands Greniers lock. To the south, the Sèvre Niortaise supplies five canals (Vienne, Clain, Cinq Abbés, Mouillepied, Vix), thus forming an important network of waterways.

Turn right at the end of the long straight road skirting the Mouillepied Canal, then left at Hutte de la Briand.
At the lock-bridge, turn right onto N 137 to return to Marans.

④ Le Marais maritime

70km/44mi round tour – allow 3hr

St-Michel-en-l'Herm – There is an old **Benedictine abbey** ⓥ here dedicated to archangel St Michael. Notice the elevated placement of statues of this saint in local churches and sanctuaries; this is a reflection of his reputation for appearing from on high. The abbey, founded in the 7C by Ansoald, Bishop of Poitiers, prospered until the 9C when it was devastated by the Normans. Wars with the English during the 14C and 15C, the Wars of Religion in the 16C and the Revolution brought only more destruction. It was rebuilt each time, though only partly the last time, in the late 17C, when François Leduc was involved. Of particular note are the Gothic chapter-house and calefactory, with a refectory and the monks' building by Leduc.

Musée André Deluol Ⓥ – Paintings, drawings, pastels and sculptures by a local artist.

Leave St-Michel S along D 60.

La Dive mound comes into view on the right, past a silo *(see below)*. Shortly afterwards, D 60 *(straight ahead at the crossroads)* crosses several dikes and polders (reclaimed from the sea). The road ends at the foot of the **Digue du Maroc** (1912), bristling with strange perches intended for birds of prey (falcons, owls).

Return to the crossroads and turn left.

La Dive – This was still an island in the 17C. From the entrance of a former quarry, the road rises and runs along the mound, above the marsh, over a distance of 700m/0.4mi. The view extends from Pointe d'Arçay to the Aiguillon creek, encompassing Île de Ré and its viaduct-bridge. Back at sea level, one can see the cliffside indented by the sea, now partly covered over with ivy.

Continue towards the sea then turn left at the crossroads.

Digue de l'Aiguillon – The famous dike, conceived and built by Dutch engineers, is a slender 6km/3.6mi tongue of land protected by a breakwater. To the left are former salt-marshes turned into oyster beds; from Les Sablons, there is a succession of beaches bordered by sand dunes.

Go to the end of the dike.

* **Pointe de l'Aiguillon** – The south-east extremity of the dike where there is a wildfowl hunting reserve (Réserve de Chasse Maritime), projects into the grey waters of the silting-up bay. The wide **view** extends from the narrow estuary of the River Lay and Pointe d'Arcay (north-west) to the Île de Ré (south-west) and the port of La Pallice (south). The famous mussel beds are visible only at low tide.

Baie de l'Aiguillon

Esnandes – *On the other side of the bay; accessible from Marans along D 105.* The inhabitants of the low, whitewashed houses here farm mussels and oysters. The first **bouchots** were installed in the 13C, when the captain of a ship wrecked in the bay, an Irishman named Walton, settled here. To survive, he caught birds by fixing a net between two posts planted in the silt, and soon he noticed that the posts became covered in small mussels which grew more rapidly than those on the natural banks. The **Maison de la Mytiliculture** Ⓥ traces the history of Aiguillon Bay and the developments in mussel farming since the 15C.
Fortified in the 14C and 15C, the **church** looks more like a castle than a sanctuary.

Follow the dike in the other direction.

L'Aiguillon-sur-Mer – The low-built houses overlooking the estuary of the Lay face a denuded countryside, bleak beneath an immense sky. The local economy is based on nursery gardening, coastal fishing and the cultivation of oysters and mussels.

Cross the Lay.

La Faute-sur-Mer – Although it boasts a casino, La Faute remains basically a small family seaside resort, with a long beach of fine sand. The string of dunes stretches southwards to **Pointe d'Arççay** (national hunting reserve).

☖ **La Tranche-sur-Mer** – This seaside resort, with a wide beach of fine sand, stretches for 13km/8mi. Behind, pine woods extend over an area of 600ha/1 483 acres. Maupas Lake offers facilities for learning various water sports, including windsurfing, boogie-boarding, and sailing. A flower festival takes place in the spring (see Calendar of events).

Parc des Floralies ⊙ – The shady 7ha/17-acre park is crisscrossed by numerous paths and dotted with multicoloured flower beds of begonias, hyacinths, narcissi, tulips etc.

Drive N out of La Tranche-sur-Mer along D 747.

Angles – One of the gables on the old abbey church here is adorned with the representation of a large bear which, according to legend, was changed into stone by a hermit named Martin. Inside the church, the chancel and transept are Romanesque whereas the nave is in the Plantagenet style.

Return to the crossroads and continue straight ahead.

Tour de Moricq – This large 15C square tower standing isolated in the middle of a field once guarded a small harbour on the River Lay.

Follow D 25 towards Grues. Continue for 2km/1.2mi beyond St-Denis-du-Payré.

Réserve naturelle de St-Denis-du-Payré ⊙ – The nature reserve (2km/1mi east) encompasses 207ha/512 acres of marshland frequented by large numbers of birds, both nesting and migratory. A diorama with slides which can be viewed at the **Maison de la Réserve**, situated at the heart of the village, illustrates the various species which can be identified through telescopes from the nearby **observatory**.

Continue along D 25. In Triaize, turn right onto D 746.

Just before crossing the Chenal Vieux, note the former limestone islet on the right, at La Dune; 500m/547yd further on, a farmhouse stands on a mound made up of oyster shells, said to be going back a very long time; this curious pile of shells, once crushed to powder to feed poultry, can be seen from the roadside.

Continue along D 746 to return to St-Michel-en-l'Herm.

MARENNES

Population 4 685
Michelin map 324: D-5 or 233 fold 14

Marennes, once an island in the Gulf of Saintonge, is today the French oyster capital.

Marennes-Oléron – This is the name distinguishing the renowned, greenish oyster fattened in the *claires* (special beds) of the Marennes-Oléron basin, which lies between the mouth of the River Seudre, the coast north of Marennes and the eastern coast of the Isle of Oléron. Oysters grow to maturity in *parcs à huîtres*, but it is only in the *claires* of this region that the adult mollusc is fattened, refined and subjected to the effects of microscopic algae known here as Navicules Bleues which give the seafood its delicate perfume and subtle hue.

SIGHTS

Église St-Pierre-de-Sales – This 15C church is built in a style known here as English, with a tall square tower, buttressed at the corners, crowned by a spire decorated with crockets. The spire, rising to a height of 85m/279ft, is a landmark visible from miles away and used as a navigation mark by sailors.
The interior is noteworthy for its wide nave flanked by chapels beneath balustraded galleries. Eight-branched rib vaulting arches above the bays.

Terrasse de la Tour ⊙ – Accessible up 291 steps, this tower platform offers an impressive **panorama**★ – 55m/180ft high – over the oyster farms, the islands, the Avert peninsula and a stretch of the marshes.

Vidéorama de l'huître ⊙ – *In the tourist information centre.* The video (in French) focuses on ostreiculture in the Marennes-Oléron basin, showing interesting material on its history and the activities of oyster farmers.

SEA VIEW

Grand Chalet – *2 av. La-Cèpe – 17390 Ronce-les-Bains – 9km/5.4mi SW of Marennes via D 728ᴱ –* ☎ *05 46 36 06 41 – closed 15 Nov to 1 Feb. – 28 rooms: 44.21/57.93€ –* ☐ *6.10€ – restaurant 18.29/38.11€.* Facing the Île d'Oléron, this 1850s hotel has kept its amusing chalet façade. But its best feature is undoubtedly its situation: on the water's edge, the garden stretches all the way to the sea. The dining room and bedrooms are somewhat outmoded, but benefit from a lovely view.

Château de la Gataudière –
1.5km/1mi N. The château was
built c 1749, in the Louis XIV
style, by François Fresneau
(1703-70), an engineer who
studied the production of rubber
from the hevea tree in French
Guyana and returned to France to
lay the base for its industrial use.
The château stands on the site of
a medieval house in the heart of
an old marsh village known as Les
Gataudières. On the garden front,
a terrace with a wrought-iron
balustrade runs the length of the
façade. A Classical pediment
embellished with a Triumph of Flora
(the goddess of flowers) surmounts
a central block decorated with
trophies symbolising the
resources of the region (oyster
farming, salt-marsh agriculture,
winemaking etc).

Oystermen near Fort Louvois

Inside, the main reception floor is notable for the Grand Salon with its stone walls
set with fluted Corinthian pilasters representing the arts, the sciences and the four
seasons. Fine Louis XV furniture can be seen in the dining hall and the Blue Salon.
A building in the courtyard houses an exhibition of horse-drawn vehicles.

EXCURSION

* **Brouage** – *6.5km/4mi NE. See BROUAGE*.

* **Fort Louvois** – *7km/4mi N*. Access to the fort (also known as Fort Chapus) is by
foot at low tide, and by boat when the tide is in.

MAULÉON

Population
Michelin map 322: B-3 or 232 fold 43

Located north-west of Deux-Sèvres, and straddling the neighbouring *départements* of
Vendée and Maine-et-Loire, Mauléon looks down from its rocky outcrop over the Ouin
Valley. From May to October 1793, Mauléon, (then called Châtillon-sur-Sèvre), was the
capital of the military resistance in Vendée, a stronghold of Royalist support during the
Revolution *(see Introduction, Historical notes)*. Royal vouchers, corresponding to the
promissory notes issued by the French Revolutionary government, were even printed.

Musée du BRHAM – The local Historical and Archaeological Research Society
(French acronym BRHAM) is housed in the beautiful granite Abbaye de la Trinité,
remodelled in the 19C in the Louis XIV style.
One of the rooms in the abbey contains eight **engraved rocks★** from Les Vaux. In the
19C, more than 200 of these slabs, carved with various motifs, such as crosses,
stars, circles and stylised figures, the date and meaning of which remain an enigma,
were discovered in the surrounding area. The other rooms contain exhibits on the
Vendée Wars and folk traditions (religious art, Poitou headdresses, local cabinetry).

La vie des jouets – An attractive naive fresco of children playing in a public garden
welcomes visitors to this toy museum. The collection includes nearly 3 000 items tracing
the 150 years of toy history since 1830. Children are delighted to discover these
unfamiliar objects devoid of any electronic components, while adults linger over them
with nostalgia. Seven rooms present different themes – dolls, tea sets, toy cyclists from
the Tour de France and other figures, aeroplanes, boats, cars and numerous board games.
The main street leads up to the front door of the old feudal castle (12C). Flanked by
two towers, it opens onto an esplanade featuring a 17C mansion, a cinema with a highly
original glass façade and a belvedere offering a panoramic view of the Vendée hills.

EXCURSIONS

St-Aubin-de-Baubigné – *5km/3mi E via D 759*. A statue by Falguière was erected
in 1895 in honour of **Henri de La Rochejaquelein** *(see below)*, who was buried in the
funerary chapel of the church near his cousin, the Marquis de Lescure, head of the
Vendée armed forces.

MAULÉON

La Rochejaquelein

Château de la Durbelière – *2km/1mi N of St-Aubin-de-Baubigné via D 153.* The old 15C-17C château, now in ruins, formed part of a vast rural development. The seigniorial lodgings, surrounded by a water-filled moat, were flanked by massive square pavilions. In one of these, in 1772, **Henri de la Rochejaquelein** was born.

It was in the courtyard of this château that Monsieur Henri, at the age of 21, rallied 2 000 peasants, calling upon them to follow him to the Vendée Wars under the Royalist flag with the memorable words:

If I advance, follow me;
If I retreat, kill me;
If I die, avenge me!

In October 1793 the very young and handsome La Rochejaquelein was appointed General of the Royalist-Catholic army. After the army moved into Brittany, he was killed by a Republican at Nuaillé, near Cholet, in 1794.

MAULÉON-LICHARRE

Population 3 533
Michelin map 85 folds 4 and 5 or 234 fold 38

Mauléon is an old stronghold and the smallest capital in the seven Basque provinces. It rises on the right bank of the River Saison, at the foot of a hill where the ruins of the old castle stand. Licharre sits on the west bank of the river and is home to the Renaissance **Château d'Andurain** ⊙, which was built c 1600.

EXCURSIONS

Navarrenx – *16km/10mi NE along D 2. Bastide* (fortified town) founded in 1316 on the way to Santiago de Compostela, Navarrenx has retained part of its fortifications, in particular **Porte St-Antoine** which offers a fine view of the river and the bridge. The town is the rendezvous of anglers keen to catch trout and salmon.

★LA SOULE

The province, which shares many cultural influences with Béarn – including, for instance, the types of houses – has retained the dances and folk traditions most characteristic of the region.

The Lower Soule

1 Round tour starting from Mauléon-Licharre

78km/49mi – allow 3hr

This area is rich in souvenirs of the famous musketeers who inspired Alexandre Dumas to write his classic story of d'Artagnan and his three friends.

Leave Mauléon to the S, along D 918.

Gotein – This Pyrenean village has a church and belfry-calvary typical of the region.

Trois-Villes – The name of the village recalls the military career and the personality of Mr de Tréville, Captain of the King's Musketeers under Louis XIII. The château was built by François Mansart (1598-1666), the great classicist architect. The **Barétous**, a transitional region between Béarn and the Basque provinces, offers the visitor a checkerboard of maize fields and magnificent meadows punctuated by thickets of oak trees, with the limestone summits of the mountains in the background.

Lanne – The pretty church, with its double porch, was originally the chapel attached to the château owned by Isaac de Porthau (Porthos in Dumas' *The Three Musketeers*).

Gotein – Belfry-calvary

Aramits – This village was once the capital of the Barétous. Aramis, another of d'Artagnan's musketeers, was a lay brother at an abbey here which has now disappeared (Athos, the third musketeer, was named after a village of that name near Sauveterre).

Arette – The small town was rebuilt after an earthquake on 13 August 1967. A mountain road leads to **Arette-Pierre-St-Martin**, a small winter sports resort.
After a pleasant, twisting climb above the Arette basin, the road traverses a slope of the Aspe Valley.

At Asasp, cross the Aspe torrent.

St-Christau – *See Le BÉARN, Gave d'Aspe.*

The road runs down to Oloron along the east bank of the river.

Oloron-Ste-Marie – *See OLORON-STE-MARIE.*

Take D 936, NW, for 12km/7mi then turn left on D 25.

★★**L'Hôpital-St-Blaise** – A tiny village on the Basque-Béarn border. The **church**★ ⓥ – a rare example of Hispano-Moorish art on the northern side of the Pyrenees – is in the form of a Greek cross, the four arms radiating from a central tower.

Return to Mauléon-Licharre.

★★The Upper Soule

2 Round tour starting from Mauléon-Licharre

130km/80mi – allow one day

Upper Soule is a magnificent region of forests and pastures, separated from the St-Jean-Pied-de-Port depression by the massifs of Iraty and Arbailles – a difficult barrier because of the rough terrain and the density of the woodland covering it. This is a region particularly suitable for forest rambles, fishing and, in winter, cross-country skiing.

Leave Mauléon S along D 147.

Eating out

BUDGET

Le Chalet Pedro – *In the Iraty Forest (near the D 18) – 64220 Mendive – ☎ 05 59 28 55 98 – open Easter to 11 Nov, school holidays and Sat-Sun in winter – closed Tue in Apr-May – ⊠ – 12.96/23.63€.* A stone's throw from the Spanish border, this charming chalet is nestled in a small valley in the middle of the forest. Family bistro style, simple decor with oak tables. River trout in season. Apartments to let in the house across the way.

Auberge du Lausset – *64130 L'Hôpital-St-Blaise – 13km/8mi E of Mauléon-Licharre via D 24 and D 25 – ☎ 05 59 66 53 03 – closed 1-28 Nov, Sun evening and Mon off-season – 13.72/26.68€.* Across from the handsome Romanesque church, here is a quiet, family style inn. Modern dining room in shades of pastel. A few small but functional, well-kept rooms. Shaded terrace.

Le Pont d'Abense – *Abense-de-Haut – 64470 Tardets-Sorholus – 13km/8mi S of Mauléon-Licharre via D 918 – ☎ 05 59 28 54 60 – closed Jan, 1-15 Dec, Wed evening and Thu except summer – reserv. required – 14.94/27.44€.* This venerable, two centuries-old family residence inspires respect. You'll be pleasantly surprised by the quality of the well-prepared fare and the affordable prices. A few comfortable rooms, two with a terrace, others simpler but all well-kept. Terrace in the shade.

Where to stay

BUDGET

Maison Elichondoa Bed and Breakfast – *64120 Pagolle – 13km/8mi W of Mauléon-Licharre via D 918 and D 302 – ☎ 05 59 65 65 34 – jeanwalter@online.fr – ⊠ – 4 rooms: 38.11/44.21€ – meals 15.24€.* In a small village perched in the mountains, this well-restored 17C farm is the perfect place to go meditate in the bosom of nature. A landscape of countryside and hills, old beams and exposed stone inside – an unusually charming and bucolic environment!

★★ Forêt des Arbailles – This is an upland forest carpeting the higher reaches of a limestone bastion standing clear of the gullies carved by the Saison, the Laurhibar and the Bidouze torrents. The forest rises to a height of 1 265m/4 150ft at Pic de Behorléguy. The beech groves, hiding slopes strewn with boulders, riddled with hollows, give way in the south to a pastoral zone ending in a sheer drop facing the Spanish frontier.

Turn right onto D 117.

Ahusquy – There is a *(restored)* mountain inn standing on this **panoramic site★★**, once a gathering place for Basque shepherds, whose piercing cries echoed off the surrounding hills. Further uphill, clearly visible at the top of a footpath, is a drinking trough filled with clear Ahusquy spring water. The water was at one time popular as a cure for kidney and bladder complaints.

Col d'Aphanize – Wild horses can be seen grazing on the slopes around the pass. The pastureland here is the summer home of many flocks of sheep. East of the pass the **view★★** opens out wide: from Pic des Escaliers, immediately south, to Pic de Ger on the south-eastern horizon, by way of Pic d'Orthy, Pic d'Anie and the Massif de Sesques between Aspe and Ossau. Ossau-Iraty is a refined local cheese made from ewe's milk; gourmets like to eat it with black cherry jam.

In Mendive, turn left onto D 18.

Chapelle St-Sauveur – From a distance this chapel looks like a sheepfold. It was once a hostel-chapel on a pilgrimage route followed by the Knights of the Order of Malta on Corpus Christi day. A line of small columns outside marks the Stations of the Cross. A number of naïve statuettes are housed inside.

Col de Burdincurutcheta – Alt 1 135m/3 724ft. *Park 1km/0.6mi below the north side of the pass, where the road approaches a rocky crest. Walk to the edge.* The view extends over the jagged foothills, extensively lacerated, of the frontier massif, gashed by bleak, deserted valleys; in the distance the basin of St-Jean-Pied-de-Port, centre of the Cize region, opens out.

Plateau d'Iraty – Horses and cattle roam here in summer along with the sheep; locally made sheep's cheese is a fresh delight.

★ Forêt d'Iraty – This forest of beech groves straddling the frontier supplied wood for masts for the French and Spanish navies from the 18C onwards; it is one of the largest wooded areas in Europe (in France alone 2 310ha/5 710 acres).

Ski area – The small resort village of Chalets d'Iraty was built in the 60s in the heart of Iraty Forest. At an altitude of 1 200m/4 000ft to 1 500m/5 000ft, the 109km/68mi of cross-country ski runs and numerous hiking paths offer a unique view of the mountain.

★ **Col Bagargui** – There is a **view**★ to the east of the Upper Soule mountains and the High Pyrenees in the Aspe and Ossau regions. In the foreground, on the right, is the heavy mass of Pic d'Orthy; further away are the elegant limestone summits of the Pic d'Anie chain, and behind them the silhouette of Pic du Midi d'Ossau. Scattered among the forest trees below are the buildings of the picturesque village of Iraty.

Continue towards Larrau then along the road to Port-de-Larrau (usually blocked by snow from November to June).

★ **Col d'Erroymendi** – *Alt 1 362m/4 469ft. 7.5km/4mi from Larrau, by the Port de Larrau road (generally blocked by snow from November to June).* From here there is a vast mountain **panorama**★ which highlights the pastoral and woodland activities in the Upper Soule region. A few yards east of the pass there is a different view: the fan of the Upper Saison valleys and, on the horizon, the rocky mass of Pic d'Anie.

★ **Crevasses d'Holçarté** – *1hr 30min round trip on foot, via the footpath marked GR 10, which is visible soon after the café and the Laugibar Bridge. At Pont de la Mouline, leave GR 10 on the left and take the right-hand alternative.*
After a steep, stiff climb, the entrance to the crevasses is reached: these are in fact very narrow gorges sliced from the limestone to a depth of 200m/656ft. The path rises to the top of the Olhadubi tributary gorge, which is crossed by a dizzily impressive footbridge slung 171m/561ft above the torrent in 1920.

★★ **Gorges de Kabouetta** ⓥ – *Access via D 113, which leads to Ste Engrâce. Take the footbridge across the Uhaïtxa, climb up the opposite bank and go down into the gorge. This excursion is a demanding one, best undertaken when the water level is low (early June through late October). Stout footwear is essential as the ground can be slippery.*
These gorges sunk vertically in the limestone are beautiful as well as impressive, with the beginning of the Grand Étroit (the Great Narrows), the most grandiose of all: this splendid canyon, more than 200m/656ft deep, is no more than 3m/11ft to 10m/33ft wide at the top of its sheer sides. The torrent roars through the long fissure with its dense clumps of vegetation. The path, frequently difficult, eventually arrives at the water's edge, crossing the stream by a number of footbridges here and there. It ends within sight of a 20m/65ft-high waterfall sustained by a resurgent spring, where a cave, replete with giant stalactites and stalagmites, marks the end of the walk.

Ste-Engrâce – This is a shepherds' village, surrounded by wooded mountains fissured by steep valleys. The Romanesque **church**, a former 11C abbey church, stands with its asymmetric roof and its heavy masonry on a pastoral **site**★ in the upper coomb of the Uhaotxa, marking one of the ancient routes to Santiago de Compostela. The chancel, closed off by a robust 14C grille, has richly ornamented capitals. These include (left) scenes involving buffoons and jesters; hunting scenes and a Resurrection in the centre; and (right) **Solomon and the Queen of Sheba**, the royal visitor's elephant bearing on its back a palanquin in the Indian manner.

Return to Mauléon along D 113, D 26 and D 918.

Gorges de Kakouetta

Melle is tucked into the angle where the narrow, heavily wooded Béronne gorge meets a smaller valley. The best view of the town is from D 950, driving north-east from St-Jean-d'Angély.

The town owes its existence to silver-bearing veins of lead mined in the hills of St-Hilaire, on the west bank of the Béronne, and used in medieval times for the production of coins in a local mint. Melle was won over at the time of the Reformation and enjoyed a certain prosperity after the foundation of its college in 1623.

Melle was once famed for raising the local breed of donkey, the Poitou Baudet *(see DAMPIERRE-SUR-BOUTONNE)*.

Melle is unusual in having three Romanesque churches. Two of them, originally attached to Benedictine monasteries, accommodated pilgrims on the road to Compostela.

SIGHTS

★ Église St-Hilaire – St Hilary's Church, built in the Poitou Romanesque style at its purest, was part of St-Jean-d'Angély Abbey. The sober east end and the west front with its coned pinnacles are particularly attractive.

Above the north doorway stands a carving of a **horseman** *(le cavalier de Melle)* which is famous in the history of religious art for the controversy the figure has provoked: the crowned rider has been identified at various times as Charlemagne, as Jesus Christ suppressing the Ancient Law, or even as the Emperor Constantine triumphing over paganism.

The east end includes three apsidal chapels with buttress-columns and carved modillions radiating from an ambulatory joined to the transept. Two more chapels lead off the transept itself; above the crossing rises a belfry-tower.

Interior – The scale of the nave, aisles and ambulatory indicates that the church was designed as a place of pilgrimage. The barrel-vaulting is supported by pillars, quadrilobed in section, with interesting carved capitals; the third on the right, entering from the west front, depicts a wild boar hunt. A doorway leading into the south aisle is – most unusually – decorated on its inner side: on the archivolt, Jesus and the Saints accompanying Him overcome fantasy animals representing the forces of evil. At the far end of this aisle a sound system diffuses a continuous programme of sacred or ritual music from all over the world.

Église St-Pierre – This church dedicated to St Peter once belonged to a priory attached to St-Maixent Abbey. It was built, like St Hilary's, in the Poitou Romanesque style, and stands on a hill overlooking the Béronne. The east end and the side entrance are remarkable for their carved ornamentation: a cornice above the south doorway is supported by historiated modillions (symbols of the Evangelists) between which are carved Signs of the Zodiac, and Christ in Glory occupies a niche above this cornice. The east end is noteworthy for the decoration

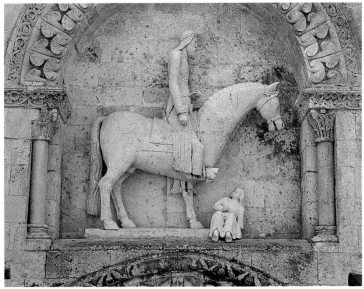
Le Cavalier de Melle

S. Sauvignier/MICHELIN

Les Glycines – *5 pl. R.-Boussard* – ☎ *05 49 27 01 11* – *closed 5-13 Jan, Sun evening from Oct to 1 May, Fri evening and Mon from Oct to Apr* – *12.50/35.06€*. In the past, this was the village café. It has evolved with the town of Melle and is now an attractive restaurant where locals and visitors savour traditional French fare. A few rooms are available.

of the bays, the charming modillions of the axial chapel, and – crowning one of the buttress-columns – a capital featuring two peacocks, the symbols of immortality.

Interior – Inside, the aisles are topped with barrel-vaulting, again like St Hilary's. The capital of the third pillar on the north side represents Christ entombed.

Ancienne église St-Savinien – This former church, dating from the 12C and deconsecrated in 1801, was for many years used as a prison. Today it serves as an exhibition hall and is also the home of Melle's annual **music festival**. The lintel roof overhanging the doorway is unusual for the region; on it, Christ stands between two lions.

Mines d'Argent des Rois Francs (Kings' Silver Mines) ⊘ – The porous limestone on which Melle stands harbours a quantity of geodes – pockets or cavities containing crystallised minerals, in this case lead ore with a small proportion (3%) of silver. The mine from which the ore was extracted, which had been worked since the 5C, became, under Charlemagne, the supplier of silver to a local mint designed to strike the royal coinage. In the 10C the mint was moved elsewhere and the disused mine was forgotten until the 19C.

Since then the build-up of rubble has been cleared from the ancient galleries to render them accessible to visitors. During the underground tour, primitive ventilation chimneys can be seen, along with a number of concretions, a small lake and traces of the oxidisation caused by the firing which broke up the rock. Sound effects within the galleries evoke an atmosphere of mining.

Outside, the **Carolingian garden** contains species of edible and medicinal plants cultivated at the time the mine was in use.

Chemin de la Découverte – ⚐ **Arboretum** – This pedestrian-only trail, which follows stretches of disused railway line, encircles nearly the whole of the old town within its 5km/3mi circuit. Vegetation native to the region alternates with zones in which 650 different species of foreign and exotic trees and shrubs have been planted, all of them labelled for identification purposes. Of particular interest is the **Bosquet d'Écorces** (Bark Grove) north of St Hilary's Church.

EXCURSIONS

Chef-Boutonne – *16km/10mi SE along D 948 and D 737*. The name of this town refers to its location at the source of the River Boutonne. The church, in the Javarzay district, dates from the 12C and 16C; it was once part of a Benedictine priory. Nearby are the ruins of the former **château** (built c 1515) of the Rochechouart family. Of the original fortified enclosure, once marked out with 12 towers, there remains one round tower with machicolations and an elegant fortified entrance flanked by turrets and pierced by Renaissance windows. The Gothic chapel is entered through a Renaissance doorway.

Pers – *20km/12mi E along D 950 then D 14 and D 15*. In a cemetery adjacent to the Romanesque church in this tiny village stands a tall structure dating from the 13C; the **Lanterne des Morts** (Lantern of the Dead). The monument, elegant in its simplicity and its sobriety, comprises a central shaft of stone flanked by four small columns with capitals, the whole supporting a lantern surmounted by a cross. Beneath the pyramid roof, four arched openings reveal the space in which an oil lamp would burn during burial ceremonies. East of this monument is a group of five sarcophagi, probably 11C and 12C, some of them adorned with carved rosettes.

MIMIZAN

Population
Michelin map 335: D-9 or 234 folds 13 and 14

Ségosa-la-Mimizan, which dates back to Gallo-Roman times, was buried by sand in the 6C. The township of Mimizan was built at the end of the 10C, at the foot of a Benedictine abbey. Buried again by the remorseless advance of the sand hills in the 18C *(on the road to Mimizan-Plage)*, the ruins were saved by a local man called Teixores, who was the first to use couch-grass and rushes to consolidate the shifting dunes. The belfry of the **old abbey church**, built in the 13C, is still standing. Richly sculpted, it is surmounted by a Christ in Glory surrounded by statues of the saints, including St John, which is the oldest of its kind in the region of Aquitaine.

THE RESORT

Mimizan-Plage – *At the very end of D 626, turn right on rue de la Poste and then left on rue Assolant-et-Lotti*. At the end of the street, on the left, a short flight of steps leads to a monument commemorating the landing of the aviators Lefèvre, Assolant and Lotti on 16 June 1929, after their epic North Atlantic flight. The view in all directions from the top of the dunes is superb.

Eating out

BUDGET

L'Auberge de St-Paul – *Quartier Villenave – 40200 St-Paul-en-Born – 7km/4.5mi E of Mimizan via D 626 –* ☎ *05 58 07 48 02 – ste.s@wanadoo.fr – closed Oct to Mar and Mon – 10.67€ lunch – 13.72/38.11€.* This auberge amid the pines is a nice place to go with the family. Everyone will be satisfied; after a good meal featuring south-west specialities, you can all meet the farm animals and discover the neighbouring park. Children's play area.

Ferme-auberge Lesca – *428 chemin du Stucs – 40260 Castets – 18km/13mi E of Léon via D 142 then N 10 dir. Bordeaux –* ☎ *05 58 89 41 45 – closed late Sep to Easter – reservations required – 13/23€.* Ah! the good cookery of the Landes. Savour the regional specialities in this former barn. You'll appreciate the country style atmosphere, enhanced by the view of the landscape from the small terrace in the back.

Where to stay

BUDGET

Hôtel Atlantique – *38 av. de la Côte-d'Argent (Mimizan-plage) –* ☎ *05 58 09 09 42 –* 🅿 *– 38 rooms: 21,34/41,92€ –* ☲ *5.34€ – restaurant 12.04/23.63€.* This Landaise house from the early 20C is near the beach yet far from the bustle of tourist crowds. Rooms of two comfort standards are available; the nicer ones come with a balcony. Beams and pink bricks adorn the dining room.

MODERATE

Hôtel Airial – *6 r. de la Papeterie –* ☎ *05 58 09 46 54 – closed Nov to Apr –* 🅿 *– 16 rooms: 42.69/45.73€ –* ☲ *5.34€.* A small family hotel built in the 1970s in a rather quiet residential neighbourhood. Friendly reception, simple, well-kept rooms and reasonable prices. Pleasant garden.

A few ideas for camping on the coast

Camping Parc de Couchoy – *40260 Lesperon – 12km/7.5mi N of Castets via D 5 and D 331 –* ☎ *05 58 89 60 15 – open Apr to Sep – reservations recommended – 71 sites: 14.03€.* Pitch your tent in the shade of the pines in this Landaise forest campground, then cool off in the pool. Volleyball court. Mobile home rental.

Camping Les Vignes – *40170 Lit-et-Mixe – 2.7km/1.7mi SW of Lit-et-Mixe via D 652 and D 88 (rte du Cap-de-l'Homy) –* ☎ *05 58 42 85 60 – camping.vignes@wanadoo.fr – open Jun to 15 Sep – reservations recommended – 420 sites: 28.20€.* Come unwind in this campground in the Landes where you can put your suitcases down and leave your worries behind. Children of all ages will enjoy playing their favourite sports in the omnisport field. Pools and waterfalls. Kids' club. Mobile home and bungalow rentals.

Camping La Paillotte – *40140 Azur – 7km/4.5km N of Soustons via D 50 –* ☎ *05 58 48 12 12 – la.paillotte@wanadoo.fr – open 7 Apr to Sep – reservations recommended – 310 sites: 30.49€.* Fixed up like a Tahitian island, with its straw bungalows lost in the tropical jungle (try the Faré for the total South Seas experience), this is not your run-of-the-mill campground. Enjoy the water surrounded by luxurious greenery. Mini-club and beach.

Mimizan-Plage has four beaches along the ocean with supervised bathing and one along the Mimizan channel. Cycle tracks link the ocean and Lac d'Aureilhan as well as Mimizan-Plage and Contis. A footpath runs along the Mimizan channel.

Lac d'Aureilhan-Mimizan – There are pleasant perspectives on this lake from the roadway.

FROM MIMIZAN TO COURANT D'HUCHET

50km/31mi itinerary – allow 2hr

Follow D 652 S and turn right just before St-Julien-en-Born.

Courant de Contis – The Contis channel takes the waters of several local streams down to the ocean through areas of vegetation as dense as they are varied. It winds slowly through the marshes and on through the dunes, beneath a cool canopy of leaves or between high natural hedges of bracken, reeds and alder bushes, intermingled with wild vines. Cypress trees, poplars, cork-oaks and pines mark the contrasting landscape above the high banks, whereas closer to the sea, downstream from Pont Rose, pines predominate.

At St-Julien-en-Born take D 41 to Lesperon.

Lévignacq – This charming village, typical of the Landes, boasts an ancient church and low, timber-framed houses with tiled roofs. The church, fortified in the 14C, is unusual with its porch and doorway in the Louis XIII style and its belfry-tower. The **wooden vaulting★** inside was decorated in the 18C with paintings. In the chancel is an altarpiece surrounded by cabled columns, whereas in front of the altar itself there is a gilt wood representation of Jesus in the Garden of Olives.

Return via D 105 to D 652, turning left at Miquéou. At Vielle a little road leads to Étang de Léon.

Étang de Léon – The cool, clear water in a peaceful countryside setting attracts tourists and water sports enthusiasts.

Return to Vielle and follow D 328 to Moliets-et-Maa.

The road circling the lake goes through rough terrain, alternating between pine forests and marshes, and revealing typical Landes houses with their diagonal brick facing. Just before the hamlet of Pichelèbe, a bridge crosses the River Huchet. A small path provides a delightful walk through peaceful surroundings (30min there and back).

★Courant d'Huchet – This capricious coastal river, popular with eel fishermen, runs through lush, exotic-looking vegetation and makes for lively **boat trips** Ⓥ, especially enjoyable on hot summer mornings. Its winding course meanders beside rushes and water-lilies, black cypresses, vines and wild hibiscus.

MONT-DE-MARSAN
Population 29 489
Michelin map 335: H-11 or 234 fold 23 – Local map see Introduction, Armagnac

The town lies at the confluence of the River Douze and River Midou, which join to form the River Midouze, and is the capital of the Marsan region in the south-east of the Landes. It enjoys a climate that is hot in summer and mild in winter. Palm trees, magnolias and oleanders flourish in the open air, spiced with the tang of pines carried on the breeze from the forest nearby.

Mont-de-Marsan is an important administrative centre, with a curious collection of public buildings (prefecture, town hall, theatre, prisons) in the style known as Empire-Restauration. The market held at place St-Roch every Tuesday and Saturday morning is one of the most picturesque in France.

To the north of the town there is a huge racecourse, with local stabling for 300 horses. The 12 meetings a year here include flat racing, steeplechases and trotting events.

The bullfights and contests pitting men against combative cows (the animals are not put to death in these events), a popular tradition in this region, are held in the town arena.

SIGHTS

★Musée Despiau-Wlérick Ⓥ – The two sections of this museum in the heart of the old town are housed in a pair of beautifully restored 12C-14C buildings, linked by a gallery where temporary exhibits are held.
Prehistoric discoveries and collections of natural history are housed in the **Musée Dubalen** *(temporarily closed to the public)*. The monumental sculptures in the garden are by Charles Despiau (1874-1946), a native of Mont-de-Marsan who was among the artists promoting the revival of interest in sculpture at the beginning of the 20C.

Where to stay

BUDGET

Le Domaine de Paguy – *40240 Betbezer-d'Armagnac – 5km/3mi NE of Labastide d'Armagnac – take D 11 and D 35 –* ☎ *05 58 44 81 57 – closed 25 Mar to 7 Apr; B&B: open all year; meals: open Sun lunch from Easter to 1 Jul and daily except Wed 1 Jul to 15 Sep –* ✉ *– reserv. required – 4 rooms: 36/46€ – meals 29€.* A charming reception awaits you in this noble 16C house surrounded by grapevines frequented by wandering ducks and chickens. Generous, home-made cuisine; visit of the Armagnac *chai*. Pretty garden with pool. Pleasant bedrooms. Four self-catering cottages.

MODERATE

Hôtel Abor – *2287 av. du Prés.-John-Kennedy – 40280 St-Pierre-du-Mont – 3km/1.8mi S of Mont-de-Marsan via rte de Grenade –* ☎ *05 58 51 58 00 –* 🅿 *– 68 rooms: 45.43/55.64€ –* ⊆ *8.23€ – restaurant 14.94/18.29€.* This hotel is on the edge of town near the ring road. Its simple furnishings and modern decor make it a convenient stop on the way to your final holiday destination. Pool.

On the town

American Rock Café – *Allée Brouchet –* ☎ *05 58 75 41 88 – daily 7am-2am except Sun 11am.* A popular hang-out where the local young people mix with soldiers and everyone drinks beer. During the war in Bosnia, many of the Americans working at the Mont-de-Marsan airbase came here for the decor, reminiscent of the US in the 1950s.

La Cidrerie – *7 r. du 4-Septembre –* ☎ *05 58 46 07 08 – Mon 6pm-2am, Tue-Sat 10am-2am.* Set in an old stable, this auberge carries on the Basque cider tradition. The big wooden tables foster discussion among customers and the atmosphere is patently good-natured. Mature clientele.

La Rhumerie – *13 pl. St-Roch –* ☎ *05 58 75 76 83 – Mon-Sat 5pm-5am.* This bar is specialized in house punches and rum, gin, whisky and champagne cocktails.

Le Havanita – *9 r. du 4-Septembre –* ☎ *05 58 85 29 63 – Tue-Sat 5pm-2am, Sun 6pm-2am – closed Aug.* Music, rum, cigars – each detail contributes to the island atmosphere of this bar where everything comes from Cuba. Admire the cigar cabinet: one whiff and the pungent scent transports you to Caribbean shores. Clientele of mature globetrotters.

Le Divan – *5 pl. du Gén.-de-Gaulle –* ☎ *05 58 75 00 87 – Mon-Sat 7:30am-10pm, Sun 10am-2pm.* No, this divan is not a psychiatrist's couch but one of the oldest city bistros, open since 1912. Some of the venerable regulars have been coming here since they were old enough to have a glass. The terrace opens onto *La Place des Halles* and the veranda offers an unbeatable view of Mont-de-Marsan's three rivers.

Showtime and sporting events

10 bis – *10 bis r. Montluc –* ☎ *05 58 75 98 84 – Tue-Sat 7pm-2am.* This bar with a cultural vocation frequently organizes plays, blues and jazz concerts and philosophy evenings. It's absolutely packed during the Flamenco festival and the *Semaine de la Madeleine*. Pretty little enclosed courtyard.

Arènes de Plumaçon – *Pl. des Arènes –* ☎ *05 58 75 39 08/05 58 75 06 09 – Mon-Fri 8:30am-noon, 2pm-6pm.* Corridas, Landaise cow contests, concerts, *la fête de la Madeleine* (mid-July), these arenas have it all! A guided visit of the arenas, the chapel and operating theatre is proposed daily.

Hippodrome des Grands Pins – *614 av. de l'Hippodrome –* ☎ *05 58 75 15 75 – gate time 2pm.* Each year, 12 races are held in this hippodrome (gallop and obstacles). This is also where jockeys and their 250-odd horses come to train. There's a young jockeys' training school as well.

Comité des Fêtes – *39 pl. Joseph-Pancaut –* ☎ *05 58 75 39 08 – Jun-Aug: Mon-Sat 9am-noon, 2:30pm-7pm; Aug-Mar: Mon-Fri 8am-noon; Apr-May: Mon-Fri 8:30am-noon, 2pm-5:30pm.* This committee runs the city corrida ticket office.

Espace Coluche – *4 r. Bosquet-cale de la Marine –* ☎ *05 58 06 14 56 or 05 58 85 92 92 – amac.cafemusic@free.fr – office hours: Tue and Sun 3pm-7pm, Wed 1pm-8pm, Thu-Fri 3pm-11pm, Sat 1pm-10pm – closed Jul-Aug.* Located on the banks of the Midouze, this cultural centre caters to the young. Baptized *café-musique*, it frequently organizes rap, reggae, rock, pop and salsa concerts. Nationally known groups come play here.

Espace François Mitterrand – *480 r. de la Ferme du Conte* – ☎ *05 58 46 62 40* – *performance evenings: ticket office run by the Service Culturel Municipal.* This cultural centre with a 3 500-seat capacity is where major concerts, operas and ballets are held, as well as sports events.

Théâtre Municipal – *9 pl. Charles-de-Gaulle* – ☎ *05 58 75 30 71* – *performance evenings: ticket office run by the Comité des Fêtes.* Plays, dance, song shows and children's entertainment figure on this theatre's programme.

Parks, Zoos, Attractions

Parc des Nahuques – 🖼 – *Rte de Villeneuve* – ☎ *05 58 75 94 38* – *summer: daily 9am-7pm; rest of the year: Mon-Fri 9am-noon, 2pm-6pm, Sat-Sun 3pm-7pm.* This animal park has an educational calling. Children come here to observe goats, sheep, Corsican mountain goats, llamas, deer, emus, swans and pink flamingos roaming freely over 4ha of land.

Parc Walibi Aquitaine – 🖼 – *Château de Caudouin – 47310 Roquefort* – ☎ *05 53 96 58 32* – *www.walibi.com* – *May: Wed, Sat and Sun 10am-6pm; Jun to mid-July and Sep: 10am-6pm; mid-July to Aug: daily 10am-7pm.* Close to Agen, this amusement park set in 30ha of greenery is dominated by an 18C château. You're guaranteed a thrill on the Fandango and the Drakkar...

Prepare your picnic basket

Guy Puyo – *3 r. Frédéric-Bastiat* – ☎ *05 58 75 00 44* – *Tue-Sat 8am-12:30pm, 3pm-7:30pm.* The first stop will be this delicatessen where every product tempts the tastebuds – the hams hanging from the ceiling, the Chalosse beef, the milk-fed veal, the free-ranging Basque hog, the milk-fed Axuria lamb...

La Tourtière – *7 allée Raymond-Farbos* – ☎ *05 58 75 77 00 or 05 58 75 84 33* – *Tue-Sat 8am-7pm, Sun 7am-12:30pm.* You can learn a trick or two in this pastry shop where the *tourtière* (Armagnac-flavoured apples or prunes in a light flaky crust), the *pastis landais* (aniseed-flavoured brioche), and the *nid d'abeille* (cream cake) are prepared before your eyes.

Lafitte – *62 r. Léon-Gambetta* – ☎ *05 58 06 06 91* – *Tue-Sat 8:30am-12:30pm, 2:30pm-7pm.* Top off your picnic hamper with a selection of fine regional products: *foie gras*, vintage white wines (Jurançon, Sauterne), jam...

The **Musée Despiau-Wlérik**, located in the old keep, is devoted to modern figurative sculpture. Over 700 works by 100 different artists are on display, most of them dating from the 1930s.

The sculptors include Orloff *(Pregnant woman)*, Bourdelle, Bouchard, Zadkine *(Seated Melancholy)*, Manolo and Gargallo *(Urano)*. The upper floors are reserved for local artists. The stairway linking them is adorned with fine examples of glazed earthenware from Samadet.

Works by Charles Despiau occupy one whole floor: they include several female busts, among them *Paulette*, a marble which was admired by Rodin, and a strikingly naturalistic *Liseuse (Woman reading)*.

On another floor *The Child in Clogs* is an early work by Robert Wlérik (1882-1944), the Mont-de-Marsan sculptor responsible for the equestrian statue of Marshal Foch in place du Trocadéro, Paris.

Viewpoint – From the bridge just downstream from where the two rivers meet there is a pleasant view, upstream, of the old houses beside the river banks.

Parc Jean-Rameau – Extending for some distance north of the town, beside the Douze, this shady riverside park with its flower gardens, its fine magnolias and plane trees is a favourite place for a stroll. At one time it was the garden of the prefecture, and a footbridge *(private)* still links the two.

EXCURSIONS

Villeneuve-de-Marsan – *17km/11mi E via D 1.* Villeneuve-de-Marsan, a former 13C *bastide*, still has its original church and ancient tower. The imposing brick church of **St-Hyppolite** is flanked by buttresses and surmounted by a beautiful square fortified tower. Inside, a 1529 fresco recounts the life and martyrdom of St Catherine of Alexandria. The top of the ancient crenellated tower (beautiful brick decoration) looks out over the vineyards which produce Grand Bas Armagnac (brandy).

Drive SE along D 1 towards Eauze for 2km/1.2mi then turn right to Perquié.

Court dress from the period of
Louis XVI (Château de Ravignan)

A. Thuillier/MICHELIN

The **Château de Ravignan** ⓥ, built on a classical plan, is surrounded by a French garden. The interior is richly furnished and decorated with family portraits and engravings of Henri IV and a particularly beautiful collection of costumes from the court of Louis XVI.

Roquefort – *22km/14mi NE via D 933.*
The home of the Vicomtes de Marsan in the 10C, Roquefort with its 12C and 14C ramparts and towers was once a fortified town. Founded by the Benedictines of St-Sever in the 11C, the **church** later housed an order of Antonites, a hospitalier order who cared for people suffering from St Anthony's Fire (ergot poisoning). The building is mainly Gothic, with fortifications such as arrow slits in the apse and a square tower used as a keep. On the south side, a Flamboyant Gothic portal leading into the church is decorated with the Roquefort arms (three rocks and three stars). Nearby stands the former priory with its Flamboyant Gothic doors and windows.

▶▶ Aire-sur-l'Adour – 35km/21mi SE: Église St-Pierre-du-Mas (sarcophagus of Ste-Quitterie in the crypt) ⓥ; Labastide d'Armagnac – 29km/18mi NE: **picturesque 13C bastide** ⓥ; Barbotan-les-Thermes – 43km/26mi via Labastide d'Armagnac: Hot springs resort nestling in a wooded valley.

MOUILLERON-EN-PAREDS
Population 1 177
Michelin map 316: K-7 or 232 fold 42

Two of the most outstanding men in the recent history of France, **Georges Clemenceau** and **Jean-Marie de Lattre de Tassigny**, were born in this small village typical of the Vendée *bocage*. It was also the birthplace of the celebrated 19C astronomer **Charles-Louis Largeteau** (1791-1857).

Jean-Marie de Lattre de Tassigny (1889-1952) – The life of Jean de Lattre is interwoven with the history of the first half of the 20C. Scion of an aristocratic Vendée family, he was admitted to the elite St-Cyr military academy; he became a dragoon and then an infantry officer during the First World War. In 1920 he was posted to Morocco, where he distinguished himself in the Rif War. A brilliant tactician, he was promoted to Colonel, and then General in 1939. After the fall of France in the Second World War, he was arrested by the Germans in 1942 but escaped a year later and made his way to London to join the Free French, and from there went to Algiers. In 1944 he led the French 1st Army during the invasion of Provence, subsequently liberating Alsace, crossing the Rhine and advancing as far as the Danube. He was among the Allied leaders who signed the German Act of Capitulation on 8 May 1945. In 1950 he was appointed High Commissioner of Indo-China. De Lattre died in Paris in January 1952; four days later he was posthumously elevated to the rank of Marshal of France.

NATIONAL MUSEUMS ⓥ

The town hall, which stands not far from the **church** with its 12C belfry (the 13-bell carillon rings daily on the hour), houses the **Musée des Deux Victoires**. As much a memorial as a museum, this establishment reviews in parallel the destiny and the career of two extraordinary men, Clemenceau and De Lattre, caught in the maelstrom of two world wars. Among the documents, souvenirs, trophies and other items on display are a walking stick presented to Tiger Clemenceau by his *poilus* (soldiers; the handle is carved in the shape of a tiger's head), as well as the eagle's head once surmounting the pediment of the Reichstag, which was presented to De Lattre in 1945 by the Soviet Marshal Zukov.

In the village, commemorative plaques identify the birthplaces of Clemenceau and De Lattre, who was called *Le Roi Jean* (King John) by his troops. The birthplace of the latter is now the **Musée Jean-de-Lattre-de-Tassigny**. The De Lattre family's lifestyle, characteristic of that enjoyed by a generation of Vendée notables, has been carefully recreated. The house retains its original furniture and there are a number of display cases evoking both the home life and the career of the Marshal.

Opposite the house is the cemetery where the body of De Lattre lies beside his son, who was killed in Indo-China.

Two sites are devoted to the memory of De Lattre: the **Mémorial** at La Boinière and the **Oratoire** (memorial chapel) housed in an old windmill situated on **Colline des Moulins** *(2km/1mi E)*. From this quiet hillside there is a fine view of the *bocage*.

Musée Jean-de-Lattre-de-Tassigny

B. Kaufamann/MICHELIN

NIORT★

Population 56 663
Michelin map 322: D-7 or 233 folds 5 and 6

Niort rises beside the green waters of the Sèvre Niortaise, distilling a charming air of placid bourgeois prosperity, especially in season when the many flowers around the town come into bloom.

Local gastronomic specialities include eels and *petit-gris* (snails) from the nearby marshes, *tourteau fromager*, a cake made with fresh goat's cheese, and **angelica** treats made from *angelica archangelica*, an aromatic plant whose stalks are crystallised (confectionery), cooked (jam) or distilled (angelica liqueur).

The town is the departure point for excursions in the Poitou marshlands *(see MARAIS POITEVIN)*.

Madame de Maintenon – **Françoise d'Aubigné**, the granddaughter of the poet Agrippa d'Aubigné, was born in Niort in 1635, in a house in rue du Pont which stood in the shadow of the castle where her father was locked up for non-payment of debts. Sent in disgrace to an Ursuline convent at the age of 14, she escaped and eventually married the poet Scarron, 25 years her senior. After his death the young widow became part of the Court, as governess to the children born to Louis XIV by his mistress Madame de Montespan, and soon caught the king's eye herself; he subsequently created her Marquise de Maintenon. Françoise and the king were secretly and morganatically – that is, her rank remained unchanged – married in 1683, the year Madame de Montespan fell from favour.

When the Sun King died in 1715, Madame de Maintenon retired to the establishment she had founded in St-Cyr in 1685: an institution for the education of impoverished daughters of the nobility. After a remarkable ascension from barnyard to palace, she died there in 1719.

Local activities – Today, while still a centre of glove-making and *chamoiserie* (tanning and oiling skins to make them supple), Niort is home to more modern activities including insurance. A number of French *mutuelles* (mutual insurance companies) have established their headquarters in the town, and the industry has made Niort one of its French capitals.

TOWN WALK

The town is built on the slopes of two facing hillsides: on one stands the castle keep and the Church of Our Lady; on the other the former town hall and the St-André district. The heart of the town, rue Victor-Hugo, crosses the site of the old medieval market in the lowest part of the valley. At the eastern extremity of place de la Brèche, a huge square bordered with trees, the main roads leading to the town centre converge. Here ancient houses roofed with round tiles line the narrow, twisting streets climbing the slope, many of which have retained their original names: rue de l'Huilerie (oil mill street), rue du Tourniquet (turnpike lane), rue du Rabot (wood plane street) etc. Rue du Pont and rue St-Jean were once shopping streets bustling with market stalls.

Leave the car in the car park on place des Halles where the walk starts.

Eating out

BUDGET

La Table des Saveurs – *9 r. Thiers* – ☎ *05 49 77 44 35 – closed Sun except holidays – 12.20/34.30€.* With a name like *The Table of Flavours*, this restaurant's vocation is all mapped out. The classic menu is inspired by the renowned cuisine of the Lyons region. A cloth shop in the past, three cosy stories of this late 19C house welcome the gourmet wayfarer.

MODERATE

La Belle Étoile – *115 quai M.-Métayer – 2.5km/1.5mi W of Niort (near the West ring road)* – ☎ *05 49 73 31 29 – closed 6-21 Aug, Sun evening and Mon – 24.39/66.32€.* Interested in having a spot of lunch in the country? This pretty house on the banks of the River Sèvre is just the place: on the terrace or in one of its elegant dining rooms, you can enjoy the well-prepared cuisine with gentle regional accents in a relaxing, tranquil setting.

Where to stay

BUDGET

Avenue – *43 av. St-Jean-d'Angély* – ☎ *05 49 79 28 42 – 20 rooms: 19.82/41.92€ –* ☲ *5.03€.* The warmth of the welcome and the impeccable cleanliness of the rooms make up for the modest comfort in this little family hotel. Renovations planned.

MODERATE

Hôtel Le Moulin – *27 r. Espingole* – ☎ *05 49 09 07 07 –* 🅿 *– 34 rooms: 41.16/45.73€ –* ☲ *4.57€.* Welcome to an architect's home! The owner, architect by profession, created the blueprints for this modern hotel, built in 1988. Somewhat removed from the old city, not far from the Sèvre, its simple rooms are pleasant even though the interior soundproofing could be better.

★**Donjon** ⊘ – This keep was the most important element in a fortress begun by Henry II Plantagenet in the 12C and completed by his son Richard the Lion Heart. It was surrounded by a defensive perimeter 700m/770yd in circumference. The ensemble formed a small town within the town, which included houses, gardens and a parade ground flanked by the collegiate church of St-Gaudens, destroyed during the Wars of Religion. Under the Bourbons the keep was used as a state prison.

Today its unusual silhouette still towers over the Sèvre. The plan and elevation are original; two tall, massive bastions, square in shape and linked by a 15C building which replaced the primitive curtain walls, are bordered by turrets which also act as buttresses.

Inside the keep, at the entrance level, the **Hall of Glove-making and Chamoiserie**★ focuses on Niort's traditional trades. The lower rooms, vaulted in the 18C, house the town's **archaeology collection**. This includes stone tools, an early Bronze Age gold necklace, ceramics discovered during excavations at Bougon, a 9C BC chariot wheel, Merovingian sarcophagi, coins from the Carolingian era found at Melle, a late Gauloise stele, and a 14C knife-handle of carved ivory representing a shepherd playing the bagpipes.

The ethnology department on the upper floor has a reconstructed Poitou interior (c 1830) complete with costumes, furniture, domestic utensils etc.

From the platform at the top of the keep there is a view of the town and the river.

From place des Halles, take the pedestrianised rue du Rabot and turn left onto rue St-Jean.

Rue St-Jean – The oldest and most interesting houses in Niort stand in rue St-Jean and adjacent streets. Among them are the 15C Governor's residence (no 30) and, at no 3 rue du Petit-St-Jean, the Hôtel Estissac, an elegant Renaissance mansion.

Turn right onto rue Notre-Dame which leads to the church.

Église Notre-Dame – The elegance of this church's 15C belfry is due in part to a lightening of the square tower by the addition of serrated pinnacles to the buttresses; four of the niches hollowed from these still contain statues. The difference in size between the tower and the spire is further emphasised by the placing of dormers and more pinnacles at the base of the latter. Finally the steeple itself, rising to a height of 76m/250ft, is reinforced by superimposed relief arches forming a chevron design.

The north façade, on rue Bion, has a fine doorway in Flamboyant Gothic style.

Inside the church – the layout was reversed in the 18C – the first chapel off the north aisle contains some curious tombs dating from 1684: Charles de Baudéan-

Parabère, Governor of Niort, his wife and his son, also Governor in his day, are all represented climbing out of their graves on Resurrection Day. In the third chapel hangs *St Bernard Trampling the Decree of Pope Anaclet*, an 18C painting by Lattainville. The early-16C font was used for the baptism of Françoise d'Aubigné. A Way of The Cross and the carved wood pulpit in the Gothic style date from 1877.

Follow rue Mellaise, then rue Pérochon which leads to the tourist office. From there, walk to the vast place de la Brèche then turn left towards the Pilori.

★ **Le Pilori** – This odd structure is the old town hall, built on the site of a medieval pillory, a public means of punishment consisting of a wooden frame, with holes in it, mounted on a post upon a platform, which was clamped over the stooped offender's neck and wrists. The building, on a ground plan that is practically triangular, was modified in the 16C by the architect Mathurin Bertomé, who bordered it with semicircular towers, crowned it with machicolated parapets and pierced it with mullioned windows. The upper part of the belfry dates from the 17C and the pinnacle from the 19C. Le Pilori is now used for displaying temporary exhibitions.

Logis de l'Hercule ⓥ – It was in this hostelry, which at one time traded under the sign of Hercules, that the first case of the plague epidemic that was to decimate the population of Niort over seven months was reported in May 1603.
On the ground floor, vaulted 16C rooms have been furnished in the style of the early Middle Ages, and contain items unearthed in digs (coins, ceramics) and a series of tableaux, with commentaries chronicling the town's past.
A miniature **museum** in one room is dedicated to angelica – with the reminder that the plant, brought to Niort by nuns in the 17C, was long believed by pharmacists to be the sole effective remedy against the plague.

Le Pilori

Rue du Pont – Old houses with projecting upper storeys line this street and at no 5, out of sight in a courtyard, is the house where Françoise d'Aubigné was born.

It is possible to continue this stroll through green spaces lining the opposite bank of the Sèvre Niortaise, or to return to place des Halles.

Coulée Verte – This promenade comprises the renovated Cronstadt, La Regratterie and La Préfecture quays and is a pleasant place for a quiet riverside stroll. From the **old bridges** (Vieux Ponts) linking the two halves of the town there is a splendid view of the castle keep.

ADDITIONAL SIGHT

Musée Bernard d'Agesci ⊘ – *28 avenue de Limoges*. Currently being set up in the former Lycée Jean Macé (secondary school), the museum will eventually contain all the exhibits from the town's various museums. The Fine Arts Museum and the Natural History Museum will be the first to be relocated. A few rooms are already open to visitors including one dedicated to the contemporary local sculptor, Pierre-Marie Poisson.

Forêt de Chizé

EXCURSIONS

Forêt de Chizé – *20km/12mi S via* ④. The Forêt de Chizé south-east of Niort, once part of the vast Argenson Forest which covered the whole region in the Middle Ages, contains more than 5 000ha/13 500 acres of oak and beech which grow in a chalky soil ideal for the cultivation of meridional species. This picturesque forest, crossed diagonally by D1, offers numerous starting points for forest walks; the road is also lined with attractive picnic areas.

★ **Zoorama Européen** ⊘ – ◉ The zoo, in the heart of the forest, occupies a former military base sealed off by the Americans during the last world war.

The aim of the zoo is to facilitate the observation and study of European fauna including nearly 600 animals in a 25ha/62-acre forest setting. The first part of the park is devoted to predatory mammals (wild cats, marten, civet, wolves, otter, lynx, brown bears and red fox), birds (diurnal and nocturnal predators, web-footed species and waders), reptiles and amphibians (vivarium), all of whom live in conditions resembling their original habitat as closely as possible.

The rest of the zoo is inhabited by larger mammals free to roam in huge wooded enclosures – graceful spotted deer, skia, roe-deer, agile ibex, chamois and moufflons (wild mountain sheep from Corsica) and an imposing herd of rare European bison and wild boar. The park also has a number of auroch (wild bulls) and tarpan (wild horses), two almost extinct species which have been re-established. A distinctly local animal is the delightful Poitou donkey, which has successfully escaped threatened extinction here.

Moulin de Rimbault ⊘ – Built in 1682 on the north-east edge of Forêt de Chizé, the windmill, overlooking the Niort plain, was abandoned 1928. It is being restored, complete with a revolving cap on a greased wooden rail, a *guivre* (long pole used to turn the sails to the wind), part of the internal machinery and sails with adjustable wooden slats using the Berton system.

Les Ruralies – *9km/6mi SE along A 10 (both ways) or D 948 (a minor road branches off D 174 S of Vouillé*. This enormous complex, conceived mainly as a rest area for motorway users, groups together not only the usual restaurants, shops selling regional specialities, and petrol and service stations but also a hotel, an exhibition centre, the local agricultural Chamber of Commerce and a couple of museums.

Maison des Ruralies ⊘ – A permanent exhibition entitled **L'Aventure humaine en Poitou-Charentes** evokes, with the use of photos, documents, period material, models and reconstructions, life in the region from prehistoric times to the present day. Temporary exhibitions on a variety of different themes are also held.

Musée agricole ⊘ – The museum illustrates the development of farming techniques through the tools, implements and machinery involved: ploughs and harrows, olive oil presses, stills, harvesters, tractors etc. In the section devoted to apiculture, a hive in full production buzzes behind a transparent panel. Video films are shown.

★ **Château du Coudray-Salbart** ⊘ – *11km/7mi N by D 743. The path up to the ruins starts near the bridge over the river*.
The castle, which rises on an escarpment overlooking the Sèvre Niortaise, is an unusual and fascinating example of 13C military architecture. Its construction (1202-25) is linked to the final phase of the battle between the Capetians (Philippe Auguste, Louis VIII) and the Plantagenets (King John, Henry III) for possession of the Guyenne region.

Château de Cherveux ⊘ – *15km/9mi NE along D 8*. This castle is a fascinating example of 15C military architecture with its keep and machicolated towers.

Île de NOIRMOUTIER★

Michelin map 316: C-5 or 232 folds 25, 26, 37 and 38

The long thin isle of Noirmoutier frames the western margin of a gulf south of the Loire estuary, separated from the mainland only by a narrow channel which recedes at low tide. The mainland facing the island is quiet marshland steeped in traditional ways (*see MARAIS BRETON-VENDÉEN*).
The low-lying island, blessed with a mild climate, luminous skies and numerous beauty spots, is a delightful and popular holiday retreat. Auguste Renoir, having stayed here with paintbrush and palette, wrote to a friend: "It is an admirable place, lovely as the South, but the sea is beautiful in a different way".
However, this haven of peace was not spared by the Vendée War, since it was of strategic importance for both sides. The island changed hands several times, which led to the inevitable massacres.
A 700m/2 300ft-long prestressed concrete bridge on 9 twin piers has spanned the Fromentine Channel since 1971.

DUNES, SALT AND MIMOSA

Since Roman times successive subsidence has been reducing the area of Noirmoutier so that although the island is still 20km/12mi long, it is now scarcely 1km/0.6mi wide at La Guérinière – where, in 1882, heavy seas almost cut the place in two.

Noirmoutier comprises three sectors. To the south, the Barbtre dunes stretch towards the Vendée coast, from which they are separated by the **Fosse de Fromentine**, a gap only 800m/880yd across but scoured by violent currents. The centre of the isle is similar to the Dutch landscape, with **polders** (stretches of land reclaimed from the sea) and salt-marshes below sea level, protected by dikes. The area is crisscrossed by canals, the most important of which, the Étier de l'Arceau, crosses the island from one side to the other.
To the north, a series of creeks indent a rocky coast carpeted with oak, pine and acacia – the flowers, commonly sold as mimosa, are exported each year by the tonne. Here again there are dunes, planted this time with maritime pines, on which several windmills stand.

Eating out

BUDGET

L'Océane – *Chemin de la Matte* – *85740 L'Épine* – *4km/2.4mi S of Noirmoutier via D 948* – ☎ *02 51 39 42 87* – *closed 15 Sep-1 Jun, Sun evening and Mon in Jun and Sep* – 🗌 – *5.34/7.62€*. A plate full of seafood or a dozen oysters washed down with a glass of Muscadet – that's the menu in this cabin set up right next to the oyster farmer's hangar. Blue and white walls, absolutely basic decor, price and freshness unbeatable. Take-out available.

La Marine – *5 r. Marie-Lemonnier* – *85330 L'Herbaudière* – ☎ *02 51 39 23 09* – *closed Oct, Tue evening and Wed except school holidays* – *12.80/38.10€*. Across from the fishing docks, this white house with blue shutters is run by a young couple. Under its exposed frame ceiling, amid old brass and wood fishing contraptions, you can savour fresh cuisine that's a blend of land and sea. Small garden-terrace in the summer.

Le Grand Four – *1 r. de la Cure* – *behind the château* – *85330 Noirmoutier-en-l'Île* – ☎ *02 51 39 61 97* – *closed 23 Dec to 1 Feb, Sun evening and Mon off-season* – *15.09/32.01€*. Don't miss this little restaurant behind the château. In a vine-covered house, it's as quaint as can be with its comfortable armchairs, fresco-painted ceiling, knick-knacks and omnipresent flowers. The cookery, based on seasonal produce, marries regional flavours with the sea.

MODERATE

Le Bistrot des Îles – *Pointe de la Fosse, at the foot of the Noirmoutier bridge* – *85630 Barbâtre* – *15.5km/10mi S of Noirmoutier via D 948 and D 38* – ☎ *02 51 39 68 95* – *closed Nov to Feb, Mon evening and Tue except Jul-Aug* – *17.53/38.11€*. A complete change of scenery awaits you in this restaurant across from Fromentine and next to the docking pier for boats to l'Île d'Yeu. In a decor inspired by the big blue, luminous and pleasant, you can opt for contemporary cuisine or the bistro-type menu, depending on your desires.

Where to stay

BUDGET

Le Caravan'Île Camping – *R. de la Tresson* – *85680 La Guérinière* – ☎ *02 51 39 50 29* – *camping-caravanile@wanadoo.fr* – *open Feb to Nov* – *reservations recommended* – *385 sites: 18.60€*. After having pitched your tent behind the dunes, dive right into the pleasures of swimming in the sea or the large heated pool. Direct access to a gigantic beach of fine sand, children's playground, mini-golf, games room and mobile home rentals.

Baranger Bed and Breakfast – *8 r. de la Mougendrie* – *85330 Noirmoutier-en-l'Île* – ☎ *02 51 39 12 59* – 🗌 – *5 rooms: 36.59/42.69€*. In a peaceful side street of downtown Noirmoutier, two steps from the château, this house offers guests simple rooms that open onto a small enclosed garden. One studio with kitchen and terrace, perfect for independent-minded travellers.

EXPENSIVE

Hôtel Fleur de Sel – *85330 Noirmoutier-en-l'Île* – ☎ *02 51 39 09 07* – *closed mid-Oct to 28 Feb* – 🅿 – *35 rooms: 85.37/112.81€* – 🍽 *8.69€* – *restaurant 29.73/35.83€*. Right near the Sableux beach, this low house with white walls and round tiles is quite charming. The rooms are posh, decorated with yew or waxed pine furniture and matching draperies, creating an island-type atmosphere. Terrace service in summer and pool.

Château du Pélavé – *9 allée de Chaillot* – *Bois de la Chaize* – *85330 Noirmoutier-en-l'Île* – ☎ *02 51 39 01 94* – 🅿 – *18 rooms: 88/120€* – *restaurant 22/45€*. In the bosom of the *bois de la Chaize* forest, this sizable late-19C granite villa is surrounded by a pretty park landscaped with trees and flowers. Its sunny rooms, four of which have big private terraces, are decorated with modern furniture. Lower rates off-season.

Resources – The **salt-marshes** ⊘ glittering beneath the sun yield several hundred tonnes of salt per year. This production is largely due to the unusually high proportion of sunshine, to the generous tidal range and, paradoxically, to bad weather. Of the 700ha/1 730 acres of salt-marsh on the island, only 100ha/247 acres are exploited, by 40 *paludiers* – proprietors grouped into syndicates or co-operatives which manage the upkeep of the channels and oversee the extraction and sale of the salt.

The island's resources are mainly agricultural. The soil, enriched with seaweed and other marine vegetation washed ashore, favours the production of new potatoes and forced fruit and vegetables which are highly prized. Dry-stone walls, embankments, tamarisk hedges or rows of cypress trees protect the crops from the sea winds.

The riches of the ocean itself, however, are not neglected: oysters are farmed in the Baie de Bourgneuf; fishermen from the port at L'Herbaudière are famed for their catches of sea bass as well as crab, lobster and other crustaceans. The harbour at Noirmoutier-en-l'Île serves mainly as a haven for wintering craft.

The islanders live in low-built houses with red-tiled roofs and whitewashed walls. Since 1959 an undersea pipeline has supplied them with fresh water from the mainland.

NOIRMOUTIER-EN-L'ÎLE

Noirmoutier is the island capital, a white town with sun-bleached buildings extending parallel to a canal-port drained of water at low tide. The 1km/0.6mi-long Grande-Rue (main street) ends at a former parade ground opening onto the port.

Place d'Armes – The royalist **General d'Elbée** was executed by a Republican firing squad on this parade ground in 1794. A little way back from the esplanade, the castle and the church stand side by side on a slight rise. Two fine 18C buildings are nearby: on the right, facing the castle, the Lebreton des Grapillières mansion (now a hotel); on the left the Jacobsen house, named after a Dutch family who worked on the draining of the island during the 18C.

Château ⊘ – The 15C defensive perimeter, bare and austere, forms a rectangle interrupted only by two corner towers with bartizan turrets. Picturesque views of the town, the salt-marshes and the sea can be seen from the covered way running around the castle's circumference. Inside the enclosure are the old Governor's residence and a square 11C keep which houses a **museum**.

Ground floor – Local history: archaeology and the Vendée Wars. The armchair in which General d'Elbée was shot is on display; incapable of moving because he had not recovered from wounds suffered in the battle of Cholet, the General was transported in this chair to place d'Armes, where the executioners waited. A 19C painting by Julien Le Blant illustrates the drama.

First floor – This section contains a diverse assortment of items connected with the ocean: ships' figureheads, model boats, a pirate's axe and sabre, an early-19C cross made from seashells.

Second and third floors – These floors, devoted to the fine arts, contain works by artists attracted by the beauty of the island (A Baudry, F Palvadeau, O de Rochebrune); temporary exhibitions are held during the high season.

The salt marshes, the church
and château in the distance

M. Thierry/MICHELIN

Logis du gouverneur – This floor houses a splendid collection of English **Staffordshire pottery**★ (18C and 19C), some of it known as **Jersey pottery** because it was there that the pieces were stored. The variety of shapes, the decorative motifs and the colours used lend this collection a particular brilliance.

From La Vigie turret there is a **panorama** of Noirmoutier and the coast: the view extends as far as La Baule on the mainland to the north and Île d'Yeu to the south.

Église St-Philbert – This former Benedictine abbey church combines the Romanesque (chancel) and Gothic (nave) styles. Beneath the chancel, flanked by sumptuous Baroque altars, a fine 11C **crypt** occupies the site of the original Merovingian chapel. The crypt houses the cenotaph of St Philbert – an empty tomb installed in the 11C, the original sarcophagus having been transferred at the time of the Norman invasions.

Aquarium-Sealand ⊘ – 🖼 Local and tropical sea creatures are on show here in a setting featuring underwater caverns and the hulks of sunken ships. A huge pool is reserved for sea-lions.

Musée de la construction navale ⊘ – This museum, housed in a former *salorge* (salt loft) once used as a yard by local artisan boat-builders, illustrates the traditional techniques of boat-building.

Plans, blueprints, templates, sails and rigging, and demonstrations of wood-sawing and the construction of hulls faithfully reproduce the atmosphere of the old marine workshop.

ADDITIONAL SIGHTS

★**Bois de la Chaize** – *2km/1.2mi NE via D 948 (follow the signs towards Plage des Dames)*.
This fragrant, harboured wood overlooking the sea could be a corner of the French Riviera: clumps of umbrella pines, ilex trees and flowering mimosa thickets, scenting the air during the mild February weather, combine to give the place its deservedly exotic reputation.

Plage des Dames owes its name to the fact that Gallic Druidesses practised their rites here in ancient times. The sheltered beach, an elegant curve of fine sand, is the starting point of the **Promenade des Souzeaux**★, a charming walk *(45min round trip)* past the rocky, wooded creeks of the island's north-eastern coast.

Leave the beach via the footpath under the ilex trees on the left of the small landing-stage, then follow the first track climbing upwards, again on the left.

After the lighthouse, pines are again interspersed with the ilex. The rocky cliffs here overlook a sea studded with reefs and there are views of the Côte de Jade (Jade Coast), west of Pornic on the mainland. The clifftop path passes above the pretty Anse Rouge (Red Cove), dominated by Plantier Tower, before leading to Souzeaux beach.

L'Herbaudière – *5km/3mi NE along D 5*. A busy traffic of brightly coloured boats animates this small fishing port where the catch (lobsters, crawfish and various white fish) is sold daily at quayside auctions. The multicoloured pennants which serve to mark the position of lobster-pots out at sea give a festive air to the vessels which carry them. A forest of masts rises above the pleasure craft moored in a neighbouring basin.
From the jetty separating this marina from the fishing port there is a view of l'Île du Pilier, a small island crowned by a lighthouse, which was once linked to Noirmoutier by a causeway.

La Guérinière – *4km/2.5mi S along D 948*. The Port du Bonhomme with its oyster-breeders' cabins shelters on the north coast of the village, whereas the south coast is lined with sand beaches overlooked by the Bois des Éloux and a row of windmills.

The **Musée des arts et traditons populaires** presents a survey of local activities and folk art in the late 19C and early 20C: agriculture, fishing, crafts and life around the salt-marshes are among the subjects treated. The museum also houses reconstructed local interiors, collections of costumes and headdresses, and such local folk art as seascapes painted on fragments of sail-canvas by *cap-horniers* (Cape-Horners) – sailors who had worked aboard the full-rigged clippers navigating the dangerous seas around Cape Horn in the cargo races of the 19C.

★★ **Passage du Gois** – *12km/7.5mi SE via D 948*. This 4.5km/3mi submersible causeway was the only way for vehicles to reach the island until 1971, when the toll bridge was opened. Shoals formed the Gois causeway; the name is derived from a local term, *goiser*, meaning to wade, which is what you will have to do if you don't read the tide tables correctly. Floats are provided at regular intervals along the way so that people caught by the rapidly rising waters can hoist themselves to safety until the waves subside.

It is a busy spot for fishermen, oyster and mussel farmers.

Passage du Gois

Abbaye de NOUAILLÉ-MAUPERTUIS★
Michelin map 322: I-5 or 233 fold 8 – 11km/7mi SE of Poitiers

The remains of this ancient Benedictine abbey, half hidden from the road in a small wooded valley, convey the charm and austerity of great Romanesque buildings.

Battle of Poitiers (1356) – It was not far from the abbey, on the north bank of the River Miosson, west of the minor road to Les Bordes, that one of the bloodiest battles of the Hundred Years War took place. Known to historians as the Battle of Poitiers, this was the encounter in which the French King **Jean II le Bon** (1319-64) was defeated and taken prisoner by the **Black Prince**, son of Edward III of England. The King, surrounded by a few companions, had advanced onto a knoll known as Alexander's Field when he was attacked by the Anglo-Gascon army. Jean, wearing the royal armour garnished with gold fleurs-de-lis, resisted long and bravely, helped by his youngest son Philippe, still only a child, who called out to him warning him of oncoming blows. Eventually, however, totally exhausted and wounded in the face, the King was obliged to give in. To regain his freedom he had to abandon to the English the western half of his kingdom, pay an enormous ransom and allow two of his other sons to be taken as hostages to London. When one of them escaped, Jean himself went to the English capital to replace him, and died there soon afterwards.

TOUR

Route D 12 from Poitiers offers an attractive view down over the abbey; the old defensive perimeter has been cleared and renovated. Aside from these defensive walls and towers – some have been partly levelled – the abbey was protected by moats fed from offshoots of the River Miosson.

A small, charming drawbridge leads to the vaulted north gate and through to the abbey courtyard beyond. The 15C abbot's residence attached to the entrance is served by an attractive staircase turret.

Abbey church – On the right, the 12C belfry-porch is lightened by a large bay pierced in the 15C. The lateral wall in the centre has a curious elevation: two levels of arching, superimposed, are themselves surmounted by arches and bays; both sets of features are Romanesque but the lower date from the 11C and the upper from the late 12C. The upper parts of the transept and chancel were altered in the 17C: it was then that the semicircular apse was replaced by a flat east end. The impressive dome on squinches, reinforced by ribs, rises above the first bay of the nave, which is framed by very narrow aisles and has 12C barrel vaulting. Note, near the north entrance, the Romanesque column of blue-grey marble, it was relocated here when the church was remodelled. A fine ensemble of 17C woodwork (rood screen, choir stalls, lectern eagle) adorns the middle of the church. At the far end of the chancel, behind the 17C high altar, stands an enormous mass of carved and painted stone: the 9C **tomb**★ known as the Shrine of St Junien. Staircases on each side of the chancel (restored in the 17C) lead down to the crypt *(not open to the public)* in which the relics of the saint were venerated.

M. Thierry/MICHELIN

The abbey behind its walls

Monastic buildings – There remains, south of the church, one wing crowned with a strange Romanesque chimney (said by some to have been a former *Lanterne des Morts*) and, beyond, a 17C building facing the Miosson.

OIRON★★

Population 945
Michelin map 322: F-3 or 232 fold 45

The small village of Oiron is the home of two splendid but little-known architectural monuments: the château of the Gouffier family and a delightful Renaissance collegiate church.

The Gouffier family – Artus Gouffier, chamberlain to François I, accompanied his sovereign to Italy and was so overwhelmed by Italian art that on his return, in the early 16C, he began building a church in the Renaissance style. At the same time he organised the construction of a tower and one wing of the château. Both church and château were completed under the direction of his eldest child, Claude, who also began collecting the works of art to be displayed in the residence. Master of the King's Horse and extremely wealthy, Claude Gouffier held the title of Comte de Caravas: in legend he became the Marquis de Carabas (the fictitious title given to his impoverished master by *Puss in Boots*, the hero of Charles Perrault's fairy tale of 1697).
In 1705 Mme de Montespan acquired the château; she stayed here often until her death in 1707.
Part of a project combining **contemporary art** and historical monuments, the château now houses a collection of specially commissioned works. The contemporary artists drew inspiration from the 16C fashion of cabinets of curiosities – or miscellanea, assembled by scientifically minded people – and the theme of the five senses and four elements, as well as the château itself.

SIGHTS

★ **Château** ⏰ – Beyond two small pavilions stands the main body of the château, a central block flanked by two square pavilions crowned by balustrades, and two wings – one 16C with an upper floor, the other 17C with a terrace – framing the central courtyard. On the left, the first floor wing, begun by Artus Gouffier in 1515, was completed by his son, Claude. Of Gothic inspiration, the **galerie des Chevaux** with its basket-handle arcades is surmounted by marble medallions depicting Roman emperors in profile. On the walls of the gallery, the Master of the King's Horses commissioned paintings of Henri II's best mounts. Over the years, the paintings slowly decomposed, leaving behind only a yellowish colour where they hung on the wall, and the brands of the stud farms (still visible) where the horses were bred. In 1992, these ochre panels framed by the arcades were painted in pure, dancing lines by Georg Ettl; the elegant horses they depict trot gaily down the length of the gallery.

A beautiful staircase, its ramp formed by the spiral moulding of the central newel, leads to the next floor forming a majestic **gallery**★★. Here, 14 paintings of remarkable composition and draughtsmanship, their colours now faded, line the walls with subjects taken from the history of Troy and the Aeneid. The Louis XIII ceiling was commissioned by Louis Gouffier. Its 1 670 caisson panels depicting various subjects – mammals, birds, weapons etc – are like an overhead encyclopaedia. The gallery leads to the Pavillion des Trophées and the former chapel of Claude Gouffier.

The **central pavilion**, begun by Louis Gouffier and completed by La Feuillade, still contains its original 16C works. The admirable Renaissance staircase, with its hollow central newel and straight flight of stairs, was inspired by that of Azay-le-Rideau. The **Salle du Roi** (also known as the *Salle des Armes*), has a remarkable polychrome ceiling, dizzying in its multitude of images. Rather than the usual hunting trophies, the walls here are hung with surprising works by Daniel Spoerri, 12 *Corps en Morceaux* (1993), compositions of objects reflecting the diversity of nature, chaos controlled.

The **Pavillon du Roi** houses two rooms with the decorative exuberance characteristic of the Louis XIII style. The King's Chamber has an extraordinary ceiling overloaded with heavy gilt motifs framing painted caissons.

The *Salon des Ondes* houses the highly original *Étuis d'Or* by Hubert Duprat (1993), gold and pearl cases which appear to be the chrysalises of insects undergoing metamorphosis.

Reflecting the Renaissance passion for the study of nature, the tower's *Cabinet des Monstres* includes imaginary animals (such as a bird's head on a fish's body) created by Thomas Grünfeld in 1992.

Sol Lewitt's *Wall Drawings Room* on the second floor is worth a detour and so are the ground-floor rooms.

In the **Tour de Madame de Montespan** (south wing), from the **Salles des Ouvrières de la Reine** wafts a penetrating fragrance, emanating from a wall of beeswax erected by Wolfgang Laib. Under the domed tower, one of the most marvellous pieces in the château is the *Decentre Acentre* (1992), by Tom Shannon. The smooth aluminium forms fit perfectly into the luminous, round room: a disk is suspended from the ceiling, it slices a sphere in two (the upper half is floating on a magnetic field), creating an image reminiscent of planets and galaxies.

Surprising works of contemporary art await inside the Renaissance château

★**Collegiate Church** – The Renaissance façade includes twinned doors and a large arch surmounted by a pediment bearing the arms of the Gouffier family.

In the transept lie the family tombs, executed by sculptors from Tuscany named Juste, who had settled in Tours. The two largest date from 1537; the smaller pair, from the studio of Jean II Juste, from 1559. In the northern arm of the transept is the tomb of Philippine de Montmorency, second wife of Guillaume Gouffier, who died in 1516. Her recumbent effigy is represented clothed in the garments of a widow. Nearby is the mausoleum of her son, the Amiral de Bonnivet, killed in 1525 while fighting with François I during the French defeat after the siege of Pavia.

The tomb of Artus Gouffier, founder of the church and brother of the admiral, is in the south transept, beside that of his son Claude; the figure of Artus is clothed in armour. A 16C painting after Raphael represents John the Baptist.

The seigneurial chapels, on either side of the chancel, are magnificently decorated in the Renaissance style. The south chapel contains a 16C portrait of St Jerome; the painting of the *Holy Family* in the north chapel dates from the 18C. The keystones in each chapel are very elaborately worked. Also noteworthy are the picturesque 16C statues of the Apostles on the high-altar reredos, the portrait of Claude Gouffier on the north wall of the chancel, and a fine Resurrection, painted in the Flemish mannerist style of the 16C, on the south wall.

Île d'OLÉRON*

Michelin map 324: C-4 or 233 folds 13 and 14

The Isle of Oléron, which lies just off the coast between Royan and La Rochelle, is a popular holiday resort with families in search of sun, sea, fresh air and the spicy tang of pines and, of course... the famous oysters.

Since 1966, Oléron has been linked to the mainland by an elegantly curving road bridge, the longest in France at 3 027m/almost 2mi. The viaduct is built of prestressed concrete in simple, modern lines and rests on 45 rectangular piles; the central spans, 79m/259ft wide, rise 23m/75ft above the highest of high tides. A 7m/23ft carriageway, two cycle lanes and two walkways for pedestrians are incorporated in the viaduct's total width of 10.6m/35ft.

From the mainland, the best view of the bridge is from the old ferry landing-stage at Le Chapus.

GEOGRAPHICAL AND HISTORICAL NOTES

Oléron, a prolongation seawards of the old province of Saintonge, is except for Corsica, the biggest of all the French islands (30km/18mi long and 6km/3.6mi wide). The Pertuis (Straits) of Antioche and those of Maumusson, ravaged by dangerous currents, separate it from the Charente coast.

The limestone foundation of the low-lying isle is streaked with areas of sand forming long strings of dunes, wooded in the north (Saumonards Dune) and west (on the Côte Sauvage). The white houses of Oléron are surrounded by mimosa, oleander, tamarisk, fig trees and the grey-green spines of agave. Windmills sprout up unexpectedly on the hill tops.

Natural resources – To the east, the coastline and the lowlands between Boyardville and St-Trojan are exclusively reserved for oyster farming – the island's principal economic asset, along with early fruit and vegetables and the cultivation of vines. The vineyards, mainly grouped around St-Pierre and St-Georges, produce white or rosé wines with an agreeable, slightly iodized flavour characteristic of the region. The salt-marshes, once numerous near Ors, St-Pierre and La Brée, have largely been transformed into oyster claires.

A more recent development on the island is the establishment of several fish farms raising eels, trout and clams.

The most important fishing port on Oléron is La Cotinière on the west coast but an unusual form of coastal fishing also survives around the Chassiron headland at the isle's northernmost extremity. Here, visitors may see the local catch caught in specialised **fish locks** – walled enclosures fitted with grilled apertures at the seaward end, through which the water filters as the tide goes out. At low tide the fishermen wade out in the shallow water which remains and capture their prey with the aid of *fouënes* (a kind of harpoon) or *espiottes* (a type of sabre).

On the Côte Sauvage (Wild Coast), locals go spear fishing – especially in June and September – for bar and meagrest.

There is a treatment centre specialising in salt-water and sea-air cures at St-Trojan.

The Rules of Oléron – In 1199, the 76-year old **Eleanor of Aquitaine**, now a penitent following her turbulent life and scandalous youth, returned to her island possession and stayed in the château here before retiring to Fontevraud Abbey where she died in 1204.

Aged but not resigned, she set about restoring law and order to the island she ruled. The dangerous Côte Sauvage, for instance, had long been at the mercy of wreckers who looted and pillaged ships driven ashore and robbed any survivors from their crews – a practice euphemistically known as *le droit d'aubaine* (windfall rights). Eleanor decreed that henceforth such brigands must be punished: "They must be put in the sea and plunged under water repeatedly until they are half dead, and then taken out and stoned to death as one would dispose of wolves or mad dogs".

Subsequently the dowager drew up a set of rules "concerning the seas, the vessels sailing upon them, their masters, crew companions and also merchants". This maritime code, known as *Les Rôles d'Oléron*, served as a base for all subsequent charters regulating conduct on the high seas.

After the reign of Eleanor (a statue of her stands in the museum in St-Pierre) Oléron was coveted both by the French and the English. In 1372 the English abandoned the isle, taking away with them all the official documents.

The Oléron Pocket – The island was occupied by the Germans in 1940 and liberated on 30 April and 1 May 1945, though not without difficulty: overcoming the stubborn resistance of the 15 000-strong occupiers' garrison and forcing a German capitulation required a large-scale combined operation, which was code-named Jupiter and involved Allied land, sea and air forces.

ST-PIERRE-D'OLÉRON

St-Pierre is situated in the centre of the island, on the edge of the marshes, and is both the commercial and the administrative capital of the island. In the summer months the town, with its attractive pedestrian precincts, becomes extremely busy.

Church – A pale-coloured octagonal belfry dating from the 18C serves as a landmark for sailors at sea. On each side of the chancel, a chapel is preceded by clover-leaf arching supported by black marble pillars.

From the platform at the top of the tower (32m/105ft high), the whole of the island is visible in the foreground of a **panorama**★ embracing the Île d'Aix, the Île de Ré and the estuary of the River Charente.

Lanterne des Morts – This Lantern of the Dead, rising to a height of 30m/98ft, stands in place Camille-Memain on the site of a former cemetery. The monument was built at the time of the English occupation in the 13C and its slender, sober lines are typical of the early Gothic style. It is crowned by an 18C pyramid roof. Inside, a staircase still leads to the beacon at the top where the priest used to light the flame symbolising the immortality of the soul. An altar stands against one of the walls.

Maison des Aïeules – It was in this ancestors' house, home of his maternal grandparents at no 13 in the street now bearing his name, that the novelist **Pierre Loti**, member of the French Academy, spent many of his school holidays. In 1923 Loti was buried – like his Huguenot ancestors – in the family garden, here "beneath the ivy and the oleanders". His childhood bucket and spade were placed near his body, following his wishes. In front of the town hall a bust of Loti, who was born in Rochefort, commemorates the writer's link with St-Pierre.

Eating out

BUDGET

Le Bout au Vent – *Le Port* – *17370 St-Trojan-les-Bains* – ☎ *05 46 76 05 43* – *leboutauvent@club-internet.fr* – *open 15 Jun to 15 Sep* – ⊠ – *14.50/21€*. If you follow the right bank of the port, you will happen upon this amusing fisherman's house on piles. You can't beat the view of the Oléron bridge from its covered terrace. Leave your hurries behind, the owner works alone. *Eglade de moules* (mussels cooked with pine needles) on demand.

MODERATE

Les Bains – *On the harbour* – *17190 Boyardville* – ☎ *05 46 47 01 02* – *closed 24 Sep to 23 May and Wed in Jun* – *14.03/51.53€*. You can enjoy the liveliness of the Boyardville yachting harbour from the terrace of this modest restaurant as soon as the weather obliges. Rustic dining rooms and appetizing menu. Spic-and-span bedrooms from another era.

Le Relais des Salines – *On the Salines harbour, Petit Village* – *17370 Grand-Village-Plage* – ☎ *05 46 75 82 42* – *closed 15 Oct to 15 Mar, Sun evening except Jul-Aug and Mon* – *18.29/22.87€*. On the harbour, this wooden oyster-breeder's cabin is a pleasant stopping place. Colourful walls and tablecloths and bistro chairs for a lovely view of the salt-marshes, their grasses billowing in the wind. Simple à la carte seafood menu.

La Campagne – *D 734* – *17310 St-Pierre-d'Oléron* – ☎ *05 46 47 25 42* – *closed early Nov to Easter, Sun evenings off-season and Mon* – *43.45€*. Set up in the out buildings of an old farm, this restaurant is surrounded by a lovely garden. An ideal spot in the summer, the tables on the terrace welcoming the sun, whereas wintertime the cosy dining room with its round tables and venerable wooden furnishings is just the thing. Well-prepared cooking.

Where to stay

BUDGET

Le Verébleu Camping – *17190 St-Georges-d'Oléron* – *1.7km/1mi SE of St-Georges-d'Oléron via D 273 and rte de Sauzelle* – ☎ *05 46 76 57 70* – *verebleu@wanadoo.fr* – *open Apr to 23 Sep* – *reservations recommended* – *360 sites: 23.02€*. They've got it all! A big aquatic theme park based on Fort Boyard, a mini-golf, a children's playground, a tennis court, archery, bike rentals… and if you've forgotten your tent, mobile homes, chalets and cottages are also available.

Les Trémières Bed and Breakfast – *5 rte de St-Pierre* – *17310 La Cotinière* – ☎ *05 46 47 44 25* – ⊠ – *4 rooms: 31/39€* – ☐ *4.60€*. Only 200m from the Cotinière port and its shops, this early-20C house is charming indeed. The pocket garden, hidden behind the blond stone wall façade with its blue shutters, is the perfect place for a delicious summertime breakfast under the horse-chestnut. Bedrooms and suites.

Micheline Denieau Bed and Breakfast – *20 r. de la Legère* – *La Menounière* – *17310 St-Pierre-d'Oléron* – *3km/1.8mi W of St-Pierre-d'Oléron* – ☎ *05 46 47 14 34* – *denieau-jean-pierre@wanadoo.fr* – ⊠ – *5 rooms: 35/43€*. Simple, well-cared-for bedrooms have been built in the outbuildings of this typical regional-style house. There's a common room with an additional kitchen. Your hosts, who make wine and *pineau* for a living, will invite you into their own dining room for breakfast.

MODERATE

Hermitage – *17190 Sables Vignier* – ☎ *05 46 76 52 56* – *closed 14 Oct to 30 Mar* – ☐ – *34 rooms: 47.26/66.32€* – ☐ *6.10€* – *restaurant 16.77/40.40€*. A good address for family holidays, 800m from the beach. The main building is dedicated to meals whereas the pine-furnished bedrooms are in ground-level bungalows. Simple cuisine served in a pleasantly rustic setting.

Hôtel L'Albatros – *11 bd du Dr-Pineau* – *17370 St-Trojan-les-Bains* – ☎ *05 46 76 00 08* – *closed 5 Nov to 6 Feb* – ☐ – *13 rooms: 51.22/60.98€* – ☐ *7.01€* – *restaurant 25€*. This old oyster breeder's house on the edge of the public forest has its toes in the water. Its double-decker terrace opens onto the deep – the ideal place to savour a seafood meal before retiring in one of the hotel's colourful rooms.

Musée de l'Île d'Oléron Aliénor-d'Aquitaine ⊘ – *31 rue Pierre-Loti.* The museum, built in the local style and named after Eleanor of Aquitaine, focuses on the arts and traditions of the island. The reconstruction of a period kitchen (furniture, utensils, domestic ware, figures in costume) evokes home life in days gone by. There is a section on agricultural and maritime activities, another on vine-growing and winemaking. A collection of sea shells illustrates species of molluscs and crustaceans found around the coast. Documents relating to Pierre Loti and a model of Fort Boyard (1867) are also on display.

ST-TROJAN-LES-BAINS

St-Trojan is a pretty seaside resort with Mediterranean-like vegetation. Warm water from the Gulf Stream laps its four sandy bathing beaches; the attractive villas scattered among the trees on the edge of a magnificent pine forest are fragrant with the scent of mimosa flower from January to March.

A thalassotherapy centre (salt-water and sea-air cures) treats rheumatism and other complaints.

Forêt de St-Trojan – This huge stretch of woodland, thickly carpeted with parasol pines relieved here and there by an undergrowth of ilex or clumps of broom, covers an area of 2 000ha/almost 5 000 acres. Much of the forest, commercially harvested, grows on dunes, cresting as high as 36m/118ft.

Grande Plage – *3km/1.8mi W of St-Trojan via D 126E1.* This splendid fine sand beach rising to a line of dunes, exposed to the west wind and the Atlantic rollers of the Côte Sauvage, stretches as far as the eye can see in every direction.

Pointe de Manson – *2.5km/1mi SE of St-Trojan.* The road to the Point ends by an *estacade* (dike). From the top of this there are **views** of the

Oysterman's cottage

M. Thierry/MICHELIN

viaduct, the headlands of Ors and Le Chapus, the Seudre estuary and La Tremblade peninsula – which frame what is in effect a small inland sea.

Plage de Gatseau – *4km/2mi S of St-Trojan.* The road leads to a delightful beach of fine sand, very popular with bathers. On the way there are fine **views** of the Arvert headland, Ronce-les-Bains and the landmark tower of the church at Marennes on the mainland.

Pointe de Gatseau – This isolated promontory at the southern extremity of Grande Plage, separating it from the more sheltered beach at Gatseau, is one of the most evocative spots on the Côte Sauvage (Wild Coast). Access is by a small **tourist train** ⊘ which runs between St-Trojan and the Côte Sauvage.

TOUR OF THE ISLAND

Round tour from St-Trojan-les-Bains

85km/53mi – allow 1 day

St-Trojan-les-Bains – *See ST-TROJAN-LES-BAINS.*

Le Grand-Village-Plage – This seaside resort combines leisure, sport and cultural activities.

La Maison Paysanne de la Coiffe et du Costume ⊘ – This local costume museum has preserved the island's folk history by recreating the atmosphere of country life in the past. The farmhouse with its single room and window is fully furnished in the local style. The outbuildings – wine stores, stables and barns – contain exhibits of traditional activities relating to the sea and vine-growing.

The neighbouring **Maison de la Coiffe et du Costume oléronais**★ includes an attractive display of traditional costumes (both everyday and festive wear) worn on the island during the last century.

Port des Salines ⊙ – Set in an enclave formed by the road to the viaduct, oyster beds and a forest, this port is a revival of the old salt-marshes.

🔲 Two well-marked trails allow visitors to discover the site. At the entrance, brightly coloured **oyster huts** contain exhibits retracing the island's recent history: salt production in Saintonge, fish locks and oyster farming.

Visitors can learn how salt is collected in a salt-works developed around a **cabane à Sau** designed to store up to 200t of salt (the island's last salt maker retired in 1990). Fine examples of trawlers and oyster boats are anchored in the waters of a small port which provides access to a channel encircling the tidal reservoir. **Boat trips** provide the opportunity to discover the flora and fauna of the salt-marshes. Quai des Hôtes offers visitors a selection of regional food products.

Return to the road bridge. In Ors, follow D 275.

Le Château-d'Oléron – The remains of a 17C fortress, a citadel originally built on Richelieu's orders, stand here. In 1666 the construction of the port at Rochefort led Louis XIV to order the establishment of a *ceinture de feu* (girdle of fire) to protect the Charente estuary leading to this new port. Fouras and the Île d'Aix were therefore heavily fortified and the Oléron citadel redesigned and reinforced. Numerous deportees, both lay and religious, were imprisoned here during the Revolution.

The town is arranged geometrically around a huge central square containing a pretty Renaissance fountain with four cabled columns. The port penetrates the built-up area: a picturesque local sight is the arrival and departure of boats bound for the oyster farms.

The small coast road heading north towards Les Allards is known locally as the **Route des Huîtres** (the oyster road). This narrow roadway permits the servicing of the many canals, sheds and ports strung out opposite the east-coast oyster farms – and gives visitors a fascinating insight, especially at low tide, into the island's ostreicultural activity.

Le Marais aux Oiseaux (Bird Marsh) ⊙ – *At Les Grissotières.* 📷 This area of former salt-marshes surrounded by oak trees is now a **bird sanctuary** and nature reserve, providing a winter retreat for some species of migratory birds and a nesting site for others. Herons, egrets, pelicans and wild geese are among the numerous species enjoying the swamp conditions of their natural habitat.

Return to Les Allards and continue along D 126.

Boyardville – The name of the resort derives from a hutted camp established here for the army of workmen building **Fort Boyard**. Boyardville, once a training centre for the crews of torpedo boats, is today enlivened with a small marina. The 8km/5mi beach is in fact the seaward side of the Dune des Saumonards, an undulating 450ha/1 100-acre sand mass covered with plantations of pine trees – an ideal site for ramblers. A forest track leads to the old Saumonards Fort (military territory).

Fort Boyard – *Not open to the public.* This is a curious stone structure rising, offshore, from the shallow sea in the middle of the Straits of Antioche, between the Île d'Oléron and the Île d'Aix. The fort, another project designed to protect the mouth of the Charente, was started in 1804 and completed in 1859 under Napoleon III; progress in the science of artillery, however, which was developing much more rapidly than work on the fort, made it militarily out of date before it was even finished. In 1871 it was used as a prison: a large number of Communards (members of a Parisian workers' rebellion who were savagely crushed after the Franco-German War of 1870-71) were incarcerated there before their trial and deportation to New Caledonia.

At the beginning of the 1990s, astute television producers turned the abandoned fort into the striking setting of a televised game which brought international fame. In high season, boats take visitors to within a short distance of the fort.

Continue along D 126.

St-Georges-d'Oléron – The façade of the 11C-12C Romanesque church in this small town is attractively decorated with geometric motifs. The crowned arch of the central doorway was rebuilt in the 13C and the Gothic vaulting over the nave dates from the same period. The church as a whole was restored in 1618 and again in 1968. There is a fine covered market in the town square.

Drive NE to join the coast road and turn left towards St-Denis-d'Oléron.

Phare de Chassiron ⊙ – This black and white lighthouse built in 1836 is 50m/164ft high. The 224-step climb to the top is worthwhile for the huge **panorama★** it reveals: apart from the Île d'Oléron itself, the view takes in the Île d'Aix, the Île de Ré, the port of La Rochelle, La Pallice and, offshore, the Rocher d'Antioche with its warning beacon, which looks like a town swallowed up by the sea. Below the lighthouse, at low tide, the fish locks around the cape are visible.

Follow the coast road S towards Chaucre via Les Trois-Pierres.

The road, running above low cliffs which mark the beginning of the **Côte Sauvage**, is flanked inland by a plain scattered with market gardens.

Fort Boyard

Plage des Sables Vigniers – The beach, between two rock spurs at the foot of wooded dunes, offers views of the Côte Sauvage and over a sea that is frequently stormy.

Continue along the coast road and turn left in La Biroire.

St-Pierre-d'Oléron – *See St-Pierre d'Oléron, above.*

Leave St-Pierre-d'Oléron S along D 274.

Parc Ornithologique de Maisonneuve Ⓥ – 📷 Over 200 species of birds can be seen in this sanctuary, including, among the brightly coloured exotics, the crowned yellowcrest crane, the toucan, the macaw and the blackheaded lory of New Guinea.

★ **La Cotinière** – This is a busy, picturesque port half way down the Côte Sauvage. Thirty small trawlers are based in the harbour, fishing mainly (in summer) for shrimps, prawns, lobster, crab and sole. Once landed the catch is sold immediately at **La Criée** Ⓥ – the local term for a fish auction in the covered market. A Sailors' Chapel (1967) stands on the dune overlooking the port.
The route crosses the Côte Sauvage dunes, passes **La Remigeasse** and then penetrates an area of woodland (pines and holm oaks) offering tantalising glimpses of the ocean.

Plage de Vert-Bois – The road follows a one-way system to loop through another patch of tree-covered dune-land fringed with reeds before arriving at this beach; from here is an impressive **view**★ of the ocean, with long lines of breakers rolling shorewards every time the wind rises.

Continue along the same road via Grand-Village-Plage and follow D 126 back to St-Trojan-les-Bains.

OLORON-STE-MARIE
Population 11 067
Michelin map 342: I-5 or 234 fold 38
Local maps see Le BÉARN

Oloron was once two separate towns, joined together in 1858. It is believed to have been originally an Iberian outpost and subsequently a late Roman citadel surrounded by ramparts on the present-day hillside quarter of Ste-Croix. Rebuilt into a military stronghold at the end of the 11C by the viscounts of Béarn, it served as a staging post along the route of the Reconquista – the wars against the Sarrasins in northern Spain. It is located at the junction of the Aspe and Ossau which join to form the River Oloron. The river's name derives from *Iluro*, an Iberian place name and a local mountain deity. Ste-Marie, which was both a rural and episcopal town, developed around the middle of the 11C on the terrace overlooking the west bank of the Aspe. Originally a Roman town, it became a bishopric at the beginning of the 6C before it was destroyed during the Basque incursions in the late 7C.
In the past Oloron and Ste-Marie were an important stage on the pilgrim's route to Santiago de Compostela, one of the last before the climb to Col de Somport, the pass on the Spanish border. In memory of this tradition, contemporary sculptures by artists including Guy de Rougemont, Carlos Cruz-Dies and Michael Warren have been placed at strategic points of historic interest around the town. This unusual urban initiative is part of an overall project to mark out the ancient pilgrims' road, to be continued along Vallée d'Aspe and from there into Galicia via Hecho (Spain). Other sculptures can now be seen in Agnos, Gurmençon, Sarrance and on the Sebers Bridge.

Eating out

BUDGET

Ferme-auberge Estrem – *64360 Cardesse – 11km/6.8mi N of Oloron-Ste-Marie via D 9 – ☎ 05 59 21 40 04 – closed 16-30 Sep, 23-31 Dec and weekdays from Oct to May – ✉ – reserv. required – 9.90/30.48€*. The entire gamut of Béarn cookery can be found in this old family farm, but the recipes have been kept secret for 17 generations. Authentic local cuisine is concocted here from timeless ingredients; try the *cassoulet fermier*, the *poule au pot au chou farci*, the *omelettes aux grattons...*

Chez Château – *64400 Esquiule – 10km/6mi W of Oloron via D 24 – ☎ 05 59 39 23 03 – closed Sun evening and Mon – 9.15€ lunch – 13.72/33.54€*. This 19C house is near the village fronton. In the front room, the fireplace was certainly used for stewing *garbure* in times past. Two other dining rooms are decorated in the regional style. Mini-terrace under a reed screen.

MODERATE

Chilo – *64130 Barcus – 16km/10mi W of Oloron-Ste-Marie via D 59 – ☎ 05 59 28 90 79 – closed 3-18 Jan, Feb school holidays, Sun evening and Mon from Oct to May and Mon lunch in season except Aug – 19.82/38.11€*. A large traditional house with blue shutters right in the village centre, facing the mountains. Cosy dining room with woodwork and fireplace. Garden terrace. Cuisine tenderly prepared from fresh ingredients. Snug, comfortable rooms; pool.

Where to stay

BUDGET

Marie Lavie Bed and Breakfast – *Quartier Auronce – 64360 Lucq-de-Béarn – 10km/6mi N of Oloron-Ste-Marie via D 9 and D 110 – ☎ 05 59 39 18 39 – ✉ – 3 rooms: 31/37€ – meals 14€*. This renovated farm in the heart of the countryside is near the Gave d'Oloron. The rooms are classic and sparkling clean. A lovely touch: you can pick your vegetables from their garden for your evening meal.

Maison Rancesamy – *64290 Lasseube – 15km/9mi E of Oloron via D 24 dir. Lasseube then secondary road – ☎ 05 59 04 26 37 – missbrowne@wanadoo.fr – ✉ – 5 rooms: 38.11/47.26€ – meals 19.82€*. If you fancy the idea of opening your bedroom windows onto the rolling landscape, this perfectly renovated 18C Bearnaise farm is for you. Spacious, sober rooms. Breakfast room with a pretty, exotic decor. Delightful flower-filled garden.

MODERATE

Le Château de Boues Bed and Breakfast – *64570 Féas – 8km/5mi SW of Oloron-Ste-Marie via D 919 – ☎ 05 59 39 95 49 – closed late Sep to 1 May – ✉ – 4 rooms: 56.41€*. This 18C château seems quite posh, with its white façade overlooking the road, but your hosts will receive you with simplicity and *joie de vivre*. Nice view from the bedrooms of the countryside and the garden with pool and vegetable plot.

SIGHTS

Église Ste-Marie ⊘ – This former cathedral dates from the 12C and 13C.
The belfry-porch shelters a magnificent Romanesque **doorway**★★, one of the rare examples of its period which, miraculously, has suffered no serious damage in spite of local invasions and religious wars. The exceptional hardness of the Pyrenees marble used in its construction is responsible for the well-preserved condition: over the centuries the stone has become as smooth as polished ivory.
Among the doorway's most impressive features are:
Two atlantes in chains (thought by 19C archaeologists to be Saracens – an allusion to the Moors Gaston found installed in France on his return from the Holy Land, and whom he subsequently drove out);
A *Deposition*;
Daniel in the Lion's Den (left) and the *Ascension of Alexander (right)*, both of which were reconstructed in the 19C;
Coving representing Heaven: the 24 elders of the Apocalypse, carrying long-necked jars of perfume, are playing violas or rebecs – three-stringed violins used by minstrels – as they worship the divine Lamb, which carries the Cross. Evil is represented by a dragon's head. This is a literal translation into sculpture of the *Vision of St John in the Apocalypse*.
Coving representing Earth. The craftsmen used local models to recreate the entire peasant life of the place and the period: boar hunting, salmon fishing and filleting (from 1 000 to 1 500 salmon were caught then each day at Oloron), cheese-making, preparation of hams, barrel-making, goose-plucking etc.

An equestrian statue of the Emperor Constantine trampling on paganism;

A monster devouring a man.

Interior – *There are two light switches, one behind the third pillar of the nave on the left and one at the entrance to the chancel on the left.* A lepers' stoup is inset into the first pillar supporting the organ loft on the north side (capital originally from the cloisters). At the entrance to the chancel, note the 18C gilded oak sanctuary lamp and 16C lectern carved from the trunk of a single tree.

Other features of note include the 16C pulpit, the fine organ loft (1650), a 17C crib with carved wood figures (north aisle).

Elders of the Apocalypse

B. Kaufmann/MICHELIN

Quartier Ste-Croix – The Holy Cross district, the old town surrounding the château of the Vicomtes (destroyed in 1644), is built on a projecting spur between the two torrents.

Église Ste-Croix – Inside, there is an unusual Spanish-Moorish dome, added in the 13C, above the 11C transept crossing. Inspired by the mosque at Cordoba, Spain, the architects of this dome mounted it above star vaulting supported by columns with historiated capitals.

Old houses – Near the church are two fine Renaissance houses; lower down in rue Dalmais is the stately **Grède tower** (14C) with its twinned bays. Beside it is a 17C building which houses the **Maison du Patrimoine** ⊘ – departments of archaeology, ethnography and mineralogy relating to the town and the Upper Béarn region occupy three floors of this museum, together with paintings and souvenirs of the wartime internment camp at Gurs.

Promenade Bellevue – West of the church, by the terrace overlooking the Aspe torrent and the Ste-Marie district. Follow, on the right, the route along the top of the old ramparts. From here there is a striking **view** up the Vallée d'Aspe to the mountain chain beyond it, which extends westward as far as the Basque country.

ORTHEZ

Population 10 121
Michelin map 342: I-5 or 234 fold 30

Orthez was the capital of Béarn before Pau; today it is a busy and picturesque town and its most interesting architectural feature is an ancient fortified bridge. Gaston VII Moncade, Vicomte of Béarn, was behind the town's development in the 13C. After the union of Foix and Béarn, Gaston Fébus held court here. The writer and court poet Jean Froissart (c 1337-c 1400) described in his *Chroniques* the brilliance of the château receptions after he had been a guest there in 1388 and 1389.

Francis Jammes (1868-1938) was another poet of note associated with Orthez. He lived in the town from 1897 to 1907; the wooden-balconied house that was his home can be seen on the way out of town, on the route to Pau.

SIGHTS

Old town – In the days of Gaston VII and Gaston Fébus the ground plan of Orthez did not lie parallel to the river, as it does now: the main axis of the town then was at right angles, clustered on each side of a line drawn from the fortified bridge to Château Moncade. Reminders of this period remain in the dignified old houses, some with decorated porches, which line rue Bourg-Vieux, rue de l'Horloge and rue Moncade.

*Pont Vieux – The 13C bridge, guarded by a tower pierced with an arched gateway guarded the entrance to the town. The tower was still in use as a defence feature in 1814, at the time of the struggle against Wellington. From the bridge there is an attractive view of the Pau torrent, tumbling past the huge blocks of limestone half-blocking the river bed.

Tour Moncade – This tower is all that remains of the grandiose fortress built by Gaston VII in the late 13C and early 14C.

283

Au Temps de la Reine Jeanne – *44 r. du Bourg-Vieux –* ☎ *05 59 67 00 76 – closed 1 Mar to 15 May – 20 rooms: 38.11/48.78€ –* ⌂ *5.03€ – restaurant 13.72/28.20€.* Located in the heart of the old city, this hotel is comprised of an 18C and a 19C house. The small, quiet rooms are reached by climbing the handsome old staircase surrounding a glass-roofed veranda. Traditional French fare.

Église Saint-Pierre – Once connected to the town's ramparts, this 13C church was a defensive post, as in the arrow slits in the north wall. Inside the original double nave is devoid of side aisles; along with the chancel with its ribbed vaulting (four very fine carved keystones), this is all that remains of the 13C building.

A. Thuillier/MICHELIN

Keystone in Saint-Pierre

Maison Jeanne-d'Albret – On the corner of rue Roarie and rue Bourg-Vieux. The elegant 16C mansion once belonged to Jeanne d'Albret, the mother of Henry IV. The building has an octagonal tower which adds to the charm of the main entrance, leading to a paved inner courtyard. The steeply sloping tiled roof is typical of the region. The carefully restored façades reveal the warm tones of the stonework.

Monument du Général Foy – *3.5km/2mi N, on the road to Dax.* The monument is a memorial recalling the Battle of Orthez (1814) in which Marshal Soult's 30 000 men were defeated by Wellington's army of 45 000. The monument sits in a pleasant location surrounded by fine Béarnaise farms crowned by tall sloping roofs, with views of the distant Pyrenees.

ZONE INDUSTRIELLE DE LACQ

A group of factories and industrial complexes, all connected with the development of natural gas fields in the Lacq area, are located between Orthez and Pau on the banks of the Gave de Pau.

Mourenx – *20km/12mi SE of Orthez via D 9.*
The modern high-rise buildings in this housing development, built in the early 1960s to provide accommodation for some 3 000 technicians employed on the Lacq industrial estate, are a somewhat incongruous site in the middle of the rolling Béarn hills.

Viewpoint – This is the town's highest hill. The car park of Le Club discotheque offers a sweeping view of the industrial estate.
There is a panoramic view of the mountains, with the Béarn hills in the foreground, followed by the Central Pyrenees from Pic d'Anie to Pic du Midi de Bigorre and due south, the Vallée d'Aspe.

The Lacq gas field

In December 1951, during exploratory drilling by La Société Nationale des Pétroles d'Aquitaine, the Lacq 3 borer hit one of the largest known gas fields at that time, at a depth of 3 500m/11 500ft.

Le Haut OSSAU★★

Michelin map 342: J-7 to J-8 or 234 folds 43 and 47

Upstream from the village of Eaux-Chaudes, the Vallée d'Ossau separates into three different branches – the Bious, Soussouéou and Brousset valleys – which together are known as Le haut Ossau (the Upper Ossau region), over which towers the imposing silhouette of the Pic du Midi d'Ossau. The greater part of the Upper Ossau region lies within the Parc national des Pyrénées.

★VALLÉE DU GAVE DE BIOUS

1 Itinerary starting from Gabas

4.5km/2mi, then 45min on foot.

Gabas – This is a mountain village lying in the hollow where the torrents rushing down from Pic du Midi d'Ossau meet. Sheep's cheese prepared (pressed) in a special way is a local delicacy. The 12C village chapel, with vaulting supported by semi-cylindrical pillars and thick, crossed joints, has been redecorated in a modern style.
From Chêne de l'Ours *(2km/1.2mi beyond Gabas)* there is a fine view of the Pic du Midi.

Drive 5km/3mi N along D 34. A wide forest track starts on the left, just before the bridge spanning the Bitet.

Gorges du Bitet – *1hr round trip on foot, via the forest track.*
A climb through this shady gorge takes the visitor past a series of fascinating cascades, rapids and pools. A hydroelectric pressure pipeline marks the end of the walk.

Turn back, drive through Gabas then turn right on D 231.

The road climbs very steeply, leading to the dam which has effectively drowned the Bious amphitheatre.

★ Lac de Bious-Artigues – Looking south from the west bank of the lake, not far from the dam, there are superb **views★** of Pic du Midi d'Ossau: at sunset the andesite rock-faces fade through every shade of red to deep violet. To the south-west is the impressive bulk of Pic d'Ayous.

Pic du Midi d'Ossau – Alt 2 884m/9 462ft. This mountain peak, recognisable from as far away as Pau, is in the form of a fang – a silhouette which contrasts with the normal Pyrenean crestline, and which is striking less for its boldness than for its delicacy.
A tour of the peak starting at Artigues *(signposted as an alternative to GR10)* is a walk which should be attempted only by fit and experienced climbers. It can be broken by an overnight stop at the **Pombie CAF Refuge**.
Hundreds of chamois live on the slopes of the peak's eastern foothills.

★★ Lacs d'Ayous – *Climb (on foot): 2hr 30min; descent: 1hr 30min; difference in altitude: 560m/1 837ft. Follow the Parc National signs and the red-and-white markers of the GR10 trail.*
From the refuge west of these three mountain lakes there are grandiose **views★★★** of Pic du Midi reflected in the waters.

Lacs d'Ayous

A. Thuillier/MICHELIN

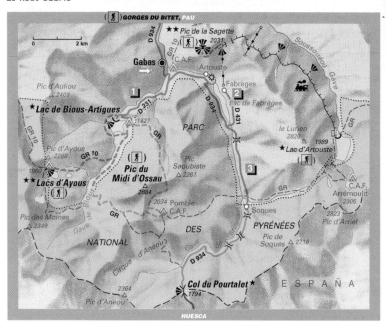

★VALLÉE DU SOUSSOUÉOU

② Excursion to Lac d'Artouste

Allow 4hr

This excursion combines a ride in a gondola to La Sagette, leaving from the eastern side of the Fabrèges reservoir (Lac de Fabrèges), and a trip on the Lac d'Artouste mountain railway.

Gondola to La Sagette ⊘ – From the upper station (alt 1 950m/6 398ft) a marvellous **view★★** of the glaciated valley of the Brousset far below – partly drowned now by the reservoir – forms part of the same mountain panorama dominated by the silhouette of Pic du Midi d'Ossau.

A look at the **Pic de la Sagette★★** viewing table is worth the climb (1hr on foot round trip).

In winter, there is gondola service to the slopes of the small family style ski resort of Artouste.

From La Sagette to Lac d'Artouste ⊘ – *This scenic train journey is not suitable for persons with respiratory problems: the engine gives off fuel smells, particularly in the tunnel at the start of the trip.* The little train winds and twists its way among the mountain slopes at a height of 1 950m/6 398ft. The 10km/6.2mi **journey★★** offers striking views of the Vallée du Soussouéou, 500m/1 640ft below.

From the terminus *(stop limited to 1hr 30min)* a footpath leads to **Lac d'Artouste★** *(30min round trip)*. A dam has now raised the surface level of the lake, which laps the granite slopes of an amphitheatre surrounded by peaks which rise to 3 000m/9 850ft.

VALLÉE DU GAVE DE BROUSSET

③ Itinerary starting from Gabas

15km/9mi

The road skirts the Fabrèges and Artouste hydroelectric power stations then climbs to the level of the Fabrèges reservoir. Ahead, on the Spanish frontier, are the slopes of Pic de Soques – a mountain with a particularly contorted geological structure. Still climbing, the road runs through a narrow channel and leads finally to the Anéou cirque.

★**Col du Pourtalet** – Alt 1 794m/5 886ft. *This border pass is normally blocked by snow from November to June.* Looking back towards the north there is a fine **view★** of the immense pastoral Anéou cirque – dotted in summer with countless sheep – and, further north still, of Pic du Midi d'Ossau.

Zoo de La PALMYRE★★★

Michelin map 324: C-5 or 233 fold 25

This 14ha/33-acre zoo is set in undulating land in La Palmyre Forest, at the eastern end of the seaside resort of La Palmyre. Shaded by maritime pines and oaks, visitors can admire the scenery from one of the many benches along the path winding through the zoo.

TOUR ⊙

☺ Pink flamingos at the foot of a waterfall welcome visitors to La Palmyre. In order to avoid missing something, it is advisable to follow the marked 4km/2.5mi trail; all along the way, panels explain the habits and characteristics of the various species.

More than 1 600 animals from every corner of the globe are scattered throughout the pine forest with its numerous lakes and hills, in areas similar to their natural habitat.

Here, it is easy to observe the astonishing variations which exist in nature and the animal world.

Carnivorous species – The most dangerous predators (cheetahs, lions, wolves, Siberian tigers) live next to smaller mammals (small pandas, suricates)

Birds – A great variety of species are represented here (ostrich, stork, hornbill and crested pigeon from Oceania). Visitors will be captivated by the magnificent plumage of exotic birds such as parrots, cockatoos and midnight blue macaws who use their beak as a third foot!

Hoofed animals – The large species (elephant, hippopotamus, rhinoceros) offer a striking contrast with the more agile species (blesbok, impala and zebra).

Polar bears – Otters and sea-lions are often seen showing off in their pond, but to see polar bears swimming and playing about is certainly unusual. The polar-bear pond is a huge pool (1 000m³/1 308cu yd) set up as an ice floe. Below, a wide glass panel enables visitors to see the agility and ease of these 450kg/992lb giants.

Reptiles – A vivarium houses crocodiles from the Nile, royal pythons and tortoises from the Seychelles Islands.

Monkeys – Visitors will be fascinated by the infinite variety of shrewd little monkeys such as the silky golden lion marmoset from Brazil with its bright orange fur or the male emperor marmoset with its magnificent white moustache. Only a sheet of plate glass separates visitors from families of African gorillas, the most imposing of all monkeys, with their highly amusing antics.

This polar bear is not just another tourist

S. Sauvignier/MICHELIN

Shows – Added attractions are the lions' feeding time, a sea-lion show, during which these delightfully playful animals demonstrate their amazing agility, and performing parrots and cockatoos, riding bicycles, driving cars and roller skating.

Feeding at the zoo – 250t of hay, 180t of fruit and vegetables, 70t of straw, 50t of meat, 20t of fish and 7 000l of milk are used every year.

Breeding – The zoo also breeds species threatened with extinction (elephants, cheetahs etc), while the lion cub nursery brings pleasure to young and old alike.

PARTHENAY★

Population 10 466
Michelin map 322: E-5 or 232 fold 44

Parthenay is picturesquely sited on a rocky spur circled by the River Thouet. The town is the capital of the Gâtine region, an agricultural area renowned for its sheep farming, dairy products, apple orchards and above all cattle-breeding. The **cattle market** ⊙, held every Wednesday in the Bellevue district (behind the railway station), is the second largest in France for animals destined for slaughter. The town is also home to a number of aeronautical, mechanical and electronics industries, and its importance is reflected in the number of trade fairs held each year in the Parthenay Palais des Congrès (conference hall and exhibition centre). From Pont-Neuf there is a fine **view**★ of the oldest part of Parthenay, in particular of the picturesque architectural group formed by Pont-St-Jacques and the ancient fortified gateway beside it.

HISTORICAL NOTES

Ubiquitous Mélusine – The legendary **Mélusine**, the beautiful maid with a serpent's tail, is said to have created the castle at Parthenay in the wink of an eye, – as she is supposed to have done in the case of many fortified towns in the Poitou region. Parthenay is, nevertheless, different; the seigniors here remained directly descended from Mélusine until the Middle Ages, being members of the Larchevêque family, the younger branch of the Lusignans, themselves supposedly issue of the potent fairy.

Pilgrims' Way – In medieval times Parthenay was one of the important stops on the pilgrims' route to Santiago de Compostela. Arriving from Thouars, the exhausted travellers would go first to the church hospital (a chapel still exists on the road to Thouars). Having left there those who had fallen ill on the journey, the pilgrims would cross the bridge, go through the fortified gateway and enter the town. Once they had found accommodation in the inns and taverns of rue de la Vaux-St-Jacques they would then pay ritual visits to the local sanctuaries (there were 16), churches such as Notre-Dame-de-la-Couldre and Ste-Croix. Once these devotions were completed, the pilgrims were free to disperse among the taverns in the town or to admire the charms of the graceful women of Parthenay, so renowned for their looks that they were celebrated in a popular folk song of the day.

MEDIEVAL TOWN *1hr*

The walk starts from the town hall.

Citadel – Perched high up at the extremity of the promontory, the citadel protected the castle keep, the seigneurial residence and two churches behind its massive ramparts (12C). Down below, the fortifications were strengthened by the natural barriers of the river and the Vaux-St-Jacques Valley. In the Middle Ages Parthenay had the reputation of being impregnable.
Porte de la Citadelle (or Porte de l'Horloge) – a powerful Gothic fortification framed by pointed towers – leads into the fortress. In the 15C the gateway served also as a belfry; a huge bell dating from 1454 still hangs here. Further on along rue de la Citadelle, on your right are the collegiate church of Ste-Croix (12C) then **Église Notre-Dame-de-la-Couldre**, which has retained a fine Romanesque doorway characteristic of

The old town by night

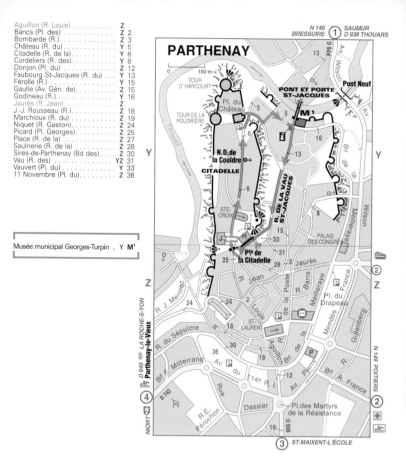

PARTHENAY

the Poitou region. The street leads to the vast esplanade where the castle used to stand (only two towers remain) and which offers bird's-eye **views** of the River Thouet meandering below and the Vau-St-Jacques district.

Take the steps down and follow the narrow rue du Château.

★**Pont and Porte St-Jacques** – The narrow 13C bridge across the River Thouet was, and is, the entrance to the town from the north. A drawbridge unites it with the St-Jacques gateway, dating from the same period, which retains its tall, twin towers and its machicolated watch-path.

★**Rue de la Vau-St-Jacques** – This was once Parthenay's main shopping street and links the two town gateways, Porte St-Jacques and Porte de la Citadelle. The street's medieval aspect still recalls the days of the pilgrims. Some of the ancient half-timbered houses with projecting upper storeys have wide bays at street level, marking the location of former shops and stalls.
The road continues up through place du Vau-Vert (Green Vale Square), skirting the walled citadel – although the towers were long-since levelled, their remains are still visible.

A footpath running below the ramparts leads back to Porte de la Citadelle.

ADDITIONAL SIGHTS

Musée Municipal George Turpin ⓥ – Housed in the **Maison des Cultures de Pays**, a contemporary building, the museum has two entrances, one from Porte St-Jacques and the other from the north bank of the Thouet *(car park)*.
Animated models retrace the history and development of Parthenay. Numerous display cases (archaeology, coin collections, furniture etc), as well as temporary exhibits, offer the visitor a broad picture of the past in Gâtine. One of the rooms is entirely devoted to **Parthenay earthenware** represented by pieces (1882-1916) made by the Jouneau-Amirault duo, who revived this popular art.

Cattle market ⓥ – The cattle market taking place on Wednesday mornings (behind the railway station) is the second most important beef market in France. Sheep and local produce are also sold here.

Eating out

BUDGET

La Truffade – *14 pl. du 11-Novembre -* ☎ *05 49 64 02 26 - closed 3 weeks in spring, 3 weeks in autumn, Tue evening and Wed - 12.50/28€.* Does a plentiful *truffade, tripous* or some Auvergne ham sound good? Then step on the brakes – here you'll find authentic Auvergne cuisine served among photos of the region, cow bells and the famous Laguiole knives... Come hungry!

Where to stay

EXPENSIVE

Château de Tennessus Bed and Breakfast – *79350 Amailloux - 9km/5.4mi NW of Parthenay via N 149 dir. Nantes then D127 dir. Lageon -* ☎ *05 49 95 50 60 - tennessus@csi.com - closed 20 Dec to 8 Mar -* ✉ *- 2 rooms: 110/125€.* A magnificent fortified 14C castle in all its outrageousness! With its moats, drawbridge, waiting rooms and ancient stairwells, it's an absolute prototype. You'll slumber in enormous, superbly decorated medieval rooms with canopy beds. One self-catering cottage with a garden.

EXCURSION

Parthenay-le-Vieux – *1.5km/0.9mi W.* The octagonal tower of the village church can be seen from afar.

Église St-Pierre – The symmetry of the Romanesque façade is most remarkable; note the presence of Melusine the enchantress among the carved scenes and motifs decorating the archivolt of the doorway.

The interior comprises a barrel-vaulted nave flanked by half-barrel-vaulted aisles. The crossing is surmounted by a cupola supporting the tower. The capitals on either side of the chancel are carved with lions and goats.

PAU★★

Population 78 732
Michelin map 342: J-5 or 234 fold 35 – Local maps see Le BÉARN

Pau, the most elegant and most pleasantly situated of all the towns on the fringe of the Pyrenees, was highly prized as a tranquil winter resort by the British in the 19C, but its consistently soft and healing climate is still appreciated today.
Pau's main tourist attractions are its historical links with Henry of Navarre (Henri IV of France), its particularly fine mountain views and excellent recreation and sports facilities including golf, horse racing, fox hunting and other pastimes introduced by the British in the 19C.
Regular events include the **Grand Prix de Pau**, a tough challenge for drivers and their vehicles competing on the 3km/1.8mi circuit through the main streets of the city, and the **Festival de Pau**, which attracts high quality performers every summer.

HISTORICAL NOTES

Gaston Fébus – In the 14C he built a wall around Pau and laid the foundations of the present castle. His successors continued his work and, in 1450, the town followed Lescar, Morlas and Orthez as the provincial capital of Béarn. It was, however, modest as capitals go: each time the States (provincial assembly) met, there were always some deputies who had to sleep under the stars owing to the shortage of lodgings.

Marguerite of Marguerites – In 1527 Henri d'Albret, King of Navarre, sovereign lord of Béarn and Comte of Foix and Bigorre, married Marguerite of Angoulême, the sister of the French king François I. The celebrated Marguerite of Marguerites transformed the castle in accordance with Renaissance taste, surrounded it with luxuriant gardens and used them as background for pageants and plays which she composed herself, and turned the castle into the foremost intellectual centre of the time.

Birth of Henri IV – Henri and Marguerite's daughter **Jeanne d'Albret** married a descendant of St Louis, and her son, Henry of Navarre, later became Henri IV of France as a consequence *(see BÉARN)*.

Jeanne returned from campaigning in Picardy to Pau for the birth of her son. She arrived on 3 December 1553 and was confined 10 days later. As Jeanne's father had advised, she sang songs in the Béarnaise tongue during labour so that the child "might neither cross nor tearful be". According to custom, directly Henri was born Grandfather d'Albret rubbed his lips with a clove of garlic and then moistened them with the local Jurançon wine, before laying the baby in the turtle-shell that was to be his cradle.

An English discovery – As early as the July Monarchy of 1830 there were English residents in Pau, and they gradually grew in numbers to form a colony. Some of these expatriates were retired officers who had fought with Louis XVIII on

Henri IV

RMN – © SPADEM 1995

his victorious return from Britain in 1814. It was however a Scot, Doctor Alexander Taylor (1802-79), who brought the town fame and fortune: in 1842 he published his theory – which was rapidly translated into most European languages – that Pau could serve as a winter resort providing cures for various ills, and many visitors came to test his claim; many did indeed find a stay here beneficial.

The local enthusiasm for sports dates from the same period the colony introduced the steeplechase in 1841 (the racetrack at Pont-Long is, along with the Grand National course at Aintree in England, one of the most important in Europe). Fox-hunting followed a year later and, in 1856, the first golf links on the continent were inaugurated. The year 1889, when Queen Victoria instead chose Biarritz for a one-month visit, saw the start of Pau's decline as an international winter resort.

TOWN WALK

★★★ **Boulevard des Pyrénées** – At the initiative of Napoleon I, place Royale was extended to form a splendid terrace overlooking the valley and the fast-flowing waters of the Gave de Pau, which was aptly named boulevard des Pyrénées.

At the end of the boulevard, the municipal casino stands in the middle of **Parc Beaumont**, with its many varieties of trees and ornamental lake. The boulevard overlooks terraced gardens and a funicular connecting place Royale to the railway station below and offers a spectacular view of the Pyrenees described with great lyricism by many writers.

★★★ **Panorama** – Beyond the vine-covered slopes of the Gelos and Jurançon foothills, the sweeping view stretches from Pic du Midi de Bigorre to Pic d'Anie, with Pic du Midi d'Ossau standing out clearly in the background. In fine weather, particularly in the early morning and evening and notably in winter, the view can be quite spectacular. Plaques indicating the altitude of each peak are fixed to the railing exactly opposite each summit.

An English town

The English, drawn to the warm climate, settled in Pau from 1840, building sumptuous villas around the town centre. Eclectic architectural styles were adopted, similar to numerous 19C public and private buildings. Each villa has its own grounds and outbuildings: greenhouses and stables, both essential parts of the British lifestyle. Villas, usually private, can still be seen today in the area around Lawrence Park, north of the town centre and the Trespoey district due east.

PAU

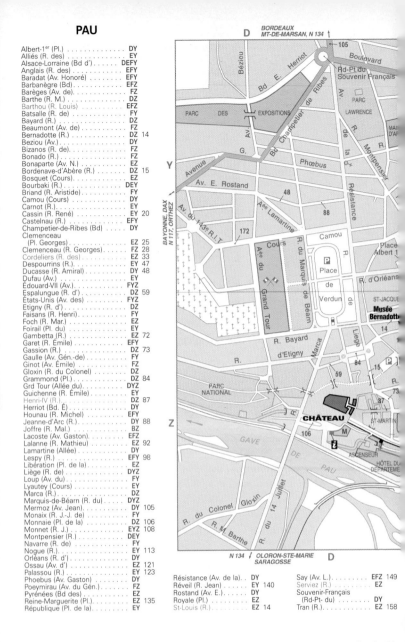

BORDEAUX
MT-DE-MARSAN, N 134

N 134 / OLORON-STE-MARIE
SARAGOSSE

Historical quarter – East of the castle, a network of picturesque streets lined with antique shops and restaurants offers a pleasant stroll. Maison Sully, built in the 17C, stands opposite the castle, whereas next door stands the former building of the Navarre parliament, restored in the 18C. The adjoining tower is the old belfry of Église St-Martin, built in the 15C. The arcaded place Reine-Marguerite was once the market place where the gallows and wheel were erected for capital punishment.

SIGHTS

★★ Château ⊘ – The castle, built by Gaston Fébus in the 14C on a spur overlooking the river, has lost its military aspect despite the square, brick keep – in typical Sicard de Lordat style – which still towers over it. Transformed into a Renaissance palace by Marguerite d'Angoulême, the building was completely restored in the 19C in the time of Louis-Philippe and Napoleon III.

Royal Apartments – This fine suite of rooms sumptuously redecorated in the 19C includes a superb collection of **tapestries★★★** removed from the royal storehouse during the reign of Louis-Philippe (numerous Gobelins tapestries). The tour starts in the elegant 16C kitchen, where a scale-model of the whole castle is on display.

A 64 - E 80
BAYONNE, TOULOUSE

MUSÉE DES BEAUX-ARTS

LOURDES, TARBES

Parc Beaumont

PALAIS DES PYRÉNÉES

ST-LOUIS-DE-GONZAGUE

CENTRE DES CONGRÈS CASINO

THÉÂTRE DE VERDURE

DES PYRÉNÉES

GROTTES DE BETHARRAM

The **hundred-place dining hall** – with a table large enough to accommodate that number of revellers – has a ceiling with exposed joists. Splendid Gobelins tapestries from the early 18C representing *The Hunts of Maximilian*, and part of the series of 17C tapestries showing the *Labours of the Months* – known, after its creator, as the Lucas Months Tapestries – hang on the walls. Elsewhere, note the large and lavish first-floor reception hall, the rest of the Lucas tapestries, Sèvres porcelain vases, neo-Gothic chandeliers and 18C Japanese-style vases.

In the **royal bedroom** stands an unusual, monumental bed fashioned in the Louis XIII style.

The **Empress' Apartment** has been restored to its second Empire style; a washstand complete with toiletries can be seen in the boudoir. Also displayed is the turtle shell from the Galapagos Islands, which is said to have been Henri IV's cradle. The historical rooms contain portraits of Henri IV (16C-17C) and stories relating his life.

★ **Musée des Beaux-Arts** ⊘ – In the Fine Arts Museum old masters are exhibited next to local little-known artists in tasteful thematic displays of old and contemporary works. For instance, El Greco's *St Francis in Ecstasy* (1590), a feverish expression of mystical fervour, hangs next to an abstract work dating from 1993, *Metaphysical Reflections*.

Eating out

BUDGET

La Gousse d'Ail – *12 r. du Hédas* – ☎ *05 59 27 31 55* – *closed Sat lunch and Tue* – *11.89€ lunch* – *16.31/19.82€*. You'll find this venerable brick and stone house in the Hédas quarter, the oldest part of Pau. Enjoy the simple cuisine skilfully made of local ingredients and served in a decidedly rustic setting.

MODERATE

Au Fin Gourmet – *24 av. G.-Lacoste* – ☎ *05 59 27 47 71* – *closed 23 Jul to 5 Aug, Nov school holidays, Sun evening and Mon* – *16.77/36.59€*. Across from the train station and at the foot of the *funiculaire*, this restaurant with a big, glass-walled dining room is reminiscent of a music pagoda. Brick tiles on the floor and pleasant hues make for a genteel ambience. Contemporary cuisine.

Les Pyrénées – *9 pl. Royale* – ☎ *05 59 27 07 75* – *closed Sun-Mon* – *19,82/26,68€*. On the ground floor, a bar resembling an English pub and the plane tree shaded terrace. Upstairs, a dining room with original table decor. And on your plate, a meal made of tasty local ingredients to be washed down with a bottle selected among 150 vintages.

La Concha – *36 r. de Liège* – ☎ *05 59 27 55 09* – *24.39/33.54€*. This restaurant is a haven for seafood lovers. The colourful, spacious dining room is decorated in the Hispano-Basque style. Grilled fish and seafood platters or dishes *à la plancha* arrive every other day from St-Jean-de-Luz.

Auberge Labarthe – *behind the church* – *64290 Bosdarros* – *15km/9mi SW of Pau via D 100 and D 285* – ☎ *05 59 21 50 13* – *closed 4-30 Jan, Tue lunch, Sun evening and Mon except Jul-Aug* – *reserv. required Sat-Sun* – *16.46/48.78€*. This flowery *auberge* is a lovely spot indeed, with a hint of the bistro in the lively, *tomette*-tiled dining room. Brick fireplace in the bar. The delectable cuisine is an excellent value.

Where to stay

BUDGET

Hôtel Central – *15 r. L.-Daran* – ☎ *05 59 27 72 75* – *28 rooms: 28.20/53.36€* – ☕ *5.34€*. A friendly reception in this modest hotel right downtown. The rooms, of varying comfort and sizes, are very clean and well-soundproofed. Salon with billiards table.

Hôtel Montpensier – *36 r. Montpensier* – ☎ *05 59 27 42 72* – ▯ – *22 rooms: 51.83/56.41€* – ☕ *6.10€*. This imposing pink house 500m from the château is set back from the street. Although the decor in the classic rooms is somewhat outmoded, you'll have space to move about in.

Hostellerie de l'Horizon – *64290 Gan* – *9km/5.5mi S of Pau via N 134* – ☎ *05 59 21 58 93* – *closed Feb, Christmas to New Year's day, Sun evening and Mon* – *10 rooms: 38.11/44.21€* – ☕ *5.34€* – *restaurant 24.39€*. This pleasant pavilion with its blue and ochre façade overlooks a pretty park with many trees. The structured rooms are furnished in the style of the 1930s-40s, and the dining room has a Japanese flavour. Nice view of the neighbouring hills from the terrace.

On the town

The Triangle, at the crossroads of rue Émile-Garet and rue Arribes, is the heart of Pau night-life. Put on your dancing shoes before checking out the bars here, such as La Luna (bodega), Le Garage, St-Patrick (pubs), Txalupa (Basque), L'Angle (techno), or the Canyon Café (country). After the Triangle, the **Boulevard des Pyrénées** is the second artery for night owls, with the terraces of its numerous cafés and *brasseries* affording a great view of the Pyrenees mountain range. The more discrete place Reine-Marguerite with its pebbled stone arcades has its own charm – this is where you'll find the West Side bar and its weekly jazz concerts.

Baracuba – *16 r. des Orphelines* – ☎ *05 59 82 82 83* – *www.baracuba.com* – *Tue-Sat 5:30pm-2am; summer: Tue-Sat 5:30pm-3am* – *closed the week of 15 Aug*. Havana lives in this Cuban bar where Afro-Cuban music and a rhythm professor unite to create an absolutely convincing ambience. Beginners and confirmed dancers come dance the salsa every weekend before indulging in the pleasure of throwing their empty peanut bags on the floor as they drink a glass of *mojito* at the bar. Try the cigars.

Black Bear – *1 bd Aragon* – ☎ *05 59 27 52 67* – *www.blackbear.fr* – *daily 9am-2am*. Run by rugbyman Robert Paparemborde's sister, this bar resembles a sports shrine, thanks to the many souvenirs (Michel Platini's and Bernard Hinault's shirts, for example) honouring its walls. Too bad you can't be sure to find Pierrette Paparemborde, often absent, behind the bar – she's the real star of this citadel of Pau merriment.

Le Boucanier Ferrand José – *64 r. Émile-Garet* – ☎ *05 59 27 38 80* – *Sep-Jun: Mon-Sat 6pm-2am; Jul-Aug: Mon-Sat 9pm-3am*. One of Pau's handsomest bars, fitted out like a ship's hold. Over 130 kinds of beer on the menu.

Casino Municipal de Pau – *Allée Alfred-de-Musset* – ☎ *05 59 27 06 92* – *www.groupetranchant.com* – *Sun-Thu 10am-3am, Fri-Sat and pre-holiday evenings until 4am*. This casino boasts 100 slot machines in addition to a traditional games room, a restaurant and a bar. Music programme Fridays and Saturdays.

Showtime

Zénith – *Bd du Cami-Salié* – ☎ *05 59 80 77 66* – *www.zenith-pau.fr* – *ticket office: Mon-Fri 9am-noon, 2pm-6pm*. This enormous, up-to-the-minute performance hall can seat as many as 6 500 spectators. Operas, classical and pop music concerts, cabarets, circuses, ice shows – they've got it all.

Speciality shops

Au Parapluie des Pyrénées – *1 r. de Laussat* – ☎ *05 59 27 53 66* – *Mon-Fri 8am-noon, 2pm-7pm, Sat 8am-noon*. Since 1890, the enormous *parapluies des Pyrénées*, or Pyrenees umbrellas, capable of sheltering one from the worst of south-west storms, have been made here. It is the last remaining enterprise of its kind in France.

Confiseur-chocolatier Verdier – *6 r. des Druides* – ☎ *05 59 72 70 30* – *Mon-Fri 9am-noon, 2pm-6pm, Sat 9am-noon* – *closed 2nd and 3rd wks of Aug*. Monsieur Verdier wanted to be a musician, but he bowed to his father's wishes and became a pastry and confectionery chef instead, specializing in chocolate making. Today, his talented hands create symphonies of succulent *raisins au jurançon*, *cailloux au chocolat* and *dents d'ours*.

Francis Miot – *Uzos roundabout* – *D 37* – ☎ *05 59 35 05 56* – *www.feerie-gourmande.com* – *Mon-Fri 10am-noon, 2pm-6pm; Sat-Sun and public holidays variable*. Francis Miot has been making jam since 1985. World's Best Jam and Jelly Maker, 1991, winner of the French Confectionery Cup in 1995 and Best Bonbon of France 2000 titleholder for his creation, *les coucougnettes*, he concocts his sweet spreads for more than 30 heads of State.

Josuat – *2 r. du Mar.-Joffre* – ☎ *05 59 27 45 93* – *Tue-Sat 9am-noon, 2:30pm-7:15pm, Mon 2:30pm-7:15pm*. Founded in 1880, this chocolate-manufacturing institution makes home-made pastries, chocolates and other sweets.

Henri Burgué – *Chemin des Bois* – *64110 St-Faust* – ☎ *05 59 83 05 91 or 06 85 20 53 23* – *daily 9am-noon, 2pm-7pm*. Mr. Burgué makes small quantities of sweet or dry Jurançon wine in oak casks closed with round stones from the river. The wine evaporates for three years before he takes the stone off, decants and fills the cask anew.

Sports and leisure

Hippodrome du Pont Long – *462 bd de Cami-Salié* – ☎ *05 59 13 07 07* – *open racing and training days*. This is one of the biggest French racetracks. Some 26 obstacle races are held here every year. This is also where the Centre d'Entraînement de Sers, with its 600 horses, is located. Wintertime, when hundreds of jockeys train on the track, the sweat and breath of their horses combine to produce veritable steam clouds that rise above the hippodrome.

Le Haras National de Gelos – *1 r. du Mar.-Leclerc* – *64110 Gelos* – ☎ *05 59 62 89 81* – *visits Jul-Sep: Mon-Sat 10am-noon, 2pm-5pm; Oct-Jun by appointment*. This is one of the most beautiful national stables of France. It's located in a 13ha park presided by the Château de Gelos. Founded in 1808 during a visit of Napoleon I, this equestrian farm was intended to create a new race of Anglo-Arab horses. The 80 stallions in residence have varying occupations – races, equestrian sports, maintenance of natural areas... Horse shows take place here in July, August and November.

Le Plantier de Pau – *5 allée du Grand-Tour* – ☎ *05 59 62 37 96* – *Mon-Sat 2pm-7pm*. Played in the Landes, the Pyrénées-Atlantiques and the Hautes-Pyrénées by 650 card-carrying members, the *quilles de neuf* (nine pin) game is bowling's ancestor. It is played with a 6.2kg ball and nine 96cm-high pins. The players, most of them retired, gather here for a game every afternoon.

Palais des Sports de Pau – *R. Suzanne-Bacarisse* – ☎ *05 59 02 54 69*. This is the temple of the Elan Béarnais basketball team, five-time champion of France and once of Europe. The ultra-modern building, capable of seating 8 000 spectators, is considered to be one of the finest sports arenas in Europe.

Stade Nautique – *Av. Nitot* – ☎ *05 59 11 20 16* – *schedule varies according to school calendar* – *closed mid-Sep to mid-Jun*. This outdoor swimming pool has two sections – one olympic-style pool for swimming and one for diving.

Boulevard des Pyrénées

Paintings from the French, Italian, Dutch, Flemish, Spanish and English schools from the 15C to the 20C include the works of Jordaens, Rubens, José de Ribera, Zurbaran, Nattier, Van Loo...

In 1878, the Fine Arts School of Pau purchased Degas' *Cotton Exchange in New Orléans*, marking the entry of Impressionism into the museum. The modern era is also represented, with paintings by Berthe Morisot, Armand Guillaumin and André Lhote.

The museum also displays numerous examples of the various trends in contemporary art. Sculpture is particularly worthy of mention, with works by Jean Arp, Gillioli, Lasserre etc.

A regional tone is given by the romantic paintings of Eugène Devéria (1805-65) – mountain landscapes, *Birth of Henri IV* – and visions of fast-flowing mountain streams with the sublime ring of the Pyrenees on the horizon by his pupil Victor Galos (Pau 1828-79), an exceptionally talented painter from Béarn.

Musée Bernadotte ⊘ – The museum is in the birthplace of Charles Bernadotte (1763-1844), the Marshal of France who succeeded to the Swedish throne in 1818 under the name of Charles XIV. The salons on the first floor are devoted to the display of family magnificence; on the second floor is an old Béarnaise kitchen and the room where the future monarch was born. The Bernadotte family rented the second floor of this house, built in a traditional style, of beaten cob.

EXCURSIONS

Haras national de Gelos Haras ⊘ – *1 rue Maréchal-Leclerc in Gelos. Leave Pau S on the road to Oloron then follow the road to Nay.*

⊙ The Haras de Gelos is a equestrian breeding and rearing centre, founded in a former 18C château by Napoleon in 1807 – there are breeds ranging from pure-blood Arabs and Anglo-Arabs, breeds from Brittany, the Ardennes and Franche-Comté, Pottok ponies and ponies from the Landes.

La Cité des Abeilles (City of Bees) ⊘ – *11km/7mi W. Leave Pau by D 2 to Mourenx. At Laroin, take the D 502 hairpin road towards St-Faust-de-Bas and continue for 2km/1mi.*

⊙ This fascinating, open-air museum, which is undergoing continuous development, is devoted to the bee and its existence. Visitors follow a footpath climbing a slope planted with sweet-smelling, nectar-bearing flowers to discover the world of apiculture, ancient and modern: traditional old beehives from different regions of France; a covered apiary from a monastery; a glass-walled observation hive in which the workers can be studied tending their allotted honeycombs.

PEYREHORADE

Population 3 056
Michelin map 335: E-13 or 234 fold 30

Peyrehorade is the main town in Pays d'Orthe in the Landes *département*. A particularly interesting example of architectural development in southern France, Peyrehorade marks the beginning of river navigation on the converging mountain streams of Pau and Oloron known as the Gaves Réunis, which flow into the Adour. Along the quays, yachts are gradually replacing the sailing barges of the past. It is best to visit the town on Wednesdays when the long central market place is busy with stalls and vendors.

Peyrehorade is one of only four fish-auction centres dealing with *pibales* (tiny elvers), a great delicacy particularly appreciated by Spanish gourmets.

The Château d'Orthe with its four corner towers (16C-18C) stands on the riverbank. Nearby, on the main square is the tourist office where a leaflet describing the walk to the Aspremont castle ruins (11C) is available.

BANKS OF THE GAVES REUNIS AND THE RIVER ADOUR

58km/36mi – allow half a day. Leave Peyrehorade via the bridge over the river and the D 19. Just before the rise, turn right.

Abbaye d'Arthous ○ – The abbey, converted into farm buildings in the 19C, was founded in the second half of the 12C and served as a staging post for pilgrims on the route to Santiago de Compostela. The abbey buildings were restored in the 16C and 17C recreating the charm of the traditional half-timbered houses of the Landes region. The church is especially noteworthy for its completely restored east end. Note the decoration in the apse and two apsidal chapels; billet-moulding is supported by modillions: figures often in pairs, geometrical designs reminiscent of a bed of reeds or a pan-pipe, interwoven patterns etc. The modillions in the south apsidal chapel depict the seven capital sins. The chancel still has a few patterned capitals with interlaced designs. The south-west pillar in the crossing is surmounted by a carved capital depicting a centaur with an elephant's body (late 12C).

Under the half-timbered gallery of the monastic buildings are two beautiful 4C mosaics from a Gallo-Roman villa in Sarbazan.

A museum in the northern part of the abbey presents the results of archaeological digs in the region (bone tools from the Magdalenian Era).

Turn back along D 19 which becomes D 10 and goes through Vallée de la Bidouze at the foot of the ruins of Château de Gramont in Bidache.
Turn right onto D 936 towards Bayonne.

The road climbs into the open countryside of the Basque foothills. When Bardos comes into sight, pull over onto the left for a **view**★★ of the Basque Pyrenees with Pic d'Anie in the background, the first summit (alt 2 504m/8 238ft) in this high chain of border mountains.

After Bardos, continue along D 936 to Séquillon. Turn right on D 123, and after about 3km/1.8mi, go left to Urcuit.

Urcuit – Like the neighbouring town of Urt, this little town has a very strong Basque character, featuring a fine Basque-style **church** with an outer gallery. Typical discoid Basque headstones can be seen in the adjoining cemetery.

Return to Urt via D 257, then take D 261.

The road follows the River Adour alongside orchards of kiwi trees grown on trellises.

After 6km/3.6mi, turn right towards Guiche.

Guiche – Above the entrance to the cemetery is an amusing house on stilts known as Maison du Fauconnier (Falconer's House) which was once the town hall. A little further along, in Guiche-Bourgade, are the ruins of a castle with a square keep.

The church in Urcuit

A. Thuillier/MICHELIN

Go down to the old port on the Bidouze and take D 253 to Aire Hastingues.

Aire d'Hastingues – On the A 64 motorway in the Pau-Bayonne direction. Access to the rest area is possible from Bayonne and the neighbouring villages.

Eating out

BUDGET

La Vieille Auberge – *40300 Port-de-Lanne – 6km/3.6mi W of Peyrehorade via N 117 –* ☎ *05 58 89 16 29 – closed end Sep to early May, Mon lunch and Tue lunch –* ✍ *– 18.29/38.11€.* This auberge has the charm of a well-cared-for family home. The dining room with veranda opens onto the flower-filled garden. Rooms in cottages around the pool. Visit the museum of local traditions.

Where to stay

BUDGET

Camping La Comtesse – *40300 Bélus – 6km/3.6mi N of Peyrehorade via D 417 –* ☎ *05 58 57 69 07 – open 15 Mar to 15 Oct – reserv. recommended – 115 sites: 15.55€.* A modern campground, with roomy sites well defined by hedges, two fine pools and a nice lake where you can angle for carp and eel.

Birds of prey

Volerie du Château – *Château de Bidache – 64520 Bidache –* ☎ *05 59 56 08 79 – show from mid-Apr to mid-Jun: Mon-Fri 3:30pm, Sat-Sun 3:30pm and 5pm; mid-Jun to mid-Sep: daily 3:30pm and 5pm – closed end Sep to mid-Apr.* In the courtyard of the château of the Ducs de Gramont, unfortunately in ruins, thirty-some unusual actors of the birds of prey ilk (eagles, falcons, vultures, buzzards, kites and owls) put on a unique flying performance.

Its geometric layout, which includes the service station, symbolises the nearby intersection of the French roads leading to Santiago de Compostela. Pathways lined with box hedges and panels illustrating well-known sites, lead to a circular building given over to the history of the famous pilgrimage. Inside, information panels, reproductions of art works, slide shows and interactive terminals recount the history of St James the Apostle and the daily lives of the pilgrims as they faced the many trials and tribulations of their journey. An exhibit entitled *La Fin des Terres* (World's End), featuring the *Tree of Jesse* which decorates the pillar of the structure dedicated to the *Glory of Saint Jacques*, recounts the end of the pilgrimage.

Take D 3 on the right; the road follows the river.

Hastingues – This tiny *bastide* is named after the King of England's seneschal, John Hastings, who founded the town in 1289 under the orders of Edouard I Plantagenet, Duc d'Aquitaine. All that remains of the upper town, perched on a headland overlooking the meadowland of Arthous below, is a single fortified gateway to the south-west and several 15C and 16C houses. Take time to admire the charming place de l'Église, shaded by cypresses from the old cemetery.

Return to Peyrehorade via D 23.

POITIERS★★

Population 83 448
Michelin map 322: H-5 or 233 fold 8

The most impressive view of Poitiers is from the Plâteau des Dunes in the St-Saturnin suburb east of the town, below the cliff on the east bank of the River Clain. The town, perched on a promontory isolated between the Clain and the Boivre, offers lovers of art and architecture a rare choice of fine buildings to admire, whereas the medieval districts in the heart of the city have much of general interest to sightseers; a busy student life centring on the nearby university additionally lends the district a particular animation, especially around the square in front of the town hall.

HISTORICAL NOTES

Dawn of Christianity – The earliest Christians in the region gathered together in the centre of the Roman city here in the 3C and 4C: St John's Baptistery was one of their sanctuaries. Their first important bishop, the gentle **St Hilaire** (St Hilary, died AD 368), was an outspoken champion of orthodoxy; he also taught St Martin, who was his favourite disciple. Arriving uninvited at the Council of Séleucée, Hilaire found that the monks refused to make room for him – "when suddenly, miraculously, the earth itself rose up and assumed the form of a splendid chair, higher than the others, and all those present were lost in wonderment," according to the chronicler of La Légende Dorée (The Golden Legend).

Another renowned name in the history of the Church in Poitou was **St Radegund**, the wife of Clotaire I, who fled to Poitiers in 559 and founded Holy Cross Monastery – where her confidant, St Fortunat, would recite poems he had written in Latin.

A momentous date – Of the three conflicts known as the **Battle of Poitiers**, that in which Charles Martel vanquished the army of the invading Arabs in AD 732 and saved Christianity is by far the most famous – and the most important.

The Arabs – Moors, Saracens – having conquered Spain flooded into Gaul from the south. Checked for the first time by Eudes, Duke of Aquitaine, they decimated his forces near Bordeaux and continued towards the centre of the country, sacking and pillaging everything on their way. Eudes asked for help from the Merovingian leader Charles Martel; the Arabs, who had just burnt down Église St-Hilaire in Poitiers, found themselves confronted by the Frankish troops a few miles north of the town. Martel's cavalry cut the Moslem army to ribbons, and little by little the invaders began to retreat from Aquitaine. The year 732 remains as an important symbol of Western Christianity's first true victory over the Moslems.

Jean de Berry's Court – The city of Poitiers, having twice fallen under English domination – in the 12C by Henry Plantagenet and Eleanor of Aquitaine, in the 14C after the second Battle of Poitiers in 1356 – was finally restored to the French crown after General Bertrand du Guesclin (c 1320-80) had chased the English from the region. The royal representative was the brother of Charles: Jean, Comte de Poitou and holder of the Berry and Auvergne dukedoms.

De Berry's rule, which extended from 1369 to 1416, brought fame and prosperity to Poitiers. Jean de Berry was ostentatious and sophisticated, a generous patron of the arts, and never travelled anywhere without his menagerie and a retinue of talented artists.

Poitiers during the Renaissance – The intellectual reputation of the renowned 4 000-student university drew many thinkers and writers to Poitiers.

Following his patron and protector Geoffroy d'Estissac, **Rabelais** stayed here several times between 1524 and 1527; Calvin was also a visitor. This city of monks and priests (there were 67 churches then) – "A big town and confident, teeming with scholars" as it was described at the time – became for a while France's third most important cultural centre after Paris and Lyon. Certain members of the humanist philosophical and poetic group known as Les Pléiades came to rub shoulders with the learned at the university. They included the mathematician Jacques Pelletier, Ronsard, the leading light of the group, the poet Jean-Antoine de Baïf and Joachim du Bellay, another poet who modelled his style on the Hellenistic lyricism of antiquity.

Four hundred years of sleep – Poitiers was not spared by the Wars of Religion. Destruction, misery, famine were visited upon the town, which in addition twice suffered the rigours of a siege. From then on life in Poitiers went into decline; even the university, despite the fame of some of its students – Descartes for instance – shared the same fate.

Despite the strenuous efforts of the Intendant **Comte de Blossac**, this slumber persisted until after the Second World War.

Since then the influence of a younger generation has injected a new dynamism into the town and has enabled it to reclaim its position as capital of the Poitou-Charentes region.

★★ ÉGLISE NOTRE-DAME-LA-GRANDE

The name of this former collegiate church stems from S. Maria Maggiore Church in Rome. The building, with its perfect lines and the aesthetic balance of its architectural features, stands as a supreme example of Romanesque art in France. The west front, which has blackened over the centuries, is one of the most famous in the country.

The dimensions of the church are: length 57m/187ft, width 13m/43ft, height 16.6m/54ft.

M. Thierry/MICHELIN

The west front of Notre-Dame-la-Grande

Eating out

BUDGET

Poitevin – *76 r. Carnot* – ☎ *05 49 88 35 04* – *closed 9-24 Apr, 8-29 Jul, 23 Dec to 2 Feb and Sun* – *10.67€ lunch* – *18.29/35.06€*. Here's an establishment that's been discretely doing a fine job for several years... Its regional recipes and reasonable prices have won over the local gourmands. Several small dining rooms for a delightful repast.

Les Bons Enfants – *11 bis r. Cloche-Perse* – ☎ *05 49 41 49 82* – *closed 1-15 Aug and Mon* – *8.99€ lunch* – *18/23€*. Amid the many schools of this neighbourhood, this little green restaurant boasts a large painting of a group of late-19C schoolchildren. Customers sit elbow to elbow to sample, among other delicacies, the Poitevin specialities served with candid good humour.

MODERATE

La Table du Sommelier – *19 r. Arthur-Ranc* – ☎ *05 49 41 16 33* – *closed 15 Aug to 3 Sep, 24 Dec to 4 Jan, Sat lunch, Sun evening and Mon* – *18.29/22.87€*. This restaurant across from the post office is a favourite meeting place for natives who tuck into veal heads, *farcis poitevins* and fresh market cuisine. The owner, whose passion for jazz is mirrored by the album covers on the walls, organizes music evenings once or twice a month...

La Chênaie – *6km/3.6mi S of Poitiers via N 10, Hauts-de-Croutelle exit* – ☎ *05 49 57 11 52* – *closed 21-27 Jan, Sun evening and Mon except holidays* – *19.06/35.06€*. Protected from the road by a garden, this old farm run by an affable young couple has been nicely decorated. The dining room with its lovely wooden beams, yellow walls and elegant tables, is pleasant indeed. Well-prepared food, served on the terrace in the summer.

Le St-Hilaire – *65 r. T.-Renaudot* – ☎ *05 49 41 15 45* – *closed 1-15 Jan, Mon except lunch in Jul-Aug and Sun* – *21.34/25.61€*. How surprising to enter this modern-looking building only to find oneself in a vaulted 12C room with massive pillars, thick stone walls and oak tables. The medieval decoration underlines the picturesque flavour of this Middle Ages *chantrerie* where monks used to chant. Several reasonable fixed-price menus.

Le Chalet de Venise – *In the village* – *86280 St-Benoît* – *4km/2.4mi S of Poitiers via D 88* – ☎ *05 49 88 45 07* – *closed Feb school holidays, 27 Aug to 4 Sep, Sun evening, Tue lunch and Mon* – *19.06/44.97€*. You have to leave Poitiers to locate this pretty house in verdant surroundings. As soon as the sun warms a bit, you can spend a delicious moment on the terrace while enjoying the quietude of the stream-crossed garden. Cosy in the winter. Pleasant rooms.

Where to stay

BUDGET

Hôtel Gibautel – *Rte de Nouaillé* – ☎ *05 49 46 16 16* – 🅿 – *36 rooms: 38.11/47.26€* – 🍵 *5.34€*. It's true that this modern hotel is not in the centre of town, but it answers the needs of travellers on the move. Basic little rooms, practical and well-equipped; clinic across the street.

MODERATE

Mondial – *6km/3.6mi from Poitiers via N 10 (Hauts-de-Croutelle exit)* – ☎ *05 49 55 44 00* – 🅿 – *40 rooms: 41.16/68.60€* – 🍵 *5.79€*. The architecture with galleries set around the pool is inspired by the hotels of Florida. Small rooms, except for the family suites that have a living area.

Château de Vaumoret Bed and Breakfast – *R. du Breuil Mingot* – *10km/6mi NE of Poitiers via D3 dir. La Roche-Posay, then D 18 to Sèvres-Anxaumont* – ☎ *05 49 61 32 11* – 🍽 – *3 rooms: 46/68€*. Although only a few miles from Poitiers, this B&B is deep in the countryside! Calm guaranteed in the 15ha park surrounding this delightful little 17C château, not to mention in the bright bedrooms, nicely furnished with old pieces. The perfect place to unwind.

Hôtel Château de Périgny – *Périgny* – *86190 Vouillé* – *17km/12mi NW of Poitiers via N 149 and secondary road* – ☎ *05 49 51 80 43* – 🅿 – *42 rooms: 64.03/131.11€* – 🍵 *9.15€* – *restaurant 25.15/44.97€*. Right in the middle of a park, this 15C château will definitely satisfy your longing for tranquillity. Opt for the larger third-floor rooms under a handsome wooden frame; rooms in the wing are more functional. Contemporary cuisine.

Get the blues

Le Pince-Oreille – *11 r. des Trois-Rois* – ☎ *05 49 60 25 99* – *Tue-Thu 5pm-2am, Fri 5pm-3am, Sat 9pm-3am* – *closed Christmas, 14 Jul and 15 Aug.* The decor of this hyperactive café-concert changes constantly (it was a sand beach when last we visited) and the music is varied and dynamic. 20 shows (jazz and blues concerts) a month plus 40 different cocktails to help you handle so many melodious sensations!

Showtime

Le Confort Moderne – *185 r. du Fg-du Pont-Neuf* – ☎ *05 49 46 08 08* – *www.confort-moderne.fr* – *following show schedules: 6pm-2am; ticket office: daily* – *closed Jul to Sep.* No, Modern Comfort is neither a new brand of bourbon nor an appliance store. This association is fully dedicated to promoting current music and contemporary arts through concerts (from the Négresses Vertes to Maceo Parker), art shows (Arman, Ben, César) and impertinent, original events. Unique in Europe, the *fanzinothèque* has collected some 20 000 fanzines, comics etc to read there or borrow. Bar open during concerts.

Take a break

Buck Mulligan's Irish Pub – *5 r. du Chaudron-d'Or* – ☎ *05 49 30 11 48* – *daily 3pm-2am.* A real Irish pub, appropriately dark, with real Irish bartenders who toast the memory of James Joyce's character Buck Mulligan. Have a mug of Guinness, (recommended to expecting Irish mothers because of the high iron content) or another of the Emerald Isle's specialities while listening to one of the frequent concerts or partaking in one of the bi-monthly quizzes.

Chez Cul de Paille – *3 r. Théophraste-Renaudot* – ☎ *05 49 41 07 35* – *Mon-Sat 9am-11pm* – *closed Aug.* For a second or two, you'll think you're the first customer to discover this paved *auberge*, with its straw stools and aged varnished tables. But if you happen to glance at the graffiti covering the old ocre walls, you'll discover an anthology of famous signatures, including Arletty, Brel and Coluche...

Maison de L'Île Jouteau – *5 chemin du Tison* – ☎ *05 49 60 06 33* – *Tue-Sun noon-11 :30pm (midnight during events); open-air café Sun 2pm-7pm.* In an island of green, this charming house is run by a helping-hand association full of original ideas to bring back the fun of the Poitiers Beach of the 1950s. The programme of festivities includes boat rides, mini-golf, open-air café, concerts...

*** West front – The elegant west front, magnificently restored in recent years, dates from the 12C and typifies the Poitou Romanesque style – even if the architects were influenced by the art of the Saintonge area. It is densely carved and the lively figures are further accentuated, according to the time of day, by the play of light and shade. In the centre, at ground level, is an arched doorway with four receding lines of coving, flanked by arcades framing twinned arches within. Above these three arched elements are bas-relief sculptures of (read from left to right and from the lower level to upper) *Adam and Eve*; *Nebuchadnezzar on his Throne*; the *Four Prophets Moses, Jeremiah, Isaiah and Daniel*; the *Annunciation*; the *Tree of Jesse*; the *Visitation*; the *Nativity*; the *Bathing of the Infant Christ*; the *Meditation of St Joseph*.

The central doorway is surmounted by a large, very tall arched window bay, itself flanked by a double row of blind arcades housing the Apostles and (at the extremities of the upper row) two figures said to be St Hilary and St Martin. The coving of the arcades is decorated with fine carvings representing plants and fantastic creatures. *Christ in Majesty* gazes down from an oval-shaped frame in the great gable above. The figure is surrounded by the symbols of the Evangelists and crowned by a stylised sun and moon, metaphors for eternity in the Romanesque period.

At each side of the west front a cluster of columns supports a pierced lantern with straight or arched cornices and a roof in the shape of a pine-cone, covered with scales.

North Wall – The chapels flanking this side of the church were added in the 15C *(against the chancel)* and the 16C *(along the aisle)*. Note the unusual silhouette of the square-sectioned 12C belfry with a pierced turret, again topped by a pine-cone roof.

Interior – The interior of the church, which is in the Poitou style but without a transept, was unfortunately repainted in 1851. On each side of the barrel-vaulted nave are very high rib-vaulted aisles.

A 17C copper goblin can be seen in the chancel. Behind the high altar stands a 16C statue of Notre-Dame-des-Clefs (Our Lady of the Keys), installed to replace the original which was destroyed in 1562: the statue recalls a miracle said to have occurred in 1202, when the keys of the town were spirited away from the traitor who was going to hand them over to the besieging English. The oven vault above the chancel – painted in the 12C with a fresco depicting the *Virgin in Majesty* and *Christ in Glory* – is supported by six heavy, round columns arranged in a semicircle. The original apsidal chapel, on the south side of the ambulatory, was replaced in 1475 by another, now dedicated to St Anne. This was founded by Yvon du Fou, the Seneschal (Steward) of the city, whose armorial bearings can be seen above the fine Flamboyant funerary niche where his tomb was lodged. In its place now is an Italian version of the *Entombment*, in polychrome stone, which dates from the 16C. The work was once in Trinity Abbey in Poitiers.

TOWN WALK

At the initiative of the town hall, three coloured itineraries drawn on the ground, starting from Église Notre-Dame-la-Grande, enable visitors to explore the town without getting lost. Below you will find two short walks and some additional sights which cover the town's main centres of interest.

1 City Centre

Starting from Église Notre-Dame-la-Grande (place Charles-de-Gaulle), follow rue de la Regratterie then turn left onto rue du Palais.

Palais de Justice ⓥ – The Restoration façade of the law courts masks the Great Hall and the original keep of the ancient ducal palace, rare examples of urban civic architecture dating from the Middle Ages.

The **Great Hall**★ (47m/154ft long and 17m/55ft wide) was reserved for important trials, solemn audiences and sessions of the Provincial Estates. In 1418, four years before he was proclaimed king, the fleeing Charles VII set up his court and parliament here. In March 1429 Joan of Arc was subjected to a gruelling interrogation by an ecclesiastical commission, to emerge after three weeks with an enhanced sense of her sacred mission – and official recognition that the mission was religiously inspired.

Although construction of the vast hall had started under the Plantagenets, it was De Berry who commissioned the architect Dammartin to build the great gable wall with its three monumental chimneys, its balcony and Flamboyant windows. Up above, four fine statues represent (left to right) Jean de Berry, his nephew Charles VI, Isabeau of Bavaria, and Jean's wife Jeanne de Boulogne.

The early-12C keep, known as **Tour Maubergeon**, which was transformed into a residence for Jean de Berry in the 14C, are visible from rue des Cordeliers. Remains of the original Gallo-Roman defensive wall can be seen in the adjacent square.

Walk from the Palais de Justice along rue Gambetta then turn left onto rue Paul-Guillon.

Hôtel de l'Échevinage – This 15C building with its contemporary chapel was once the town hall. It originally housed first the university's Grandes Écoles (seats of higher learning) and then the local magistrate *(échevinage)*.

Return to rue Gambetta.

Église St-Porchaire – All that remains of the original 11C church built on this site is the belfry-porch with its four-sided pyramid roof.

Three tiers of arcades and bays stand above the great Roman arch, decorated with Romanesque capitals, which serves as an entrance to the two-aisle church restored in the 16C.

Up in the belfry hangs the great bell of the university, which was cast in 1451. At one time it was used to announce the start of student classes.

▶ **Musée de Chièvres** ⓥ – Fine 16C-18C furniture, also tapestries, ceramics, and enamels from Limoges. **Hôtel Jean-Beaucé** – Handsome Renaissance building.

2 Trois Quartiers

Walking through this pleasant but steep district requires a certain amount of energy! Starting from place Charles-de-Gaulle, follow rue de l'Université and walk past the multimedia library.

Médiathèque ⓥ – The multimedia library is one of the most attractive modern buildings in Poitiers. Inaugurated in 1996, it contains a fine medieval collection and works in close association with the Bibliothèque Nationale de France in Paris.

Walk down rue Cloche-Perse on the right until you reach place de la Liberté then follow rue Pierre-Rat.

Église de Montierneuf – This church belonged to an abbey of the Cluniac order. The sanctuary dating from the 11C was completely remodelled during the Gothic and Classical periods. The west front was rebuilt in the 17C.

Walk along the north side of the church to the garden situated behind the east end.

In the lower Romanesque part of the edifice, note the east-facing transept chapels and the radiating chapels of the apse. The Gothic upper part is flanked by graceful flying buttresses.

Walk up rue Jean-Bouchet and rue de la Chaine which leads onto rue René-Descartes.

Hôtel Fumé – Note the Flamboyant dormer windows adorning the restored façade of no 8 rue Descartes, a 16C building belonging to the university. The courtyard looks most attractive with its stair turret, its **gallery** and corbelled balcony.

Return to place Charles-de-Gaulle via place Charles-VII and rue de la Regratterie.

ADDITIONAL SIGHTS

Quartier épiscopal

★**Cathédrale St-Pierre** – St Peter's Cathedral was begun at the end of the 12C and almost completed by the end of the 14C – the date of its consecration; it is most striking for its huge dimensions.

Exterior – The wide west front, with its rose window and three 13C doorways, is flanked by two asymmetric towers. That on the left *(northern)* side, supported by a series of engaged colonnettes, retains an octagonal storey topped by a balustrade. The tympana of the doorways are carved with fascinating sculptures, among them the *Crowning of the Virgin (left)*; the dead hurrying from their graves and the heavenly elect separated from the damned delivered to Leviathan *(centre)*; the teaching of St Thomas, patron of stone-carvers – the miraculous building of a mystical palace for the King of India *(right)*.

Walk around the northern flank of the cathedral as far as rue Arthur-de-la-Mauvinière.

Note on the way around the massive strength of the buttresses and the absence of flying buttresses. At the far end of the building the dizzy height (49m/161ft) of the flat **east end** can be appreciated – especially as this is emphasised by a falling away of the land.

Interior – On entering, visitors are struck by the sheer power of the architecture: the wide shell of the cathedral is divided into three aisles of almost equal height, and the impression of a perspective soaring away towards the east is accentuated by a progressive narrowing of the aisles and a lowering of the central vault from the chancel onwards.
Twenty-four domed rib vaults – a Plantagenet influence – crown the eight spans of each of the three aisles. Despite its flat exterior, the east end is hollowed out enough to form three apsidal chapels. A cornice embellished with historiated modillions supports a narrow gallery running around the walls above a series of blind arcades. Among the stained-glass windows at the far east end is a late-12C representation of the *Crucifixion* showing a radiant Christ flanked by the Virgin and St John. Above and below this are: the Apostles, with their faces raised towards a Christ in Glory, set in a mandorla; the crucifixion of St Peter and the beheading of St Paul.

The **choir stalls**★, dating from the 13C, are said to be the oldest in France. The carved corner-pieces represent the Virgin and Child, angels carrying crowns, the architect at work etc.
The 18C organ, built by François-Henri Clicquot (1732-90), member of a celebrated dynasty of organ-makers working in Reims and Paris in the 17C and 18C, is located on the inner side of the west front, within a beautiful shell-shaped loft with basket-handled arching.

Walk along rue Ste-Radegonde which starts behind the cathedral then continue along rue Arthur-de-la-Mauvinière.

★**Église Ste-Radegonde** – This former collegiate church was founded around AD 552 by Radegund with the idea that it would eventually become the last resting-place of her nuns from Holy Cross Abbey. The church is characterised by a Romanesque apse and a belfry-porch which stand at opposite ends of a nave in the style known as Angevin Gothic. The belfry-porch, majestic and massive in its proportions, square in plan and then octagonal, was enhanced in the 15C with a Flamboyant portal in the niches of which today stand modern statues of the patron saints of Poitiers. At the base of the tower there remains a chamber, lined with stone benches, where ecclesiastical justice used to be dispensed.
A small garden east of the church offers an agreeable view of the **east end** and the pleasing lines of the church as a whole.

★**Baptistère St-Jean** ⓥ – St John's Baptistery, dating from the middle of the 4C, is the oldest example of Christian architecture in France. It is now buried to a depth of 4m/13ft owing to a progressive series of landslides over the centuries and work on embankments carried out in the 18C. The ditches surrounding the site were dug in the middle of the 19C.
Originally the baptistery comprised two rectangular chambers: the baptismal hall and a narthex, preceded by an entrance corridor framed by two changing-rooms.
The rectangular baptismal hall still exists, together with a 6C-7C quadrangular apse and two apsidal chapels, originally square but changed to a semicircular shape in the middle of the 19C. The former narthex, however, which was restored in the 10C, is now polygonal. Panels of Romanesque brickwork brace the window embrasures, which are partly blocked up and pierced with oculi. Beneath the gables are strange pilasters with capitals carved in bas-relief.

Interior – Inside, the baptistery is notable for the intricately carved capitals of its marble columns, covered with beading, strapwork and foliage in the antique manner; for the colonnettes supporting the arcades; for the three tall arcades, pierced in the wall set back from the entrance doorway, which link the narthex and the baptismal chamber. The apse and its two chapels are surmounted by oven vaults.

In the centre of the baptismal chamber is the **octagonal pool** which was used for baptism by total immersion: the novice convert, whose clothes would have been removed in one of the changing rooms, was first lowered into the water to receive the ritual unction from the bishop, then dressed in a white tunic and solemnly received in the cathedral. In the 7C use of the pool was superseded by baptism by affusion (holy water poured over the head) following the installation of a cistern supplying the font; until the 12C this was the only place in Poitiers where baptisms could be consecrated.

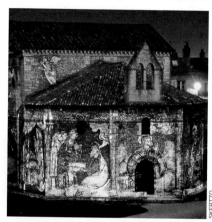

Frescos projected on the walls of St-Jean

SKERTZO

The building now houses an interesting lapidary museum. The exhibits include a fine collection of Merovingian sarcophagi discovered in Poitiers and the surrounding area, inscribed pillars, an ancient *dimière* (a measure used when collecting tithes) carved in stone, and the moulds which were used to produce the decorations adorning the outer walls of the baptistery itself.

Romanesque frescoes – partly over-painted in the 13C and 14C – adorn the baptistery walls: an *Ascension* above the apse; *Christ in Majesty* decorating its oven vault; four horsemen, including the Emperor Constantine, on one of the walls in the rectangular chamber; peacocks, the symbol of immortality, on the left-hand wall. Between 10pm and midnight in summer, the frescoes are projected onto the outer wall of the edifice *(the show lasts approximately 30min)*.

** Musée Ste-Croix Ⓥ – The museum is housed in a modern building standing on the site of the former Holy Cross Abbey (Abbaye Ste-Croix).

Archaeology – *Basement: access down a staircase at the far end of the first hall.* The collections here concentrate on the Poitou of prehistory to medieval times. The chronology of the Palaeolithic Era is set out, with displays of flint implements, tools and other items discovered during digs (fragments of a bronze roasting spit from the 7C BC, an ingot of pure copper, objects buried c 700 BC). A number of Gallo-Roman finds are presented against a backdrop of the remains of antique walls: inscriptions, fragments of columns, bas-relief sculptures and statues, among them the head of a man and a famous **Minerva** in white marble (1C AD) unearthed in Poitiers. Fine funerary stones from Civaux, including Man as a Child, are also on show.

The rest of the collections are displayed in a number of rooms on several different levels linked by stairways or steps.

Painting – The staircase at the end of the archaeology gallery leads to a fine series of paintings from Abbaye Ste-Croix by the Dutch painter Nicolas Van der Maes depicting the 17C **Mysteries of the life of Christ**.

Other paintings include works from the **late 18C**: the local artist, J-A Pajou *(Oedipus cursing Polynices)*, Géricault's circle *(Masculine Anatomy)*. The **19C** is represented by Alfred de Curzon, a local painter *(The Convent Garden)*, Octave Penguilly-l'Haridan *(The Parade of Pierrot)*, Charles Brun *(Portrait of Germaine Pichot)*, and Léopold Burthe *(Ophelia)*. A number of works by **Orientalists** are grouped together, they include: *Jewish Fête in Tangier* by Alfred Dehodencq, *Fantasia* by Eugène Fromentin and *A Street in Constantinople* by André Brouillet.

Sculpture – The collections include a medieval bas-relief, the *Stone-cutter*, found near St-Hilaire-le-Grand, a Renaissance medallion embossed with the features of Christ, a marble bust of Louis XIII from the Château de Richelieu as well as 19C exhibits: an Auguste Ottin marble, a Carrier-Belleuse terracotta, a recumbent plaster effigy of Mademoiselle de Montpensier by James Pradier and a marble by Jean Escoula symbolising Sleep. There is also a reconstruction of the studio of sculptor Jean-René Carrière (1888-1982).

Bronzes include small works by Rodin *(The Man with the Broken Nose* and *The Despairing Adolescent)*, Maillol *(Prairie Nymphs)* and Camille Claudel. A room recently refurbished and devoted to Camille Claudel displays *Desertion* (1888), *The Waltz* (1893), *Deep Thought* (1900) and *Fortune* (1900-04).

Note the bust of the writer Colette by Sarah Lipska.

Ethnological Collections – The first floor houses an exhibit on trades in the urban areas, such as cobbler, wood turner or textile worker, and a curious carousel made by a local postman, Mr Bonnet.

Espace Mendès-France Ⓥ – This modern building houses scientific, technological and industrial exhibitions. The **planetarium** Ⓥ offers a multimedia show about the town.

▶ Faubourg St-Saturnin *(east of the city centre on the opposite bank of the River Clain)*.

★★ St-Hilaire-le-Grand

Archaeological enthusiasts consider this ancient church dedicated to St Hilary to be the most interesting in Poitiers. Before going inside, it is worth walking around the church to admire the group of chapels grafted onto the transept and ambulatory. Each chapel is surrounded by columns with intricately worked capitals, and boasts a cornice decorated with modillions carved with horses' heads, small monsters, foliage...

Interior – The church of St-Hilaire-the-Great, which was completed in 1049, was always an important sanctuary as well as being a large one; the three aisles, covered

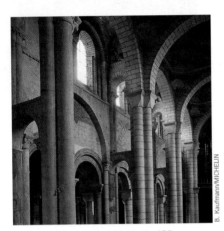

Columns were added in the 12C
to support the vaulting

with timber ceilings, frequently sheltered members of the earliest pilgrimages to Santiago de Compostela. Unfortunately in the 12C the church was ravaged by fire and the gutted timbers were replaced by stone vaults; however, as the distance it was possible to span in stone was naturally less than it was with wooden beams, the architects charged with the restoration were obliged to narrow the aisles. They solved the problem by dividing each of the original side aisles longitudinally in two, adding central columns to support the ribbed vaulting above; at the same time two rows of columns were added to the nave, linked ingeniously to the original walls and bearing a whole series of small domes. The final arrangement – the church as it is today – has a central nave bordered by three aisles on either side – the only seven-aisle church in Europe.

Two of the northern aisles incorporate the 11C belfry, the base of which forms an impressive room with massive columns and remarkable archaic capitals. The vaulting is reinforced with huge string courses.

It is from the transept that the vision and originality of the architecture can best be appreciated. Both transept and **chancel** are raised some way above the level of the aisles. The floor at the front of the chancel is covered with a fine mosaic. The pillars framing it have interesting capitals, notably, on the north side, that representing the burial of St Hilary himself. The ancient frescoes on the four pillars preceding the transept represent bishops of Poitiers. In the chapels, more frescoes illustrate episodes in the lives of St Quentin and St Martin.

The chancel is separated from the ambulatory by a semicircle of eight columns, linked at the base by fine 12C wrought-iron grilles. In the ambulatory, on the main axis of the church, is an unusual statuary group of the *Holy Trinity*: God the Father presenting his Son on the Cross, above which stands the dove of the Holy Spirit. In the **crypt** is a casket (19C) containing the relics of St Hilary.

PONS

Population 4 427
Michelin map 324: G-6 or 233 fold 27

The attractive little town of Pons (pronounced Pon) is built on a hillside, its keep and ramparts overlooking the languid waters of the Seugne, a tributary of the Charente, as it branches out into a myriad of streams flowing through meadows, poplars and willows.

A staging post on the road to Santiago de Compostela in the Middle Ages, Pons became a stronghold of military radicalism and anticlericalism at the turn of the 20C, in the person of its mayor, Émile Combes (1835-1921).

SIGHTS

Castle – It once covered the area now occupied by the square and public gardens. Its owners, the lords of Pons, answered to no one but the King of France; they commanded more than 60 towns and villages and more than 600 parishes and domains, giving rise to the motto, "What the King of France cannot be, the lord of Pons will".

Where to stay

BUDGET

Hôtel Bordeaux – *1 av. Gambetta* – ☎ *05 46 91 31 12* – *closed 15-28 Feb, Sun from Oct to Easter* – 🅿 *– 15 rooms: 30.49/39.64€* – 🍽 *6.10€ – restaurant 13.72/48.78€*. In an old building, this hotel's doors open onto a rather recent decor. Its small rooms are simple and functional. Don't overlook the fare – the reasonable prices and gourmand cooking are worthy of notice. Terrace in the summer.

MODERATE

Auberge Pontoise – *23 av. Gambetta* – ☎ *05 46 94 00 99* – *closed Sun evening and Mon from Oct to Easter* – 🅿 *– 21 rooms: 38.11/60.98€* – 🍽 *6.10€ – restaurant 14.48/35.06€*. Set right in the village, this cosy *auberge* is a popular address with the natives, whether for a fine meal or a good sleep. The cuisine, a blend of traditional and contemporary flavours, features some tasty specialities that justify its reputation.

The 12C **keep★** ⊙ is 30m/100ft high; it was reached by ladders which could be withdrawn if there was a threat. Although the roof ridge, renovated in 1904, is rather fanciful, the rest of the building, supported by narrow buttresses, gives a powerful impression. From the top, there is a **panorama** of the town and valley.

At the foot of the slope, the old seigneurial abode includes a main 17C building flanked by an older staircase turret. It now houses the town hall.

Further on, the charming public gardens forming a terrace along the ramparts offer attractive views overlooking the streams branching out from the Seugne.

Église St-Vivien – *South of the town, near cours Jean-Jaurès*. This former priory chapel with its 12C façade is interesting for its very deep Romanesque door with receding arches and two small belfry arcades; built in the 18C, they provide a serendipitous frame for the gable on the façade.

Église Notre-Dame de l'Hôpital-Neuf – *1km/0.6mi SW of Pons on the old Bordeaux road*. The church was built in the early 12C, and served as the burial place for the lords of Pons until 1793. Today, the building is a mausoleum and a **historical museum** ⊙ devoted to the lords who played such an important role in the history of France.

A hospice was built across from the church in the 12C. These religious establishments, so numerous in the Middle Ages, have rarely survived to the present day. This one, outside the city walls, offered refuge to travellers or pilgrims who arrived at night, after the city gates were closed.

★Vaulted passage – The passage crosses the road to link church and hospice. The entrance to the hospital wards opens under a semicircular arch embellished with designs both organic and geometrical. The eel carved in the stonework is reminiscent of a local legend concerning the slipperiest eel of all, one no one could ever catch.

Along the walls, stone benches allowed pilgrims to rest or wait out storms. The graffiti still visible on the walls recall their passage.

Château d'Usson ⊙ – *1km/0.6mi S on D 249*. A fine example of Renaissance architecture, the château was built by the Rabaine family near Lonzac, two leagues east of Pons. Threatened with destruction at the end of 20C, it was transported and rebuilt, stone by stone, on its present site.

The courtyard is interesting for the variety of its ornamentation: at the back, the gallery with its basket-handle arches is remarkable for its medallions (the 12 Caesars), statues of marmosets, engraved maxims etc. At the end of one of the wings, a tower with its original roof is carved with coats of arms and emblems (shells and crescents from the Rabaine arms) and, just under the edge of the roof, a frieze divided into panels by short, hollow columns.

Inside, note the drawing room decorated with fine Regency **wood panelling★**, white with gold borders, from the château in Choisy-le-Roi and, in the main hall, the door of the former chapel, sculpted by Nicolas Bachelier, a pupil of Michelangelo.

▶ Pérignac, Échebrune, Lonzac, Chadenac, Dolmen de St-Fort-sur-le-Né, Marignac, Abbaye de la Tenaille, Château de Plassac, Fléac-sur-Seugne, Avy.

PORNIC ♨

Population 11 903
Michelin map 316: D-5 or 232 fold 26

A narrow inlet sheltering a small fishing port, historical quarters clustered on a hillside, stately homes with gardens full of parasol pines, a golf course, sheltered sandy beaches, a large marina and a thalassotherapy centre make Pornic a popular seaside resort, which boasts a long list of famous visitors from the 19C onwards: George Sand, Gustave Flaubert, Auguste Renoir, Lenin, Marc Elder, Max Ernst...

SIGHTS

Old town – Once a fortified town, it was naturally protected to the south by the port and to the west by the valley known today as the Jardin de Retz. The castle and ramparts, now replaced by promenade de la Terrasse and Rue de la Douve, constituted the defence system.

The fishing port – From the end of the port which mainly shelters fishing boats and an occasional coastal vessel, see the buildings of town cluster on the hillside, and directly opposite, the cove and the silhouette of the castle at its entrance.

Castle – Hidden deep in the greenery, Pornic Castle, of granite construction, overlooks Plage du Château below. Once surrounded by water, access was via a drawbridge later replaced by a fixed bridge over rue des Sables.
Built in the 13C-14C, it belonged to the famous Gilles de Rais or Bluebeard *(see TIFFAUGES)*; it was renovated in the 19C.

Promenade de la Terrasse – Built on the site of the old ramparts, the view from the walkway is lovely: the castle and the Jardin de Retz, with its many plant nurseries.

★ **Corniche de la Noéveillard** – *30min round trip on foot. Take the path along the coast from Plage du Château.* It joins another path jutting out over the sea; as you walk along, the view over Pornic cove, the rocks and ocean changes. Eventually, the path overlooks the facilities of the large marina, before winding its way to the fine sandy beach of Plage de la Noéveillard.

Corniche de Gourmalon – The road runs along the edge of the corniche, above Anse aux Lapins Beach, then on to Pointe de Gourmalon headland. Views of Pornic, the castle, Corniche de la Noéveillard.

Dolmen des Mousseaux – *Signposted from Plage du Château.* This double walkway, covered by stones arranged in tiers, apparently doubled as a tomb and a prestigious monument for Neolithic farmers in about 3500 BC. The two chambers have a characteristic commonly found near the Loire Estuary: a corridor joins the side chambers, somewhat like the transept of a church.

CÔTE DE JADE

From Pornic to Pointe de St-Gildas

14 km/8.4mi via D751 – 45min

From Pornic to St-Brévin-les Bains, popular seaside resorts adorn the coastline of the Pays de Retz, known as the **Jade Coast**, in honour of the deep green colour of the water there. Between Pornic and St-Gildas, the line of schist cliffs is broken by creeks and sandy alcoves, making the landscape especially appealing.

Pornic – View of the old town from Gourmalon

BED AND BREAKFAST …

Cupidon Bed and Breakfast – *Plage du Portmain – 44210 Ste-Marie – 6km/3.5mi W of Pornic on the coast road* – ☎ *02 51 74 19 61* – ✉ *– 4 rooms: 42/50€.* Only 50m/55yd from Portmain Beach, this contemporary house was designed as a shore chalet, made of wood and snug as can be. The beach begins across the street, but if it's too crowded you can always take a dip in the pool or borrow a bicycle!

LUNCH AND DINNER

La Godille – *La Noëveillard – Port de Plaisance* – ☎ *02 40 82 44 67 – closed 11 Nov to 3 Jan, Tue evening and Wed except during the high season – reservations recommended weekends and summertime – 10.37/21.04€.* This restaurant's bay windows open onto a tangle of sailboat masts. On the wharf, its well-groomed decor of wood and polished metal evokes a boat deck so that sailors can feel at home and would-be adventurers can make believe… Air-conditioned.

Ste-Marie – Near Mombeau Beach, a cliff top path provides a pretty **view** of the rocky coastline speckled with sandy beaches. Fishing nets hang from poles upright in the water.

Follow the signs Le Porteau par la Côte.

From Sablons beach to Porteau, the road goes along the sea above the ragged coastline. From Porteau to Préfailles, the road leaves the coast; ramblers can continue on the Tour de Pays de Retz trail high above the ocean.

* Pointe de St-Gildas – *Leave the car in the car park near the marina.* The point of land is covered with short grass, growing fitfully over the vestiges of the Atlantic wall; shell cliffs extend out to meet the breakers. It was off Pointe St-Gildas that the steamship *St-Philibert* sunk in June of 1931, drowning 500 day trippers returning from Noirmoutier Island. From the far end of the point, the view opens up to the coast of Brittany, between St-Nazaire and Le Croisic and all the way to Noirmoutier, sitting low on the horizon.

PAYS DE RETZ

Round tour from Pornic

130km/80mi – allow one day

Drive SE out of Pornic.

The road runs along the coast to Moutiers-en-Retz which offers fine views of Bourgneuf Bay and Noirmoutier Island.

Bourgneuf en Retz – Important crossroads on the way to the beaches of Bourgneuf Bay (north) and the oyster beds of the Vendée region (south).

The **Musée du Pays de Retz** Ⓥ *(6 rue des Moines)* is housed in the 17C buildings of an old monastery. It includes sections on archaeology, collections of local headdresses and costumes, reconstructions of traditional workshops etc.

Leave Bourgneuf E along D 13.

Machecoul – The historic capital of Pays de Retz stages shows illustrating the history of the region.

Drive NE on D 64, turn right onto D 71 2km/1.2mi beyond St-Même-le-Tenu and right again onto D 61 in St-Lumine-de-Coutais.

St-Philbert-de-Grand-Lieu – The ancient abbey church and the Maison du Lac are both accessible via the tourist office.

Abbatiale St-Philbert Ⓥ – Erected in the 9C, the abbey church was altered during the Revolution and again in 1870 but was later partly restored to its original aspect. Inside, note the austere nave with its massive pillars; it was built of brick and stone, a technique inherited from the Romans… and some of the stones date from the Roman period. The crypt has openings designed to enable the congregation to see the 7C marble sarcophagus which, until 858, contained the remains of St Philbert.

Maison du Lac Ⓥ – This ornithological museum is devoted to the 225 species of sedentary and migratory birds living close to Lac de Grand-Lieu. There is an audio-visual presentation of the local fauna and flora.

Drive N out of St-Philbert along D 65.

Lac de Grand-Lieu – This was once a true lake but over the past 100 years, an insidious invasion of vegetation has gradually converted it into an immense and forbidding swamp-like marsh. The shores are thick with rushes, reeds and clumps of furze making it an exceptional ornithological site.

The lake, which is linked to the Loire estuary by the Achenau (*cheneau* is a local word for canal), was officially declared a nature reserve in 1980. It covers 4 000ha/10 000 acres in summer and 8 000ha/20 000 acres in winter. The rocky bottom, at depths ranging from 1m/3ft- to 2m/6ft depending on the season, is sometimes covered with a thick bed of silt. It is said that the ancient town of Herbauge, cursed for its dissolute morals, is buried beneath this shroud. According to legend, the muffled tolling of its church bell can be heard in the middle of the swamp at midnight on Christmas Eve.

The lake lies directly below one of the regular Atlantic migration routes and is the temporary home of more than 200 species of birds, including ducks, geese, teal, snipe, corncrake, rail and grebe. It is also an important nesting site for grey heron and the rare spoonbill.

Boat trips ⓥ are allowed only very rarely on the lake, whose natural beauties can be discovered by visiting the local museums (La Maison du Pêcheur and La Maison du Lac in St-Philibert-le-Grand-Lieu). The annual Fête des Pêcheurs *(15 August and the following Sunday)* is the occasion for a colourful regatta and water games.

Passay – This typical inland fishing hamlet is the only place from which it is possible to approach the mysterious Lac de Grand-Lieu.

Maison du Pêcheur ⓥ – This small museum, housed in an **observation tower** overlooking the marsh and its surroundings, reveals the secrets of an unusually rich ecosystem. The fauna and flora of the area, as well as associated activities – especially local fishing techniques – are clearly and simply presented and explained. Indigenous species (perch, pike, carp and eel) can be viewed in the museum's aquariums.

Continue NE along D 65 and, in Pont-St-Martin, turn W onto D 11. In Bouaye, take the road to the S, which leads to St-Mars-de-Coutais.

★★ Planète sauvage ⓥ – More than 2 000 animals roam freely through the sparsely wooded hills and plains, interspersed with lakes and ponds. The park consists of two tours: one by car and the other on foot.

Safari track – ⚙ After passing through the disinfecting basin, the driver must proceed very slowly along the 10km/6mi of tracks winding through bushland and savannah. There are 13 enclosures, where visitors can discover different animals at close

quarters: hippopotami and elephants playing water games, a herd of galloping bison, agile impalas and springboks, majestic stags in full-antler combat, bears napping on the rocks, tigers wrestling, lions regally sprawling in the sun, painted hyenas snarling, giraffes placidly nibbling greenery, and more. While car windows must be closed at all times, it is still quite exciting to see wild animals at such close range, in natural habitats.

Safari Village – The village has various leisure facilities including a playground, a picnic area, restaurants, shops, cultural facilities (a very· attractive thematic exhibition room), and walking paths through a replica of a bush village.

Pachyderms at play

S. Sauvignier/MICHELIN

The tour can begin with the **Arche des Reptiles** (a vivarium containing snakes and crocodiles in a dimly lit environment) and a miniature animal farm (20 species), followed by the **Sea Lion show** and **Île des Siamangs** where screeching monkeys mingle with flocks of pink flamingos, marabou and pelicans along the banks of the lake. An exotic garden leads to the **Forêt de Singes** (keep to the marked footpaths), inhabited by rhesus monkeys.

Drive to Port-St-Père and continue N on D 103.

Le Pellerin – Here you can catch a ferry across the River Loire.

Drive westwards along D 58 via Rouans to D 266 and turn left. The road runs through Princé Forest. Turn right to Chauvé and pick up D 6 which leads back to Pornic.

POUZAUGES

Population 5 473
Michelin map 316: K-7 or 232 fold 42

Pouzauges stands at the heart of the hills of the Vendée, on the slope of a hill crowned by the Bois de la Folie and overlooking the expanse of the *bocage*.

SIGHTS

Château – This medieval fortress comprises walls incorporating 10 ruined towers, and a square keep, flanked by turrets, which protected the entrance. A cross recalls the 32 Vendée Royalists who were shot here during the Revolution.

Église St-Jacques – St James' Church was built of granite in the Vendée style with a square tower over the crossing; it has a short nave and a 12C transept which is in a transitional Romanesque-Gothic style. The large, Flamboyant Gothic chancel with three bays is 15C.

EXCURSIONS

★ **Moulins du Terrier-Marteau** – *1km/0.6mi along D 752 and a minor road on the right; not open to the public.* On the right-hand side are the quaint white windmills of the region with their shingle roofs. It is pleasant just to watch the canvas sails go round. These two windmills, built in the 19C, have been restored and still have their mobile roof, so that the sails can be turned to catch the wind, using a *guivre* (long pole). Attractive **view**★ of the farmland crisscrossed with trees and hedges to the west.

Bois de la Folie – *Near Le Terrier-Marteau.* This was probably a *luccus*, or sacred wood, in Roman times, after being a meeting place for the Druids who gathered mistletoe and performed ritual sacrifices.
The wood, situated on a mound of granite, has oak, pine and beech trees. This thick, isolated clump of trees, visible from afar, was known to the locals as *Pouzauges Bouquet*, or the Vendée Lighthouse. It affords a **view**★ of the typical farmland to the north-east.

BETWEEN SÈVRE NANTAISE AND GRAND LAY

Round trip 75km/145mi – 6hr

Leave Pouzauges SW along D 43 and turn right onto D 113.

Château du Bois-Tiffrais – The château houses the **Musée de la France protestante de l'Ouest** ⓥ which traces the trials and tribulations of Protestantism in western France, especially in the region of Poitou. Well-documented explanatory panels illustrate the major events – Calvin's sermon in Poitou (1534), the Edict of Nantes (1598), revocation of the Edict of Nantes (1685), which led to Protestant emigration and the practice of secret worship during the period known as The Desert, and finally, the Edict of Tolerance (1787). Various exhibits, including Bibles and copies of *méreaux* (medals which enabled the pastor to identify the clandestine faithful) and a collapsible pulpit (for assemblies held in secret), recall the days of oppression.

Continue along D 113 then follow the Chantonnay road, turning right after 2km/1.2mi.

Sails to the wind

Prieuré de Chassay-Grammont ⓥ – This monastery founded by Richard the Lionheart in c 1196, has been massively restored. It is a good example of the architecture of the Order of Grammont, a community of hermits who lived in secluded spots and attached great importance to poverty. Their monasteries were sober and without ornamentation.

At Chassay, all of the monastic buildings as well as the church, are built around a cloistered courtyard. The church has a single nave stripped of all embellishments. The only light came from three windows in the apsidal chapel. On the ground floor, the chapter-house with its Romanesque vaulting and the large refectory, whose 13C Anjou-Gothic vaulting has been restored, have a certain elegance. The monks' dormitory is on the first floor.

Return and cut across D 960bis. Turn left in Sigournais then right in Chavagnes onto D 89.

Mouilleron-en-Pareds – *See MOUILLERON-EN-PAREDS.*

Leave Mouilleron NE along D 8.

Église de Pouzauges-le-Vieux – The granite **church** dates from the Romanesque period, apart from the chancel which was remodelled in the 14C, and stands in an attractive landscape dotted with cypresses. The pure lines of its architecture – its strong, simple doorway, extended transept and short, square tower over the crossing – became a model for many other churches in the region. Beneath the broken-barrel vaulting of the interior are a floor paved with funerary stones and walls painted with 13C **murals**: note in particular the *Conversation between the Virgin and an Angel*.

Take D 49 in the direction of Montournais.

Puy Crapaud – At an altitude of 270m/885ft, it is one of the highest points on the Vendée hills. It is crowned with the remains of a windmill, converted into a restaurant. *For access to the viewing table (steep staircase), ask at the local bar.* From the top of the windmill, there is a vast **panorama**★★ of the whole of the Vendée region as far as the sea. The view of the hills stretching out between Pouzauges and St-Michel-Mont-Mercure is particularly attractive.

Continue on D 49; at Montournais, take D 8 N to St-Mesmin.

About 1km/0.6mi beyond St-Mesmin, on the road to Cerisay, are the medieval ruins of the picturesquely located **Château de St-Mesmin** – the machicolations of the keep are still intact.

At the crossroads, turn left on the small road which joins D 27.

La Pommeraie-sur-Sèvre – In the Gothic **church**, with its elegant Plantagenet vaulting in the nave, 15C frescoes depict the seven capital sins, symbolised by figures on animals. There is a Roman bridge across the Sèvre.

Leave La Pommeraie-sur-Sèvre and take D 43 W to return to Pouzauges.

Le PUY DU FOU★★

Michelin map 316: K-6 or 232 fold 42 – 2.5km/1.5mi NE of Les Herbiers

On summer evenings the château sparkles under the lights of its famous Son et Lumière show in which a cast of hundreds stages an open-air historical pageant; by day the museum evokes the entire past of the Vendée region, while various attractions lure visitors into the 12ha/30 acres of grounds.

The name Puy du Fou is derived from the Latin: *puy* (from *podium*) means an eminence, a knoll; *fou* (from *fagus*) designates a beech tree. Thus a hill where a beech tree grows or, less lyrically, Beechmount.

★★★CINÉSCÉNIE ⓥ

Not open to the public during the day. 13 500 seats. The terrace below the rear façade of the château, together with the ornamental lake below it, makes an agreeable background for the Cinéscénie spectacular, in which the story of Jacques Maupillier, peasant of the Vendée, and the history of the Vendée region come to life with the help of 800 actors and 50 horsemen in a dazzling show, including an impressive array of special effects, fountains, fireworks, laser and other lighting displays.

Where to eat

MODERATE

Restaurant L'Auberge – *Domaine du Puy du Fou – 85590 Les Épesses –* ☎ *02 51 57 68 68 – reservation required – 19.82/33.54€.* In the north end of the Puy du Fou grounds, this *auberge* proposes meals prepared with tasty regional products in a convivial setting. Costumed service and a tempting fixed-price Gourmets menu.

SPECIAL EFFECTS INCLUDED

La Halle Renaissance – *Grand Parc du Puy du Fou – 85590 Les Épesses –* ☎ *02 51 64 11 11 – www.puydufou.com – May: Sat-Sun; early Jun to mid-Sep – closed holidays – adults: 21.34€, children: 10.67€.* Situated behind the *Espace Souvenir*, this enormous room is where dinner shows are staged. Three rooms, one on top of the other, face a stage where the Puy du Fou emcee introduces each of the dishes served by the eager pages. The grand master comes to thank visitors on horseback.

Le Relais de Poste – *Grand Parc du Puy du Fou – 85590 Les Épesses –* ☎ *02 51 64 11 11 – from beginning Jun to mid-Sep: 11:45am, 1:30pm; additional sittings on Cinéscénie evenings: 6:30pm and 8:15pm; May: Sat-Sun – 16.01€.* In the north end of the site, a handsome room with exposed beams opens onto tables in a courtyard where feast lovers gather to enjoy meals animated by musicians and dancers.

CHÂTEAU

It is likely that the original castle, built in the 15C and 16C, was never completed; it was in any case partly destroyed by fire during the Vendée Wars. A fine late Renaissance pavilion remains at the far end of the courtyard, preceded by a peristyle with recessed Ionic columns. This now serves as the entrance to the museum. The left wing of the château is built over a long gallery.

★**Écomusée de la Vendée** ⓥ – In the museum entrance there is a fine staircase with straight flights of steps, and a coffered ceiling.
The first section of the museum proper is concerned with the region's past, from its geological formation to the end of the Ancien Régime: each main period is evoked thematically, with complementary displays of contemporary objects and reconstructions (a Megalithic tomb, a Gallo-Roman kitchen, a Romanesque façade).
The second (post-Revolution) section begins with an examination of the Vendée Wars, an audio-visual montage tracing the military operations from 1793 to 1796.
Following this, the emergence of a local folk memory based on local fables, memoirs and accounts written in the 18C and early 19C – a corpus of material structured and given official approval under the Restoration – is explained; it found expression in an abundant iconography (portraits of Vendée heroes), a recognisable literary current and indeed royal rewards.

G.IE/Le Puy du Fou

Le Puy du Fou – Cinéscénie

The legend of Saint Philibert

By the end of the 19C, however, a Republican vision opposed to this view had appeared. Revolutionary heroes such as Bara and Hoche were revered, while official art imposed a Breton image on the combatants in the west.

Finally the museum includes a review of the industrial heritage of the Vendée. One of the most interesting exhibits is an early-20C steam engine designed by Piguet which drives a carding machine.

★★ GRAND PARC ⊙

The entire Puy du Fou estate extends over 35ha/86 acres. Numerous paths surrounding the château, skirting lakes or crossing dense woods of chestnut trees offer pleasant walks with a choice of interesting diversions.

Fauna

On the way up to the castle, explanatory panels line the path linking several **aviaries**★★ containing birds of prey.

Farm animals★, among them the famous *baudets*, graze inside large enclosures and a peasant can be seen guiding his team of oxen in and out of the old stables.

Reconstructed **underground galleries** show the life and habits of rabbits and foxes.

In the **wolves' lair**, you can hear the story of the last wolf who roamed the area in 1908...

Flora

A pleasant trail through the **Arboretum de France**★ provides useful information about a great variety of plants.

There is also a **heather trail** and a **Renaissance rose garden**★ containing 100 different species.

Another trail, known as the **Vallée fleurie**★★, lined with various plants and trees, winds round ponds and waterfalls.

Remembering the Vendée Wars

This historic trail can upset young children and sensitive persons.

The underground trail is lined with dramatic scenes of massacres perpetrated during the Vendée Wars.

Music

Every 15min, a **peal** of 21 bells plays ancient melodies and regional characters come alive every 30min.

Costumed musicians forming a **brass quintet**★ play Baroque music.

It is possible for visitors to control the play of **fountains** from a distance.

Shows

★★ **Fête de Chevalerie** – *25min show; 3 500 seats.* Knights in splendid costumes take part in tournaments and jousting displays to attract the attention of the beautiful Catherine du Puy du Fou. Parades and riding feats complete this colourful show.

Bataille du Donjon – *30min show; 3 500 seats*. Reconstruction of the battle which led to the first Puy du Fou castle being taken by the English in 1429. Stunts and special effects.

★★ **Grand spectacle de Fauconnerie** – *30min show; 1 700 seats*. The ruins of a 13C **castle** provide the background for a display of falconry – free-flying trained birds – with running commentary by a falconer in period costume.

★★★ **La légende de St-Philibert** – *30min show; 3 000 seats*. Spectacular special effects (a longship emerging from the water), cavalcades and fighting illustrate the story of this monk who died in Noirmoutier in 685.

★ **Le magicien-ménestrel** – *20min show; 800 seats*. Jugglers vie for the applause of bystanders with feats of skill and virtuosity beneath the ramparts of the medieval city.

★★ **Théâtre d'eau** – *20min show; 600 seats*. A fairy like display of 1 500 computer-controlled fountains enhanced by spectacular light effect.

Théâtre pour enfants – *15min show; 400 seats*. Puppet show for children.

Villages

Three villages of different periods have been reconstructed north of the site.

Inside the **Fort de l'an Mil**★★, craftsmen can be seen at work in their thatched stone houses.

A drawbridge leads to the **Cité médiévale**★★★ protected by its ramparts. Inside, craftsmen and minstrels walk about their business along the narrow lanes.

In the **18C village**★★, the work of craftsmen in period costume can be admired while musicians perform a serenade and jugglers demonstrate their virtuosity.

Île de RÉ★

Michelin map 324: C-3 or 233 folds 2, 13 – off the coast near La Rochelle

The Île de Ré points a long finger seawards just off the port of La Rochelle, cutting in two the gulf between the Île d'Oléron and the Vendée coast. The island is bordered to the north by the Breton Straits (Pertuis Breton) and to the south by the Straits of Antioche.

This unspoilt island, its surface broken only by vineyards and an occasional pinewood, has become a favourite retreat for summer holiday-makers in search of sunshine, sea air and wide open spaces. Although a bridge now links it to the mainland it retains most of its insular character and its famous salt-marshes. Numerous blazed cycle-tracks allow visitors to crisscross the island in peace and quiet.

WHITE ISLE, RED-COATS

Anglo-French rivalry – From the Hundred Years War to the fall of Napoleon, the Île de Ré was closely involved in the conflict between the English and the French, during which the "red-coats" (the English) made many attempts to storm its shores: it would have been an invaluable base so close to mainland France. Nor was the isle spared during the Wars of Religion, which brought misery and deprivation to the inhabitants.

Dunes on pointe du Fier

S. Sauvignier/MICHELIN

In 1625 the brave Marquis de **Toiras** (1585-1636), a deeply spiritual and fiercely warlike man, was governor of the island, which he had wrested from the Protestants and then reinforced by building the St-Martin citadel and the fort of La Prée. At that time, the whole island was under arms. An English fleet commanded by the Duke of Buckingham anchored off Les Sablanceaux and columns of infantry poured ashore to lay siege to the town of St-Martin, defended by 1 400 French, and the fort of La Prée. In no time there was an acute shortage of provisions. There were rations for less than a single day left when the miracle occurred: a squadron of 30 ships from the French fleet appeared in the Breton Straits and, with a favourable wind, managed to penetrate the harbour at St-Martin.

The siege, nevertheless, continued. On 6 November 1625, 6 000 Englishmen, encouraged by a mass singing of psalms, hurled themselves at the town walls. After a bloody hand-to-hand battle they were however repulsed.

It was then that Louis XIII, arriving at La Rochelle, despatched a contingent of reinforcements to the island, under the leadership of Marshal de Schomberg. The English, caught between two fires, were attacked at Pont de Feneau, near Loix, and massacred, leaving 2 000 dead on the field together with 6 cannon and 46 flags. Toiras was created Marshal of France in 1630.

The land and its inhabitants – L'Île de Ré, sometimes known as "L'Île Blanche", extends in a northwesterly direction for almost 30km/18mi. It largely comprises a series of Jurassic limestone outliers forming islets – principally Loix, Ars and Ré proper – which have become linked together.

In the north the deeply indented bay of Fier d'Ars, and the marshes surrounding it, constitute the **Réserve Naturelle de Lilleau des Niges**, the home of thousands of different species of birds including grey curlews, widgeon, teal, silver plovers and geese. In the south a line of sand dunes has formed on a rocky plateau which stretches far away beneath the sea; the jagged cliffs eaten away by the encroaching tides have given rise to the name of this area: La Côte Sauvage (The Wild Coast).

The southeastern part of the Île de Ré, the widest and most fertile, is broken up into tiny smallholdings producing early fruit and vegetables, asparagus and above all vines (the wine, red, white and rosé, is full-favoured, with a hint of algae in the after-taste). The fortified apéritif-wine made here on the island is as good as the better-known Pineau des Charentes.

To the north and west the vines share the land with pines, as far as La Couarde. Beyond that, Ars-en-Ré is salt-marsh country – although the marshes are fast disappearing.

Quichenotte headdress

S. Sauvignier/MICHELIN

The people of Ré – the Rétais – are landlubbers rather than seafaring folk. Of the riches of the ocean they deal only in *sart* (seaweed and other wrack), harvested with huge rakes, shellfish and the prawns which teem on the rocky *platin* exposed at low tide. In addition, oyster farming has been introduced to the Fosse de Loix and Fier d'Ars inlets.

In the past the women of the island wore a long, narrow headdress to protect them against the fierceness of the sun; its name, the **quichenotte**, is said to derive from "kiss not", as its function was also, allegedly, to discourage the advances of amorous invading Englishmen. Today this tradition, like many others, has all but vanished – the island donkeys, for instance, which have disappeared entirely, were bedecked with straw hats and picturesque striped or plaid "trousers" to keep away flies and mosquitoes in the salt-marshes. Such things can now be seen only on postcards in the village shops. The villages are scattered all over the island, their single-storey houses, dazzling white, with typically green shutters, are brightened with hollyhocks, delphiniums and scarlet salvia, or a wisteria on a trellis.

ACCESS AND BOAT TRIPS

Boat trips ⊙ – There are cruises in season, and direct links to the Île d'Aix.

The viaduct ⊙ – This gracefully-curving toll bridge, opened in 1988, is one of the engineering marvels of Europe, carrying the road 2 960m/nearly 2mi across the narrows separating the Île de Ré from the suburbs of La Rochelle. The viaduct reaches a maximum height of 32m/105ft above the level of the highest tides.

ST-MARTIN-DE-RÉ

★ST-MARTIN-DE-RÉ

The island capital, formerly an active port and a military stronghold, has turned gracefully into a charming tourist centre. The narrow streets, quiet, spotlessly clean, still bumpy with cobblestones, have largely managed to retain the atmosphere of the Grand Siècle (the 17C in France).

★Fortifications – These date back to the early 17C but were entirely refashioned by Vauban after the siege of 1625 *(see above)*. Vauban came to inspect the Île de Ré in 1674 with the aim of strengthening the defences of the naval installations created by Colbert at Rochefort in 1666; the fortifications he designed for St-Martin were completed in 1692.

The walled enclosure was pierced by two monumental gateways, Porte Toiras and Porte des Campani, preceded by ravelins (half-moon defences) and with guard-rooms on the inner face.

The **citadel**, built in 1681, was used as a prison under the Ancien Régime (19C) and later became a religious penitentiary.

The citadel is not open to the public but a walk around the bastions on the seaward side reveals pleasing **views** of the Breton Straits and the mainland; note also the interesting watch-turrets and the cannon embrasures. The defensive point's main entrance takes the form of a majestic Classical gateway with a pediment bearing carved military emblems. The citadel has its own small port, between two bastions in front of this gateway.

Beyond the citadel and the tennis courts below it lies a beach of fine sand.

Parc de la Barbette – This park, sheltered by the fortifications, is a pleasant place for a shady stroll, looking down on the sea and the distant southern coast of the Vendée. Holm oaks, acacias, parasol pines and locust trees lend the park an almost Mediterranean air.

Hôtel de Clerjotte – Tall slate roofs crown this fine building constructed in a style midway between Flamboyant Gothic and Renaissance. It was originally the headquarters of an organisation owing allegiance to the local ruler, the Officiers des Seigneurs de Ré, and was at one time used as the town arsenal.

Today the building houses a museum and the tourist information centre. In the courtyard, bordered with Renaissance galleries, stands a staircase-tower at the foot of which is an elegant Flamboyant doorway.

Musée Ernest-Cognacq ⊘ – The maritime history of St-Martin and the island as a whole is presented through models, ships' figureheads, ancient weapons and tableaux (combat scenes, portraits of mariners, Napoleon's return from the Isle of Elba

Eating out

BUDGET

Les Embrums – *6 r. Chay-Morin – Îlot – 17410 St-Martin-de-Ré – ☎ 05 46 09 63 23 – closed 6 Jan to 4 Feb, Sun evening and Thu except Jul-Aug – 14.48/19.82€.* Behind its green shutters, this little restaurant serves food fresh from the marketplace with a spotlight on fish. Chalked onto a slate menu, it changes with the seasons and blends perfectly with the fishing paraphernalia decor on the obligatory white and blue background.

MODERATE

Le Chat Botté – *r. Mairie – 17590 St-Clément-des-Baleines – ☎ 05 46 29 42 09 – closed 10 Jan to 15 Feb, 22 Nov to 21 Dec and Mon from 15 Sep to 1 Apr – 19.82/56.41€.* You go through the bar to enter this regional-style house near the church. Its large, recently renovated dining room gives onto a terrace and garden. Decor in shades of wood and modern furniture for traditional cuisine, proposed in fixed-price menus.

Le Bistrot de Bernard – *1 quai de la Criée – 17590 Ars-en-Ré – ☎ 05 46 29 40 26 – closed 7 Jan to 28 Feb, 12 Nov to 19 Dec, Mon evening and Tue in Mar, Oct and Nov – 19.82/26.68€.* On the wharf, this old, typical house has charm to spare...With its terrace in front in the summer and its pretty dining room looking out on a courtyard garden, this is a very pleasant place to dine. Marine decor in keeping with the fish on the menu.

L'Auberge de la Rivière – *17880 Les Portes-en-Ré – 1km/à.6mi W of les Portes-en-Ré on D 101 – ☎ 05 46 29 54 55 – closed Jan, 15 Nov to 15 Dec and Wed off- season – 19.82/56.41€.* At the tip of the island, this relatively recent establishment is separated from the road by a garden. The well-prepared cuisine is a favorite with the locals. Choose the second room, more attractive with its round tables in white laquered wood. Interesting set-price menu during the week.

Lavardin – *r. H. Lainé – 17630 La Flotte – ☎ 05 46 09 68 32 – closed Tue-Wed off-season – 19.06€ lunch. – 25.15/51.83€.* The dining room has painted wood sidings and paintings showing island landscapes. Contemporary cuisine and a few Danish specialities.

La Bouvette – *Le Morinand – 17580 Le Bois-Plage-en-Ré – 2km/1.2mi SE of St-Martin-de-Ré via D 201E2 – ☎ 05 46 09 29 87 – closed 3 weeks in Jan – 13.72€ lunch – 27.44€.* Next to the Morinand mill, this former wine storehouse is now a restaurant. Step inside and try just-caught fish grilled on a wood fire or a meat dish. The slate menu changes with the seasons. Very relaxed atmosphere.

Where to stay

BUDGET

Hôtel L'Hippocampe – *r. du Château des Mauléons – 17630 La Flotte – ☎ 05 46 09 60 68 – 14 rms: 20.58/38.11€ – ☲ 4.57€.* This 1927 house profits from the calm of a peaceful street in the village. Albeit modest, the interior design is slowly evolving. The small and simple rooms are still somewhat out-moded. Breakfast served outside in the summer.

Camping La Tour des Prises – *rte d'Ars – 17670 La Couarde-sur-Mer – 4km/2.4mi E of Ars-en-Ré via D 735 – ☎ 05 46 29 84 82 – open Apr to Sep – reservations recommended – 150 sites: 27.44€.* Trees and cypress hedges lend a shady, natural feeling to this stone-walled campground. Heated pool, games room and mobile home rental. Grab a bicycle, queen of the island, for the 5 minute ride to the *plage des Prises*.

Sénéchal – *6 r. Gambetta – 17590 Ars-en-Ré – ☎ 05 46 29 40 42 – closed 13 Nov to 19 Dec and 3 Jan to 29 Mar – 16 rms: 35.06/99.09€ – ☲ 6.40€.* This old island hotel just got a facelift. White stones, blond wood and colourful textiles in the renovated rooms. Pleasant patio.

Camping Interlude-Gros Jonc – *Plage de Gros Jonc – 17580 Le Bois-Plage-en-Ré – 4km/2.4mi S of St-Martin. Take D 201E2 then rte de Gros Jonc – ☎ 05 46 09 18 22 – interlude@iledere.com – open 31 Mar to 22 Sep – reservation recommended – 300 sires: 35.52€.* Just 150m from the beach, in a landscaped park, you can choose between your tent, a mobile home or a chalet. Sports and leisure include covered and open-air pools, *pétanque*, ping-pong and a fitness room. Plenty of games for the kids, too.

MODERATE

Français – *cours F. Faure – 17630 La Flotte – ☎ 05 46 09 60 06 – closed 16 Nov to 30 Mar – 29 rms: 42.69/73.18€ – ☲ 5.34€.* Amid the lively ambience of the port, this modest hotel offers small and impeccably tidy rooms. Those of the nearby annex buildings are calmer.

Le Clos Bel Ébat – *17 r. de la Grainetière – 17630 La Flotte* – ☎ *05 46 09 61 49 – closed Jan to Mar* – 🗇 – *3 rms: 60.98/83.85€.* The pretty little rooms (two-night minimum in season) of this ancient spirit storehouse are perfect for a romantic sojourn as well as for large families because they have communicating doors. A nice touch: the breakfast basket set in front of your bedroom door each morning.

Domaine de la Baronnie Bed and Breakfast – *21 r. Baron de Chantal – 17410 St-Martin-de-Ré* – ☎ *05 46 09 21 29 – closed 4 Nov to 28 Mar* – 🗇 – *5 rms: 116/146€* – 🍽 *10€.* A unique address on the island! This superb registered mansion, tastefully restored, offers calm rooms of refined comfort. One of them, a duplex in the tower, has a splendid view of the garden and roofs of St. Martin. Breakfast served in a charming room.

aboard the brig Inconstant...). These seafaring displays are supplemented with a collection of pottery from Delft and porcelain from China, a reminder of the island's former maritime trade with the rest of the world.

The Port – Trade with Canada and the West Indies brought the port of St-Martin great prosperity during the 17C. Pleasure craft and a few fishing boats have now, however, replaced the tall ships sailing from the north in search of salt or wine, and the schooners from the Caribbean laden with spices. Port and harbour between them girdle the old sailors' district, now busy with shops, forming a picturesque islet which is popular with visitors. The quays are paved with the ballast of long-gone merchant ships.

Église St-Martin ⓥ – The church dates from the 15C and was nicknamed "the big fort" because of the fortifications (still visible from the transept) which protected it. Ruined by the Anglo-Dutch naval bombardment of 1696, it was restored in the early 18C. A chapel dedicated to sailors contains 18C and 19C votive offerings.

Ancien Hôtel des Cadets de la Marine – This building houses both the town hall and the post office. It was built in the 18C to be used as barracks for a company of naval cadets. At the beginning of the 20C Ernest Cognacq, a merchant who founded the famous La Samaritaine department store in Paris, made a gift of it to his native town.

TOUR OF THE ISLAND

Round tour from Pointe de Sablanceaux

75km/47mi – allow one day

The road, D 735, follows the coast as far as Fort de La Prée, built as part of the ring of defences around La Rochelle. Take the first road to the right.

Ancienne Abbaye des Châteliers – The ruins of this Cistercian abbey founded in the 12C and destroyed in 1623 stand, with the wind whistling through them, on the bleak moorland carpeting Les Barres promontory. The remains of the abbey church include the west front and walls tracing the outline of a nave and a flattened east end in the style of Citeaux Abbey. The chancel was lit via an elegant window. On the left of the church a series of pillars crowned with the beginnings of ribs indicate that cloisters once stood here. Excavations have unearthed capitals, coins, even skeletons.

Continue along this minor road through the seaside resort of **La Flotte**⌂.

Port de St-Martin-de-Ré

★ **St-Martin-de-Ré** – *See above.*

Leave St-Martin and drive west along D 735.

⌂ **Ars-en-Ré** – This small port with a network of lanes and alleys so narrow that the corners of houses had to be shaved off to allow carriages to turn into them was once frequented by Dutch and Scandinavian vessels loading cargoes of salt.
In the main square, once a cemetery but now covered over and planted with elms, stands **Église St-Étienne** (St Stephen's Church), its needle-sharp belfry spire, painted black and white as a landmark to sailors. A fine Romanesque entrance, partly below the new ground level, leads to a nave of the same period reinforced with thick ribs. The Gothic chancel, longer than the nave, is flanked by wide side aisles. The domed vaulting here is in the Angevin style.
Just south of the church is the Seneschal's (Steward's) House, dating from the Renaissance period and embellished with two corner turrets.

Réserve naturelle de Lilleau des Niges ⊙ – 🔲 This nature reserve is inhabited by thousands of birds: curlews, grey plovers, teals, barnacle geese...which you can observe from the cycle track which skirts the southern part of the reserve.

Bear right towards D 101.

Les Portes-en-Ré – This former salt-marsh workers' village is known locally as the "tip end of the island". Note the Chapelle de la Redoute, which is in fact a former powder magazine.

Bois de Trousse-Chemise – This pleasant wood planted with pine trees surrounds the vast beach of **Pointe du Fier**.

Conche des Baleines – A forest track leads to this wide bay backed by dunes which describes a graceful curve indenting the coast. The use of the word *baleine* (whale) in names in this area derives from the fact that, in Roman times, hundreds of whales were washed up on these shores.

Vertigo

★**Phare des Baleines** ⊙ – The lighthouse, rising 55m/180ft above the headland, was built in 1854 to replace a 17C beacon-tower which had a light that did not carry very far. The tower can be seen from the shore and reached by a pathway.
A spiral staircase of 257 steps leads to the gallery of the lighthouse. From here there is a splendid **panorama**★ over the Breton Straits, the Vendée coast and Pointe de l'Aiguillon to the north and east, over the Île de Ré to the southeast and the Île d'Oléron to the south. At low tide it is possible to see the **fish-locks** around the cape.

M. Thierry/MICHELIN

L'Arche de Noé – This "Noah's Ark" **amusement and culture park** not far from Phare des Baleines offers visitors a trip through a magical world which presents the history of navigation at sea through models and dioramas, a collection of crustaceans and corals ("Océanorama"), displays of stuffed birds native to ële de Ré, a maze and exotic animals. The **Naturama★** houses a remarkable collection of stuffed animals from all over the world, grouped according to their habitat; decoratively-presented exotic butterflies and insects; a number of aquariums, and a turtle weighing 537kg/1 175lbs which was washed up on one of the island's beaches in 1978.

St-Clément-des-Baleines – The **Maison des Marais** *(16 Rue de l'École)* is an information centre specialising in the island's flora and fauna.
🚶 Guided walks are organised to explore the dunes, the coastline and the marshes.

Continue along D 735 then, at La Couarde, bear right onto D 201 and return to Pointe de Sablanceaux via Le Bois-Plage-en-Ré and Ste-Marie-en-Ré.

Château de la ROCHE-COURBON★
Michelin maps 324: F-4 or 233 fold 15 – 2km1.2mi N of St-Porchaire

This château, which stands isolated at the heart of the oakwoods that novelist **Pierre Loti** loved so much, overlooks a graceful series of balustraded terraces and formal gardens in the French manner.

"Sleeping Beauty's Castle" – This was the title of an article written by Loti in 1908, which appeared in Le Figaro newspaper, to stimulate interest in his campaign to save the woods around the old château, itself long abandoned. Loti recalled the memories of his youth, when his holidays were spent with a friend – later to be his brother-in-law – who became the tax-collector in nearby St-Porchaire. Often as an adolescent, he wrote years later, he would stray "into the density of these oaken groves" sliced by a ravine buried beneath the foliage and pitted with small grottoes where "the greenish half-light filtered through leafy branches".
The campaign – harnessed to another run by fellow writer André Hallays – was a success: not only was the forest saved from the woodsman's axe; from 1920 onwards the château was restored and its gardens brought back to life.

TOUR ⓥ

The estate is entered via Porte des Lions (Lions' Gate), a monumental 17C structure with three arches, adorned with caryatids on the inside. Having crossed a moat, which was bordered with balustrades in the 17C, visitors pass below the "keep", an ancient machicolated tower.

Château – The château, like the keep, dates from the 15C but was substantially altered by Jean-Louis de Courbon in the 17C when windows, dormers and skylights were refashioned and arcades added at the foot of the garden façade to support a balcony. This façade is remarkable for the balance of its elements and its balustraded stairway. Inside, the tour of the château starts with a library-cum-study furnished in Louis XIII

Does a princess sleep within?

style which serves as a gallery for the paintings, most of them from the old chapel: they include biblical episodes, allegories, landscapes and a series of painted panels illustrating *The Labours of Hercules* which date from the time of Louis XIV.

The 18C Grand Salon, with panelling and furniture from the same period, contains a bust of Hubert Robert after Pajou, and a painting by the Dutch artist Hackaert which shows the château as it was in the 17C.

Visitors then pass through a Louis XVI vestibule hung with rare, early 19C, illustrated panoramic wallpaper, and landscapes painted by Casanova, the brother of the notorious libertine. The tour finishes with two 17C rooms with Louis XIII ceilings: in the first of these is an enormous stone fireplace bearing the Latin inscription: *Fide, Fidelitate, Fortitudine* (By Faith, Fidelity and Courage); the second room is a kitchen-banqueting hall with regional furniture and faience and a curious, very old roasting jack.

★ Gardens – Beyond the château formal parterres and basins, separated by clipped yew hedges and graced with statues, form a magnificent and colourful perspective focusing on a double stairway flanking an ornamental waterway. Partially laid over marshland, these gardens were preserved from flooding by havin their supporting piles regularly rebuilt (works lasting 17 years).

Skirting these waters and the nymph at their far end, visitors reach a terrace offering a stunning **view★★** of the château, reflected in the smooth surface of the pool below it. The wide tree-lined walk leads to a column surmounted by a sphere; from here, by turning suddenly around, it is possible to experience that same sense of magic and surprise that so stimulated Pierre Loti.

Salle des Fêtes – Within this "festival hall" there is a superb late 16C stone stairway with balustrades.

Grottoes – *30min round trip on foot.*

The woodland walk ends in an avenue of holm oaks which leads to the narrow valley carved out by the Bruant, a tributary of the River Charente. It is this stream which feeds the pools and waterways in the castle gardens.

The caves in the steep wall of the ravine which intrigued the young Loti were inhabited by prehistoric man.

ROCHEFORT★★

Population 25 797
Michelin map 324: E-4 or 233 folds 14, 15

Rochefort, known as the "town of Pierre Loti", on the border of the Aunis and Saintonge regions, between the right bank of River Charente and the marshes at a short distance from the Atlantic coast, takes pride in its illustrious maritime past. There is still something very exotic in the air around the arsenal in which the great expeditions of the time were masterminded.

Despite its air of severity, due to the grid pattern of its rectilinear roads set at right-angles to each other (some of which still have their original blue Quebec cobblestones), Rochefort, created by Colbert in the 17C, is famous for the dignity and harmony of its architecture: one and two-storey buildings, private mansions (highly decorated façades, wrought-iron balconies) and Royal Rope Factory, built of fine pale-coloured dressed stone. Its excellent museums, such as La Maison de Pierre Loti, Le Centre International de la Mer, which is laid out in the Rope Factory, Le Musée de la Marine and many others, add interest to the town.

Rochefort's thermal springs were reopened in 1953.

HISTORICAL NOTES

In the days of sailing ships – In the middle of the 17C Jean-Baptiste Colbert (1619-83), Louis XIV's minister in charge of the Navy, was looking for a base from which the Atlantic coast could be defended against the incursions of the English. Brouage was silting up and the roadstead of La Rochelle was not sufficiently sheltered. Rochefort, 15km/9mi upriver from the mouth of the Charente, seemed the ideal choice. It was protected off-shore, moreover, not only by the Île de Ré, Île d'Aix and Île d'Oléron, but also by the Fouras and Le Chapus promontories – all of them easy to fortify.

It was decided therefore, starting from scratch, to turn Rochefort into a military port with an arsenal as powerful as the one in Toulon, and from 1666 onwards work started on the docks and fortifications. By 1671 Rochefort could boast a population of 20 000, and 13 men-of-war, a galley and several brigantines had been launched.

The town, originally constructed of wood, was rebuilt in stone in 1688 on the orders of the naval governor Michel Bégon – the man who gave his name to the begonia family: these exotic plants discovered in the West Indies by a priest, Father Plumier, were brought back to France at the governor's request *(see below)*.

Arsenal – Colbert's arsenal was, by 1690, "the biggest, the most complete and the most magnificent in the kingdom": 47 warships had been armed and provisioned there with ammunition, among them several three-deckers such as the famous *Louis-le-Grand*. Between 1690 and 1800 three hundred new vessels sailed into the waters of the Charente from Rochefort's naval yards.

The *Sphinx*, the French navy's first steam-powered warship, was built in the first half of the 19C, followed by the *Mogador*, the most powerful paddle-wheel frigate ever to be built in France. The arsenal was closed in 1926.

Between 5 000 and 10 000 workmen were employed in the arsenal. Every morning and evening the flagship fired a cannon shot to signal the opening or closing of the gates.

It was from Rochefort, on 21 March 1780, that General La Fayette set sail for the second time to reinforce the "Insurgent" troops in America onboard a brand new frigate, *L'Hermione*, built at the arsenal.

In 1816 the frigate *La Méduse* sailed from Rochefort for Senegal in West Africa, only to be wrecked off the coast of what is now Mauritania. The loss of the ship inspired Géricault to paint his celebrated dramatic work *The Raft of the Medusa*.

The Hulks of Rochefort – In the autumn of 1792 the Republican "cleansing" of the clergy began. Hundreds and hundreds of priests who had refused to swear that they accepted the "civil" status of the Church under the new Constitution were sent to Rochefort, where they were destined to embark on ships taking them to the Guyana penal colony in South America. Anchored in the Charente were two decrepit ships (known as *pontons* or hulks) awaiting them. In the event the prisoners were transferred to two even more dilapidated slave traders. The "villains" were crammed between decks in batches of 400, lying on filthy straw, with nothing but sea-water to wash in. A communal tub of broth with a few broad beans floating in it was all they had for food, the *sans-culottes* (revolutionaries) having already sold part of the rations destined for the prisoners. One day, after a short voyage, the hulks weighed anchor. Instead of deportation to Guyana, the priests found they were kept aboard ship off the Île d'Aix. On deck shots were fired and cries of "Long live the Republic! Long live Robespierre!" rang out over the water. By now the deportees, lacking everything, had only one aim: to survive. In January 1794, however, typhus made its grim appearance. Twelve or thirteen priests died every day; at each death there was a noisy celebration by the crew. The corpses, at first thrown into the sea, were later transported to Aix or Île Madame – a tiny off-shore islet linked to the mainland at low tide: fatigue parties drawn from the surviving priests were forced to carry out this gruesome task; many of them died doing it. Transferred at last to Île Madame, all of those still living were freed in 1795.

★ THE ARSENAL DISTRICT

The arsenal was built on the banks of the River Charente in two sectors which still exist, interspersed with launching slipways and entrances to dry docks. From 1830 the entrance was via the famous Porte du Soleil. The arsenal contained 11 shipbuilding yards and four refitting basins, including **La Vieille Forme**, the oldest masonry dry dock (1669) in the world. The complex also housed a foundry specialising in copper-plated nails, a boilermaking shop, forges, sawmills, rope-makers and a cooperage works producing barrels for gunpowder etc. as well as enormous warehouses for quartermasters' stores. Huge mast pits could contain up to 50 000m^3/65 400yd^3 of wood rendered rot-proof by the briny water. A workshop of "Naval sculptors" carved figureheads and embellished poops and prows.

Porte du Soleil – This entrance to the arsenal, dating from 1830, is built in the form of a triumphal arch. Vigorously-carved seafaring emblems adorn the side of the entrance facing the town.

Graving docks – Excavated from the Charente, opposite the Porte du Soleil, these immense shells, now empty, were used for ship repair.

Pierre Loti (1850-1923)

The author Pierre Loti, whose real name was Julien Viaud, was born in Rochefort at No 141 of the street that now bears his nom-de-plume. He was the son of a municipal official. Loti, a much-travelled naval officer, accomplished sportsman and something of a dandy with a distinguished bearing, was also a novelist of great sensitivity and an exceptional story-teller. Inspired by his voyages to exotic destinations, he wrote *Pêcheur d'Islande* (Iceland Fisherman), *Aziyadé*, *Ramuntcho* and *Madame Chrysanthème*, books that were instrumental in his acceptance as a member of the élite Académie Française at the unusually young age of 41.

Maison de Pierre Loti, Rochefort

ROCHEFORT

Chantier de reconstruction de l'Hermione ⊘ – The double dock (1728) was specially restored and equipped for the construction of a replica of the *Hermione*, the frigate (fitted with guns using 12lb cannonballs) in which La Fayette sailed to America *(see above)*. Work began on 4 July 1997 using the same techniques as in 1779, when the *Hermione* was first built.

Hôtel de Cheusses – A magnificent gateway leads to the courtyard of this 17C mansion which was once the local Admiralty headquarters. Today the building is a naval museum.

Musée de la Marine ⊘ – Model ships, ships' figureheads, navigational equipment, paintings, charts, weapons and flags evoke the history of the French Navy from the 17C to the 20C. Maps, documents and explanatory models illustrate the story of Rochefort's old naval dockyard. Particularly impressive are the very large ship models (and those of windmills) in the outer hall.
Of particular note is the enormous capstan from the privateer commanded by René Duguay-Trouin (1673-1736), whose great exploit was the capture of Rio de Janeiro in 1711 with "a feeble fleet".

Eating out

BUDGET

Ferme aquacole de l'Île Madame – *17730 Port-des-Barques* – ☎ *05 46 84 12 67 – closed Feb, Sun evening and Wed from Sep to Jun – reservation required – 12.20/24.39€*. Caution ! This farm on an island is only accessible at low tide. Surrounded by pools and salt marshes, you can savour seafood and congers raised here. Occasionally, the sea covers the passage to *terra firma* at lunchtime, but don't fret, it doesn't last!

Where to stay

MODERATE

Hôtel La Belle Poule – *3km/1.8mi S of Rochefort via rte de Royan* – ☎ *05 46 99 71 87 – closed 29 Oct to 18 Nov, Sun evening and Fri off-season* – ℙ *– 20 rms: 44.21/47.26€ –* ☕ *5.64€ – restaurant 18.29/28.97€*. Just next to the Martrou bridge, this house in a flower-filled garden is an enjoyable stop. A cable's length from the islands, the centre of Rochefort and therefore of Pierre Loti's house, it offers big rooms and a pleasant dining room with a fireplace...for a family holiday.

Hôtel Corderie Royale – *r. Audebert – near la Corderie Royale* – ☎ *05 46 99 35 35 – closed 26 Jan to 27 Feb, Sun evening and Mon from 1 Nov to 1 Apr* – ℙ *– 45 rms: 75.46/149.40€ –* ☕ *9.15€ – restaurant 22.87/48.78€*. This hotel accross from the port has been constructed out of the magnificent 17C buildings of the Royal Artillery. An excellent halt in the very centre of the Arsenal quarter, even if the 1980s decor doesn't suit everyone's fancy. Superb view of the Charente river from the restaurant. Pool.

Hôtel de la Marine – Napoleon Bonaparte once stayed here, and the oldest part of the building dates back to the time of Louis XIV. In front of it is a monumental 18C gateway. A tall, square-sectioned tower at one side was formerly used for the exchange of visual signals with ships.

Jardin de la Marine – The tree-lined riverside walks and terraced lime trees of this quiet, sheltered garden date back to the 18C. A handsome staircase terminating in a doorway with three arches leads down to the former royal rope factory.

** Corderie Royale – This rope factory below the garden and overlooking the Charente was founded by Colbert in 1666 and completed four years later; it stands on a kind of "raft", a grid of heavy oak beams, because of the nature of the soil. The factory supplied all the rigging for the entire French fleet from the time the factory was opened until the Revolution; once steam took over from sail, however, its activity declined and it was closed at the same time as the arsenal.

The Corderie Royale was severely damaged during World War II but has been the subject of an extensive restoration programme which has replaced the original lengthy and very harmonious façade (374m/1 227ft long). This is surmounted by a blue slate mansard roof with pediment dormers. The rear façade is reinforced by elegant scrolled buttresses. The building as a whole is a classic – and rare – example of 17C industrial architecture.

Rebuiling the *Hermione*

The **Centre International de la Mer** houses a permanent exhibit on ropes and rigging: once the hemp had arrived from the Auvergne it was spun, assembled in strands and then twisted into its final form before being tarred – the length of the building both limiting and conditioning that of the rigging. Among the exhibits is an imposing 19C machine corder (twisting machine) which runs on rails. Temporary exhibits on maritime themes are also held here.

Surrounding the Corderie is the **Jardin des Retours**. Its rare and exotic species make it easy to imagine great expeditions returning to the port, laden with unknown plants such as begonias and magnolias. The riverside **Jardin des Amériques** includes the **Aire des Gréements** (Rigging Zone), evoking the vessels of the past; while the **Labyrinthe des Batailles Navales** is a maze of clipped yew hedges.

Magasin aux Vivres – This late 17C naval storehouse, next to the provisioning dock and facing the marina, was the site of a bakery able to produce 20 000kg/ 44 100lbs of bread each day.

Ancienne École de médecine navale – 18C building standing in the middle of a park. The chapel, crowned with a pinnacle, lies behind a faïade with a carved pediment. The École de médecine navale et tropicale was established in 1722. The library and various collections of anatomy, surgery and natural history can be visited.

Thermal springs – Nearby is a small centre for thermal cures: the springs were first tapped after Napoleon I's visit in 1808 and rehabilitated once again in 1953, when the virtues of thermal treatment regained their popularity. The naturally hot waters (42 °C/ 108 °F) gush forth from the depths of the marshes. La **Source de l'Empereur** (Emperor's Spring) is especially effective in the treatment of rheumatism, osteoarthritis, dermatitis, etc.

Opposite stands the old **water tower**, a fine quadrangular structure in stone, dating from 1900, which at one time supplied the whole town.

Former royal forges – This imposing complex of technical buildings housing the Charente Maritime Regional Council.

ADDITIONAL SIGHTS

Église St-Louis – The church, built on the site of a chapel belonging to an old Capuchin monastery (1672), is imbued with the majesty of the Classical style.

Place Colbert – This fine square, huge and rectangular in shape and bordered by elegant façades, is the true city centre. On the western side, the town hall is installed in the Hôtel d'Amblimont. The 18C monumental fountain on the other side of the square represents the Ocean and the River Charente mingling their waters.

Many of the scenes in the 1967 Jacques Demy musical film, *Les Demoiselles de Rochefort*, were shot in this square.

★**Musée d'Art et d'Histoire** – The museum is housed in the former Hôtel Hèbre-de-Saint-Clément.

A large picture gallery and an adjoining exhibit room contain a sketch by Rubens (*Lycaon Changed into a Wolf* by Jupiter), a number of 17C flower paintings, portraits from the 16C Italian School, and others by Roques (Ingres' teacher) and a series of landscapes, portraits and sentimental scenes from the Empire and Romantic epochs. These include Gauffier's *Return of the Prodigal Son* and work by Belloc, Rouget *(Portrait of Lola Montès)* and Michallon. More recent paintings hang nearby. Fine collections of ethnographic interest from Africa and the South Pacific, including superb Polynesian masks, may be found in the Lesson Gallery.

Maison de Pierre Loti, Rochefort

Pierre Loti's House, Rochefort

In the following room hang seascapes and a copy of Géricault's dramatic work inspired by the Medusa tragedy (see above). The Local History department has an extraordinary plan of Rochefort, in relief, from 1835, and Vernet's painting, *The Port of Rochefort*. The Camille Mériot Room is reserved for collections of shells.

★**Maison de Pierre Loti** – Loti's house is in fact two intercommunicating buildings – his birthplace and the house next door, which he acquired as soon as he was able – concealing a remarkable interior behind a relatively plain façade. The rooms are sumptuously furnished and decorated, and full of souvenirs from his many voyages.

There are two salons on the ground floor. Loti's piano stands in the first, which is hung with family paintings, some by his sister; the second houses Louis XVI furniture and a number of mementoes and objets d'art. The **"Renaissance" Dining Room** – furnished in the Spanish style and hung with five 17C Flemish tapestries – includes a huge chimney piece and a dais for musicians. On the mezzanine floor, the former studio used by the author's painter sister, transformed into a "15C salon", was the site of a famous "Louis XI dinner" in April 1888.

The spartan furnishings of the first-floor master bedroom are in striking contrast to the three apartments around it: the **Mosque**, with décor largely from a mosque in Damascus (collection of prayer mats, candelabra, weapons, a painted cedarwood ceiling); the **Turkish Salon** with its sofas, cushions, exotic wall hangings and a stucco ceiling inspired by the Alhambra in Granada; the **Arab Room**, glittering with enamel-work and adorned with a *moucharabieh* (a carved wood screen placed in front of a window).

Église St-Louis – The church was built on the site of a chapel belonging to an old Capuchin monastery (1672). The enormous entrance (Corinthian columns surmounted by a triangular pediment), the three aisles with their vast pillars, the vaults above, are imbued with the majesty of the Classical style.

Four more Corinthian columns support the canopy above the high altar.

Musée des commerces d'autrefois ⊙ – Here a series of workshops and stores dating from 1900 to 1940 have been re-created in meticulous detail within an old warehouse dating from the turn of the century. The picturesque evocation of life in days gone by includes a Rochefort bar with its Belle Époque façade, a pharmacy, a hatter's, a grocery store, a forge, dyer's workshop etc.

Conservatoire du Bégonia ⊙ – *Take Avenue du 11-Novembre-1918 to the south, turn left into Avenue de la Charente and right into Rue Charles-Plumier.*

Plumier was the botanist priest who first brought begonias back from the West Indies in the 17C. The plant was not, however, commercially available in France until the end of the 18C. Here, in a huge hothouse, over 850 species, natural and hybrid, are grown, cared for and brought to perfection.

Pont Transbordeur de Martrou ⊙ – *2.5km/1.5mi S, rue Jacques-Demy which becomes avenue du 11-Novembre.*

This iron transporter bridge, a splendid example of industrial art dating from 1900, is 176m/577ft long and stands more than 50m/164ft above the surface of the Charente. Five of these bridges were built in France by the engineer Ferdinand Arnodin: in Marseille, Rouen, Brest, Nantes and Rochefort. Transporter bridges enabled both pedestrians and vehicles to cross from one side of the river to the other, without sea-going ships being hindered by the structures of a fixed bridge. Martrou is the only one to have been re-instated (1994). It can be used by cyclists and pedestrians. A new toll-bridge for vehicles was opened in 1991.

Station de Lagunage ⊙ – *Access via avenue du 11 Novembre.* This water treatment station consisting of 35ha/84 acres of basins along the banks of the river, is used to treat Rochefort's wastewater using environment-friendly processes. It attracts numerous species of aquatic birds and is a migratory stopping-place (herons, small river bank waders and ducks). Using a pair of binoculars, you can get a closer look at these birds from the observatory.

La ROCHEFOUCAULD

Population 3 228
Michelin map 324: M-5 or 233 fold 30

La Rochefoucauld is a small town on the banks of the River Tardoire which is lent a picturesque quality by the beauty of its old half-timbered houses.

Near the old fairground (Champ de Foire) is a 17C **bridge**, slightly humpbacked, with two half-moon ravelins, face to face, built so that pedestrians could get out of the way of carts and carriages. From here there are pleasant views of the river and the old château rising grandly above it.

The prosperity of La Rochefoucauld depends on several small industries, among them the production of *charentaises* – a comfortable form of slipper. It was in the time of Louis XIV that this began as a cottage industry; the slippers were partly made from fabric left over from the manufacture of sailors' reefer jackets while the soles were cut from felt used to dry paper pulp in the paper factories of Angoulême. The slippers were so successful that they even found their way into the Court.

SIGHTS

★ **Château** ⊙ – The Château de La Rochefoucauld was the home of an illustrious line whose chief has traditionally always had the Christian name of François; the best known is probably **François VI de La Rochefoucauld** (1613-80), the pessimistic author of the famous *Maxims*. The château, still the property of the same family, is constructed of soft white stone. The remains of a square Romanesque keep are still visible, but the place as a

La ROCHEFOUCAULD

Eponymous château

whole, with its elegant Renaissance façade and beautiful **main courtyard**★★, recalls the châteaux of the Loire more than any military stronghold. Note in particular the **spiral staircase**★ (108 steps) and it elegant vaulting, as well as Marguerite d'Angoulême's **boudoir**★, decorated with 17C painted panels depicting the French properties of the La Rochefoucauld family.

The river front is framed by a medieval tower and the castle chapel. Noteworthy here are the pedimented dormers with their candelabra and their tabernacle motifs stamped with a shell.

Ancien Couvent des Carmes – *Rue des Halles*. A restored chapter-house and huge cloisters with groined vaulting and trefoil arching supported by delicate small columns comprise the main points of interest in this former Carmelite monastery. Part of the building has been turned into a laboratory of paleontology.

Église Notre-Dame-de-l'Assomption-et-St-Cybard – The church is built in a style rarely found in the Angoulême region: 13C Gothic.

Ancienne Pharmacie de l'Hôpital ⊘ – *Place du Champ-de-Foire*. The old pharmacy of the hospital, which dates back to the 17C, houses an interesting collection of chemist's pots, flasks, mortars (16C and 17C) and a complete surgeon's instrument case from the Empire period; its original owner was attached to the army of Napoleon. Also on display, a fine 17C Christ fashioned from ivory, etc.

EXCURSIONS

Chasseneuil-sur-Bonnieure, Memorial de la Résistance et Cimetière National ⊘ *11km/6.6mi NE along N 141*. This monument to the French Resistance occupies the centre of a cemetery laid out in terraces on the hillside – 2 026 soldiers and members of the Resistance, killed between 1940 and 1945, rest in peace beneath the rose-bush covered lawns.

Église de Ste-Colombe – *12km/7.5mi NW along D 6 and D 91*. The church in this typical little Charente village has an interesting Romanesque façade adorned with statue-columns (St Colombe, St Peter) and bas-reliefs with symbols from the gospels.

Forêt de la Braconne – The Braconne massif (around 4 000ha/9 884 acres) is a limestone plateau extensively carved by underground waters which have produced dolines or sink-holes caused by subsidence of the surface. The best-known – and the most spectacular – is **La Grande Fosse** (the big pit), a huge funnel-shaped depression 55m/180ft deep and 250m/820ft in diameter. Although it is smaller, **La Fosse Limousine** *(south-east of the Grande Combe roundabout)*, hidden by tall beech trees, is also attractive. As for **La Fosse Mobile** *(not open to the public)*, legend has it that a wicked son who had murdered his father tried in vain to dump the body in this sink-hole – but the nearer he approached the edge of the depression, the more it moved away from him. In fact the depths of this abyss, which lies in an isolated spot in the silence of the woods, are used as a training centre for local cavers.

Return to La Rochefoucauld via D 88.

La Rochelle is the capital of the Aunis – a region, once a Roman colony, which changed hands several times between the English and the French in the Middle Ages. It is a town popular with painters, seduced by its atmosphere, the hustle and bustle of its daily life.

The old fortified port, the hidden streets lined with arcades, the ancient wooden houses and stately mansions, whether under the brilliance of summer skies or the most romantic of drizzles, all combine to make La Rochelle the most attractive town on the coast between Nantes and Bordeaux.

HISTORICAL NOTES

The English connection – Henry II of England, who was Eleanor of Aquitaine's second husband, granted La Rochelle its charter in 1199, thus liberating the city of its feudal and ecclesiastical ties. Ramparts were erected as early as the 13C and La Rochelle entered into commercial agreements with England and Flanders, importing canvas and wool, exporting wine and salt. The town became an international trading centre, with banks and merchants from Spain, England and Flanders. From the 15C onwards, La Rochelle prospered through the fur trade with Canada and the slave trade with the West Indies.

A Protestant stronghold – La Rochelle was sometimes known as "the French Geneva" as it was, like its Swiss counterpart, a haven for numerous disciples of Calvin before 1540; in the early days of the Reformation his teachings were even preached in the city churches. Between 1562 and 1598 the Wars of Religion brought a bloodbath to the region. In 1565 priests were hurled into the sea from the top of the tall Lantern Tower. Three years later a National Synod was held here under the presidency of Calvin's follower, the writer and theologian Théodore de Bèze. The staunchly Calvinist queen Jeanne d'Albret, her son Henri de Navarre (the future Henri IV) and the Prince de Condé took part in the debates.

In 1573 the royal army, led by the Duc d'Anjou, laid siege to the city. But La Rochelle held out. The inhabitants made use of a machine, derisively known as *L'Encensoir* (the censer), which drenched the assailants with boiling water and melted pitch. After six months of continued attacks the city still had not fallen, and the royalists had lost 20 000 men, when the siege was lifted.

The siege of La Rochelle (1627-28) – Some 55 years later a second royalist army stood at the gates of La Rochelle – though this time the town was allied with the English, who had invaded the Île de Ré.

Two equally determined figures were pitted against each other on this occasion: outside was **Cardinal Richelieu**, determined to impose a unity on France, whatever the cost; inside was **Jean Guiton** (1585-1654), a small, abrupt man, uncultivated yet fanatic in temperament, who had been an admiral in the navy and was now Mayor of La Rochelle.

Unfortunately for Guiton the blockade was organised by a masterly hand, both on land and at sea, from where help for the besieged from the English was expected: Richelieu himself took charge of the siege.

Siege of La Rochelle, by H. Motte

LA ROCHELLE

What was in effect a gigantic dike was erected across the bay to block the entrance to the harbour. Both infantry and artillery were posted on top of the dike with the result that the English fleet was unable to sail through and relieve the beleaguered garrison. At first the people of La Rochelle were not overly concerned at the building of the dike: storms, they were convinced, would sweep it away. In fact it held, though it took the besiegers 15 months to starve the town into submission. Richelieu made his victorious entry on 30 October 1628, followed two days later by Louis XIII.

From Rabelais to Fromentin – La Rochelle has always been a popular town with writers. **Rabelais**, one of the first, broke his journey here and described the light from the Lantern Tower in Pantagruel. **Choderlos de Laclos**, the author of *Les Liaisons Dangereuses*, was garrisoned here c1786 as an engineer officer overseeing the construction of the arsenal. He lived in a house linked, via a concealed stairway and an underground passage, with the mansion owned by Admiral Duperré *(see below)*. It can only be guessed at whether de Laclos' marriage to Solange, the Admiral's sister, was in any way connected to this ease of access...

The writer associated more than anyone with La Rochelle is **Eugène Fromentin** (1820-76), who was a painter and an art critic as well as a novelist. He was influenced by the artists Corot and Delacroix, and his painter's eye is obvious everywhere in his beautiful romance, *Dominique*, published in 1862 and dedicated to George Sand. In this novel he describes with the precision of a naturalist the life in 19C La Rochelle; the landscapes, the skies and the light of the Aunis are suggested with an incomparable lightness of touch.

Fromentin was a native Rochelais but many other eminent men from other parts of France were also associated with the town. They include Voltaire and Laclos, Corot, the Impressionist painters Signac and Marquet, Joseph Vernet who painted the port, and distinguished naturalists and scientists like Lafaille, d'Orbigny and Bonpland. Jean-Paul Sartre was at school in La Rochelle; Georges Simenon lived here for a while: his novel *Le Voyageur de la Toussaint* (The All Saints Day Traveller) is set in the town. An annual convention, held since 1732, brought together some of these eminent figures.

Sailing – The port of La Rochelle is on the route of several sailing races (Open UAP, Le Figaro, Hong Kong Challenge) and will be on the route of the Whitebread, the future Volvo Ocean Race, in 2002. The port's main asset is the presence of shipyards, renowned sail-makers and specialists in outfitting of ships' superstructure. It is therefore not surprising that several famous sailers should have chosen La Rochelle as their base: Philippe Poupon, Isabelle Autissier, etc.

TOWN WALKS

★★ Vieux Port

This walk starts from the tourist office and lasts 1hr 30min.

The old harbour (the modern harbour has been transferred to La Palice) is located deep inside a narrow bay. You can see the forward harbour, the old harbour, the small dock used by yachts, the outside dock used by trawlers, the reservoir supplied by a canal with water from the River Sèvre.

Gabut District – A picturesque residential and shopping development has been built on the site (east of Tour St-Nicolas) of an old bastion which was once part of the town's ring of fortifications (demolished in 1858). The façades with their wood cladding recall the fish-lofts and sheds of old-time sailors, while vivid colours and wide windows lend the place a Nordic air.

★**Tour St-Nicolas** – *See additional sights.*

Turn south, cross a small bridge and turn right onto the alleyway running alongside avenue Marillac.

Walk along the quayside past the multimedia library inaugurated in 1998 and admire the view of the towers and Vieux Port. Take the small boat which ferries passengers to the foot of Tour de la Chaîne.

Eating out

BUDGET

L'Océan – *121 bd de la République – 17340 Châtelaillon-Plage – ☎ 05 46 56 25 91 – closed mid-Dec to mid-Jan, Sun evening and Mon. – 10.98/35.06€.* Don't be put off by the outdated facade of this very hospitable restaurant decorated in red faux leather chairs, flowery walls and a linoleum floor. The service is pleasant, the seafood as fresh as can be. Good value for the money.

Le Café de la Mer – *Port du Plomb – Lauzières – 17137 Nieul-sur-Mer – Take D 106E1 4km/2.5mi W of Nieul-sur-Mer – ☎ 05 46 37 39 37 – closed Dec-Jan and Mon – 15.24/22.87€.* Mouclades (mussels in a spicy cream sauce), oysters and crepes in the summer, hearty simmering dishes in the winter. This little restaurant opens its bay windows onto a view of the Île de Ré bridge. Enthusiastic appetites will be more than satisfied with the generous portions.

MODERATE

Le Belvédère – *At the l'Île de Ré Bridge – 7km/4.2mi W of La Rochelle – ☎ 05 46 42 62 62 – closed Mon, Tue and Wed evenings from Oct to Easter – 15.24/32€.* You'll have a good view of the bridge and the Port de la Pallice when you sit down to dine in one the restaurant's two rooms. Brasserie-type decor for lunch, more comfortable in the evening for the one and only bill of fare featuring fixed-price menus with a spotlight on fish dishes.

Le Boute-en-Train – *7 r. des Bonnes-Femmes – ☎ 05 46 41 73 74 – closed 15-31 Oct, Sun and Mon – 19.82€.* Near the markets, this charming restaurant serves a variety of quiches and food fresh from the marketplace. Children's drawings adorn the walls of the bistro dining room…grab a crayon and add to their collection. More mature customers may prefer to visit the vaulted cellar to choose their bottle of wine.

Le Petit Rochelais – *25 r. St-Jean-du-Pérot – ☎ 05 46 41 28 43 – closed Sun except public holidays – 22.87€.* A friendly and competent team has taken over this ex-pizzeria cum bistro. The menu chalked on slate and the inviting atmosphere complement food prepared with brio, cooked fresh each day and served with enjoyable wines.

André – *pl. de la Chaîne – ☎ 05 46 41 28 24 – 22.87/60.98€.* A visit to La Rochelle is not complete without a meal at André! On the old docks, facing the Tour de la Chaîne, this enormous restaurant is comprised of a dozen bistro-style dining rooms where customers sit elbow to elbow to feast on seafood. Nautical ambience, marine paintings and objects de rigeur.

À Côté de chez Fred – *30 r. St-Nicolas – ☎ 05 46 41 65 76 – closed 23 Oct to 15 Nov, Sun and Mon – 22.87/33.54€.* Here the fish couldn't be fresher! And no wonder – this little restaurant gets its provisions from its neighbour and sister…the fishmonger. Result: a slate menu that changes as the fishing boats come to moor and an authentic atmosphere just behind the docks.

Where to stay

BUDGET

Margorie Bed and Breakfast – *17139 Dompierre-sur-Mer – 8km/4.8mi NE of La Rochelle on N 11, then take the road to Mouillepied – ☎ 05 46 35 33 41 – ✉ – 4 rms: 31/40€.* A relaxing stop in the local countryside, this isolated old farm is surrounded by stone walls and its inviting garden is full of flowers and trees. In the outbuildings, the rooms are arranged around a second courtyard; some come with a mezzanine.

Hôtel de la Plage – *bd de la Mer – 17340 Châtelaillon-Plage – ☎ 05 46 56 26 02 – closed 3 Jan to 10 Feb, Sun evening and Mon – 🅿 – 10 ch.: 38.11/57.93€ – ☕ 5.79€ – restaurant 11.43/22.56€.* This tiny hotel facing the beach is nothing fancy, but it is impeccably managed and conveniently located. The small rooms are appealing and soundproofed, and their very reasonable prices should win over the wariest wayfarer. A sure bet.

MODERATE

Hôtel France-Angleterre et Champlain – *20 r. Rambaud – ☎ 05 46 41 23 99 – 🅿 – 36 rms: 53.36/91.47€ – ☕ 8.38€.* A spot of the country in the city. On a busy street near the historic district, this old 16C convent features a discrete, pleasant garden – a marvellous place to unwind after a busy day in town. In this genteel setting, the rooms, some quite spacious, are decorated with period pieces.

Hôtel Les Brises – *chemin digue Richelieu, (av. P.-Vincent)* – ☎ *05 46 43 89 37* – 🅿 – *46 rms: 65.55/100.62€* – ⊊ *8.54€.* How delightful to open one's windows in the morning, contemplate the ocean and breathe the sea air...This 1960s hotel is well situated between earth and water. Lovely view from the panoramic terrace and most of the rooms.

Hôtel de la Monnaie – *3 r. de la Monnaie* – ☎ *05 46 50 65 65* – 🅿 – *31 rms: 74.70/99.09€* – ⊊ *8.84€.* Right behind the Tour de la Lanterne, this splendid 17C mansion where coins used to be made is an agreeable address. You'll appreciate the serenity of the rooms between courtyard and garden, as well as their modern furnishings and spaciousness.

Going out

Casino de la Rochelle – *Allée du Mail* – ☎ *05 46 34 12 75* – *www.lucienbarriere.com* – *casino: daily 10am-5am; le Cosy: Wed-Sat 10:30pm-5am; traditional games: 9pm-5am; restaurant: daily for lunch and dinner.* Le Casino Barrière de la Rochelle awaits you with its 120 slot machines. From 9pm on you can also try your hand at traditional gambling games: blackjack, roulette or boule. After 10pm you can catch your breath at the Cosy with a cocktail while planning your next bet. This chic bar merits its name – note the tartan carpet, marble counter, leather armchairs and terrace overlooking the ocean.

Cave de la Guignette – *8 r. St-Nicolas* – ☎ *05 46 41 05 75* – *Tue-Sat 9:30am-1:30pm, 3:30pm-8pm – closed holidays except Ascension Thursday and 8 May.* This charming and colourful wine bar used to be the watering hole of the local fishermen (who have since changed towns). Try the house speciality, *la Guinguette*, an aperitif made of wine and fruit.

Cour du Temple – *Cour du Temple.* All of the city's beer bars are gathered around this eminently genial tree-lined courtyard. Tradition requires visiting one after the other until the break of dawn.

Le Saoufé – *12 r. du Port* – ☎ *05 46 41 46 96* – *Oct-Apr: Mon-Sat 5pm-3am; May-Sep: daily 5pm-3am – closed Christmas and New Year's.* This little regulars' bar deserves its name – *saoufé* means 'everything's fine' in Creole. Laughter and good humour are always on the menu, the walls are covered with graffiti and the rum is excellent. Be careful not to overindulge – at night the nearby docks can be awfully slippery!

All aboard

Cours des Dames – *Cours des Dames.* This is the place to go if you want to discover the Charantais archipelago by boat. In this part of the port, several ventures offer cruises to Fort Boyard, l'île de Ré, l'île d'Oléron or l'île d'Aix. You can also charter a journey up the Charente river, amid verdant landscapes.

Cheers!

Bar du Musée – *Pl. Bernard-Moitessier* – ☎ *05 46 44 71 70* – *daily 11am-2am – closed Nov-Feb.* No, this is not a cafeteria! Despite its ho-hum name, this little bar on the deck of the France 1 (the boat of the Maritime Museum) never stops partying. There's no sign to point you to it, so follow the music and cast off!

Café de la Paix – *54 r. Chaudrier* – ☎ *05 46 41 39 79* – *Mon-Sat 6:45am-9:30pm, Sun 10am-8pm.* Behind its carved wood facade, this big café covered with mirrors and mouldings has a long history. A hospital in 1709, a theatre during the Revolution, since 1900 it has been a café popular with visiting artists such as Colette, Jean Gabin and Lino Ventura

Le Comptoir de Belgique – *13 r. St-Nicolas* – ☎ *05 46 50 51 40* – *Tue-Sat 5pm-2am.* Beer barrels have been transformed into the bar and tables of this hop-happy watering hole. Surrounded by aficionados of a good mug of the frothy stuff, you can choose your brew among the 200 bottles exposed on a rail attached to the cask-shaped ceiling.

Le Morgane Pub – *99 bd de la Mer – 17340 Châtelaillon-Plage* – ☎ *05 46 56 39 19* – *lemorganepub@free.fr* – *Apr-Sep: daily 9am-2am; rest of the year: daily except Tue – closed Jan.* No evil spells cast by the fairy queen of this spot! Instead, the enchantment of enjoying a glass of potion while gazing at the sea from the pub's terrace.

The old port

Cour des Dames – Once the haunt of sardine mongers and fishermen repairing their nets, this esplanade, which is one of the most animated parts of the old port, now features a cinema, a museum (Grévin) and terrace restaurants.

La Coursive – Now a theatre, formerly the Ancienne Chapelle des Carmes (chapel), has an imposing 17C doorway surmounted with a scallop shell. Inside, there is a fine arcaded courtyard.

Tour de la Chaîne – *See additional sights.*

Rue Sur-les-Murs – The tower is linked with Tour de la Lanterne by this narrow street which follows the top of the old medieval rampart – the only section not demolished by Richelieu, who hoped to use it as a defence against the English (at that time the foot of the wall was at the water's edge).

★ **Tour de la Lanterne** – *See additional sights.*

Continue along the sea front then through the gardens.

★ **Parc Charruyer** – This park, built on the mounds and ditches of the old fortifications, encircles the town (2km/1mi long and 200m/658ft wide); alongside, runs a river – home for swans and herons – and winding avenues. To the west, the park become the **mail** – a favourite with strollers – finishing up at the monument to the dead, one of Joachim Costa's major works. Between this majestic avenue of elms and the sea, stretch the gardens and terrace of the casino and Parc d'Orbigny, followed by Parc Delmas.

Préfecture – The *préfecture* (administrative headquarters of the *département*), housed in the former Hôtel Poupet, built in the period of Louis XVI presents architecture typical of local private buildings; the magnificent doorway crowned with balustrades faces onto the square.

From the Préfecture, walk to Porte de la Grosse-Horloge; here you have the choice of starting on the second walk or returning to the Gabut district via quai Duperré.

Quai Duperré – The cafés lining this quay offer a fine view of the waterfront activity. Beyond the masts and the rigging, the embarkation and disembarkation and the manoeuvring of small boats, the perspective is closed by the two towers guarding the harbour mouth – Tour St-Nicolas on the left, Tour de la Chaîne on the right. On the extreme right, the conical roof of the Lantern Tower is visible.
The picturesque Rue du Port and Petite-Rue du Port, inhabited mainly by fishermen and sailors, lead to the quay. On the western side, facing the big clock, stands a statue of **Admiral Duperré**, who was born in La Rochelle in 1775 and commanded the French fleet at the time of the taking of Algiers in 1830.

★★ Old Town

The oldest district of La Rochelle, which was built to a regular plan and protected, until 1913, by Vauban's fine ramparts, still exudes an atmosphere part mercantile and part military. The busy, lively **shopping centre** is based around the town hall, its principal axes Grande-Rue des Merciers and Rue du Palais. Narrow streets still paved with ancient stone slabs, secret passages, some of them vaulted, arcades and darkened "porches" where passers-by can stroll sheltered from bad weather – all these give the area plenty of character.

Many of the houses are designed on a plan particular to La Rochelle. Almost all of them have two entrances, one on the main street, the other on a lane parallel to it. At ground-floor level, these buildings have one huge room – often converted into a shop – an interior courtyard with a staircase leading to a balconied gallery, and a rear courtyard surrounded by outhouses. On the upper floor, above the shop, is a room looking out on the street, a kitchen overlooking the courtyard, and a "dark room" with no direct light from outside. **Half-timbering** on the oldest houses is over-hung with slates to protect the wood from the rain.

The **beaux quartiers** – the fashionable areas – are west of Rue du Palais. The most stately are Rue Réaumur and Rue de l'Escale. Here, behind high walls pierced with imposing gateways and sometimes (Rue Réaumur) topped with balustrades, the old families live in their solemn 18C mansions midway between courtyard and garden.

Follow the itinerary marked in green on the town plan.

* **Porte de la Grosse-Horloge** – This gateway with its outsize clock was the entrance to the town, coming from the port. The original Gothic tower was modified in the 18C by the addition of a belfry surmounted by a dome and lantern. The turrets on either side are decorated with nautical emblems.

Porte de la Grosse Horloge

On the far side of the gateway is Place des Petits-Bancs, a small square with a statue of Fromentin in the middle. On the corner of Rue du Temple stands a charming house (1654) with a Renaissance façade.

* **Rue du Palais** – This is one of the most important streets in La Rochelle, linking the shopping centre with the residential district. On the right, lines of shops extend beneath a succession of galleries varying in style according to the period in which they were built. Public buildings alternate with galleries on the left-hand side, and there are some fine old houses – the fourth one along, for example, has windows adorned with miniature arches and carved masks.

* **Hôtel de la Bourse** – This 18C Stock Exchange building, the seat of the local Chamber of Commerce since its founding, is an example of the early Louis XVI style. The attractive courtyard has an unusual layout which includes a portal and peripheral galleries. The inner façade is adorned with the sterns of ships and other maritime emblems. In a corner on the left is a fine wrought-iron staircase.

A passageway across the road from the Stock Exchange (by no 29 Rue du Palais) leads via Cour de la Commanderie to Cour du Temple (old half-timbered houses).

Palais de Justice – The law-courts façade, majestic with its fluted Corinthian columns and frieze of carved foliage, was completed in 1789. The inscription on the pediment reads "Temple of Justice"; it is flanked by the two traditional symbols of justice, the sword and the scales.

At the intersection of Rue Chaudrier and Rue E.-Fromentin stands a fine 17C house with a corner turret and staircase on carved corbels. Opposite, at the entrance to Rue Dupaty, is an old half-timbered house protected by slates.

Turn left onto rue E.-Fromentin.

Maison Venette – The picturesque **Rue de l'Escale★** is paved with pebbles which were once used as ballast by ships from Canada, and is bordered partly by arcades and partly by the projecting porches behind which the homes of 18C nobles were

> "La Rochelle is a strange town, yet full of character, with its labyrinthine streets and pavements passing under arcaded galleries such as the Rivoli. These low galleries and stunted, mysterious arcades could easily have been the setting for a conspiracy, a captivating backdrop for the wars of bygone days – the heroic, yet savage wars of religion."
>
> Guy de Maupassant

concealed. Maison Venette was built in the 17C for a doctor of that name. The façade of the house is rhythmically sculpted with motifs representing celebrated doctors from antiquity to medieval times: Hippocrates, Galen, Avicenna etc.

Return to Rue du Palais.

★ **Rue Chaudrier** – At No 6 stands an old half-timbered house with slate cladding. A plaque in front of the building bears an inscription glorifying Chaudrier, a famous and heroic defender of La Rochelle.

Turn right into Rue des Augustins and continue to No 11 bis.

Maison Henri II – *See additional sights.*

Return to Rue Chaudrier.

Cathédrale St-Louis – The cathedral, sober and severe in aspect, was constructed in part on the site of a church dedicated to St Bartholomew. The plans were drawn up by the architects Gabriel, father and son. The west front, a little heavy in style, is surmounted by a scrolled pediment in the Louis XVI manner.
In the third chapel of the north aisle simple votive paintings by sailors contrast with the "literary" and academic compositions by A D Bouguereau (1825-1905), a native of La Rochelle, which cover the dome above the axial chapel. The **treasury** ⊘ contains 18C and 19C liturgical items.

Café de la Paix – This is the sole remaining example in La Rochelle of those opulent, flamboyant cafés of the last century, gleaming with gilt and glass, where the local burghers read their newspapers or played billiards. Glass panels in the form of arcades, decorated with designs in frosted glass, adorn the façade. The resplendent interior is decked out with carved wood and gilded designs, and huge arched mirrors beneath glittering chandeliers and ceiling medallions painted in trompe-l'œil (1895).

Rue du Minage – Old **arcades**★ on each side of the street are irregular in shape – which brings an eccentric element into the perspective down the street. Some of the very old houses are adorned with friezes and sculptures, others with windows beneath a triangular pediment (nos 43, 22, 4 and 2). At the end of the street stands the **Fontaine du Pilori**, which dates from the 16C but was rebuilt in the 18C.

Continue, via rue Pas-du-Minage, towards the market.

Place du Marché – At the entrance to the Tout-y-Faut cul-de-sac two well-preserved old houses face one another. The half-timbered one, with mullion windows and a high-up dormer, dates from the 15C; the other (16C) is stone-built with narrow, pedimented window bays.

★ **Grande-Rue des Merciers** – This shopping street is one of the most characteristic arteries of La Rochelle, bordered by numerous galleries and houses built in the 16C and 17C. The medieval buildings, half-timbered under the familiar slate covering, alternate with Renaissance homes built of stone and distinguished by fantastic gargoyles.

Francofolies: when music takes the town by storm

Every year, around 14 July, a musical storm hits La Rochelle. For 6 days, the old port resonates with music and applause.
The idea of the festival originated in Quebec where Jean-Louis Foulquier, a radio broadcaster, was captivated by the lively success of a "Francofête" of French songs. In 1985, he chose his home town to host the Francofolies, hanging a bright banner between the towers of the old port. The first year, 25 000 people attended the outdoor celebration. Over the years, a wide variety of entertainers, including Jacques Higelin, Charles Aznavour, Francis Cabrel, Johnny Halliday, Larra, MC Solar, Rita Mitsouko, Samson, Sapho and Alain Souchon, have enchanted the eclectic audience.
The festival is open to every style of music from hard rock to jazz and rap. At the foot of Lanterne tower, on Esplanade Jean-d'Acre, a huge stage welcomes big names in the entertainment business (decibels and lighting effects guaranteed). A few yards away, La Coursive, Le Grand Théâtre and La Salle Bleue are better suited to more intimate performances and new talent. Le Carré Amelot (regional venue), l'Encan (the hip-hop spot) and Magic Mirrors (improvisation and jam sessions until the wee hours) complete the official Francofolies. Unofficially, the beat on the street goes on and on. An autograph session is held in Cours des Dames every afternoon, so be sure to take your camera!

The wood-and-slate house on the corner of Rue du Beurre, and those at nos 33, 31, 29 and, at the far end, no 17, are all 17C buildings with pedimented windows. no 8 is late 16C, with very narrow windows and heavy pediments; no 5 is early 17C with strange carved figures. No 3 dates from 1628. Mayor Jean Guiton lived in the last two.

Take rue de la Grille on the right, then turn left onto rue de l'Hôtel-de-Ville.

Hôtel de ville – *See additional sights.*

Follow rue de la Ferté on the left. The Protestant church is on your left, on the corner of rue St-Michel.

Protestant Church – This church has a charming façade, with sculpted palm leaves and drapery. It is the former Récollets chapel, constructed in 1708. It houses the Musée Protestant *(see additional sights).*

Cloître des Dames Blanches – These cloisters, located next to the Protestant Temple, are part of the former Récollets' Convent. It has now become a cultural centre, and beneath the 32 arches exhibits and concerts are held (in season).

Église St-Sauveur – 17C and 18C edifice with a tall 15C bell tower.

Follow rue St-Sauveur then rue du Temple to return to Porte de la Grosse-Horloge.

ADDITIONAL SIGHTS

★★ Vieux Port

★**Tour St-Nicolas** ⊙ – This slightly leaning tower, 42m/138ft high, and dedicated to the patron saint of sailors, is a fortress in itself. It was built in the 14C on a pentagonal plan, its five corners reinforced by three engaged circular turrets, a rectangular turret and a higher square tower forming a keep. An outside staircase forming a buttress leads to the main room, octagonal beneath elegant ribbed vaulting. From here, other staircases built in the thickness of the walls lead to a second chamber, which branches off into

S. Sauvignier/MICHELIN

Tour St-Nicolas

several rooms including a chapel, and out onto the lower parapet, surrounded by merlons. Scale models, dioramas and water-colour maps *(from the Musée Maritime, see below)* trace the development of the port from the 12C to the present day. The upper parapet, surrounded by high machicolated walls with arrow-slits, affords views of the entrance to the harbour, the bay and Île d'Aix.

Tour de la Chaîne ⊙ – The tower owes its name to a huge and heavy chain which used to be stretched across the harbour mouth between this tower and Tour St-Nicolas at night, closing the port to ships. According to Rabelais the chain – still visible at the foot of the tower – was used to keep the giant Pantagruel in his cradle.
Tour de la Chaîne, built in the 14C, was for a long time used as a powder magazine. Originally there was a turret attached to it but this was demolished in the 17C to widen the narrow channel. Inside, a superb vaulted chamber houses an exhibition devoted to the siege of La Rochelle.

★**Tour de la Lanterne** ⊙ – The Lantern Tower is not as old as the other two (it dates from the 15C), and was built with strictly functional concerns in mind, eschewing aesthetic considerations in favour of military imperatives. The great mass of the building, its walls 6m/20ft thick at the base, contrasts starkly with the elegant octagonal spire and the fine lantern – originally used as a beacon – which surmount it. At ground level is the old guard-room in which the history of La Rochelle is now recounted through illustrated panels.
Within the spire are four rooms one above the other, the walls of which bear **graffiti**★ scrawled by soldiers as well as prisoners, mostly dating from the 17C and 18C. The most interesting are protected by glass.
At the second level of the spire a projecting balcony affords a remarkable **panorama**★★ embracing the roofs of the old town, the port, the ocean and the off-shore islands. At low tide it is possible to make out the foundations of Richelieu's dike, level with Fort-Louis, beyond the promenade.

Old Town

★ Maison Henri-II ⓥ – This grand house, built in 1555 for Hugues de Pontard, the Seigneur de Champdeniers, rises at the far end of a garden. The façade, with its twin pavilions, gallery and loggia, is in the Henri II style. It includes a frieze sectioned by triglyphs (tablets with vertical grooves), medallions and bucranes (carved oxen masks). At ground-floor level two buttresses supporting the left-hand pavilion are decorated with (right) a satyr playing a guitar and (left) a winged woman grappling with a serpent.

★ Hôtel de ville ⓥ – The town hall, a late 15C-early 16C composite building, is notable for its rich decoration. The rectangular central courtyard is protected by a walled Gothic enclosure surmounted by a machicolated watch-path reinforced by a belfry-tower.

The **main façade★**, built in the reign of Henri IV in the Italian style, overlooks the courtyard. Behind its fluted columns the ground-floor gallery of the façade hides a fine coffered ceiling. The decoration includes trophies, medallions and monograms entwining the initials of Henri IV and Mary de' Medici.

Finer still is the upper level, reached via a balustraded stairway. Here there are pillars and niches in the Tuscan manner, the niches housing effigies representing the four cardinal virtues: (left to right) Prudence, Justice, Fortitude and Temperance.

The **interior** contains Jean Guiton's study, complete with his armchair in Cordoba leather and the desk he struck forcefully with his dagger to emphasise his famous pronouncement before the siege; the walls are hung with Aubusson tapestries.

Henri Motte's 19C painting of the siege can be found in another room, along with a Jacques Callot engraving and a 1628 canvas by Van der Kabel depicting the same tragic event in the town's history.

The rear **façade** looks out over rue des Gentilshommes and also dates from the time of Henri IV; it includes a door studded with bosses which is known as the "Porte des Gentilshommes" because it was through here that the city aldermen filed on the day that the mandate granting them each "the style and title of Gentleman" expired.

Musée Protestant ⓥ – The museum relates the history of Protestantism, particularly around La Rochelle. Among documents and objects on display: copy of the Confession of Faith of La Rochelle (1571) with ministers' signatures; a bible from 1606 printed in La Rochelle; A collapsible altar and pulpit and a collection of *méreaux* (medals worn by Protestants for mutual recognition), reminders of the period of clandestine meetings, known as the *désert*.

★★ Musée d'Histoire Naturelle ⓥ – The museum stands by the entrance to a park, the Jardin des Plantes, and is housed in two separate buildings facing one another:

Musée Lafaille – This fine 18C building, once the home of the Governor, still contains much of its Louis XV woodwork. On the ground floor is the **Cabinet Lafaille**, a study-room in

Cabinet Clément Lafaille

which Clément de Lafaille, a War Controller and natural history enthusiast, assembled a collection of curiosities which he bequeathed to the La Rochelle Royal Academy in 1770; the collection, furniture included, was transferred here in 1832. Against a backdrop of magnificent panelling and woodwork inlaid with coral and carved with scientific objects are glass-fronted cabinets, display-cases and a *coquillier* – an 18C cupboard with numerous small drawers, designed to house a collection of shells – said to be the last one remaining in France. The rare crustaceans, molluscs and other shellfish are worth a close examination.

Stags' heads, antlers and other trophies adorn the wide stone stairway leading to the first floor. The landing is occupied by the stuffed figure of the first giraffe ever brought to France, a gift to Charles X from Mahomet Ali, the pasha of Egypt.

The **Zoological Hall**, created in 1832, is an interesting example of the museological thinking of curators of the period, anxious to offer a complete cross-section of the animal kingdom, which was only then beginning to be classified in a rational manner. The **Ethnology Rooms** contain some exceptional exhibits: a statue of the god Terriapatura brought back from the Gambier archipelago in Polynesia, a two-headed statuette, *Moaï-Kava-Kava*, from Easter Island, a large Kwele mask from the Congo, and terracotta works from Chad.

Musée Régional Fleuriau – This second building focuses on the natural history of the La Rochelle area: geology, paleontology, pre-history and zoology. There is an interesting reconstruction of part of a forest with such local fauna as wild boar, otters, roe deer and stags.

★ **Musée du Nouveau Monde** Ⓥ – The Hôtel Fleuriau, acquired by a ship-owner of that name in 1772, houses within panelled Louis XV and Louis XVI salons a number of collections tracing the relationship between La Rochelle and the Americas since the Renaissance. Ship owners and merchants grew rich trading with Canada, Louisiana and especially the West Indies, where they possessed huge plantations producing spices, sugar, coffee, cocoa and vanilla. They prospered enormously too in the "black gold" trade, known more politely as "triangular commerce": sale of cloth and purchase of slaves on the African coast; sale of these slaves and purchase of colonial products in America; sale of the latter in Europe.

Among the displays, ancient maps, coloured engravings, allegories of America, wallpapers (*The Incas* by Dufour and Leroy) and everyday objects used by the Indians are of particular interest. Note also the section on slavery, the fall of Quebec, West Indian engraving and relevant literary themes, including Chateaubriand's novel *Atala*, about the impossible love between an Indian and a Christian girl.

★ **Musée des Beaux-Arts** Ⓥ – The Fine-Arts Museum occupies the second floor of the old bishop's palace, which was built during the reign of Louis XVI; following local custom the courtyard is separated from the gardens by a high balustraded wall. A wrought-iron staircase with ovoli leads to the alcoved gallery and rooms in which the paintings hang. The rest of the palace houses a library, an *artothèque* (a lending department for engravings and photographs of paintings) and a study section. The most interesting work among the older paintings is an *Adoration of the Magi*, the last known painting by Eustache Le Sueur (17C French School). Portraits by local artists dating from the 18C include works by Brossard de Beaulieu and Duvivier. The 19C is represented by Bouguereau, Corot, Chassériau and Eugène Fromentin – including several evocative studies of Algeria.

A separate department is devoted to 20C work (glass by Maurice Marinot, Georges Rouault's **Miserere**), some of which is displayed in rotation.

★ **Musée d'Orbigny-Bernon** Ⓥ – This museum specialises in local history and ceramics from Europe and the Far East. Mementoes of the siege of La Rochelle include liturgical items used by Cardinal Richelieu when he celebrated the first Mass after the fall of the town. A number of documents relate to the economic prosperity and intellectual life in the Aunis capital during the 18C.

On the first floor an exceptional collection of ceramics centres on the faïence (glazed earthenware) of La Rochelle but there are fine pieces also from Marseille, Nevers, Strasbourg and Moustiers. An interesting series of pharmacy flasks and bowls is displayed in a number of 18C medicine cabinets.

The second floor is devoted to the Far East (precious Chinese porcelain from the Sung to the Ch'ing dynasties and musical instruments), while the basement houses an archaeology section including a celebrated 12C tomb, attributed to Laleu but probably work of a monk.

▶▶ **Musée Grévin** Ⓥ *(cours des Dames)* – waxworks illustrating the town's historic events; **Musée du Flacon à Parfum** Ⓥ *(rue du Temple)* – charming collection of perfume bottles and powder boxes.

The Wooden Town

The wooden town lies to the west of the larger tidal basin; it is an area of low wooden houses mainly used in the past as workshops for ships' repairs or chandlers and spare-part shops. Reorganised after a fire, this district has added cultural activities (university, museums) to its handicraft tradition.

★ **Neptunéa : Maritime Museum** Ⓥ – Spreading along the eastern quays of the Chalutiers docks, the entrance to this complex is distinguished by a slipway. Two separate museums tell the tale of maritime history in La Rochelle.

Musée à Flot – A small armada of boats of all shapes and sizes are anchored along the quays (rowing boats, trawlers, open-sea tugs and yachts), including **Joshua**, the elegant red ketch manned by Bernard Moitesier in the Golden Globe Challenge, the first round-the-world solo race (1967-68). Formerly a meteorological frigate, the 80m/263ft long **France 1** is the fleet's most impressive ship; visitors are free to wander up and down its five decks and take a closer look at interesting exhibits on life onboard, meteorology and ships in bottles. The latest arrival is Commandant Cousteau's **La Calypso** *(not yet open to the public)*.

Musée à Quai – This museum, located in the refurbished buildings of the Encan (fish auction rooms), houses the Comptoir des Océans (maritime boutique and bookshop), Cinévague (nautical cinema), the Peintures sur Mer exhibit (seascapes) and the Halle à Marée (exhibition on fishing methods and a pool for sailing remote-controlled model boats.

Musée des Automates Ⓨ – 🖼 Three hundred figures move to the sound of music against a sumptuous backdrop, ingeniously vying with each other for the attention of visitors. The astonishingly life-like figures are animated by a cam system, demonstrated on a Harlequin figure cut in cross-section. Note, in particular, some more recent works, one of which evokes the inventor de Vaucanson and his famous duck, as well as animated shop windows, exhibits for children and historical reconstructions.

An imitation Paris metro entrance leads to **"Place de Montmartre"**★★ where the cosmopolitan atmosphere is faithfully recreated. Children will marvel at the mechanical billboards decorating the shops while adults can stroll in the cobbled, lamplit streets and be taken by surprise as an overhead metro rattles by.

Musée des modèles réduits Ⓨ – 🖼 *A miniature train takes children through the museum.* The tour starts with a collection of superb model cars and lorries, some remote-controlled. The inside of a galleon tells the story of the great sea-going expeditions while a fabulous water setting provides the backdrop for a **naval battle**. An underwater world plunges the visitor into the ocean depths while train-spotters can admire model trains circuits, one of which includes a model of La Rochelle railway station, and gleaming locomotives of every shape and size, some of which are steam-operated.

Underwater encounter

Aquarium de la Rochelle

★ **Aquarium** Ⓨ – 🖼 This very large, ultra-modern aquarium founded by René Coutant presents a vast panorama of underwater fauna and flora from around the world in 65 tanks. Several rooms are devoted either to a particular ocean or to a specific marine area (the Atlantic, the Mediterranean, tropical seas etc.), their species displayed in superbly arranged tanks. A tunnel with transparent walls allows visitors to wander freely through a tropical marine environment, while an immense basin containing 2 500hl/55 000 gallons of water accommodates turtles and sharks. There is a large tropical house, a shop and a café with a terrace.

Port des Minimes

Three thousand two hundred craft of all types can be accommodated at Minimes marina, on the southern side of the bay sheltering La Rochelle, which makes it the largest pleasure port in Europe on the Atlantic side. Three deep-water tidal basins – Bout-Blanc, Marillac and Lazaret – have been developed. Around the port is a zone of artisans: ship-fitters, sail-makers, painters and experts in repair work provide every service needed by the owners of yachts and cruisers. A sailing school of repute is based here, and there is also a residential area with apartment blocks and holiday homes.

A regular waterbus service operates between Les Minimes and Vieux Port.

La ROCHE-SUR-YON

Population 49 262
Michelin map 316: H-7 or 232 fold 40

This unusual town, built on a plateau overlooking the River Yon and the *bocage*, was born out of an imperial wish to install – if necessary by force of arms – a strategic military stronghold designed to prevent further uprisings in the Vendée. In 1804 Napoleon transferred the provincial capital from Fontenay to La Roche-sur-Yon, a modest small town which was subsequently renamed "Napoléon-Vendée". Plans for a military transformation were drawn up by the engineer Duvivier but the lack of stone in the region constrained him to build in cob; as a consequence, when Napoleon passed through in 1808 to have a look at the new fortifications, Duvivier was sacked, being reproached for having created "a mud-walled town".

It was in fact during the Restoration that La Roche found its definitive shape: a geometric, straight-line plan with a grid of streets crossing each other at right-angles, the wide main arteries converging on a huge esplanade which served as a parade ground or barrack square. This town took the form of an irregular pentagon from which six main routes permitted a rapid rectilinear deployment of troops. This innovation in urban planning reflected precisely the politico-architectural thinking in France in the middle of the 19C. The name of the town was nevertheless changed several more times: it became Bourbon-Vendée under the Restoration and the July Monarchy, Napoléon-Vendée at the time of the Second Empire and returned to La Roche-sur-Yon in 1870.

SIGHTS

Place Napoléon – The great esplanade, designed to accommodate 20 000 soldiers, is surrounded by neo-Classical buildings. In the centre of the square stands an equestrian statue (1854) of Napoleon I.

Hôtel du Département – This comprises an old Napoleonic hospital in which exhibitions are held and, just behind it, a modern building (1990) by Roland Castro and Jean-Luc Pellerin. The latter, with its immense glass façade scarcely hiding a large pink tower, cuts vividly across the austerity and rigour of the 19C town-planning.

Museum ⊙ – As well as archaeological collections from the prehistoric, Gallo-Roman and medieval periods, the museum offers a panorama of 19C Parisian academic painting and a series of canvases by local artists of the same period – Milcendeau, for instance, who recorded the life around the marshes (a museum is devoted to his work in Soullans), and Baudry, who was created the decor in the Paris Opera House.

The museum has a collection of works by contemporary artists (Beuys, Boltanski, and others) based on photographic material and holds temporary exhibits highlighting works by living painters.

Haras (Stud Farm) ⊙ – This is one of the most important stud-farms in France. A number of thoroughbred stallions and French trotting horses are stabled here.

ROYAN ✿✿✿

Population 17 102
Michelin map 324: D-6 or 233 fold 25

The town of Royan, capital of the **Côte de Beauté** (Coast of Beauty), was rebuilt after the bombardments which flattened it in 1945 and has once more found, in the guise of a modern town, the popularity and prosperity which characterised it at the end of the 19C. In the holiday season there is a substantial increase in the population.

THE SITE AND ITS HISTORY

A privileged place – Royan is ideally located on a headland at the entrance to the Gironde. The town is flanked by choice holiday resorts: the stately Pontaillac, **Meschers-sur-Gironde** and the more family-orientated St-Palais and **St-Georges-de-Didonne**. Beaches of fine sand curve enticingly at the inner end of the town's four **conches** (coves or bays indenting the coastline). The largest cove harbours a strand 2km/1mi long; the smaller ones, warm and sheltered from the wind, are separated by cliffs or dunes carpeted with a forest of holm oaks and parasol pines which give out a pleasant summer fragrance.

Apart from the natural beauty of the area and a particularly mild climate, Royan also benefits from a seaweed-cure centre and numerous other attractions, hence its popularity.

The Royan Pocket – At the time of the Liberation of France, in the autumn of 1944, Nazi troops stationed in the southwest withdrew to a number of coastal enclaves – St-Nazaire, Verdon, Royan – and dug themselves in with the intention of holding out as long as possible. Royan was besieged by the French forces of General de Larminat when, on 5 January and 14-15 April 1945, two violent aerial bombardments almost totally destroyed the town. The Germans surrendered on 17 April, only three weeks before the armistice on 8 May.

Royan today – Anyone who knew Royan before World War II will remember, not without a certain nostalgia, its ornate villas and chalets half-hidden among the palms, its great Victorian hotels with their heavily decorated façades, the casinos like Baroque temples or palaces from the Renaissance. All that has gone: only the Pontaillac area today can evoke such memories; Royan town centre has been rebuilt following the norms of late 20C town planning. Huge perspectives have been opened up, bordered by apartment blocks with wide balconies and red-tiled roofs in the Charentais manner.

ROYAN

SIGHTS

★**Église Notre-Dame** – The church was built between 1955 and 1958 to plans by the architects Guillaume Gillet and Hébrard. It is a structure of reinforced concrete coated with resin to protect it from wind erosion.

From Place Notre-Dame, at a slightly lower level, the ascending perspective of the east end, forming a kind of prow, is accentuated by the belfry which soars to a height of 65m/213ft.

On the left, detached from the nave, is a pyramidal baptistery.

Inside the church, visitors are at once struck by the weightless quality of the single nave, flying away, spacious and light. The great organ, the work of the Poitou master Robert Boisseau, has a case of hammered pewter and is renowned for the quality of its tone.

Two contrasting statues face one another beneath the northern gallery: a 14C carved wood St Joseph with a recumbent Christ, and a modern, copper figure of Joan of Arc.

★**Front de Mer** – Royan's seafront curves around the northern end of the **Grande Conche** – an imposing crescent of buildings, commercial as well as residential, its line emphasised by a columned peristyle in the shelter of which people can shop or admire the view of the Gironde estuary. Off to the right the distinctive silhouette of Cordouan lighthouse can be recognised.

At the western end of the seafront is the port. This comprises a dock for trawlers and the sardine boats which fish for the famous *royan*, a marina for yachts and cruisers, and a tidal basin with the jetty from which the ferry to Pointe de Grave leaves.

Boat trips ⓥ are organised in summer, especially out to Cordouan lighthouse.

Corniche de Pontaillac – *This walk should be taken at high tide for the best views. Follow Boulevard Carnot and Boulevard de la Côte-d'Argent.*
Having skirted the tennis courts and the old Fort du Chay, the route runs above a number of small coves (Conche du Chay, Conche du Pigeonnier) from which there are fine views of the Gironde and the Côte de Beauté, from Pointe de Suzac (south east) to Pointe de la Coubre (northwest). The walk ends at the **Conche de Pontaillac★**, a sheltered inlet surrounded with smart villas scattered among the sub-tropical foliage. This small beach fringed with a perfect curve of fine sand is the most popular in Royan.

▶▶Église Réformée, Marché Central – Market with original fine-concrete dome, Palais des Congrès – Glass-walled building.

EXCURSIONS

Saujon – *11km/7mi N along N 150*. The church of this small spa town situated on the banks of the River Seudre contains four elaborately carved Romanesque **capitals**★ *(in the nave, on the left side)*.
The **Chemin de fer touristique de la Seudre** Ⓥ (tourist train), linking Saujon to La Tremblade, runs along the Seudre estuary offering fine views of the oyster beds and oyster breeders' huts lining the west bank.

★**Pointe and Forêt de la Coubre** *31km/19mi NW – allow 3hr.*

Drive north-west out of Royan along D 25.

Vaux-sur-Mer – On one side of the valley stands a charming Romanesque church rising from an old cemetery planted with elms and cypress trees. Inside, note the capitals at the transept crossing, especially the figure of the bear trainer on the southern side.

Continue south to Nauzan.

Nauzan – A cove with a beach of fine sand, sheltered from the wind by cliffs on either side.

St-Palais-sur-Mer – This small, popular resort with its stylish elegance is surrounded by smart villas scattered among the pines and ilex trees. The **Parc du Marais du Rhâ** (behind the covered market), laid out around a lake, is well equipped for leisure activities (miniature golf, cycle-track, tennis, boating, fishing etc.). From the cove there is a view of the Cordouan light.
At the far end of the beach (on the right, looking at the cove), take rue de l'Océan and then **Sentier de la Corniche**★ *(signposted, 45min round trip on foot)*.
🚶 The path, also known as the Sentier des Perrières (path of the slate quarries), twists through the woods and then crosses a gash in the cliff into which, at high tide, the ocean rollers hurl themselves with a thunderous noise. The path ends at a promontory where the jagged rocks have been smashed into bizarre shapes: Monk's Rock, the Devil's Bridge, the Quarrymen.

★★**La Grande Côte** – *Park in the car park, on the left, where D 25 turns away from the coast and plunges into the woods. Walk to the rock platform. Telescope.* From this viewpoint, when the weather is bad – or even unsettled – sightseers can enjoy the grandiose spectacle of huge waves breaking violently on the rocks, sending bursts of spindrift jetting high in the air. From left to right, the **view** embraces the Gironde, Pointe de Grave, the Cordouan light, and the promontory and light-house of La Coubre.

Eating out

BUDGET

La Siesta – *140 r. Gambetta* – ☎ *05 46 38 36 53* – *closed mid-Dec to mid-Jan and Wed* – *9.50/23€*. This restaurant, rebuilt on the exact site of the Brasserie des Bains where Pablo Picasso sojourned, faces a sailing harbour. Try the *bruschetta*, a slice of good Italian toast with a choice of toppings, before moving on to some fish, Italian pasta or a Tex-Mex dish.

Le Relais de la Mairie – *1 r. du Chay* – ☎ *05 46 39 03 15* – *closed Feb school holidays; 4-12 Nov; Sun, Tue and Thu evenings, except Jul-Aug* – *14.48/29.73€*. Appearances can be deceiving! Behind the rather gloomy exterior, this retaurant's narrow dining room is colourful and pleasant. Interesting fixed-price menu offered daily. A la carte menu a bit pricey.

Le Petit Poucet – *La Grande Côte* – *17420 St-Palais-sur-Mer* – ☎ *05 46 23 20 48* – *closed Jan, 1-15 Dec and Wed from Oct to late Mar* – *12/30€*. A gripping view of the sea, especially from the terrace! This is the best feature of this strange 1950s edifice built over the beach. Served in a modern blue and white decor, the cuisine is nothing special but the prices are quite affordable. Bar in the back.

MODERATE

La Jabotière – *espl. de Pontaillac* – ☎ *05 46 39 91 29* – *closed 2 Jan to 2 Feb, Christmas school holidays, Sun evening and Mon* – *22.87/53.36€*. White and blue parasols, wooden terrace and big bay windows looking out on the Conche de Pontaillac – this shoreside restaurant a stone's throw from the casino is a very enjoyable stop. Summertime, a less expensive fixed-price menu makes dining on the terrace at lunch a pleasure.

Where to stay

BUDGET

Hôtel Pasteur – *40 r. Pasteur* – ☎ *05 46 05 14 34* – *15 rms: 27.44/45.73€* – ☐ *4.27€*. In a calm Royan neighbourhood, this big, renovated post-war house has reasonable prices for the area. The rooms are tidy and sensibly furnished, even if the style is a bit out-moded. Family boarding-house ambience.

MODERATE

Hôtel Téthys – *plage de Nauzan* – *17420 St-Palais-sur-Mer* – *1.5km/1mi SE of St-Palais via rte de Royan* – ☎ *05 46 23 33 61* – *closed Oct to Apr* – 🅿 *– 23 rms: 45.73/60.98€* – ☐ *6.10€* – *restaurant 15.24/30.49€*. Across from the *plage de Nauzan*, this family hotel is both quiet and near the centre. Its relatively recent rooms of varying sizes are impeccably well-kept. Half of them open onto the sea as does the dining room, solemnly decorated with garden furniture.

Hôtel Primavera – *12 r. Brick, via ave.de la Grande Côte* – *17420 St-Palais-sur-Mer* – ☎ *05 46 23 20 35* – *closed 15 Nov to 15 Dec and Feb school holidays* – 🅿 *– 45 rms: 83.85/121.96€* – ☐ *9.15€* – *restaurant 19.06/36.59€*. Built in the late 19C, this elegant seaside villa is enhanced by its peaceful park. Whether in the old building or the new wing, the decor is bourgeois and most of the rooms have a view of the sea. Two simpler annexes, a covered pool and a tennis court.

On the town

La Maison Blanche – *Av. de la plage de Nauzan* – *17640 Vaux-sur-Mer* – ☎ *05 46 38 01 06* – *daily 9am-2am* – *closed Nov-Feb*. An unbeatable view of the sea, a big pool surrounded by palm trees, a labyrinth of benches scattered throughout a huge 'casbah' decorated with African cloths and masks…This establishment with three bars is jam-packed until closing.

L'Astoria – *42 av. du maréchal-Leclerc* – ☎ *05 46 05 85 75* – *pub.astoria@libertysurf.fr* – *summer: daily 8am-2am; rest of the year: 4pm-2am*. Here is where a night on the town begins in Royan. This little café-expo can't compare with the opulence of its peers, but everyone enjoys convening in this intimate haunt, halfway between a working-class bistro and a chronicle of imaginary travels.

Le Koud à Koud – *Plage du Chay* – ☎ *05 46 38 51 99* – *from mid-Sep to Halloween, Apr-Jun: daily except Tue morning and evening; Nov-Dec, Mar: Thu-Sat from 6pm; Jun to mid-Sep: 11am-2am*. Whether you opt for the wild atmosphere of the main room, the intimacy of the billiards corner or the tranquility of the terrace dominated by an enormous fig tree, you'll have a terrific evening in this extraordinary rendezvous overhanging the sea.

Cast off

Gispier 5 – Deep Sea Fishing – *Quai du 13ᵉ Dragons* – ☎ *05 46 39 86 51* – *by reservation only*. Bass, sea bream, sole, eels but also tuna and sharks (until now limited to a certain élite)…This is your chance to discover deep-sea fishing and the big blue aboard this 11m Merry Fisher equipped in a style (radar, sounder, sonar, GPS…) that would have done the Cousteau team proud!

A few yards away, on the right, there is a view sideways down onto the beaches and dunes of La Grande Côte, where long lines of breakers roll shorewards and bathing is very dangerous. Rod and reel fishing with cast weights is practised along the almost-deserted strand, especially for bass.

★★★ **Zoo de la Palmyre** – *See Zoo de la PALMYRE*.

The route emerges from the forest to pass the resort of **La Palmyre** then skirts **La Bonne Anse** – a lagoon refuge for small boats during bad weather, where coastal currents have turned the extremity of Pointe de La Courbe back on itself to form a spit shaped like a shepherd's crook.

★ **Phare de La Coubre** – La Coubre Lighthouse has had to be rebuilt several times because the dune on which it stands is "mobile". The present version dates from 1905 and rises to a height of 60m/199ft. Its slender, soaring, two-tone tower overlooks the Point from a position near the semaphore station. This is one of the most powerful lighthouses in France, with a beam that carries 53km/33mi, signalling the approaches to the Gironde. The walls inside are coloured an opaline blue. From the top – 300 steps and then a metal ladder – there is an extensive **panorama**★ over La Coubre Forest and the Isle of Oléron (north and east); the extremity of the point and its coastal spit, La Bonne Anse, and Cordouan lighthouse standing alone on the horizon (south). In the distance Pointe de Grave and the Côte de Beauté as far as the cliffs of Meschers-sur-Gironde are visible.

★ **Forêt de la Coubre** Ⓥ – Most of this 8 000ha/19 768 acre forest is composed of maritime pines and ilex trees; there are still a few deer to be seen. Extensive reforestation has all but eradicated the traces of the devastating fire which ravaged the area in 1976.
The forest serves to stabilise the dunes along the Arvert coast, better known as the **Côte Sauvage** (Wild Coast), which was studded during World War II with bunkers built by prisoners of war under the German Todt Organisation. Bike paths wind through the woodlands and lead to the beaches.
Half a mile north of La Coubre lighthouse *(car park)* a sandy track twists through the dunes to the strand, from which there is an impressive view of Atlantic rollers crashing against the shore.
8km/5mi further north, beyond the metallic Gardour tower, there is a wooded knoll on the right of route D 25. Crowning this rise, at the end of a forest road known as Chemin des Fontaines, is a panoramic tower made of wood: this is the **Tour des Quatre Fontaines**. From it there are wide-ranging views over the forest and the ocean beyond.

Enjoy the sea spray at La Grande Côte

S. Sauvignier/MICHELIN

Les SABLES-D'OLONNE☆☆☆

Population 15 532
Michelin map 316: F-8 or 233 fold 1

Les Sables-d'Olonne is an important seaside resort on the **Côte de la Lumière** (Coast of Light), built on the sands of what was once an off-shore bar. The town stretches between a small port and an immense beach of fine sand running for more than 3km/1.8mi at the foot of the *Remblai* (an embankment-promenade).

The only time visitors will see the local girls in their traditional, ancestral costume is during the summer season's folklore festivals: dark-haired, light on their feet and dressed in short skirts with pleated petticoats, black stockings, sabots with heels, and tall headdresses with quivering "wings".

Port Olona is the starting point for the round-the-world yacht race held every four years known as the "Vendée Globe" – a tough challenge for single-handed sailing boats with no ports of call allowed and no help on the way (the next race will take place in November 2004).

PRIVATEERS AND FISHERMEN

Origins – In the Middle Ages the site here was no more than an outer port for Olonne, a small town on the Vertonne estuary now a little way inland. Then, little by little, the inlet silted up, finally turning into a swamp and then a salt-marsh; Les Sables-d'Olonne (the sands of Olonne) was created.

Under the patronage of Louis XI, who visited the area with the chronicler Commynes, the Seneschal (Steward) of Poitou, the port was dredged out and shipyards were built. Some of the vessels launched here took part in the great voyages of discovery. In the 17C a local sailor, **Nau the Olonnais**, distinguished himself in the West Indies during the bloody guerrilla warfare waged against the Spaniards by the buccaneers of Turtle Island and the privateer-pirate gang known as the "Brothers of the Coast". The seafarer met a gruesome fate, devoured by hostile natives.

La Grande Plage

Economic life – The harbour comprises a dock for fishing boats, a wet dock (Bassin flot) for cargo ships, and a marina known as **Port Olona** with 1 100 berths for yachts and cruisers which lies further upriver, just south of the long, straight by-pass road linking Les Sables with the ancient fishermen's district of La Chaume west of the town.

Trawlers with their modern gear are engaged in both coastal and deep-sea fishing, generally in the southern part of the Bay of Biscay, although vessels sometimes travel as far north as St George's Channel, between Great Britain and Ireland. Because of the tonnage landed the town ranks 12th among France's fishing ports.

The **salt-marshes** north of the town are no longer exploited: plans have been approved to transform them into a zone of aquaculture. Market gardens in La Chaume, on the other hand, well-fertilised with marine compost, continue to produce high-quality early strawberries, artichokes etc.

Eating out

BUDGET

L'Affiche – *21 quai Guinée* – ☎ *02 51 95 34 74* – *closed Jan, Wed from 15 Jun to 15 Sep, Sun and Thu evenings and Mon all day from 15 Sep to 15 Jun* – *10.55/26€*. You can't miss this little eatery on the fishing docks – its sunshine yellow exterior catches the eye! Pleasant, simple decor and a varied menu, with an accent on – what else? – seafood.

MODERATE

La Pêcherie – *4 quai Boucaniers – la Chaume* – ☎ *02 51 95 18 27* – *closed 7 Jan to 8 Feb, 18-23 Jun, 15-30 Oct, Mon in Jul-Aug, Tue and Wed from Sep to Jun* – *20.58/35.83€*. Across from Port Olona, this small restaurant with a veranda is run by a dynamic young chef. In the yellow- and blue-toned dining room, you can savour a cuisine made from the harvest of the sea, well-prepared and served with a smile.

Auberge Robinson – *51 r. du Puits-d'Enfer – La Pironière – 85100 Château-d'Olonne – 4km/2.4mi SE of Les Sables; take the coast road* – ☎ *02 51 23 92 65 – closed 5- 21 Mar, 3-21 Dec; Sun evening and Mon from Sep to Jun, Mon and Wed lunch in Jul-Aug – 19.06/44.97€*. Follow the coast road out of Les Sables d'Olonne, it will lead you to this charming auberge with its sweet little garden and awnings. Barbecued meat on the terrace in the summer and delicious cuisine in the candy-pink dining room full of trinkets and curios in the winter.

Cayola – *76 prom. de Cayola – Anse de Cayola – 85100 Château-d'Olonne – 7km/4.2mi SE of Les Sables on the coast road* – ☎ *02 51 22 01 01 – closed Jan, Sun evening from Sep to Jun, Wed lunch in Jul-Aug and Mon 22.11/53.36€*. Perched high upon a cliff, this handsome contemporary villa has a majestic view of the ocean. Its large modern dining room gives on to a teak terrace, an overflowing swimming pool and, on the horizon, the deep…Vertigo guaranteed! Tasty, well-prepared contemporary cuisine.

Where to stay

BUDGET

Alizé Hôtel – *78 av. A.-Gabaret* – ☎ *02 51 32 44 90 – closed 20 Dec to 20 Feb.* – **P** – *24 rms: 33.54/50.31€* – ☲ *4.57€*. On a busy avenue a short distance from the centre of town, this modest hotel is well-suited to small budgets. Its rooms are somewhat out-moded but clean and tidy. Very reasonable prices for the area.

MODERATE

Hôtel Antoine – *60 r. Napoléon* – ☎ *02 51 95 08 36 – closed mid-Oct to 28 Feb.* – **P** – *20 rms: 53.36€* – ☲ *5.34€ – restaurant 15.24/19.82€*. Between the harbour and the beach in the old fishermen's quarters, this swank-looking hotel doubles as a family boarding house where regulars come for an annual visit. Spick-and-span rooms of varying sizes, friendly reception. Half-board available in season.

Atlantic Hôtel – *5 prom. Godet* – ☎ *02 51 95 37 71 – 30 rms: 70.13/118.91€* – ☲ *8.08€ – restaurant 15.09/39.64€*. This 1970s hotel is on the promenade, directly across from the Sables d'Olonne bay. Its pleasant rooms are spacious. Ask for a seaside room – you'll get a balcony as well as a view. Le Sloop restaurant and covered pool.

Château de la Millière Bed and Breakfast – *85150 St-Mathurin – 9km/5.4mi NE of Les Sables via N 160* – ☎ *02 51 22 73 29 – closed Oct to Apr –* ⊠ *– 5 rms: 84/90€*. This elegant 19C residence is nestled in a 25ha park. The large rooms, decorated with period furniture, overlook the trees in the park. The pool is set in a pretty garden with pavilions. French billiards for fans. Two self-catering cottages available year round.

Going out

Casino des Pins – *Av. Rhin-et-Danube – Casino des Pins bus (line 6)* – ☎ *02 51 21 69 00 – mini-golf: daily 10am-4am; tennis: from mid-Jun to mid-Sep: daily 8:30am-11pm*. In addition to its 90 slot machines and traditional games, this casino claims a classy and comfortable pub with a big shady flower-filled terrace around an ornamental pool. One concert per week in the summer.

Hot Blues Café – *24 prom. Clemenceau* – ☎ *02 51 95 91 01* – *hot-blues-cafe@wanadoo.fr* – *winter: Mon-Fri 12 :30pm-2am, Sat-Sun 12:30pm-3am; summer: daily 10am-3am.* The walls of this little basement hideout are painted with a big fresco of a blues concert. Locals come here to escape the agitation of the city. An authentic blues lovers' lair.

Le Navarin – *18 pl. Navarin* – ☎ *02 51 21 11 61* – *Jul-Aug: daily 9am-2am; Sep-Jun: 9am-midnight.* Facing the ocean, this café boasts a flower-filled terrace seating 120 that becomes a heated veranda in the winter. The interior is from a 16C galleon.

Sports and leisure

Les Circaètes – *Base de mer (petite jetée)* – ☎ *06 09 80 28 70* – *www.chez.com/les circaètes* – *daily 10am-8pm* – *open from mid-Jun to mid-Sep.* In the sailing centre on the sea, a wooden garden shack serves as an office for the well-qualified husband-and-wife team who run the place. Water-skiing and para-boating for the daring – at 80 metres above the sea, it's a real high!

Vendée Plongée – *Quai de l'Amiral de la Gravière-Port Olona* – ☎ *02 51 21 51 51* – *vendee.plongee@wanadoo.fr* – *daily 8:30am-7:30pm* – *closed Dec-Feb (depending on offshore weather).* This school's curriculum includes an introduction to diving and exploration of shipwrecks. Although some vessels were intentionally sunk for tourism, others are more authentic and all the more impressive, like the Alizé that has lain under 35m of water since 1940.

Le Ranch – *56 r. des Rochers* – *85340 Olonne-sur-Mer* – ☎ *02 51 90 76 96* – *summer: daily 7:30am-noon, 2pm-9pm; rest of the year: 9am-noon, 2pm-5pm.* Come winter or summer, this ranch offers rides through the forest, in the wetlands and along the shore for riders of all levels. Summertime, two 2-hour trips are organised on the beach, at 7:30am and 7:30pm.

Base Canoë – Les Salines – *120 rte de l'Aubraie* – ☎ *02 51 90 87 74* – *Jun-Aug: 9am-7pm; rest of the year: on demand (call ahead)* – *closed Nov-Apr.* Discover 1400ha of untamed marshlands by canoeing along the saline river. Several different itineraries are proposed depending on your wishes and the desired length of your outing.

Le Lys – *Quai Guiné* – ☎ *02 51 23 54 88 / 06 68 40 33 39* – *Jul-Aug: daily 9:30am-7pm* – *closed from mid-Oct to Apr.* Quick as a cannonball, this catamaran, jet-propelled at a speed of up to 80 km/h by two 250hp engines, will blow your jaunty sailor's cap right off your head. Fishing and sightseeing on the agenda.

Le Kifanlo-Organisme de Culture, d'Étude et d'Action Maritimes – *48 r. Parisse* – ☎ *02 51 95 53 11 ou 02 51 96 85 85* – *www.multimania.com/OCEAM* – *from mid-Mar to Oct: Mon-Sat; sign up at the l'Office du tourisme (02 51 96 85 85); schedule follows the tides.* Aboard this superb trawler, listed as a historical monument, learn all the ins and outs of the great and terrible profession of deep-sea fishing. Twelve participants at a time.

Les Salines – *Port-Olona-Nord* – ☎ *02 51 21 01 19* – *www.lessalines.fr* – *Jun-Sep: 9am-7pm; from mid-Mar to the end of May and Oct: daily 10am-12:30pm, 2pm-7pm* – *closed Nov-Mar.* The genuine Olonnais region can only be discovered by boat, following the saline river. The guided tour lasts 2hr 30min and winds up with a halt at the Jardin des Salines (historical site with sound; commentaries about the salt marshes) in the company of saltworkers. A bird sanctuary now occupies one whole side of the marsh.

Paint ball – *1 r. Marchais* – *Le Puits d'Enfer* – ☎ *02 51 21 48 91* – *daily 10:30am-12:30pm, 3pm-9pm* – *closed from early Sep to the end of Jun.* Australian shepherds invented this game as a way to mark sheep while having fun. Children of all ages can play this amusing and vigorous version of hide-and-seek on a big field along the sea.

Vedettes Sablaises: L'Aigue Marine – *Quai Guiné* – ☎ *02 51 21 31 43* – *www.inter-iles.com* – *schedules vary following the seasons* – *closed from mid-Sep to early Apr.* The Côte Sauvage (Wild Coast) used to be swarming with pirates. To discover this now peaceful coastline, nothing beats a 50min sea cruise complete with commentary. Moreover, if you're a rod-and-reel fishing buff, a boat will take you towards the Barges lighthouse, where the fish are plentiful. Equipment and bait are provided.

SIGHTS

In the summer season organised **boat trips** leave from the port.

★ **Le Remblai** – This embankment was built in the 18C to protect the town from the incursions of the sea. Today the fine promenade along its top is bordered by shops, hotels, cafés and luxury apartment blocks with splendid views of the beach and the bay. At the western extremity of Le Remblai is the municipal swimming pool and one of the casinos (Casino de la Plage, which includes a 700-seat theatre and a conference hall which can accommodate 1 000). Behind the modern blocks, the narrow streets of the old town beckon.

La Corniche – This southerly prolongation of Le Remblai leads to the new residential district of La Rudelière. After 3km/1.8mi the clifftop route arrives at **Le Puits d'Enfer** (Hell's Well) – a narrow and impressive cleft in the rock, where the sea foams and thrashes.

La Rudelière District – The development is near the **Lac de Tanchet**, with its lakeside sailing school. In the same area are the town's second casino, Casino des Sports, a sea-water cure centre (Centre de Thalassothérapie), sports grounds and a zoo.

Parc Zoologique de Tranchet – In this pleasantly laid out "green belt" environment, visitors can observe a variety of wildlife including camels, llamas, kangaroos, monkeys and rare birds.

Église Notre-Dame-de-Bon-Port – The church was built in 1646 by Richelieu. In the nave, which is an excellent example of late Gothic architecture, the Gothic vaults are perfectly complemented by the pilasters of the Corinthian order supporting them.

Musée de l'Abbaye Ste-Croix – The old Holy Cross Abbey, founded in the 17C by Benedictine monks, is now a cultural centre. The ground floor of the museum is devoted to the last works of Victor Brauner: *Mythologies et Fêtes des Mères* (1965) On the first floor are works by Gaston Chaissac (one of the leaders of the Art Brut (Outsider or Raw Art) movement, 1910-64). a second room is devoted to temporary exhibitions.

The second floor houses works by contemporary painters: Baselitz, Beckmann, Cahn, Magnelli, Marquet etc. The 17C attics contain collections of **popular art and traditions** including a marshland domestic hut interior, traditional costumes from Les Sables and the surrounding marshlands, seascapes by the local painter Paul-Emil Pajot, and a number of model boats.

OLONNE COUNTRY

40km/25mi round tour – allow half a day

Drive west out of Les Sables-d'Olonne.

La Chaume – The redeveloped, former fishermen's district has retained its small houses with tiled roofs which contrast starkly with the planned modernism of the resort. A shuttle service links La Chaume to Les Sables *(departure from quai Guiné)*.

Tour d'Arundel – This tower, once the keep of a fort built in the 12C for Lord Arundel, is used today as a lighthouse. There is a fine view of the bay from the top.

Prieuré St-Nicolas – The 11C priory chapel, transformed into a fort in 1779, stands on a pleasant site commanding the entrance to the port and offering a splendid view of the bay.
A garden has been laid out around the building, with a **mosaic memorial** (1971) to sailors lost at sea. Fine view of the bay.

Leave La Chaume and follow D 87 A northwards.

On your right lies the abandoned **salt-marsh zone**.

Forêt d'Olonne – This stretch of woodland standing alone between the ocean and the Vertonne marshes shimmering beneath the sun extends for 15km/9mi north of Les Sables. Oak thickets beneath clusters of tall pines carpet over 1 000ha/2 470 acres of dunes crisscrossed by footpaths; the quick eye may catch sight of one of the herds of deer wandering freely.

M. Thierry/MICHELIN

Lighthouse on the jetty

At Champclou turn left onto D 80.

St-Nicolas-de-Brem – The church here is curious. It was built in the 11C and partially reconstructed in the 17C. There is a statue of St Nicolas above the entrance. Nearby is a tumulus, an ancient medieval mound probably thrown up to protect the port.

Drive south-east out of St-Nicolas-de-Brem along D 38. At L'Île-d'Olonne, turn right onto D 87.

The road crosses the **Olonne marsh**, the eastern part of which has been transformed into a bird sanctuary. The marsh was originally formed because of the gradual silting up, in prehistoric times, of what was the Bay of Olonne.

Observatoire d'Oiseaux de l'Île-d'Olonne – ⓥ Well-placed on a rise overlooking the marsh, the observatory allows visitors, with the help of telescopes, to study the birds in the **Chanteloup Hunting Reserve**. Every summer the 38ha/94 acre reserve accommodates, among many other species, an important colony of avocets.

Return to L'Île-d'Olonne and continue along D 38.

Olonne-sur-Mer – This one-time coastal port now stands a little way inland, the effect of the silting up of the Bay.

Leave Olonne-sur-Mer east via D 80.

Château de Pierre-Levée – This charming 18C folly in the Louis XVI style was built by Luc Pezot, a tax collector for Les Sables district.

N 160 leads back to Les Sables-d'Olonne.

ST-ÉMILION★★

St-Émilion is a delightful town built on the slopes of a limestone plateau overlooking the Dordogne Valley, and surrounded by its famous vineyards. Ancient ramparts, monuments, a maze of narrow streets and stone stairways linking picturesque small squares combine to form an overall picture that never fails to impress visitors. In fine weather the sun accentuates the golden tones of the old stone walls, while the ever-changing contrasts of light and shade enliven a stroll through the medieval quarters. The town is known not only for its fine wines but also for the local macaroons (small crushed almond cakes).

Peace Lovers – Centuries after the Latin poet Ausonius settled in the locality – he had property on the hillside, and his name today remains allied to one of the prestigious wine "houses" – it was a hermit named **Émilion** who found here the peace and tranquillity necessary for meditation. Émilion, originally from Brittany, was a baker by trade before embracing the monastic life at Saujon, near Royan. Withdrawing subsequently to the limestone slopes of the Dordogne Valley, he discovered a grotto watered by a natural spring in the rocky centre of what is now the town bearing his name, and lived there until his death towards the end of the 8C.

Ten centuries later it was a fugitive who sought sanctuary in St-Émilion: **Élie Guadet**, a native of the town and a prominent member of the Girondin Party at the beginning of the Convention. Suspected of "Moderantism" – what today would be termed deviation from the party line – Gaudet became a victim of the Revolutionary leader Robespierre's hatred for the Girondins, and was obliged to flee Paris disguised as an upholsterer. He took refuge first in Normandy and later rejoined a couple of Girondin colleagues in St-Émilion. It was here, one day in 1794, that he was discovered, arrested, and taken to Bordeaux, where he died on the scaffold.

Jurats and the Jurade

In the Middle Ages the famous red wines of St-Émilion *(see Vignoble de BORDEAUX)* were qualified as "honorific" because it was the custom to offer them to royalty and persons of note. From then on it was decided that, in order to maintain the excellence and reputation of wines permitted to bear that name, they should be subject each year to evaluation by a committee of professionals. The body appointed by the town council to carry out this task was called the Jurade and its members the Jurats. The Jurade was reformed in 1948 and still operates today.

In the spring of each year, a procession of Jurats wearing scarlet, ermine-trimmed robes and silken hoods attends a solemn mass and then proceeds towards the cloisters of the collegiate church for ceremonial events. At the end of the afternoon, the Jurade pronounces its judgement on the new wine from the top of the King's Tower.

In the autumn these same Jurats assemble at the top of the King's Tower to proclaim the official start of the grape harvest. Such solemn rites are accompanied by ritual banquets – suitably washed down with local wines – held in the Dominican Room of the local wine-growers' association.

TOWN WALK

★★ **Site** – St-Émilion faces due south, nestling within a horse-shoe between two hillsides. At the junction of the two slopes, a tall belfry rises above a rocky spur honeycombed with caves, catacombs, a hermitage, a chapel and an extraordinary underground church. At the foot of this promontory, below the church, lies Place du Marché, the main square at the heart of this busy small town. The square acts as a link between the districts sprawled over the two hills, one the site of the royal castle, the other the site of a deanery (clerical residence), reflecting the age-old rivalry between civil and religious powers.

This walk takes in St-Émilion's main sights; however, one can easily adapt it to one's taste and stroll at random through the picturesque network of narrow streets.

Le petit train touristique, which has been operating since 1992, is a good alternative for those who want to tour the town but can't do it on foot. The 35-min trip (Easter to mid-November) carries vistors past some presitigioius wine-growing châteaux and the main monuments of the town. Departures every 45min from in front of the Collégiale church (upper town) from 10.30am-6.30pm (4.57€).

Eating out

Le Bouchon – *1 pl. du Marché* – ☎ *05 57 24 62 81* – *lebouchon@wanadoo.fr* – *closed Nov to Feb* – *14.48/28.20€*. One of the nicest addresses on the marketplace. The recently repainted dining room has aerial photos and Botero prints on the green and blue walls. Traditional fare prepared with care and an interesting selection of wines.

MODERATE

L'Envers du Decor – *11 r. du Clocher* – ☎ *05 57 74 48 31* – *closed 22 Dec to 9 Jan and Sat-Sun in winter* – *15€ lunch* – *23/31€*. With its back against the collegiate church, a lovely, peaceful terrace graced with a fig tree and flowers prolongs the sober dining room of wood and metal. Fine St-Emilion vintages complement your *tournedos de magret sauce miel et badiane* or other market-fresh dishes.

Where to stay

BUDGET

Château Meylet – *1.5km/1mi W of St-Émilion, rte de Libourne via D 243* – ☎ *05 57 24 68 85* – ⊟ – *4 rms: 42.69/50.31€*. Built in 1789, this Girondin residence is situated among 2ha of grapevines. The charming, rustic rooms are furnished with fine period pieces. Breakfast is served on the veranda in the winter, and under the garden bower in the summer.

Auberge de la Commanderie – *R. des Cordeliers* – ☎ *05 57 24 70 19* – *closed 15 Jan to late Feb* – 🅿 – *17 rms: 53.36/83.85€* – ☕ *7.62€*. This 17C *commanderie* (officer's residence) is located in the centre of the city. The rooms are compact but well soundproofed. Ask for one in the annex across the way; embellished with exposed stones, they are more modern. Sitting room with fireplace.

Château Monlot Capet – *33330 St-Hippolyte* – *3km/1.8mi E of St-Émilion dir. Castillon via D 245* – ☎ *05 57 74 49 47* – ⊟ – *5 rms: 53.36/83.85€*. The foundations of this château with its chalky facade and handsome tiled roof were laid when the Capets ruled the land. Old photographs hang in the rooms, each of which is named after a different vintage. The breakfast room is decorated in a grapevine theme.

On the town

Au Bois de l'Or (BDL) – *4 Champs du Rivalon* – ☎ *05 57 51 35 43* – *Fri-Sat 11pm-5am*. A very popular disco. Theme evenings weekly. Terrace.

Place du Marché – *Pl. du Marché*. Come enjoy yourself in one of the many cafés and restaurants of the Place du Marché, at the foot of the monolithic church.

Place du Marché – St-Émilion's main square and market place, in a picturesque setting at the foot of the spur, offers a fine view of the troglodyte church and its great belfry soaring heavenwards (fine view from the top).

A ramp leads to Porte de la Cadène.

Porte et logis de la Cadène – This gateway stands at the end of a street off the main square, with a 15C timber-framed house beside it. The name of the arch derives from the Latin word *catena* ("chain"), and is a reminder of nights past, when access to the town centre was blocked by a chain across this gateway. The span frames the church belfry.

Turn right onto rue de la Porte-Brunet.

Of the old **Logis de la Commanderie** (the abbot's lodgings), nothing remains but a covered watch-path and a corner bartizan.

Cloître des Cordeliers ⊘ – The Cordeliers – Franciscans of a strict order distinguished by a knotted cord worn around the waist – built this sanctuary in the 14C. The handsome ruins of their square **cloisters**★ include slender twinned columns supporting Romanesque arches. At the far end, on the right, a 15C Gothic archway precedes the stairway which led to the monks' cells.

On the left, the belfry of the old church (15C) is supported by two unusual super-imposed arches. Inside, the nave is separated from the apse by a triumphal arch in the Flamboyant Gothic style, which gives access down to a series of caves quarried out 20m/66ft deep in the bedrock where sparkling white and rosé wines are left to age.

There is an interesting view of St-Émilion from the Esplanade nearby (place du Cap-du-Pont).

Continue along rue de la Porte-Brunet to the ramparts.

Porte Brunet – It is one of the six gates which allowed access through the ramparts erected in the 13C and reinforced later by a machicolated watch-path. It was through this gate, one night in January 1794, that the outlawed Girondins escaped from Robespierre's men after the arrest of their companion Guadet

From Porte Brunet, there are impressive views of the vineyards. The Tour du Roi (the king's tower) and the spire of the church tower can be seen rising above the narrow winding streets

Head for the Tour du Roi via ramps, steps and culs-de-sac.

Château du Roi ⊙ – The King's Castle, founded according to some by Louis VIII and to others by Henri III Plantagenet in the 13C, was used as the town hall until 1720. From the top of the **King's Tower** (a rectangular keep with latrines on its outer face, standing on an isolated spur of rock) there is a fine **view**★ over the huddled rooftops of the town and across to the valleys of the Dordogne and the Isle rivers.

Follow rue de la Grande-Fontaine then the steep ruelle du Tertre-des-Vaillants which wends its way between houses dug out of the rock.

Collégiale – *Place Pioceau.* This huge church (*collégiale* is used to refer to churches which are endowed for a chapter of canons, but do not host the bishop's see) has a Romanesque nave with a Gothic chancel. The entrance is on the north side of the chancel, via a superb 14C porch built at a time when Gaillard de Lamothe, the nephew of Pope Clement V, was Dean of the resident canons. The carved tympanum represents *The Last Judgement.* Below, only the lower parts of the statues of the Apostles remain in their niches, the figures having been mutilated during the Wars of Religion and during the Revolution. The 15C choir stalls in the chancel are carved with an entertaining variety of characters.

Inside the nave, two 12C mural paintings – *The Virgin* and *The Legend of St Catherine* – adorn the far end of the right-hand wall.

Logis de Malet de Roquefort – Opposite the *église collégiale*, a 15C mansion is incorporated into the ramparts; the old covered watch path of the fortified town with its corbelled crenellations passes beneath the roof of the house.

Cloître de la collégiale ⊙ – *Enter via the tourist information centre.*

The cloisters, which lie to the south of the church, date from the 14C and are still in very good condition; they have much in common with the Cordeliers' Cloisters, particularly in the design of their twinned columns, which are extremely elegant.

Arches reinforce the corners separating the galleries – one of which houses an impressive series of covered niches formerly used as tombs.

The deanery – comprising the old refectory and the monks' dormitory – has been restored and is occupied today by the tourist information centre.

Return to place du Marché.

St-Émilion vineyards

ROUND PLACE DU MARCHÉ

Combined tours ⏱ of the sights below.

Ermitage St-Émilion – Enlarged to form of a Greek cross, this grotto contains "St Émilion's Bed", his armchair carved from the limestone, and a spring, now guarded by a 17C balustrade; right at the end is an altar surmounted by a statue of the saint.

Catacombes – Near the chapel the cliff face opens out into catacombs – rock galleries once used as an ancient burial ground, with tombs gouged from the rock. Later, the main part of this subterranean maze was used as an ossuary: at the top of a central dome is an opening through which bones from a cemetery on top of the cliff were disposed of. At the base of the dome is a primitive representation depicting the resurrection of the dead: three carved figures emerging hand in hand from their sarcophagi.

Chapelle de la Trinité – Holy Trinity Chapel, a miniature sanctuary built by Benedictine monks in the 13C, includes a harmonious – and, in the southwest, rare – example of a timber-framed Gothic apse (frescoes). Inside, elegant High Gothic ribbed vaulting converges on a keystone embossed with the symbolic Lamb.

★ **Église Monolithe** ⏱ – The church, the largest monolithic sanctuary in France to be carved from a single solid block of rock, is a great rarity. It was fashioned between the 8C and the 12C by enlarging natural grottoes and caverns which already existed in the porous strata. The main entrance was through a tall 14C Gothic porch decorated on the tympanum with a *Last Judgement* and a *Resurrection of the Dead*.
The interior of the church is impressive as much for the size of those three aisles carved from the rock as for the perfect symmetry of its vaulting and squared pillars – only two of which support the belfry *(concrete supporting posts have been added temporarily, during restoration work)*. At the back of the central nave, beneath the arcade of the bay, there is a bas-relief of two four-winged angels or cherubims.
The majestic **belfry** (198 steps) offers a fine view of the town, its monuments and the neighbouring vineyards.

EXCURSION

St-Émilion Vineyards – *Round trip of 52km/32mi. See Vignoble de BORDEAUX.*

ST-GILLES-CROIX-DE-VIE ⌂

Population 6 797
Michelin map 324: E-7 or 232 folds 38, 39

The lively fishing port of **Croix-de-Vie** and the town of St-Gilles-sur-Vie, on the south bank of the Vie estuary, north-west of Les Sables-d'Olonne, combine to make the single commune of St-Gilles-Croix-de-Vie. When St-Hilaire-de-Riez (northeast) is included, the combined area is also known as Havre-de-Vie. The fishing boats here supply wholesale fish merchants and factories with lobsters, crabs, tuna fish and sardines for canning or freezing. A sheltered marina can accommodate up to 600 craft.

CREPES

La Crêperie – *4 r. Gautté – ☎ 02 51 55 02 77 – closed Sun lunch and Mon off season except school holidays – 9.45€.* This pretty 17C house is embellished by visible stones, period floor-tiles, wooden tables, cast iron chairs, fishing nets and ropes and modern art. The batter is hand-beaten in the kitchen and the galettes cooked before your eyes. Covered terrace in the back.

The Vie estuary is a geographical curiosity. Approaching the sea, the stream first runs up against a line of sand dunes, the Pointe de la Garenne, and then against the rocky headland known as the Corniche Vendéenne, looping itself as a result into a number of meanders. It finally emerges into the Atlantic between the beaches of Croix-de-Vie (Plage de Boisvinet) and St-Gilles (Grand-Plage) via a bottleneck at the harbour mouth. In the summer **boat trips** ⏱ are organised around the coast, leaving from the port.

B. Kaufmann/MICHELIN

St-Gilles-Croix-de-Vie

EXCURSIONS

From the shore to the first hedgerows – *60km/36mi round tour, allow 3hr; see Le Marais BRETON-VENDÉEN.*

Coëx – *14km/8mi E via D 6.* A fragrant garden lies at the heart of this village.

★ **Jardin des Olfacties** ⊘ – The Gué-Gorand stream runs through this pleasantly undulating floral garden. A path takes visitors through a series of "fragrant chambers" combining different plants and scents. Colourful flower beds giving off various fragrances (artemisia, varieties of mint, sage, sweet-smelling geraniums, roses, etc.) encircle an attractive pond surrounded by sculptures, cultural exhibitions and leisure facilities, open to the public from June through October.

ST-JEAN-DE-LUZ★★

Population 13 247
Michelin map 342: C-4 or 234 folds 29, 33

As a smart summer and winter seaside resort, St-Jean-de-Luz dates back only to 1843; as a fishing port, however, the town is ancient, though only one house survives from before the great fire of 1558, when the place was sacked by Spaniards. The sea-front is determinedly modern.

Ste-Barbe headland, which can be reached on foot via Promenade de la Plage and Boulevard Thiers, offers a fine view southwards across the bay to Socoa fort on its rocky promontory.

St-Jean-de-Luz, the most Basque of the towns lying north of the Spanish border, offers all the attractions and amenities of a beach resort together with the picturesque and briny delights of a busy fishing port.

The Marriage of Louis XIV – The outstanding historical event connected with St-Jean-de-Luz is the marriage of Louis XIV and Maria Theresa. The wedding between the King of France and the Infanta of Spain, provided for in the Treaty of the Pyrenees, was delayed because of the monarch's passion for Marie Mancini, the niece of Cardinal Mazarin. The situation was resolved when the Cardinal – successor to Richelieu and Louis XIV's chief minister – eventually sent the young girl into exile and the King yielded for "reasons of State". Louis arrived in St-Jean-de-Luz on 8 May 1660 and was lodged, together with the royal retinue, in an imposing mansion which had been built for the shipowner Lohobiague; Maria Theresa stayed in an elegant brick and stone house nearby.

On the morning of 9 June the King presented himself at the Infanta's house to claim his bride. The procession moved off towards the church between the Swiss Guards lining the route, and was led by two companies of Gentlemen-at-Arms followed by Cardinal Mazarin dressed in sumptuous robes. Behind him came Louis XIV, in black with lace trimmings, and then the Infanta who wore a dress of spun silver and a cloak of heavy purple velvet, with a gold crown on her head. The King's brother, known in royal circles simply as "Monsieur", was a few paces behind with their mother, the imposing Anne of Austria. They were followed by the rest of the court.

The marriage was solemnised by the Bishop of Bayonne and the service lasted until halfway through the afternoon. The door through which the royal couple left the church was walled up after the ceremony.

The cortège returned to the Infanta's house. From the balcony there the King himself and Mazarin threw commemorative medals to the crowd below. Later the newlyweds dined with the court in Lohobiague's mansion.

Following a strict etiquette they were then led to the nuptial couch, and given the traditional blessing by the Queen Mother as she drew its curtains.

Louis XIV found in Maria Theresa a gentle and worthy wife, and when she died the King remarked: "This is the first and only time she has ever made me unhappy."

Wedding Gifts – The young Queen was showered with gifts worthy of the Thousand and One Nights. From her husband she received six dazzling sets of jewellery encrusted with diamonds and other precious stones; from Monsieur, twelve jewelled dress ornaments. The present from Mazarin, who was phenomenally wealthy, outshone them all: 1 200 000 *livres*-worth of diamonds and pearls, a great dinner service in solid gold, and two state coaches, one drawn by six Russian horses, the other by six Indian horses, each with trappings and livery to match the colours of the carriages.

TOWN WALK

★**Port** – With whaling a thing of the past, local fishermen nowadays rely on hauls of sardines, anchovies and especially tuna fish for their livelihood.

The port is at the inner end of the only anchorage to break the long straight line of the Atlantic coast between Arcachon and the Bidasoa River. The estuary, nestling between the Socoa and Ste-Barbe headlands, is further protected from westerly gales by massive dikes and the Artha breakwaters.

From the quays there are picturesque views across the busy harbour of the old town and inland, in the distance, the great pyramid bulk of La Rhune.

The imposing **Maison de l'Infante** seems to be guarding the boats. This elegant building in the Louis XIII style, constructed of brick and stone with Italian-style galleries overlooking the port, belonged to the rich Haraneder family. The Infanta stayed here with her future mother-in-law, Anne of Austria.

Rue Mazarin – 17C shipowners used to live on the strip of land separating the roadstead from the harbour. The area has retained a few elegant houses; note in particular **Maison St-Martin** at no 13 rue Mazarin.

Town centre – Modernised now with many pedestrian precincts (rue de la République, rue Gambetta) – the town centre has a special charm of its own. The famous "oldest house", its solid dressed-stone construction contrasting with the red-roofed, white-walled Basque buildings nearby, is at 17 rue de la République, near the harbour.

La Maison de l'Infante

B. Kaufmann/MICHELIN

Eating out

Salon de thé L'Acanthe – *31 r. Garat* – ☎ *05 59 26 85 59* – *lacanthe@lacanthe.com – closed mid-Nov to Mar and Mon off-season – 9.15€.* Has swimming in the sea given you an appetite? Here's a very down-to-earth, practical address just 50m from the shore. You can have breakfast, a simple meal, tea or a snack at any time, or sample the superb ham on show in the dining room.

Muscade – *20 r. Garat* – ☎ *05 59 26 96 73 – closed 7 Nov to 1 Apr and Mon off-season – 12.20€.* Gourmands beware: this is a dangerous window to tarry by. Quiches, pies and tarts of all varieties are tantalizingly exposed, enticing one to enter the spruce pastel dining room for a bite. A pleasant, affordable pause.

Restaurant Ibaïa – *39 r. Tourasse* – ☎ *05 59 51 12 21 – closed Jan, Sun evening off-season and Mon – 12.96/16.77€.* A handful of tables are set on the pavement in front of this old house a few steps from the beach. The fireplace, exposed beams and hot pepper garlands hanging in the windows pay homage to the pleasures of the region. Local cuisine.

Venta Insola – *Col d'Ibardin – 64500 Vera de Bidasoa – after the Venta Gloria, take the first left after 3km/1.8mi* – ☎ *00 349 48 63 12 28 – closed weekdays in winter and Mon in summer –* ✍ *– 10.67/12.50€.* How to resist this authentic *venta* nestled in the bottom of the valley? The dining room has retained its traditional flavour with its large wooden counter and shelves presenting liquors, cigarettes and foodstuffs. Terrace by a stream.

Les Trois Fontaines – *64310 Col de St-Ignace – 11km/6.6mi SE of St-Jean-de-Luz via D 918 and D 4* – ☎ *05 59 54 20 80 – closed end Jan to mid-Feb, mid-Nov to early Dec and Wed from Oct to Mar – 11.43/22.11€.* Right near where the Rhune train departs, this little auberge is a tranquil halt in a fertile valley. If weather permits, take a seat on the terrace and enjoy the decor and quietude. Simple cuisine.

Chez Théo – *25 r. de l'Abbé-Onaindia* – ☎ *05 59 26 81 30 – closed Mar, Nov, Sun evening in season and Mon except evening in season – 12.04/14.64€.* A family auberge in Spanish Basque country where you'll find *azulejos*, posters of ferias, cob walls, solid wood furniture as well as a wide choice of tapas and more substantial fare whipped up with zeal and served in a convivial ambience.

Au Chipiron – *4 r. Etchegaray* – ☎ *05 59 26 03 41 – closed Dec to mid-Jan, Tue-Wed off-season – 17.99/24.39€.* This restaurant calls itself a "house of fish and regional specialities", the most celebrated of which is their *chipirons à l'encre* (squid in ink). The communicating dining rooms, decorated in Basque country colours, are agreeable. Games corner for the children.

Petit Grill Basque « Chez Maya » – *4 r. St-Jacques* – ☎ *05 59 26 80 76 – closed 20 Dec to 20 Jan and Wed – 16.77/23.63€.* This small, hospitable neighbourhood restaurant has been run by the same family for three generations. The Basque time-honoured interior is quite stylish with its old plates and wall frescos. Plentiful regional cuisine.

Where to stay

Arrayoa Bed and Breakfast – *at the village edge – 64310 Ascain* – ☎ *05 59 54 06 18 – closed 1-7 Oct –* ✍ *– 4 rms: /45.73€.* This peaceful duck farm is located outside the village. The charming reception, big common room with a corner kitchen and bookshelves, country-style bedrooms, private fronton and reasonable prices make this a popular address indeed. Take some home-made *confit* or *foie gras* back with you.

Hôtel Bolivar – *18 r. Sopite* – ☎ *05 59 26 02 00 – closed Oct to Apr – 16 rms: 34.30/53.36€ –* ⊆ *5.34€.* If you've come here to spend most of your time by the sea, this family hotel 50m from the beach is for you. The rooms, though smallish, are simple and clean, and the bathrooms well equipped.

Mme Itzala's Rooms – *64310 Ascain* – ☎ *05 59 54 02 90 – closed Jan – 4 rms: 36.59€ –* ⊆ *4.57€.* Built in 1720, this Basque building used to house a presbytery. The thick walls of the cool rooms shut out excess noise. Order a generous salad, an omelette or one of a few regional dishes to enjoy on the shaded terrace.

Villa Argi-Eder Bed and Breakfast – *Av. Napoléon III, – Plage Lafitenia – 5km/3mi NE of St-Jean-de-Luz. Take N 10 dir. Biarritz then secondary road – ☎ 05 59 54 81 65 – villa-argi-eder@wanadoo.fr – ⊠ – 4 rms: 46€ – ☐ 4.50€.* A Basque house (as one would expect), a lawn, flowers, quietude and the surfers' beach 100m away: what else could a holidaymaker possibly desire? The big, simple rooms open onto private terraces on the garden side.

Olhabidea Bed and Breakfast – *64310 Sare – 13km/8mi SE of St-Jean-de-Luz via D 918 and D 4 – ☎ 05 59 54 21 85 – closed Dec to Feb – ⊠ – 4 rms: 46/60€.* This typical 17-18C house was restored by local craftsmen. The rooms, with their pretty Basque colours and waxed furniture, are quite smart. Warning! This B&B's reputation has travelled beyond the region – better to come off-season or reserve well in advance.

MODERATE

Hôtel Le Petit Trianon – *56 bd Victor-Hugo – ☎ 05 59 26 11 90 – closed Jan – 26 rms: 38.11/60.98€ – ☐ 6.10€.* An address without pretence, but well managed. The rooms, rather cramped, come with 1960s-style bathrooms. In season, you can have breakfast in the inner courtyard decorated with an immense Basque fresco.

Château d'Urtubie Bed and Breakfast – *r. Bernard-de-Coral – 64122 Urrugne – 2km/1.2mi S of St-Jean-de-Luz via N 10 (dir. Hendaye) – ☎ 05 59 54 31 15 – closed 15 Nov to 15 Mar – ▣ – 9 rms: 70/130€ – ☐ 10€.* Have a taste of château life in the handsome, appealing bedrooms of this historic monument that has belonged to the same family since 1341. Don't be put off by the nearness of the road – the air-conditioned rooms are well insulated against sound. Park and museum.

On the town

La Pergola – *Pl. Maurice-Ravel – ☎ 05 59 51 58 58 – daily 11am-3am.* This casino has a traditional games room, a slot machine section, a *brasserie* and a piano bar. Music Fridays and Saturdays in the *brasserie*.

Place Louis XIV – *Pl. Louis-XIV –* The terraces of numerous bars, *brasseries* and restaurants are to be found around St-Jean-de-Luz's central square. The meeting place of local guys and dolls, the square becomes even more animated in the summer when concerts and other shows are performed here on a regular basis.

Sports

Association Sportive de la Nivelle – *Pl. William-Sharp – 64500 Ciboure – ☎ 05 59 47 18 99 – golf.nivelle@etxe.fr – summer: daily except Thu 7am-8:30pm; off-season: daily except Thu 8am-7pm or 7:30am-7:30pm.* While the general French enthusiasm for golf is a recent phenomenon, it has always been one of the most popular sports in the Basque country, exempt of the snobbism one might fear to find elsewhere. In addition to the 18-hole golf course, this association has 3 tennis and 2 squash courts.

Fronton Municipal – *1 av. André-Ithurralde – ☎ 05 59 26 13 93 – Jul-Sep: Mon, Thu 7:30pm-11pm.* From July to September, you can watch chistera matches played on Mondays and grand chistera matches on Thursdays (9:15pm). Open to the public except during competitions, the fronton is often used by local children coming to hit their *pelotes* (balls) against the *fronton* (wall) with their *palas* (wooden rackets).

Jaï Alaï – *Av. André-Ithurralde – ☎ 05 59 51 65 30 – www.saintjeandeluz.fr – during professional Cesta Punta competitions, Mon-Fri 9am-7pm. Cesta punta* is the emblematic sport of the Basque country. It is played against a covered Spanish fronton *(jaï alaï)* of three walls – in front, behind and to the left. From June to September, professional cesta punta matches take place here Tuesdays and Fridays.

Le Spot – *16 r. Gambetta – ☎ 05 59 26 07 93 – lespot64@aol.com – Mon-Sat 9:30am-12:30pm, 2:30pm-7:30pm; Jul-Aug: Mon-Sat 9:30am-9pm – closed Feb.* This sports shop organizes surf and bodyboard lessons. Two other shops in the same street, Bakea (n° 37) and H2O (n° 72) offer similar deals.

Sports Mer – *7 bd Thiers – Digue aux Chevaux – ☎ 05 59 26 96 94 or 06 80 64 39 11 – Jul-Aug: daily 10am-8pm; office open year round.* Thrill seekers of all ages can come stimulate their adrenaline by trying para-boating (solo or tandem) or other adventures.

Trinquet Maïtena – *42 r. du Midi* – ☎ *05 59 26 05 13* – *daily 9am-10pm*. The Basques practice many sports, like squash, tennis and golf, but their heart belongs to *pala*, played in a *trinquet* (small covered court). After a game, they come here to cool down and sing together.

École de Voile Internationale – *Parking de Socoa – 64500 Ciboure* – ☎ *05 59 47 06 32 or 06 80 13 79 22 – Easter to 1 Nov: Tue-Sun 9:30am-noon, 2pm-7pm; Jul-Aug: daily 9:30am-7pm – Price for a session of water-skiing: 17,53€*. This school offers sailing and water-skiing courses and rents boats and windsurf boards.

All aboard

Le Marie Rose – *100 r. Gambetta* – ☎ *06 08 25 49 74 or 05 59 26 39 84 – www.bateau-marirose.com – Apr to mid-Oct: daily 8am-noon (deep-sea fishing), 2pm-4pm (Spanish cruise), 4pm-5pm (cliff cruise), 5pm-5:30pm (short cruise)*. On board the Marie Rose, an old pilot boat built in 1932, you can discover the shale cliffs of the Basque coast or go fishing in the ocean. Just down the docks, the Nivelle III offers similar services.

Take a break

Bar Xaia – *R. de la Fontaine – 64500 Ciboure* – ☎ *05 59 47 02 10 – Mon-Thu 7am-10pm, Fri-Sun 9am-2am*. An old, dim and humid house with exposed beams is the setting for this 'snack bar'. This is where the old salts have a drink with fishermen gathering their strength before the next expedition at sea. In the evening, their children come take their seats at the bar.

Le Brouillarta – *48 prom. Jacques-Thibaud* – ☎ *05 59 51 29 51 – summer: daily 9am-3am; off-season: Tue-Sat 9am-2am, Sun 9am-6pm – closed mid-Nov to mid-Dec and early Jan to early Feb*. An unbeatable view of the ocean and the hundred-year-old Artha dike make this the perfect observation point for watching the dark and fearsome *brouillarta*, the storm that comes suddenly from the sea, make its way towards the shore. Sober, classic decor.

Le Duke – *Pl. Maurice-Ravel* – ☎ *05 59 51 12 96 – summer: daily 'til 3am; off-season: 8am-2am*. This contemporary bar is run by Michel Chardié, a former surfing champion who named it after his idol, The Duke, a Hawaiian surfing star who rode the waves in the 1950s. Hip music and clientele.

Maison Adam – *6 r. de la République* – ☎ *05 59 26 03 54 – Tue-Sun 7:45am-12:30pm, 2pm-7:30pm; from mid-Jun to mid-Sep: daily – closed beg. Jan to mid-Feb*. Since 1660, La Maison Adam has been carrying on the tradition of making the same *macarons* that Louis XIV was so fond of. Indeed, it was in 1660 that the Sun King and his wife Marie-Thérèse d'Autriche resided across the way from the boutique.

Pariès – *9 R. Gambetta* – ☎ *05 59 26 01 46 – paries@wanadoo.fr – daily 8:30am-1pm, 2:30pm-7:30pm; summer: 'til 11pm – closed mid-Jan to mid-Feb*. Robert Pariès is a master chocolate-maker, and his turn of the century pastry shop is paradise for sweet-toothed gourmands. Among his specialities, note the *mouchou basque* (macaroon made of almonds, sugar and egg whites), the soft caramel *Kanougas* and the chocolates made in the Bayonne tradition.

Pub du Corsaire – *16 r. de la République* – ☎ *05 59 26 10 74 – Jul-Aug: daily 4pm-3am; off-season: 5pm-2am*. The *patronne* has been part of the bar scene since she was 15; today she's at the helm of this pub decorated like a boat's hold. Her renowned establishment, a beacon of St-Jean-de-Luz nightlife, lists 130 kinds of beer and 100 whiskies on the menu.

ADDITIONAL SIGHTS

★Maison Louis-XIV ⓥ– The house now named after the monarch who stayed here was built by the shipowner Lohobiague in 1643. It is an imposing building beside the port, with the façade facing the town distinguished by corbelled turrets at the corners. Inside, the "Old Basque" character of the house is evident in the sturdy, straight-flight staircase which was built by ship's carpenters: like the original floorboards in all the rooms, the treads are kept in place by large, visible, heavy-headed nails which make sanding or planing impossible. From the second-floor landing a passage leads to the apartments where Lohobiague's widow received Louis XIV in 1660; a south-facing, arcaded gallery here offers a splendid view of the Basque Pyrenees.

The huge kitchen boasts an impressive fireplace. The green-panelled dining-room contains a marble Directoire table and – a gift from the royal guest to his hostess – a three-piece service in silver-gilt with inlaid enamel work.

Musée Grévin ⓥ – *Tour with headphones*. 🎧 The museum is housed in the Pavillon de l'Infante, an outbuilding of the Maison de l'Infante, and traces some of the major historical episodes which occurred in the 17C in the Basque Country, particularly in St-Jean-de-Luz. The main events are the Treaty of the Pyrenees which was solemnly ratified on 6 June 1660 on Île des Faisans (Pheasant Island) in the middle of the River Bidassoa, and the marriage of Louis XIV celebrated three days later in Église St-Jean-Baptiste (the scene has been reconstructed according to a painting by Laumosnier).

★★ Église St-Jean-Baptiste – This is the biggest and most famous of all the Basque churches in France; it was founded in the 15C and was being enlarged at the time of Louis XIV's wedding. The bricked-up doorway through which the royal couple left can be seen just inside the main entrance, on the south side.

Externally the architecture is sober, even severe, with high walls and small windows. A vaulted passageway tunnels beneath the massive tower. A fine wrought-iron stairway leads to the galleries.

Interior – The sumptuous, largely 17C interior presents a striking contrast to the church's exterior.

Three tiers of oak galleries (five on the end wall) surround the broad, single nave; these, traditionally, are reserved for men. The vaulted roof above the nave is lined with remarkable painted panels. The chancel, raised high as in all Basque churches, is separated from the nave by a handsome wrought-iron screen. The dazzling gold **altarpiece★** dates from c 1670 (restored 1987). Between the columns and entablatures that divide it into three levels, shallow niches hold statues of the Apostles, angels and local saints.

Among other items of interest are the 17C pulpit supported by sphinxes and – in the embrasure of the walled-up doorway – a statue of **Notre-Dame-des-Douleurs** (Our Lady of Sorrows). Beside this is a small Virgin of the Rosary in ceremonial dress.

CIBOURE

Ciboure (in the Basque language, *Zubiburu:* bridge-head) lies opposite St-Jean-de-Luz, on the west bank of the Nivelle; in fact the two towns form a single conurbation, sharing the port between them. One of the local landmarks is no 27 quai Maurice-Ravel, which is where the composer was born. **Rue Pocalette** just behind it presents a contrast between half-timbered houses in the Labourd style (corbelled house dating from 1589 on the corner of rue Agorette) and the more gentrified stone-built mansions, such as that at no 12 by the east end of the church.

Église St-Vincent – *Rue Pocalette*. The church was built in the 16C. It has an unusual bell tower terminating in two wooden lantern storeys of decreasing size. The side entrance to the church is across a fine flagstone square (18C stone cross).

Villa Leïhorra ⓥ – *1 impasse Muskoa*. The villa, decorated both inside and outside in Art Deco, was built from 1926 to 1928 by the architect Hiriart for his family. The gardens and part of the house facing onto the patio (in particular a magnificent bathroom) are open to the public.

EXCURSIONS

Socoa – *3km/1.8mi W via D 912. Park at the port and continue (45min round trip on foot) towards the jetty.*

🚶 The beginning of the dike offers a good view of the harbour and the town.

Entrance to the anchorage at St-Jean-de-Luz was formerly defended by Socoa fort, which was built under Henri IV and improved by the celebrated military architect Vauban.

Turn right, leaving the port, and climb to the lighthouse along Rue du Phare, then follow Rue du Sémaphore to the coastal signal station: to the southwest there is a superb **view★★** of the Basque coastline from Cape Higuer (Cabo Higuer) in Spain all the way to Biarritz. Below, in the foreground, the foliated strata of the cliffs drop steeply down to the crashing waves of the Atlantic.

★★ La Corniche Basque (The Basque Coast Road)

⓵ *30km/19mi round trip – allow 1hr.*

Leave St-Jean-de-Luz west via D 912.

The route approaches the cliffs of Socoa, offering superb sea **views★★**. Before snaking down to Hendaye, it passes near **Domaine d'Abbadia**, the Second Empire home of Antoine Abbadie (1810-97) which the scholar left to the French Academy of Sciences *(see HENDAYE, Pointe Ste-Anne)*.

Hendaye – *See HENDAYE.*

Leave Hendaye by N 10 east towards Béhobie and St-Jean-de-Luz.

Parc Florénia ⊘ – *3km/1.8mi before Urrugne.* The park contains a hilly footpath which takes visitors through various floral themes, ranging from woodland (Montherey pines and giant rhubarb) to Mediterranean terraces (eucalyptus, palm trees, jasmine), a small enclosed garden (aromatic plants), a rose garden, and a water garden on the banks of a lake (water lilies, lotuses). The park is illuminated in the evenings.

Urrugne – The church at the centre of the town presents an almost military aspect, with high walls and few windows. The face of the adjoining belfry-porch bears a sundial.

From the main square in Urrugne, take the hill leading up to Notre-Dame-de-Socorri.

Socoa

Notre-Dame-de-Socorri – This pilgrimage chapel dedicated to the Virgin lies in a lovely **setting★**: the shady clearing on the site of the former cemetery offers views of the undulating countryside dominated by the great spur of La Rhune and, on the horizon, the heights of Jaozkibel and Les Trois Couronnes.

Beyond Urrugne, **Château d'Urtubie** ⊘ can be seen *(left, below the road).* This castle was built in the 14C with the authorisation of King Edward III of England; it has undergone many changes since.

Return to St-Jean-de-Luz by N 10.

★ Le Labourd

2 *116km/72mi round tour – allow 1 day*

The Labourd coastline offers a picturesque alternation of rugged cliffs and sandy coves; away from the ocean rollers the landscape is one of gentle hills and wide moors known as *touyas*. Mountains stand out against the clear skies but they are not high: La Rhune, the culminating peak in the range, rises to no more than 900m/2 953ft above sea level. This excursion will lead you through the traditional villages and rolling hills of this picturesque region.

Leave St-Jean-de-Luz via N 10, drive as far as Urrugne and turn left on D 4 to Ascain.

Petit train de la Rhune

361

★ Ascain – The pretty village square, with its church, pelota court, traditional houses and welcoming hotels, has a great deal of character. The Basque church with its three-tiered galleries is preceded by a massive belfry-porch; on the right of the cemetery behind it is an interesting disk-shaped stele dating from 1657. In one of the Ascain restaurants there is a *trinquet* – a rectangular indoor court marked out for a variant of *pelota*, reminiscent of the English game of fives.

Continuing south through a moorland landscape, the road (D 4) rises beside an attractive valley to reach Col de St Ignace (St Ignatius Pass), at an altitude of 169m/555ft.

★★ La Rhume ⊘ – *From Col de St Ignace* – ⌨ *1hr round trip by rack railway. The journey aboard the wooden train dating from 1924 is well worth it. It is possible to come back on foot (wear suitable walking shoes). Enquire before leaving about the visibility on the summit.*

La Rhune (in Basque *larrun* means good pastureland) is regarded as the symbol of the French Basque country. From the summit (alt 900m/2 952ft; television transmitter) of the frontier-mountain there is a superb **panorama★★★** over the ocean (Bay of Biscay), the Forest of the Landes, the Basque Pyrenees and, southwards, the Bidasoa valley.

The road down through the *touyas* has cut through and exposed the red sandstone of the mountain, which is used as the local building stone. There are views of the Artzamendi and the upper Nivelle to the east.

★ Sare – This charming village was described, under the name of Etchezar, by the author Pierre Loti in his novel *Ramuntcho* (1897). The high fronton wall of the pelota court, the shaded streets, and the fine church with its galleries, raised chancel and Baroque altarpieces are all typical of the Basque country.

Sare is also known as "wood pigeons' hell" due to the local method of snaring the migratory birds as they fly south in the autumn.

The upper Sare valley, a pastoral landscape of sheep, dairy cattle and *Pottok* ponies between scattered hamlets with some fine dovecotes is particularly appealing.

Take D 306 south.

Grotte de Sare ⊘ – The grotto or *lezea* (a Basque word meaning cave) is part of a vast series of galleries gouged from the limestone at the beginning of the Quaternary era by waters hurtling down from Pic d'Atchouria. Corrosion, abrasion and dissolution of some of the rock's mineral constituents have produced over the millennia every kind of karstic cavity. The discovery here of flint tools and the remnants of bones shows that many of these caves were at one time occupied by humans, particularly during the Upper Perigordian period (20 000 BC).

The enormous entrance, which opens to the northeast, leads into a subterranean labyrinth illuminated by blue lights. The natural marvels to be seen on the tour (900m – about half a mile) are explained in an audiovisual presentation *(in French)*.

Return to D 306 and turn left.

The road continues beside attractive undergrowth flourishing on the banks of a stream, then rises into the oak-filled Forêt de Sare.

Col de Lizarrieta – Alt 441m/1 447ft. The pass, with its hides and snare centres all along the crests, is a hive of activity during the pigeon-shooting season.

Return to D 4 and continue eastwards.

★ Aïnhoa – *See AÏNHOA.*

Head northeast along D 20.

★ Espelette – *See ESPELETTE.*

Before the road plunges down into the valley of the Nive, the view opens out again onto the Basque Pyrenees, La Rhune and the Artzamendi *(behind)*, and the heights of Cambo-les-Bains and the gentle green slopes of Mont Ursuya *(ahead)*.

Turn left (D 20) to Larressore.

La Rhune stone

Houses in the Basque country are surrounded by an unusual type of wall made of large stone slabs, just under one metre high (3 feet), driven into the ground. This beautiful red and beige sandstone, known as *rhune*, is quarried in Ascain. Commonly used for the door and window frames of traditional Basque houses, it is also used nowadays for the restoration of historical monuments. Several towns in northern France have even ordered it to pave their pedestrian precincts.

Larressore – From 1733 to 1906 a seminary founded in this village by Abbot Daguerre trained many Basque priests. Beside the *pelota* court is the **Atelier Ainciart-Bergara** (⊙); this workshop was established before the French Revolution by a craftsman of that name and is still family-operated today. Using their own time-honoured methods, the workshop produces the traditional Basque staff or *makhila*, from the wood of the medlar tree. The canes are seasoned and decorated with a pattern of dried sap which has oozed from incisions cut in the fresh wood.

Follow D 932 towards Bayonne and turn left onto D 3 just before reaching the motorway.

Arcangues – This picturesque village is particularly attractive around the church, the inn and the pelota court. Inside the church, with its carved galleries, there is a large Empire-style chandelier and a bas-relief representing the beheading of John the Baptist, patron saint of the parish. The landscaped cemetery with its characteristic Basque tombstones (a stone disc on a plinth) offers a panoramic **view**★ of the Basque Pyrenees.

The Arcangues cemetery contains the tomb of the popular crooner Mariano Eusebio Gonzalez Garcia, better known as Luis Mariano. The Prince of Operettas died of hepatitis on 14 July 1970, after receiving inadequate medical care. Ever since, crowds of admirers have descended upon the cemetery to pay homage to their idol.

Continue along D 3.

The winding road snakes through Ustaritz Forest. Beyond, the descent towards St-Pée offers distant glimpses of La Rhune, the Irun depression, the promontory of Jaizkibel and the sea. To the east, the minor Artzamendi range closes off the upper Nivelle basin.

In St-Pée-de-Nivelle, turn right (west) on D 918 to St-Jean-de-Luz.

ST-JEAN-PIED-DE-PORT★

Population 1 417
Michelin map 342: E-6 or 234 fold 37

This pretty little town, once the capital of Lower Navarre, lies in a mild, picturesque basin watered by the Nive and Petite Nive rivers, its red sandstone houses grouped around a spur crowned by the old citadel. The old or upper town on the north bank of the Nive is encircled by 15C ramparts dating from the time of Navarrese domination; the citadel and fortifications on the south bank, built to defend the road to Spain after the Treaty of the Pyrenees, are part of the 17C military complex designed by Vauban.

The name St-Jean-Pied-de-Port is a reminder that the town lies at the foot of a *port* or pass: for travellers heading for Spain it was the last stop before the climb to Puerto Ibaêeta, or Port de Roncevaux as it is known on the French side (alt 1 058m/3 468ft), 25km/16mi away on Spanish territory. Beyond the crest, the monastery of Roncesvalles (Roncevaux to the French) has maintained a tradition of Christian hospitality since the 12C – and preserved the memory of the brave hero Roland, who fell in the year 778 when the rear guard of Charlemagne's army was overwhelmed by Basque mountain people on the way back from a campaign against the Saracens in Spain. According to the tale, Roland, though urged to do so by his councillors, was too proud to blow his horn to sound the retreat in time to save his men. In the ancient epic of The **Song of Roland** the mountain people themselves are transformed into Saracens. In one version of the legend, the cleft in the rock formed when Roland tried to break his magic sword is near the Cirque de Gavarnie; in another it is here at Roncesvalles.

Pilgrims' Way – In the Middle Ages St-Jean was a great rallying centre for *Jacquets*, the pilgrims en route for Santiago de Compostela, who journeyed from all over Europe. They wore a heavy grey cloak, a broad-brimmed felt hat turned up at the front and marked with three or four scallop shells (the emblems of the pilgrimage), and carried a bread bag and an eight-foot stave with a water flask attached.

Whenever a devout procession of the pious was announced, the town became a hive of activity: church bells pealed, priests intoned prayers, children ran out to escort the pilgrims, and the inhabitants, standing on their doorsteps, offered provisions. Then the pilgrims would move on, chanting the responses; those too tired to continue could stop in rue de la Citadelle, where the monks from Roncesvalles had organised a refuge for them.

★FOLLOWING THE PILGRIMS' WAY

Rue de la Citadelle – The street, sloping down towards the river, is bordered by charming 16C and 17C houses with rounded doorways and carved lintels.

Église Notre-Dame – The Gothic church, dedicated to the Virgin, has handsome sandstone pillars.

ST-JEAN
PIED-DE-PORT

Eating out

BUDGET

Chez Arbillaga – *8 r. de l'Église* – ☎ *05 59 37 06 44 – closed 1-15 Jun, 3 wks in Oct, Tue evening and Wed except from Jul to Sep – 12.96/25.92€.* Set against the ramparts, this restaurant plays the regional repertory. Wintertime, *la garbure, les pibales* or milk-fed lamb with green garlic cooked in the fireplace; springtime, the *omelette aux mousserons de la St-Georges* or the *lamproie à la bordelaise;* other local specialities all year round.

Pecoïtz – *64220 Aincille – 7km/4.2mi N of St-Jean-Pied-de-Port via D 933 and D 18* – ☎ *05 59 37 11 88 – closed 1 Jan to 10 Mar and Fri from Oct to May – 13.72/28.20€.* This restaurant in a Basque house next to the village church is a pleasant place to stop. Ask to be seated next to the bay windows and take advantage of the view. Generous, well-prepared family cuisine. A few basic but clean rooms.

Cidrerie Aldakurria – *64220 Lasse – 3.5km/2.2mi W of St-Jean-Pied-de-Port. Take D 918 and D 403* – ☎ *05 59 37 13 13 – cidrerie-aldakurria@wanadoo.fr – closed Jan, Sun evening and Mon 15 Sep to 15 Jun – reserv. recommended – 15.24/22.86€.* This cider-house offers cod omelettes and beef ribs with as much cider as you care to drink, Spanish-style. A rustic decor in this house amidst the fields: wagon wheels, beams, stuccoed walls, big tables with wooden benches. Comfortable rooms.

Where to stay

BUDGET

Ferme Etxeberria Bed and Breakfast – *64220 Ispoure – 0.8km/0.5mi NE of St-Jean-Pied-de-Port via D 933* – ☎ *05 59 37 06 23 – closed Dec-Jan –* ⧄ *– 4 rms: 38.12€.* You'll sleep in what used to be the barn of this rural farm a short distance from St-Jean-Pied-de-Port. Modern rooms, plain but pretty. Breakfast is served on the pleasant veranda with a view of the Irouleguy vineyards. Unforgettable family outings on donkeyback for the daring.

MODERATE

Hôtel Central – *Pl. Ch.-de-Gaulle* – ☎ *05 59 37 00 22 – closed 15 Dec to 1 Mar – 14 rms: 53.36/74.70€ –* ⌑ *7.32€ – restaurant 16.77/35.06€.* This rather old-fashioned hotel with 1960s decor is conveniently located in centre city. Have a seat on the small terrace above the river for an outdoors meal or try the recently smartened up dining room.

Hôtel Arcé – *Rte du col d'Ispéguy – 64430 St-Étienne-de-Baïgorry – 11km/6.6mi W of St-Jean-Pied-de-Port via D 15* – ☎ *05 59 37 40 14 – closed mid-Nov to mid-Mar –* ▯ *– 23 rms: 74.70/118.91€ –* ⌑ *7.62€ – restaurant 16.77/27.44€.* This Basque house facing the village is peacefully situated by the river flowing at the edge of its terrace. The rooms are dissimilar, some a bit outmoded, but those in the front have a lovely view of the water. Garden with pool.

Houses along the River Nive

Rue de l'Église – This street leads from the church to Porte de Navarre, passing the **former hospital** which now houses a library and the **house of the Jassu family**, paternal ancestors of St François-Xavier (1506-52).

Return to the church, pass through the vaulted passage beneath the belfry and cross the river.

Vieux Pont – From the Old Bridge there is a picturesque view of the church, which is incorporated into the ramparts, and the old riverside houses.

Rue d'Espagne – The street, which climbs uphill to Porte d'Espagne through which the pilgrims left the town, has always been one of the main shopping areas.

Follow avenue du Fronton to the left, cross the river again, walk to the back of the church and take the steps up to the citadel.

Citadelle – *Access via the church or from Porte St-Jacques.*

From the bastion facing the entrance to the citadel, the view stretches over the St-Jean basin and the neat little villages within it.

Return to Porte St-Jacques.

Abbaye de ST-SAVIN★★

Michelin map 322: L-5 or 233 fold 10 – 17km/11mi N of Montmorillon

St-Savin rises on the west bank of the River Gartempe; it is famous for its Romanesque abbey church which is decorated with the finest and most complete series of mural paintings in France, now on UNESCO's World Heritage List.

HISTORICAL NOTES

Part of the legend – Towards the middle of the 5C in Macedonia, two brothers, Savin and Cyprien, were summoned to appear in front of the proconsul Ladicius for having refused to worship certain idols. The brothers were condemned to death, and all pleas for mercy were in vain. They were imprisoned but managed to escape and left for the Gauls, though their executioners caught up with them on the banks of the Gartempe: the brothers were decapitated on the spot. Savin's body was buried by priests on a height known at the time as Three Cypresses Mount, not far from where the town of St-Savin stands today.

The building stages – The first abbey church was erected in the 9C, near the sacred burial site, and placed under the patronage of the martyr Savin. Louis the Debonair installed twenty Benedictine monks in the abbey under the tutelage, it is said, of Benoît d'Aniane.

In 878 the abbey was pillaged by the Normans, despite it being protected by a line of fortifications. Reconstruction did not begin until the 11C but was finished in a relatively short space of time. The painted decoration, which completely covered the interior of the church, was added as the building work progressed.

Decline and rebirth – The Hundred Years War brought to an end the period of relative prosperity enjoyed by the monks up to that time; the abbey was caught up in violent battles between soldiers loyal to the King of France and those fighting for the Black Prince. In the 16C the Wars of Religion saw the Catholics and the Huguenots in furious conflict over possession of the abbey: it was devastated in 1562 and 1568 by the Huguenots, who burnt the choir stalls, the organ and the timber roof, and pillaged six years later by the Royal army. Most of the buildings were later demolished as their upkeep was too expensive.

From 1611 to 1635 an adventurer who liked to call himself the Baron of the Francs installed himself in the church as though it were a stronghold. The arrival, in 1640, of monks from Saint-Maur finally brought an end to the profanities to which the abbey had been subjected for three centuries. However, though the monks saved the buildings from total ruin, the wall paintings suffered from various efforts to restore them.

In 1836 Prosper Mérimée, the writer and Inspector of Historic Monuments, had the church listed as a historic monument and organised important restoration works which continued for almost a century.

An unrelated historical anecdote: it was an engineer from St-Savin, Léon Edoux, who in 1867 invented the hydraulic elevator and perfected it in trials within the bishop's lodgings; he gave it the name *ascenseur*.

ABBEY ⊘

★★★ **Wall Paintings** – Some of the paintings were destroyed during the devastation visited on the abbey, others were damaged by whitewash which the monks applied, still others suffered as a result of the first phases of restoration.

Unlike most frescoes painted from a preliminary sketch, the paintings here were drawn directly onto the wall, using a process halfway between the fresco technique and distemper-painting: the colours were applied to old plaster, thereby penetrating only the top level of this coating and forming a very thin layer. The few colours used include yellow-ochre, red-ochre and green, mixed with black and white.

The overall effect is one of gentle tones but avoids being insipid through the use of contrast: the different characters are portrayed with great liveliness, their feet suggesting movement, their forms revealed by the moulding of their clothes, their hands often disproportionately long, accentuating the expressive qualities.

This dancing, rhythmic allure is also found in Romanesque sculpture. Faces have large, simple, bold features, with red and white marks describing cheeks, nostrils and chins.

M. Thierry/MICHELIN

The nave

In the **narthex** the various painted scenes recount episodes from the Apocalypse: Christ in Majesty in Celestial Jerusalem, Combat between the Archangel and the Beast, the New Jerusalem, the Plague of Grasshoppers. The predominantly pale tones (green, yellow-ochre, red-ochre) allow the scenes to be clearly read despite the darkness inside the porch.

The **nave**, however, is the setting for the true masterpiece which is highlighted by the purity of the architecture. The stories told in the carefully-restored paintings on the vaulting unfold at a height of over 16m/52ft and cover an area of $412m^2/1\ 351sq\ ft$. The most striking thing initially is the soft tones – beige and pink – of the columns supporting the vaulting. The vaulting itself is covered with famous scenes from the Book of Genesis and the Book of Exodus, ranged in two rows along either side of the centre ridge, which forms a decorative band. A painting behind the main door shows the Triumph of the Virgin.

Two sections are distinguishable in the nave. The first three bays, which make up the first part of the nave, are separated by transverse ribs, while the rest of the vaulting is a continuous barrel which made painting that section of the ceiling easier; the painter nevertheless added a false rib between the 5th and 6th bays.

Stand in the south aisle to see the frescoes on the left-hand side of the nave.

The following scenes are recognisable:

1) Creation of the stars (God adds the Sun and the Moon to the firmament).

2) Creation of Woman – God presents Eve to Adam – Eve and the serpent.

3) Eve, seated, spins.

4) The offerings of Cain and Abel (Abel, God's chosen one, is the only one haloed).

5) Abel's murder – Cain's curse.

6) Enoch, his arms raised to heaven, invokes God – God tells Noah of the forthcoming flood and invites him to build the ark.

7) Noah's Ark during the flood.

8) God blesses Noah's family leaving the ark (showing the famous "Beau Dieu" representation of God).

9) Noach sacrifies a pair of birds and a lamb in thanksgiving.

10) Noah's vineyard.
Before continuing with the story of Naoh on the right-hand section, note the scenes on the lower register which tell the end of Exodus and include the life of Moses.

11) Passage through the Red Sea: the waters swallow up the Egyptian cavalry and Pharaoh's chariot.

12) The Angel of God and the column of fire separate the Egyptians and the Hebrews and protect the latter who march in rows, led by Moses.

13) Moses receives the Tables of the Law from God.

Cross the transept crossing and stand at the beginning of the left-hand aisle to view the paintings on the right-hand side of the ceiling.

TRANSEPT	14	15	16	17		18	19	20	21	22
	31	30	29	28	27	26	25	24	23	

14) Noah drinks and dances, a gobelet in hand.

15) Drunken Noah lies asleep, his robes in disarray; Ham mocks his father, while his brothers Shem and Japhet cover him with a banket.

16) Noah curses Canaan in front of Shem and Japhet.

17) Construction of the Tower of Babel.

18) The call of Abraham *(see illustration)*.

19) Abraham and Lot's separation.

20) Announcement of the combat of the kings and call for help from Lot of Abraham.

21) The combat of the Kings *(removed)*.

22) Meeting between Abraham and Melchizedeck, King of Salem and priest of the Most

High, who brings him bread and wine *(removed)*.

23) Death of Abraham.

24) Isaac blesses his son Jacob.

25) Joseph sold by his brothers.

26) Joseph bought by Potiphar, one of Pharaoh's officers.

27) Joseph, Potiphar and his wife (the Temptation of Joseph).

28) Joseph in prison.

29) Joseph explains Pharaoh's dream.

30) Pharaoh puts his ring of Joseph's finger and makes him his administrator.

31) Joseph's Triumph.

* Abbey buildings – These were rebuilt in the 17C in the extension of the church's transept arm; they have since been restored.

The old **refectory**, to the right of the entrance, houses exhibits of contemporary mural art organised by CIAM, the International Centre for Mural Art, which is based within the abbey.

To the left, in the **chapter house**, photographs reveal the appearance of the church crypt *(temporarily closed)*.

From the garden, which the river runs through, there is an attractive view over the elegant rear face of the abbey buildings, from the bishop's lodgings *(on the left)*, which are of medieval origin, although remodelled in the 17C and 19C, across to the east end of the church with its apse, apsidal chapels and belfry.

** Abbey Church – The church, a handsome combination of harmony and sobriety, is also striking for its sheer size: 76m/250ft long with a transept 31m/101ft across and a spire rising to 77m/252ft.

Inside the church, in the nave, there are fine **capitals** deeply-carved with foliage and animals; those by the chancel are decorated with acanthus leaves and lions.

The best **view*** of the church is from the far side of the river. On the left extend the abbey buildings and the elegant belfry-porch – overshadowing the apse, the apsidal chapels and the squat belfry; it is crowned by a crocketed spire surrounded by turrets. On the right stands **Vieux Pont** (the Old Bridge), which dates from the 13C and 14C.

SAINT-SEVER

Population 4 455

Michelin map 335: H-12 or 234 fold 27

St-Sever offers good views of the River Adour and the enormous sea of pines which covers the neighbouring Landes. The one-time "city of scholars" is a useful base for excursions through the Chalosse region and the departure point of a corniche *(D 32)* winding above local meadows bordering the course of the Adour.

TOWN WALK

Église – The Romanesque abbey church (partly restored in the 17C and 19C) features a chancel with 6 apsidal chapels of decreasing depth, and transept arms which end in galleries resting on a single column which develops, above, into a purely decorative arcade. The marble columns of the chancel and transept were taken from the old palace of the Roman governors of Morlanne; their remarkable **capitals*** include water-leaf (11C) and lion designs, historiated capitals (inside the west front) showing Herod's banquet and the beheading of John the Baptist, and a mixture of figures symbolising the predominance of the New Testament over the Old. The **sacristy** leads to the cloisters, only two sides of which remain.

Outside, the **east end** of the church is crowned with a dome and a lantern, and surrounded by the Romanesque apsidal chapels which have amusing modillions.

From the church, follow rue des Arceaux.

Rue du Général-Lamarque – This street is lined with a few 18C mansions (nos 6, 18, 20 and 26); others dating from the 19C include General Lamarque's former residence at nos 8 and 11; note the neo-Classical doorway of the edifice and the two pavilions flanking it. 16C mansion at no 21. The former **Jacobin convent**, which has been turned into a cultural centre, has late-17C brick-built cloisters.

Promenade de Morlanne – *Access by car.* From the viewpoint, the panorama encompasses the River Adour below and the vast "sea of pine trees" offering a striking contrast with the rolling hills of the Chalosse.

A. Thuilier/MICHELIN

A historiated capital

★CHALOSSE

Chalosse, a hilly region nestling within the great curve of the River Adour, has yet to be discovered by the crowds. Fertile patches of "wild" sand – visible in cuts and ditches – stud the region. Despite the modest aspect of the smallholdings and villages, which are in the Landes style, the agriculture is productive and well-balanced. Chalosse has a long history: it is in this region that Palaeolithic man fashioned such primal masterpieces as the celebrated Lady of Brassempouy; later, pilgrims passed through on their way to Santiago de Compostela.

Round tour from St-Sever

71km/44mi – allow half a day

Drive south-west out of St-Sever along D 21.

Audignon – The village has an interesting church enclosed within a seemingly fortified cemetery. Note, in the chancel, the remarkable stone altarpiece with its coloured frescoes. The Romanesque east end contrasts with the belfry-porch and its octagonal Gothic spire. In the 14C, the medieval keep became the church tower.

Continue along the narrow D 21 which winds through the wooded hills.

Brassempouy – See HAGETMAU.

Between Brassempouy and Bastennes, D 58 runs through rolling hills.

Château de Gaujacq ⓥ – The elegant château is visible behind a screen of magnolias, with the Pyrenees in the distance. The courtyard forms a cloister with a garden and a gallery. Several rooms are open to the public.
The **Plantarium** ⓥ, located at the back of the castle *(entrance on the right)*, is divided into eight colourful and fragrant flower beds.

In Castelnau-Chalosse, turn north onto D 7 to Montfort.

Eating out

BUDGET

Auberge du Moulin – *Rte de Dax – 40330 Amou – 11km/6.6mi S of Gaujacq. Take D 158 then D 15 towards Dax – ☎ 05 58 89 30 09 – closed Nov to May – ✍ – 12.20/27.45€.* Canard gras (fattened duck), prepared in every manner imaginable, is the speciality of the "Mill Inn". The dining room, rather outmoded but charming, features coloured tiles and Basque tablecloths. Peace and quiet guaranteed on the terrace under the parasols. A few rooms are available.

MODERATE

Le Relais du Pavillon – *2km/1.2mi N of St-Sever at the crossroads of D 933 and D 924 – ☎ 05 58 76 20 22 – closed 2-14 Jan, 3-10 Sep, Sun evening and Mon except from 14 Jul to 15 Aug – 13.72/38.11€.* Here's a traditional restaurant in a building dating from the sixties, just outside the centre city. If weather permits, have a seat on the terrace near the pool. Luminous dining room with bay windows. A few renovated, well-kept rooms.

La Ferme aux Grives – *111 r. des Thermes – 40320 Eugénie-les-Bains – ☎ 05 58 05 05 06 – closed 3 Jan to 8 Feb, Mon-Tue except public holidays and 16 Jul to 26 Aug – 33.54€.* In the heart of this famous spa town, this prettily restored farm has stones walls, wooden floors, old furnishings and a friendly atmosphere. Good rural cuisine. A few tastefully decorated rooms.

Where to stay

BUDGET

Hôtel Alios – *40500 Bas-Mauco – 4.5km NE of St-Sever via rte de Mont-de-Marsan – ☎ 05 58 76 44 00 – ▣ – 10 rms: 33.54/45.73€ – ☲ 4.57€ – restaurant 12.96/24.39€.* Here's a practical address for a simple, affordable halt on the holiday road. The rooms, all based on the same model, are functional. Bright contemporary dining room. Traditional French cuisine.

Montfort-en-Chalosse – The nucleus of this small town is a hillock criss-crossed by narrow lanes and steep, stepped streets. **Musée de la Chalosse** ⊘ and the nearby Médiathèque are both devoted to country life and the economy of this pleasant rural region.

Continue along D 7 then D 10, passing the 17C Poyanne Château to Laurède.

Laurède – The village **church** ⊘ boasts a striking Baroque interior. Of particular note are the monumental high altar surmounted by a baldaquin, the pulpit and lectern, and the woodwork in the sacristy.

Mugron – This small town is the "county town" of the region and is heavily involved in the development of agriculture in the Chalosse (wine co-operative, grain silos). At the time of the *Intendants*, the small port on the Adour nearby used to export the local wine as far as Holland. From the public gardens around the town hall, once the hillside home of a rich bourgeois family, there are fine **views★** of the valley.

Between Mugron and Montaut there are frequent views of the rear of the plateau, the promontories dropping down in succession towards the Adour and the *pignada* (a local term for the forest of maritime pines).

Montaut – The main street of this old fortified village runs along the crest crowning the last fold of the Chalosse plateau; its charming houses look out over the plain of the Adour and the forests of the Landes. The church tower, which is also the gateway to the town, was rebuilt after the ravages perpetrated by the bands under Montgomery. The two altarpieces inside the church reveal interesting stylistic differences: that on the right-hand (south) side features a strict rhythm of perpendiculars, in contrast with the sinuous, flowing lines of the Baroque reredos on the left. The former dates from the early 17C, the latter from the 18C.

D 32 leads back to St-Sever.

ST-VINCENT-SUR-JARD

Population 871

Michelin map 316: G-9 or 233 fold 2 – 9km/5.6mi SE of Talmont-St-Hilaire.

St-Vincent, a seaside village on the Vendée coast, evokes the fighting spirit of the French political leader **Georges Clemenceau** (1841-1929) who spent the last years of his tumultuous life here.

Clemenceau, the son of a bourgeois family in the Vendée, launched himself into politics in 1869 after studying medicine and visiting the United States. He was Mayor of Montmartre by 1870 and a member of the National Assembly (Parliament) a year later. Representing the extreme Left of the time, he earned a reputation as a fighter of duels and a destroyer of ministers (he earned the nickname "the Tiger" because of the ferocity of his parliamentary attacks).

In 1906 Clemenceau became a minister (for Home Affairs) and also President of the *Conseil* (Cabinet), and instituted a vigorous policy of reform. Ousted by the Radicals in 1909 after he had harshly repressed a series of strikes in the South, he founded a newspaper which bitterly attacked every government until 1917, when he was recalled to the Presidency of the *Conseil*. It was then that he began to mobilise the enthusiasm of the French, visiting the Western Front, encouraging the troops, sustaining the morale of the civilians: the Tiger had become the Father of Victory. He presided over the 1919 peace conference, resigned his chairmanship in 1920 and retired to his house in St-Vincent after more than half a century of political life.

MAISON DE GEORGES CLEMENCEAU ⓥ

The house is a short distance from the village, at the end of route D 19A.

The site, facing the ocean and the Île de Ré, has a hint of grandeur about it, and is a suitable resting-place for the wild and restless spirit of the old warrior.

The low building, typical of the Vendée, has been preserved exactly as it was when Clemenceau died. The tour includes the salon, Clemenceau's bedroom-study, a kitchen-dining room containing a hammered copper watering-can which is believed to have belonged to Marie-Antoinette, and the thatched summer-house, all of which are filled with souvenirs recalling his political life.

In the garden, which flowers with the roses Clemenceau always loved, there is an expressive portrait bust of the grand old man.

Clemenceau's house

TALMONDAIS COUNTRY: CLIFFS AND MEGALITHS

Round trip of 55km/34mi – 3hr

Leave St-Vincent-sur-Jard by the west.

The road follows a line of dunes covered in maritime pines.

Abbaye Notre-Dame-de-Lieu-Dieu ⓥ – *Closed to the public owing to damage caused by the storms of December 1999.* The imposing mass of this ancient abbey, founded in 1190 by Richard the Lionheart, lies between the marshes of Talmont and the coastal pine woods of Jard. Sacked and pillaged during the Hundred Years War, ruined by the Protestants in the 16C, the abbey was rebuilt by Premonstratensian monks in the 17C, when the storey with octagonal corner bartizans was added. By the end of that century, however, the abbey was again abandoned. Today the fine Plantagenet vaulting can still be admired in the chapter-house, which opens onto a garden laid out on the site of the old cloisters.

Follow the road to a car park in front of a farm called St-Nicolas.

★Pointe du Payré – The best way to explore this nature reserve is on foot *(2hr 30min round trip).* A path leads through a forest of evergreen oaks, holly and ivy, among dunes and marshes. Closer to the shorelines, the sea winds and salt spray have twisted the evergreen oaks into fantastic shapes. The view from the water's edge takes in the charming sandy Plage des Mines on the right and the cove of St-Nicolas framed by cliffs overlooking the rocky foreshore on the left. On the way

Eating out

BUDGET

Le Chalet St-Hubert – *rte de Jard* – ☎ *02 51 33 40 33* – *closed 15 Nov to 15 Dec, Sun evening and Mon from 15 Sep to 15 Jun* – *13.57/28.97€*. A spotless house run by an affable woman. Her son is master of the kitchen, where he prepares flavoursome food served at reasonable prices. If you choose to sleep there, ask for one of the ground-level rooms – they're bigger and open onto the garden.

Le Menhir – *av. du Gén.-de-Gaulle* – *85440 Avrillé* – ☎ *02 51 22 32 18* – *closed 15 Jan to 28 Feb, Sun evening from Sep to Jun and Mon* – *14.48/33.54€*. A convivial auberge siuated in a village famous for its menhir, the tallest of Vendée. Country-style decor with an inviting fireplace; traditional, simple cuisine.

Where to stay

BUDGET

Camping Les Écureuils – *rte des Goffineaux* – *85520 Jard-sur-Mer* – *3km/1.8mi W of St-Vincent on a secondary road* – ☎ *02 51 33 42 74* – *camping-ecureuils@wanadoo.fr* – *open 24 May to 9 Sep* – *reservation recommended* – *261 sites: 20.43€*. In a live oak and pine forest 300m from the ocean, this campground has a warm welcome, a well-conceived composition and agreeable furnishings that make up for the slight lack of space. Pool and kids' club.

MID-RANGE

Hôtel de l'Océan – *1km/0.6mi S of St-Vincent* – ☎ *02 51 33 40 45* – *closed 16 Nov to 14 Feb and Wed off season* – **P** – *37 rms: 51.83/68.60€* – ⌨ *5.79€* – *restaurant 12.96/38.11€*. Right next to G. Clemenceau's house and 50m from the beach, this family hotel is appreciated by a clientele of regulars who come back year after year to enjoy a holiday spent between pool and sea. Decor from another epoch, calm and friendly ambience.

---

back through the undergrowth along the shoreline, it is important to keep to the footpath in order to protect the ecosystem. The view can be admired from the rocky outcrops along the way. The path sometimes passes beneath curious canopies formed by the criss crossed branches of the evergreen oaks on either side. Pointe de Payré affords a fine view of Le Veillon cliffs.

Return via Jard-sur-Mer then take D21 northwards. After 2km/1mi, turn left.

La Boulière marshes run along the side of the road to the left.

Turn left along D180.

The road leads to the **port** which marks the beginning of a zone of oyster farms at the junction of the Île Bernard and Payré channels.

RejoinD108 and continue northwards.

Talmont-St-Hilaire – The town is in the marshy alluvial zone of the Payré Estuary, east of the Sables-d'Olonne. The **château** ⊙ in ruins (11C) rises up above the former port; the view from the top of the keep extends as far as the sea. Tourists can also admire the nearly 140 vehicles in the **Musée Automobile de Vendée★** ⊙, 2.5km/1.5mi northwest of town. The vintage automobiles on display, made between 1885 and 1970, are restored and in working condition. Among the many models built before the First World War are a Léon Bollé (with an odd resemblance to a railway car), a 1906 Renault, 1908 Monobloc and a Peugeot Lion from 1910.

Leave Talmont east along D949 for 4km/2mi. At Poteau, turn right.

St-Hilaire-la-Forêt – This little village is the gateway to the Talmondais megalithic region with its astonishing number of dolmens and menhirs. Together with Île d'Yeu *(see Île d'Yeu)* this area has the richest collection of Neolithic upright stones in Vendée. The Neolithic period, in which these megaliths were erected, is the focus for **CAIRN** (Centre Archéologique d'Initiation et de Recherche sur le Néolithique) ⊙. Explanatory panels convey information on this ancient civilisation and there is a fine display of photographs illustrating the principal sites in western France. A visit to the centre is completed by a diorama presentation on the Neolithic megaliths of the Talmont *(illuminated map)* and a video-recording. Outside, in season, there are **demonstrations of prehistoric techniques★**: the building of a dolmen, stone polishing techniques, etc A number of plants known to have been flourishing in Neolithic times have been sown.

Bicycles may be hired for exploring the megalithic sites in the area *(the trail is indicated by arrows)*.

Leave St-Hilaire north-east via D19.

Avrillé – In the municipal park behind the town hall stands the **Caesar's Camp Menhir**. This, the tallest menhir in Vendée and one of the biggest in France (rising 7m/23ft above ground), is the sole survivor of what was once a group of stones.

Leave Avrillé west via D 949.

Château de la Guignardière ⓥ – The château was founded in c 1555 by Géhan Girard, the *Panetier* (officer charged with the safeguard and distribution of bread) of Henri II, but was never finished because Girard was murdered.

The original garden façade is in the Renaissance style with granite courses and tall, double-mullioned windows. The high chimney stacks are built of brick. A number of alterations – in the same style – were made in the 18C.

Of particular note inside are the monumental chimney pieces in granite; a fine stairway, also in granite, which is halfway between a spiral staircase and one with half-landings; the attics with their magnificent three-stage rafter-work in oak; the vaulted cellars.

A trail through the grounds leads to a series of ponds fringed by bald cypress, with unique structures called "knees" (conical outgrowths of lateral roots) projecting upwards, and – hidden in Fourgon Wood – to three groups of menhirs which were once part of an ancient alignment. The tallest of these megaliths measures about 6m/20ft.

Return to Avrillé and take D 105 south-east, then turn left along D91[A]. At Bernard, turn left along D 91, then left again at the calvary.

The three **Savatole dolmens** can be seen on the right-hand side of the road *(explanatory panel)*.

Dolmen de la Frébouchère – This impressive granite monument, of the so-called Angevin type, consists of a stone portico leading to a rectangular chamber. The single slab of rock (now cracked) covering the chamber weighs about 80 tonnes.

Continue south along D91. At Longeville-sur-Mer, take D105 for 1km/0.6mi towards La Tranche-sur-Mer, then turn right.

The road along the north side of the Longeville forest leads back to St-Vincent-sur-Jard.

Frébouchère dolmen

SAINTES★★

Population 25 595
Michelin map 324: G-5 or 233 fold 27

To those hurrying through the town via avenue Gambetta, cours National and cours Lemercier (busy shopping streets shaded by plane trees), Saintes offers the straightforward appearance of a prosperous, well laid-out regional capital; for those prepared to visit Saintes, however, there are attractive discoveries in store as the local monuments date from every period since the Romans. From the bridge onwards, visitors can stroll enjoyably beside the River Charente as far as the public gardens and beyond.

The town has given its name to the Saintonge, an old province in the western Charentes.

HISTORICAL NOTES

Origins – "Mediolanum Santonum", capital of the Santons during the Roman domination of the Vendée, was built on the hillside sloping up from the west bank of the Charente; the river was spanned by a bridge on which the Arch of Germanicus was erected. The Latin poet Ausonius died in this town, in his Villa Pagus Noverus, at the time St Eutrope was beginning to preach the Gospel. In the Middle Ages, when Saintes was under Plantagenet rule, religious buildings sprang up all over the town; pilgrims on the way to Santiago de Compostela *(see Introduction, The Way of St James)* filed continuously across the bridge. They were welcomed and sent on their way to two suburbs which had developed around religious establishments: St-Eutrope and, on the east bank of the Charente, the Abbaye aux Dames.

Until the Revolution – under which Saintes became the county seat of Lower Charente but was deprived of its bishopric – so many luxurious mansions were built by local nobles and lawyers that the town could serve as a lesson in the evolution of Classical architecture.

Town planning had its place in 18C Saintes, laying out the thoroughfares on the perimeter of the old town along the site of the ancient ramparts. In the 19C Cours National (the principal axis of the modern town) was bordered with neo-Classical public buildings; among them, on opposite sides of the avenue, are the law courts and the theatre.

A determined man – In c1539 a man called **Bernard Palissy** (1510-90) was working in Saintes as a surveyor. He decided, however, to renounce this profession and devote his time to the art of ceramics, and set up a studio-workshop near the ramparts. Here, in a state of complete privation, he struggled day and night to survive until he discovered the secret of enamelling. "Maistre Bernard, the worker in earth", as he was known, became celebrated for his enamelled terracotta work.

A philanthropist – Against his will perhaps, **Joseph Ignace Guillotin** (1738-1814), a doctor living in Saintes, lent his name to France's notorious machine for judicial executions. Until then, decapitation had been reserved for those of noble birth. The doctor believed that all men should be equal at death – and he was anxious to spare the condemned unnecessary suffering. He therefore proposed to the National Assembly in 1789 "a rapid-action beheading machine". Guillotin, himself a deputy, was gratified when the invention was approved; he was less pleased when the death machine was not unnaturally christened, in 1792 when it was first used, La Guillotine.

The old town along the Charente

★OLD TOWN

Park the car on the market square where the walk begins.

The Old Town district around the cathedral on the west bank of the river is characteristic of Saintes, proud of its distinctive image.

Cathédrale St-Pierre – St Peter's Cathedral was built on the site of a Romanesque church; all that remains of the early building is a dome above the south transept. Its construction, under the direction of three successive Bishops of Saintes, all members of the Rochechouart family, dates in the main from the 15C. It was severely damaged by the Calvinists in 1568. The massive bell tower, made heavier still by enormous buttresses with projecting features, was never completed: a dome with lead panels replaced the spire proposed in the original plans. Angels, saints and prophets adorn the Flamboyant doorway within the porch at the foot of the tower.

Unity and simplicity characterise the architecture of the interior. This impression of coherence is accentuated by rays of light slanting through tall windows, making the stone walls even whiter. Stripped of ornamentation, the large round columns of the nave, like the Gothic pillars in the chancel, support a bare upper wall roofed with visible timbers. Only the side aisles are vaulted in stone.

Both nave and aisles date almost in their entirety from the 16C, the great organ from the 16C and 17C. A door in the south transept opens onto the former canons' cloisters (13C), of which two galleries and the ruins of the chapter house remain. The axial chapel, with its niches surmounted by elaborately carved canopies, exemplifies the final effervescence of the Flamboyant Gothic style; the credences were already Renaissance. The **treasury** ⊘, in an annex chapel, displays a collection of sacred vessels and vestments.

Leave place du Marché, which is beside the cathedral, and follow the whole length of rue St-Michel then turn left onto rue Victor-Hugo.

A succession of pretty stone houses in the characteristic Saintonge style, can be seen in Rue Victor-Hugo, once known as Grande-Rue, which follows the course of the old road which led via the Germanicus arch to the bridge across the river.

Présidial (Musée des Beaux-Arts) ⊘ – At no 2 rue Victor-Hugo; set back at the far end of the garden, the mansion, a former presidential residence (President Le Berthon, 1605), today houses a fine arts museum mainly devoted to paintings from the 15-18C (Flemish, Dutch and French schools). Architecturally its façade, with wide bays and dormers topped by triangular pediments, marks the beginning of the Classical period.

Continue along rue Victor-Hugo as far as rue d'Alsace-Lorraine. Turn left here and continue to place de l'Échevinage.

Eating out

BUDGET

Auberge des Glycines – *4 quai des Gabarriers – 17350 Taillebourg – 16km/10mi N of Saintes. Take D 114 dir. St-Savinien –* ☎ *05 46 91 81 40 – closed 15 Feb-1 Mar, 2-15 Nov and Wed from 15 Sep to 30 Jun – 16.01€ lunch – 21.34€.* This bourgeois house is in a charming village on the banks of the Charente. You can enjoy the view from the windows of its cosy dining room or have your meal in the secret garden behind the house in the summer. A genteel halt for sampling tasty regional cuisine.

MODERATE

Le Bistrot Galant – *28 r. St-Michel –* ☎ *05 46 93 08 51 – closed Sun except for lunch from Apr to Aug and Mon – 14.94/30.18€.* This little restaurant in a calm pedestrian street downtown is a sure bet. Interesting fixed-price menus, contemporary cuisine and two small, colourful dining rooms.

Where to stay

BUDGET

Hôtel Avenue – *114 av. Gambetta –* ☎ *05 46 74 05 91 – closed 23 Dec to 2 Jan –* 🅿 *– 15 rms: 29.73/44.21€ –* ☲ *5.64€.* The rooms of this 1970s hotel in the centre of town are relatively calm because they all face away from the street. Attractive breakfast room.

Anne et Dominique Trouvé Bed and Breakfast – *5 r. de l'Église – 17810 St-Georges-des-Coteaux – 9km/5.4mi NW of Saintes. Take N 137 dir. Rochefort then D 127 –* ☎ *05 46 92 96 66 – closed 15 Nov to 28 Mar –* ⊠ *– 4 rms: 35/43€.* Bookworms are going to love this age-old farm where the bedrooms are named after authors and contain their works. One can snuggle up for a good read among old furnishings or venture outside to see the '*bujour*', the erstwhile washing-place.

MODERATE

Messageries – *r. des Messageries –* ☎ *05 46 93 64 99 – closed 21 Dec to 7 Jan –* 🅿 *– 34 rms: 44.21/57.93€ –* ☲ *6.25€.* Near the historic district, this old stagecoach inn built around a courtyard dates from 1792. Soundproofed bedrooms, big breakfast room.

Ancien Échevinage – Beyond the Classical gateway, an 18C façade is attached to a turret dating from the 16C. The spiral staircase of this former belfry leads to the **Musée des Beaux Arts de l'Échevinage** ⊘, a fine arts museum housing 19C and 20C paintings as well as a splendid collection of Sèvres porcelain from 1890 to 1910.

Return to place de l'Échevinage and take rue du Dr-Mauny. Pass through the triple-arcade porch to the Hôtel Martineau courtyard.

Hôtel Martineau – This mansion is now the home of the municipal library.

Chapelle des Jacobins – This chapel has an elegantly designed bay in the Flamboyant style.

Rue des Jacobins. The route passes the rear façade of Hôtel Martineau. Turn left to reach the steps leading up to the hospital.

Hôpital – 16C pavilion in the middle of gardens overlooking the old districts.

Go back down the steps and walk past the cathedral to quai de Verdun.

Quai de Verdun is lined with the terraced gardens of some 17C and 18C mansions adorned with wrought ironwork and balusters.

Take the footbridge across the River Charente.

Jardin public – These public gardens, laid over the town's former parade ground, are decorated with Roman ruins. One end is closed off by a façade built in 18C style and an orangery.

* **Arc de Germanicus** – This fine Roman arch with its twin arcades stood until 1843 on the bridge that carried the main thoroughfare in Saintes across the River Charente. Threatened with destruction when the bridge, itself Roman, was about to be demolished, the arch was saved by the intervention of the writer Prosper Merimée, who held the post of Inspector of Historic Monuments. It was dismantled and rebuilt on the east bank of the river.

The structure, built of local limestone and erected in the year AD19, was a votive – not a triumphal – arch. Inscriptions still visible dedicate it to Germanicus, to the Emperor Tiberius, and to his son Drusus. The name of the donor, Caius Julius Rufus, also appears. In the centre of the arch the groins of the three pillars supporting the double arcade are emphasised by fluted columns with Corinthian capitals.

Musée Archéologique ⓥ – The museum houses an interesting lapidary collection, deriving mainly from discoveries made when the wall of the ancient Gallo-Roman *castrum* (fort) was demolished. It includes columns, capitals, architraves and remarkable bas-reliefs.

Further traces of Roman remains can be seen in the neighbourhood of the museum.

From here it is possible to make a detour to Abbaye aux Dames and to come back to the market square via the footbridge.

ABBAYE AUX DAMES ⓥ

This "Ladies' Abbey", which stands on the east bank of the Charente, was consecrated in 1047. The abbey was dedicated to St Mary, and owed its prosperity to Agnès de Bourgogne, whose second husband was Geoffroy Martel, Comte d'Anjou and seigneur of the Saintonge. The Abbey, placed in the hands of Benedictine nuns, was directed by an Abbess – customarily chosen from among the most illustrious families in France – who then bore the title "Madame de Saintes". Charged with the education of young daughters of the nobility, the convent counted among its boarders at one time Athenaos de Rochechouart, the future Marquise de Montespan and mistress to Louis XIV. After the Revolution and during the Empire period the Abbey fell into decline. It was transformed into a barracks, freed after World War I, but required a great deal of restoration before it could be returned to the Church for religious use.

★ **Abbey Church** – The Abbey Church is in the local Saintonge Romanesque style; it is reached via an 18C porch leading to the Abbey's first courtyard, where it is surrounded by the usual convent buildings. The most remarkable features of the church are the façade and the bell tower.

The **façade** presents a richly-ornamented **doorway** at the centre, flanked by blind arcades. The carved coving in the doorway shows, from bottom to top: six angels adoring the Hand of God; the symbols of the Evangelists around the Lamb; the suffering of the martyrs, menaced by a whip, an axe or the Sword of Justice; 54 old men wearing crowns, facing each other two by two as they play music. The coving of the right arcade portrays the Last Supper; that on the left, the presence of a divine Christ facing five other figures suffused with light whose significance is uncertain. Note also the historiated capitals (a knight, monsters) and, on the gable, the arms of Françoise I de La Rochefoucauld, Abbess from 1559 to 1605.

The lower level of the **bell tower** *(illustration in Introduction, Art and Architecture)*, situated above the transept crossing, is square in section and pierced with three arcades on each face. Above this is a shallow octagonal level flanked by pinnacles which is in turn surmounted by a dome pierced by 12 twinned bays separated by small columns. The whole tower is topped by a scaled conical roof, the slopes of which are slightly convex.

Interior – In the first half of the 12C the interior was the subject of alterations, generally thought to have been made by the architect Béranger (an inscription carved into the outside of the north wall dates the work as pre-1150). The quadripartite vaulting in the transept arms – and the Gothic chapel in the northern arm – are later (15C) additions. The two-bay nave, lined with six heavy 12C pillars erected in front of the 11C walls, is covered with a timber ceiling which replaced the two original domes on pendentives, destroyed by fire in 1648. On the southern side of the transept entrance, a console supports a 12C head of Christ.

At the intersection of the nave and the transept, before the transept crossing and the belfry above it, four more heavy pillars support a dome on squinches.

Half-barrel vaulting over the Romanesque chancel is prolonged by a slightly recessed, terminal oven vault.

Convent buildings – The façade of the long 17C central block has been restored to its original purity of line: two storeys pierced by narrow windows and surmounted by an upper level punctuated by dormers with pediments.

On the left, adjoining three renovated bays of the old 14C cloisters, is a fine 17C doorway, the pilasters of which are adorned with exuberant sculptures that contrast strikingly with the severity of the façade.

ADDITIONAL SIGHTS

★ **Arènes** ⓥ – *West of the town centre.* A short distance from the centre, the Roman arena – in reality an amphitheatre – owes part of its sylvan attraction and evocative atmosphere to the fact that grass covers a large proportion of the stepped terracing. This is one of the oldest amphitheatres of the Roman world – it was built in the 1C AD – but is relatively small. Overall dimensions of the ellipse are 125m long x 102m wide (413ft x 335ft), while the actual arena, where performances took place, measures 64m x 39m (210ft x 128ft). The terraces could accommodate 20 000 spectators.

Halfway up the terraced slope, on the southern side, there is a gap in which a small fountain plays. This is dedicated to St Eustelle, a young female disciple of St Eutrope who was beheaded here.

The Roman Amphitheatre

▶▶**Église St-Eutrope** ⓥ – 11C church, with lower **church★**; **Musée Dupuy-Mestreau** ⓥ – assorted collections in an 18C mansion; **Thermes St-Saloine** (north of the town centre); **Musée Éducatif de Préhistoire** ⓥ (east of the town centre) – includes the giant Grézac tool-polishing stone; **Haras** ⓥ (east of the town centre) – Stud farm.

EXCURSIONS

★**Romanesque churches in the Saintonge**

Round trip of 75km/47mi – 4hr

Leave Saintes heading west (N 150 then D 728).

Église de Corme-Royal – The church, a dependency of Abbaye aux Dames in Saintes, is noted for its two-storey west front decorated with a profusion of delicate carvings. The interior, which has regained its original vaulting, is lit by modern stained-glass windows.

Return via D 728. At Nancras go left along D 117.

Abbaye de Sablonceaux ⓥ – This abbey was founded in 1136 by Guillaume X, the father of Eleanor of Aquitaine. Partially destroyed five times since the 14C, the abbey church with its Romanesque nave and tall Gothic tower has been restored to something like its original splendour. The convent buildings are being restored.

Take D 243^{E1} to St-Romain-de-Benet.

Hameau de Pirelonge – The hamlet, which has a number of historical houses renovated using traditional methods, boasts a series of small museums which together preserve the local heritage: **Musée des Alambics**, installed in a distillery, displays a collection of alembics (stills) from the Charente region, of the type still in use for the refinement of cognac. The museum also shows a series of "mobile" stills used by home distillers to make alcohol from wine or fruit. A collection of alcoholmeters is interesting.

Musée Charentais de l'Imprimerie – An immense workshop containing about 30 machines (linotype machines and old printing presses) are used to demonstrate the printing methods of the past. Young visitors will discover the amazing history of the printing industry before the age of the computer, when lead still reigned supreme.

Some of the houses have displays of **church vestments** (albs, copes and chasubles), paper money (from promissory notes issued during the French Revolution to modern bills) and reconstructions of **craftsman's workshops** (blacksmith's, weaver's, barrel-maker's, etc.).

In the autumn, the **Alembic and Harvest Fairs** held in the hamlet revive local traditions (numerous demonstrations – *see Practical Information*).

About 200m/218yd from the hamlet *(behind the railway line)* the **Tour de Pirelonge**, a Roman tower, is still partially roofed with carved stones. Between vineyards and woods, the tower stands on the edge of an old Roman road but its function remains a mystery – boundary marker or religious monument?

Return via N 150 towards Saintes. After 500m/550yd turn right on D 243^{E1}.

Église de Meursac – The Gothic church, shored up by powerful buttresses, ends in a Romanesque chancel with half-barrel vaulting. Romanesque capitals in the chancel depict birds pecking lions and a human figure strangling two lions. The altarpiece and tabernacle are of carved and gilded wood. A 5C crypt was discovered beneath the church in 1972; the large chamber was hollowed from the bedrock and has a domed roof *(access via a narrow spiral staircase near the chancel).*

Follow D 243^{E1} south-east.

Église de Thaims – The modest church was built on the site of a Gallo-Roman villa (remains of the villa walls, up to a height of 2.5m/8ft, can be seen at the foot of the octagonal church tower, on the north side). In the garden

East end of
the church in Rioux

on the southern side of the church are a number of Merovingian sarcophagi. The cornices of the transept crossing inside are Merovingian too, although scenes engraved there, including the Flight of St Peter, are later (Carolingian).

A lapidary museum has been installed between the nave and the chancel. Among other exhibits are the remains of two Gallo-Roman sculptures.

Leave Thaims north-east via D 114.

Église de Rétaud – The 12C church is worth seeing for the decorative frieze of its west front, the octagonal belfry above the transept crossing, and especially for the richly carved, faceted walls of the apse. The consoles, fashioned into grotesques, are interesting. Noteworthy features inside include the two capitals at the entrance to the apse, the small columns framing its bays, and part of a funerary litre (a black band on the church wall decorated with the armorial bearings of the dead).

Leave Retaud heading south via D 216.

Église de Rioux – This simple rural church with a low nave and belfry-porch, is known to art enthusiasts for its brilliant sculptured décor; the **east end★** is particularly noteworthy.

Leave Rioux north-east via D 129.

On the way to Chermignac the road passes within view of the Château de Rioux, which belonged in the Middle Ages to the family of the Seigneurs of Didonne, vassals of the Comtes de Poitou.

Église de Chermignac – Frightening animals and different types of human characters adorn the covings above the church entrance. Near the church is a fine example of a **hosanna cross** *(see Introduction, Art and Architecture).*

Return to D 129 which leads back to Saintes.

Woodland tour through northeastern Saintonge

Round trip 39km/24mi – allow 4hr. Leave Saintes heading east along N 150.

Château du Douhet ⓥ – The 17C château, with its sober lines, is thought to have been built from plans drawn up by Jules Hardouin-Mansart (1646-1708), the brilliant classicist architect responsible for the Grand Trianon at Versailles and Place Vendôme in Paris. The château and its dependencies, together with the gardens, park and pools, extend over an area of 20ha/49 acres.

Don't miss the tour of the grounds (1hr on foot), from the Renaissance dovecote to the two mirrored pools of the southern esplanade. These elegant, square, balustraded basins are still fed by the 1C Gallo-Roman aqueduct which once serviced the thermal baths at Saintes. Stop to admire and breathe in the fragrance of the centenary **boxwood**★. Beyond the trees, from the terrace which overlooks the pools, there is a beautiful view across the water to the majestic south face of the château. Inside the château *(access via the steps below the south front)* – where the period furniture and fittings have only partly been preserved – interest centres mainly on the curious salon named The Lantern, with its 17C woodwork. In the right wing a museum of local traditions has been installed, with the reconstruction of an early 19C bourgeois interior in the Saintonge style, and collections of regional prehistoric, Gallo-Roman and mineralogical items.

Drive east along D 231 which soon crosses N 150.

Écoyeux – The church here is an imposing 12C building, fortified in the 15C – witness the two turreted watchtowers framing the west front.

Leave Écoyeux south-east via D 231.

Abbaye de Fontdouce ⓥ – This prosperous Benedictine abbey, half hidden in a steep, wooded valley, was sacked by the Huguenots. All that remains today is a small collection of monastic dependencies: a 12C cellar, a heating house with a 15C campanile, the main block dating from the 12C and 13C, and a Charente-style residential hall added to it in the 19C.

Visitors can tour the parlour, the two Romanesque chapels one above the other, and especially the magnificent **chapter house**★, with its twelve bays in which the ribbed vaulting rests on a forest of pillars. Notable here are the finely carved keystones, among them a curious three-faced head with four eyes, probably symbolising the Holy Trinity. The abbey church is now only a few ruined columns and a huge pillar base which would have been at the transept crossing.

Take D 131 towards Saintes.

La Chapelle-des-Pots – Locally fashioned ceramics, in a tradition dating back to the 13C, are still made in this village today.

D 131 joins N 141 which leads back to Saintes.

SAUVETERRE-DE-BÉARN★

Population 1 304
Michelin map 342: G-4 or 234 fold 34

The small town lies on a picturesque **site**★ above an escarpment overlooking the Oloron Torrent.

The Judgement of God – In the year 1170 Sancie, the widow of Gaston V of Béarn was accused of having killed a child born after her husband's death and was submitted to a trial known as the Judgement of God. On the orders of her own brother, the King of Navarre, she was bound hand and foot and thrown into the river from the top of the town's fortified bridge *(see below)*. However, the strong current cast her up on the bank, safe and sound, further downstream – so Sancie was pronounced innocent and had her rights restored.

SIGHTS

Terraces by the Church and the Town Hall – From here there is a wonderful view: the old bridge, the torrent, a tree-covered island, a ruined tower, the Romanesque belfry of the church, the outline of the distant Pyrenees – a most romantic landscape.

Vieux pont – One arch of the ancient bridge remains, surmounted by the town's 12C fortified gateway. The legend of Sancie is explained *(in French)* on a panel. From here again there is a magnificent **view**★★ of the river, the fortifications, the church and the splendid Montréal Tower.

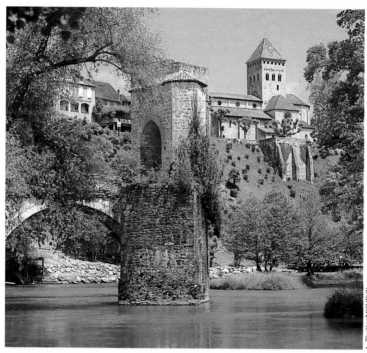

Sauveterre-de-Béarn

Église St-André ⓥ – The tympanum above the entrance to St Andrew's Church depicts Christ in Glory surrounded by the four Evangelists. The ribbed vaulting harmonises perfectly with the Romanesque design of the interior. A pillar on the north side of the chancel is topped by a historiated capital representing Scandal-Mongering and Gluttony. The east end, flanked by two apsidal chapels, is surmounted by a quadrangular bell tower pierced by twinned windows.

EXCURSION

Château de Laàs ⓥ – *9km/5mi SE via D 27.* This is an extraordinary château-museum: by collecting together **furniture★**, objets d'art and family paintings from three different homes, Monsieur and Madame Serbat, the last owners, created a decorative arts museum which also serves to illustrate the art of living in the Hainaut region (in the north of France) during the 18C.
Louis XVI panelling adorns the bedchambers and salons. Mme Serbat's room is decorated with illustrations of the *Fables* of La Fontaine. Tapestries and hand-painted fabrics (music room) set off the fine Northern School paintings (Watteau de Lille). Nor is historical anecdote forgotten: a first-floor bedroom recalls the aftermath of Waterloo, for here is the bed Napoleon slept in at Maubert-Fontaine on 19 June 1815.

Musée du Maïs – This small, specialised museum in the château outbuildings concerns itself exclusively with the subject of maize. Exhibits touch on methods, implements and the nutritional valve of this crop, known as corn to Americans.
The cereal, cultivated in central and southern America since 5 000 BC, was introduced into Europe at the end of the 15C immediately after the discovery of America. It filtered into France via Spain and by the 17C had become an essential component of the traditional Béarn agricultural system. Together with the Basque country, the province became the cradle of maize production throughout France.

SOULAC-SUR-MER

Population 2 720
Michelin map 335: E-1 or 233 fold 25

This seaside resort is sheltered by pine-covered dunes on one side, and from the surging surf on the other, by a high sand bank, once the site of the ancient city of Noviomagus, which was swallowed up by the sea in the 6C. Until the 16C, Soulac had a large natural harbour giving on to the Gironde estuary, where pilgrims would come ashore on their way to Santiago de Compostela. It was overrun by marshes in the 17C.

From the waterfront there is a fine view of the Phare de Cordouan. Bathing is supervised along the resort's four beaches and there are numerous possibilities for water sports, hikes and cycle tours.

SIGHTS

Basilique Notre-Dame-de-la-Fin-des-Terres – was a Benedictine abbey church which, at the end of the 18C, was almost entirely covered by sand. It was uncovered and restored in the 19C. The church includes elements of 12C Romanesque architecture and has a 14C belfry which replaced the original one which stood over the transept crossing. The Poitou style of building is apparent in the windowless nave, and dimly lit by tall bays in the side aisles which are almost as high as the nave itself. Some of the historiated capitals remain. Three capitals show the tomb and shrine of St Veronica *(left pier before the chancel)* who evangelised the Médoc region and died in Soulac; one portrays St Peter in prison *(at the entrance to the chancel, left)*, and another depicts Daniel in the lions' den *(inside the chancel)*. A polychrome wood statue of Our Lady of Land's End, to whom the church is dedicated, stands in the south transept.

Musée d'Art et Archéologie ⊙ – The town boasts an Archaeological Museum displaying flint axes, chisels, decorated pottery, arrow heads from the Neolithic and Bronze Ages, and military ensigns, money, ceramics and glassware from the Gallo-Roman period.

The museum also houses the **Fondation Soulac-Médoc**. On view, inside, are paintings and sculptures by contemporary local artists.

UNDER THE STARS ...

Camping Les Lacs – *126 rte des Lacs – 33780 Soulac-sur-Mer – 3km/1.8mi S of Soulac via D 101 – ☎ 05 56 09 76 63 – camping-les-lacs@wanadoo.fr – open 30 Mar to Sep – ✉ – reserv. recommended – 152 sites: 19,82€.* Real holidays in a convivial, lively atmosphere. Two pools, one covered and one outdoors, a games room, a bar, a pizzeria and activities. Fun for the whole family, whether you stay in your tent, a camping car or a mobile home.

... IN THE WHISPERING PINES

Hôtel des Pins – *92 bd Amélie – 33780 L'Amélie-sur-Mer – 4.5km/2.8mi SW of Soulac via D 101E – ☎ 05 56 73 27 27 – closed 6 Jan to 16 Mar, Sun-Mon from 15 Oct to 1 Apr – ▫ – 31 rms: 36,59/73,18€ – ☲ 7,01€ – restaurant 20,58/38,11€.* Just a hundred-metre stroll and you're on the beach. This is a tranquil hotel with well-kept, albeit somewhat outdated, rooms. Dining room with terrace. Traditional cuisine with shellfish on the menu.

EXCURSIONS

Pointe de Grave ⊙ – *10km/6.2mi N. Park the car by the monument.* Pointe de Grave is the tip of a headland at the northernmost limit of the Landes, which curves across to narrow the mouth of the Gironde. It lies directly across the water from the beach resort of Royan.

The present monument replaces a 75m/246ft pyramid erected to commemorate the landing of American troops in 1917 and demolished by the Germans in 1942. The Point was a strategic coastal defensive position. German forces occupying western France held on to it after the Allied landings in 1944; and it was not recaptured until April 1945, only weeks before the armistice.

The old blockhouse on top of the dune offers a vast **panoramic view★** of the Cordouan lighthouse 9km/5mi out to sea, the peninsula and lighthouse of La Coubre, the Gironde and the harbour at Le Verdon, the coves around Royan and the splendid expanse of the Atlantic Ocean.

Another lighthouse, on the Point itself, houses the **Musée du phare de Cordouan** ⊙ (120 steps). This museum highlights the exceptional architecture of the off-shore Cordouan lighthouse and gives some idea of the daily life of the keepers. Children's drawings on the theme of lighthouses, and an aquarium with exotic marine species complete the exhibition; from the gallery, admire the view of the estuary.

* **Phare de Cordouan** – *See Phare de CORDOUAN*. As well as providing access to the lighthouse, Pointe de Grave is the departure point for various **boat trips**. There is also a **scenic railway**.

Le Verdon-sur-Mer – Le Verdon is a large container terminal in an advantageous location at the mouth of the estuary, protected from the ocean by Pointe de Grave. It has a deep-water port unrestricted by locks or tides, and offers direct access up the Gironde. Its disposition, combined with the excellent facilities (fast cargo handling, ample warehouse space), makes it particularly suitable for the huge container ships and oil tankers which dock here before sailing for Central America, South America, West Africa and the Indian Ocean.

Moulin de Vensac ⓥ – *From Soulac take D 101E⁶ left and follow the orange signposting to the mill*. This traditional 18C windmill, consisting of a stone tower with a conical roof, was moved to its present location in 1858. Visitors can follow the different stages of flour-making from the grinding of corn to the final sifting. Some of the machinery, fashioned from oak, is as old as the mill itself.

TALMONT-SUR-GIRONDE★

Population 83
Michelin map 324: E-6 or 233 fold 26 – 16km/10mi southeast of Royan

The charming "walled town" of Talmont, modelled on the *bastides* of Aquitaine, was built in 1234 on a peninsula by Edward I of England. Talmont is famous for its Romanesque church dedicated to St Radegund; walk along the ramparts and through streets lined with hollyhocks.

SIGHTS

* **Église Ste-Radegonde** – St Radegund's church, a fine example of the Saintonge Romanesque style, stands on an impressive **site★** at the tip of the promontory, on the edge of a sheer cliff dropping into the Gironde. It is continually threatened by the tides which unceasingly attack the horizontal strata of the sedimentary beds it rests upon. The cliff face has more than once been consolidated and the church restored to its original 12C appearance. This stone sentinel standing apart from the village and its tiny port is surrounded by a small cemetery from which there is a fine **view** of the estuary and, off to the right, the white chalk cliffs of Meschers.

Fishing piers and Saint Radegund's

Eating out

L'Estuaire – *au Caillaud – 1 av. de l'Estuaire –* ☎ *05 46 90 43 85 – closed 1 Oct to 28 Feb, Tue-Wed off-season – 16.01/32.01€.* Diners enjoy a rare view of the estuary and village from this superb location. The decor is plain (but who cares?); the regional cuisine prepared by the owner delicious. A few well-kept rooms are let in season.

L'Auberge des Monards – *16 Le Port des Monards – 17120 Barzan – 4.5km/3mi SE of Talmont via D 145 –* ☎ *05 46 90 44 44 – closed 15 Nov to 15 Dec, Wed evening and Thu off season – 14.48/27.44€.* Located in one of the small ports typical of the estuary, here's an address favoured by the locals. Fish and meat are grilled all year round in the big fireplace stoked under the veranda. Simple decor and dancing evenings based on culinary themes, like *piballes* or spare rib of beef.

The building is squat and compact, with a traditional apse and apsidal chapels. A square tower with a shallow pyramid roof surmounts the transept crossing. One bay of the nave was lost to the sea in the 15C.

From the mud flats and seaweed-covered rocks exposed at the foot of the cliff when the tide is out, the spectacular site of the church can be admired to the full, along with the particular elegance of its east end. Rhythmically punctuated by buttress-columns, this is enlivened by a ring of tall, blind arcades which frame windows at first-floor level; a neat row of smaller blind arcades with small columns decorates the second storey.

The fine doorway in the northern arm of the transept has coving adorned with angels adoring the Lamb, acrobats, and men pulling a rope tethering two lions. Note the dome on pendentives, and the capitals around the half-domed apse.

Musée d'Histoire locale ○ – Near the seamen's cemetery, the old school houses a museum designed to provide visitors with detailed information of the town and the traditional fishing activities practised in the lower estuary of the Gironde.

EXCURSION

Site gallo-romain du Fâ ○ – *Barzan, 2km/1.2mi SE.* Excavations have revealed the ancient ruins (baths and sanctuary) of a Gallo-Roman city extending beneath a cultivated area of 150ha/371 acres. An exhibition introduces the site and the latest archaeological finds.

THOUARS★

Population 10 656

Michelin map 322: E-3 or 232 folds 44, 45

The best view of the **site★** of this old town is from the southern approach (D 39), across the bridge over the River Thouet. From Pont Neuf (New Bridge) there is a fine view of the rocky promontory, cradled by the river on the Poitou-Anjou border, and of the roofs – a mixture of Romanesque tiles and Angevin slates – of the houses clustered below the castle walls. Celebrations in traditional and medieval costume bring life to the town in summer.

For many years Thouars remained faithful to the Plantagenets but the town eventually fell to **Bertrand du Guesclin** (1320-80), one of the generals who chased the English from the region, after a memorable siege in 1372. Having purchased Thouars from the Amboise family, Louis XI stayed here several times, and his wife, Margaret of Scotland, expressed a wish to be buried here. Charles VIII gave the town to the House of La Trémoille, and the family remained seigneurs of Thouars until the Revolution. The Protestant faith had been embraced by the inhabitants; after the Revocation of the Edict of Nantes Thouars lost fifty per cent of its population.

OLD TOWN *1hr.*

The walk starts from place St-Médard, where it is possible to park the car.

★**Église St-Médard** – The church, standing adjacent to a 15C square tower with overhanging corner turrets, is a Romanesque building despite the Gothic rose-window adorning its fine Poitevin **west front★★**. The extensively-decorated entrance is surmounted by a Christ in Glory worshipped by angels. The archivolts – the last one breaks the ranks with a resurrected Christ Rising from the Tomb – spring from historiated capitals depicting the Punishment of the Vices. Splendid effigies of St Peter, St Paul, the Prophets and the Sibyls stand above the lateral arcades. The Romanesque doorway with festooned arches on the north side of the church is of Moorish inspiration. Inside, the three original Romanesque naves were replaced in the 15C by a single nave with lowered vaulting.

Chapelle St-Louis (on the north side) with its lierne-and-tierceron vaulting was built in 1510 by Gabrielle de Bourbon, the wife of Louis II of La Trémoille.

Follow rue du Château which prolongs rue St-Médard. The two streets once formed the town's high street and led to the old bridge.

* **Old houses** – Rue du Château boasts two brick-and-timber houses including the Hostellerie St-Médard, flanked by a vaulted passageway, and several corbelled façades beneath sharp, steep gables – notably that of the 15C Hôtel des Trois-Rois (Three Kings Mansion) at no 11. It was here that the future Louis XI slept when he was still *dauphin* (heir to the throne). A moulded corbel on the façade supports a bartizan where guards could mount to keep watch over the street.

Opening onto the esplanade, that was once the seigneurial courtyard, are the Chapelle Notre-Dame and the Château.

Chapelle Notre-Dame – This chapel was built above a series of crypts, one of which is still the family tomb of the La Trémoilles. The superb Flamboyant Gothic façade is surmounted by a Renaissance gallery with shell decorations.

Château (Collège Marie-de-La-Tour-d'Auvergne) ⊙ – A domed pavilion housing a monumental staircase projects from the central block and there are two other pavilions at the extremities.

Walk up avenue de La-Trémoille to Abbaye St-Laon.

View of Thouars

Ancienne Abbaye St-Laon – This former abbey first staffed by Benedictine monks and then, after 1117, by Augustinians includes a 12C-15C church with a fine, square Romanesque belfry. Margaret of Scotland is buried here. The present town hall is installed in the old (17C) monastic buildings.

Follow rue Régnier-Desmarais, rue St-Médard and turn right towards Chapelle Jeanne-d'Arc.

Chapelle Jeanne-d'Arc – Built in 1892, the chapel now houses regular exhibitions of contemporary art.

Walk along rue Du-Guesclin to Porte au Prévôt.

Porte au Prévôt – This is the gateway forced by Du Guesclin when he penetrated the town in 1372 to end the siege. It is framed by two projecting ravelin towers on octagonal bases.

Follow rue du Président-Tyndo.

Tour du Prince-de-Galles ⊙ – The Prince of Wales Tower, also known as the Granary Tower because it was used as a grain store when it formed part of the town's defensive perimeter, is round and massive and capped with small bartizans. It has also gone under the name of Faux-Sauniers, in reference to unscrupulous salt dealers who were locked up here by members of the "salt police". Before its

DINING IN POMPOIS

Le Logis de Pompois – *(Centre d'Aide par le Travail), Pompois – 79100 Ste-Verge – 5km/3mi NW of Thouars. Travel towards Doué-la-Fontaine and Pompois –* ☎ *05 49 96 27 84 – Closed Sun evening, Mon and Tue – 13.74€ lunch – 23.64/39.65€.* Set in a hamlet, the tables of this old vineyard farm from the 18 and 19C are arranged across from the fields in the summer. In the winter, guests have their meals in the elegant dining room, a blend of modern and traditional styles. "Jazzy" dinners two Saturdays a month. Well-prepared cuisine.

BACK TO NATURE IN MASSAIS

Le Moulin Bernard – *79150 Massais – 13km/8mi W of Thouars, towards Argenton then secondary route –* ☎ *05 49 96 84 64 – closed 15 Nov to 15 Mar, Tue from 15 Mar to 15 Jun, Sat lunch from 15 Jun to 31 Aug and Mon except evenings from 15 Jun to 31 Aug – 4 rms: 31.25/36.60€ – meals 10/17.50€.* This is an address for nature lovers and sports aficionados. Meals on the banks of the Argenton, camping in a natural environment, rooms in the self-catering cottage or B & B – a varied choice in a simple setting. Numerous activities too – canoeing, rock-climbing, fishing, etc…

abolition in 1709, the highly unpopular and iniquitous salt tax spurred vast smuggling operations; hapless bandits ended up in narrow cages visible on the second floor of the tower. Contemporary artists Ange Leccia and Jacques Vielle were inspired by this aspect of the building's history to the produce the works on exhibit within, transforming the mood from carceral to creative.

Rues Prince-de-Galles and Saugé lead back to place St-Médard.

EXCURSION

▶▶ **Airvault** – 21km/13mi south – Église St-Pierre (12C Poitevin and 13C Angevin styles; porch★), **Musée des arts et traditions populaires** ⊙.

TIFFAUGES
Population 1 328
Michelin map 316: J-5 or 232 fold 41

Tiffauges is a small town built on a promontory overlooking the confluence of the Sèvre Nantaise and the River Crume, and is best known for the romantic ruins of a castle which once belonged to the man who is said to have inspired Charles Perrault to write the tale of **Bluebeard**.

Gilles de Rais – or Retz (1404-40) – was a fine horseman and a serious scholar in his youth. Early on he also demonstrated unusual qualities of leadership and military prowess (or, by some analyses, bloodthirsty, violent tendencies), acting as a lieutenant to Charles VII in the war against the English and fighting beside Joan of Arc for the recovery of the crown. He accompanied her to Paris for the consecration of the king. In recognition of his valour, Charles awarded him the title of Maréchal at the age of 25. He was at Joan's side when Paris was attacked; after her capture he retired, disconsolate, to his lands.

In 1420 he married Catherine de Thouars, who brought him as a dowry the domain of Pouzauges, adding to his own inherited wealth and making him one of the richest men in France. De Rais was a big spender, keeping a retinue of 200 horsemen in his lavish court, decorating his château, maintaining heralds, servants and priests. He sponsored elaborate pageants in which he himself performed, recreating his own role in Joan's army.

With his vast fortune depleted and compromised, his family secured a decree from the king in 1435, preventing him from mortgaging or selling any more property. In an effort to find some way of making money, the dissolute seigneur of Tiffauges turned to alchemy and sought the help of demons. He was later accused of the satanic abduction, torture and murder of as many as 200 children.

In 1440, Rais was arrested on an unrelated charge and, on pain of torture, confessed to heresy before the ecclesiastical court and to murder before civil judges, who condemned him to death by hanging. His body was then burned in Nantes, in the presence of an eager crowd.

Truth or fiction? Sceptics point out the Duke of Brittany's financial interest in de Rais' ruin, the irregularities of the proceedings, and unbelievable scope of his alleged crimes. Yet the details of his "confession" leave little to the imagination.

CHÂTEAU ⊙ 1hr

The ruins of the castle cover a huge area (3ha/7acres) within a defensive wall.
The parts in the best condition are the 12C keep, still protected by a deep ditch,
and the 15C Vidame Tower with its enormous machicolations. Guardroom, latrines
and an ancient chimney piece can be seen here, as well as a night-duty room linked
to the watch path around the ramparts (there is a curious acoustic effect from the
circular bench where watchmen sat).
The 13C chapel, built over an 11C crypt, has retained its oven-vaulted apse.

Le Conservatoire des machines de guerre: Animation – In a reconstruction of
a 15C siege camp, full-scale engines of war, rebuilt according to authentic
documents, have been erected on the inner esplanade. Cannon balls are fired a
distance of 150m/500ft. The **trebuchet**, the most powerful medieval engine of war,
is the château's prize exhibit. A mortar spits fire and giant wooden catapults are
fired by men in medieval costume (a belfry, giant cross-bows, cannon and a
battering ram are also on display). Armoured horsemen wield their mighty swords
while visitors can try their hand at firing bows and arrows and cross-bows.

Château de Tiffauges – Tour du Vidame

VILLENEUVE-SUR-LOT
Population 22 782
Michelin map 336: G-3 or 235 fold 13

The town, which has preserved numerous alleys and ancient houses from the Middle
Ages (especially around Place La Fayette, a typical old square) is today largely spread
around the banks of the River Lot. The fertile alluvial valley, which produces plentiful
crops of fruit and early vegetables, has made Villeneuve into a busy trading centre and,
like Agen, a regional market for plums.

The town, founded in 1253 on the borders between Périgord and Guyenne by Alphonse
de Poitiers, was built to serve as a "support centre" for the strongholds scattered
throughout the upper Agenais region; Villeneuve was one of the largest and most
powerful *bastides* in the southwest.

SIGHTS

Town gates – The two town gates – **Porte de Paris** north-east of the old town and
Porte de Pujols south-west – are the only traces of the old ramparts. The gates are
both built of brick and stone, are both crowned with crenellations and
machicolations, and both covered by a roof of brown tiles. Porte du Pujols is three
storeys high with mullioned windows; Porte de Paris was instrumental in the fierce
resistance to Mazarin's troops during the siege of 1653.

Eating out

BUDGET

Auberge Lou Calel – *47300 Pujols – 4km/2.5mi SW of Villeneuve-sur-Lot. Take D 118 and C 207 –* ☎ *05 53 70 46 14 – closed 3-17 Jan, Tue evening, Wed, and Thu lunch – 12,96/32,01€.* A traditional auberge with a superb view as a bonus – the dining room's bay windows open onto Villeneuve-sur-Lot. Weather allowing, you can enjoy the lovely scenery from the terrace. Affordable cuisine prepared with care.

Where to stay

BUDGET

Hôtel La Résidence – *17 av. L.-Carnot –* ☎ *05 53 40 17 03 – closed 23 Dec to 5 Jan –* 🅿 *– 18 rooms: 21,19/47,26€ –* ☲ *4,42€.* A small family hotel that won't bust your budget. The rooms in the main house are very basic; those in the building just behind are quieter and more comfortable.

MODERATE

Château de Seiglal Bed and Breakfast – *47380 Monclar-d'Agenais – 6km/3.6mi N of Fongrave. Take D 238 then D 667, kilometre post n° 25 –* ☎ *05 53 41 81 30 – decourty-chambres-hotes@wordline.fr –* ✉ *– 5 rooms: 50,31/54,88€ – meals 15,25€.* Well-being and hospitality define this handsome 19C edifice surrounded by century-old trees. You'll appreciate the comfortable rooms, named after the owner's five sisters, with a view of the park and fields. Convivial *table d'hôte* meals served in the dining room with sculpted furniture and fireplace.

Disco

La Loco – *2 pl. du 4-Septembre –* ☎ *05 53 40 09 27 – Thu-Sun from 11pm; school holidays: Wed-Sun from 11pm.* Located downtown, this discotheque is very fashionable with the young crowd. Many theme evenings.

Shopping

Place Lafayette – *Pl. Lafayette – markets Tue and Sat morning.* La Place Lafayette, a.k.a. la Place des Cornières, in the centre of Villeneuve-sur-Lot, is always a very lively spot. The streets leading from the square are full of shops as well as a few bars where the late-night crowd seeks refuge.

La Boutique des Pruneaux – *Pl. de la Libération –* ☎ *05 53 70 02 75 – www.boutiquedespruneaux.com – Mon-Sun 8am-12h15, 2pm-7:45pm.* One tends to forget that most of the famous *pruneaux d'Agen* are grown and conditioned in Villeneuve-sur-Lot and vicinity. This boutique, at the foot of the Porte de Paris, is specialized in prunes (natural or filled...) and vintage Armagnacs (40 to 50 years old).

Sports and recreation

Aviron Villeneuvois – *Quai d'Alsace –* ☎ *05 53 49 18 27 – office hours: Mon-Fri 9am-noon, 2pm-5pm.* This rowing club, situated in the heart of the city, organizes boat trips up the Lot river during summer months.

Haras National – *R. des Haras –* ☎ *05 53 70 00 91 – www.haras-nationaux.fr – visit by appointment: Mon-Sat 2pm-5pm – closed public holidays.* Founded in 1804 in the bosom of the city, this national stud farm was originally meant to provide military mounts. Today, horses are bred here principally for use in sports. Breeds include pureblood saddle horses (Anglo-Arab, French Saddle, Arab...) and draft horses (Breton, Percheron and Comtois).

Stade de la Myre Mory – *Rte d'Agen –* ☎ *05 53 70 08 35 – daily 8am-dusk.* Rugby fans, hold your breath: this is the stadium of the Villeneuve-sur-Lot rugby team, oft-times French champion and 1999 European title holder. A 1.7km track circles the park.

Centre de Plein Air de Rogé – 🖽 *– D 661 –* ☎ *05 53 70 48 13 – Jul-Aug: daily 10am-6pm.* Surrounded by greenery and bordered by a bend of the Lot, this children's outdoor centre is blessed with an idyllic setting. Kayak, rowing, water-skiing, horseback riding, archery, trampoline and mountain biking courses are held here. Course price is 61€ per week.

Église Ste-Catherine – *North bank of the river.* This brick-built church, in Romanesque-Byzantine style, resting on a granite plinth, was consecrated in 1937. Its north-south orientation is extremely unusual. The interior is decorated, apart from the chancel, with a series of restored stained-glass windows; those dating from the 14C and 15C – which came from the old church – have been attributed to the school of **Arnaud de Moles**, the master-enameller and painter who worked on the cathedral in Auch. Beautiful 17C and 18C gilt wood statues (of Our Lady of the Rosary, St Joseph, Mary Magdalene and St Jerome) adorn the four pillars of the nave above the doorway into the baptistery. The marble font stands bathed in blue-tinged shafts of light. The paintings in the nave show a procession moving towards the chancel.

Bell tower, St Catherine's

B. Kaufmann/MICHELIN

Pont des Cieutats (or Pont-Vieux) – This old bridge with uneven arches, which was built by the English in the 13C, offers a picturesque view over the banks of the river and over the 16C chapel at the end of the bridge, with its east end jutting over the water.

Musée de la Vallée du Lot – The new municipal museum of Villeneuve, housed in an old windmill overlooking the Lot, mainly contains collections of paintings from the 18C (Lebrun school), the 19C (Hyppolyte Flandrin, Eva Gonzalès and André Crochepierre) and the 20C (Henri Martin, Brayer) as well as a prints and graphic art (Piranesi). A large archaeological collection and a section on the history of the Lot and the *bastide* are also open to the public.

EXCURSIONS

★ Penne d'Agenais – *10km/6mi E via D 661.*
This stronghold was once the fief of the kings of England, and so suffered during the wars of religion that it was nothing but ruins by the mid-20C. Greatly restored, it is now a lively summer tourist attraction.

Place Gambetta – This shady terrace is an excellent starting point for a tour of Penne. The "gateway to the town" opens onto two fine 16C houses, one of which served as a local prison for many years.

Notre-Dame-de-Peyragude – This modern sanctuary (in Romanesque-Byzantine style) is built on the top of a hill offering a scenic view of the valley. Very popular pilgrimages in honour of the Virgin are held here.

★ Viewpoint – The orientation table overlooks the valley of the Lot, from Villeneuve to Fume: the view extends as far as the Upper Quercy in the distance.

Porte de Ferracap – The gallows used to be erected close to this gate.

Rue de Ferracap – This, and the adjacent streets, are lined with very fine renovated houses (some with half-timbering and corbelling).

Place Paul-Froment – A remarkable brick house preceded by a house with Gothic arches contains a café and exhibit rooms.

Porte et Fontaine de Ricard – This old fortified gate and the fountain below are named after Richard the Lionheart who was responsible for building the town's first fortifications.

The Lower Lot Valley

65km/41mi round trip – allow all day

Leave Villeneuve north-west via D242 towards Casseneuil.

Casseneuil – The pretty brown-tiled roofs of Casseneuil, built in a bend at the junction of the Lède and the Lot, are clustered around the church. After living off the river trade for many years, the town has now turned to preserved foods as its chief source of revenue. Many fine old houses, their loggias leaning towards the Lède and surrounded by terrace gardens, are arranged throughout the village and on the roads to St-Pastour and Hauterive.

Go south-west via D 217 to Ste-Livrade and turn left along D 667. After 1km/0.6mi, turn left to Fongrave.

Fongrave – Fongrave priory was founded in 1130 and placed under the rule of Fontevraud, only accepting nuns of noble birth. The **church** has a monumental 17C carved oak **altar piece★** with snake-infested vines writhing around its cabled columns; an Adoration of the Magi occupies the centre.

Go west to Castelmoron-sur-Lot. Take D 249 then D 263 to Laparade.

Laparade – The ramparts of this *bastide* overlooking the Lot Valley offer a sweeping **view★** from Villeneuve-sur-Lot on the left to the junction of the Lot and Garonne on the right. The river meanders companionably through a checkerboard of crops and orchards.

From Laparade, take D 202 west, then D 911.

Clairac – Picturesque half-timbered houses with brick facings are witness to Clairac's rich past. The seat of a Benedictine abbey, it was destroyed and rebuilt many times during the Wars of Religion. The Crusaders won the town back from the Cathari (also known as Albigenses, a heretic sect seeking to achieve purity through complete ascetic renunciation), in 1224; it became a Protestant stronghold in 1560. Today, it is home to three museums that will delight children in particular.

Plum delicious

The **Musée du Train** ⊘ presents miniature trains chugging through animated scenes.

The **Forêt Magique** ⊘, also based on animated figures, plunges the visitor into a world of elves and forest animals.

L'abbaye des Automates ⊘ – Set in the former Benedictine Abbey, this astonishing museum of automated figures explains the daily life of the abbey monks (it is said that the Clairac monks introduced prunes to the region and brought in tobacco from Brazil in 1555) and retraces the history of the town, which boasts such illustrious figures as the poet Théophile de Viau (born in Clairac in 1590) and Montesquieu, whose wife came from Clairac.

Take D 911 east and follow the signs to "Le Musée du Pruneau", just before Granges-sr-Lot.

Granges-sur-Lot – The **Musée du Pruneau** ⊘, in the Grabach estate, surrounded by plum trees whose fruit is used for prunes, presents various tools used up until very recently to pick and prepare the dried fruit. A film explains the age-old production process and, at the end of the tour, the visitor is invited to taste the estate's home-made specialities, all derived from plums and prunes, of course.

Return to Villeneuve via D 911.

Les Serres du Bas Quercy

49km/31mi round trip – allow all day

Leave Villeneuve south-west via D 118.

The region of Lower Quercy consists of peaceful countryside with low elongated plateaux, cut across by chains of hills *(les Serres)* stretching between the fertile valleys.

Pujols – This very old village is perched on a hill providing an attractive **view★** of Villeneuve-sur-Lot and the broad valley of the Lot, dotted with market gardens and fruit trees.

A passageway under the St-Nicolas bell tower leads to the old village which is still surrounded by the remains of its 13C ramparts. The main street is lined with timber-framed houses with canopy roofs. The nave of the church of St-Nicolas has rib vaulting, while that of Ste-Foy-la-Jeune, currently used as an exhibit hall, is decorated with 15C frescoes *(in poor condition)*. An old well, vestiges of fortifications, and Renaissance houses add to the pleasure of the tour.

Turn left on D 118, then on D 220.

Grottes de Lastournelles ⓥ – Bones found in the caves are displayed in glass cases at the entrance. Galleries have been hollowed out by the seepage of underground water. Small stalactites are forming on the roof. Seven chambers are open to visitors; Les Colonnes is named for the massive pillars within.

Join D 212, then turn left, then left again towards St-Antoine-de-Ficalba.

Grottes de Fontirou ⓥ – The galleries and rooms hollowed out in the grey limestone of the Agenais region are decorated with reddish ochre concretions (due to the clay content), contrasting with a number of lovely white stalagmites.
Animal bones from the Tertiary era found in the caves are displayed in one of the rooms.

Go back to N 21, turn right, then left on D 110.

The road goes through the Serres, limestone hills rising above the wide valleys, and through. **Laroque-Timbaut**, a small village which has retained a number of historical houses (on its southern side) and an old covered market.

Take D 10, then D 656 to the left, take the third road on the left, towards Frespech.

Frespech – Surrounded by 11C walls (reinforced during the Hundred Years War), this charming little village's Romanesque church dates from the 11C, as do a few of the stone houses.
Souleille farm (3.5km/2.2mi from Frespech) houses an attractive **Musée du Foie Gras** ⓥ.

Turn right, following the signs to Hautefage-la-Tour.

Hautefage-la-Tour – Near the Gothic-style **Notre-Dame-de-Hautefage** ⓥ, whose Flamboyant porch is surmounted by a canopy, there is a beautiful hexagonal tower used as a belfry. A round turret topped by a pinnacle turret is part of the tower, pierced with mullion windows on some of its sides. The upper section is decorated with an open-work balustrade, gargoyles and pinnacles. On the square below, planted with beautiful plane trees, is an old wash-house. Against the church, also below, is a pilgrims' fountain.

D 103, D 223 left, then N 21 right lead back to Villeneuve-sur-Lot.

VOUVANT★

Population 867
Michelin map 316: L-8 or 233 fold 4

The hedgerows of the *bocage* and the dense woodland of the forest combine with the rippling waters of the River Mère to confer on this village, perched behind ancient ramparts on a bluff, an atmosphere of silence and safety, steeped in the past – an atmosphere resulting perhaps from the intervention of the Fairy **Mélusine**, who is said to have built Vouvant Château in a single night.

SIGHTS

★**Church** ⓥ – The church was founded by the monks of Maillezais Abbey. The 11C nave was very badly damaged by partisans of the Reformation in 1568 and only the walls of the first three bays remain. The original three apses were rebuilt in the 12C (restored in 1882) along with the crypt below (also restored in the 19C) and the great doorway of the northern transept, which is in the Romanesque style; this doorway, the main **façade★**, flanked by clustered columns and topped by a sharp gable, form a rich and readable page of sculpture.

Main Doorway – The doorway consists of arched doors twinned beneath a common archivolt, surmounted on the tympanum by two interesting stone carvings in relief. On the right, partly damaged by weather, is the figure of Samson overcoming the lion; on the left is Delilah shearing Samson's hair. The covings above the two doors are decorated with floral motifs and the capitals with animals and fantastic figures.
The first coving of the **archivolt** features a line of supporting atlantes, the second a finely carved succession of characters, biblical and mythological. On the left above the arch is a Virgin and Child, balanced on the right by an

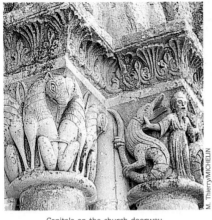
Capitals on the church doorway

effigy of John the Baptist. Higher still are two **friezes** on modillions: the Last Supper (below); the Apostles witnessing the Ascension (above).

Château – The old fortress, home of the Lusignans in medieval times, bars the neck of the promontory girdled by a loop of the river. Its defensive walls demarcate Place du Bail, a grassy esplanade planted with chestnut trees now used as a site for country fairs. From the edge there are attractive views over the lazy curve of the River Mere, which widens here upstream from the Pierre-Brune dam.

★**Tour Mélusine** ⊙ – Once a keep, the tower was built in 1242. The walls, up to 3m/10ft thick, enclose two chambers, one above the other, with curious pyramid vaulting. The top of the tower can be reached by a stairway of 120 steps. From here, 36m/118ft above the ground, there is a vast **panorama**★ to be admired – from the picturesque site of the village itself to the sombre mass of the forest-covered plateau in the south and the chessboard of *bocage* farmland in the north.

Île d'YEU★★
Population 4 788
Michelin map 316: B-7 to C-7 or 232 fold 37

The Isle of Yeu off the Atlantic Coast has managed to preserve all the advantages of its insularity – unspoiled nature, mild temperature, sunny climate and limited motor traffic. Highly contrasting in terms of scenery, often grandiose, its has two totally different coastlines. A tour of the island begins with a sometimes choppy crossing from the mainland. The visitor can step out of the boat and immediately begin to explore the sunny isle on foot or by bicycle (rental on the island).

BELLE-ÎLE'S LITTLE SISTER

Natural contrast – Its geographic location and geology have earned it many affectionate nicknames such as the Corsica of the Atlantic and the Grain of Granite. Standing watch over the mainland, the 10km/6mi long and 4km/2mi wide island, is one of the furthest from the west coast of France (10 nautical miles).
Where the unspoilt "Côte Sauvage" faces the open sea, crystalline schist rock formations make the island look much like Belle-Île. The eastern and southern coasts, however, look more like Vendée: pine trees, evergreen oaks, dunes and long, wide beaches of fine sand.

History and activities of the islanders – The island has been inhabited since prehistoric times (there are a large number of dolmens and menhirs) and it is not impossible that this was the island where, according to the Greek geographer Strabo, a religious "college" of Druidesses was established.
A monastery was founded on Yeu in the 6C. The future St Amand, the "Apostle of Flanders", was drawn here at the beginning of the following century. In the 8C the island was given the enigmatic name of *Insula* (isle) *Oya*. In the 16C the entire population of a village in Cornouaille, south-west Brittany, led by its priest, disembarked on Yeu with the idea of settling here. The prefix *ker-*, attached to certain villages is a distortion of the Lower Poitou dialect word *querry*, meaning a village. Île d'Yeu was ruled by various seigneurs, including Olivier de Clisson, the brilliant warrior who became Commander-in-Chief of the French army, before it was sold to the Crown in 1785.
Aside from tourism, the islanders' main resource is fishing. Specialising in high quality fish, the island's fishermen hold the national record for white tuna (101 tonnes). With a fishing fleet of 81 boats equipped with special trawling nets, the port of Île d'Yeu supports nearly 260 fishermen. Often forced to travel far from their home port to fish using their traditional methods, a number of islanders have been in the news as a result of clashes with other fishermen in southern Europe.

A Marshal detained – On 16 November 1945 a naval escort vessel landed an old man of 90 on the island. He was to be incarcerated in the citadel at Pierre-Levée. The old man was the "ex-Marshal" Pétain, head of Vichy (collaborationist) France from 1940 to 1944, whose death sentence had been commuted to life imprisonment In 1951 he was struck by a double pulmonary congestion and removed to hospital. He died on 23 July. Men who had fought under him at Verdun, in the First World War, carried the coffin to the cemetery at Port-Joinville, where he lies.

TOUR OF THE ISLAND *allow 1 day*

Cliff paths around the coast offer visitors a succession of splendid views – especially in the south and west – as well as the opportunity to explore the attractive coves and beaches below.

* **Port-Joinville** – This, the largest town on the island, was originally called Port-Breton; the present name derives from Admiral de Joinville, the third son of Louis-Philippe I, who brought Napoleon's body back to France in 1840. It is one of the most important tuna fishing ports in France. Tourists arriving from Fromentine or

Île d'Yeu – Port-Joinville

Eating out

BUDGET

La Burette – *1 r. du Petit-Moulin – 85350 Port-Joinville –* ☎ *02 51 58 31 34 – closed Jan-Feb, Sun evening and Mon – 18.29€ lunch – 20.73/22.11€.* Leave the port behind you and come have a seat in the pretty blue and yellow dining room of this nice and simple restaurant. The cuisine doesn't put on airs, and the prices and reception are friendly. A few specialities, like the *patagos*, *vénus à la crème* or fish sauerkraut...

MODERATE

Le Père Raballand – *6 pl. de la Norvège – 85350 Port-Joinville –* ☎ *02 51 26 02 77 – closed 5 Jan to beginning Feb, Sun evening and Mon except from 15 Jun to 15 Sep and school holidays – reservation recommended summer and weekends – 19.51/26.22€.* A very popular address in the port. From your table on the grand terrace, you'll have a front-row seat for admiring the boats and enjoying the animation. Off season, diners converge in the dining room decorated with marine paraphernalia. Listless cuisine based on seafood.

Where to stay

BUDGET

Hôtel l'Escale – *La Croix de port – 85350 Port-Joinville –* ☎ *02 51 58 50 28 – closed 15 Nov to 15 Dec – 28 rms: 28.97/50.31€ –* 🍽 *5.34€.* A stopover in island colours, somewhat removed from the activity of the wharf. White walls and yellow shutters for the house, teak furniture and marine-inspired decor for the breakfast room. Rooms simple and tidy.

Mr. and Mme Cadou Bed and Breakfast – *10 r. Ker-Guérin – 85350 St-Sauveur –* ☎ *02 51 58 55 13 – closed Oct –* 🍽 *– 3 rms: 30.49/48.78€.* This house is one of the rare places to stay in the picturesque village of Saint-Sauveur. All blue and white, the decor of the spacious rooms is inspired by ship rooms and no wonder – Monsieur is a naval carpenter. In fine weather, breakfast is served in the garden.

MODERATE

Villa Monaco Bed and Breakfast – *85350 Pointe-des-Corbeaux –* ☎ *02 51 58 76 56 – closed Oct to Mar –* 🍽 *– 5 rms: 53.36/114.34€ – meals 16.77€.* Situated on the eastern tip of the island, this blue-shuttered Vendée house is in an unbeatable location – the view of both coasts from the garden is just splendid. Simple rooms tastefully decorated, let by the week in the summer. Self-catering cottage available only in the winter.

Atlantic Hôtel – *quai Carnot – 85350 Port-Joinville –* ☎ *02 51 58 38 80 – closed 6-29 Jan – 15 rms: 59.46€ –* 🍽 *5.34€.* On the fishing docks above a fishmonger's, this hotel is one of the island's better addresses. Access by a narrow stairway next to the shop. Its small modern rooms are simple but functional and well-kept. Friendly reception.

Noirmoutier can enjoy a picturesque view of the tiny port crammed with fishing boats and small trawlers, their multicoloured pennants, dressed above a series of buoys, fluttering in the breeze. Behind the masts and rigging is a quay bordered by white houses.

With the exception of the outer harbour, the port is left dry at low tide. Beyond the waterfront there is one shopping street and a network of lanes close-packed with fishermen's cottages.

The house where Mme Pétain lived while her husband was imprisoned is now **Le Musée-Historial** ⓥ. One room is reserved for the exhibit of Pétain mementoes: in the remainder of the small museum the history of the island is illustrated. The Marshal's tomb, a simple white stone slab in a grove of yews and cypress trees, faces the mainland from the local cemetery.

Grand Phare ⓥ – The upper platform (201 steps) of the lighthouse is 41m/135ft above the ground (and 56m/184ft above sea level). There is a splendid **view**★ looking out over the island to the ocean and, in clear weather, to the coast from Noirmoutier to St-Gilles-Croix-de-Vie.

Dolmen de La Planche à Puare – This megalith stands on a stretch of moorland near the **Anse des Broches** cove, at the northwestern tip of the island. It is constructed of schistose granite blocks and is unusual in that it has a central passage with lateral chambers (two each side of the passage in this case). Ancient bones have been found.

★★Côte Sauvage – The rocky coast, extending in a northwest-southeast line from Pointe de But to Pointe des Corbeaux, is indented in an irregular fashion. The ocean views are magnificent. Two of the best are from a cliff path linking the old castle with Port-de-la-Meule. Perched above sheer rock-faces plunging into the sea, the path leads walkers eventually to a picturesque **view★★** looking down over the creek.

★Le Vieux Château – This old castle occupies an imposing site at the seaward end of a moor. Its ghostly silhouette, almost indistinguishable from the rock on which it is built, is both romantic and spectacular. Its walls rise from a granite spur gashed by a narrow crevasse 17m/56ft deep; down below, the ocean waves boom and echo like thunder.

It was built in feudal times (possibly the 11C) and remodelled in the 16C, and this wild pirates' lair now forms a rough trapezoid flanked by defensive bastiontowers. A foot-bridge, replacing the old drawbridge, leads inside the walls. From the top of the keep *(beware: there is no parapet)* there are marvellous **views★★** of the Côte Sauvage and the sea.

★★Port-de-la-Meule – A long, narrow inlet penetrating the coast. At the inner end is the slipway of the crabbers and lobster boats which sink their pots along the rocky depths of Côte Sauvage.

From the moorland heights above, the small white **Chapel of Notre-Dame-de-Bonne-Nouvelle** watches over the tiny port. The local sailors take part in an annual pilgrimage here.

The cliff path continues beyond the chapel as far as **la Pierre Tremblante**, an enormous boulder perched above the sea which can be made to rock gently by pressing on a certain spot.

★Pointe de la Tranche – A number of rocky creeks surround this headland: Anse des Fontaines, so-called because of its freshwater spring, and another two, particularly calm, sheltered and suitable for bathing: the Anse des Soux, where there is a marine grotto, and the **Anse des Vieilles**, the prettiest beach on the island.

Pointe des Corbeaux – This is the south-eastern extremity of Île d'Yeu, forming the dividing line from which the astonishing contrast between the island's two different landscapes can best be appreciated – the rocky, storm-tossed, Breton-style coast on the west; a calm, sandy, pine-clad shoreline on the east.

St-Sauveur – This is commonly referred to simply as "the Town" as it was once the island capital and residence of the Governor. There is a Romanesque church with a square tower above the transept crossing.

Île d'Yeu – Le Vieux Château

S. Sauvignier/MICHELIN

Admission times and charges

Every sight for which times and charges are listed is indicated by the symbol ⊙ in the main part of the guide.

Admission times and charges are liable to alteration without prior notice; the information below is given only as a general indication. Dates given are inclusive. The information was, as far as possible, correct at the time of going to press. Information shown in italics indicates that current details were not available.

The admission charges quoted here are full price for one adult; there are usually reduced rates or free entry for children and often reductions for family groups or students; proof of age may be required. In some cases admission is free on certain days (Wednesdays, Sundays or public holidays). Last admission is often 30-45min before the actual closing time.

Churches and chapels are usually closed during the lunch period from noon to 2pm and do not admit visitors during services; tourists should therefore refrain from visits when services are being held. Visitors to chapels are often accompanied by the person who keeps the key; a donation is welcome.

Many sights are closed on public holidays (listed in the Practical information section).

Most guided tours are conducted by French-speaking guides but in some cases the term "guided tour" may cover group-visiting with recorded commentaries. Some of the more popular sights may offer guided tours or printed information in other languages. Enquire at the ticket office or book stall.

Enquire at the local tourist office or Tourist Information Centre (Office de Tourisme, Maison de Tourisme or Syndicat d'Initiative) – the address of which is shown following the 🖪 below – for local religious holidays, market days etc.

The symbol ও indicates places which are accessible to persons of reduced mobility.

A

AGEN
🖪 107 bd Carnot, 47000 AGEN, ☎ 05 53 47 36 09.

Guided tours of the town – The guided tours take place from mid-July to Aug: tours of the old town (1hr 30min) Mon at 6.30pm; visits of the illuminated monuments (2hr) Thurs at 9pm. No charge. The tourist office distributes a small pamphlet to visitors who wish to make a tour of the town unaccompanied.

Musée des Beaux-Arts – Daily except Tues 10am-5pm (May to Sept: 6pm). Closed 1 Jan, 1 May, 1 Nov, 25 Dec. 3.05€. ☎ 05 53 69 47 23.

AINHOA

Chapelle Notre-Dame-de-l'Aubépine – Pilgrimage Whit Monday with mass said in the Basque language at 10.30am. Mr Audiot. ☎ 05 59 29 90 16.

Île d'AIX

Access – Regular service (30min) leaving from Fouras (Pointe de la Fumée). 9.15€ (children: 6.40€). ☎ 05 46 41 76 24. Regular seasonal liaison with Île de Ré, Île d'Oléron and La Rochelle (see under these names) and cruises leaving from La Tranche-sur-Mer (see under this name), with a sighting of Fort Boyard.

Horse-drawn carriage ride – ও From Apr to Sept, two friendly teams in harness wait quietly at the entrance to place Austerlitz for the boats to arrive. ☎ 05 46 84 07 18.

Musée Napoléonien – Apr to Oct: daily except Tues (June to Sept: daily) 9.30am-12.30pm, 2-6pm (last admission 30min before closing); Nov to Mar: daily except Tues 9.30am-12.30pm, 2-5pm. Closed 1 May. 2.44€, no charge 1st Sunday in the month. ☎ 05 46 84 66 40.

Musée Africain – Apr to Oct: daily except Wed (June to Sept: daily) 9.30am-12.30pm, 2-6pm (last admission 30min before closing); Nov to Mar: daily except Wed 9.30am-12.30pm, 2-5pm. Closed 1 May. 2.99€, no charge 1st Sunday in the month. ☎ 05 46 84 66 40.

ANGLES-SUR-L'ANGLIN

🛈 Le Bourg, 86260 ANGLES-SUR-L'ANGLIN. ☎ 05 49 48 86 87.

Castle ruins – July to end of Aug: daily except Tues 10.30am-12.30pm, 2.30-6.30pm; May, June, Sept and Oct: Sat 2.30-6.30pm, Sun and public holidays 10.30am-12.30pm, 2.30-6.30pm. 1.52€. ☎ 05 49 48 61 20.

ANGOULÊME

🛈 7bis r. du Chat - pl. des Halles, 16007 ANGOULÊME, ☎ 05 45 95 16 84.

Guided tours of the town – Contact the tourist office.

Musée municipal des Beaux-Arts – Mon-Fri noon-6pm, Sat-Sun 2-6pm. Closed public holidays. 2.29€, no charge on weekdays between noon and 2pm. ☎ 05 45 95 07 69.

Musée de la Société archéologique – Daily except Tues 2-5pm (Aug: daily except Sat-Sun). Closed between Christmas and New Year's Day and public holidays. No charge. ☎ 05 45 94 90 75.

Hôtel de Ville – July and Aug: guided tours (1hr) by appointment at 3pm, 4pm, 5pm and 6pm, Sun at 4pm; June and Sept: daily at 4pm; Mar to May, Oct and Nov: Sat-Sun at 3.30pm. 3.81€. ☎ 05 45 38 70 79.

Hôtel St-Simon-FRAC Poitou-Charentes – Daily except Mon and Sun 10.30am-noon, 2-7pm, public holidays 3-6pm. Closed 1 Jan and 25 Dec. No charge. ☎ 05 45 92 87 01.

CNBDI: Musée de la Bande dessinée – Daily except Mon (except school holidays) 10am-6pm, Sat-Sun 2-6pm (summer: 7pm). Closed public holidays. 4.57€ (children: 3.05€). ☎ 05 45 38 65 65.

Musée du Papier "Le Nil" – Daily except Mon 2-6pm (July and Aug: noon-6.30pm). Closed public holidays. No charge. ☎ 05 45 92 73 43.

Excursion

Grottes du Queroy – Apr to end of Oct: guided tours (45min) Sun and public holidays 2-6pm (July and Aug: daily 11am-7pm; mid to end of June: daily 2-6pm). 4.88€ (children: 3.35€). ☎ 05 45 70 38 14 or ☎ 05 45 65 47 09.

ARCACHON

🛈 Esplanade Georges-Pompidou - BP 137, 33310 ARCACHON, ☎ 05 57 52 97 97.

Winter Resort – End of June to beginning of Sept: guided tours (1hr) Tues, Thurs, Fri at 10.30am. Meet at the tourist office; minimum 3 persons. 3.81€.

Aquarium and museum – Apr to end of Oct: 10am-12.30pm, 2-7pm (June to Aug: 9.30am-12.30pm, 2-8pm; July and Aug: open in the evening 8-11pm). 3.96€ (children: 2.44€). ☎ 05 56 83 33 32.

Bassin d'ARCACHON

The Banc d'Arguin Nature Reserve – Guided tours. SEPANSO, 1 r. Tauzia, 33800 Bordeaux, ☎ 05 56 91 33 65.

Cap Ferret:

🛈 Pl. de l'Europe, 33970 LE CANON, ☎ 05 56 60 86 43

Lighthouse – July and Aug: 10am-7pm; Jan to Mar and Oct to Dec: daily except Tues 2-5pm; Apr and May: daily except Tues 10am-noon, 2-5.30pm; June and Sept: daily except Tues 10am-1pm, 2-6pm. Closed mid-Nov to mid-Dec. 1.83€. ☎ 05 56 03 94 49.

Plage de l'océan: narrow-gauge railway – Hourly departures in season starting from around 11am; Apr-May at 3.15 and 4.15pm. Rates posted in the station. ☎ 05 56 60 60 20.

Parc Ornithologique du Teich – ♿ July and Aug: 10am-8pm; mid-Apr to June and beginning to mid-Sept: 10am-7pm; mid-Sept to mid-Apr: 10am-6pm. 5.64€ (children: 3.96€). ☎ 05 56 22 80 93.

Gujan Mestras: Maison de l'huître – ♿ Mar to Sept: guided tours (45min) 10am-noon, 2.30-6.30pm; Oct to Feb: daily except Sun 10am-12.30pm, 2.30-6pm. Closed between Christmas and New Year's Day. 2.44€. ☎ 05 56 66 23 71.

Parc de loisirs de la Hume:

Medieval mini-Golf – ♿ July and Aug: 2-7pm. 4.57€. ☎ 05 56 66 16 76.

Aqualand – July and Aug: 10am-7pm (mid-July to mid-Aug: 9.30am-8pm); June and beginning to mid-Sept: 10am-6pm. 15.55€ (children under 12: 13.11€). ☎ 08 92 68 66 13.

La Coccinelle – ♿ End of May to beginning of Sept: 10am-6.30pm (July and Aug: 10.30am-7.30pm). 7.17€ (children: 5.64€). ☎ 05 56 66 30 41.

AUBETERRE-SUR-DRONNE

🛈 R. St-Jean, 16390 AUBETERRE-SUR-DRONNE, ☎ 05 45 98 57 18.

Monolithic church – 9.30am-12.30pm, 2-7pm (mid-Oct to end of May: 6pm). 3.35€. ☎ 05 45 98 65 06.

B

BAYONNE

🛈 Pl. des Basques, 64100 BAYONNE, ☎ 05 59 46 01 46.

Guided tours of the town – Listed as a "Town of Art and History", Bayonne offers visitors the services of guide-lecturers approved by the Ministry of Culture, who give guided tours of the town (2hr) covering six different themes. July to Sept: daily at 10am; Oct to June: Sat at 3pm. 4.60 €. Contact the tourist office.

Cathédrale Ste-Marie: Cloisters – ♿ 9.30am-12.30pm, 2-5pm (May to Sept: 9am-6pm). Closed 1 Jan, 1 May, 1 and 11 Nov, 25 Dec. No charge. ☎ 05 59 46 11 43.

Musée Bonnat – ♿ Daily except Tues 10am-12.30pm, 2-6pm. Closed public holidays. 3.05€, no charge 1st Sunday in the month. ☎ 05 59 59 08 52.

Musée Basque – Daily except Mon 10.30am-12.30pm, 2-6pm (Apr to Oct: 10am-6.30pm). Closed public holidays. 5.50€, no charge 1st Sunday in the month. Combined ticket with the Musée Bonnat 9€. ☎ 05 59 59 08 98.

BAZAS

🛈 1 pl. de la Cathédrale, 33430 BAZAS, ☎ 05 56 25 25 84.

Guided tours of the town – A 1-3hr tour will be sufficient for you to see all the town has to offer. By appointment at the tourist office. 5€ .

Cathédrale St-Jean – Guided tours available, ask at the tourist office.

Excursions

Collégiale d'Uzeste – Apr to mid-Oct: guided tours Sat-Sun 9.30am-noon, 2-6pm and by appointment with Mr de Richecour or Mrs Capeyron. ☎ 05 56 65 22 47 or 05 56 25 87 48.

Château de Villandraut – July and Aug: 10am-7pm; June: 10am-12.30pm, 2-6pm; Sept to Nov and Feb to May: 2-6pm; Dec to Jan: by appointment. 3€. ☎ 05 56 25 87 57.

Château de Roquetaillade – Easter to All Saints: guided tours (1hr) 2.30-6pm (July and Aug: 10.30am-7pm); All Saints to Easter: Sat-Sun, public and zone B school holidays 2.30-5pm. Closed 25 Dec. 6.15€. ☎ 05 56 76 14 16.

Château de Cazeneuve – Easter to All Saints: guided tours (1hr 15min) Sat-Sun 2-6pm, grounds 11am-6pm (June to Sept: daily). 6.86€ (children: 3.81€). ☎ 05 56 25 48 16.

Le BÉARN

Nay: Musée du Béret – ♿ Apr to mid-Nov and school holidays: daily except Mon 10am-noon, 2-6pm; mid-Nov to end of Mar: Tues and Thurs 2-6pm. Closed 1 Jan and 25 Dec. 3.05€. ☎ 05 59 61 91 70.

Asson: Zoo – 8am-8pm. 6.86€ (children: 4.58€). ☎ 05 59 71 03 34.

Arudy: Maison d'Ossau – July and Aug: 10am-noon, 3-6pm; Jan to June and Sept: Tues to Fri 2-6pm, Sun 3-6pm; winter and spring school holidays: Tues to Fri 2-6pm, Sat-Sun 3-6pm. 2.44€. ☎ 05 59 05 61 71.

Aste-Béon: Falaise aux vautours – Apr and June to Aug: 9am-12.30pm, 2-7pm; May and Sept: 2.30-6.30pm; school holidays: daily except Sat 3-6pm. Closed 1 Jan and 25 Dec. 5.95€ (children: 3.81€). ☎ 05 59 82 65 49.

BÉTHARRAM

Chapelle-rotonde de St-Michel-Garicoits – Apr to Sept: 10am-noon, 2-6pm (July and Aug: 9am-7pm); Oct to Mar: 2-5pm (Feb and Mar: 2-6pm). Closed 1 Jan and 25 Dec. 0.76€. ☎ 04 67 43 02 80.

Grottes – End of Mar to end of Oct: guided tours (1hr 30min) 9am-noon, 1.30-5.30pm; beginning of Jan to end of Mar: daily except Sat-Sun at 2.30pm and 4pm. Closed from end of Oct to beginning of Jan. 7.93€. ☎ 05 62 41 80 04.

BIARRITZ

🛈 Javalquinto, square d'Ixelles, 64200 BIARRITZ, ☎ 05 59 22 37 10.

Pointe St-Martin – Easter to Christmas and school holidays: Sat-Sun 3-7pm (July and Aug: daily except Mon 10am-noon, 3-7pm). 1.52€. ☎ 05 59 22 37 10.

Musée de la Mer – ♿ 9.30am-12.30pm, 2-6pm (July and Aug: 9.30am-midnight); Easter school holidays: Sat-Sun and public holidays in May; June and Sept: 9.30am-7pm; Christmas and Feb school holidays: 9.30am-6pm. Closed second week in Jan, 1 Jan (morning), 25 Dec (morning). 7.17€ (children: 4.57€). ☎ 05 59 22 75 40.

Musée du Chocolat – ♿ 10am-noon, 2.30-6pm (July and Aug: 7pm). Closed Sun outside of school holidays, 1 Jan and 25 Dec. 4.57€ (children: 1.83€). ☎ 05 59 41 54 64.

Excursion

Guéthary: Church – Guided tours available by appointment with Mr Delmas. ☎ 05 59 26 51 75.

BISCAROSSE

Musée historique de l'Hydraviation – & 2-6pm (July and Aug: 10am-7pm). 3.81€ (children: 0.76€). ☎ 05 58 78 00 65.

Excursions

Sanguinet: Archaeological Museum – & July to end of Aug: 10am-12.30pm, 2.30-7pm. 2.74€. ☎ 05 58 78 54 20.

Parentis-en-Born: Musée du Pétrole – & July to end of Aug: at 11am and 3pm. 2.29€. ☎ 05 58 78 43 60.

BLAYE

🔲 Allées Marines, 33390 BLAYE, ☎ 05 57 42 12 09.

Citadel – Guided tours Sun and holidays (1hr 15min) Apr to Sept. Contact the tourist office. 5€

Château de BONAGUIL

July and Aug: 10am-5.45pm; June: 10am-noon, 2-5pm; Sept to May: 10.30am-noon, 2.30-4.30pm; Christmas school holidays: 2.30-4.30pm. Closed Jan. 4.58€. ☎ 05 53 49 59 76.

BORDEAUX

🔲 12 cours du XX-Juillet, 33080 BORDEAUX, ☎ 05 56 00 66 00.

🔲 Pl. Gambetta (Kiosque Bordeluche), 33700 BORDEAUX, ☎ 05 56 92 89 86.

🔲 St-Jean railway station (arrivals), 33000 BORDEAUX, ☎ 05 56 91 64 70.

🔲 Bordeaux airport, 33700 MERIGNAC, ☎ 05 56 34 39 39.

Guided tours of the town – Listed as a "Town of Art and History", Bordeaux offers visitors the services of guide-lecturers approved by the Ministry of Culture, who give guided tours of the town (2hr) covering different themes and circuits. Daily at 10am (and at 3pm from mid-July to mid-Aug). 6.10 €. Contact the tourist office.

Palais Gallien – June to Sept: guided tours at 3pm. 1.52€. Contact the tourist office, ☎ 05 56 00 66 00.

Exposition Porte Cailhau – June to end of Sept: 3-7pm. 2.29€. ☎ 05 56 00 66 00.

Tour St-Michel – June to end of Sept: 3-7pm. 2.29€. ☎ 05 56 00 66 00.

Église Ste-Croix – Weekdays 9am-6pm.

Quartier des Quinconces

Grand Théâtre – Guided tours (1hr) according to the rehearsal schedule. 4.57€. Booking essential. Contact the tourist office.

Église Notre-Dame – & Closed Mon morning. From June to end of Sept: possibility of guided tours Sun to Fri 2.30-5.30pm.

Quartier de la Bourse

Musée des Douanes – & Daily except Mon 10am-6pm. Closed 1 Jan and 25 Dec. 3.05€, no charge 1st Sunday in the month. ☎ 05 56 48 82 82.

Basilique St-Michel – Weekdays: Guided tours 1st Saturday in the month 2.30-6pm.

Quartier Pey-Berland

Cathédrale St-André – Low season: closed Sun afternoon.

Pey-Berland Tower – June to Sept: 10am-6.30pm; Oct to May: daily except Mon 10am-12.30pm, 2-5.30pm. Closed public holidays. 3.81€. ☎ 05 56 81 25 26.

Centre Jean-Moulin – Daily except Mon 11am-6pm, Sat-Sun 2-6pm. Closed public holidays. No charge. ☎ 05 56 79 66 00.

Hôtel de ville – Guided tours (1hr) Wed at 2.30pm (except 15 Aug). 2.29€. ☎ 05 56 00 66 00.

Musée and Galerie des Beaux-Arts – & Daily except Tues 11am-6pm. Closed public holidays. 3.81€, no charge 1st Sunday in the month. ☎ 05 56 10 20 56.

Musée des Arts décoratifs – Daily except Tues 2-6pm. Closed public holidays. 3.81€ (5.34€ temporary exhibitions), no charge 1st Sunday in the month. ☎ 05 56 00 72 52.

Musée d'Aquitaine – & Daily except Mon 11am-6pm. Closed public holidays. 3.81€, no charge 1st Sunday in the month. ☎ 05 56 01 51 00.

Musée Goupil – & Daily except Mon 11am-6pm. Closed public holidays. 5.34€ (3.81€ when no exhibition), no charge 1st Sunday in the month. ☎ 05 56 01 69 40.

Quartier des Chartrons

Musée d'Art contemporain – ♿ Daily except Mon 11am-6pm, Wed 11am-8pm. Closed public holidays. 5.34 €, no charge 1st Sunday in the month. ☎ 05 56 00 81 50.

Musée des Chartrons – Daily except Sat-Sun 2-6pm (May to Oct: 9am-noon, 2-6pm). Closed public holidays. 3.05€. ☎ 05 57 87 50 60.

Vinorama – July and Aug: daily 10am-noon, 2-6pm, Sat-Sun and public holidays 2-6pm; Sept to end of June: daily except Sat-Sun 10am-noon, 2-6pm. Closed 1 May, 14 July, 15 Aug, 25 and 31 Dec, 1 Jan. 5.30€. ☎ 05 56 39 53 02.

Croiseur Colbert – Apr to Sept and zone C school holidays: 10am-6pm, Sat-Sun 10am-7pm (June to Aug: 8pm); Oct to Mar: 1-6pm, Sat-Sun, public and school holidays 10am-6pm. Closed from beginning of Dec to mid-Dec except Sat-Sun, 1 Jan, 25 Dec. 7.30€. ☎ 05 56 44 96 11.

Musée d'Histoire naturelle – Daily except Tues 11am-6pm, Sat-Sun 2-6pm. Closed public holidays. 5.34€, no charge 1st Sunday in the month. ☎ 05 56 48 29 86.

Basilique St-Seurin – Unaccompanied visits daily except Mon morning 8.30-11.30am, 2-7pm, Sun 8.30am-12.30pm, 5-8pm. ☎ 05 56 93 89 28.

Site paléochrétien de St-Seurin – June to end of Sept: 3-7pm. 2.29€. ☎ 05 56 00 66 00.

Vignoble de BORDEAUX

Château de Langoiran – Sept to June: Sat 2-6pm, Sun 10am-8pm; July and Aug: daily 10am-8pm. Closed 1 Jan and 25 Dec. 3.05€. ☎ 05 56 67 12 00.

Cadillac: Château des Ducs d'Épernon – July and Aug: daily 9.30am-1pm, 2-7pm; Apr to June and Sept: daily except Mon 9.30am-12.30pm, 2-6pm; Oct to Mar: daily except Mon 10am-noon, 2-5.30pm. Closed 1 Jan, 1 May, 1 and 11 Nov, 25 Dec. 3.96€. ☎ 05 56 62 69 58.

Ste-Croix-du-Mont: Cave de dégustation – Apr to mid-Oct: daily except Wed 2.30-6pm, Sat-Sun and public holidays 10am-12.30pm, 2.30-8pm. No charge. ☎ 05 56 62 01 54.

St-Macaire: Église St-Sauveur – Guided tours possible by appointment. ☎ 05 56 63 34 52

Verdelais: Basilique Notre-Dame – Guided tours possible by appointment. ☎ 05 56 76 70 45.

Sadirac:

Maison de la Poterie – ♿ Daily except Mon 2-6pm, Sun 3-6pm. Closed public holidays. 1.52€. ☎ 05 56 30 60 03.

Ferme parc Oh! Légumes Oubliés – ♿ Mid-Apr to mid-Dec: 2-6pm. 5.33€ (children: 3.81€). ☎ 05 56 30 61 00.

La Sauve: old abbey – June to Sept: 10am-6.30pm; Oct to May: 10am-1pm, 2.30-5.30pm, Sun and public holidays 10am-1pm, 2.30-6pm. Closed 1 Jan, 1 May, 1 and 11 Nov, 25 Dec. 3.96€. ☎ 05 56 23 01 55.

Église de Castelviel – Guided tours Sun by appointment with the mayor, Mr Jaumin. ☎ 05 56 61 97 58

Ancienne abbaye de Blasimon – ♿ Mid-June to mid-Sept: Thurs at 5pm; rest of the year: guided tours by appointment with the tourist office. 1.52€. ☎ 05 56 71 59 62.

Rauzan: Château des Duras – Contact the tourist office. ☎ 05 57 84 03 88.

Barsac: Church – Guided tours by request. ☎ 05 56 27 15 39.

Château de Malle – Apr to end of Oct: Guided tours (30min) 10am-noon, 2-6.30pm. 6.86€. ☎ 05 56 62 36 86.

Montagne: Écomusée du Libournais – ♿ 10am-noon, 2-6pm. Closed from beginning of Dec to end of Feb. 4.57€ (children: 1.98€). ☎ 05 57 74 56 89.

Château Siran – ♿ Guided tours (30min, last tour leaves 45min before closing time) 10.15am-6.30pm. Closed 1 Jan and 25 Dec. No charge. ☎ 05 57 88 34 04.

Château Margaux – Guided tours (45min) daily except Sat-Sun 10am-noon, 2-4pm by appointment two weeks in advance with Mrs Bizard, Château Margaux, 33460 Margaux. Closed Aug and during the grape harvest. No charge. ☎ 05 57 88 83 93.

Château Maucaillou – ♿ June to Sept: guided tours (1hr 30min) 10am-7.30pm; Oct to May: 10am-12.30pm, 2-6pm. It is advisable to book in advance. 6.86€ (children under 12: no charge). ☎ 05 56 58 01 23.

Fort Médoc – Daily except Mon 10am-7pm. Closed 14 and 15 July. 1.83€. ☎ 05 56 58 98 40.

Château Lanessan – Guided tours (1hr 15min) 9am-noon, 4-6pm. Closed 1 Jan and 25 Dec. 5.34€ (children: no charge). ☎ 05 56 58 94 80.

Château Beychevelle – Guided tours (1hr) daily except Sat-Sun 10am-noon, 1.30-5pm. Closed public holidays. No charge. ☎ 05 56 73 20 70.

Château Mouton Rothschild – Apr to Oct: guided tours (1hr 15min) 9.15-11am, 2-4pm, Sat-Sun and public holidays 9.15-11am, 2-3.30pm; Nov to Mar: daily except Sat-Sun. Closed 1 May, All Saints and between Christmas and New Year's Day. 4.57€. Book two weeks in advance with Miss Parinet, Château Mouton Rothschild, 33250 Pauillac. ☎ 05 56 73 21 29.

Château Lafite Rothschild – Guided tours (1hr) daily except Sat-Sun 9-10.30am, 2-3.30pm. Closed public holidays. No charge. Book two weeks in advance through: Domaine des Barons de Rothschild, 33 r. de la Baume, 75008 Paris. ☎ 01 53 89 78 00.

Tumulus de BOUGON

Museum – ♿ July and Aug: daily except Wed morning 10am-7pm, Sat-Sun and public holidays 10am-8pm; Sept to Dec and Feb to June: daily except Wed morning 10am-6pm; Jan: Sun 2-6pm. Closed 1 Jan and 25 Dec. ☎ 05 49 05 12 13.

La BRÈDE

Château – ♿ July to Sept: guided tours (30min) daily except Tues 2-6pm; Apr to June: Sat-Sun and public holidays 2-6pm; Oct to mid-Nov: Sat-Sun and public holidays 2-5.30pm. Price information not provided.

BRESSUIRE

Musée municipal – Feb to end of Dec: daily except Mon and Tues 2-6pm, Sat-Sun and public holidays 2.30-6.30pm (mid-June to end of Sept: daily except Mon 2-6pm, Sat-Sun and public holidays 2.30-6.30pm). Closed Easter and Whitsun. No charge. ☎ 05 49 65 26 79.

Château – Unaccompanied visits permitted all year round. July and Aug: guided tours 2.30-6.30pm; Sept to June: by appointment two weeks in advance. No charge. ☎ 05 49 65 26 79.

C

CAMBO-LES-BAINS

Villa Arnaga (Musée Edmond Rostand) – Apr to Sept: guided tours (45min) 10am-12.30pm, 2.30-7pm; mid-Feb to end of Nov: Sat-Sun 2.30-6pm; from Oct to autumn half-term and Christmas school holidays: 2.30-6pm. Closed 1 Jan and 25 Dec. 4.88€. ☎ 05 59 29 70 57.

CELLES-SUR-BELLE

Abbaye – Guided tours (1hr) by appointment with the tourist office. Entrance to the grounds and unaccompanied tours of the outside of the abbey are permitted at any time.

Excursions

Temple de Beaussais – Apr to mid-Nov: Sat-Sun, public and school holidays 2.30-6pm (July to mid-Sept: daily except Sun morning and Mon 10.30am-noon, 2.30-7pm). 3.81€. ☎ 05 49 32 83 16.

La Couarde: Maison du Protestantisme Poitevin – ♿ Apr to mid-Nov: Sat-Sun, public and school holidays 2.30-6pm (July to mid-Sept: daily except Mon 2.30-7pm). 3.81€ (ticket combined with the Temple de Beaussais). ☎ 05 49 32 83 16.

Logis de la CHABOTTERIE

Tour of the Manor – 9.30am-6pm, Sun and public holidays 10am-7pm (July and Aug: 10am-7pm). Closed last 3 weeks in Jan. 4.57€ (children: no charge). ☎ 02 51 42 81 00.

Excursions

Château du Bois-Chevalier – From beginning of July to beginning of Aug: guided tours (1hr) 10am-4pm. 2.29€. ☎ 02 40 26 62 18.

Refuge de Grasla – ♿ Mid-Apr to end of Sept: guided tours (2hr) 2-6pm (mid-June to mid-Sept: 11am-1pm, 2-6pm, Sun and public holidays 11am-1pm, 2-7pm). 3.81€. ☎ 02 51 42 96 20.

Le Chemin de la Mémoire des Lucs – July and Aug: 10am-7pm; Sept to June: 9.30am-6pm, Sun and public holidays 10am-7pm. Closed last 3 weeks in Jan. No charge. ☎ 02 51 42 81 00.

🄸 2 rue de Chatain, 86250 CHARROUX, ☎ 05 49 87 60 12.

Abbaye St-Sauveur – ♿ July and Aug: 9.30am-7pm; May, June and Sept: 9.30am-12.30pm, 2-6pm; Oct to Apr: daily except Mon 10am-12.30pm, 2-5.30pm. Closed 1 Jan, 1 May, 1 and 11 Nov, 25 Dec. 3.96€. ☎ 05 49 87 62 43.

Thermes de CHASSENON

Roman baths – Beginning of Apr to mid-Nov: guided tours (1hr, last departure 45min before closing time) 2-5.30pm (June to mid-Sept: 10am-noon, 2-7pm). 4.57€. ☎ 05 45 89 32 21.

CHÂTELLERAULT   🄸 1 av. Treuille, 86100 CHÂTELLERAULT, ☎ 05 49 21 05 47.

Guided tours of the town – Contact the tourist office.

Musée municipal – Daily except Tues 2-6pm. Closed public holidays. 2.63€ ☎ 05 49 21 01 27.

Musée Auto-Moto-Vélo – ♿ May to Sept: 10am-12.30pm, 1.30-7pm; Oct to Apr: daily except Mon 2-6pm. Closed 1 Jan and 25 Dec. 4.57€ (children under 18: no charge). ☎ 05 49 21 03 46.

CHAUVIGNY

Guided tours of the town – Contact the tourist office.

Falconry show – Apr, May and Sept to beginning of Nov: show (45min) at 2.30pm and 4pm; June to Aug: at 11am, 2.30pm, 4pm and 5.30pm. Closed 14 July. 7.32€ (children: 4.88€). ☎ 05 49 46 47 48.

Donjon de Gouzon: Espace d'Archéologie industrielle – ♿ Apr to mid-Oct: 2-6pm (mid-June to end of Aug: 10am-12.30pm, 2.30-6.30pm, Sun 11am-6.30pm); mid-Oct to Mar: Sat-Sun and public holidays 2-6pm. Closed 1 Jan and 25 Dec. 4.57€. ☎ 05 49 46 35 45.

Musée de Chauvigny – Mid-June to end of Aug: daily 10am-12.30pm, 2.30-6.30pm, Sat-Sun and public holidays 2.30-6.30pm; Apr to mid-June, Sept and Oct: daily 2-6pm; Nov to Mar: Sat-Sun and public holidays 2-6pm. Closed 1 Jan and 25 Dec. 1.52€. ☎ 05 49 46 40 31.

Église St-Pierre-les-Églises – July to end of Aug: possibility of guided tours Fri at 10.30am; school holidays: 9am-6pm (winter: 9am-5pm).

Excursions

Château de Touffou – Mid-June to mid-Sept: guided tours (1hr 30min) daily except Tues 10am-noon, 2-6.30pm; May to mid-June: Thurs to Sun and public holidays 2-6.30pm; mid-Sept to end of Apr: Sat-Sun and public holidays 2-6pm. Closed 1 Jan, 25 and 31 Dec. 6.10€. ☎ 05 49 56 08 48.

Archigny: Ferme Acadienne – ♿ Apr to end of Oct: guided tours (45min) Sat-Sun and public holidays 3-7pm (July and Aug: daily except Mon). 1.52€. ☎ 05 49 85 57 46.

Civaux: Musée archéologique – ♿ Beginning of Apr to end of Sept: Thurs to Sun and public holidays 3-6pm (mid-Apr to mid-Sept: daily except Tues 10am-noon, 3-6pm). 0.76€. ☎ 05 49 48 34 61.

CLISSON   🄸 Pl. du Minage, 44190 CLISSON, ☎ 02 40 54 02 95.

Guided tours of the town – Contact the tourist office.

Château d'Olivier de Clisson – Daily except Tues 9.30am-noon, 2-6pm (last admission 20min before closing). Closed during Christmas school holidays. 2.29€. ☎ 02 40 54 02 22.

Park – Apr to Sept: 9am-8pm; Oct to Mar: 9.30am-6.30pm. Guided tours possible by appointment. Unaccompanied visits: no charge, guided tours: 3.05€. ☎ 02 40 54 75 85.

Villa Lemot – Mar to Oct: daily except Mon 10am-noon, 2-6pm (June to Sept: 10am-noon, 2-7pm, Mon 2-7pm); Nov to Feb: daily except Mon 10am-noon, 2-5pm, Sat 2-5pm. Guided tours Sun at 3pm and 5pm; 14 and 15 July at 4pm; July and Aug: Tues and Thurs at 4pm. Closed 1 Jan, 1 May and 25 Dec. Unaccompanied tours: no charge, guided tours: 2.29€. ☎ 02 40 54 75 85.

Maison du Jardinier – Mar to Oct: daily except Mon 10am-noon, 2-6pm (June to Sept: 10am-noon, 2-7pm, Mon 2-7pm); Nov to Feb: daily except Mon 10am-noon, 2-5pm, Sat 2-5pm. Closed 1 Jan, 1 May and 25 Dec. No charge. ☎ 02 40 54 75 85.

Le Pallet: Musée du Vignoble Nantais – ♿ Apr to mid-Nov: 10.30am-1pm, 2.30-6pm. Closed 1 Nov. 3.05€. ☎ 02 40 80 90 13.

Vallet: Château de la Noë de Bel Air – Unaccompanied visits of the grounds and surrounding areas of the château 11am-6.30pm. No charge. ☎ 02 40 33 92 72.

Le Loroux-Bottereau: Église St-Jean-Baptiste – For guided tours, contact the tourist office. ☎ 02 40 03 79 76.

Marais de Goulaine: Boat trips – Apr to end of Sept: boat hire 10.30am-noon, 3-6pm. Closed during the hunting season. Keys and oars available at the tourist office. 7.62€ per boat (half day), 15.24€ (full day). ☎ 02 40 03 79 76.

Goulaine: Château – End of Mar to end of Oct: guided tours (1hr 30min) Sat-Sun and public holidays 2-6pm (mid-June to mid-Sept: daily except Tues 2-6pm). 7€. ☎ 02 40 54 91 42.

La Haye-Fouassière: Maison des Vins de Nantes – July and Aug: daily 8.30am-12.30pm, 2-5.45pm, Sat-Sun 10am-12.30pm, 2-6pm; Sept to June: daily except Sat-Sun. Closed public holidays. No charge. ☎ 02 40 36 90 10.

COGNAC

🖥 16 r. du 14-Juillet, 16100 COGNAC, ☎ 05 45 82 10 71.

Guided tours of the town – Mid-July to end of Aug: Thurs evenings from 9.30pm. 6.10€. Contact the tourist office.

Église St-Léger – Daily except Sun afternoon. Possibility of guided tours in July and Aug.

Les Chais Camus – May to end of Oct: guided tours (1hr 15min) daily except Sat-Sun 10am-noon, 1.45-4.30pm. Closed public holidays. No charge. ☎ 05 45 32 72 96.

Les Chais Hennessy – ♿ Mar to end of Dec: guided tours (1hr 15min) 10am-5pm (June to Sept: 10am-6pm). Closed 1 Jan, 1 May and 25 Dec. 4.57€. ☎ 05 45 35 72 68.

Les Chais Martell – June to Sept: guided tours (1hr) 9.30am-5pm, Sat-Sun and public holidays noon-5pm; Mar to May and Oct: Mon to Thurs at 9.30am, 11am, 2.30pm, 3.45pm and 5pm, Fri at 9.30am and 11am. 3.81€ (children under 16: no charge). ☎ 05 45 36 33 33.

Les Chais Prince Hubert de Polignac – ♿ From end of June to end of Aug: guided tours (1hr 30min) daily except Sun 10am-6pm. No charge. ☎ 05 45 82 09 98.

Les Chais Rémy Martin – Mid-July to mid-Sept: guided tours by train (1hr 30min) 10am-5.30pm; Apr to mid-July and beginning of Sept to beginning of Nov: 9.30-11am, 1.30-5.15pm. Closed Nov to Mar and 1 May. It is advisable to book. 4.55€. ☎ 05 45 35 76 66.

Ancien château: Les Chais Otard – Apr to Oct: guided tours (1hr, last departure 1hr before closing time) 10am-noon, 2-6pm (July and Aug: 10am-noon, 1.30-7pm); Nov to Dec: daily except Sat-Sun and public holidays at 11am, 2.30pm, 3.45pm and 5pm, Fri at 11am, 2.30pm and 4pm. Closed Jan to Mar, 1 May, 1 and 11 Nov, 25 Dec. 3.81€. ☎ 05 45 36 88 86.

Musée municipal de Cognac – June to Sept: daily except Tues 10am-noon, 2-6pm: Oct to May: daily except Tues 2-5.30pm. Closed 1 Jan, 1 and 8 May, 14 July, 15 Aug, 1 and 11 Nov and 25 Dec. 2.13€. ☎ 05 45 32 07 25.

Excursions

Richemont: Church – July and Aug: guided tours 3-7pm.

Migron: Écomusée de Cognac – Discovery game: June to end of Sept: 10am-12.30pm, 2.30-6.30pm (June and Sept: closed mornings). Guided tour and audio-visual show (1hr 30min): July to end of Aug: daily at 4pm. 3.05€ (game), 3.81€ (tour). ☎ 05 46 94 91 16.

CONFOLENS

🖥 Pl. des Marronniers, 16500 CONFOLENS, ☎ 05 45 84 22 22.

Château de Rochebrune – July and Aug: guided tours (45min) 10am-noon, 2-6pm; June and Sept: daily except Tues 2-6pm. 4.57€. ☎ 05 45 89 08 29.

Phare de CORDOUAN

Access – Departure from Verdon-sur-Mer depending on the tide and weather conditions, enquire at the tourist office. 22.87€ (boat crossing and entrance to the lighthouse).

Tour – Visits are governed by the tide and weather conditions. For information, contact the following companies: La Sirène, ☎ 05 46 05 30 93; Cap Cordouan, ☎ 05 46 06 42 36; La Bohème II, ☎ 05 56 90 62 93; or the tourist office, ☎ 05 56 09 61 78. 22.87€ (boat crossing and entrance to the lighthouse).

D

DAMPIERRE-SUR-BOUTONNE

Château – Mid-Mar to 11 Nov. guided tours (45min) Sun and public holidays 2-5pm (June to Sept: daily 2-6.30pm; July and Aug: 10.30am-6.30pm). 5.34€. ☎ 05 46 24 02 24.

Maison du Baudet de Poitou – Contact the Maison du Baudet du Poitou - La Tillauderie, 17470 Dampierre-sur-Boutonne. ☎ 05 46 24 68 94.

DAX

🛈 Pl. Thiers - BP 177, 40100 DAX, ☎ 05 58 56 86 86.

Guided tours of the town – Guided tours (3hr) once a week at 2pm (visit of the thermal installations) and 2.30pm (visit of the town's monuments and buildings). 4.57€. Contact the tourist office.

Musée de Borda – Daily except Tues and Sun 2-6pm. Closed public holidays and during the Dax festival. 3.05€ (ticket includes access to the crypt and the Chapelle des Carmes). ☎ 05 58 74 12 91.

Crypte Archéologique – Feb to end of Nov: guided tours daily except Tues and Sun at 4pm leaving from the Musée de Borda. Closed public holidays. 1.52€. ☎ 05 58 74 12 91.

Parc du Sarrat – ♿ Guided tours (1hr 30min) Tues, Thurs and Sat at 3.30pm. Closed Dec, Jan and public holidays. 3.05€. ☎ 05 58 56 85 03.

Musée de l'Aviation Légère de l'Armée de Terre – ♿ Daily except Sun 2-6pm. Closed Dec, Jan and public holidays. 5.03€. ☎ 05 58 74 66 19.

E

ESPELETTE

Ancien château – ♿ Daily except Sun 8.30am-12.30pm, 1.30-6pm, Sat 8.30am-12.30pm (June to Oct: 3-6pm as well on Sat). Closed public holidays. No charge. ☎ 05 59 93 95 02.

F

FONTENAY-LE-COMTE

🛈 Tr de l'Octroi, quai Poey-d'Avant, 85200 FONTENAY-LE-COMTE, ☎ 02 51 69 44 99.

Guided tour of the town – Contact the tourist office.

Église Notre-Dame – Daily except Sun.

Belfry – July to end of Aug: guided tours (30min) daily except Sun and Mon at 11am, 11.30am, 3pm, 4pm and 5pm, Sat at 3pm, 4pm and 5pm. No charge. ☎ 02 51 69 31 31.

Crypt – July and Aug: Tues at 10.30am, 3pm and 4.45pm, Sat at 3pm and 4.45pm. No charge. ☎ 02 51 69 44 99.

Musée Vendéen – ♿ Mid-June to mid-Sept: daily except Mon 10am-noon, 2-6pm, Sat-Sun 2-6pm; mid-Sept to mid-June: daily except Mon and Tues 2-6pm. Closed 1 Jan, 1 and 8 May, 25 Dec. 2.06€. ☎ 02 51 69 31 31.

Château de Terre-Neuve – May to end of Sept: guided tours (45min) 9am-noon, 2-7pm. 4.88€ (children: 1.52€). ☎ 02 51 69 17 75.

Forêt de Mervent-Vouvant:

Pierre-Brune: amusement park – June to mid-Sept: 10am-8pm; mid-Apr to end of May: 11am-7pm; mid-Sept to beginning of Nov: Sun and public holidays 11am-7pm. 9.15€. ☎ 02 51 00 20 18.

La Jamonière: Musée des Amis de la Forêt – Mar to Oct: daily except Sat 10am-noon, 2-5.30pm, Sun and public holidays 2.30-5.30pm (July and Aug: daily 10am-noon, 3-6pm, Sat-Sun and public holidays 3-6pm); Nov to Easter: Mon to Fri 2-5pm. Closed between Christmas and New Year's Day. 1.98€. ☎ 02 51 00 00 87.

Parc Animalier de Pagnolle – ♿ May to Sept: 10am-8pm; mid-Feb to end of Apr: Sat-Sun and school holidays 2-6pm; Oct to mid-Nov: Sat-Sun 2-6pm. 5.79€ (children: 3.35€). ☎ 02 51 69 02 55.

Le FUTUROSCOPE

Le Parc Européen de l'Image – Apr to beginning of Nov: 9am-10pm (midnight with show); beginning of Nov to beginning of Jan: 9am-6pm, school and public holidays and certain weekends: 9am-7pm. 32.01€ (children: 22.11€), low season: 22.11€ (children: 15.24€). ☎ 05 49 49 30 80.

H

 HAGETMAU   **🛈** Pl. de la République, 40700 HAGETMAU, ☎ 05 58 79 38 26.

Crypte de St-Girons – July and Aug: daily except Tues 3-6pm; Sept to June: Sat 2.30-5.30pm. 1.52€. Contact the town hall. ☎ 05 58 05 77 77.

Excursions

Brassempouy:

La Grotte du Pape – From beginning of July to beginning of Aug: guided tours (1hr) Mon, Wed, Fri 5-6pm. No charge.

Musée de la Préhistoire – ♿ Apr to Oct: daily except Mon 3-6pm (July to Sept: daily); Nov to Mar: 2.30-5.30pm. 2.50€. ☎ 05 58 89 21 73.

Samadet: Musée de la Faïencerie – ♿ May to Sept: daily except Mon 10am-noon, 2-7pm; Oct to Apr: daily except Mon 2-6pm. Closed Jan, 1 May, 11 Nov, 25 Dec and New Year's day. 3.81€ ☎ 05 58 05 40 92.

HENDAYE   **🛈** 12 r. des Aubépines, 64700 HENDAYE, ☎ 05 59 20 00 34.

Château d'Antoine Abbadie – June to mid-Sept: guided tours (45min) daily except Sun 3-5.30pm; Feb to May and mid-Sept to mid-Dec: at 3pm and 4pm. Closed mid-Dec to end of Jan and public holidays. 6€. ☎ 05 59 20 04 51.

Les HERBIERS

Chemin de Fer de la Vendée – ♿ July to mid-Sept: breakfast and dinner in an "Orient Express" dining car, leaving from Mortagne-sur-Sèvre Sat-Sun at noon and 7pm. 17.53€. Passengers must book two weeks in advance. ☎ 02 51 63 02 01.

Abbaye Notre-Dame-de-la-Grainetière – 9am-7pm. 1.52€. ☎ 02 51 67 21 19.

St-Michel-Mont-Mercure: Belfry – Apr to Sept: 8am-8pm, Sat 8am-6pm, Sun and public holidays 1-8pm; Oct to Mar: 8am-7pm, Sat 8am-6pm, Sun and public holidays 1-7pm. 0.46€. ☎ 02 51 57 20 32.

Moulin des Justices – Closed for renovation work. ☎ 02 51 64 98 64.

Mallièvre: Maison de l'Eau – Apr to mid-Oct: Sun and public holidays 2-7pm (mid-June to mid-Sept: daily 10am-noon, 2-7pm). 4.57€. ☎ 02 51 65 33 99.

Mont des Alouettes: Mill – Apr to Sept: daily 9.30am-7pm (beginning to mid-Sept: 10am-12.30pm, 2.30-7pm, Sat-Sun and public holidays 9.30am-7pm). Closed from end of Sept to end of Mar. 2.28€. ☎ 02 51 66 80 32.

HOSSEGOR   **🛈** Pl. Pasteur - BP 6, 40150 HOSSEGOR, ☎ 05 58 41 79 00.

Capbreton:

Écomusée de la Pêche et de la Mer – ♿ July and Aug: 9.30am-noon, 2-6.30pm; Apr to June and Sept: 2-6pm; Oct to Mar: Sun, public and school holidays 2-6pm. Closed 1 Jan and 25 Dec. 4.26€. ☎ 05 58 72 40 50.

La Pinède des Singes – ♿ May to end of Sept: 10am-7pm. 6.10€ (children: 3.05€). ☎ 05 59 45 43 66.

I

Grottes d'ISTURITS et d'OXOCELHAYA

Caves – July and Aug: guided tours (45min) every 30min, 10am-noon, 1-6pm; June to Sept: at 11am, noon, 2pm, 3pm, 4pm and 5pm; mid-Mar to end of May and Oct to mid-Nov: at 2pm and 5pm, extra tour Sun and public holidays at 11am. Closed mid-Nov to mid-Mar. 5.40€ (children: 2.80€). ☎ 05 59 29 64 72.

J

JARNAC   **🛈** Pl. du Château, 16200 JARNAC, ☎ 05 45 81 09 30.

Donation François-Mitterrand – ♿ Apr to end of Sept: daily except Tues 2-6pm (July and Aug: daily 10am-noon, 2-7pm). 3.05€. ☎ 05 45 81 09 30.

Maison Courvoisier: Museum – ♿ May to Sept: 11am-7pm. Closed 1 May. 3.05€. ☎ 05 45 35 55 55

Maison Louis Royer – ♿ For opening times, contact the Maison Louis Royer directly. No charge. ☎ 05 45 81 02 72.

Abbaye de Bassac: Monastery buildings – ♿ Guided tours (1hr) 10am-noon, 3-6pm, Sun and public holidays 3-6pm. No charge. ☎ 05 45 81 94 22.

L

Étang de Cousseau – Apply to the Sepanso for a guided tour. ☏ 05 56 91 33 65.

Maubuisson: Musée des Arts et Traditions populaires – ♿ Mid-June to mid-Sept: daily except Sat-Sun 3.30-7.30pm. 3.05€. ☏ 05 56 03 41 96.

Parc naturel régional des **LANDES DE GASCOGNE**

Moustey: Musée du Patrimoine Religieux et des Croyances Populaires – Apr to beginning of Nov: Sat-Sun and public holidays 2-6pm (July and Aug: 10am-noon, 2-7pm). 3.81€. ☏ 05 58 08 31 31.

Marquèze – ♿ Tourist steam train from Sabres every 45min from beginning of June to mid-Sept: 10am-noon, 2-5.20pm; beginning of Apr to end of May and mid-Sept to beginning of Nov: 2-4.40pm, Sun and public holidays 10am-noon, 2-4.40pm. Closed from beginning of Nov to end of Mar. 7.32€. ☏ 05 58 08 31 31.

Luxey: Jacques et Louis Vidal Resinous Products Workshop – July and Aug: 10am-noon, 2-7pm; June and Sept: 10am-noon, 2-6pm; Apr, May and Oct: 2-6pm, Sun and public holidays 10am-noon, 2-6pm. Closed Nov to Mar. 3.81€. ☏ 05 58 08 31 31.

Abbaye de **LIGUGÉ**

Galerie d'Émaux – Daily except Mon morning 9-11am, 3-5.30pm, Sun and public holidays 11.15am-noon, 3-4.15pm, 5.15-6pm. No charge. ☏ 05 49 55 21 12.

Museum – As for the Galerie d'Émaux.

LUÇON 🛈 Sq. Édouard-Herriot, 85400 LUÇON, ☏ 02 51 56 36 52.

LUSIGNAN 🛈 Pl. du Bail - BP 10, 86600 LUSIGNAN, ☏ 05 49 43 61 21.

Church – Guided tours available, ask at the tourist office.

M

MAILLEZAIS 🛈 R. du Dr-Daroux, 85420 MAILLEZAIS, ☏ 02 51 87 23 01.

Abbey church – Apr to Sept: 9am-12.30pm, 2-7pm (July and Aug: 9am-8pm); Feb to Mar and Oct: 9am-noon, 2-6pm; Nov to Jan: 9am-noon, 2-5.30pm. 2.29€. ☏ 02 51 00 70 11.

Boat trip – Abbey landing-stage, ☏ 02 51 87 21 87; Aria-Loisirs, ☏ 02 51 87 14 00; or Le Pichet de Gargantua, ☏ 02 51 00 71 77.

Niel-sur-l'Autise:

Abbey cloisters – ♿ Feb to Oct: 9am-noon, 2-6pm (July and Aug: 9am-8pm); Nov to Jan: 9am-noon, 2-5.30pm. 2.29€. ☏ 02 51 50 43 00.

Maison de la Meunerie – June to Sept: 10.30am-12.30pm, 2-7pm; Easter and Nov school holidays: 3-6pm; May: Sat-Sun 3-6pm. 3.35€. ☏ 02 51 52 47 43.

MARAIS BRETON-VENDÉEN

Moulin de Rairé – July and Aug: guided tours (45min) 10am-noon, 2-6.30pm; Feb to May, June, Sept and school holidays: 2-6pm. 3.05€. ☏ 02 51 35 51 82 or ☏ 06 85 42 07 87.

La Bourrine à Rosalie – Mid-June to mid-Sept: 3-6pm (July and Aug: 10.30am-12.30pm, 2.30-6.30pm); Apr to Aug: Sat-Sun 3-6pm; Easter school holidays: 3-6pm. 1.52€. ☏ 02 51 68 73 61 or ☏ 02 51 49 43 60.

Salle panoramique – ♿ May to Sept: daily except Mon 10am-noon, 2-6pm (last admission 1hr before closing time), Sat-Sun and public holidays 3-7pm (July and Aug: daily 10am-7pm, Sun and public holidays 3-7pm); Feb to Apr and Oct: daily except Mon 2-6pm. 3.13€. ☏ 02 51 58 86 09.

Écomusée de Daviaud – ♿ May to Sept: 10am-7pm, Sun and public holidays 2-7pm; Feb to Apr, Easter and Christmas school holidays: daily except Mon 2-6pm. Closed 1 Jan and 25 Dec. 4.27€. ☏ 02 51 93 84 84.

Châteauneuf: Le Petit Moulin – Feb to beginning of Nov: 2-7pm (July and Aug: 10am-noon, 2-7pm). 2.74€. ☏ 02 51 49 31 07.

Abbaye de l'Île-Chauvet – June to end of Sept: daily except Sat 1-6pm. 3.81€. ☏ 02 51 68 13 19.

La Garnache:

Château – ♿ July and Aug: guided tours (1hr) 10.30am-6.30pm (open in the evenings Wed from 9pm), Sun and public holidays 2.30-6.30pm; mid-June to beginning of July and mid to end of Aug: daily except Sat-Sun and public holidays 2-6pm. Closed Sept to June. 4.57€. ☎ 02 51 35 03 05.

Musée Passé et Traditions – Mid-June to mid-Sept: 2.30-7pm. 2.29€. ☎ 02 51 68 12 81.

St-Hilaire-de-Riez: Church – July and Aug: possibility of guided tours Tues at 10.45am. ☎ 02 51 54 33 89.

Bourrine du Bois Juquaud – ♿ May to Sept: daily except Mon 10am-noon, 2-6pm, Sun and public holidays 3-7pm (July and Aug: 10am-7pm, Sun and public holidays 3-7pm); Feb to Apr, Easter and Christmas school holidays: daily except Mon 2-6pm. Closed 1 Jan, All Saints and 25 Dec. 2.13€. ☎ 02 51 49 27 37.

Musée Milcendeau-Jean-Yole – ♿ May to Sept: daily except Mon 10am-noon, 2-6pm, Sun and public holidays 3-7pm (July and Aug: 10am-7pm); Feb to Apr and Oct: daily except Mon 2-6pm. 3.13€. ☎ 02 51 35 03 84.

MARAIS POITEVIN

Coulon:

Boat trips – With or without a guide. Contact Mr Prada, ☎ 05 49 35 97 63; La Pigouille, Mrs Agnès, ☎ 05 49 35 80 99; La Roselière (specially equipped and approved boats available for the handicapped), Mr Jubien, ☎ 05 49 35 82 98; La Trigale, DLMS Tourisme, ☎ 05 49 35 02 29; Préplot "La maison aux volets bleus", Mr Ravard, ☎ 05 49 35 93 66; "Les bords de Sèvre", ☎ 05 49 35 58 34; Cardinaud, ☎ 05 49 35 90 47.

Miniature train – Easter to All Saints: commented tours of the Marais Poitevin with Pibalou, regular departures daily. Contact DLMS Tourisme, 6 r. de l'Église. ☎ 05 49 35 02 29.

Aquarium – ♿ Mid-Apr to mid-Oct: 9am-7pm. 2.40€ (children: 1.52€). ☎ 05 49 35 90 31.

Maison des Marais mouillés – July and Aug: 10am-8pm; May, June and Sept: 10am-noon, 2-7pm, Sat-Sun 10am-1pm, 2-7pm; school holidays: 10am-noon, 2-7pm; outside school holidays: daily except Mon 10am-noon, 2-7pm; Nov: 2-7pm. Closed Dec and Jan. 4.57€ (children: 3.51€). ☎ 05 49 35 81 04.

L'Espace Marais – ♿ May to end of Sept: 10am-7pm. 3.20€. ☎ 02 51 00 72 20.

Maison du Petit Poitou – ♿ Apr to Sept: daily except Sun morning 10am-6pm. 3.35€. ☎ 02 51 56 77 30.

St-Michel-en-l'Herm:

Benedictine Abbey – July to end of Aug: guided tours (30min) Tues, Thur, Fri 10am-noon, 3-7pm. Closed public holidays. 2.74€. ☎ 02 51 30 21 89.

Musée André Deluol – ♿ Mid-June to mid-Sept: daily except Tues 3-7pm; Oct to mid-June: Sat-Sun and public holidays 3-5pm. 3€. ☎ 02 51 30 25 15.

Esnandes: Maison de la Mytiliculture – Apr to mid-Sept: daily except Tues 2-7pm (mid-June to end of Aug: daily 10am-12.30pm, 2-7.30pm); Feb and Mar, mid to end of Sept and Nov school holidays: Mon, Wed, Sat 2-6pm; Oct and Nov: Sat 2-5pm. 3.05€. ☎ 05 46 01 34 64.

La Tranche-sur-Mer: Parc des Floralies – June to Sept: 10am-6pm; Mar to May: 10am-12.30pm, 2-6pm, Sat-Sun 10am-6pm. 5.18€, no charge in summer. ☎ 02 51 30 33 96.

St-Denis-du-Payré: Réserve Naturelle M.-Brosselin – July and Aug: guided tours (2hr) 9am-12.30pm, 3-7pm; Mar to June: Sun 2-6pm; Dec to Feb: 1st Sun in the month 2-6pm; Feb and Easter school holidays: 9am-noon, 2-6pm. 5.34€ (children 3.05€). ☎ 02 51 27 23 92.

MARENNES   🅱 Pl. Chasseloup-Loubat, 17320 MARENNES, ☎ 05 46 85 04 36.

Église St-Pierre-de-Sales: Terrasse de la tour – July and Aug: 10am-12.30pm, 2-7pm; Sept to June: daily except Sat-Sun 2-6pm. 1.52€. ☎ 05 46 85 03 86.

Vidéorama de l'huître – ♿ Apr to Sept: daily except Sun 9.30am-noon, 2-6pm (July and Aug: Sun 10.30-11.30am); Oct to Mar: daily except Sun 10-11.30am, 2-3.30pm, Sat 9.30am-noon. Closed 1 Jan, 1 May, Ascension, Easter, 1 Nov, 25 Dec. 1.68€. ☎ 05 46 85 04 36.

Château de la Gataudière – Apr to Nov: guided tours (45min) daily except Mon 10am-noon, 2-6pm (Oct and Nov: closing time: 5pm; June to Sept: daily). Closed Dec to Mar. 5.34€ (children: 3.81€). ☎ 05 46 85 01 07.

i 27 Grande Rue, 79700 MAULÉON, ☎ 05 49 81 95 22.

Musée du BRHAM – 10am-noon, 2-6pm, Sat-Sun and public holidays 2.30-6pm. 1.52€. ☎ 05 49 81 86 23.

Vie des Jouets – Daily except Mon and Tues 2-6pm, Sun and public holidays 2.30-6pm (July and Aug: daily 10am-noon, 2-7pm, Sun and public holidays 2.30-6pm; school holidays: daily 2-6pm, Sun and public holidays 2.30-6pm). 4€ (children: 2.40€). ☎ 05 49 81 64 12.

MAULÉON-LICHARRE

Château d'Andurain – July to mid-Sept: guided tours (45min) daily except Thurs 11am-noon, 3-6pm, Sun 3-6pm. 3.81€. ☎ 05 59 28 04 18.

L'Hôpital St-Blaise: Church – Apply to the town hall in St-Blaise for guided tours. ☎ 05 59 66 11 12.

Gorges de Kakouetta – Mid-Mar to mid-Nov: 8am to dusk. 3.81€. ☎ 05 59 28 73 44 (Bar La Cascade) or ☎ 05 59 28 60 83 (town hall).

MELLE

i Pl. de la poste - BP 51, 79500 MELLE, ☎ 05 49 29 15 10.

Mines d'Argent des Rois Francs – Mar to mid-Nov: guided tours (1hr 15min) Sat-Sun and public holidays 2.30-6.30pm (June to Sept: daily 10am-noon, 2.30-7.30pm). 4.88€ (children: 2.90€). ☎ 05 49 29 19 54.

MONT-DE-MARSAN

i 2 pl. du Général-Leclerc - BP 305, MONT-DE-MARSAN, ☎ 05 58 05 87 37

Guided tours of the town – The tourist office proposes a discovery tour of the town (1hr 30min) all year round (except Sun) by appointment. 4.57€.

Musée Despiau-Wlérick – Daily except Tues 10am-noon, 2-6pm (last admission 30min before closing). Closed public holidays. 3.05€, no charge Mon. ☎ 05 58 75 00 45.

Excursions

Villeneuve-de-Marsan: Château de Ravignan – ♿ July to Sept: guided tours (1hr) Sat-Sun and public holidays 3-7pm, Mon to Fri by appointment; Apr to June and Oct: by appointment. 4.57€. ☎ 05 58 45 22 04.

Labastide d'Armagnac: Bastide – Contact the town hall or the tourist office. 3.05€. ☎ 05 58 44 81 06 or 05 58 44 67 56.

MOUILLERON-EN-PAREDS

National Museums – Mid-Apr to mid-Oct: daily except Tues 9.30am-noon, 2-6pm; mid-Oct to mid-Apr: daily except Tues 10am-noon, 2-5pm. Closed 1 Jan and 25 Dec. 3.35€. ☎ 02 51 00 31 49.

N

NIORT

i Pl. de la Poste, 79000 NIORT, ☎ 05 49 24 18 79.

Guided tours of the town – Contact the tourist office.

Donjon – Daily except Tues 9am-noon, 2-5pm (beginning of May to mid-Sept: 6pm). 2.67€, no charge Wed. ☎ 05 49 78 72 00.

Logis de l'Hercule – July to end of Aug: guided tours (1hr 30min). 4.57€ (children under 12: no charge). Contact the tourist office, ☎ 05 49 24 18 79.

Musée Bernard d'Agesci – Daily except Tues 9am-noon, 2-5pm (beginning of May to mid-Sept: 6pm). 2.67€. ☎ 05 49 78 72 00.

Excursions

Forêt de Chizé:

Zoorama Européen – ♿ Apr to Sept: daily except Tues (except in May and June) 9am-7pm (July and Aug: daily 9am-8pm); Oct to Mar: 9am-noon, 2-6pm. Closed Dec and Jan. 6.86€ (children: 3.20€). ☎ 05 49 77 17 17.

Moulin Rimbault – Closed for an unspecified period of time. ☎ 05 49 09 73 05.

Les Ruralies:

Maison des Ruralies – ☎ 05 49 75 80 70.

Musée de la Machine Agricole – ♿ 10am-6pm (mid-June to mid-Sept: 10am-7pm). Closed 1 Jan and 25 Dec. 4.57€, low season: 3.05€. ☎ 05 49 75 68 27.

Château du Coudray-Salbart – Mid-Feb to beginning of Nov: daily except Tues 10am-6pm (mid-June to mid-Sept: daily 9am-7pm). Closed from beginning of Nov to mid-Feb. 3€ (children: 1.50€). ☎ 06 08 66 84 02.

Château de Cherveux – Apr to Sept: Sat-Sun 10am-noon, 3-7pm. 4.57€. ☎ 05 49 75 06 55, www.chateau-de-cherveux.com.

Île de NOIRMOUTIER

🛈 Rte du Pont-Barbâtre, 85330 NOIRMOUTIER-EN-ÎLE, ☎ 02 51 39 80 71.

Guided tours of the town – Contact the tourist office.

Salt-marshes – July and Aug (late afternoon), seven of the island's salt producers open their salt-marshes to visitors (tours last 1hr): Bernard Chamley, ☎ 02 51 39 32 89; Michel Gallois, ☎ 02 51 39 52 72; Véronique Gendron, ☎ 02 51 39 58 67; Stéphane Leffondré, ☎ 06 03 07 48 15; Didier Magadur, ☎ 02 51 39 53 29, Philippe Martineau, ☎ 02 51 35 93 93, Denis Veille, ☎ 02 51 39 68 23.

Château – Mid-June to mid-Sept: 10am-7pm; Feb to Nov: daily except Tues 10am-12.30pm, 2-5.30pm. Closed Dec and Jan. 3.66€. ☎ 05 51 39 10 42.

Aquarium-Sealand – Feb to mid-Nov: 10am-12.30pm, 2-7pm (July and Aug: 10am-8pm). 7.62€ (children: 5.34€). ☎ 02 51 39 08 11.

Musée de la Construction navale – ♿ Mid-June to mid-Sept: 10am-7pm; Apr to mid-June and mid to end of Sept: daily except Mon 10am-12.30pm, 2.30-6pm. Closed Oct to Feb. 3.05€. ☎ 02 51 39 24 00.

La Guérinière: Musée des Arts et Traditions populaires – ♿ Apr to mid-Oct and school holidays: 2.30-5.30pm (July and Aug: 10am-7pm). Closed 1 May. 3.05€. ☎ 02 51 39 41 39.

Abbaye de NOUAILLE-MAUPERTUIS

Abbey – July and Aug: possibility of guided tours at 10.30am and 3pm, Sun at 3pm and 7pm. Tours leave from the visitor's meeting point near the town hall. ☎ 05 49 55 35 69.

OIRON

Château – Apr to Sept: 10.30am-6.30pm (last admission 1hr before closing), Sat-Sun and public holidays 10.30am-5.30pm; Oct to Mar: 10.30am-5.30pm. Closed 1 Jan, 1 May, 1 and 11 Nov, 25 Dec. 5.48€ (children: no charge). ☎ 05 49 96 51 25.

Île d'OLÉRON

🛈 Pl. Gambetta, 17310 Île d'OLÉRON, ☎ 05 46 47 11 39.

🛈 Carrefour du Port, 17370 Île d'OLÉRON, ☎ 05 46 76 00 86.

St-Pierre-d'Oléron: Musée de l'île d'Oléron Aliénor-d'Aquitaine – ♿ Mid-June to mid-Sept: daily except Sun 10.30am-noon, 2-6pm, Sat 2-6pm; Easter school holidays: daily except Sat-Sun 3-6pm. Closed public holidays. 4€. ☎ 05 46 75 02 77 or ☎ 05 46 47 39 88 (museum).

Pointe de Gatseau: tourist train – From Easter school holidays to end of Oct: enquire for times (train at dusk in July and Aug). 8.38€ (children: 5.34€). ☎ 05 46 76 01 26.

Le Grand-Village-Plage: Maison Paysanne de la Coiffe et du Costume orléannais – ♿ Mid-June to mid-Sept: guided tours daily except Sun at 10am, 11am, 3pm, 4pm and 5pm; Apr: at 10am, 11am, 2pm and 3pm. 4.57€. ☎ 05 46 47 43 44.

Port des Salines – Apr to end of Sept: 10am-12.30pm, 2.30-6.30pm (beginning of June to beginning of Sept: 9.30am-1pm, 2-7.30pm, Sun 9.30am-1pm, 2-6pm). 4.30€. ☎ 05 46 75 82 28.

Le Marais aux Oiseaux – ♿ July and Aug: 10am-8pm; June and Sept: 10am-1pm, 2-7pm; Apr and May: daily except Sat 10am-1pm, 2-7pm; Oct to Mar: during school holidays, daily except Mon 2-6pm. Closed 1 Jan and 25 Dec. 3.81€ (children: 2.29€). ☎ 05 46 75 37 54.

Phare de Chassiron – Mid-June to mid-Sept: 10am-7pm; Apr to mid-June: 10am-12.30pm, 2-6pm; mid-Sept to end of Mar: 10am-12.30pm, 2-5pm. 1.52€ ☎ 05 46 75 18 62.

Parc Ornithologique de Maisonneuve – ♿ June to mid-Oct: 10am-8pm; Jan to May: daily 10am-7pm. 5.24€ (children: 3.05€). ☎ 05 46 47 10 32.

La Cotinère: "La Criée" – Daily except Sun at 6am and 4pm. Closed public holidays. ☎ 05 46 76 42 42.

OLORON-STE-MARIE

🛈 R. du Bourg-Vieux, 64300 ORTHEZ, ☎ 05 59 69 02 75.

Église Ste-Marie – June to end of Sept: guided tours possible daily except Sun 3-6pm. ☎ 05 59 39 04 15.

Quartier Ste-Croix: Maison du Patrimoine – June to Nov: daily except Mon 10am-12.30pm, 3-7pm; Dec to May: by appointment. 3.05€. ☎ 05 59 39 98 00 or 05 59 36 12 05.

Le Haut OSSAU

Gondola to la Sagette – End of May to beginning of Oct and Sat-Sun in Oct: every 30min, 9am-4pm. Combined ticket with the tourist train. ☎ 05 59 05 36 99.

Artouste train – Beginning of June to end of Sept: excursion 3hr 30min. Combined ticket with the gondola: end of July to end of Aug 15.24€ return (children: 10.98€); June, Sept 10.52€ return (children: 7.47€). ☎ 05 59 05 36 99.

P

Zoo de la PALMYRE

&. Apr to Sept: 9am-7pm; Oct to Mar: 9am-noon, 2-5pm. 10,67€ (children: 7.62€). ☎ 05 46 22 46 06 or 08 36 68 18 48.

PARTHENAY   🛈 8 r. de la Vau-St-Jacques, 79200 PARTHENAY, ☎ 05 49 64 24 24.

Guided tours of the town – Parthenay, which is listed as a "Town of Art and history", offers discovery tours conducted by guide-lecturers approved by the Ministry of Culture and Communication. Information available from the Association Atemporelle, ☎ 05 49 63 13 86 or on www.vpah.culture.fr

Musée municipal Georges Turpin – &. June to Sept: daily except Tues 10am-noon, 2.30-6.30pm, Sat-Sun 2.30-6.30pm; mid-Apr to end of May: daily except Tues and Sat 10am-noon, 2.30-6.30pm, Sun 2.30-6.30pm; Oct to mid-Apr: daily except Mon, Tues, Wed and Sat 2-6pm. Closed public holidays except 14 July and 15 Aug. No charge. ☎ 05 49 64 53 73.

Cattle market – Unaccompanied visits Wed 7.30-10.30am. Enquire at Parthenay market. ☎ 05 49 94 03 44.

PAU   🛈 Pl. Royale, 64000 PAU, ☎ 05 59 27 27 08.

Château – Beginning of Apr to mid-June and mid-Sept to end of Oct: guided tours (1hr) 9.30am-11.45am, 2-5pm; mid-June to mid-Sept: 9.30am-12.15pm, 1.30-5.45pm; Nov to May: 9.30am-11.45, 2-4.15pm. Closed 1 Jan, 1 May, 25 Dec. 3.81€. ☎ 05 59 82 38 19.

Musée des Beaux-Arts – Daily except Tues 10am-noon, 2-6pm. Closed public holidays. 1.52€. ☎ 05 59 27 33 02.

Musée Bernadotte – Daily except Mon 10am-noon, 2-6pm. Closed 1 Jan, 1 May, Whitsun, 14 July, 1 Nov, 25 Dec. 1.52€. ☎ 05 59 27 48 42.

Excursions

Gelos: Haras National – &. July to end of Sept: guided tours (1hr 30min) daily except Sat-Sun 2.30pm; Oct to June: guided tours by request. Closed public holidays. 3.81€. ☎ 05 59 06 60 57.

"La Cité des Abeilles" – Apr to mid-Oct: daily except Mon 2-7pm (last admission 1hr before closing, July and Aug: daily); mid-Oct to end Mar: Sat-Sun and public holidays 2-7pm. Closed mid-Dec to mid-Jan. 5.35€ (children: 3.05€). ☎ 05 59 83 10 31.

PEYREHORADE   🛈 147 quai du Sablot, 40300 PEYREHORADE, ☎ 05 58 73 00 52.

Abbaye d'Arthous – Closed for renovation work. ☎ 05 58 05 40 92.

POITIERS   🛈 45 pl. Charles-de-Gaulle, 86009 POITIERS, ☎ 05 49 41 21 24.

Guided tours of the town – Poitiers, which is listed as a "Town of Art and history", offers discovery tours conducted by guide-lecturers approved by the Ministry of Culture and Communication. Information at the tourist office or on www.vpah.culture.fr

Palais de Justice – Daily except Sat-Sun 8am-6pm. Closed public holidays. No charge. ☎ 05 49 50 22 00.

Musée de Chièvres – June to Sept: 10am-noon, 1.15-6pm, Mon 1.15-6pm, Thurs 10am-noon, 1.15-9pm, Sat-Sun and public holidays 10am-noon, 2-6pm; Oct to May: 10am-noon, 1.15-5pm, Mon 1.15-5pm, Sat-Sun and public holidays 2-6pm. Closed 1 Jan, Easter, Whitsun, All Saints, 25 Dec. 3.05€, no charge Tues and 1st Sunday in the month. ☎ 05 49 41 07 53.

Médiathèque – &. June to Sept: Tues 11am-8pm, Wed to Fri 11am-6pm, Sat 11am-5pm; Oct to May: Tues and Thurs 11am-10pm, Wed and Fri 11am-6pm, Sat 11am-5pm. Closed public holidays. No charge. ☎ 05 49 52 31 51.

Baptistère St-Jean – July and Aug: Tues, Sun and public holidays 10am-12.30pm, 2.30-6pm; Apr to June and Sept to Oct: 10.30am-12.30pm, 3-6pm; Nov to Mar: daily except Tues 2.30-4.30pm. Closed 1 Jan and 25 Dec. 0.61€. ☎ 05 49 52 54 65.

Musée Ste-Croix – June to Sept: daily except Mon morning 10am-noon, 1.15-6pm (Tues 8pm), Sat-Sun and public holidays 10am-noon, 2-6pm; Oct to May: daily except Mon morning 10am-noon, 1.15-5pm (Tues open throughout lunchtime), Sat-Sun and public holidays 2-6pm. Closed 1 Jan, Easter, Whitsun, 25 Dec. 3.05€, no charge Tues (ticket combined with the Musée des Chièvres). ☎ 05 49 41 07 53.

Espace Mendès-France: exhibitions – &. 9.30am-6.30pm, Sat-Sun and Mon 2-6.30pm. Closed 1 Jan, 1 May, 14 and 15 July, 15 Aug, 25 and 31 Dec. 4€ (children: 2.50€). ☎ 05 49 50 33 08.

Planetarium – &. Daily except Sat 9.30am-6.30pm, Sun, Mon and public holidays 2-6.30pm. Closed 1 Jan, 1 May, 14 and 15 July, 15 Aug, 25 and 31 Dec. 5.50€ (children: 4€). ☎ 05 49 50 33 08.

PONS

Keep of Pons Castle – Mid-June to mid-Sept: 9.30am-12.30pm, 1.30-6.30pm (last admission 5.45pm); mid-Sept to mid-June, enquire at the tourist office. Closed Nov to Mar, 1 May, 14 July and the afternoon of 15 Aug. 2.29€. ☎ 05 46 96 13 31.

Église Notre-Dame-de-l'Hôpital-Neuf: Historical Museum – The site appears on the UNESCO World Heritage list. Mid-May to mid-Sept: Sat 2-5pm. All year round by appointment two weeks in advance. No charge. Européenne d'Histoire et d'Archéologie, Église N.-D.-de-l'Hôpital-Neuf, BP 83, 17800 Pons, Fax 05 46 92 06 23.

Château d'Usson – Apr to Oct: 10am-7pm. 7.62€ (children: 6.10€). ☎ 05 46 91 09 19.

PORNIC

🖪 La Gare - BP 1119, 44210 PORNIC, ☎ 02 40 82 04 40.

Bourganeuf-en-Retz: Musée du Pays de Retz – &. End of Mar to end of Oct: daily except Mon 10am-noon, 2-6pm (July and Aug: daily 10.30am-1pm, 2-6.30pm). 3.05€. ☎ 02 40 21 40 83.

Saint-Philibert de Grand-Lieu:

Abbatiale St-Philbert – Apr to Sept: 10am-noon, 2-5.30pm; Oct to Mar: 10am-noon, 2-5.30pm, Sun 2-5.30pm. ☎ 02 40 78 73 88.

Maison du Lac – 10am-noon, 2-5.30pm (Apr to Sept: 6.30pm). Closed during Christmas school holidays. 2.44€ (combined ticket with the abbey). ☎ 02 40 78 73 88.

Lac du Grand-Lieu: Boat trips – During the annual Fishermen's Festival which takes place at Passay on 15 Aug and the following Sun.

Passay: Maison du Pêcheur – Apr to Oct: 10am-noon, 2.30-6.30pm; Nov to Mar: 10am-noon, 2-6pm, Sun, Mon and public holidays 3-6pm. Closed 1 Jan and 25 Dec. 2.29€. ☎ 02 40 31 36 46.

Planète sauvage – &. End of Mar to 11 Nov: 10am-5pm. 14.50€ (children: 9.15€). ☎ 02 40 04 82 82.

POUZAUGES

Château du Bois-Tiffrais: Musée de la France Protestante de l'Ouest – &. Mid-June to mid-Sept: 10am-1pm, 2-7pm, Sun and public holidays 2-7pm. 2.29€. ☎ 02 51 66 41 03.

Prieuré de Chassay-Grammont – Mid-June to mid-Sept: 10am-7pm. 2.29€. ☎ 06 74 94 89 95 or ☎ 02 51 42 81 00 (low season).

Le PUY DU FOU

Cinéscénie – &. Last Sat in May: show (1hr 15min) at 10.30pm (last admission 10pm); beginning of June to end of July: Fri and Sat at 10.30pm; Aug: Fri and Sat at 10pm; first two Sat in Sept. 19.82€ (children: 7.62€). Visitors must reserve. ☎ 02 51 64 11 11.

Écomusée de la Vendée – &. Daily except Mon (last admission 30min before closing time) 10am-noon, 2-6pm (May to Sept: daily except Mon 10am-7pm). Closed Jan and 25 Dec. 2.29€. ☎ 02 51 57 60 60.

Grand Parc – &. June to mid-Sept: 10am-7pm; May: Sat-Sun and public holidays 10am-7pm. 21.34€ (children: 10.67€). ☎ 02 51 64 11 11.

R

Île de RÉ

Boat trips – Easter to end of Sept: regular crossings to Aix Island (with a sighting of Fort Boyard). Inter-isle cruises. In high season, there are regular cruises along the coast of the island and to La Rochelle and the Île d'Oléron. ☏ 05 46 09 87 27.

Pont viaduc – Mid-June to mid-Sept: vehicle toll 16.77€ return tariff covering driver and passengers (mid-Sept to mid-June: 9.15€); two-wheelers: 2.29€.

Hôtel de Clerjotte: Musée Ernest-Cognacq – July and Aug: 10am-1pm, 2-7pm; June and Sept: daily except Tues 10am-noon, 2-6pm: Oct to June: daily except Tues (apart from school holidays) 10am-noon, 2-5pm. Closed 1 Jan and 25 Dec. 3.51€. ☏ 05 46 09 21 22.

Église St-Martin – July and Aug: 9.30am-midnight; Apr to June and Sept: 9.30am-11pm; Feb, Mar, Oct and Christmas holidays: 9.30am-8pm; Nov to Dec: Sat-Sun 9.30am-8pm. Closed Jan. ☏ 05 46 09 58 25.

Réserve Naturelle de Lilleau des Niges – ♿ Guided tours (2hr 30min) by appointment. Unaccompanied tours of the reserve's peripheral areas. 4.57€ (children: 1.52€). ☏ 05 46 29 50 74.

Phare des Baleines – June to Sept: 9.30am-7.30pm; Jan, Feb and Oct to mid-Nov: 10am-12.30pm, 2-5.30pm; mid-Nov to end of Dec: 10am-12.30pm, 2-5pm. 1.52€. ☏ 05 46 29 18 23.

L'Arche de Noé – ♿ June to Aug: 10am-7pm; Apr, May and Sept to Nov school holidays (inclusive): 2-5pm. 6.86€ (children: 4.57€). ☏ 05 46 29 23 23.

Château de la ROCHE-COURBON

♿ Apr to Oct: guided tours (45min) 10am-noon, 2.30-6.30pm (closed Thurs from mid-Sept to Oct), gardens daily 9am-6.30pm; Nov to Mar: daily except Thurs 10am-noon, 2-5.30pm, gardens daily 9am-5.30pm. Closed mid-Jan to mid-Feb, 1 Jan, 25 Dec. 6.40€, 4.42€ gardens only. ☏ 05 46 95 60 10.

ROCHEFORT

🛈 Av. Sadi-Carnot, 17300 ROCHEFORT, ☏ 05 46 99 08 60.

Guided tours of the town – Contact the tourist office.

Chantier de reconstruction de l'Hermione – Apr to Sept: 9am-7pm; Oct to Mar: 10am-6pm. Closed 1 Jan and 25 Dec. 4.12€. ☏ 05 46 87 01 90.

Hôtel de Cheusses: Musée de la Marine – Summer: daily except Tues 10am-6.30pm; winter: daily except Tues 10am-noon, 2-5pm. Closed mid-Nov to mid-Dec, 1 Jan, 1 May, 25 Dec. 4.57€ (ticket combined with the Musée de l'Ancienne École de Médecine Navale). ☏ 05 46 99 86 57.

Corderie Royale: Centre International de la Mer – ♿ Apr to Sept: 9am-7pm; Oct to Mar: 10am-6pm (last admission 1hr before closing). Closed 1 Jan and 25 Dec. 4.57€. ☏ 05 46 87 01 90.

Ancienne École de médecine navale – Apr to Sept: guided tours (1hr) daily except Sat-Sun 10am-6pm; Oct to Mar: daily except Tues and Sat-Sun 10am-noon, 2-5pm. Closed mid-Nov to mid-Dec, 1 Jan. 4.57€ ☏ 05 46 99 59 57.

Musée d'Art et d'Histoire – Closed for renovation work. Call ☏ 05 46 99 83 99.

Maison de Pierre Loti – Guided tours (45min) daily except Tues at 10.30am, 11.30am, 2pm, 3pm and 4pm (July to mid-Sept: from 10am, departure every 30min). Closed Jan, 1 and 11 Nov, 25 Dec. It is advisable to book. 7.32€, 6.40€ low season. ☏ 05 46 99 08 60.

Musée des commerces d'autrefois – Daily except Tues 10am-noon, 2-7pm, Sun and public holidays 2-7pm (July and Aug: daily 10am-8pm, winter: 6pm). Closed Jan and 25 Dec. 5€. ☏ 05 46 83 91 50.

Conservatoire du Bégonia – Guided tours (1hr) daily except Sun and Mon at 2pm, 3pm, 4pm and 5pm (Nov to Jan: no visit at 5pm). Closed public holidays. 3€. ☏ 05 46 99 08 26.

Pont transbordeur de Martrou – ♿ May to Sept: 10am-noon, 2-7pm, Mon 2-7pm (June to Aug: 8pm); Apr: 2-6pm, Sat-Sun 10am-noon, 2-6pm; Oct: Sat-Sun 10am-noon, 2-5pm; Nov: Sat 2-5pm, Sun 10am-noon, 2-5pm. Closed Dec to Mar. 1.83€. ☏ 05 46 99 08 60.

Station de lagunage – ♿ July and Aug: guided tours (2hr 30min) Mon and Fri 2-5pm (open in the evening Tues and Thurs at 8pm). 4.57€. ☏ 05 46 82 12 44.

La ROCHEFOUCAULD   🛈 1 r. des Tanneurs, 16110 La ROCHEFOUCAULD,
☎ 05 45 63 07 45.

Château – Apr to end of Nov: 10am-7pm; Dec to Mar: Sun and public holidays from 2pm. 6€. ☎ 05 45 62 07 42.

Ancienne Pharmacie de l'Hôpital – June to Sept: daily except Sun and Mon; low season: Tues to Sat 9.30am-12.30pm, 2.30-6pm. Closed public holidays (except 1 May). Guided tours (30min) by appointment with the tourist office. No charge. ☎ 05 45 63 07 45.

Chasseneuil-sur-Bonnieure: Mémorial de la Résistance et Cimetière National – Unaccompanied visits of the memorial daily, guided tours of the crypt. No charge. ☎ 06 83 53 68 98.

La ROCHELLE   🛈 Quartier du Gabut, pl. de la Petite-Sirène, 17000 La ROCHELLE, ☎ 05 46 41 14 68.

Guided tours of the town – Contact the tourist office.

Cathédrale St-Louis: Treasury – Daily except Sun and public holidays 8.30am-6pm. No charge.

Tour St-Nicolas – Apr to Sept: 10am-1pm, 2-7pm (July and Aug: 10am-7pm); Oct to Mar: daily except Tues 10am-12.30pm, 2-5.30pm. Closed 1 Jan, 1 May, 1 and 11 Nov, 25 Dec. 3.96€, 6.86€ ticket combined with the Tour de la Chaîne and Tour de la Lanterne. ☎ 05 46 34 11 81.

Tour de la Chaîne – Apr to Sept: 10am-1pm, 2-7pm (July and Aug: 10am-7pm); Oct to Mar: daily except Tues 10am-12.30pm, 2-5.30pm. Closed 1 Jan, 1 May, 1 and 11 Nov, 25 Dec. 3.96€, 6.86€ ticket combined with the Tour de la Lanterne and the Tour St-Nicolas. ☎ 05 46 34 11 81.

Tour de la Lanterne – Apr to Sept: 10am-1pm, 2-7pm (July and Aug: 10am-7pm); Oct to Mar: daily except Tues 10am-12.30pm, 2-5.30pm. Closed 1 Jan, 1 May, 1 and 11 Nov, 25 Dec. 3.96€, 6.86€ ticket combined with the Tour de la Chaîne and the Tour St-Nicolas. ☎ 05 46 34 11 81.

Maison Henri-II – Closed to the public.

Hôtel de Ville – ♿ June to Sept and school holidays: guided tours (45min) at 3pm (July and Aug: at 3pm and 4pm); Oct to May: Sat-Sun and public holidays at 3pm. 3.05€. ☎ 05 46 41 14 68.

Musée Protestant – July to mid-Sept: daily except Sun 2.30-6pm; mid-Sept to end of June: by appointment. 1.52€. ☎ 05 46 41 67 07.

Musée d'Histoire naturelle – ♿ Daily except Mon 10am-12.30pm, 1.30-5.30pm, Sat-Sun and public holidays 2-6pm. Closed 1 Jan, 1 May, 14 July, 1 Nov, 25 Dec. 3.51€ (children: no charge). ☎ 05 46 41 18 25.

Musée du Nouveau Monde – Daily except Tues 10.30am-12.30pm, 1.30-6pm, Sun and public holidays 3-6pm. Closed 1 Jan, 1 May, 14 July, 1 and 11 Nov, 25 Dec. 3.50€. ☎ 05 46 41 46 50.

Musée des Beaux-Arts – Daily except Tues 2-5pm. Closed 1 Jan, 1 and 8 May, 14 July, 1 and 11 Nov, 25 Dec. 3.50€. ☎ 05 46 41 64 65.

Musée d'Orbigny-Bernon – Daily except Tues 10am-noon, 2-6pm, Sun and public holidays 2-6pm. Closed 1 Jan, 1 May, 14 July, 1 and 11 Nov, 25 Dec. 3.50€. ☎ 05 46 41 18 83.

Musée Grévin – 10am-7pm (June to Sept: 9am-11pm). Closed mid-Nov to end of Feb except during school holidays. 4.57€ (children: 3.05€). ☎ 05 46 41 08 71.

Musée du Flacon à parfum – Daily except Sun 10.30am-12.30pm, 2-7pm, Mon 3-7pm. Closed public holidays. 4.27€ (children under 10: no charge). ☎ 05 46 41 32 40.

Neptunéa: Maritime Museum – July and Aug: 10am-7.30pm; Apr to June and Sept: 10am-6.30pm; Oct to Mar: 2-6.30pm. Closed mid-Nov to beginning of Feb (except Christmas school holidays). 7.69€. ☎ 05 46 28 03 00.

Musée des Automates – ♿ July and Aug: 9.30am-7pm; Feb to June, Sept and Oct: 10am-noon, 2-6pm; Nov to Jan: 2-6pm. 6.10€ (children: 3.81€). ☎ 05 46 41 68 08.

Musée des Modèles réduits – ♿ July and Aug: 9.30am-7pm; Feb to June, Sept and Oct: 10am-noon, 2-6pm; Nov to Jan: 2-6pm. 6.10€ (children: 3.81€). ☎ 05 46 41 68 08.

Aquarium – ♿ July and Aug: 9am-11pm; Apr to June and Sept: 9am-8pm; Oct to Mar: 10am-8pm. 9.91€ (children: 6.86€). ☎ 05 46 34 00 00.

🛈 R. Clemenceau, 85000 La ROCHE-SUR-YON, ☎ 02 51 36 00 85.

Museum – Daily except Sun and Mon 1-6pm, Wed 10am-7pm, Sat 10am-6pm. No charge. ☎ 02 51 47 48 50.

Haras – July and Aug: guided tours (1hr) daily except Sun at 10.45am, 2-5pm; June and Sept: daily except Sat-Sun at 3pm. 3.81€ (children: 2.29€). Closed public holidays. ☎ 02 51 46 14 47.

🛈 Palais des Congrès, 17200 ROYAN, ☎ 05 46 23 00 00.

🛈 1 bd de la Grandière, 17200 ROYAN, ☎ 05 46 05 04 71.

Guided tours of the town – Contact the tourist office.

Boat trips – The "La Bohême II" (99 passengers) offers trips along the foot of the Meschers cliffs and around the Talmont headland. ☎ 05 56 09 62 93 (Mr Grass). Meschers harbour landing-stage.

Excursions

Saujon: Chemin de fer touristique de la Seudre – Aug: Wed, Fri, Sun; beginning to mid-Sept: Wed, Sun; July: Wed, Sun; June: last two Sundays. Departure from Saujon at 11.05am, 2pm and 5.15pm; departure from La Tremblade at 9.20am, 3.20pm and 6.40pm. Diesel train or autorail depending on the times. The Schneider steam engine dating from 1891, at present being restored, can be seen at Chaillevette station at 11.50am and 3.50pm. 9.15€ (children: 4.57€), bicycles are carried free of charge. ☎ 05 46 36 64 59.

Forêt de la Coubre – July and Aug: guided tours (2hr 30min) daily except Sun and public holidays (Tues, Thurs, Sat: ecology of the dune, Mon, Wed, Fri: knowledge of the forest). Meet at 10am on the Bouverie car park (CD 25 - CD 268 crossroads). 3.81€. ☎ 05 46 67 80 80 or ☎ 05 46 90 65 53.

S

🛈 1 prom. Joffre, 85100 Les SABLES-D'OLONNE, ☎ 02 51 96 85 75.

Guided tours of the town – Contact the tourist office.

Boat trips – Easter to end of Sept: trip (50min) in the afternoon. Locally built launches belonging to the Compagnie Croisières Inter-Îles. ☎ 02 51 21 31 43.

Parc Zoologique de Tranchet – ♿ May to mid-Sept: 9.30am-7pm; mid-Feb to end of Apr and mid-Sept to beginning of Nov: 10am-noon, 2-6pm; beginning of Nov to mid-Feb: 2-6pm. 9.15€ (children: 4.57€). ☎ 02 51 95 14 10.

Musée de l'Abbaye Ste-Croix – Mid-June to mid-Sept: daily except Mon 10am-noon, 2.30-6.30pm; Oct to mid-June: daily except Mon 2.30-5.30pm. Closed public holidays. 4.57€, no charge 1st Sunday in the month. ☎ 02 51 32 01 16.

Observatoire d'Oiseaux de l'Île d'Olonne – July and Aug: 9.30am-7pm; Easter school holidays, mid to end of June and beginning to mid-Sept: 10am-5pm. 2.29€. ☎ 02 51 33 12 97.

🛈 Pl. des Créneaux, 33330 ST-ÉMILION, ☎ 05 57 55 28 28.

Cloître des Cordeliers – June to Oct: guided tours 10.30am-7pm; Mar to May: 10.30am-12.30pm, 2-6pm; Nov to Feb: 2-6pm. Closed 1 Jan and 25 Dec. No charge. ☎ 05 57 24 72 07.

Château du Roi – 10.30am-12.45pm, 2.15-6.45pm (June to Aug: 8.30pm), entrance at the top of the Tour du Roi. 0.91€. ☎ 05 57 24 61 07.

Cloître de la collégiale – ♿ Same as for the Monolithe church bell-tower. No charge.

Tours – Apr to Oct: guided tours (45min) 9.30am-12.30pm, 1.45-6.30pm (July and Aug: 9.30am-8pm; mid to end of June and beginning to mid-Sept 9.30am-7pm); Nov to Mar: 9.30am-12.30pm, 1.45-6pm. 5.03€. ☎ 05 57 55 28 28.

Église Monolithe – Apr to Oct: 9.30am-12.30pm, 1.45-6.30pm (July and Aug: 9.30am-8pm; mid to end of June and beginning to mid-Sept: 9.30am-7pm); Nov to Mar: 9.30am-12.30pm, 1.45-6pm. 0.96€. ☎ 05 57 55 28 28.

🛈 Bd de l'Égalité, 86800 ST-GILLES-CROIX-DE-VIE, ☎ 02 51 55 03 66.

Boat trips – Trips (1hr) aboard the "Mephisto" or the "Ami du Pêcheur": July and Aug every afternoon; 6.86€. Sea-fishing trips aboard the "Mephisto": July and Aug

7am-noon; 19.82 €. 3hr trip aboard the "Class Europ" (racing/cruiser sailing boat) to learn the rudiments of sailing, 30.49 €. Contact Parenthèse, 34 bis bd de l'Égalité, 85800 St-Gilles-Croix-de-Vie.

Excursion

Coëx: Jardin des Olfacties – ♿ Mid-June to end of Aug: 10.30am-7pm; mid-Apr to mid-June and beginning to mid-Sept: daily except Sat 2-7pm. 6,10€. ☎ 02 51 55 53 41.

ST-JEAN-DE-LUZ
🅸 Pl. du Mar.-Foch, 64500 ST-JEAN-DE-LUZ, ☎ 05 59 26 03 16.

Guided tours of the town – The tour (1hr 30min to 2hr) gives you the opportunity to discover the town's principal monuments and main districts. July and Aug: Tues, Thurs and Sat at 10am (in French and English on Thurs). 5€. Contact the tourist office.

Maison Louis-XIV – June to end of Sept: guided tours (30min) 10.30am-noon, 2.30-5.30pm (July and Aug: 10.30am-12.30pm, 2.30-6.30pm), Sun 2.30-5.30pm (July and Aug: 6.30pm). Closed 14 July and 15 Aug in the morning. 3.81€. ☎ 05 59 26 01 56.

Musée Grévin – Apr to end of Oct and school holidays: 10am-noon, 2-6.30pm. 5.34€ (children: 2.67€). ☎ 05 59 51 24 88.

Ciboure: Villa Leïhorra – Apr to Oct: guided tours (45min) daily except Mon, Wed and Fri 3-6.30pm; Jan to Mar: Tues and Sat-Sun 2-5pm; Nov to Dec: Sat-Sun 2-4.30pm. Closed public holidays. 3.81€, 0.76€ unaccompanied tours of the gardens. ☎ 05 59 47 07 09.

Excursion

Parc Florénia – Mid-Mar to end of June and Sept: daily except Mon 10am-7pm (July and Aug: daily 10am-9pm); Oct and Nov holidays: daily except Mon 2-6pm. 6€. ☎ 05 59 48 02 51.

Château d'Urtubie – Mid-Mar to mid-Nov: guided tours (1hr) 2-6pm (and at 11am daily except Wed and Thurs). 5.34€. ☎ 05 59 54 31 15.

Le Labourd:

La Rhune – Mid-Mar to mid-Nov: departures according to weather conditions and numbers, generally every 30min from 9am. 9.95€ return (children: 6.10€). ☎ 05 59 54 20 26 or 05 59 47 51 16.

Grotte de Sare – Apr to Oct: 10am-6pm; Nov to Mar: 2-5pm. Closed 1 Jan and 25 Dec. 5.34€ (children: 3.05€). ☎ 05 59 54 21 88.

Larressore: Atelier Aincart Bergara – Daily except Sun 8am-noon, 2-6.30pm. Closed public holidays. No charge. ☎ 05 59 93 03 05, www.makhila.com

ST-JEAN-PIED-DE-PORT
🅸 14 pl. Charles-de-Gaulle, 64220 ST-JEAN-PIED-DE-PORT, ☎ 05 59 37 03 57.

Abbaye de ST-SAVIN
🅸 20 pl. de la Libération, 86310 ST-SAVIN, ☎ 05 49 48 11 00.

Apr to Oct: 9.30am-12.30pm, 1.30-6.30pm (July and Aug: 9.30am-7pm); Feb, Mar, Nov and Dec: 2-5.30pm. Closed Jan, 1 May and 25 Dec. 4.57€. ☎ 05 49 84 30 00.

SAINT-SEVER

Château de Gaujac – ♿ Mid-Feb to mid-Nov: guided tours (45min) daily except Wed at 3pm, 4pm and 5pm (July and Aug: at 11am, 2pm, 3pm, 4pm, 5pm and 6pm); June: daily except Wed at 3pm, 4pm, 5pm and 6pm. 4.60€ (children: 1.60€). ☎ 05 58 89 01 01.

Plantarium – ♿ Daily except Wed 2.30-6.30pm. Closed mid-Dec to mid-Jan. 4.57€ (children: 1.52€). ☎ 05 58 89 24 22.

Monfort-en-Chalosse: Musée de la Chalosse – Nov to Mar: daily except Mon 2-6pm; Apr to Oct: daily except Mon 10am-noon, 2-6.30pm, Sat-Sun 2-6.30pm. 4.57€. ☎ 05 58 98 69 27.

Laurède: Church – Possibility of guided tours of the sacristy, ask at the presbytery. ☎ 05 58 97 97 39 or Mr Dubos. ☎ 05 58 97 74 39.

ST-VINCENT-SUR-JARD
🅸 Pl. de l'Église, 85520 ST-VINCENT-SUR-JARD, ☎ 02 51 33 62 06.

Maison de Georges Clemenceau – ♿ Apr and May: guided tours (30min) 9.30am-12.30pm, 2.15-6.30pm; June to Sept: 9.30am-7pm; Oct to Mar: daily except Tues 10am-12.30pm, 2-5.30pm. Closed 1 Jan, 1 May, 1 Nov, 25 Dec. 3.96€. ☎ 02 51 33 40 32.

Abbaye Notre-Dame-de-Lieu-Dieu – Closed to the public for restoration work. Reopening planned for the summer 2002.

Talmont-St-Hilaire:

Château – July and Aug: daily 11am-7pm; Apr to June: 10am-12.30pm, 2-6.30pm; Sept to beginning of Nov: 2-6pm. Price information not provided. ☎ 02 51 90 27 43.

Musée Automobile de Vendée – ♿ Apr to Sept: 10am-noon, 2-7pm (June to Aug: 9.30am-7pm); Oct to Mar and school holidays: 2-6pm. Closed 1 Jan, 25 Dec. Price information not provided. ☎ 02 51 22 05 81.

St-Hilaire-la-Forêt: CAIRN – ♿ July and Aug: 10am-1pm, 3-7pm, Sat-Sun 3-7pm; Apr to June and Sept: daily except Sat 3-6pm. 5.49€. ☎ 02 51 33 38 38.

Château de la Guignardière – June to end of Aug: guided tours (1hr) daily 10am-7pm; Easter to end of May and beginning to end of Sept: Sun and public holidays noon-6pm. 5.95€. ☎ 02 51 22 33 06.

SAINTES   🛈 Villa Musso, 62 cours National, 17100 SAINTES. ☎ 05 46 74 23 82

Guided tours of the town – Saintes, which is listed as a "Town of Art and history", offers discovery tours conducted by guide-lecturers approved by the Ministry of Culture and Communication. Information is available at the Heritage workshop. ☎ 05 46 92 06 27 or on www.vpah.culture.fr

Cathédrale St-Pierre: Treasury – July and Aug: daily except Sun morning 10.30am-1pm, 2.30-6pm; Easter: daily except Sun morning 10am-noon, 2-6pm. No charge. ☎ 05 46 74 20 97.

Présidial: Musée des Beaux-Arts – May to Sept: daily except Mon 10am-noon, 2-6pm; Oct to Apr: daily except Mon 10am-noon, 2-5.30pm, Sun and public holidays 2-6pm. Closed 1 Jan, 1 May, 1 Nov, 25 Dec. 1.52€, no charge Sun. ☎ 05 46 93 52 39.

Musée des Beaux-Arts de l'Échevinage – May to Sept: daily except Mon 10am-noon, 2-6pm; Oct to Apr: daily except Mon 10am-noon, 2-5.30pm, Sun and public holidays 2-6pm. Closed 1 Jan, 1 May, 1 Nov, 25 Dec. 1.52€, no charge Sun. ☎ 05 46 93 52 39.

Musée Archéologique – May to Sept: daily except Mon 10am-noon, 2-6pm; Oct to Apr: daily except Mon 10am-noon, 2-5.30pm, Sun and public holidays 2-6pm. Closed 1 Jan, 1 May, 1 Nov, 25 Dec. 1.52€. ☎ 05 46 74 20 97.

Abbaye aux Dames – Apr to Sept: 10am-12.30pm, 2-7pm; Oct to Mar: 2-6pm, Wed and Sat 10am-12.30pm, 2-7pm (beginning of Nov to end of Mar: daily except Mon). Closed between Christmas and New Year's Day. 3.05€. ☎ 05 46 97 48 48.

Arènes – Apr to Oct: 9am-7pm; Nov to Mar: daily except Mon 10am-12.30pm, 2-4.30pm. 0.76€.

Église St-Eutrope – Summer: possibility of guided tours.

Musée Dupuy-Mestreau – May to Sept: daily except Mon 2-6pm (July and Aug: additional tour at 11am); Oct to Apr: daily except Mon 2-5.30pm. Closed 1 Jan, 1 May, 1 Nov, 25 Dec. 1.52€. ☎ 05 46 93 36 71.

Musée Éducatif de Préhistoire – Guided tours (1hr) in the afternoon by appointment. ☎ 05 46 93 43 27.

Haras – ♿ Daily except Sat-Sun 2-5pm. Closed public holidays. No charge. ☎ 05 46 74 80 13.

Excursions

Abbaye de Sablonceaux – July and Aug: daily except Tues 3-6.30pm; Sept to June: daily except Tues 3-6pm. Sound and light show in summer, enquire for information. No charge. ☎ 05 46 94 41 62.

Hameau de Pirelonge – ♿ Guided tours (2hr) daily except Mon 2-7pm (by appointment). Closed Feb. 4.57€ (children: 1.52€). ☎ 05 46 02 00 14.

Château du Douhet – Closed for renovation work. ☎ 05 46 02 30 00 or 05 46 97 78 14.

Abbaye de Fontdouce – Easter to All Saints: guided tours (45min) Sun and public holidays 2.30-6.30pm (July to mid-Sept: daily 10am-noon, 2-6.30pm, Sun and public holidays 2-6.30pm). 3.81€ (children: 2.29€). ☎ 05 46 91 55 24.

SAUVETERRE-DE-BÉARN

Église St-André – Possibility of guided tours. Contact the tourist office. ☎ 05 59 38 58 65.

Excursion

Château de Laàs – Apr: daily except Tues 2-7pm; May to Oct: daily except Tues 10am-7pm (July and Aug: daily). 3.81€ (ticket gives access to all parts of the château). ☎ 05 59 38 91 53.

SOULAC-SUR-MER

Musée d'Art et Archéologie – ♿ June to mid-Sept: 3-6pm (July and Aug: 3-7pm). No charge. ☎ 05 56 09 83 99.

Excursions

Pointe de Grave: Musée du phare de Cordouan – Easter to end of Oct: Sat-Sun and public holidays 3-6pm (July and Aug to mid-Sept: daily 10am-noon, 2-6pm). 2.29€. ☎ 05 56 09 61 78.

Moulin de Vensac – June to Sept: guided tours (45min) Sat-Sun 10am-12.30pm, 2.30-6.30pm (July and Aug: daily); Apr, May and Oct: Sun 2.30-6.30pm. Closed Nov to Mar. 2.74€. ☎ 05 56 09 45 00.

T

TALMONT-SUR-GIRONDE

Musée d'Histoire locale – Apr to mid-June: Sat-Sun, public and school holidays 2-6pm (mid-June to end of Aug: daily 10.30am-1pm, 2-7pm); Sept: daily 2-6pm. 1.60€. ☎ 05 46 90 43 87.

Site gallo-romain du Fâ – ♿ Apr to Sept: guided tours (45min) 2-6pm (July and Aug: 10am-1pm, 2-7pm); Oct to Mar: Sat-Sun, public and school holidays 2-5pm. 3.05€. ☎ 05 46 90 43 66.

THOUARS

🛈 3 bis bd Pierre-Curie, 79100 THOUARS, ☎ 05 49 66 17 65.

Guided tours of the town – Contact the tourist office.

Château – July to end of Aug: guided tours (2hr) Tues and Sat at 3.30pm. 4 57€ (children under 12: no charge). Contact the tourist office, 05 49 66 17 65.

Tour du Prince de Galles – July to beginning of Sept: daily except Tues 10am-noon, 3-7pm; beginning to end of Apr: daily except Tues 3-7pm; end of Apr to end of June and mid-Sept to end of Oct: Sat-Sun 3-7pm. Closed end of Oct to beginning of Apr and public holidays. No charge. ☎ 05 49 67 93 79.

Excursion

Airvault: Musée des Arts et Traditions populaires – Mid-Apr to end of Sept: 2-6pm; Oct to Easter: Wed, Sun and public holidays 2-5pm. 2.29€. ☎ 05 49 64 71 42 or 05 49 70 84 07.

TIFFAUGES

Château – ♿ Apr to mid-Sept: 10am-12.30pm, 2-6pm, Sat-Sun and public holidays 2-7pm (July and Aug: 11am-7pm). 6.10€. ☎ 02 51 65 70 51.

V

VILLENEUVE-SUR-LOT

 1 bd de la République, 47300 VILLENEUVE-SUR-LOT, ☎ 05 53 36 17 30.

Église Ste-Catherine – Mid-July to mid-Aug: possibility of guided tours Tues 9am-6.30pm, contact the tourist office.

Musée de la Vallée du Lot – ♿ 2-6pm (July and Aug: 10am-noon, 2-6pm). 3€. ☎ 05 53 40 48 00.

Musée du Train – Wed, Sat-Sun, public and school holidays 10am-6pm (Apr to Oct: daily). 3.84€ (children: 3.07€). ☎ 05 53 88 04 30.

Forêt Magique – ♿ Wed, Sat-Sun, public and school holidays 10am-6pm (Apr to Oct: daily). Closed Jan and 25 Dec. 3.07€. ☎ 05 53 84 27 54.

Clairac: L'abbaye des Automates – Wed, Sat-Sun, public and school holidays 10am-6pm (Apr to Oct: daily). 6.15€ (children: 4.61€). ☎ 05 53 79 34 81.

Granges-sur-Lot: Musée du Pruneau – ♿ Apr to Oct: 9am-noon, 2-7pm, Sun and public holidays 3-7pm; Nov to Mar: 9am-noon, 2-6.30pm. Closed mid to end of Jan, 1 Jan, 25 Dec. 3.05€. ☎ 05 53 84 00 69.

Grottes de Lastournelle – Guided tours (45min) by appointment (July and Aug: daily without appointment). 4.57€. ☎ 05 53 40 08 09.

Grottes de Fontirou – Apr to mid-Sept: guided tours (45min) 2-5.30pm (beginning of May to mid-June: Sun and public holidays; July and Aug: 10am-12.30pm, 2-6pm). 5.10€ (children: 3.60€). ☎ 05 53 41 73 97 or ☎ 05 53 40 15 29.

VILLENEUVE-SUR-LOT

Frespech: Musée du Foie Gras – ♿ 3-7pm (mid-June to mid-Sept: 10am-7pm). Closed Jan and 25 Dec. 3€. ☎ 05 53 41 23 24.

Église d'Hautefage-la-Tour – Closed for renovation work.

VOUVANT ⓘ Pl. du Bail, 85120 VOUVANT, ☎ 02 51 00 86 80.

Guided tours of the town – Contact the tourist office.

Church – To visit, ask at the tourist office.

Château: Tour Mélusine – Open all year round, ask for the keys at the tourist office (or at the "Café du centre" if the tourist office is closed). 1.22€. ☎ 02 51 00 86 80.

Y

Île d'YEU ⓘ Pl. du Marché, 85350 YEU (ÎLE D'), ☎ 02 51 58 32 58.

Port-Joinville: Musée-Historial – By request. Contact Mr Nolleau, hôtel des voyageurs, Port Joinville, 85350 Île d'Yeu. 3,05€. ☎ 02 51 58 36 88.

Grand Phare – ♿ July to end of Aug: 9.30am-5pm; low season: 9.30-11.45am, 2-5pm. 1.52€. ☎ 02 51 58 30 61.

Index

Notes

Notes

Notes

Please write to us !
Your input will help us to improve our guides.

Please send this questionnaire to the following address:
MICHELIN TRAVEL PUBLICATIONS, The Edward Hyde Building
Hannay House, 39 Clarendon Road Watford, Herts WD17 1JA

1. Is this the first time you have purchased THE GREEN GUIDE? yes   no

2. Which title did you buy? :

3. What influenced your decision to purchase this guide?

	Not important at all	Somewhat important	Important	Very important
Cover				
Clear, attractive layout				
Structure				
Cultural information				
Practical information				
Maps and plans				
Michelin quality				
Loyalty to THE GREEN GUIDE collection				

Your comments :

4. How would you rate the following aspects of THE GREEN GUIDE?

	Poor	Average	Good	Excellent
Maps at the beginning of the guide				
Maps and plans throughout the guide				
Description of the sites (style, detail...)				
Depth of cultural information				
Amount of practical information				
Format				

Please comment if you have responded poor or average on any of the above:

5. What do you think about the establishments provided in the guide?

HOTELS:	Not Enough	Sufficient	Too many
All categories			
"Budget"			
"Moderate"			
"Expensive"			
RESTAURANTS:	Not Enough	Sufficient	Too many
All categories			
"Budget"			
"Moderate"			
"Expensive"			

Your comments:

6. On a scale of 1-20, please rate THE GREEN GUIDE (1 being the lowest, 20 being the highest):

How would you suggest we improve these guides?

1. Maps and Plans:

2. Sights:

3. Establishments:

4. Practical Information:

5. Other:

Demographic information: (optional)

Male   Female   Age

Name:

Address: